THE
ONENESS
HYPOTHESIS

Beyond the Boundary of Self

EDITED BY

PHILIP J. IVANHOE,

OWEN J. FLANAGAN,

VICTORIA S. HARRISON,

HAGOP SARKISSIAN, AND

ERIC SCHWITZGEBEL

Columbia University Press
New York

Columbia University Press
Publishers Since 1893
New York   Chichester, West Sussex
cup.columbia.edu

Library of Congress Cataloging-in-Publication Data
Names: Ivanhoe, P. J., editor.
Title: The oneness hypothesis : beyond the boundary of self / edited by Philip J.
    Ivanhoe, Owen J. Flanagan, Victoria S. Harrison, Hagop Sarkissian, and
    Eric Schwitzgebel.
Description: New York : Columbia University Press, 2018. | Includes
    bibliographical references and index.
Identifiers: LCCN 2018007434 | ISBN 9780231182980 (cloth : alk. paper) |
    ISBN 9780231544634 (e-book)
Subjects: LCSH: Whole and parts (Philosophy) | Concord. | Monism. |
    Self (Philosophy) | Other (Philosophy) | Philosophy. | Religion.
Classification: LCC BD396 .O54 2018 | DDC 111/.82—dc23
LC record available at https://lccn.loc.gov/2018007434

Columbia University Press books are printed
on permanent and durable acid-free paper.
Printed in the United States of America

Cover design: Chang Jae Lee

Cover image: Ma Yuan, *Viewing plum blossoms by moonlight*, The Metropolitan
Museum of Art, Gift of John M Crawford Jr., in honor of Alfreda Murck, 1986.

CONTENTS

CONVENTIONS

For the first occurrence of Chinese, Korean, or Japanese names, we provide the Romanization in the relevant language, followed by the Chinese characters, for example, Zhu Xi 朱熹, Cheondo 天道, Bukyō仏教.

ACKNOWLEDGMENTS

W e, the editors, thank all of the contributors for their participation in the two international conferences that served as the original basis for this anthology: "Oneness in Philosophy and Religion," organized by the Center for East Asian and Comparative Philosophy and held April 25–27, 2015, at City University of Hong Kong, and "Oneness in Philosophy and Psychology," also organized by the Center for East Asian and Comparative Philosophy and held May 14–16, 2016, at City University of Hong Kong. We also thank them for their subsequent work revising and refining their contributions in conversation with us. The conferences served as the origin of all the papers collected here, and the lively, extensive, and insightful conversations that took place during and after this event helped to hone and polish these works into this splendid anthology. The editors gratefully acknowledge and express our sincere gratitude for the generous support of the John Templeton Foundation, which sponsored not only the conference but also the subsequent work compiling and editing this volume all as parts of a larger project titled *Eastern and Western Conceptions of Oneness, Virtue, and Human Happiness* (Grant ID 41879).

THE
ONENESS
HYPOTHESIS

INTRODUCTION

PHILIP J. IVANHOE, OWEN FLANAGAN,
VICTORIA HARRISON, HAGOP SARKISSIAN, AND
ERIC SCHWITZGEBEL

The Oneness Hypothesis

A number of East Asian and Western thinkers argue that, in various ways, the self is inextricably intertwined with, a part of, or in some sense identical with the rest of the world. In recent interdisciplinary work, this general idea has been described as the "oneness hypothesis" (Ivanhoe 2015). The relationship between the self and the rest of the world at issue is more than the simple claim that we are connected with other people, creatures, and things—a claim that is not only in some sense obviously true but practically and morally ambiguous. At times, we find ourselves connected with other parts of the world to which we would strongly prefer not to be connected and have no obligation to be so united (think of malignant bacteria or tumors). The connections the oneness hypothesis advocates are those that conduce to the health, benefit, and improvement of both individuals and the larger wholes of which they are parts. This is why, as we shall see, the ideal of oneness often gets expressed by metaphors of natural organic unity and spontaneous activity, for example, about how a healthy person is connected to the various parts of her own well-functioning body.

While the oneness hypothesis is often described in terms of a "loss" of independence, self, or autonomy, the idea of organic unity shows this to be mistaken; the oneness that serves as the ideal is more accurately and helpfully understood as an argument for, or as providing ways to imagine and achieve, a more expansive conception of the self—a self that is seen as intimately connected with other people, creatures, and things in ways that conduce to their greater happiness, advantage, and well-being. In contemporary analytic philosophy, psychology, and cognitive science, this general issue is more commonly discussed in terms of the "boundaries of the self," and versions of a oneness view are found in such areas as epigenetics and process ontology for organisms (Dupré 2014) in biology. Eric Scerri draws upon a notion of oneness that he rightly sees as an "aspect of Eastern philosophy" to propose an alternative account of the history of science in which "the development of science should be regarded as one organic flow in which the individual worker bees are all contributing to the good of the hive" (Scerri 2016, xxiv, xix). Kathleen M. Higgins, developing R. G. Laing's insights about the importance of being "ontologically secure," argues that music has the capacity to engender a greater sense of connection between the self and the world, including "feelings of being at home in and supported by the world" (Higgins 2012, 147). Recent work in the field of extended cognition also challenges traditional assumptions that the proper scope of the mind and by implication the self stops at the boundaries of the skin and skull (Chemero 2009, Menary 2010). The implications of such a view are quite remarkable and directly challenge accounts of the self that are found in a broad range of disciplines including (but not limited to) philosophy, religion, political theory, sociology, environmental studies, and psychology. This volume focuses on philosophy, religion, and psychology but draws upon other disciplines, such as evolutionary theory and cognitive neuroscience, when these are revealing or otherwise analytically helpful. This more expansive view of the self challenges widespread and uncritically accepted views about the strong (some would say, hyper) individualism that characterizes many contemporary Western theories of the self, but it also has profound implications for a range of practical concerns such as how we conceive of and might seek to care for the people, creatures, and things of the world.

The aim of this volume is focused on describing versions of the oneness hypothesis as found in a variety of philosophical, religious, and psychological writings, evaluating their plausibility, and exploring some of their major implications. We intend this anthology to serve as an important first step in the larger project of developing a new and psychologically well-grounded (Flanagan 1991) model for reflecting on conceptions of the good human life and, in particular, our relationship to and responsibility for the rest of the natural world that can inform and guide a wide range of disciplines in the humanities and social sciences. How would our view of ourselves change, and how would our approach and views about ethical, social, political, or spiritual life change, if we begin with the belief that we all are deeply and inextricably interconnected with other people, creatures, and things, and that our own flourishing and happiness is bound up with the well-being of the rest of the world?

Two aspects of the oneness hypothesis can be distinguished: a metaphysical aspect and a normative aspect. Metaphysical oneness involves an expansive conception of the self as a metaphysical object—a self that extends to include or partly include family, community, or large parts of the environment. Normative oneness rejects the idea that rationality depends on an individualistic conception of one's "self-interest." The metaphysical and normative aspects of oneness are separable. For example, a philosopher might accept a strict metaphysical individualism while embracing normative oneness. However, they are also related in that commitment to a strong form of metaphysical oneness renders the normative individualistic conception of "self-interest" incoherent.

Indeed, much contemporary ethical, political, economic, and social theory assumes, without evidence or argument, a picture of the self that is strongly individualistic, what we call the *hyperindividualistic* conception of the self (Freud 1949, Nozick 1974, O'Neill 1993, Rawls 1999). Such a self is thought to pursue largely self-centered calculations and plans and to enter into agreements and contracts with others in a strategic effort to maximize its own best interests. Even though this model has been shown to be extremely poor at predicting how people actually behave (Sen 1977), and is even less successful in leading people to actually track their best interests (Haybron 2008, 225–51), it is still widely employed and largely regarded as representing not only the best way to be but also *the way people are*. The first of these claims is highly dubious and the last is patently false. Many cultures around the world, especially those in Africa, South and East Asia, Southern Europe, and South America have developed and employ conceptions of the self that are relational—organically and inextricably interrelated with other people, creatures, and things. Similar views have been and are defended in regard to ethical and political forms of life.

Buddhism, a complex, venerable, and influential global religion, is well known for its view that there is no separate and enduring self, and that the delusion that such an enduring self exists is the source of all suffering. While the expression of this core claim about the nature of the self varies across the different strands of the tradition, the idea can be understood as describing the polar opposite of the hyperindividualist view. People in Buddhist societies throughout time and around the world have lived perfectly normal lives in light of such a conception of the self, and many have lived lives of exemplary virtue and especially of immense compassion. Daoism is another of the several East Asian traditions that maintain the world is a grand interconnected whole, with each and every aspect enjoying the same moral status; as Zhuangzi (370–287 BCE) describes it, conceiving the world in such a fashion is a "sorting that evens things out." Many Daoists believe that it is only humanity's propensity to puff itself up and see itself as the only locus of genuine value among things that leads it to disrupt the natural harmony of the world and prey upon one another as well as other creatures and things. Like Buddhists, Daoists do not deny the genuine and healthy everyday regard we have for our own interests; the object of their criticism is not so much a concern with the self but a *mistaken* conception of the self that leads to self-centeredness and even selfishness (a related but different failing). Confucians agree with Buddhists and Daoists that the self is more a corporate than isolated entity, that human beings are familial, social, and cultural creatures whose natural state is community, and whose innate tendencies for cooperation and compassion have made their distinctive form of life possible. Such a view of human nature highlights the degree to which meaningful, satisfying, and happy human lives require recognizing, respecting, and caring not only for other people, but for other creatures and things as well. Under the influence of Daoism and Buddhism, later Confucians, known collectively as neo-Confucians, developed a dramatic version of such a view based on the idea that morally cultivated people "regard heaven, earth, and the myriad things as one body" (*tiandi wanwu wei yiti* 天地萬物為一體) (Cheng and Cheng 2004, Wang 1997, Zhang 2004, Zhu 1986).

Such a conception of the self is by no means exclusively South or East Asian. In the West, the notion of the Great Chain of Being (*scala naturae*), an idea with a long and venerable history, offers another example of this kind of view. It finds some of its earliest forms in the writings of Plato and Aristotle, and was later dramatically developed into a powerful new form by Plotinus, the founder of Neoplatonism, in the third century CE. Primarily through Neoplatonism, it became an important part of a great deal of Christian, Jewish, and Islamic thought, evolving into its most mature expression in the early modern Neoplatonism of the Middle Ages. For our purposes, the Great Chain of Being is important because it links every part of the natural world—living and nonliving—as well as every feature of the supernatural world in a strict, hierarchical structure believed to have been designed and decreed by God. At the top of the hierarchy stands God and below God are all supernatural beings—the different forms of angels and demons. Farther down the hierarchy one finds the stars, planets, moon, and other celestial bodies, then kings, princes, nobles, commoners, domesticated and wild animals, plants, precious stones and metals, and more mundane and common minerals. Setting aside the strictly hierarchical ordering, the crucial thing to note in this grand scheme is that not a single thing exists in isolation, and each and every thing has a form and function within the whole. Human beings are not independent individuals who set and pursue ends that are largely of their own design; rather, they too have a distinct and normatively binding role to play in the great drama that is the cosmos.

Modern thought has generated several wholly naturalized versions of the oneness hypothesis, and the present project reflects several of these. In general, environmental ethics begins with the recognition that human beings are related in complex and intricate ways not only to other people, but also to other creatures and things as well. We are not separate from but integral parts of the greater environment or world, both historically and relationally, and through recognizing this connection and its implications for all concerned we come to see that we have moral obligations that are not evident or salient from the hyperindividualist perspective (Leopold 1968, Callicott 1989). Political philosophy too arguably begins with some kind of recognition of at least our relationship with and obligations toward other people (though the strength and degree to which this insight is maintained and defended varies considerably). Political theories like communitarianism express a view of the self that is closely related to the general form of the oneness hypothesis, insisting that human beings are inevitably embedded within, and partly defined by, the complex set of relationships they find themselves suspended within—simply by virtue of being human. We are not—as hyperindividualist theories of politics would have it—"unencumbered selves" (Sandel 1984) but beings who are to a significant extent constituted by our relationships. More directly and fundamentally, some modern theorists of the self take their inspiration from recent work in evolutionary biology, arguing that environment—from cytoplasm, to uterus, to family and social setting—plays a dominant and underappreciated role in the formation of the self: epigenetic factors take precedence over things like genes. A related, social-scientific expression of such a view is found in those theorists—American Pragmatists (James 1890, Dewey 1925, and Mead 1934) as well as advocates of the dialogic self (Bakhtin 1981)—who emphasize the primacy of the social over the individual.

Brief Descriptions of the Contributions to This Volume

In our first contribution to part 1 of this volume, "Oneness: A Big History Perspective," Victoria S. Harrison explores the oneness hypothesis from the perspective of big history, seeking to place the idea that we are intertwined with other people, creatures, and things in the "broad context of global intellectual and cultural history." Big history conceives of human history as marked by a fairly small number of dramatic and large-scale transformations in social and cultural paradigms, patterns, and practices. Such transformations result from complex processes that often build up gradually over time but then profoundly and fundamentally alter the way human life is conceived, lived, and experienced. On such a view, history is seen more in terms of paradigm shifts, which punctuate the course of historical events and alter its trajectory. Most big historians recognize at least three examples of such major historical transformation. The first occurred about fifty thousand years ago in response to the challenges posed by the last ice age and marked by the earliest appearance of various forms of symbolic representation. The second occurred at the end of the last ice age, about eleven thousand years ago, when humans started to show a preference for more settled life, marked by things like the domestication of animals and plants. The third episode occurred around five thousand years ago, when the first cities and states began to take shape.

Harrison contends that big history can offer important insights into "ideas about the self and the significance of human life in the context of the wider cosmos," which might well lead us to conclude that "prior to the move towards urbanisation the self was predominantly experienced and understood within the framework of possibilities provided by . . . a oneness perspective." Very roughly, the thought is that prior to this time people experienced and conceived of themselves primarily in terms of the clear roles they played and the positions they held within families, tribes, and the larger biological environment; in other words, they saw themselves as intricately interconnected with other people, creatures, and things—as one with them. The Axial Age (800–200 BCE) marked a dramatic shift away from forms of life focusing on one's place in the cosmos and one's obligation to maintain it through ritual and sacrifice to those calling upon individuals to engage in different forms of more personal spiritual transformation. This change reflected a profound big history shift in how human lives were lived during this period: life in urban settings presupposed complex and fine-grained divisions of labor, opened up new vocations, and called on people to negotiate other dramatic, novel, and fast-changing social conditions that did not sit well with the earlier perspective of oneness.

Nevertheless, since these new forms of human life emerged out of and overlaid older models that had existed and shaped human beings for vast stretches of time, the old ways were never wholly effaced. As Robert N. Bellah, echoing Hegel, notes, "nothing is ever lost" (Bellah 2011, Xiao 2015). As a result, "traces of a oneness perspective can still be discerned within later philosophical and religious worldviews that do not seem immediately aligned to it." Harrison suggests that perhaps a general form of the oneness hypothesis may explain features of human experience that are embedded in "our biology and our long history as a species." This would not only leave open but to some extent *favor* the development of contemporary conceptions of the self that either are based upon or incorporate important features of the oneness perspective. In any event, if Harrison's account is true, it shows that such a perspective is not only a possible resource for contemporary people but also comes with a long, complex, and well-attested history.

In our second contribution, "Oneness and Its Discontent: Contesting *Ren* in Classical Chinese Philosophy," Tao Jiang identifies and analyzes what he sees as an important underlying tension between humaneness (*ren* 仁), which he understands as expressing a conception of oneness, and justice, which he understands as offering a contrasting picture of the self and morality, among pre-Qin Chinese philosophers and in particular among early Confucian and Mohist thinkers. He understands humaneness as an agent-relative virtue defined by the natural tendency to care more for, and on this basis show partiality toward, "those who are spacio-temporally close to us, especially our family members." In contrast, justice is an agent-neutral virtue characterized by disinterested appraisal based upon clear, publicly available standards. One of Jiang's aims is to challenge the common scholarly tendency to associate humanness with Confucianism and justice with Mohism; rather, we should note that the tension described by the juxtaposition between these two moral ideals served as a shared theme and site of contention within both schools of philosophy, with the Mohists highlighting and harmonizing the tension expressed by the Confucians.

The tension that Jiang explores is represented clearly in *Analects* 13.18, where Kongzi (Confucius) famously claims that an upright son should cover for his father if his father steals a sheep. Rather than seeking to resolve this tension, Jiang argues we should use it as a lens through which to understand and appreciate the conflicted "moral universe presented in the *Analects*." He does this by proposing readings of several passages in the *Analects* that concern *ren*, that present it as deeply and centrally concerned with justice. Another way Jiang works to make his case is by offering an interpretation of Kongzi's formulation of the Golden Rule—which explicitly concerns the concept of *ren*—that highlights the ways in which it supports an obligation to treat others with justice. In particular, Jiang notes and develops the idea that Kongzi's version of the Golden Rule insists that actions be "reversible" between agents and recipients, generating "a leveling effect . . . neutralizing the moral agent's personal preference and privileged status when it comes to the determination of what is and is not proper" and that such "reversibility lies at the heart of any conception of justice."

One of the most original and provocative aspects of Jiang's essay is his claim that members of the Mohist school "disambiguate the notion of *ren* in Confucius's teaching by putting the Golden Rule into practice and push *ren* to its logical conclusion, thereby pioneering a powerful theory of impartial care and universal justice in Chinese intellectual history." In other words, Jiang sees the Mohists as taking up Kongzi's idea of the Golden Rule, following out its implications, and developing it into a systematic and powerful moral theory. This theory is most clearly represented in their signature teaching of impartial care (*jian ai* 兼愛). Impartial care is the "logical conclusion" of applying the Golden

Rule to *ren*. The thought seems to be that we should love or care for others as we want to be loved and cared for. If we reinforce this idea with the Mohist belief that Heaven cares for all impartially, we might come to believe we should care for all in the same manner and can do so by expanding and being guided by our own desire for care. Such a view combines benevolence with justice by advocating an obligation to take care of, and perhaps even care for, all, with partiality toward none.

Many systems of ethics challenge us to give greater consideration to the needs, desires, and dignity of other people, creatures, and things and thereby to overcome a natural human tendency toward self-centeredness and selfishness. In this respect, ethics often and perhaps fundamentally ought to be concerned with encouraging a greater sense of oneness between ourselves and other parts of the world. Ethical systems that encourage care or benevolence certainly rely upon our inclination to believe that others feel, need, and value in ways quite similar to the ways in which we feel, need, and value; they thereby endorse the idea that in these respects we are one. On the other hand, those who advocate justice in its various forms insist in one way or another that we owe others many of the same basic rights and goods that not only we desire but that every creature of a certain kind merits and can demand. This leads, in thinkers like Kant, to embracing the ideal of a kingdom of ends, or in the case of the Mohists to an imperative to take care of and perhaps care for all impartially. Perhaps such views as well can be understood as more formal ways to express the normative ideal of oneness.

In "One Alone and Many," Stephen R. L. Clark provides a nuanced and original reading of Plotinus that seeks to illuminate the connection between his mysticism and his moral outlook. Clark argues that a correct interpretation of Plotinus will regard "the flight of the alone to the Alone" not as a rejection of community and morality, but rather as a turn toward these. *Monos*, as Clark explains, is often misleadingly translated as "solitary," and this leads to an unfortunate misunderstanding of Plotinus's position. Plotinus was not principally concerned with solitude, Clark avers, but with purity and undistractedness—both of which have profound implications for moral practice. In line with this interpretation, Clark provides a way of reading certain passages of Plotinus that have struck other readers as uncompassionate and as having little bearing on practical moral action.

Clark begins his argument by exploring the contours of the contrast frequently drawn between "mysticism" and "morality." Clark argues that the familiar neat contrast between the mystic, who is concerned with matters beyond this world, and the moralist, who regards the desire to improve the world as of primary importance, cannot help us to understand Plotinus. According to Porphyry, as Clark recounts, Plotinus was actively concerned with practical moral issues and acted according to his moral convictions. Clark provides the example of Plotinus looking "after the property of the orphans left in his care, in case they turned out not to be philosophers." As Clark also notes, Plotinus was not lacking in practical ambitions for the betterment of society. He wanted, for instance, to found a city. Yet this was the same man who wrote that "we should be spectators of murders, and all deaths, and takings and sacking of cities, as if they were on the stages of theatres" (*Enneads* III.2 [47].15, 44f).

The first step toward reevaluating Plotinus's moral position and coming to a more accurate appreciate of the delicate balance he achieved between "morality" and "mysticism" lies in ceasing to read him through the lenses provided by our contemporary moral assumptions, which are permeated, Clark argues, with the conviction that pain is to be avoided. As Clark points out, in the ancient world much pain simply could not be avoided. The pressing moral question concerned how it could be borne. Plotinus's answer to this question was presented within the framework of his account of the relationship between the One and the many, a relationship that Clark discusses using Plotinus's metaphor of a dance to depict the all-encompassing reality of which every individual is a part. Through this metaphor and a careful rereading of key passages, Clark persuasively argues that in Plotinus's work "we find a mystical expression of oneness that entails a practical morality of profound and universal care."

In "Oneness, Aspects, and the Neo-Confucians," Donald L. M. Baxter defends the characteristic neo-Confucian metaphysical claim of identity with the universe and everything in it as well as its related normative teaching that "this identity explains a natural concern for everyone and everything, not just for our narrow selves." Baxter sees clearly the critical and tight relationship between neo-Confucian metaphysics and ethics and recognizes that if the metaphysical picture cannot be defended, neo-Confucians will lose the primary foundation for their distinctive ethical claims. Neo-Confucian metaphysics is not self-evident and in fact seems to involve some rather challenging claims. Many of the things we encounter in the universe differ from one another in the sense that they have qualities that others lack. But if all of these apparently different things are in the end one and the same, then the one thing they all turn out to be differs from itself and this seems to involve a contradiction. Baxter draws upon his theory of aspects—a theory of qualitative self-differing—in order to resolve the apparent contradiction; according to his account "I and everyone else and everything else are aspects of the One—the universe itself." After introducing, motivating, and defending his theory of aspects, he goes on to discuss two objections concerning the ethical view that rests upon neo-Confucian and other related claims about oneness, namely, that it challenges the possibility of altruism, and that it entails equal concern for everyone and everything, including concern for unappealing or despicable aspects of the universe.

Baxter begins by introducing his theory of aspects, which explains how numerically identical things can differ qualitatively. Aspects are not entities nor are they qualities, though they possess qualities. Aspects are numerically identical to but not the same as the individuals of which they are aspects; they are not the same because they lack some of the qualities the individuals have yet they are not simply parts of these individuals. Baxter refers to such cases as "qualitative self-differing" and stipulates that what self-differs in such cases are the "aspects" of the individual. He sums up the view by saying, "For the case to be one of *differing*, one aspect must have a quality that somehow the other aspect lacks. For it to be a case of *self*-differing, the aspects must be numerically identical with the individual that self-differs."

Baxter motivates his theory of aspects by presenting an account of someone who is torn about what to do or how to feel. Euripides's Medea struggles *with herself* about whether to kill her children to punish their father, Jason, who has abandoned her. Deploying his notion of aspects, Baxter argues against any interpretation that describes this struggle in terms of different *parts* of Medea being in conflict. The struggle is within a single person, a unified consciousness; it is between two aspects of Medea, "Medea insofar as she is enraged at Jason *versus* Medea insofar as she loves her children."

One common objection to views like Baxter's theory of aspects is that it violates Leibniz's Law (also known as the Indiscernibility of Identicals), which claims, roughly, that if two things are identical then anything true of either is true of the other as well. Baxter fends off such objections by arguing that Leibniz's Law "applies only to complete entities such as individuals." Since aspects are not complete entities they escape this objection and provide a way to defend conceptions of identity or oneness like that espoused by neo-Confucians, which claims there is only one individual—one body—the universe itself and that "everyone and everything, including oneself, are aspects of the One."

Baxter then turns to address two apparently troubling ethical implications of such a view. First, if all is One, there are no others who can stand as the recipients of altruistic concern; second, even if there were such others, it would seem that our universal concern would extend to the undeserving and even the repugnant as well as the deserving good among them. Baxter defends his aspect account of oneness from both these challenges. In response to the first, he notes that, on his view, beyond the aspect of the One that is the narrow self are other aspects of the One, and these can be fitting objects of altruistic concern. In response to the second challenge, Baxter argues that the fitting concern one should have for everyone and everything as aspects of the One does not entail equal and indiscriminate concern for each and every aspect. It is fully consistent with and possible under the theory of aspects to recognize that some are more deserving than others: "Universal concern need not entail universal impartiality." This final point might appear to reintroduce grounds for excessive partiality for the narrow self and its interests and concerns. Baxter fends off such criticism by noting that the oneness that lies at the heart of his theory of aspects removes the foundation needed to justify "our overweening concern with the narrow self." Having eliminated this foundation, self-centeredness and selfishness have no basis or support.

In "One-to-One Fellow Feeling, Universal Identification and Oneness, and Group Solidarities," Lawrence Blum explores four related themes concerned with compassion or fellow feeling for other human beings, which are sometimes expressed in the language of "oneness." The first of these is whether compassion is particularized by being directed toward a specific human being or universally expressed toward all. Blum's second concern is the nature and extent to which subjects of fellow feeling are aware of, and focus upon their identities as distinct from, those toward whom they have fellow feeling. Third, he examines the relationship between oneness and different group solidarities, such as those of a racial or ethnic character. Blum's fourth and final concern picks up a theme that animates much of Flanagan's contribution: the relation between metaphysics and ethics.

Blum begins his essay by describing and analyzing the philosophy of Schopenhauer, who argued that compassion, by which he meant "an affective phenomenon involving taking the weal or woe of another as a direct motive of action to assist the other," is the basis for morality. He notes that Schopenhauer regarded compassion as psychologically mysterious—a form of "practical mysticism"—and that he offered several not wholly consistent accounts of what compassion means, ranging from recognizing and loving "his own inner nature and self in all others," which seems problematically self-centered, to "making less of a distinction" between self and other, which seems quite preferable. We need metaphysics in order to justify compassion: "In the noumenal world, everything is one, a unity, so the compassionate person is in touch with the reality of that world because he makes no distinction between himself and others." It is not altogether clear, though, whether for Schopenhauer the compassion follows from a grasp of the metaphysical truth or is simply an expression of the way things fundamentally happen to be. Here we see themes that also engaged the attention of Flanagan.

Max Scheler, who was influenced by Schopenhauer, writes on many of these same topics but emphasized, in a way Schopenhauer did not, that the person expressing compassion must have a clear sense of herself as an individual distinct from the one toward whom she feels compassion; she must not confuse herself with the target of her feelings, as compassion does not involve the identity of self and other but rather extends the self to include others, thereby transcending the self. Without this vivid recognition of the difference between self and other, the person feeling compassion will lack the appropriate sense of the other *as other* and this is necessary in order for concern to have moral worth.

Blum notes the similarity between this aspect of Scheler's views and those of a number of contemporary feminists. He also provides a careful comparison with the related but contrasting view of Iris Murdoch, who proposed a more cognitive, perceptual view grounded in a larger frame of moral realism. Her view refocuses attention on the ways in which metaphysics can and perhaps must play a role in ethics and how it does so in views, like hers, inspired by Plato.

Group solidarities present a clear example of nonmetaphysical oneness and Blum offers a range of insights based on the particular example of ethnic or racial group solidarities. One can identify with other members of such groups based on their shared group identity while being clearly aware of other differences between oneself and other members of the group—for example, through a different understanding of a shared experience. Group solidarity entails concern for a group and for members of the group as members. However, in almost all cases such concern in not all encompassing, but instead limited to particular features of shared experience or history, or to certain circumstances or times. Here we see a permeable, fungible, and complex array of different senses of oneness within groups. Blum introduces the African American philosophers Charles Johnson and Tommie Shelby as offering particularly interesting and powerful insights regarding how such group identity can offer a ground and starting point for group or universal teaching and identity. It is simply true that as a group African Americans have suffered more than most. This can be the source of solidarity within the African American community, but it can also testify to a basic condition of humanity—the fact of suffering—and inspire solidarity beyond the community.

Blum further explores the sense of oneness and solidarity by discussing aspects of the film *Selma*, about a march for voting rights led by Martin Luther King, Jr., in 1965 in Alabama. The film "vividly recreates the sense of solidarity among the marchers, all seeing themselves as part of a single entity, a movement, with which they all identify. When some marchers are beaten, others rush to help them. They do not feel a sense of separateness from one another." This sense of oneness need not be confined to race- or ethnicity-based forms of solidarity and indeed this was shown (both in history and in this film) when King reached out to those beyond the African American community to join in the pursuit of its noble ends. This example leads Blum to argue for three bases of solidarity: experience, group membership, and political commitment. Such sources of solidarity can inspire a form of universalism expressed in Martin Luther King's vision of "the beloved community," which Blum describes as "a vision of the future in which white, black, and other would live together in harmony, accepting one another as fellow citizens and fellow human beings in an overarching community of care and concern." Reprising some of the themes with which he began his contribution, Blum makes clear that King's vision did not aim to erase racial identity or the distinct individuality of members within the different communities that comprise it. In these ways, the beloved community and the different racial and ethnic groups that constitute it offer important lessons about and an ideal example of healthy forms of oneness.

It should be evident to all that the capacity for and practice of care has been critical for the success of our species and profoundly shapes the forms that human societies take and the values we find within them. Nevertheless, as Kittay points out in her contribution to this volume, "The Relationality and the Normativity of *An Ethic of Care*," a description and analysis of care "as moral theory is still in its infancy—at least in the West." Most of the work aimed at articulating different expressions of an ethics of care has been done by contemporary women philosophers; the most influential examples of such work not only explicitly address the question of the nature of the self but also challenge the dominant hyperindividualism that is characteristic of mainstream philosophical writings. Such views clearly should be understood as expressions of the oneness hypothesis; they hold, as Kittay explains, that "selves are porous and connected, situated in a web of relationships where even those far from us are bound to us with invisible but morally important threads."

At the heart of Kittay's essay is a highly original, insightful, and challenging account of the nature of care. One of the first features she argues for in crafting her account of care is the need to care about care. Drawing a parallel with Royce's analysis of loyalty, she shows how caring about care is necessary in order to ensure that one works to create and protect the conditions to pursue what we might call first-order care. Without such second-order concern, caring will lack the "moral validation that makes a practice *fully* normative." This point is related to another key feature of her account of care, which concerns attending to what she refers to as "people's CARES"; she means by this term "those things people care about, which figure in their flourishing and in the case of persons who need care, they cannot accomplish without the proper assistance." Attending to people's cares offers an example of caring about care, for it keeps us alert and attentive to creating and preserving the conditions and environment required to perform acts of first-order care. This not only honors care as our supreme and organizing good, but also keeps in focus the importance of interpersonal connection, which is part of the conception of self associated with this expression of oneness. If we recognize the priority of care, we accept the priority of relationships as constitutive of the self and will work to preserve conditions and environments conducive to such relationships as well as the particular relationships we are in.

Drawing upon her extensive and inspiring practice of care, Kittay goes on to explore another important but unrecognized dimension of caring: the ways in which the reception of care constitutes a critical part of the practice and how it completes care. The core claim here concerns what Kittay calls the "taking up of care." It is often thought that when we care for and benefit another, the recipient of our care is largely passive. This in fact is one of the reasons the reception of care often goes unnoticed. But in order for care to be "something we do *for* another's benefit" (as opposed to *to* them), it is something we must do "*with* their engagement." This feature of care distinguishes it from many other dispositions widely regarded as virtues. Caring is a distinctive type of activity. It requires that the agent providing care intend to care in a way attentive to the taking up of care; it also, though, requires that this care in fact be taken up by the recipient of care. This latter claim distinguishes Kittay's account from other theories of care; on her view, even the most well-directed and sincere effort to care is at best "partial" if not taken up by the recipient of care.

The fully normative account of care that Kittay describes and defends entails additional implications, which she points out and discusses in the closing sections of her essay. One of these involves a novel understanding of the notion of moral luck. More familiar conceptions of moral luck would accept the idea that many of the background or enabling conditions for care often involve luck: one needs the ability, resources, and opportunity to provide care. Kittay's account, though, which insists that even competent and sincerely offered care be taken up in order to be complete, entails an additional dimension of moral luck; care givers must enjoy good fortune in order for the care they offer to be received by the cared-for. This need for the reception of care leads to a final implication: whether there exists an obligation to receive care. Kittay argues that there is such an obligation, though it is limited to cases of appropriately offered care. Such an obligation is warranted "because refusing care when it is offered in good faith and with requisite competence is harmful, both to myself and to the carer." One might add that refusing such care fails to honor the imperative to care for care, for it almost certainly harms the conditions within which care can be offered.

Kittay's contribution to this collection of essays offers a trenchant and highly stimulating account of care and particularly care in regard to cases of dependency. She makes a compelling case that such dependency extends far beyond human relationships, "to the air we breathe, the water we drink, the food we consume, the animals and creatures who share the world with us." In light of such dependency, care is called for as a fundamental moral stance with universal application, founded in a view of the self as inextricably interdependent and one with the people, creatures, and things of the entire world.

Mark Unno contributes the seventh essay in our collection, "Oneness and Narrativity: A Comparative Case Study," in which he explores the relevance of conceptions of oneness within the narrative context of human life, a theme or ideal that informs and guides a person's story. This narrative approach to oneness not only enables us to see how this concept is enacted and made real in the course of different human lives but also allows us to examine some of the similarities and differences manifested in these variations on the shared theme.

Unno carefully presents and analyzes three contemporary first-person narratives for examination: one Zen Buddhist, one Pure Land Buddhist, and one Protestant Christian. The Zen Buddhist narrative describes the life path of an Irish American woman, Maura O'Halloran (1955–82), who went to study Zen Buddhism in a rural area of northern Japan. The Pure Land Buddhist narrative presents the story of a Japanese man, Shinmon Aoki (b. 1937), who, through a series of unanticipated events, finds himself making his living as a mortician, which, even more unexpectedly, ushers him on a journey that leads to Pure Land Buddhist awakening. The third and final narrative, that of a Protestant Christian, is the tale of Michael Morton (b. 1954), who after being wrongfully convicted of murder, spends nearly twenty-five years in prison, which leads him to embark upon a journey toward faith and to encountering the light of the Divine.

In each of these narratives, some element of the protagonist's dominant master narrative proves oppressive or inadequate, generating counterstories that retell, alter, or overturn it. The emergence of these counterstories hinges on critical junctures or turning points where a personal realization of oneness either erupts from "deep within" or descends from a "higher power." In the first case he explores, Maura O'Halloran sought a way to free herself from the master narrative of free-market capitalism in the global economy, which she found wholly unfulfilling. She set out on a different and demanding path, pursuing a three-year period of intensive Zen practice at Kannonji in rural Iwate Prefecture, Japan. After a prolonged and strenuous course of study, practice, and reflection, she was recognized as an awakened teacher; she fully realized the distinctive Zen understanding of oneness, the state where "'ought' issues spontaneously from 'is'-ness," as well as that great compassion "is the self-expression of the practitioner's own self-identity as inseparable from the world." Unno explores other dimensions of her life narrative and how it served as a vehicle for the expression of oneness by discussing and analyzing her struggles with the male-dominated, patriarchal culture of the Zen monastery at Kannonji, poignantly described in *Pure Heart, Enlightened Mind*, a collection of her journals and letters. This adds further richness, texture, and nuance to the story of her exemplary life and our understanding of oneness.

The next narrative, that of Shinmon Aoki, author of the memoir *Coffinman*, turns around the more lay-oriented Shin tradition of Pure Land Buddhism, the largest sectarian development of Japanese Buddhism, which focuses on the dynamic between blind passions and boundless compassion or foolish being and Amida Buddha. As a young man, Aoki finds himself facing the collapse of his business and with a family to support. Having few prospects, he answers a vaguely worded help-wanted ad, only to find out after accepting the job that it was for mortuary service, cleaning and dressing corpses for funerals. Shin Buddhism has made a special effort to embrace those on the margins of society, subject to prejudice because of "impure" livelihoods, such as morticians. And so, through the turning of fate, Aoki finds himself excluded by society's master narrative, pushing him to develop his own counterstory that resonates with and finds support and fulfillment in the Pure Land tradition.

One day, Aoki's practice leads him to a situation that holds great dread but proves to be of singular spiritual significance: he is asked to perform a coffining procedure at the home of his former girlfriend. Prospectively mortified to appear before her in this capacity, Aoki instead finds her deeply appreciative of him and his work. She becomes the conduit for boundless compassion, embracing him, a foolish being, just as he is. This acceptance and embrace lead him to see and embrace others and to understand and appreciate the work he does in a wholly different light, seeing it—and his own dignity and worth—for the first time. Aoki's story presents multiple visions of oneness that "break through the conventional or master narrative of social expectations, and . . . empower Aoki to propel his self-narrative."

In 1986, Michael Morton was wrongly convicted of his wife's murder and separated from his three-year-old son, and he spent the next twenty-five years of his life in prison. It was only because of DNA evidence produced through the work of the Innocence Project that his conviction finally was overturned, and he was released from prison. The tragic course of his incarceration and struggle, however, led him to discover and embrace a greater truth and brighter light, the truth and light of the Divine, which he experienced one night in the darkness of his prison cell: "What I had seen and felt and heard was divine light—and divine love—and the presence of a power that I had sought, in one way or another, all my life." This miraculous turning point in Morton's life was preceded and precipitated by a great deal of suffering and a bottoming-out, reaching the point of having been ground down and worn away, standing without any sense of power or hope on the edge and staring into the abyss. In that moment the experience of being bathed in the oneness of the divine light gave Morton the strength to endure and to forgive; it freed him from the master narrative that had consumed him and everything he had held dear and opened up a new path for him to follow: a path that led him to freedom, redemption, and reconciliation. The counterstory he constructed, along with those of O'Halloran and Aoki, allows us to touch in imagination different manifestations of oneness and feel its palpable presence in these three remarkable lives.

In "Kant, Buddhism, and Self-Centered Vice," Bradford Cokelet argues that the Kantian conception of treating people as ends in themselves and not mere means, while offering us an important insight into moral behavior, cannot be adequately understood much less attained within a Kantian framework, and that Buddhist philosophy has resources that can help address such shortcomings. In order to achieve the goal of treating others as ends we need to begin with a substantive account of the ideal that, Cokelet suggests, "calls on us both to reach out to others in a positive way (to treat others as ends in themselves) and to exercise self-restraint in our interactions with others (to never treat them as mere means). . . . The ideal calls on us to act with both *love/devotion* and *respect*." A full account of the ideal of treating people as final ends will also describe and explain negative motivations or vices that obstruct the attainment of (and are ruled out by) the realization of this ethical ideal. Cokelet focuses on the first requirement and is particularly concerned with the positive aspect of the ideal, which calls on us to treat others as ends in themselves by acting out of love or devotion. His view, roughly, is that realizing the moral ideal of treating people as ends requires an agent to overcome self-centeredness and that, contrary to what the Kantian account implies, self-centered people cannot be perfectly morally motivated.

Cokelet develops a line of argument described and advanced by David W. Tien (2012) and Philip J. Ivanhoe (2017) that contends that self-centeredness is distinct from selfishness and that one can be problematically self-centered while acting altruistically. Among the insights he adds to this discussion is the general point that self-centered motivation is problematic primarily because it tends to involve an undue concern with getting or meriting approval, esteem, or pride. Inordinate concern with, or false beliefs about, the worth of one's self often is manifest in self-centered patterns of thought and behavior that can impede treating others as ends in themselves. Cokelet divides such inordinate concern into three categories, "self-centered attention, self-centered judgment, and self-centered interpersonal interaction," and then shows how each of these can seriously impede our ability to behave morally. For example, excessive self-centered attention will inhibit one's ability to empathize well simply because one will not notice others at all, how they are doing or what is happening to or with them. Some forms of self-centeredness lead to disrespect, others to failing to nurture healthy independence and confidence; in such cases, self-centeredness directly undermines the ideal of treating others as ends in themselves.

Self-centered people can fail to treat others as ends in themselves because they either fail to *respect* the other person's dignity or treat the person in a *loving* way. Cokelet draws upon Iris Murdoch's rich and productive example of a mother-in-law judging her daughter-in-law to make the case that Kant's moral philosophy lacks the resources needed to explain fully how such moral failures can occur. Kant claims that self-centered vice is motivated by an agent's concern for her own happiness and that respect for the law strikes down her self-conceit and thereby curbs her self-love. But Cokelet offers an interpretation of Murdoch's case in which the mother-in-law "nonetheless has a Kantian good will because she treats the daughter-in-law with respect and benevolently wishes that she ends up happy," which shows that "good Kantian moral motivation is insufficient for treating people as ends in themselves."

In the final section of his essay Cokelet takes up the challenge of showing how certain Buddhist insights into oneness, understood here in terms of an appreciation of the true empty nature of both self and world, can help overcome self-centeredness. Roughly, his argument is that Buddhist insight into oneness undermines the efficacy of—and may even succeed in eliminating—those self-interpreting emotions that support the kind of self-centered vice he has identified in the course of his study. This is achieved through a variety of related paths having to do with Buddhist claims about the limitations of one's propositional understanding of oneself and the world and Buddhist arguments aimed at undermining a clear sense of a separately existing self. Buddhism is famous for its assault on the notion of a separately existing self and its general claim about the impermanence of all existing things, and Cokelet presents a compelling case that versions of these claims can serve us well in undermining a pernicious tendency toward self-centeredness and enabling us to attain the noble goal of treating others as ends in themselves.

Whereas most of the essays highlight the positive potential in oneness, Kendy M. Hess's "Fractured Wholes: Corporate Agents and Their Members," questions such a too-ready acceptance of oneness as tending toward the good. As she puts the point, "There are ways of forming wholes, of 'being one' that are not wholesome, and these are increasingly common and increasingly problematic." Her particular concern is the way that people come or are brought together to form collective, corporate agents. Such aggregation often produces large, powerful, efficient, and productive entities, but too often such agents are indifferent to the harm associated with their self-organization. She is careful to point out that there is no necessary connection between the formation of corporate agents and bad results; to the contrary, one of her primary points is to alert us to the potential hazards and urge us to create "'wholesome wholes' rather than the incomplete and fractured wholes we've usually created thus far."

Hess begins by sketching an account of what it is to be a collective agent that engages in action-expressing shared intentions. Such shared intentions are needed to establish the kind of agency and responsibility that distinguishes robust examples of such agents from mere groups. The members of a team usually share a number of important beliefs, commitments, and aims that help to organize and execute their collective behavior in ways that a crowd of people waiting to get into a concert do not. There are, however, collective agents—Hess refers to these as "corporate agents"—that do not share commitments or intentions in this way. (For example, the members of a modern corporation, university, or state, while governed by a shared set of commitments, need not and often do not personally hold the commitments by which they are governed and that inform and direct the action of the corporation or firm to which they belong. Often, in fact, the members of such organizations have personal commitments that conflict with those of the corporate entity to which they belong and for which they work.) And so, "the unity of a corporate agent is not the intimate, internal unity of most collective endeavor, driven by the distinctive, shared commitments of their members. . . . A corporate agent is not . . . bound by the commitments of the members and closely linked to the members' own goals and preferences." Such agents are what she calls "fractured wholes," entities that are unified from the outside or top-down rather than the inside or bottom-up.

The members of such organizations almost all have to adapt in order to fit into the preexisting structure, ethos, and aims of the corporation, and often are asked to leave many of their personal commitments and aims "at the door" while taking on its values, commitments, and style of reasoning. As Hess describes this, "the 'fractured wholes' of the title comprise 'fractured selves.' The members of corporate agents need to sever (or at least repress) those aspects of themselves that run counter to the corporate project . . . bringing only that part of the self that fits with and is valued by the corporate agent." This is where we begin to see the potential for moral hazard and in particular a threat to healthy versions of personal and social unity or oneness; anyone working in such a corporation must abandon the hope of harmonizing many of her basic values and commitments with the work that she performs each day. In many cases, she will find her personal values and commitments in deep conflict with those of the organization for which she works. This harms and may destroy any sense of personal unity or oneness and preclude enjoying the kind of psychic harmony that has been valued across a variety of philosophical and religious traditions. Moreover, there is equal threat to the aim of attaining some kind of unity between the corporation and the larger society and world. If a corporate agent acts hermetically sealed off not only from the values and commitments of its constituent members but also from those of those outside the corporation, it may and probably will often find itself in conflict with the values, commitments, and aims of society at large and perhaps humanity in general. Such conflict does not conduce to the health of the corporation any more than to that of those inside or outside of it.

In her conclusion, Hess sketches some possible response to the problems she has described and analyzed in the course of her work. She makes a good case for steering clear of more utopian approaches that seek to find a way to preserve the complete wholeness of individuals who enter into such corporate entities or that hope to reshape and refine the corporate cultures in ways that bring them into complete harmony with the rest of the world. Among other things, the former approach would undermine the organizational capacity and efficiency of corporations in ways that largely defeat their very purpose; the latter would damage the capacity of corporations to set and pursue the more limited goals, which gives them their reasons to exist. Such efforts undercut the need for individuals to, at times, suspend their personal agendas and join in cooperative ventures with others whose values and commitments they do not share, which is an important aspect of life in a pluralistic democratic society. In different ways, the aim of excessive harmony or oneness is harmful and arguably even more harmful than the current state of affairs. Instead, Hess advocates pursuing a more ameliorative approach that aims to respect the personal or private but allows for, protects, and appreciates the impersonal corporate point of view as well. Her contribution highlights some of the potential dangers of conceptions of oneness while making clear that there are healthy conceptions of oneness that not only can accommodate but also see value in tensions they allow.

In "Religious Faith, Self-Unification, and Human Flourishing in James and Dewey," Michael R. Slater compares the religious philosophies of James and Dewey with particular attention to their respective views on religious faith, self-unification, and human flourishing. Slater argues that both philosophers endorsed a version of the oneness hypothesis, understood broadly in terms of two claims: "first, human beings are capable of realizing a more expansive sense of self by making connection with, and understanding their personal identity as inextricably intertwined with, an object of faith that exceeds and transcends themselves (a descriptive claim); and second, that realizing an expanded sense of self of this kind is an important, and possibly even an essential, ingredient in human flourishing at both the individual and social levels (a normative claim)." Slater goes on to argue that the differences in their respective accounts of oneness arise primarily from differences in their metaphysical commitments and epistemological theories but that both have important insights to offer "about the relationship between religious faith and the widespread human longing for happiness and a sense of wholeness."

James is well known for insisting that religion is primarily a practical as opposed to theoretical affair with the basically therapeutic aim of providing happiness—understood not hedonically but in terms of human well-being or flourishing. This helps us understand his deep study and broad use of psychology and why he saw this as essential for addressing the question of the nature and role of religion in human life. His research and reflection led him to conclude that religion plays an important role in human happiness (a claim supported by a great deal of contemporary empirical research), that this is the result of people achieving a proper relationship with an "unseen order" or a transcendent higher power that is concerned about human happiness, and that these shared features of religion are equally present in and accessible through a variety of different traditions and experiences. The nature of the proper relation between the self and the transcendent brings us to James's conception of oneness; he thought what is needed is to identify with a higher "wider self" that incorporates the transcendent within the everyday or ordinary self. This is where James parts company with those who insist on a strict naturalism; he defended a limited appeal to the supernatural. As Slater is careful to note, though, his defense of piecemeal supernaturalism is made indirectly, on the basis of the practical importance such beliefs have in the actual lives of religious people.

Dewey argued for a wholly naturalistic conception of faith on pragmatic grounds: in terms of its power to unify the self and to strengthen commitment to a set of secular moral values and ideals. He sought to locate such faith in the territory between traditional religious belief and militant atheism by rejecting what he took to be their common focus on supernaturalism. In other words, he sought to shear supernatural claims from religion but retain what he rightly saw as the power religion has to give unity, shape, meaning, and moral direction to life. For Dewey religious faith is the expression of a strong commitment to worthy ideal ends. Such a commitment takes as its object a not-wholly-specified and open-ended moral vision, which stands in place of traditional theistic teachings about God. Dewey claimed this secular faith has the power to bring unity to the self, to connect the self with the rest of humanity and ultimately with the rest of the world. This is a sketch of the nature and function of Dewey's ideal of oneness between the self and other people, creatures, and things.

One profound challenge for Dewey's ideal, ironically, concerns the pragmatic force of his secular substitute for God. As Slater insightfully notes, "an idea of God all by itself does not plausibly have the power that Dewey wants to ascribe to it, any more than the idea of Batman all by itself could frighten criminals or make a large city a safer place to live." Just as James's defense of piecemeal supernaturalism tends to leave confirmed naturalists underwhelmed and perhaps bemused, Dewey's secular God will strike most religiously inclined people as hollow and uninspiring; Dewey promises a great show and sets an impressive stage, but in the end no one shows up to perform the main act. This by no means implies that his or James's view is without considerable merit, insight, or force. Slater's comparative study makes clear that they have much to teach us and that among the most interesting and powerful shared feature of both James's and Dewey's writings on faith and human flourishing is the critical role that conceptions of oneness play in their respective accounts.

Professor Cho Geung Ho provides our next contribution, "The Self and the Ideal Human Being in Eastern and Western Philosophical Traditions: Two Types of 'Being a Valuable Person,'" which offers a far-ranging exploration of cultural differences in terms of two contrasting conceptions of the relationship between individuals and their societies: the culture of individualism, which is the cultural type dominant in North America, Oceania, and Northern Europe, and the culture of collectivism, which is dominant in East Asian countries. Professor Cho argues that these alternative conceptions of the relationship between individuals and their societies have led to different concepts of self-hood and worldview, and to contrasting schemes of personal character and behavior among those raised and living within these respective cultures.

Professor Cho pursues two primary lines of arguments in his contribution. First, he maintains that the cultural differences just sketched between Western individualism and East Asian collectivism have their ideological roots in liberalism and Confucianism, respectively. Second, he seeks to show that Western liberalism and East Asian Confucianism develop and advocate characteristic and contrasting ideals for being a human being. These contrasting ideals in turn lead to different accounts of what is valuable in life and different conceptions of what constitutes a good person in each of these two cultural spheres.

In arguing that the culture of individualism offers the philosophical underpinnings of Western liberalism, Professor Cho defends the very strong claim that such a liberal point of view "is a system of thought that attempts to find human ontological significance in the individuality of persons who are independent and have clear boundaries from one another." He further claims that such a system of thought entails an eliminative reductionism in regard to social phenomenon resulting in the view that "society is no more than an aggregate of independent and equal individuals." In stark contrast, Professor Cho claims that collectivism provides the dominant character of East Asian societies. In this case, the correlate of Western liberalism is Confucianism, "a theoretical system whose goal is to find human ontological significance in the sociality of a person." Drawing upon a particular interpretation of the Confucian self, Professor Cho asserts that persons exist within Confucian societies only in terms of their social relations; "outside of such relations, the person loses her very ontological significance." This seems to imply not only that there is no person apart from social relationship but also that society is not an "aggregate of independent and equal individuals" but a collection of instantiated social relationships.

The contrast between Western liberalism and East Asian Confucianism supports and generates a range of differences in their respective understandings of what a human being is and what the ideal human being might be. According to Professor Cho one important difference that connects views about what a person is and can be concerns whether human beings are *stable entities* or *variable beings*. The former seems to be the view that human beings have fixed and unchanging characteristics, while the latter is that each human being "is in a constant process of changing." The precise meaning of these alternatives is not altogether clear, but at the very least the former seems to imply that people are destined to live out a particular, preassigned character and personality in the course of their lives, while the latter highlights the ongoing challenge of developing and improving oneself in the quest to realize an ideal of human goodness.

Western liberalism conceives of each and every person as free and the bearer of rights, a view that engenders and prizes attitudes such as personal independence and autonomy and focuses on the individual person's inner qualities. Professor Cho argues that this leads to more self-centered psychological and behavioral characteristics that emphasize individual uniqueness and independent action. East Asian Confucianism understands individuals in terms of their particular social relationships and Confucian societies generate and prize attitudes such as caring and harmony. As a consequence, such collectivist societies highlight and advocate emotions such as compassion, sympathy, and a sense of shame, which support and engender the building of interpersonal relationships.

Professor Cho explores other dimensions of the individualistic (Western liberal) and collectivist (East Asian Confucian) ideals he describes and concludes by discussing the degree to which such cultural differences determine one's conception of what is valuable in life and what constitutes a good person. It would of course be wrong to assume that one's cultural context determines one's values and ideals; some born and raised in Confucian cultures are more individualistic and some born in Western liberal cultures are more collectivist in orientation and action, and "Cultural differences only reflect average differences between cultures." Nevertheless, the cultural differences Professor Cho has identified, analyzed, and discussed are real and significant.

In his concluding remarks, Professor Cho poses the question of the future of the individualist and collectivist ideals he has explored. In an increasingly global and interconnected world, where ideas, values, and practices flow more quickly and widely around the world, one might be inclined to believe that such cultural differences will be mitigated over time, as cultures increasingly blend into one another and "*converge* somewhere in the middle." This is surely one possibility, but other scenarios are equally in play; for example, one or another of the two ideal types might absorb or come to dominate the other. Alternatively, societies that represent one or the other of the two ideals might hold more tightly to their distinctive ways of life or, perhaps, individuals or groups within one or another cultural type might choose or adopt or adapt the alternative view and make it their own.

In "Hallucinating Oneness: Is Oneness True or Just a Positive Metaphysical Illusion?," Owen Flanagan begins by noting some recent arguments, declarations, and initiatives dedicated to the goal of achieving what Pope Francis called a "global ecological *conversion*," in which "the oneness and indivisibility of the natural, social, and spiritual realms is fully recognized and then acted upon." Flanagan offers a novel approach to such proposals by considering—as the title of his contribution makes clear—the possibility of embracing oneness as a positive illusion: a false (or probably false) belief that brings with it good features or consequences. The chances that one will contract some debilitating disease or suffer a severe accident are what they are, but it matters, in terms of one's psychological state of mind and the myriad consequences that follow from this, whether one thinks that the good or bad objective probabilities apply to one. To think the former may be wishful thinking but tends to produce a better life for one and those around one: "positive illusions are epistemically negative, but existentially positive."

Flanagan distinguishes between metaphysical illusions and metaphysical hallucinations. Metaphysical illusions involve "false beliefs about *Being*, about *What There Is*, which have good existential effects." In contrast, metaphysical hallucinations involve "an altered state of consciousness in which the shape of reality and the structure of values are envisioned in a fantastical but entirely appealing and transformative way." There is good evidence to support the claim that certain metaphysical illusions can lead to greater good for individuals and groups, but something stronger—something along the lines of a metaphysical hallucination—seems necessary in order to "mark, announce, or motivate the life of a bodhisattva, or a Christian saint, or make possible the sort of grass roots global ecological *conversion* Pope Francis seeks." Flanagan explores the possibility that "'making believe' that certain metaphysical theses that pertain to oneness . . . that are false are true or, what is different, are worth aiming at, committing to, trying to make so."

Buddhism, in general, holds that people do not exist as separate and sub-sisting things but instead are intimately interrelated to all sentient beings through a comprehensive and infinitely extending system of causes and effects mediated through karma and stretching over a myriad of lifetimes. If we see ourselves and our relationships to other people and creatures in such terms, we will see the folly of self-centeredness; in light of an accurate picture of *Being* and *What There Is*, we will see ourselves as in some deep sense identical to all sentient beings and as a result will take up and practice great compassion and loving kindness to all. This brief account offers a sketch of the relationship between a belief in oneness and a life of compassion and loving kindness, illustrating the more general linkage one often finds between metaphysics and ethics.

Flanagan makes clear that to move from grasping the intellectual proposi-tions constituting the Buddhist view in no-self—a view that is held for the most part by Western philosophers such as David Hume, Derek Parfit, and Galen Strawson as well—to living a life of compassion and loving kindness requires a form of "noetic confidence" in the truth of the view described: "believing that *no-self* is false is compatible with thinking it good to believe (or as I should say 'make-believe') in *no-self*, and that it is even better, morally good, to hallucinate *no-self*, and then to live as if the hallucination was true." Embracing no-self is necessary if one is to successfully live the kind of life that such a view seems to imply. The question, though, is whether one needs the reasons provided by the truth of the metaphysical view in order to generate and sustain the ethical life with which it is aligned.

Things are more complicated even than this for, as Flanagan notes, there are many different conceptions of oneness even within Buddhism. He describes five possible interpretations of Buddhist-like oneness, with each making a stronger or weaker claim for metaphysical identity or connection between self and world. (Even the weakest of these, *care oneness*, which holds that we "naturally care . . . about the weal and woe of others," works to undermine self-centeredness, offering what we might describe as a "less myself" rather than "no-self" view.) None of these five, though, provide what is needed to support a life of compassion and loving kindness, for none entails that "my well-being is ONE with the fate of the universe." This highly robust form of oneness, what Flanagan tags as ONENESS*, is characteristic of religious views that link a metaphysical view of oneness with a heroic obligation to care for all the world. A question remains: Would it be good to hallucinate one's way to such a view and be able to live such a life?

Flanagan gives several examples where believing in views one deems false or highly likely to be false seems to have nothing but upside, and he notes that work in contemplative neuroscience and renewed research on hallucinogens at several leading medical centers (as part of their whole life treatment of terminally ill patients) appear to offer evidence in support his view. Yet it is important to appreciate the radical nature of his proposal, which, as he makes clear, goes beyond the ethics of belief (or right to believe) espoused by people like Clifford or James. Flanagan is proposing an existentially more strident alternative. At the very least, Flanagan's bold excursion challenges the traditional linkage between metaphysics and ethics and presses us to consider the possibility that the latter should inform or at least influence the former. This line of argument might lead one to think more about, and draw upon, Freud's helpful distinction between illusions and delusions (Yearley 1985).

According to Freud, an illusion differs from a simple error in two ways: illusions are derived from human wishes and are not necessarily contrary to reality (though they can be). More importantly, they are beneficial to oneself and those around one. In contrast, it is part of the essence of delusions that they conflict with reality and prove harmful to oneself and others. Freud was an avid advocate of the power of art and its role in good human lives, and of course art is a clear example of an edifying illusion. By contrast, Freud considered religion an infantile and largely debilitating illusion best banished from awareness or rendered impotent in ordering and motivating our beliefs and actions.

Now there are reasons, some along the lines provided by Flanagan, to take issue with Freud's view (Ivanhoe 1998). But if we are to save religion or versions of the oneness hypothesis from being delusions, we need to ground them at least to some extent in reality. Perhaps the best illusions will always involve some connection to actual states of affairs and will enlarge, extend, or embellish a feature or features of the world in ways that preserve some sense of reality within a symbolic or metaphoric expression that conduces to the human good. Perhaps even our wildest hallucinations (like all acts of imagination) can't but be grounded *at some level* in our experience of the real world. Or perhaps we should simply not remain tethered to the world but embrace metaphysical hallucinations, according to which "the shape of reality and the structure of values are envisioned in a fantastical but entirely appealing and transformative way." Whether such are good or bad may depend more or simply on the range of their application and the nature of the good they provide and not whether or to what degree they are connected to actual states of affairs.

One common theme across the contributions just discussed is that self-centeredness can interfere with a person's having such a more expansive conception of the self, or experiencing oneness. This continues in "Episodic Memory and Oneness," where Jay Garfield, Shaun Nichols, and Nina Strohminger discuss how Buddhism has traditionally tried to undermine "egocentricity," or the tendency to focus on oneself. Their contribution begins by outlining the views of the eighth-century Buddhist philosopher Śāntideva on moral progress.

Śāntideva notes that before one has realized the emptiness of the self (and, indeed, of all phenomena) one's "cognitive and conative states are still pervaded by an instinctive ego-grasping that she or he nonetheless knows—at a more reflective level—to be deluded." Put another way, coming to an inferential or "merely cognitive" understanding of the truth of no-self and the emptiness of all phenomena is by itself insufficient to dislodge one from egocentricity. The latter is only possible through direct realization or immediate awareness of these truths, after which one can start to give up the idea that one matters more than others and begin to see oneself as part of a greater whole. The process begins with an aspiration to see the world as it really is, and only ends when one directly experiences it as such.

Garfield, Nichols, and Strohminger go on to argue that at the heart of ego-centricity is a particular form of memory—namely, episodic memory or memory of experiences. "It's widely thought that when a person remembers an experience, she remembers the experience as having happened to *her*. Theorists in both Eastern and Western traditions maintain that episodic memory involves representing an event as having happened to one's *self*. The memory has to present the experience as having happened to *me*." They note the prevalence of this idea in thinkers ranging from Thomas Reid, James Mill, and William

James, on the one hand, to such Indian philosophers as Uddyotakara (of the Nyaya school) and Dignāga (a Buddhist), on the other, before pointing out that "there are within the Buddhist tradition conceptual resources for understanding episodic memory in the absence of self or of self-consciousness"—for example, in the teachings of Candrakīrti and Śāntideva in India and Tsongkhapa in Tibet. This is because one can think of an *organism*-centered egocentricity, as opposed to a *self*-centered egocentricity. Rats, plausibly, have organism-centered egocentricity, including egocentric spatial memory and recollection; representations are relative to the position of the rat as an organism, even without having any representation of the rat as a self. So even though episodic or experiential memory may inevitably be egocentric, this may not run afoul of the view that there is no self, because "Buddhists, like those in many other philosophical traditions, reject the idea that the organism is the self."

The problem, then, is not egocentricity, but rather how the self is interjected into memory during the process of recollection. "The real problem posed by experience memory . . . is that when we *reflect* on our experiences—something rats can't do—we naturally represent the experiences as having happened to the self . . . as an experience that happened to *me*." Buddhists, of course, hone in on this problem and recommend that we rid ourselves of the illusion of the self. But is this possible? Here, Garfield, Nichols, and Strohminger draw on empirical studies suggesting that it is indeed possible to recall experiences without identifying with them (that is, thinking of them as having happened to oneself) under certain conditions, and suggest that there may be legitimacy to the classical Buddhist strategies to rid one of the notion of a self—for example, through analysis and meditation. However, more recent and targeted work on Tibetan monks suggests a potential stumbling block: despite denying the reality of the self and saying that this realization helped them cope with death, these advanced Buddhist practitioners nonetheless showed great fear of death and pronounced selfishness in wanting to extend their own lives, especially when compared to Christians and Hindus. Garfield, Nichols, and Strohminger try to explain this unexpected empirical result by highlighting the stubborn recalcitrance of identity in episodic memory and the sustained effort required to overcome it, using examples drawn from autobiographies of advanced Tibetan practitioners to illustrate the point. They conclude that, "although it might be possible to have experience memories without the sense of personal identity, this seems to be a remarkably difficult feat to accomplish in an enduring way."

Several of the essays just discussed advert to notions of relational or collective selves as being ways by which to think of oneness, or more expansive notions of the self. This theme continues in "Confucius and the Superorganism," where Hagop Sarkissian articulates a particular sense of oneness that he finds operative in early Confucian thought. It is a sense of oneness that, he argues, is accessible to many persons today, as accepting it requires no commitment to any demanding metaphysical or spiritual views. It is not a sense of oneness with all of humanity, let alone with all the creatures under the sky or all the elements of the cosmos. Instead, it is a sense of oneness that stems from the existence of large, coherent, and interconnected social networks.

Sarkissian takes as his starting point a passage in the *Analects* suggesting that the *dao* of the founding sage kings of the Zhou Dynasty (mythical heroes long since dead) remains embedded within the people of Confucius's home state of Lu (the cultural inheritor of the Zhou). Drawing on this and other passages, Sarkissian claims that the people of the state of Lu comprise a latent superorganism—a term he borrows from social and natural sciences. However, this superorganism remains scattered, disorganized, and unrealized, for it lacks a central node through which it may become organized and coherent. Confucius plays precisely this role, facilitating the revival of the Zhou superorganism by threading it together. Confucius both is constituted by the larger Zhou superorganism (in the sense of being embedded, shaped, and connected with it) and constitutes it in turn (by being a central node through which its culture, practices, and ethos flow).

The superorganism, then, consists of a large social network, including all the connections and ties within it. The nodes of the network are the individual selves, and constitute both particular points *upon* which the forces of the larger network impinge and particular points *from* which various forces emanate. These forces can be understood as behaviors, norms, and information, as well as moods, dispositions, and other forms of affect. They spread from one node to another (also known as dyadic spread), but also continue to influence other nodes several links away (also known as hyperdyadic spread). Sarkissian relates these ideas back to some central passages in other key Confucian texts such as the *Daxue* (or Great Learning). He also argues that the classical Confucian concept of *de*, which refers to the particular ways in which individuals influence others in their midst through noncoercive, effortless ways, can be fruitfully compared to the ways in which nodes influence one another in the networks within which they're embedded.

Sarkissian argues that this helps us understand the great importance placed on the ruler in early Confucian thought. He points out that "one of the fundamental axioms of network theory is that the opportunities and constraints of any particular node—the degree to which it is both susceptible to network effects and susceptible of affecting the network—hinges on its *position* within the network." The ruler, being at the center of the superorganism, is positioned to have enormous effects on it, and so the power of the ruler to shape the polity (as emphasized in several early Confucian texts) can be explained by his central position, from which he had tremendous potency. A ruler's *de* influences his senior ministers, who in turn affect their subordinates, engendering a resonant chain that would extend out to villages and clans. Through his own personal excellence, and owing to his centrality, the ruler would thus bind the network together.

Sarkissian concludes by suggesting the utility in thinking of oneself as a node of influence on one's own network, and the importance of minding the ways in which one might be both influenced by it while also being a source of influence within it. A paradigmatic way of influencing others is, of course, through discrete, volitional actions. However, this corresponds to a very narrow conception of agency and a very strict and unrealistic conception of the boundaries between individuals. A more expansive notion suggests it is naïve to think that influence consists merely in such acts. Instead, influence across networks occurs automatically and effortlessly; one cannot be a node without shaping the network to some extent or other, even while being subject to influence in turn.

The relationship between death and oneness is explored again in the following chapter. In "Death, Self, and Oneness in the Incomprehensible Zhuangzi," Eric Schwitzgebel portrays the ancient Chinese philosopher Zhuangzi as having an "incomprehensible" view, that is, a view so loaded with contradiction that it defies coherent, rational interpretation. Schwitzgebel's Zhuangzi is a philosopher who openly shares his confusions and shifting opinions, inviting us to join him as he plunges into wonder and doubt, including wonder and doubt about what constitutes the boundaries of the self.

On the question of death, Schwitzgebel argues that Zhuangzi embraces three inconsistent ideas: (1) that living out one's full life span is a good thing and preferable to dying young, (2) that living out one's full life span is not preferable to dying young, and (3) that we cannot know whether living out one's full life span is preferable to dying young. All three of these views appear to be advocated more than once in the text, and although there are various ways in which they might be reconciled (including attributing the relevant passages to different authors who separately contributed to the text we now know as the *Zhuangzi*), Schwitzgebel argues that the passages have a similarity of voice, style, and vision. Although when reading most of the great philosophers in history it makes sense to attempt to render passages consistent with one another when possible, even if superficially they seem to conflict, this interpretative principle should not, Schwitzgebel says, be extended to the particular case of Zhuangzi. Both the content of the text and facts about style and presentation suggest that if any philosopher is OK with expressing contradictory views in different passages, it should be Zhuangzi. Schwitzgebel recommends that we relish, rather than attempt to resolve, Zhuangzi's inconsistency.

One advantage of this interpretive approach is that it allows the reader to take Zhuangzi's sometimes radical-seeming claims at face value, without having to tame them to render them consistent with his more moderate-seeming claims—and also without treating Zhuangzi's radical claims as fixed dogmas. (Interpreted as such, they might be indefensible.) We can instead treat the radical ideas as "real possibilities" worth entertaining, without taking those possibilities too seriously. For example, one of the many quirky sage-like figures in Zhuangzi's text speculates that after his death he might become a mouse's liver or a bug's arm. Schwitzgebel interprets this as a humorous, colorful way of imagining that after one's bodily death one might find one's consciousness continuing in some other form, perhaps in some other part of nature. Even without positive evidence for such continuation, we can entertain it as a real possibility. And doing so might help us break out of our ordinary assumptions, creating a more vivid and skeptical sense of the possibilities.

Schwitzgebel's portrayal of Zhuangzi feeds into the oneness hypothesis as follows. The ordinary reader might enter the Zhuangzi with an ordinary set of suppositions about the boundaries of the self: I begin at my birth; I end at my death; I am essentially a human being; my hands and feet are part of me but the trees and rivers and people in Yue and Chu are not part of me. Maybe the reader is hyperindividualistically committed to a picture of the self as entirely distinct from everything else, or maybe the reader is only a moderate individualist. In reading the text, the reader encounters radical possibilities presented nondogmatically, in a charming way: I might wake to find that all of what I took to be normal life was in fact a dream; I might die and become a mouse's liver; my feet are no more or less a part of me than the people in Yue and Chu; human form is just a temporary manifestation that I should be happy enough to give away. If Zhuangzi is successful, he induces doubt and wonder, shaking the reader's commitment to individualism, opening the reader to the possibility of a more radical oneness, or at least to the possibility of a moderate view with a less sharp, fixed, and certain sense of the boundaries of the self than you had before.

"Identity fusion" is an important concept in social psychology that has been explored at length over the past decade in a series of papers by William B. Swann, Jr., and collaborators. In "Identity Fusion: The Union of Personal and Social Selves," Sanaz Talaifar and Swann synthesize this work along with work by other authors, exploring the history of the concept of identity fusion and the social and psychological importance of feeling "fused" with a social group. Like Putilin in his chapter, Talaifar and Swann see their work as partly growing out of classic work by Henri Tajfel, which showed that even nominal or trivial group memberships tend to trigger in-group/outgroup favoritism. One feature of Tajfel's view is that there is a competition between personal identities and social identities, so that attention to one's status as an individual tends to diminish attention to one's status as a member of a social group. The essential insight behind the concept of identity fusion is that the personal and social selves need not compete. To the extent that one's personal identity is "fused" with one's social identity, attention to one can harmonize with attention to the other. High commitment to a social group needn't require subjugating personal identity; instead, in identity fusion, the personal self "remains a potent force that combines synergistically with the social self to motivate behavior."

Strongly fused people identify intensely with a social group—for example, their nation. They feel a visceral sense of union, or oneness, with that group. They tend to agree with statements like "I am one with my group" or "I have a deep emotional bond with my group." When asked to select a depiction of their relationship to their group, they will favor pictures in which a circle representing the "self" and a circle representing the "group" are largely overlapping rather than separate or minimally overlapping.

As Talaifar and Swann detail, high levels of identity fusion predict a range of behaviors, including whether a person is likely to undergo gender reassignment surgery (higher fusion with the future gender predicting follow-through with surgery) and extreme pronational behaviors, including fighting and dying for one's country. Evidence from a variety of sources, including observation of combat troops and controlled studies using hypothetical scenarios, suggests that highly fused people tend to reason more intuitively, emotionally, and spontaneously than less-fused people when acting on behalf of their group. Talaifar and Swann suggest that part of the underlying explanation is that people who are highly fused tend to think of other members of their group as "fictive kin," thereby drawing upon well-known, evolutionarily selected psychological mechanisms that favor loyalty to and sacrifice for one's kin group.

Talaifar and Swann acknowledge that high levels of fusion are morally bivalent. High levels of fusion can lead both to heroic action and to extreme violence against outgroups. However, they conclude with the hopeful thought that people might expand the group with which they feel fused until eventually, ideally, it includes all of humanity, giving those people an emotionally powerful reason to work toward the good of everyone.

In "Tribalism and Universalism: Reflections and Scientific Evidence," Dimitri Putilin begins with the unambiguous—and disconcerting—results of research on in-group versus outgroup attitudes and behavior. Work by Henri Tajfel and others has shown that even ad hoc, arbitrarily established groups of people immediately behave preferentially toward their in-group and discriminate against the outgroup. Moreover, those within each group "expected outgroup members to behave as they did." In-group favoritism is the dominant and default form of behavior; fairness and care tend to operate only when dealing with members of one's in-group.

Many religious and philosophical teachings around the world offer a starkly opposing view, calling on us to have equal and universal concern for all others and not just for oneself and the members of one's in-group. This, in essence, is what the Golden Rule—a principle found throughout the various religious and philosophical traditions of the world—teaches. Putilin notes and is encouraged by the ubiquity of the Golden Rule, but is interested in the question of whether such advice is "plausible as a practical guide to behavior"; he seeks to answer this question by exploring some of the psychological abilities and barriers that are relevant to the effort to live according to this high-minded moral principle.

One of the first issues he examines is whether we are psychologically *able* truly to care about another's needs at all: Are we *capable* of genuinely altruistic behavior? C. Daniel Batson's research offers compelling evidence that human beings are capable of genuine altruism. Moreover, he shows that empathic concern, by which he means the emotional state of valuing the well-being of another who is in distress, is an important source for altruistic motivation. After presenting a detailed account of Batson's work and analyzing a number of its key features, Putilin summarizes this research: "Batson and his colleagues have successfully demonstrated that, when exposed to a person in need and instructed to consider how that person is feeling, people are more likely to value his or her well-being as an end in itself, to experience the emotional state of empathic concern, and to be increasingly willing to engage in helping behavior at a cost to themselves."

In response to Batson's research, R. B. Cialdini, J. K. Maner, and others have produced research that shows that the degree of kinship or perceived similarity between an observer and observed sufferer simultaneously increases empathic concern, helping behavior, and what they called "oneness" on the part of the observer. Arguing that such "oneness" constitutes a merging of observer and observed, they conclude that "by helping the victim the participants were in fact selfishly helping themselves." If their conclusion is valid, altruism is simply an illusion masking distinctive forms of selfish behavior. Putilin shows that this conclusion is unwarranted and for a number of overlapping reasons. First, a careful examination of the research shows that observing participants recognized "both the majority of their own identity and that of the victim as unique and separate from whatever it was they shared in common." In other words, there was a sense of deep connection but no complete merging of self and other. Second, even though participants came to see the victim's problems as to some extent their own, an important asymmetry remained: "the actual victim has no choice but to deal with the aversive circumstances in which she finds herself, the potential helper (that is, the participant) has the ability to walk away from the problem." Such asymmetry would not persist in cases of genuine merging between self and other.

While Putilin shows why we should reject some of the conclusions of the advocates of oneness, he maintains that they make a compelling case for the role of a sense of interdependence or oneness and care, for "although the motivation produced when we feel empathic concern for another is altruistic—that is, focused on increasing their well-being, rather than attaining some benefit for oneself—such motivation is most likely to arise when we are exposed to the suffering of another with whom we are interdependent: a member of the ingroup." Putilin explores a number of evolutionary advantages such a predisposition seems to offer but notes that such a disposition is neither inevitable nor ideal, since a "trait evolved under one set of conditions may become maladaptive when environmental circumstances change." In our increasingly global and interdependent world, we may need to work against our evolutionary inclinations—what Putilin calls our "disinclination to altruism with outsiders"—which is reinforced by a "misguided pragmatism" concerning our interests.

To address this, Putilin draws upon the work of William James, whose ideas are insightfully discussed by Michael R. Slater in chapter 10 of the present work. Specifically, James argued that our degree of closeness with others not only can fluctuate significantly over time but also is something we can influence and control. We are capable of expanding our sense of connection or oneness with other people, creatures, and things, and thereby transforming our initially tribal altruism so that it embraces "more universally inclusive ends." Putilin goes on to explore a number of techniques for achieving this more inclusive sense of care, including recategorization (the changing of group boundaries) and identity fusion (as described by Sanaz Talaifar and William B. Swann, Jr., in chapter 16 of this work).

Putilin concludes his contribution by providing justification for the more expansive view of the self and more capacious feeling of care just described. Roughly, he argues for a richer account of what constitutes well-being and concludes that "altruism may not be the optimal way of amassing material fortunes, but it provides wealth of a different kind." So, in the end a life of care reflects a form of enlightened self-interest, though one, perhaps, that is supported by a goal one cannot aim at directly; we must in some sense give up caring about a narrowly construed conception of the self and genuinely care for others in order to nurture and enjoy the goods associated with a greater self. Putilin goes on to describe how certain exemplary individuals—specifically Mahatma Gandhi and Martin Luther King, Jr.—seem to have advocated and lived in accordance with such an expanded sense of self or oneness and its corresponding imperative to care for all the world. The encouraging implication of his analysis and discussion of our psychological resources and limitations is "that the gulf between ourselves and . . . exceptional individuals . . . may not be as unbridgeable as it appears at first glance: it may be one of degree, rather than kind."

In "Two Notions of Empathy and Oneness," Justin Tiwald explores two forms of empathy and two conceptions of oneness and, drawing upon the writings of two neo-Confucian philosophers, relates these to the moral ideal of seeing oneself as part of a larger whole and the role this might play in supporting moral motivation and other-directed moral concern. The first type of empathy, in which one reconstructs the thoughts and feelings someone else has or might have, is "other-focused" or "imagine-other" empathy. The second type, "self-focused" or "imagine-self" empathy, involves imagining how one would think or feel were one in another person's place. Tiwald explains that the Song dynasty neo-Confucian philosopher Zhu Xi朱熹 (1130–1200) insisted that other-focused empathy is more virtuous or "benevolent" (*ren* 仁) than self-focused empathy, because self-focused empathy tends to undermine the sense of oneness with others, whereas Dai Zhen戴震 (1724–77) defended the superiority of self-focused empathy because, on the one hand, he rejected Zhu's metaphysical beliefs and, on the other, he relied instead on human psychology and anthropology as the basis for ethical concern.

Tiwald begins by noting that Zhu Xi understood "being one with a larger whole" in terms of "forming one body with Heaven, Earth, and the myriad things" and believed that contributing to and caring about "widespread life-production" make us one with other people, creatures, and things, and thus warrant seeing oneself as one with them. Tiwald is careful to make clear that for Zhu, it was by virtue of caring and contributing in this way that *we are one* with the people, creatures, and things of the world. Zhu explicitly rejected subtly different views, for example, that such caring and contributing are a natural consequence of being metaphysically one or that it is some unanalyzable brute fact and intuition.

Moreover, Tiwald explains that Zhu believed attaining a proper state of oneness "requires eliminating attachment to one's own interests as such, a primarily subtractive project directed at oneself, rather than the more constructive, bidirectional project of building relationships in which one becomes more attached to others in light of the fact that contributing to their well-being tends to enhance one's own."

Like Zhu Xi, Dai Zhen rejected more mystical accounts of oneness and believed we attain oneness by contributing to the widespread production of life. But Dai insisted that the role we play in nurturing life requires a special sense of mutual identity—"mutual nourishment" and "mutual growth." In contrast to the kind of self-abnegation advocated by thinkers like Zhu Xi, he insisted that we are united with others through mutually beneficial relationships. Dai also rejected the metaphysical picture underlying Zhu's notion of oneness, which held that oneness requires the recognition of a fundamental identity between our nature and the nature of others. On Zhu's view, oneness was in some sense a discovery, an insight into the underlying oneness already there in the universe; for Dai, oneness is an achievement, something we come to through sustained and concerted efforts at developing and embracing relationships of mutual fulfillment, seeing ourselves as contributing to life-production more generally, and coming to identify ourselves with the world and our inextricably shared welfare.

Tiwald next notes that neo-Confucians were interested in the relationship between their core virtue of benevolence (*ren* 仁) and a certain kind of empathic state described in ancient texts as *shu* 恕, a term and concept associated with Confucius's formulation of the Golden Rule: "Do not do to others as one wouldn't want done to oneself." While *shu* was widely regarded by neo-Confucians as the proper method for cultivating benevolence, it was also seen as falling short of benevolence itself. Zhu Xi believed that the principal difference between *shu* and the full virtue of benevolence is that when we rely on *shu*, we need to make the effort of comparing others to ourselves in order to elicit right feelings and motivations, whereas the fully benevolent need not make such effort or refer to themselves; their care for others flows freely, unencumbered by thoughts of themselves. A number of leading psychologists focusing on empathy, such as C. Daniel Batson, Ezra Stotland, and Martin Hoffman, distinguish these two forms of empathy using paired terms such as *imagine-self* and *imagine-other* or *self-focused* and *other-focused* empathy, and their research provides solid empirical support for this conceptual distinction.

In opposition to Zhu, Dai advocates self-focused empathy. Tiwald characterizes one of Dai's most important arguments by saying, "If we really want to use empathy to understand and be motivated to act upon the interests of others, we need to simulate not just their first-order desires for things like food and shelter, but their broader-scope and often higher-order desires that their lives go well in various respects." Since Zhu strongly implies that dwelling in this way on one's own needs and interests will undermine the effort to effectively adopt another's point of view, Tiwald offers a number of responses consistent with, and in defense of, Dai's view. First, he notes that at times "our own needs and interests converge with those of others, because we want what they want." Second, as Martin Hoffman has shown, while we often learn to empathize through perspective-taking, empathy can become automatic, and so it need not rely on adopting another point of view at all.

Tiwald summarizes and concludes his essay by expressing the hope that his description and analysis of two types of oneness and empathy in light of Zhu Xi and Dai Zhen's philosophy are sufficient "to elucidate the tremendous importance of these connections between feelings of oneness and the two kinds of empathy, and to show that there are historical resources that address these issues with great subtlety, subtlety unmatched by contemporary treatments of the issue."

* * *

Among the most fundamental and important points to be learned from this collection of essays is that one's conception of oneself is not something that simply can be discovered, like the orbit of a planet or the mass of a stone, but is instead the product of a range of biological and psychological facts about the needs and capacities of human beings in combination with culture, imagination, and reflective endorsement. There are many alternative conceptions of the self to be found in philosophy, religion, and psychology (Parfit 1986, Collins 1982, Gallagher 2011) and there are yet more to be crafted; among these are various conceptions of a more expansive self connected with the oneness hypothesis. Until recently, no one has sought to press the more general point about the open nature of the self or explore the implications of conceptions of oneness in a careful and systematic manner, with the aim of ascertaining whether such alternatives might prove more conducive to human well-being, their happiness, satisfaction, and fulfilment, and thereby perhaps more attractive as personal and cultural ideals.

This volume is part of a larger, ongoing project, *Eastern and Western Conceptions of Oneness, Virtue, and Happiness* (http://www6.cityu.edu.hk/ceacop /Oneness/index.html), supported by the John Templeton Foundation. The goal of the larger project is to explore what different fields of endeavor look like when pursued with a view about the self as organically and inextricably interrelated to other people, creatures, and things as opposed to proceeding, as they often do, with the assumption of hyperindividualism. We believe this will constitute a paradigm shift or at least an important and productive disruption to many disciplines in the humanities and social sciences. It seems eminently clear that *as a matter of fact*, throughout almost all of their history and much of their prior evolution, human beings have existed and understood themselves as deeply embedded in personal, familial, social, and cultural contexts, and as systematically related to other creatures and things—in other words, as in some sense "one" with the rest of the world (Lovejoy 1936, Wilson 1984, Kellert and Wilson 1993). Equally clear, as a matter of fact, human beings are inextricably embedded in complex relationships with other people, creatures, and things; no human being exists or can clearly conceive of herself apart from these different parts of the environment. One thought motivating this far-ranging exploration of the oneness hypothesis is that our most pressing moral, political, social, and spiritual problems often arise from trying to conceive of ourselves as wholly distinct and separate from the rest of the world and to live as if there were a sharp moral and metaphysical boundary between ourselves and other people, creatures, and things. To accept hyperindividualism as self-evident, metaphysically well-founded, or psychologically inevitable is simply untrue; indeed, as has been argued in this introduction and shown in many of the contributions to this volume, to deny certain senses of oneness—for example, to deny that we are partly constituted by our relationships to the other people, creatures, and things of this world—is not only to have a bad view of the self but also to have a false one.

References

Bakhtin, M. 1981. *The Dialogic Imagination*. Austin: University of Texas Press.

Bellah, Robert N. 2011. *Religion in Human Evolution: From the Paleolithic to the Axial Age*. Cambridge: Belknap Press of Harvard University Press.

Callicott, J. B. 1989. *In Defense of the Land Ethic: Essays in Environmental Philosophy*. Albany: State University of New York Press.

Chemero, Anthony. 2009. *Radical Embodied Cognitive Science*. Cambridge: MIT Press.

Cheng Hao 程顥 and Cheng Yí 程頤. 2004. *Er Cheng ji*二程集. Beijing: Zhonghua Shuju.

Collins, Steven. 1982. *Selfless Persons*. Cambridge: Cambridge University Press.

Dewey, James. 1925. *Experience and Nature*. New York: Dover.

Dupré, John. 2014. "Animalism and the Persistence of Human Organisms." *Southern Journal of Philosophy* 52, spindle supplement, 6–23.

Flanagan, Owen. 1991. *Varieties of Moral Personality: Ethics and Psychological Realism*. Cambridge: Harvard University Press.

Freud, Sigmund. 1949. *The Ego and the Id*. London: Hogarth.

Gallagher, Shaun, ed. 2011. *The Oxford Handbook of the Self*. Oxford: Oxford University Press.

Haybron, Daniel M. 2008. *The Pursuit of Unhappiness: The Elusive Psychology of Well-Being*. Oxford: Oxford University Press.

Higgins, Kathleen M. 2012. *The Music Between Us: Is Music a Universal Language?* Chicago: University of Chicago Press.

Ivanhoe, Philip J. 1998. "Nature, Awe, and the Sublime." *Midwest Studies in Philosophy* 21, "The Philosophy of Religion," 98–117.

——. 2015. "Senses and Values of Oneness." In *The Philosophical Challenge from China*, edited by Brian Bruya, 231–51. Cambridge: MIT Press.

——. .2017. *Oneness: East Asian Conceptions of Virtue, Happiness and How We Are All Connected*. Oxford University Press.

James, William. 1890. *The Principles of Psychology*. London: Macmillan.

Kellert, Stephen R., and E. O. Wilson. 1993. *The Biophilia Hypothesis*. Washington, DC: Island.

Leopold, Aldo. 1968. *A Sand County Almanac*. New York: Oxford University Press.

Lovejoy, Arthur O. 1936. *The Great Chain of Being: A Study of the History of an Idea*. Cambridge: Harvard University Press.

Mead, George Herbert. 1934. *Mind, Self, and Society from the Standpoint of a Social Behaviorist*. Edited by C. W. Morris. Chicago: University of Chicago Press.

Menary, Richard, ed. 2010. *The Extended Mind*. Cambridge: MIT Press/Bradford.

Nozick, Robert. 1974. *Anarchy, State, And Utopia*. New York: Basic.

O'Neill, John. 1993. *Ecology, Policy and Politics: Human Well-Being and the Natural World*. London: Routledge.

Parfit, Derek. 1986. *Reasons and Persons*. New York: Oxford University Press.

Rawls, John. 1999. *A Theory of Justice*. Rev. ed. Cambridge: Belknap Press of Harvard University Press.

Sandel, Michel. 1984. "The Procedural Republic and the Unencumbered Self." *Political Theory* 12:81–96.

Scerri, Eric. 2016. *A Tale of Seven Scientists and a New Philosophy of Science*. New York: Oxford University Press.

Sen, Amartya K. 1977. "Rational Fools: A Critique of the Behavioral Foundations of Economic Theory." *Philosophy and Public Affairs* 6 (4): 317–44.

Tien, D. W. 2012. "Oneness and Self-Centeredness in the Moral Psychology of Wang Yangming." *Journal of Religious Ethics* 40.

Wang Yangming 王陽明. 1997. *Wang Yangming quanji* 王陽明全集. Shanghai: Shanghai guji chubanshe.

Wilson, E. O. 1984. *Biophilia*. Cambridge: Harvard University Press.

Xiao Yang 2015. "Culture as Habits of the Heart: Bellah on Religion in Human Evolution and History." In *Confucianism, a Habit of the Heart*, edited by Philip J. Ivanhoe and Sungmoon Kim, 183–203. Albany: State University of New York Press, 2015.

Yearley, Lee H. 1985. "Freud as Creator and Critic of Cosmogonies and Their Ethics." In *Cosmogony and Ethical Order*, edited by Robin W. Lovin and Frank E. Reynolds, 381–413. Chicago: University of Chicago Press.

Zhang Zai 張載. 2004. *Zhang Zai ji* 張載集. Taibei: Hanjing wenhua shiye youxian gongsi.

Zhu Xi 朱熹. 1986. *Zhuzi yulei* 朱子語類. Beijing: Zhonghua shuju.

CHAPTER 1

ONENESS

A Big History Perspective

VICTORIA S. HARRISON

What Is Big History?

In this essay I take a big history perspective on the oneness hypothesis: the view
that the self is inextricably linked to some larger whole. Adopting a big history
perspective allows me to take a wide-angled view of this hypothesis and to consider its significance within the broad context of global intellectual and cultural history.[1]

"Big historians" hold that human history is punctuated by a small number
of episodes of dramatic and large-scale social and cultural transformation.[2]
These episodes are thought to have occurred gradually over relatively long periods of time and in a number of geographical areas not necessarily directly
connected. Each of these episodes is regarded as a time of transition in which
human social organization crossed a threshold leading human culture to a new
level of complexity. Big historians typically identify three such episodes.

The first occurred about fifty thousand years ago in response to the challenges faced by our ancestors during the last ice age. These challenges spurred
humans toward significant technological advances that assisted them to survive in their changing environment. Many hold that we should include in this
range of technologies early forms of symbol systems (although the use of sym-
bols has a much longer history) and, in particular, the development of spoken
language.[3]

The second episode again occurred in response to a changing climate, this
time the end of the last ice age, about eleven thousand years ago. In various

parts of Afro-Eurasia, human culture was irrevocably altered by the move away from the typical lifeways of the Paleolithic—which were predominantly nomadic and based on foraging—and toward the agricultural patterns of life characteristic of the Neolithic. At around this time many humans started to show a preference for a settled life, and the domestication of animals and plants became a key feature of this.[4]

The third episode—and the one that seems much closer conceptually to our own era—occurred about five thousand years ago, when the first cities and states began to take shape.[5] Since this decisive revolution in human lifeways, our planet has continuously hosted a number of highly urbanized environments; these were first sprinkled across Eurasia and slowly spread across the globe until, not long ago, and within our own recent experience, more than 50 percent of humans had come to live in cities.

Big historians claim that these episodes of social and cultural transformations, which involved massive technological and lifestyle changes, are what make the history of humanity fundamentally different from the history of any other species on our planet. They further claim that an understanding of these dramatic episodes that have shaped our current ways of living can provide us with the long-range perspective that we need to consider the global dimensions of human history and culture. In examining these formative episodes, big historians hypothesize about their possible causes, paying particular attention to environmental influences.[6] They also consider the impact of intercultural exchange in transmitting these social and cultural transformations so widely, noting that, in areas where there has been a high level of intercultural exchange, the overall effect of the episodes of transformation has been correspondingly expedited.

In reconstructing the episodes of human history that concern them, big historians rely to a large degree on their ability to frame hypotheses using indirect evidence. Unlike historians of more recent periods, they cannot rely on documentary evidence to form their views of what human lifeways and culture were like prior to the various transformations they describe. The evidence that is available, at least with respect to the first transformation and to some extent the second, comes from the findings of paleo-anthropologists and paleo-archaeologists. Big historians are on slightly firmer ground with respect to the second transformation (that is, the transition from the Paleolithic to the Neolithic), but still the remains of human material culture from this period of transition are fragmentary at best. The material evidence is more abundant with respect to the third transformation—the move toward urbanization. We have impressive archaeological remains of ancient cities, particularly in the Indus Valley. But even where material remains are abundant, lacking documentary evidence, big historians, like archaeologists, must rely on informed intuition if they are to give an account of the cultural life of the people who dwelled in these newly urbanized environments.

Big History and the Self

Having noted the difficulties facing big historians when they seek to include the episodes of large-scale transformation that interest them into wider interpretive accounts of human cultural history, now consider the further difficulties that would face what I want to call a "big intellectual historian," one who seeks to reconstruct the intellectual transformations that accompanied the episodes of social and cultural transformation described by big history.[7] Even where material remains are accessible to us (such as the cave paintings in Lascaux, France, that date from around 15,000 BCE), lacking documentary evidence, we can only speculate about the meanings they had for the people that made and used them. In short, the remnants of material culture are silent with respect to what people of earlier times believed. Such interpretive difficulties should not be underestimated; however, we should not let them put us off the project of big intellectual history too easily.

Just as big history can provide us with a valuable perspective from which to view the past, present, and, perhaps, even the future of global human culture, so big intellectual history might be able to furnish a similarly valuable perspective by shedding new light on the intellectual options available to us today. Of particular interest to a big intellectual historian would be the possibility of identifying ideas about the self and the significance of human life in the context of the wider cosmos, as these have been transformed alongside and in the wake of the wider social and cultural transformations discussed by big historians.[8] Such ideas about the self and its significance would be intrinsically interesting, but they would also be important insofar as they could point us toward an understanding of the "self-experience" that underlay them.[9]

Modern humans had been surviving on this planet by living as nomads and foraging for food for roughly 150,000 to 200,000 years prior to the first great episode of transformation, which, as noted, took place about fifty thousand years ago and consisted of the invention of new technologies, including unprecedentedly complex symbolic systems. We have no material evidence at all to support any theory about how humans experienced and thought about themselves or their communities, such as they were, during the long period of time prior to this first wave of social and cultural transformation. Any proposal would therefore inevitably be highly speculative.

We are not in a hugely improved position with respect to the period between the first and the second social and cultural transformations, that is, between, about fifty thousand and eleven thousand years ago. Various human burial sites have been found that date from about the middle of this period, so we do have material evidence concerning such things as the configuration of bodies relative to one another within certain graves and we know exactly what goods some of these people were buried with. However, the archaeological data does not provide evidence that could support anything but a highly speculative account of what people at this time thought about themselves, the world at large, or the significance of their death.

It seems intuitively likely, however, that some change in how people thought about and experienced themselves and their environment would have been facilitated by the transition from a typically Paleolithic lifeway that was predominantly nomadic to the Neolithic lifeway of more sedentary agriculturalists. The change in lifeway was, of course, gradual, sweeping across Afro-Eurasia at different paces.[10] Many communities seem to have had a period during which they followed a mixed pattern, adopting a nomadic-foraging life for part of the year and a more stable agricultural life when conditions permitted. Again, we can only speculate about the impact of this expanded range of possible lifeways on how people thought of themselves and their communities and their relationship to the environment within which they lived.

Matters become more promising when we consider the third episode of dramatic social and cultural transformation, the development of the great urban complexes whose emergence in various areas of Eurasia was well underway around five thousand years ago. This gradual transition to an increasingly urbanized lifeway, with the complex social organization and fine-grained divisions of labor it required (not to mention the inequalities in control of material resources that it brought quickly in its wake), seems very likely to have elicited a correspondingly dramatic change both in the self-experience of the people affected by it and in the ways they thought of themselves, their communities, and their relationship to the natural world. However, just as the change in lifeway affected different regions of the planet to different degrees at different times, so we would expect that the old way of experiencing and thinking about the self and the world that was suited to the former way of life would have been replaced gradually in different areas and at different times.

The claim that there was a dramatic transformation in ways of experiencing and thinking about the self that happened gradually in different parts of Eurasia alongside the higher levels of social organization that came with urbanization invites us to ask: How did people experience and think about the self prior to this transformation? My speculative proposal is that prior to the move toward urbanization the self was predominantly experienced and understood within the framework of possibilities provided by a conceptual system that favored a oneness perspective.[11] Such a conceptual system will have informed, not necessarily at a conscious level, a self-experience that tied a person's identity to that of their family or clan and perhaps also to their local environment. For those operating with such a conceptual system, their sense of what was good for them would have been inextricably tied to their sense of what was good for those with whom they lived, and this very likely provided the context in which they understood death. The death of an individual would likely have been regarded as unfortunate but of secondary importance to the continuation of the family, and there would have been little inclination to speculate about a postmortem fate.

In the following section, I provide some reasons in support of the proposal that prior to the social and cultural transformations brought about by an increasingly urbanized environment a conceptual system that favored some form of oneness perspective was widely employed. To do so, however, I need to focus attention on a period of human history that we do know a great deal about.

The Self in the Axial Age

The term *Axial Age* (*die Achsenzeit*) was introduced by Karl Jaspers (1883–1969) and is now widely accepted as referring to the period roughly between 800 and 200 BCE.[12] This was a period of dramatic intellectual and cultural change across Eurasia.[13] The Axial Age was a pivotal turning point in human history and the ideas developed during it were the ones that came to shape the lives of subsequent humans, and many of them continue to shape our own lives today. All of the major thought forms—religious and philosophical—that came to dominate the more than two millennia separating us late moderns from the people of the Axial Age had roots in this period. It is no exaggeration to claim that the world that humans lived in before the Axial Age was fundamentally different than the one they inhabited after it.

* * *

Four major areas of Eurasia were "Axial centers": East Asia; South Asia; West Asia; and the Northern Mediterranean.[14] In each of these there was an intensification of the urbanization process that, as we have seen, had already been underway for some time. People flocked to the cities, as they do in our own day, in pursuit of enhanced economic opportunities. Their lives were changed as they came to live in closer proximity to large numbers of other people—some of whom would not have shared their own traditions and customs. However, despite the new prosperity that many enjoyed, each of the Axial centers was also characterized by extensive political and social upheaval. In China, for example, the period of the Warring States overlapped with the Axial Age. Both of these factors—more intensive urbanization and intense social and political upheaval—seem to have contributed to an increased level of anxiety about death and a new urgency to understand the human condition (although these were expressed in different ways in each Axial center).

Indeed, if we look at what issues were of central concern to key thinkers of the Axial Age, we find that many of them gave serious attention to questions about the fundamental nature of the self and its postmortem prospects. This can be seen most strikingly, perhaps, in the late-Vedic tradition. The intense intellectual energy that was focused on understanding the self and the urgent concern elicited by its postmortem fate are evident in many of the *Upaniṣads*. Many of these texts probe the limits of our self-knowledge and promote the view that obtaining such knowledge is of far greater importance than performing the ritualized acts prescribed by the earlier Vedic tradition.[15] It is in these texts that we find the first introduction into the Vedic tradition of the idea—which many now regard as a defining feature of Hinduism—that the self does not die when the body does.[16] Also in the *Upaniṣads* another idea is developed that was to have a huge impact on later Hindu traditions, namely, that the self that survives the death of the body is to be identified with the essence of reality.[17] Both of these ideas were dramatic departures from the earlier Vedic tradition and they mark the beginnings of a long process of reflection in which not only the self but also reality (which in this era came to be identified as "Brahman") came to be understood in novel ways.[18]

The dissatisfaction with older views voiced in the *Upaniṣads* is clearly associated with a loss of confidence in traditional forms of religion. The new kind of philosophical inquiry we see in these texts was symptomatic of the transformation of religion that was underway in all of the Axial centers, as the received forms of religion no longer seemed adequate to the day. Across Eurasia there was a trend that moved away from religious forms focused on ritualized acts of sacrifice (which had often included human sacrifice, the importance of which in many pre- and early Axial Age cultures points again to the view that individuals were not regarded as being of primary importance but could be sacrificed for the good of the whole), toward those with a more interior focus. John Hick has characterized this as a shift away from religious forms that were geared toward "cosmic maintenance" in favor of those that were focused on personal transformation.[19] In the older forms of religion, ritual was seen as the means by which humans and gods (variously conceived) cooperated in the project of keeping the cosmos well ordered, a cooperation that all parties needed to succeed if they were to survive. The goal of these ritual-focused religions was to maintain the cosmos and thus secure the well-being of all those who lived within it. It was this older conception of religion that gave way to the forms of religion that came to dominate later human cultures. It seems clear that the move away from this older religious conception was intimately connected to changes in the way the self, as well as its relationship with the wider cosmos, was experienced.

The intense focus on the nature of the self that accompanied and fueled the transformation of older, highly ritualized religious forms into those that are more familiar to us today is widely evident in the thought of many of the foundational figures of both Eastern and Western civilisation.[20] Consider figures such as the historical Buddha, Māhavīra, and Zoroaster, but also—and to no lesser extent—those in East Asia, such as, Kongzi, Mengzi, Xunzi, "Laozi," and Zhuangzi. We should also add to this list the great thinkers from this period from Greece—Thales, Pythagoras, Socrates, Plato, and Aristotle. Surely it is not a coincidence that across Eurasia a concern with the nature of the self, often stimulated by anxiety about death, suddenly became of vital concern to intellectuals during the Axial Age.

Despite the range of accounts of the self found within the religious and philosophical traditions of both the East and the West that had their formative moments in the Axial Age, the conviction that the self can be the subject of profound transformation is presupposed in all of them.[21] This is the case to the extent that one struggles to identify a major world religion or philosophy with roots in the Axial Age within which this conviction has no place. Of course this shared conviction is played out in very different ways within each tradition and at different stages of each tradition's evolution. Consider, for instance, the Christian's aspiration to become Christ-like and the Mahayana Buddhist's aspiration to become a bodhisattva. Although these aspirations are clearly very different in quite specific respects, each presupposes and depends upon the idea that the self is capable of undergoing deep transformation.[22]

Post-Axial religions not only teach that profound self-transformation is possible; they also require their adherents to pursue it. Those adopting a particular religion are presented with a (typically nonoptional) goal to aspire toward (to become Christ-like, to become enlightened, to achieve omniscience, and so on), along with various spiritual practices that can be understood as methods to assist them in the attainment of that goal.[23] Moreover, religious goals typically cannot be achieved without the self undergoing significant self-transformation. To become Christ-like, for example, involves more than a few superficial behavioral changes; it requires that a person's core commitments, traits, aspirations, and ideals become realigned. If a person is successfully to arrive at the goal, then a great deal of effort will be required of her. In adopting a religious goal and undertaking to follow the directions provided to reach it, a person makes a conscious choice to strive to bring about whatever core changes to herself are required for her to arrive at her goal.[24] This kind of "self-shaping" project requires that the one undertaking it already possesses a heightened sense of awareness of her individuality, precisely the sort of awareness that was facilitated by the cultural and intellectual transformations that occurred during the Axial Age. In this new style of religion, success or failure is very much an individual matter, even—and perhaps especially—within early Buddhism, which, in conjunction with the theory of *anātta* (nonself), taught that only the concrete human individual could liberate him- or herself; not even a god or goddess could accomplish this for another.[25]

The overwhelming concern to understand the self that we find in otherwise independent traditions (those emerging from the Indo-Iranian cultural nexus, on the one hand, and the East Asian, on the other)[26] suggests that this concern grew out of pressures presented by the changing social environment to which humans were, in increasingly large numbers, being expected to adapt. It seems reasonable to speculate that across Eurasia a way of thinking about and experiencing the self that had been adequate to the earlier conditions in which biologically modern humans lived was increasingly found to be inadequate to the new circumstances of life. Because this inadequacy was felt, and had to be accommodated, within the context of independent and already quite distinctive intellectual and cultural traditions, it is understandable that the oneness perspective that had informed previous self-experiences was not replaced by a single universally employed new way of experiencing and thinking about the self.

As we have seen, a number of new ways of thinking about the self emerged from the Axial Age. Many of these were eventually developed into sophisticated philosophical theories honed by centuries of debate. In the Indo-Iranian cultural nexus these rival views developed side by side, and their proponents were in vigorous debate with one another.[27] As cultural exchange, facilitated by trade along the various Silk Routes, intensified in the last century before the Common Era and the early centuries of the Common Era, this philosophical debate quickly spread across the borders of the Indo-Iranian and the Sinitic geographical and cultural worlds.

As explained earlier, my hypothesis is that the majority of humans for most of their history employed a conceptual system that framed their self-experience and self-understanding within a oneness perspective.[28] The self-experiences and self-understandings informed, probably largely unconsciously, by such a conceptual system gradually came to seem inadequate as a result of the third wave of change that dramatically transformed human society and culture. This transformation, which, as we have seen, was underway roughly five thousand years ago, climaxed in the social and political upheavals of the Axial Age. Given this history, it seems plausible to suggest that the new ways of experiencing and thinking about the self and its relations to the world that began to be developed into elaborate philosophical systems during the Axial Age were the products of a gradual cognitive shift at the level of our conceptual system. At a deep and largely unconscious level, a conceptual system favoring a oneness perspective was being transformed into one capable of generating a wider range of forms of self-experience and self-understanding that were more attuned to the new conditions.[29]

We can regard these newly emerging understandings of the self and its relationship to the world as (more or less self-conscious) departures from the oneness perspective, previously taken for granted, with some understandings moving further away from the earlier perspective than others. Because of this relationship, in which newer ways of thinking and experiencing emerged gradually out of earlier ones, traces of a oneness perspective can still be discerned within later philosophical and religious worldviews that do not seem immediately aligned with it (Confucianism and Christianity would be cases in point).[30] Perhaps before regarding these traces of a oneness perspective simply as foreign bodies, fitting badly alongside other usually more dominant elements within the newer ways of thinking, we might consider to what extent they are throwbacks to our unconscious attachment to a conceptual system that served us well in the past. More speculatively yet, perhaps the resilience of ways of thinking about and experiencing the self that are informed by a oneness perspective, along with their ability to be coopted into otherwise very different worldviews, is an indication that the appeal they have for us is based on our biology and our long history as a species.[31]

Conceptions of the Self

At first blush it might have looked as if the various theoretical conceptions of the self found in the developed philosophies of the post-Axial world were rivals; and, indeed, they are often so regarded. However, we can also see them as culturally contextualized solutions to the same problem: to provide a way of thinking about the self that is responsive to a human experience that has been altered almost beyond recognition by the social and cultural transformations identified by big history. The range of viable conceptions of the self proposed in the Axial Age is evidence that the cultural environments within which the people of that age found themselves were consistent with a number of different ways of thinking about, and experiencing, the self. It would seem likely that the same was also the case in subsequent periods, as it surely is in our own.

***

The approach I have outlined does not presume that any one theoretical conception of the self will turn out ultimately to be the correct one (whatever that might mean in this context), and hence I have not been concerned to discover which of the available conceptions is to be preferred. In fact, I don't think that it is helpful to regard conceptions of the self as correct or incorrect, as giving us a true or false descriptive account of what the self is. Rather, in my view, it is more interesting to think about broad biologically based emotional and cognitive systems that can generate a range of forms of self-experience and self-understanding that are more or less adequate, perhaps at different times and in different places, to our needs. They will be adequate if they allow us to successfully negotiate the demands placed on us, first, by our physical environment and, second, by our social environment.[32]

Prior to the third wave of social and cultural transformation, which consisted of our move to an increasingly complex urbanized social environment, the main constraint on our cognitive system was that it had to be capable of underwriting a self-experience and self-understanding that were adequate to the demands placed on a person by the need to survive in an often unforgiving physical environment. A cognitive system that did not presuppose a hard dichotomy between nature and nonnature, the natural and the artificial, the individual and the social, the good for one and the good for all would likely have been entirely appropriate to a world in which humans lived close to nature and experienced themselves as being part of it.[33] In such a world, the hard and fast distinctions, which came to seem so obvious to many later humans, between oneself and the natural world or between the human and the nonhuman, for example, may well have been relatively unimportant.[34]

But the forms of self-experience and self-understanding adequate to humans in cultural contexts that lacked high levels of social stratification would be likely to come under increasing strain as a socially simple environment was transformed into a socially complex one. It was this transformation, I have argued, that generated a fundamental change in human experience that could not be easily accommodated using ways of thinking about, and experiencing, the self previously taken for granted.[35] This is what gave rise to the urgent need for the alternative approaches that finally came to theoretical expression in the new philosophical and religious views that proliferated across Eurasia in the Axial Age. Nonetheless, old ways of thinking about, and experiencing, the self were not completely replaced by new ones; rather they often remain discernible within newer forms of thought and experience. The result is better characterized as akin to a palimpsest rather than a complete erasure and rewriting.[36]

Considering the long history of our species, it is striking that, as far as we can tell, ways of thinking about the self that are informed by a cognitive system favoring an expansive conception of the self and its relations to others and to the world seem to have only been called into question relatively recently. This should alert us to the fact that when we look at the various theories of the self that have been developed, and in some cases widely adopted by entire cultures, since the dawn of the Axial Age and beyond, we are dealing with new ideas that are radical departures from those that had probably seemed quite natural to earlier humans. From the perspective offered by big history, our current theories are young. It should not surprise us then if none is yet entirely adequate to our needs in a world whose complexity continues to increase exponentially.

* * *

I have suggested that a deep cognitive shift lies behind the emergence, during the Axial Age, of the major religious and philosophical traditions that became formative of the ways of thinking about the self that dominated the post–Axial Age, in both the East and West. This cognitive transformation was precipitated by dramatic changes in human lifeways, particularly the increasingly pronounced social stratification required by urbanized environments. The cognitive system that favored a oneness perspective, which had informed self-experience and self-understanding prior to these changes, was not well aligned with lifeways that required fine-grained divisions of labor and quickly led to significant inequalities in the distribution of material resources. Yet we have no reason to suppose that prior to these social and cultural changes the oneness perspective was unable to support forms of self-experience and self-understanding that were adequate to our needs; and I have argued that the contrary is the case. This suggests that our ability to successfully employ a oneness perspective is rooted in facts about our biological nature. If that is so, such a perspective may yet provide us with a valuable resource from which to draw as we continue the intellectual project begun in the Axial Age and try to make sense of our individual and collective experience in the rapidly changing cultural and physical environments that we now inhabit.

Notes

1. The term *big history* was first coined by David Christian, and Christian remains one of the field's main proponents. See David Christian, *Maps of Time: An Introduction to Big History*, 2nd rev. ed. (Berkeley: University of California Press, 2011).
2. "Big history" also covers the history of the cosmos prior to the evolution of our species. Here, however, I jump into the narrative of big history rather later in order to explore a big history perspective on human thought forms as these relate to the self and the world.
3. See the discussion in Robert N. Bellah, *Religion in Human Evolution: From the Paleolithic to the Axial Age* (Cambridge: Belknap Press of Harvard University Press, 2011), chaps. 1 and 2.
4. On these transformations, see Jared Diamond, *Guns, Germs, and Steel: The Fates of Human Societies* (New York: Norton, 1997).
5. As more material evidence emerges, especially from the Indus Valley, this episode is being is pushed further back into the past. However, nothing in the argument to follow depends on pinning it down more precisely.

6. Jared Diamond's work stands among the best examples of this approach. See, for example, *Guns, Germs, and Steel.*

7. Robert Bellah's mounumental *Religion in Human Evolution* can be regarded as a work of "big intellectual history." For an excellent summary of Bellah's book, see Yang Xiao, "The Bildungsroman of the Heart: Thick Naturalism in Robert Bellah's *Religion in Human Evolution*," in *Confucianism, a Habit of the Heart: Bellah, Civil Religion, and East Asia,* ed. Philip J. Ivanhoe and Sungmoon Kim (Albany: State University of New York Press, 2016), 183–203.

8. Robert Bellah has gone further than anyone in this direction. See, especially, chapters 3, 4, and 5 of *Religion in Human Evolution.*

9. I am presupposing a distinction between having a sense of what it is to be a self (what I call "self-experience") and representing that experience to oneself by conceptualizing it. I doubt that the experience and the conceptualization are in practice separable; nonetheless there does seem to be an important difference between them that should not be conflated with the related distinction often made between "self" and "self-concept." On this, see the discussion in Kristján Kristjánsson, *The Self and Its Emotions* (Cambridge: Cambridge University Press, 2010).

10. On these gradual, yet dramatic changes, see Diamond, *Guns, Germs, and Steel.*

11. A conceptual system provides us, often at an unconscious level, with the range of core concepts we need to structure our experience at the most basic level (concepts such as "inside" and "outside," "self" and "world"). This doesn't entail that people require an explicit theory in order to enjoy self-experience or to reflect upon it. A conceptual system, as I understand it here, is logically prior to any particular person's self-experience and self-understanding as it provides the necessary framework within which these take place.

12. Karl Jaspers, *The Origin and Goal of History,* trans. Michael Bullock (New Haven: Yale University Press, 1953).

13. The following discussion targets Eurasia rather than Afro-Eurasia. This is because our knowledge of the intellectual history of Eurasia is far richer and more fully developed than our knowledge of African intellectual history. Egypt aside, posterity has been less kind to the earlier civilizations of the African subcontinent than to many of those of Eurasia.

14. See S. N. Eisenstadt, ed., *The Origins and Diversity of Axial Age Civilization* (Cambridge: Harvard University Press, 1965).

15. On the earlier Vedic tradition, see William K. Mahony, *The Artful Universe: An Introduction to the Vedic Religious Imagination* (Albany: State University of New York Press, 1998).

16. *Kaṭha Upaniṣad* 2.18. Juan Mascaró, trans., *The Upanishads* (Baltimore: Penguin, 1965).

17. *Chāndogya Upaniṣad,* see 6.13.1–2.

18. Wendy D. O'Flaherty, ed., *Karma and Rebirth in Classical Indian Traditions* (Berkeley: University of California Press, 1980).

19. See John Hick, *An Interpretation of Religion: Human Responses to the Transcendent,* 2nd ed. (New Haven: Yale University Press, 2005).

20. With respect to earlier forms of religion in East Asia, see S. Allen, *The Shape of the Turtle: Myth, Art and Cosmology in Early China* (Albany: State University of New York Press, 1991). See also David Keightley, "The Religious Commitment: Shang Theology and the Genesis of Chinese Political Culture," *History of Religions* 17 (1978): 211–24.

21. See Hick, *An Interpretation of Religion.*

22. Despite the fact that the Christianity only emerged in the Common Era, it is still appropriately regarded as a product of the Axial Age because of the earlier traditions that it assimilated.

23. For some examples, see Nan Huai-chin and William Bodri, *Spiritual Paths and Their Meditation Techniques* (Nevada: Top Shape, 2010).

24. See Victoria S. Harrison, "Self-Transformation, Self-Shaping, and Exemplars," in *True to Oneself: Philosophy of Religion Comes to Life*, ed. Mark Wynn (forthcoming).

25. See Steven Collins, *Selfless Persons: Imagery and Thought in Theravada Buddhism* (Cambridge: Cambridge University Press, 1982).

26. For an archaeologically informed view of the latter, see G. L. Barnes, *China, Korea and Japan: The Rise of Civilization in East Asia* (London: Thames and Hudson, 1993).

27. On the practice of philosophical debate between the various *āstika* and *nāstika darśanas* of classical India, see Jonardon Ganeri, *Philosophy in Classical India: The Proper Work of Reason* (London: Routledge, 2001).

28. This conceptual system would have been capable of generating different forms of self-experience and self-understanding, forms that were well suited to people living a nomadic-foraging lifestyle, the material conditions and social demands of which are not widely variable across Eurasia.

29. As societies became more complex, politics assumed increased importance. The move away from the earlier conceptual system that favored a oneness perspective may have been associated with changing political circumstances that demanded that the individual's relationship to the whole be mediated through others, the leader, or the ruler. This can be seen especially clearly in East Asia from the time of the early Shang kings. See Robert Bellah's discussion of kingship and Archaic religion in *Religion in Human Evolution*, chap. 5.

30. Ways of thinking about the self that are indebted to a oneness perspective can be found embedded in many of the religious and philosophical traditions of the world. This suggests that we might be able to construct a scale of theories of the self: at one end would be the Axial and post-Axial forms of explicit oneness perspective, such as those found in Daoism and Advaita Vedānta, while at the other end we might find the (recently much maligned) theory of Western individualism (a theory that, arguably, is maximally removed from a oneness perspective). Other major religious and philosophical theories would be located at various points on the scale, according to how central a role they accorded the notion of oneness. Of course this would be a complex undertaking, as one would need to factor in variations within each philosophical and religious system across different times and places.

31. The approach developed here is convergent with what Yang Xiao describes as Robert Bellah's "guiding heuristic device," namely, the Hegelian principle that "nothing is ever lost." See Bellah, *Religion in Human Evolution*, and Xiao, "The Bildungsroman of the Heart," 194–95. I am grateful to Philip J. Ivanhoe for drawing this convergence to my attention.

32. Presumably inadequate forms of self-experience and self-understanding, and their associated theoretical expressions (for example, solipsism and extreme forms of skepticism), are selected out from our range of real choices.

33. We can only speculate about the range of self-experiences and self-understandings that may have been supported by such a cognitive system. The best evidence may well be the various oneness theories that were elaborated by religious thinkers and philosophers in the Axial and post-Axial ages. The difficulty with this proposal, though, is akin to that faced by paleo-anthropologists when they seek to reconstruct early

hominid behavior on the basis of observation of the behavior of present-day nonhuman primates. The nonhuman primates that are available for this kind of study have evolved considerably from their ancestral roots and many of them have spent their lives in highly artificial environments. In claiming that prior to the social and cultural transformation brought about by urbanization the self-experience and self-understanding of earlier humans were informed by a cognitive system favoring a oneness perspective, we should not be taken to mean that these earlier people held the sort of elaborate philosophical theory of the self and the world developed by much later neo-Confucians or Advaita Vedāntists. The oneness theories available for our scrutiny today are themselves products of highly rarefied intellectual cultures, so much so that their affinity to a much earlier and, so I have argued, ubiquitous cognitive system favoring a oneness perspective can be difficult to discern. For one thing, the later theories tend to characterize the "whole" in ways that would have been literally unthinkable to pre-Axial humans.

34. For an evocative account of how nature stimulates and informs our emotional, cognitive, and imaginative lives, see E. O. Wilson, *Biophilia: The Human Bond with Other Species* (Cambridge: Harvard University Press, 1984), especially the chapter "The Serpent."

35. Post-Axial forms of oneness theory contain sophisticated qualifications to explain the connection between the "conventional" individual self that we operate with on a day-to-day basis and the ultimately real self.

36. I am grateful to Philip J. Ivanhoe for this insightful image.

CHAPTER 2

ONENESS AND ITS DISCONTENT

Contesting Ren *in Classical Chinese Philosophy*

TAO JIANG

Oneness is a description of intimate relationships. Oneness with those close to us, especially family members, is a natural form of oneness whereas the sense of oneness with fellow citizens when one's country is under attack is also a powerful, if more temporary, form of oneness. Clearly, depending on contexts and circumstances, our sense of oneness with others can shift and our obligations to others change as a result. Importantly, oneness is both inclusive and exclusive at the same time, for example, to be one with our family can be at odds with our relationship with others or our sense of oneness with others can, under certain circumstances, jeopardize our family relationship. Consequently, oneness and its discontent are one of the most persistent problems that characterize the human condition.

The Chinese intellectual tradition has struggled with this problem since its very inception in the classical period (from the eighth century to the third century BCE). The challenge for the classical Chinese thinkers was how to negotiate the tension between the idea that oneness with one's family should be the foundation of a broader sociopolitical order and the idea that oneness with all impartially can provide a better model for an orderly world. The following two anecdotes put into sharp focus the wide gap in moral sensibility between classical Confucians and Mohists. The first is from the *Analects*:

> The Duke of She said to Confucius, "Among my people there is one we call 'Upright Gong.' When his father stole a sheep, he reported him to the authorities."

Confucius replied, "Among my people, those who we consider 'upright' are different from this: fathers cover up for their sons, and sons cover up for their fathers. 'Uprightness' is to be found in this."

(*Analects* 13.18, Slingerland's translation)

The second anecdote is recounted in *The Annals of Lü Buwei* I/5.5 (呂氏春秋):

The Mohist leader Fu Tun resided in Qin. His son murdered a man. King Hui of Qin said, "You, sir, are too old to have another son, so I have already ordered that the officials not execute him. I hope, sir, that you will abide by my judgment in this matter."

Fu Tun replied, "The law of the Mohist order says: 'He who kills another person shall die; he who injures another shall be punished.' The purpose of this is to prevent the injuring and killing of other people. To prevent the injuring and killing of other people is the most important moral principle in the world. Though your majesty out of kindness has ordered that the officials not execute my son, I cannot but implement the law of the Mohist order." He would not assent to King Hui's request and proceeded to kill his own son.

A son is what a man is most partial to. Yet Fu Tun endured the loss of what he was most partial to in order to observe his most important moral principle. The Mohist leader may properly be called impartial.

(Knoblock and Riegel 2000, 75, with slight modification)

These two narratives, to the extent they represent typical Confucian and Mohist moral instincts, vividly capture the core tension and conceptual parameters in Chinese moral thinking of the classical period. That is, classical moral thinking struggles with the tension between humaneness and justice. Humaneness is understood here to be an agent-relative virtue, referring to our natural inclination to be partial toward those who are close to us in a variety of ways, especially our family members, whereas justice is an agent-neutral virtue, referring to our exercise of impersonal judgment on the merits of persons and states of affairs irrespective of their relations to us. Importantly, both humaneness and justice are universal values. The distinction between them, in classical Chinese debate, has to do with whether or not differential treatments accorded to a family member and someone unrelated can be justified and on what ground, especially when the two treatments are in conflict. What is the proper way to treat our family when they are at fault is at the heart of the struggle between humaneness and justice. Most contemporary scholarship on classical Confucian and Mohist philosophies is built on the implicit assumption operative in these two representative narratives, with Confucians touting humaneness and Mohists extolling justice.

However, I will argue that it would be too simplistic to characterize the Confucian moral project as being exclusively oriented toward humaneness since concern for justice is also one of its core considerations. In fact, I will make the case that from the very beginning the Confucians struggle with the tension between humaneness and justice in their conceptions of ideal virtue, community, and polity.[1] In this essay, the tension is highlighted, instead of explained away, and used as a lens to look into the conflicted world of the moral universe presented in the *Analects*. I do this by drawing our attention to the concern for justice in several iterations of *ren*, a notion that is at the very center of the Confucian moral universe.

Ren, most appropriately translated as Good,[2] has been universally recognized as the singular moral ideal touted in the *Analects*. Due to the multiple definitions of *ren* in the text, the internal structure of *ren* and the order of priority among its definitions are still debated among contemporary scholars. More specifically, on different occasions, *ren* is defined as wisdom, courage, self-discipline, following ritual propriety, reverence, care, and so on. The reigning interpretative strategy among scholars of Confucianism is to treat *ren* as a kind of metavirtue that encapsulates various lower-order virtues mentioned earlier (for example, Slingerland 2003, Luo 2012). I generally agree with this interpretative strategy, although I think justice should be added to the list of qualities constitutive of *ren*. More importantly, I would argue that if the previous set of virtues listed under *ren* can be captured under "humaneness," justice is more difficult to accommodate within such an interpretation due to its agent-neutral nature. That is, the element of justice in *ren* destabilizes the humaneness-centered interpretation of the latter. Consequently, a critical question naturally presents itself: Is there a better interpretation of *ren* that can accommodate these conflicting components of this seminal concept? This essay is an attempt in such a direction.

In order to address this question, I would like to propose that, instead of treating *ren* as the settled concept of humaneness in the *Analects*, we should see it as the locus of philosophical debate whereupon contestations and competitions of visions by different thinkers on ideal virtue, community, and polity are registered during the formative period of Chinese intellectual history. Such an interpretation is more historically grounded in that, as Lin Yü-sheng (1974–75) has pointed out, it was Confucius who appropriated an earlier concept of *ren* referring to the noble qualities of an aristocratic man, removed it from its aristocratic association, and made it the central idea that anchors the emerging Confucian moral universe. Given Confucius's new and innovative way of using *ren*, it is at least reasonable to assume that it was not yet a settled concept. I will argue that central to the contestation of *ren* is the competition between two kinds of ideal virtue, community, and polity, namely a humaneness-centered vision versus a justice-centered one. The fact that *ren* is defined in so many ways in the *Analects* itself is a clear indication that Confucius and his close disciples are still trying to think through what constitutes ideal virtue, community, and polity. The unsettled nature of *ren* becomes even more evident when we bring in other thinkers from the classical period, especially the Mohists, who are widely acknowledged as the most serious challengers of the Confucians and their intellectual project.

While many occurrences of *ren* in the *Analects* warrant the interpretation of humaneness, here I argue that in certain other cases, within the *Analects* and other classical texts like the *Mozi*, it is actually preferable to understand *ren* in terms of justice, rather than humaneness. In light of this, I conclude that the prevailing translation of *ren* tends to privilege agent-dependent virtues like humaneness, with the result that the classical Confucian project has been framed with a bias toward humaneness at the expense of properly appreciating the intellectual struggle between these two kinds of concerns therein.

To make the case, let us first examine some occurrences of *ren* in the *Analects* in which it makes more semantic sense to interpret it as justice instead of humaneness. Second, and more importantly, we look into an underappreciated aspect of *ren*, namely, the constitutive role of the Golden Rule in Confucius's formulation of *ren*, and explore its implications for the component of justice in *ren*. Although there is a good deal of scholarly literature on *ren* and the Confucian Golden Rule, not much attention has been given to exploring the implications of the Golden Rule's constitutive role in *ren* articulated in the *Analects*. Furthermore, we will direct some attention to examining the Mohist exercising of the Golden Rule in developing the Confucian notion of *ren* and its extraordinary intellectual consequences, which have been largely ignored in the scholarly discussion of the Golden Rule and *ren* in Chinese intellectual history.

My central argument in this essay is that the critical role of the Golden Rule in Confucius's articulation of *ren* highlights the importance of justice in the project outlined by Confucius and that the reigning consensus on interpreting *ren* as humaneness underappreciates such a critical component in *ren*. Furthermore, I make the case that it is Mozi and the Mohists who disambiguate the notion of *ren* in Confucius's teaching by putting the Golden Rule into practice and pushing *ren* to its logical conclusion, thereby pioneering a powerful theory of impartial care and universal justice.

Instances of *Ren* as the Virtue of Justice in the *Analects*

In order to make the case that there is a conceptual tension between humaneness and justice in Confucius's articulation of *ren*, let us begin by taking a close look at certain occurrences of *ren* in the *Analects* that favor a justice-oriented interpretation, as opposed to other occurrences that favor a humaneness-oriented interpretation. Since the latter have received most of the scholarly attention, we will focus on the former as a corrective to the dominant discourse on *ren*. Specifically, we will look at three particular cases wherein translating *ren* as humaneness is both conceptually and semantically difficult: First, how can a person of *ren* both love and despise people? Second, what does *ren* mean in the case of "sacrificing oneself to realize *ren* (*shashen chengren* 殺身成仁, *Analects* 15.9)? Third, should Guan Zhong 管仲 be considered *ren* or not? Let us examine these cases more closely to see what is at stake in the interpretation of *ren*. We will see how, in different ways, the prevailing interpretive paradigm has tried to accommodate these difficulties and how such interpretive maneuvers have failed to appreciate the critical component of justice in *ren*.

The first interpretive difficulty has to do with whether a person of *ren* loves or despises/hates people. In *Analects* 12.22, Confucius famously defines *ren* in terms of loving or caring for people (*ai ren* 愛人). However, *Analects* 4.3 seems to problematize such a definition:

> The Master said, "Only a person of *ren* knows how to like people and how to hate (or despise) them."[3]
>
> (*Analects* 4.3)

This occurrence of *ren* appears to contradict the definition of *ren* in terms of loving or caring for people in 12.22, and it demands some semantic flexibility in interpreting *ren*. One way to treat the difficulty is to sharply distinguish the meanings of *ai* 愛 from *hao* 好. However, given a significant overlap in the generic meanings of these two words, such an interpretative strategy does not take the conceptual tension between the two understandings of *ren* seriously.

Conceptually, there is a clear tension between saying that *ren* is loving/caring for people and saying that *ren* is knowing how to love and despise/hate people. While loving and caring for people are indicative of the humaneness of the moral agent, knowing how to love and despise/hate people brings in the consideration of desert in the agent's treatment of others. Knowing how to treat others, whether liking or disliking, based on their moral desert points to the virtue of justice (each receiving her due)[4] that is being touted in *Analects* 4.3. It is therefore more straightforward to understand *ren* in 4.3 as the virtue of justice rather than humaneness. The *Analects* is full of disparaging remarks and observations regarding "petty men" (*xiao ren* 小人) and warns the disciples to be vigilant against (becoming) such people, with the obvious implication that petty men deserve being despised and that it is just to despise them. On the other hand, the semantic limit of humaneness is less accommodating of the elements of despising and disliking.

The second interpretative difficulty concerns the understanding of *ren ren* 仁人, those who are *ren*. In *Analects* 15.9, Confucius famously heaps praises on persons of *ren*:

> The Master said, "No scholar-officials with noble vocations or persons of *ren* would harm *ren* when trying to preserve their lives, but they could very well sacrifice themselves in accomplishing the ideal of *ren*."
>
> (*Analects* 15.9)

Again, a person of *ren* (*ren ren* 仁人) is usually translated as a humane person. However, it is rather counterintuitive to understand *ren* as humaneness in this particular context since "sacrificing oneself to accomplish the ideal of humaneness" does not work very well either semantically or conceptually. On the other hand, it is much more intuitive to translate *ren* as the virtue of justice here. That is, translating *ren ren* as humane persons is rather stretched as it is not quite intuitive to say that a humane person would sacrifice his or her life to accomplish humaneness whereas the semantic and conceptual range of justice is much more aligned with the context here, namely, a just person would sacrifice his or her life for a just cause.

Third, for the purpose of this essay the most significant of these interpretative difficulties has to do Confucius's evaluations of Guan Zhong on different occasions. There are several interesting evaluations of important historical personalities in the *Analects*, Guan Zhong being one of the most prominent and controversial figures. He was Duke Huan of Qi's 齊桓公 chief minister and was instrumental in launching critical reforms to make Qi an efficient and centralized bureaucratic state as well as an economic and military power. He was widely credited as being primarily responsible for making Duke Huan the first of the five hegemons (*ba* 霸) of the Spring and Autumn period (*chunqiu wuba* 春秋五霸).[5] Confucius, as recorded in the *Analects*, seems rather conflicted in his evaluations of Guan Zhong.

In the *Analects* 3.22, Confucius criticizes Guan Zhong as someone who does not understand ritual (*li* 禮), a damning critique of a figure with such a high stature. However, in 14.16 and 14.17 Confucius seems to take a completely different attitude toward Guan Zhong. Indeed, in those passages Confucius praises Guan Zhong rather profusely. Let us take a closer look.

Analects 14.16 records an interesting conversation between Confucius and his disciple Zilu:

> Zilu said, "When Duke Huan had his brother Prince Jiu murdered, Shao Hu died for his master, whereas Guan Zhong did not." He then added, "Does this behavior not fall short of Goodness?"

The Master replied, "It was Guan Zhong's strength that allowed Duke Huan, on many occasions, to harmoniously unite the feudal lords without the use of military force. *Ru qi ren, ru qi ren . . .*"

(Slingerland's translation with modifications)

According to established ritual norm at the time, a vassal should kill himself when his master dies as a demonstration of loyalty to his master. However, Guan Zhong did not follow this norm. Instead, he was recruited by the murderer of his master, the brother of his master, who became Duke Huan, to serve as his chief minister. Due to such a serious violation of ritual norm, Zilu asks Confucius whether Guan Zhong should indeed not be considered *ren*. Given Confucius's disapproval of Guan Zhong as someone who does not understand *li* and the importance of *li* in the virtue of *ren* (*Analects* 12.1), we would expect Confucius to dismiss Guan Zhong as someone who is not *ren*. Surprisingly, however, Confucius touts Guan Zhong's accomplishment, including his assistance in helping Duke Huan to bring peace among the warring lords without resorting to military means.

Toward the end of Confucius's remarks, he utters "*ru qi ren, ru qi ren*" 如其仁如其仁 and the precise meaning of the Master's words has been contested in contemporary scholarship. Interestingly, however, traditional Chinese commentary regarding the meaning of *ru qi ren* is a settled one. As Edward Slingerland summarizes,

> Beginning with Kong Anguo, the standard interpretation of Confucius' final assessment, *ruqiren* (lit. "like his Goodness"), has been to understand it either with an implicit "who" before it ("who could match his Goodness!") or as in the sense of "such was his Goodness!" Such high praise has caused consternation among commentators, considering the negative attitudes expressed toward Guan Zhong in 3.22, as well as the fact that he was serving a hegemon rather than a legitimate king. Zhu Xi follows Kong Anguo, but tries to explain away the contradiction by adding, "probably what he meant is that, although Guan Zhong was not quite a truly Good person, his beneficence extended to all people, and therefore his achievements were Good." A more satisfying way to reconcile 14.16–14.17 with 3.22 is to follow commentators who understand *ruqiren*—like the "Ah! That man! That man!" in 14.9—as a noncommittal "But as for his Goodness, as for his Goodness."

(160–61; "Good"/"Goodness" is Slingerland's translation of *ren*)

Slingerland makes a reasonable case for understanding *ru qi ren* to refer to Confucius's noncommittal attitude toward Guan Zhong. However, the fact that the long-standing Confucian commentarial tradition has interpreted

Confucius to be praising Guan Zhong as an exemplar of *ren* par excellence is itself telling. That is, the Confucian commentarial tradition recognizes the virtue of *ren* demonstrated by Guan Zhong, manifested in the restoration of order in the world without resorting to military force. Such a recognition should not be easily dismissed as a case of misreading or misunderstanding Confucius.

This positive reading of Confucius's evaluation of Guan Zhong in *Analects* 14.16 is strengthened by 14.17, wherein Confucius credits Guan Zhong for his effort to preserve the cultural heritage of the Chinese civilization and prevent the invasions of "barbarians."

> Zigong asked, "Guan Zhong was not a Good person, was he? When Duke Huan had Prince Jiu murdered, Guan Zhong was not only incapable of dying with his master, he moreover turned around and served his master's murderer as Prime Minister."
>
> The Master replied, "When Guan Zhong served as Duke Huan's Prime Minister, he allowed him to become hegemon over the other feudal lords, uniting and ordering the entire world. To this day, the people continue to enjoy the benefits of his achievements—if it were not for Guan Zhong, we would all be wearing our hair loose and fastening our garments on the left. How could he be expected to emulate the petty fidelity of a common husband or wife, going off to hang himself and die anonymously in some gully or ditch?"
>
> (*Analects* 14.17, Slingerland's translation)

Here Confucius is much more forthcoming in rejecting the notion that Guan Zhong was not *ren* due to his violation of the ritual norm expected of him with the death of his former master. Confucius makes a powerful case for considering Guan Zhong *ren* by listing his major accomplishments.[6] When compared with such towering achievements in bringing greater good to the world, Guan Zhong's following his master to death would have been petty and pitiful. Confucius's low regard for petty men (*xiaoren* 小人), manifestly evident in this passage, is well known. The Confucian tradition has clearly seen this as a case of sacrificing the norm of personal virtue for the greater good of bringing peace to the world.

If we restrict the meaning of *ren* to the agent-dependent virtue of humaneness, Guan Zhong was not a person of *ren* since he did not demonstrate sufficient devotion and loyalty to his former master. On the other hand, if *ren* is understood more in the direction of the agent-neutral virtue of justice, Guan Zhong can indeed be regarded as a person of *ren*. This point becomes even clearer in the third reference to Guan Zhong in *Analects* 14.9. Someone asks for Confucius's assessments of Zichan, Zixi, and Guan Zhong and Confucius's comment on Guan Zhong is again an interesting one.

They asked about Guan Zhong. The Master replied, "Now there was a man. He confiscated the three hundred household city of Ping from the head of the Bo Clan, reducing him to abject poverty, and yet to the end of his days not a single resentful word was uttered against him."

(*Analects* 14.9, Slingerland's translation)

Slingerland provides some helpful historical background to the reference Confucius makes here: "The head of the Bo Clan was a minister in the state of Qi, and apparently his fiefdom was confiscated as punishment for an unspecified crime. The most plausible way to understand Confucius' comment is to follow Kong Anguo: Guan Zhong's actions were appropriate and reasonable, and therefore even those who suffered from his decisions could find no reason to blame him" (Slingerland 2003, 157). Recall *Analects* 12.2, wherein one of the qualities of *ren* is the ability to cause no resentment in fulfilling one's official duties. In 14.9, Confucius clearly recognizes such a quality in Guan Zhong.

All of these cases point to Guan Zhong's deserving the recognition of being a person of *ren*, as a man of justice, in the eyes of Confucius. As for Confucius's dismissal of Guan Zhong as not a person of *li*, it can be more interestingly explored in terms of the tension between *li* and *ren* in the moral universe of the *Analects*. This approach, which takes seriously such tensions in the Confucian moral universe, should be more fruitful to the philosophical interpretation of the Confucian project. Seeing Guan Zhong as representing at least one kind of *ren* opens up the possibility of integrating the component of justice into a fuller understanding of *ren*.

If the case made for interpreting *ren* as the virtue of justice *in some instances* within the *Analects* is plausible, a question would follow: Are there conceptual resources for such an interpretation of *ren* in the text? In this connection, Guan Zhong's own understanding of *ren* is a useful pointer for us. In *Guanzi* 51.2, Guan Zhong is recorded as advising Duke Huan, "what one does not want do not impose it on others. That is *ren*" (非其所欲，勿施於人，仁也). As we will see in the next section, although the Golden Rule is not used by itself to define *ren* in the *Analects*, unlike in the *Guanzi*, it is nevertheless constitutive of *ren*. Indeed, I argue that Confucius's deliberation on the Golden Rule as constitutive of *ren* in the *Analects* offers a precious conceptual resource to explore the dimension of justice in *ren*.

Ren and the Golden Rule in the *Analects*

The Golden Rule is a major milestone in the historical development of human moral consciousness in that it forges a powerful and, at least prima facie, intuitive path toward a fair treatment of others that is necessary in building a flourishing community by using the self as the barometer to measure how others should be treated, especially strangers. There has also been a long-standing critique of the Golden Rule arguing that using what the self desires and wants as the criterion to measure how to treat others properly is unreliable at best and problematic at worst, given the troubling nature of the self and the great diversity of people's desires and hopes. For example, the Golden Rule logic can potentially turn a masochist into a sadist if a masochist believes that everybody shares his masochism (Ivanhoe 1990, 19), or a fanatical Buddhist can use the Golden Rule logic to justify his effort to convert others to Buddhism with the belief that everybody would be better off being a Buddhist, just like him. To be fair to the Golden Rule, it is hard to conceive of a moral principle that would be foolproof in providing guidance to our actions under any circumstance, although that has not prevented philosophers from trying to formulate one.

However, my focus here is not on an evaluation of the Golden Rule per se. Rather, I am more interested in the connection between *ren* and the Golden Rule in the *Analects* as a fertile conceptual resource for interpreting *ren* as justice in some contexts within the classical Chinese philosophical discourse and for examining its philosophical and historical implications and consequences. The clearest connection between *ren* and the Golden Rule is laid out in *Analects* 12.2, where Confucius explains *ren* this way:

> Zhong Gong inquires about *ren*. Confucius says, "When you leave home, act as though you were about to greet important guests; when you employ people, act as though you were performing the grand sacrificial ritual. Do not do to others what you do not want for yourself. Then there would be no resentment in public or at home."

In this passage, the Golden Rule is clearly understood as constitutive of *ren*. The expression "do not do to others what you do not want for yourself" (己所不欲勿施於人) is referred to as *shu* 恕 in the *Analects*. *Shu*'s constitutive role in *ren* is key to our following discussion.

Shu, commonly translated as reciprocity, is often dubbed the negative Golden Rule (or Silver Rule), in contrast with the famous Golden Rule in the biblical tradition, which has a positive formulation. Indeed, the negative formulation features so prominently in the *Analects* that, within recent scholarly discussions of the Golden Rule, it is widely regarded as a uniquely Confucian formulation. Earlier, scholars debated whether the positive or the negative formulation had the conceptual advantage, although lately there has not been much scholarly interest in adjudicating such an issue.

The negative Golden Rule appears on several occasions in the *Analects*. For example,

Zigong asks, "Is there one word that can be applied throughout one's life?" Confucius replies, "Is that *shu*? Do not do to others what you do not want for yourself."

(*Analects* 15.24)

Here *shu* is elevated to the exalted status of a lifelong guide to a moral life or "a general maxim," as Heiner Roetz puts it (Roetz 1993, 133) in Confucius's teaching. It is also a difficult one to practice, possibly beyond the capacity of some disciples like Zigong (*Analects* 5.12).

However, *Analects* 15.24 is rather controversial in current Sinological scholarship. As Mark Csikszentmihalyi points out, many interpreters are "skeptical about either the claim that reciprocity is so central or the original nature of the passage itself" (2008, 161). Indeed, many scholars of classical Confucianism, such as Bryan Van Norden, E. Bruce Brooks, and to some extent Mark Csikszentmihalyi, dismiss the central importance of the Golden Rule in the *Analects* because it does not quite "fit" with the general orientation of the text or with the Confucian tradition, which tends to be virtue-based rather than rule-based. This approach raises an important question about the general orientation of the *Analects* that is key to this essay. If we interpret the Confucian project as centering on humaneness, those justice-oriented passages might indeed appear out of place. But as a general interpretative rule I think it is preferable, to the extent possible, to resist the temptation to explain away conceptual tensions within the *Analects* through Sinological maneuvers since such an approach can potentially undermine the integrity of philosophical interpretations of Chinese classics.[7]

Another strand of contemporary discussion about the Confucian Golden Rule, represented by Fung Yulan, D. C. Lau, Herbert Fingarette, David Nivison, and Philip J. Ivanhoe, accepts its centrality in the Confucian project and tries to creatively explore ways in which the Golden Rule might fit with the general contour of the *Analects* and classical Confucian thought. Their central verse is *Analects* 4.15, the famous "one-thread" teaching that supposedly runs through all of the Master's teachings:

The Master said, "Zeng, my Way can be strung together in one thread."
Zengzi answered, "Yes."
The Master left.
Other disciples asked, "What did he mean?"
Zengzi said, "The Way of the Master is nothing more than loyalty (*zhong* 忠) and reciprocity (*shu* 恕)."

(*Analects* 4.15)

There has also been much disputation about the authenticity and the proper interpretation of this passage.[8] What is relevant to our discussion here is not so much the historical authenticity of this passage, in terms of whether it really represents the teaching of Confucius[9] himself, as the less controversial issue of its pertinence to the overall Confucian project during the classical period.

Among the second group of scholars we can see two distinct approaches to the Golden Rule, with Fung, Lau, and Fingarette favoring a universalist treatment of *zhong* and *shu* on a more egalitarian ground and Nivison and Ivanhoe paying more attention to the hierarchical subtext of the Golden Rule in the Confucian context.[10] I am more sympathetic to the effort to interpret the Golden Rule as central to the Confucian project, especially by Nivison and Ivanhoe, due to their historical and textual sensitivity to the *Analects*. However, I do not think hierarchy exhausts the Golden Rule in the *Analects* and I will argue that hierarchy is only one way Confucius's iteration of the Golden Rule can be employed and interpreted.

In many ways, the emphasis on the hierarchical subtext of Confucius's Golden Rule has to do with the juxtaposition of *zhong* and *shu* in the *Analects* as the single thread in the Master's teaching. However, leaving aside for now whether *zhong shu* is single or dual, I would note that the Confucian Golden Rule is not necessarily defined by *zhong* and *shu* together since it is the way *shu* is defined in the *Analects* that has prompted the Golden Rule comparison whereas *zhong* by itself would not have invited any obvious parallelism with the biblical Golden Rule. Furthermore, *shu* is also used independently of *zhong* in the *Analects*, so the two are hardly inseparable. This is important because if *zhong* presupposes the embedded social and ritual hierarchy, as Nivison and Ivanhoe have convincingly argued, *shu* does not carry a similar assumption. Therefore, I would like to separate *shu* from *zhong* and focus on *shu* here.

In Roetz's analysis, the Confucian Golden Rule is linked to the Axial Age discourse that highlights a spiritual and intellectual breakthrough around the time of Confucius across the globe. More specifically, Roetz treats the Confucian Golden Rule as more universalistic and less embedded in the social hierarchy of Confucius's time, at least in its aspiration and potential in the *Analects* (Roetz 1993, 145). As he perceptively observes, what is remarkable about the Golden Rule articulated by Confucius is that it alone has the status of the "one pervading all" in the *Analects* (Roetz 1993, 134–35). Such an exalted status is not accorded to any of the familiar aspects of Confucian ethics in the Western (and Chinese) scholarly iterations, such as "tradition or a casuistry which tells us to act like certain models from the past did in comparable situations, parental authority, the judgment of the community, or the conventional normality of what 'one does' or 'one does not do'" (Roetz 1993, 134–35). This can partially explain the first group of scholars mentioned earlier who dismiss the Golden Rule as not belonging to the *Analects* or at least not fitting the general orientation of Confucius's teachings.

In his article "Reweaving the 'One Thread' of the *Analects*," Ivanhoe (1990, 17) highlights reversibility in Confucius's formulation of the Golden Rule.[11] As Ivanhoe explains, "One sees that one's actions should be *reversible*—that I should treat others as I would want to be treated by them, were we to exchange our position" (17, italics in original). Such a reversal of roles between a moral agent and a moral recipient can, potentially, have a leveling effect in neutralizing the moral agent's personal preference and privileged status when it comes to the determination of what it is and is not proper. Lau relies on *Analects* 6.30 to interpret *shu* as the method of *ren* in that *shu* "consists in taking oneself—'what is near at hand'—as an analogy and asking oneself what one would like or dislike were one in the position of the person at the receiving end" (1983, xiii). This reversibility lies at the heart of any conception of justice. The constitution of the Golden Rule in some of Confucius's iterations of *ren* points to the dimension of justice in the consummate virtue of *ren*.

However, as pointed out earlier in the essay, there is another powerful sentiment expressed in the *Analects* that is also registered in *ren*, namely, a moral agent's attachment to their family (*Analects* 1.2) as well as commitment to their role in the ritual-based sociopolitical hierarchy (*Analects* 12.1) celebrated by the Master. In fact, the humaneness-centered interpretation of *ren* is the dominant approach in contemporary scholarship. In *Analects* 1.2, Confucius identifies the familial virtue of filial piety and respect for elder brothers as the root of *ren* (孝弟也者, 其為仁之本與). The implication is that from filial piety and respect for elder brothers one would gradually develop the capacity to love and care for people more generally. That is, *ren* is rooted in the familial sentiments of filial piety and brotherly love that then develop into a more general care for people. This means that *ren* is understood as both a particular virtue and a general virtue in the *Analects*, as Wing-tsit Chan (1955, 297–98) observes. Still, the tension between familial obligations (particular) and the sense of justice (general) is palpable in the *Analects*, crystallized in Confucius's endorsement of a son covering up his father's theft, cited at the beginning of this essay.

At the center of the difficulty is the extent to which the moral agent can extend their care. That is, the Golden Rule entails the actual practice of extending care to others through an imagined role reversal by putting oneself in another's shoes in order to achieve *ren*. In other words, the Golden Rule is not only a rule, but also requires the willingness on the part of a moral agent to extend care to others. This is why Confucius's definition of *ren* as caring for people (*ai ren* 愛人, *Analects* 12.22) is critical for understanding what is being extended in the practice the Golden Rule. However, it is precisely in the actual practice of extending one's care to others entailed by the Golden Rule where potentially insurmountable problems are encountered. This has to do with the scope of reversibility, constrained by the practice of extending one's care.

In the *Analects*, one's attachment to family constitutes the most serious limit in the extension of care. If the Golden Rule uses the self as the barometer for measuring how to treat others, in the Confucian moral universe family belongs to an ambiguous category between the self and other. This is because family is neither self nor other. It is in between. The Golden Rule offers a way to extend one's care to those beyond our circle of family (and friends), but the Confucians cannot give up the special status or the root of care accorded to those close to the moral agent because for the Confucians that would violate our humanity.

By contrast, Mozi and the Mohists develop an account of the general virtue of *ren* by applying the reversibility principle in the Golden Rule to *ren*, pushing the latter from "loving or caring for people" (*Analects* 12.22) to its logical conclusion of impartial care (*jian ai* 兼愛) and thereby pioneering the radical idea of universal justice in Chinese history.

Ren and the Golden Rule in the *Mozi*

To many contemporary scholars of Chinese philosophy, it is Mozi who represents the true beginning of Chinese philosophical thinking. Unlike most other major thinkers of the classical period, Mozi came from the lower strata of Chinese society, likely a craftsman and a self-made thinker. He was also the head of a major religious and social movement at the time, challenging the established social and moral norms of the aristocracy. As Chris Fraser acutely observes, "search for objective moral standards to guide action and reform society lies at the heart of the Mohist philosophical and political project" (2009, 143). This would have major implications in the ways Mohist thought develops, especially when compared with its Confucian rival. Mozi is said to have studied Confucius's teachings early on. Mozi might have seen himself as developing Confucius's teachings in some respect and his understanding of *ren* can be seen as a good example of his development of Confucius's thought.

The teaching of impartial care is universally recognized as the single most important ethical teaching of Mozi and the Mohists. There is a clear conceptual connection between *ren* qua *ai* in the *Analects* and *jian ai* in the *Mozi*. In fact, Mozi and the Mohists reach the doctrine of *jian ai* by taking reversibility in the Golden Rule much more seriously than the self-professed followers of Confucius and interpreting *ren* more as an agent-neutral virtue of justice than an agent-dependent virtue of humaneness. That is, Mozi and the Mohists vigorously apply the Golden Rule to *ren* and push Confucius's idea of loving/caring for people to its logical conclusion of loving/caring for *all*, often to the exasperation of later Confucians like Mencius, who accuse the Mohists of being unfilial (無父, *Mencius* 3B/9).[12]

If justice is an important aspect of *ren* in the *Analects*, it becomes identified with *ren* in the *Mozi*. In "Jian Ai" III 兼愛下 (16.6), the virtue of *jian* 兼 (impartiality) is explicitly linked to the virtues of *ren* and *yi* (兼即仁矣義矣). Clearly, the idea of *jian* is conceptually connected to the more established term of *ren* and pushes *ren* further in the direction of impartiality, namely, the agent-neutral virtue of justice. As an example, let us take a look at the "Fa Yi" 法儀 chapter wherein Mozi uses *ren* in the sense of justice:

> This being the case, what then is the proper model for governing? Supposing everyone were to model themselves on their parents, what would that be like? There are many parents in the world, but very few of them are *ren*. If we were to model ourselves on our parents, the model we chose would not be one of *ren*. A model that is not *ren* cannot serve as a model. Supposing everyone were to model themselves on their teachers, what would that be like? There are many teachers in the world, but very few of them are *ren*. If we were to model ourselves on our teachers, the model would not be one of *ren*. A model that is not *ren* cannot serve as a model. Supposing everyone were to model themselves on their rulers, what would that be like? There are many rulers in the world, but very few of them are *ren*. If we were to model ourselves on our rulers, then the model would not be one of *ren*. A model that is not *ren* cannot serve as a true model. Therefore of the three—parents, teachers, and rulers—not one can be regarded as the model for governing.
>
> (Knoblock and Riegel 2013, 4.2, with modifications)

In this passage, Mozi deals with the problem of standard/criterion/model in governance by refuting parents, scholars, and rulers as possible candidates. His reasoning is simple and straightforward, namely, given the plurality and heterogeneity of parents, scholars, and rulers in the world, following any of them would entail setting up standards, criteria, or models that are not *ren*. As Ivanhoe points out, "The fundamental problem [for the Mohists] is a fragmentation of values. Hence the most pressing task is to get people to agree on a single notion of what is right" (1998, 453).

However, what particularly interests us in this passage is the notion of *ren*. Given the context here, it is much more intuitive to translate *ren* as just, rather than humane. To translate *ren* as humane here is awkward since it makes little sense to say that the law/standard/model is not humane when there is no uniformity in it. On the other hand, it makes much more sense to say that the law/standard/model cannot be just if it is inconsistent, as it would then lead to differential treatments of people, which is unjust. Clearly, the idea of *ren* in the *Mozi* is a much more justice-oriented concept than it is in the *Analects*.

More importantly, for our purpose in this essay, Mozi and the Mohists can be seen as using the Golden Rule to push the element of *ai* in the Confucian moral universe to its logical conclusion, resulting in the ideal of impartial care (*jian ai*). Many scholars have pointed out the relative scarcity of *ai* in Confucius's iterations of *ren* in the *Analects*. This means that Mozi and his followers develop the seed of *ai* planted in the *Analects* into a full-blown notion of *jian ai*. For example, in "Jian Ai" I 兼愛上 Mozi appeals to the Golden Rule to explain impartial care:

> If we could induce everyone in the world to love others impartially, so that each person loved others just as he loved himself, would there be any person who failed to be obedient to superiors? If each person regarded his father and elder brothers as well as his lord just as he did himself, how could he do anything that was disobedient? And would there be any person who failed to be affectionate to inferiors? If each person regarded his younger brothers and sons as well as ministers just as he did himself, how could he do anything that was unaffectionate? Thus disobedient and unaffectionate conduct would cases to exist. And would there be robbery and murder? If each person regarded the families of other men just as he regards his own family, from whom would he steal? And if he regarded other men's bodies just as he regards his own, on whom would he inflict injury? Thus robbers and murderers would cease to exist. And would there be grand officers who bring disorder to teach other's houses and lords of the various states who attack each other's states? If a grand officer regarded other men's houses just as he regards his own, to whom would he bring disorder? If the lord of a state regarded another lord's state just as he regards his own, whom would he attack? Thus grand officers who bring disorder to each other's houses and the lords of the various states who attack each other's states would both cease to exist. If we could induce everyone in the world to love others impartially, states wouldn't attack each other, houses would not bring disorder to each other, there would be neither robbers nor murderers, and every lord and minister, father and son, would be capable of behaving obediently and affectionately. If the world were like this, then it would be well ordered.
>
> (Knoblock and Riegel 2013, 14.3)

In this passage, Mozi explicitly appeals to the Golden Rule in arguing for the impartial care of all in the world. More specifically, he states that if we could care about others the way we care about ourselves, there would be no unfilial son, no unloving parent, no theft, no attack on another's house, no aggression among states, and so on. As Carine Defoort points out, there is a major flaw in the Mohist argument "since the scope of caring is inherently ambiguous: very often, egoism or 'care for oneself' coincides with altruism or 'care for others,' such as when it benefits more than just oneself" (2013, 48).[13] Defoort does not think there are conceptual resources in the *Mozi* to deal with such a challenge.

However, the center of controversy concerning the Mohist ideal of *jian ai* has to do with its perceived impossibility and lack of a credible account for its moral motivation. Modern scholars have generally followed Mencius in interpreting the Mohist ideal of *jian ai* as incompatible with filial obligations. Against this interpretation, Dan Robins argues that the Mohist teachings of *jian ai*, rather than challenging the familial obligations, "consistently took for granted the value of the family, sometimes defending their core doctrines on its basis" (2008, 386–87). Defoort, in her recent essay, reaffirms the more traditional reading of the Mohist teaching of *jian ai* that highlights the tension between filial piety and impartial care. More interestingly, however, Defoort's study of the evolution of *jian ai* in the *Mozi* is helpful in our deliberations on the role reciprocity plays in the Mohist teachings as well as in providing an account of the moral motivation for *jian ai*.

Defoort observes a rather curious fact, that the term *jian ai* does not appear much in the three chapters with the title "Jian ai" but that it appears more frequently in later "Tian Zhi" 天志 chapters. After reviewing various hypotheses offered by A. C. Graham, Ding Weixiang, Watanabe Takashi, A. Taeko Brooks, Chris Fraser, and others to account for the differences among the three chapters, she offers her own solution to accommodate the textual and conceptual differences among the "Jian ai" triplet, which includes chapter 14, 15, and 16. Defoort argues that there is a gradual evolution from chapter 14 to chapter 16 that culminates in the notion of *jian ai* (2013, 41). As she elaborates,

> In the whole triplet, "care" in itself is never an object of controversy, but only its scope and specific content: the value of reciprocity (*xiang*) that was prominent in chapter 14 was slowly replaced by inclusiveness (*jian*)[14] from the middle of chapter 15 onward, and most explicitly so in chapter 16. The deep-rooted idea of reciprocity has not disappeared but has become a part of the explicit argument in favor of impartiality: those who are not shortsighted realize that being good to others will involve compensation for themselves (chapter 15) and for their loved ones (chapter 16). But this is clearly not the final stage of *jian ai*: its occurrence in chapter 16 as well as in other Core Chapters illustrates the inherent dynamics of the Mohist idea: the new demand for inclusive caring moves further on, almost leaving behind all reflections in terms of reciprocity.
>
> (Defoort 2013, 57–58)

The concern about the scope of care in the "Jian ai" chapters echoes our previous discussion of Confucius's take on the Golden Rule. In Defoort's observation of the doctrinal development of the notion of *jian ai* in the evolving Mohist moral thinking, reciprocity is seen as an important step from an agent-dependent moral universe to an agent-neutral moral universe. While the Mohists would make the leap to the agent-neutral moral universe, the Confucians remain reluctant to embrace the full implications of the Golden Rule and follow it to its logical conclusion.

Furthermore, Defoort argues that the idea of *jian ai* would be further radicalized in the "Tian Zhi" chapters in two ways, both having to do with reciprocity: "First, they establish a reciprocity between Heaven and all human beings, as a new way to motivate the inclusion of strangers in one's scope of caring. Second, they further radicalize their moral stance to the extent that reciprocity becomes a duty toward Heaven rather than something to be expected from others. Here the obligation of 'inclusive caring' is for the first time explicitly identified as the will of Heaven (*tian zhi yi* 天之意)" (Defoort 2013, 61). This means that *jian ai* is evolving into a transcendent notion as the will of Heaven, with the result that *jian ai* is expanded to include everybody as the expression of Heaven's will. In so doing, the Mohists put Heaven as the foundation of *jian ai* (62). Consequently, reciprocity is now considered too limited "to contain the ever-growing moral demands of the Mohists and to support the absolute duty to care for everybody without expecting anything in return" (63). In other words, truly universal justice ultimately transcends human reciprocity, which inevitably retains the residue of agent-dependency, whereas true universal impartiality is completely agent-neutral since Heaven is its true agent. Indeed, such an account of the evolution of *jian ai* in the *Mozi* can be seen as a later stage in the intellectual development of the Golden Rule in early Chinese intellectual history.

However, it is one thing to observe the power and cogency of an ethical theory, but quite another to judge whether anybody can use it to guide their moral actions. In this connection, the most frequent critique of the Mohist ideal of *jian ai* is that it lacks a credible account of the motivation for moral actions within the Mohist *jian ai* framework. That is, how can someone be motivated to embrace *jian ai*, especially when there is conflict in benefit between oneself or one's family and someone else or their family? The virtue of humaneness can more easily account for this by arguing that sentiments of partiality to those close to us, especially our family, are natural expressions of our humanity whereas it is unclear what could motivate anybody to save someone else's parents when one's own parents are in danger. The Mohists counter that if everyone can be uniformly motivated to save everybody else's parents our own parents will also be taken care of. David Wong (1989) and Van Norden (2007) have convincingly demonstrated the near impossibility of any person not morally prioritizing their loved ones over strangers. This very much echoes Mencius's accusation that the Mohists are unfilial. In other words, the consensus verdict for the Mohist teaching of *jian ai* is that it is beyond the limit of humanity (*Mencius* 3A/5).

This is where Defoort's account of *jian ai* can be helpful. What Defoort's interpretation has demonstrated is that the motivation for the Mohist vision of universal justice is fundamentally religious, with Heaven as its foundation.[15] In this connection, it is important to observe the extraordinary lengths to which the Mohists take the teaching of *jian ai*, in that they would come to the defense of a city unjustly attacked when they have no obvious ties with that city. Furthermore, the Mohists share with the Confucians the idea that there would be peace in the world if everybody treated one another's family as they would treat their own (*Mencius* 1A/7), but the Confucians do not take this idea as literally as the Mohists. As such, the Mohist teaching calls for a much more robust sense of communal and reciprocal commitment among its members whereas the Confucian position is considered more humanly possible and reasonable (and more secular by comparison). This is how we should interpret the Mohist teaching in the "Shang Tong" 尚同 chapters, wherein Mozi touts the leader of a community, whether village (*li* 里), district (*xiang* 鄉), or state (*guo* 國), as a *ren ren* 仁人 and advocates the idea that everybody in a given community conform him- or herself to the leader by taking his ideas, speech, and actions as the sole criterion in that community. Given the context here, it is much more intuitive to translate *ren ren* as a just person than as a humane person. The Mohist concern here is precisely how a robust community can be constituted with uniform standards and models such that *jian ai* can be put into practice within such a vigorously disciplined community.

✳ ✳ ✳

To conclude, in this essay I have attempted to make the case that there is serious conceptual tension between humaneness and justice in Chinese philosophical discourse during the classical period. It is done through an investigation of the relationship between *ren* and the Golden Rule in the *Analects* and the *Mozi*. Essentially, what I am proposing here is that if we problematize the tensions in the classical texts, instead of explaining them away, we can potentially open up hitherto unexplored dimensions of the projects classical thinkers like Confucius and Mozi were engaged in, and we can thereby acquire a better appreciation of the intellectual struggles they faced.

Mencius is clearly aware of the tension between humaneness and justice, as evidenced by his solution to Shun's predicament about whether to prosecute his criminal father (*Mencius* 7A/35). According to Mencius, Shun, an ancient sage king idolized in Confucianism, did not stop his justice minister's persecution of his father, but before he allowed that to happen, Shun abdicated his throne and carried his father to a faraway land to live there forever happily with no regret. Shun's refusal to stand by and allow his father to be prosecuted is humane but unjust to most people, yet his abdication removed the element of injustice since it would be the equivalent of Shun recusing himself in the case of a conflict of interest and duty, even though it has been construed as the demonstration of his selfless filial act to save his father regardless of the cost to himself (loss of empire). The example in the *Annals of Lü Buwei* cited in the beginning of this essay, wherein an ideal Mohist magistrate executed his criminal son, provides a sharp contrast to the story of Shun and his father. In the Mohist example, the magistrate is just but inhumane.

This unresolved tension between humaneness and justice has a direct bearing on the Confucian idea of moral cultivation. More specifically, in order to solve the inherent tension in the Confucian project between concerns for humaneness and justice, the Confucians eventually settled on the idea of moral cultivation, with the hope that a morally cultivated agent alone will be best positioned to handle a particular moral dilemma that might be unsolvable at the level of doctrines and generalities. In other words, the irreducibility of human subjectivity in the Confucian moral universe can be seen as directly related to their unwillingness to entertain the possibility of a singular uniform moral system that allows for no exceptions or discretions.[16] In this respect, it is perhaps not a historical coincidence that, unlike the Confucians, the Mohists did not develop an elaborate system for moral cultivation in the way the Confucians did, since they did not place all their hope on idealized moral exemplars. Rather, their hope is to establish a uniform moral standard and norm that is applicable to everyone under all circumstances and allows for no special considerations or discretions. The radicality of the Mohist moral project is simply breathtaking, especially within the context of the classical Chinese intellectual environment and the social conditions of the time. For complex social and political reasons, Mohism did not survive as a philosophical school in postclassical China. Nonetheless it would be a mistake to underestimate the impact of the Mohists within subsequent Chinese intellectual history. The ideal of universal justice heralded by the Mohists lived on through various mutations in the hands of later Chinese thinkers, including many Confucians.

Notes

I would like to thank Philip J. Ivanhoe and Victoria Harrison for their detailed comments and suggestions on this essay. I would also like to thank the participants of the "International Conference on Oneness in Philosophy and Religion," held in the City University of Hong Kong, April 25–27, 2015, for their comments on an earlier version of this article. Needless to say, all errors and inadequacies remain mine alone.

1. In her fascinating book, *Confucius, Rawls, and the Senses of Justice*, Erin Cline (2013) rightly emphasizes the role of moral cultivation in discussing the Confucian sense of justice and clearly regards justice as a personal virtue appreciated by Confucius. She lists the virtues touted by Confucius in the *Analects* as expressing the sentiment of justice, such as *yi* 義 (rightness), *shu* 恕 (reciprocity), *bu bi* 不比 (not partial or biased),

and *zhou* 周 (associate widely), and so on (2013, 152–53). Cline's book has made an important contribution to the recognition of the importance of justice in Confucius's teaching, especially the judicial aspect of personal virtues a committed Confucian should cultivate and strive for. However, her book does not address the conceptual tension between her own justice-centered interpretation and the more traditional humaneness-centered interpretation of the classical Confucian project. In fact, Cline includes humaneness as one of the expressions of justice in the *Analects*, without looking into the tension between the two. On the contrary, Cline devotes a great deal of effort to explaining away the tension in *Analects* 13.18, cited earlier, wherein Confucius famously claims that an upright son should cover for his father if his father commits theft (157–67).

2. Another common translation of *ren* is humaneness, but as we will see in the following this essay is meant to contest such an interpretation. Some early scholars also used "benevolence" to translate *ren* in the *Analects*, but more recent scholarly discussion has reached a consensus that "benevolence" is more appropriate for Mencius's use of *ren*. James Legge's translation of *ren* in the *Mencius* as benevolence has been extremely influential in modern scholarship. Legge's translation is influenced by what he perceives as striking similarities between Mencius and Bishop Butler in their understandings of human nature. Benevolence is the first natural principle of human nature in Butler's *Sermons Upon Human Nature* (Legge 1960, 60–64). I will leave *ren* untranslated in this essay in order to highlight its ambiguity.

3. All translations in this essay are mine, unless noted otherwise.

4. Ivanhoe points out to me that the kind of justice I am referring to here, each receiving his or her due, is Aristotelian rather than distributive (fairness) as the latter implies excellence in social institutions.

5. There are two versions of the five hegemons, but Duke Huan of Qi is recognized in both as the first on the list.

6. The best-known Chinese historian, Sima Qian (司馬遷 c. 145–c. 87 BCE), wrote a glowing biography of Guan Zhong (*Grand Scribe's Records*, vol. 7, pp. 9–14). The translators of volume 5.1 provide an interesting note on Sima Qian's own attitude toward Guan Zhong:

> Ssu-ma Ch'ien (Sima Qian), who himself wrote that "establishing one's fame is the endpoint of all action," certainly identifies with the alleged reasons underlying Kuan Chung's (Guan Zhong) decision to not commit ritual suicide along with Shao Hu 召忽 (d. 685 B.C.) when their lord Tzu Chiu 子糾 was killed by his brother Duke Huan. Together with Kuan Chung's great friend, Pao Shu, the Grand Scribe no doubt well understood why Kuan Chung may have said "I would not be ashamed by the trivial principle (*chieh* 節; of committing suicide), but I would be disgraced if my merit and fame were not made known to the world." Similarly, Ssu-ma Ch'ien justifies his own decision to not take the nobler path of suicide after the disgrace of castration citing reasons including he "despises leaving the world without letting the glory of [his] writings be shown to posterity." Kuan Chung would also probably agree with Ssu-ma Ch'ien's assessment of the Ch'u minister Wu Tzu Hsü (伍子胥 d. 485 B.C.) that had he "accompanied [his father] She 奢 in death, how would he differ from an ant or a mole-cricket? Casting aside the trivial rightness (*yi* 義; of committing suicide), he wiped clean a great disgrace, and his name has been handed down to later generations.
>
> (*Grand Scribe's Records*, vol. 5.1, p. 127)

7. I address the Sinological challenge to Chinese philosophy more extensively in Jiang 2016.

8. Cf. Van Norden 2007, 72–74.

9. Van Norden (2007, 75) thinks it represents more of the Zengzi's school of Confucius's teaching. See Ivanhoe's (2008) response.

10. Nivison sheds a critical light on the traditional hierarchy deeply embedded in the teaching of the Golden Rule, even though he still insists that the Confucian Golden Rule undergirds the vision of a common humanity, a conclusion Martha Nussbaum (2003) is skeptical about given the unchallenged status of hierarchy embedded in Nivison's interpretation of the Confucian Golden Rule.

11. In his more recent article on the Golden Rule, Ivanhoe interprets *shu* as having to do with moral discretion that "helps me to be sensitive to the lives of those who are directly affected by my actions" (2008, 96). I am more sympathetic to his earlier interpretation, which emphasizes reversibility. Ivanhoe points out to me that his two accounts are compatible: "The notion of discretion is connected with the obligation to do my duty as described by the rites, which is critical for making sure people get what they are due. Discretion is the ability to emend, bend, or suspend the rites when sympathetic consideration moves me to do so. But making such exceptions is what I would want others to do for me and something I discover through the practice of SHU (imaginatively putting myself in another's place)" (private comments).

12. Chad Hansen (1992, 168) is baffled by the inconsistency of Mencius's ideas in the latter's reluctance to embrace the universalist conclusion of his own teaching.

13. Ivanhoe disputes Defoort's point here: "Moral altruism is about the aim or focus of one's care. If I keep myself healthy and alive in order to donate my kidneys to my twin sisters, it would be odd to accuse me of being selfish in tending to myself" (private comment).

14. Defoort translates *jian* as inclusive or inclusiveness whereas I have used impartial or impartiality as the translation of *jian* in this essay. Ivanhoe observes that inclusiveness "describes a result of impartiality but that is not the meaning of the term *jian*. The term *jian* describes the type of *ai* ("care") being advocated, not its consequences" (private comment).

15. Ivanhoe presents a more nuanced account of the Mohist motivation. While critiquing the lack of discussion of the psychological dimension of human actions in Mohist theories, Ivanhoe (1998) takes much more seriously the religious aspect of the Mohist moral teaching.

16. In *Mencius* 7A/26, Mencius expresses his exasperation toward no allowance of discretion or taking circumstances into consideration.

References

Brooks, E. Bruce, and A. Taeko. 1998. *The Original Analects: Sayings of Confucius and His Successors*. New York: Columbia University Press.

Chan, Wing-tsit. 1955. "The Evolution of the Confucian Concept of Jen." *Philosophy East and West* 4 (4): 295–319.

Cline, Erin. 2013. *Confucius, Rawls, and the Senses of Justice*. New York: Fordham University Press.

Csikszentmihalyi, Mark. 2008. "The Golden Rule in Confucianism." In *The Golden Rule: The Ethics of Reciprocity in World Religions*, edited by Jacob Neusner and Bruce Chilton, 157–69. New York: Continuum.

Defoort, Carine. 2013. "Are the Three 'Jian Ai' Chapters About Universal Love?" In *The Mozi as an Evolving Text: Different Voices in Early Chinese Thought*, edited by Carine Defoort and Nicolas Standaert, 35–68. Leiden: Brill.

Fraser, Chris. 2009. "The Mohist School." In *History of Chinese Philosophy*, edited by Bo Mou, Routledge History of World Philosophies 3, 137–63. New York: Routledge.

Hansen, Chad. 1992. *A Daoist Theory of Chinese Thought: A Philosophical Interpretation*. Oxford: Oxford University Press.

Ivanhoe, Philip J. 1990. "Reweaving the 'One Thread' of the *Analects*." *Philosophy East and West* 40 (1): 17–33.

——. 1998. "Mohist Philosophy." In *Routledge Encyclopedia of Philosophy*, edited by Edward Craig. New York: Routledge.

——. 2008. "The 'Golden Rule' in the *Analects*." In *Confucius Now: Contemporary Encounters with the* Analects, edited by David Jones, 81–107. LaSalle, IL: Open Court.

Jiang, Tao. 2016. "The Problem of Authorship and the Project of Chinese Philosophy: Zhuang Zhou and the *Zhuangzi* Between Sinology and Philosophy Within Western Academy." *Dao: A Journal of Comparative Philosophy* (March).

Knoblock, John, and Jeffrey Riegel, trans. 2000. *The Annals of Lü Buwei* 呂氏春秋. Stanford: Stanford University Press.

——, trans. 2013. *Mozi: A Study and Translation of the Ethical and Political Writings*. Berkeley, CA: Institute of East Asian Studies.

Lau, D. C., trans. 1983. *Confucius: The Analects*. Bilingual ed. Hong Kong: Chinese University Press.

Legge, James. 1960. *The Chinese Classics, with a Translation, Critical and Exegetical Notes, Prolegomena, and Copious Indexes*. Vol. 2, *The Works of Mencius, with a Concordance Table and Notes by Dr. Arthur Waley*. Hong Kong: Hong Kong University Press.

Lin, Yü-sheng. 1974–75. "The Evolution of the Pre-Confucian Meaning of *Jen* 仁 and the Confucian Concept of Moral Autonomy." *Monumenta Serica* 31:172–204.

Luo, Shirong. 2012. "Setting the Record Straight: Confucius' Notion of *Ren*." *Dao: A Journal of Comparative Philosophy* 11:39–52.

Nivison, David. 1996. "Golden Rule Arguments in Chinese Moral Philosophy." In *The Ways of Confucianism: Investigations in Chinese Philosophy*, edited by Bryan Van Norden, 59–76. LaSalle, IL: Open Court.

Nussbaum, Martha. 2003. "Golden Rule Arguments: A Missing Thought?" In *The Moral Circle and the Self: Chinese and Western Approaches*, edited by Kim-chong Chong, Sor-hoon Tan, and C. L. Ten, 3–16. Chicago: Open Court.

Rickett, W. Allyn, trans. 1985. *Guanzi: Political, Economic, and Philosophical Essays from Early China*. Vol. 1. Princeton: Princeton University Press.

Robin, Dan. 2008. "The Moists and the Gentlemen of the World." *Journal of Chinese Philosophy* 35 (3): 385–402.

Roetz, Heiner. 1993. *Confucian Ethics of the Axial Age: A Reconstruction Under the Aspect of the Breakthrough Toward Postconventional Thinking*. Albany: State University of New York Press.

Sima (Ssu-ma), Qian (Ch'ien). 1994. *Grand Scribe's Records*. Vol. 7, *The Memoirs of Pre-Han China*, edited by William H. Nienhauser, Jr., translated by Tsai-fa Cheng, Zongli Lu, William H. Nienhauser, Jr., and Robert Reynolds. Bloomington: Indiana University Press.

——. 2006. *Grand Scribe's Records*. Vol. 5.1, *The Hereditary Houses of Pre-Han China*, edited by William H. Nienhauser, Jr., translated by Weiguo Cao, Zhi Chen, Scott Cook, Hongyu Huang, Bruce Knickerbocker, William H. Nienhauser, Jr., Wang Jing, Zhang Zhenjun, and Zhao Hua. Bloomington: Indiana University Press.

Slingerland, Edward, trans. 2003. *Confucius Analects, with Selection from Traditional Commentaries*. Indianapolis: Hackett.

Van Norden, Bryan. 2007. *Virtue Ethics and Consequentialism in Early Chinese Philosophy*. Cambridge: Cambridge University Press.

Wong, David. 1989. "Universalism Versus Love with Distinctions: An Ancient Debate Revived." *Journal of Chinese Philosophy* 16 (3–4): 251–72.

CHAPTER 3

ONE ALONE AND MANY

STEPHEN R. L. CLARK

I t is a common error—at least among philosophers—to contrast mysticism and morality, and thence to conclude that either Plotinus can have little to say about everyday moral concerns or else that what he does say is too robust and uncompassionate to convince us now. It is true that, on the one hand, Plotinus seems to suggest that we should detach ourselves from all earthly concerns, and regard events here-now as no more than children's games (*Ennead* I.4 [46].8; III.2 [47].8). On the other hand, he is confident that we should care for whatever is kin to the Father (and therefore should care for every living soul: *Ennead* II.9 [33].16), and supposes that Minos's communion with Zeus issued in laws for the proper conduct of society (*Ennead* VI.9 [9].7). My argument is that "the flight of the alone to the Alone" (*Ennead* VI.9 [9].11) is misinterpreted.[1] *Monos* does not mean "solitary," but "pure" or "undistracted." Seeking *solitude* is, on the contrary, the very essence of the fall: "as if they were tired of being together, they each go to their own" (*Ennead* IV.8 [6].4, 11f.), and the inward turn that Plotinus recommends is actually a turn toward community. "When we look outside that on which we depend we do not know that we are one, like faces which are many on the outside but have one head inside. But if someone is able to turn around, either by himself or having the good luck to have his hair pulled by Athena herself, he will see God and himself and the all. . . . He will stop marking himself off from all being and will come to all the All without going out anywhere" (*Ennead* VI.5 [23].7, 9f.).[2] Similarly those passages that now seem to us robust and uncompassionate are a recipe for a more genuine love: seeing the beauty of each living soul, but without concupiscence, sets each soul free to help the World Soul make the world. In other words, in Plotinus we find a mystical expression of oneness that entails a practical morality of profound and universal care.

Mysticism and Morality

What reasons might there be, despite my firm assurance, to contrast "mysticism" and "morality"? The mystic doubts that anything in *this* world matters much, and tries to reach outward or upward to some "condition of complete simplicity (costing not less than everything)."[3] The moralist, on the contrary, supposes that *this* life is of supreme importance, and despises those who opt out of the daily struggle. Mystics typically think *one* thing is needful; moralists that there are many good and bad things, and many rights and wrongs. Moralists—it is supposed—must *reason* to their conclusions (even if their fundamental principles have a different root), while mystics expect to transcend reason (even if they are prepared to use it in the early stages of their ascent). Our image of the mystic may be a pillar saint, and of the moralist a social activist (though in real life the pillar saint may have a daily surgery, and the activist will only sustain her efforts and avoid despair if she has some access to a realm beyond the usual). Most recent ethical philosophers have sided with the moralist against the mystic, Martha against Mary, and take it for granted that "true morality" lies in an altruistic desire to improve the world (or at least some favored section of the world—typically, humankind), or at least do it no "harm." Ancient moralists doubted that we could do more than improve ourselves, and must take the world as it came—and maybe for that reason were all more open to the "mystical."

But my intention here is to examine Plotinus—and specifically the view that, being a mystic, he could have little to say on morals. It is, on the face of it, a strange claim. Porphyry records Plotinus's fury when specious arguments were offered for the thesis that pupils should have sex with their master, if the master wished it.[4] "He refused to take medicines containing the flesh of wild beasts, giving as his reason that he did not approve of eating the flesh even of domestic animals."[5] He looked after the property of the orphans left in his care, in case they turned out not to be philosophers.[6] He argued against suicide in general,[7] and gave Porphyry good advice when the latter was afflicted with depression. And he wanted to found a city—not just a university with support staff![8] In short, he *did* involve himself in everyday affairs, and had strong views on many controversial moral issues. Far from adopting a purely quietist attitude, he urged us to "stand up against the blows of fortune like a great trained athlete" (I.4 [46].8, 25), remembering that "the law says those who fight bravely, not those who pray, are to come safe out of the wars" (III.2 [47].32, 36f.).

It is perhaps that very robustness that perturbs modern moralists. There is a sense in which, by contrast with the ancients, we are all utilitarians nowadays, since we take it for granted that suffering is an evil, and that decent people aim at least to reduce it, even if we are not all convinced that this is best done by acting upon utilitarian calculations. Even Epicureans, in the days before effective analgesics and anaesthetics, were more concerned to help us *bear* our pains than hide from them. Plotinus's blunt reminder that "as far as [the good man's] pains go, when they are very great, he will bear them as long as he can; when they are too much for him, they will bear him off" (I.4 [46].8, 1ff.) is an echo of Epicurus, who bore the pain of terminal strangury by recalling past philosophical conversations with his friends.[9] The real implication of consistent utilitarianism is that the only lives worth preserving or desiring are ones that provide a surplus of pleasure over pain (not necessarily to themselves). Plotinus, like other ancients, held that "a man has not failed if he fails to win beauty of colours or bodies, or power or office or kingship even, but if he fails to win [the vision of the Good]" (I.6 [1].7, 34f.). He has not failed in that case even if he does not realize he has succeeded.

"And when the pains concern others?" (I.4 [46].8, 13f.). Decent people nowadays care about others' pains. It is therefore a shock to learn that Plotinus, like the Stoics, thought it weakness to feel for others: "There is evidence for this in the fact that we think it something gained if we do not know about other people's sufferings, and even regard it as a good thing if we die first" (I.4 [46].8, 14f.). That at least *is* weakness, to be avoided by facing up to what "ordinary nature normally finds terrible" (I.4 [46].8, 23f.). But modern moralists, and all of us, are likelier to feel that virtue lies in pity and fear, rather than in knowing that "though some natures may not like [such evils], one's own can bear them, not as terrors but as children's bogies." In the very next treatise that he wrote he added that "we should be spectators of murders, and all deaths, and takings and sacking of cities, as if they were on the stages of theatres" (III.2 [47].15, 44f.). Such things are no more than children's games: "one must not take weeping and lamenting as evidence of the presence of evils, for children, too, weep and wail over things that are not evils" (III.2 [47].15, 61).

If some boys, who have kept their bodies in good training, but are inferior in soul to their bodily condition because of lack of education, win a wrestle with others who are trained neither in body or soul and grab their food and their dainty clothes, would the affair be anything but a joke? Or would it not be right for even the lawgiver to allow them to suffer this as a penalty for their laziness and luxury? . . . Those who do these things are punished, first by being wolves and ill-fated men. . . . But the wicked rule by the cowardice of the ruled; for this is just, and the opposite is not.

(III.2 [47].8, 16–21, 26–28, 51–52)

On the one hand the genuinely virtuous cannot be bullied. On the other, such virtuous persons will probably not intervene to prevent such bullying. More than a little alarmingly—to our taste—he is also willing to consider that "there is no accident in a man's becoming a slave, nor is he taken prisoner in war by chance, nor is outrage done on his body without due cause, but he was once the doer of that which he now suffers; and a man who made away with his mother will be made away with by a son when he has become a woman, and one who has raped a woman will be a woman in order to be raped" (III.2 [47].13, 11ff.). So though the agent in these cases is wicked (and will suffer in his turn), he has done no real harm—he has indeed, in a sense, done justly. The whole is beautiful, or as beautiful as it could be, despite or even because of its evil-seeming parts, "just as the public executioner, who is a scoundrel, does not make his well-governed city worse" (III.2 [47].17, 87f.).

> A manifold life exists in the All and makes all things, and in its living embroiders a rich variety and does not rest from ceaselessly making beautiful and shapely living toys. And when men, mortal as they are, direct their weapons against fighting in orderly ranks, doing what they do in sport in their war-dances, their battles show that all human concerns are children's games, and tell us that deaths are nothing terrible, and that those who die in wars and battles anticipate only a little the death which comes in old age—they go away and come back quicker. But if their property is taken away while they are still alive, they may recognize that it was not theirs before either, and that its possession is a mockery to the robbers themselves when others take it away from them.
>
> (III.2 [47].15, 31–43)

Flight of the Alone

So maybe the critics are correct. Virtue matters, but not virtuous *acts* in any sense familiar to the modern moralist. "For what can true [self-possession] (*sophrosune*) be except not keeping company with bodily pleasures, but avoiding them as impure and belonging to something impure? Courage, too, is not being afraid of death. And death is the separation of body and soul; and a man does not fear this if he welcomes the prospect of being alone (*monos genesthai*) [better, "being stripped"]. Again, greatness of soul is despising the things here: and wisdom (*phronesis*) is an intellectual activity that turns away from the things below and leads the soul to those above" (I.6 [1].6, 7–13; see also I.2 [19].5, 6ff.). "And if you are wronged, what is there dreadful in that to an immortal?" (II.9 [33].9, 15f.).

Even *righteous* action is a sort of weakness, a failure—in a way—to live up to contemplative virtue. All action is subject to the enchantments of the flesh

(IV.4 [28].44). Someone properly united to the intellect and its vision does not *need* to make things different here: what better image of the intelligible could there be than the one that exists already (II.9 [33].4, 26), and so what need to improve or interfere with it? On the other hand, if there are indeed this-worldly evils to be remedied, the virtuous do not wish this to be so. A truly courageous person (say) would not actually want to display courage—since that depends on there being wrongs to resist or even wars to fight "as if a physician were to wish that nobody needed his skill" (VI.8 [39].5, 13–21). "Pity would be no more, if we did not make somebody poor"[10]—unless pity (or better, liberality) is the name of something better than its practical performance. And finally, neither accomplishment nor performance is entirely in our power (as the Stoics also recognized). All that we can ourselves achieve is to "love and serve the Lord" (*ton theon theorein kai therapeuein*),[11] without expecting any merely earthly reward, whether for ourselves or others.

The higher, noncontingent principles themselves, "absolute justice or any other moral absolute," are not strictly virtues, "but a kind of exemplar: virtue is what is derived from it in the soul" (I.2 [19].6, 18f.). If there were no such rightness we could not even reason about the right, nor do right when we had to (V.1 [10].11).[12] "So the higher justice in the soul is its activity toward intellect, its self-[possession] (*sophronein*) is its inward turning to intellect, its courage is its freedom from affections (*apatheia*), according to the likeness of that to which it looks which is free from affections by nature" (I.2 [19].6, 23f.).[13] The lesser, "civic" virtues may be a necessary stage on the way upward, but they are not themselves the virtue that Plotinus wishes. True virtue lies in gathering up the energies we have invested in the outward, sensual world. We may or even must begin from beautiful sights, then beautiful ways of life, "beautiful works, not those which the arts produce, but the works of men who have a name for goodness, then look at the souls of the people who produce the beautiful works" (I.6 [1].9, 4ff.). But the goal is to go back into yourself and see. "Never stop working on your statue till the divine glory of virtue shines out on you, till you see self-possession (*sophrosune*) enthroned upon its holy seat."[14]

Even other Platonists were not altogether convinced by Plotinus's final gloss. The higher soul to which we should awaken is already There, and exists in its felicity, whatever happens here (IV.8 [6].8). Even if the good man were asleep or mad, he would still be *eudaimon* (I.4 [46].9), just as he could be healthy or handsome without knowing it. Even in the bull of Phalaris, even in the utmost agony, "there is another which, even while it is compelled to accompany that which suffers pain, remains in its own company and will not fall short of the vision of the universal good" (I.4 [46].13, 6ff.). So the higher soul's existence and essential goodness are unaffected by anything that the composite or lower being does or suffers. Heracles's shadow might recall his earthly life, but *Heracles himself*—who often represents our own true self—does not remember it

(IV.3 [27].27).[15] The point then is not even the stern doctrine that we *shouldn't* pay attention to these corporeal events or passions, but that our higher soul is always already free, whatever happens here. So what reason can it have for caring?

> The man who belongs to this world may be handsome and tall and rich and the ruler of all mankind (since he is essentially of this region), and we ought not to envy him for things like these, by which he is beguiled. The wise man will perhaps not have them at all, and if he has them will himself reduce them, if he cares for his true self. He will reduce and gradually extinguish his bodily advantages by neglect, and will put away authority and office. He will take care of his bodily health, but will not wish to be altogether without experience of illness, nor indeed also of pain.[16]
>
>   (I.4 [46].14, 14ff.)

But if we are all already There, what does it matter what we do about things here? Correspondingly, if this world is a game, how can we take it seriously enough even to play it properly?

The Dance of Immortal Love

Plotinian philosophy is not the only doctrine that creates a problem. Stoics must somehow combine the habit of giving advice on how best to live with the conviction that everything is already perfect. The wise man regrets and repents *nothing*, since he knows that nothing ever happens against God's will, but still prepares precepts for those who are not wise even though their actual, fore-known *disobedience* to those very precepts will be what God requires. Plotinus is much clearer than the Stoics that each individual soul does make a real con-tribution, and that not everything that happens should: "If all things are well done, can the doers act unjustly or err? And how can we assert that some things are according to nature, but others against nature, if all things that happen and are done are according to nature?" (III.2 [47].16, 3ff.).[17] Beauty is woven, in this world, from brighter and darker threads, and even if there is no prospect of making a new, "better" world (II.9 [33].5, 24f.), it is our task here-now to aim for the higher. "In this city [of the world] virtue is honoured and vice has its appro-priate dishonour, and not merely the images of gods but gods themselves— [that is, presumably, the stars]—look down on us from above" (II.9 [33].9, 19ff.). This world here, in short, is not entirely empty, and "becoming solitary" is not to be understood as an absolute withdrawal from it. Correspondingly, though Plotinus sometimes speaks of the soul's *fall* into this world here, he is also con-fident that the soul did right in coming. It is in every nature "to produce what comes after it, and to unfold itself as a seed does" (IV.8 [6].6, 8f.).

So what does aiming for the higher amount to? How are we to ascend?

> It does no good at all to say "Look to God," unless one also teaches how one is to look. . . . In reality it is virtue which goes before us to the goal and, when it comes to exist in the soul along with wisdom, shows God; but God, if you talk about him without true virtue, is only a name. Again, despising the universe and the gods in it and the other noble things is certainly not becoming good. . . . For anyone who feels affection for anything at all shows kindness to all that is akin to the object of his affection, and to the children of the father that he loves. But every soul is a child [specifically, a *daughter*] of That Father.
>   (II.9 [33].15, 33—16.10)

"When [the soul] is there [that is, in the intelligible realm] [she] has the heavenly love, but here love becomes vulgar; for the soul there is the heavenly Aphrodite, but here becomes the vulgar Aphrodite, a kind of whore. And every soul is Aphrodite. . . . The soul then in her natural state is in love with God and wants to be united with him; it is like the noble love of a girl for her noble father" (VI.9 [9].9, 28ff.).

The original and ever-present truth is a community—but to realize it we must go within, shaking free of sensory illusions.

> If one likens it to a living richly varied sphere, or imagines it as a thing all faces, shining with living faces, or as all the pure souls running together into the same place, with no deficiencies but having all that is their own, and universal Intellect seated on their summits so that the region is illuminated by intellectual light—if one imagined it like this one would be seeing it somehow as one sees another from outside; but one must become that, and make oneself the contemplation.
>   (VI.7 [38].15, 25–34)

It would be premature (presumptuous, pretentious) to attempt any outline or description of what that transformation could be like. It is enough to suggest that we should take seriously the intellectual image of the One, and recognize that the path to it is through multiplicity. Our Fall is by desiring our own world, and the ascent is by acknowledging that there are many faces, facets of reality "and universal Intellect seated on their summits." The "inward turn" is not a turn *away* from company. It is when we recall the *real* world in which we live that we can have companions: concentrating instead on the sensory and sensual phenomena that we do *not* share with others is to lose them. Most of us may occasionally realize this obvious truth, that the world you and I inhabit is not structured as our senses would suggest. My body is not the center of the world, and "over there" and "here" are merely part of my (our) illusion. Most of us forget this truth at once, "as if people who slept through their life thought the things in their dreams were reliable and obvious, but, if someone woke them up, disbelieved in what they saw with their eyes open and went to sleep again" (V.5 [32].11, 19ff.).[18] It is for this reason that an assembly has more chance of achieving truth than any singleton (VI.5 [23].10), unless that singleton is inspired, as Minos was, who brought the laws down from his colloquy with Zeus (VI.9 [9].7).[19] The best image of the divine intellect, the intelligible world, to which we are native, is a community. In Armstrong's words, "Plotinus's divine mind [which is also the totality of intelligible being] is not just a mind knowing a lot of eternal objects. It is an organic living community of interpenetrating beings which are at once Forms and intelligences, all 'awake and alive,' in which every part thinks and therefore is the whole; so that all are one mind and yet each retains its distinct individuality without which the whole would be impoverished."[20]

So what becomes of that misleading description, as commonly remembered, of a "flight of the alone to the Alone"?[21] What is it to be *monos*? I suggest that the better parallel is with Jerome's injunction: "*nudus nudum Jesum sequi.*"[22] *Monos* here means "pure," freed from unnecessary passion and transient opinion, and so at last enabled to return to the common truth, to wake up, to have *Nous* as our king: *Nous* is King (alongside the One), "but we too are kings (*basileuomen*), when we are in accord with it; we can be in accord with it in two ways, either by having something like its writing written in us like laws, or by being as if filled with it and able to see it and be aware of it as present."[23] We need to strip.

Modern moralists of course may still object to Plotinus's implicit account of what it is like to mirror that intellect. Disturbingly to modern tastes (and perhaps fallaciously), Plotinus concludes that it would be wrong to make our ordinary cities only out of obvious equals: cities, like the world itself, need all sorts and ranks of creatures, multiple visions of a transcendent whole (III.2 [47].11.13ff.). Such cities can avoid corruption, but only if we all acknowledge that more is real than we can individually sense, and that there is an inner self that tyrants cannot touch, or popular opinion wholly master. The ancients were right after all: each of us has many parts to play. It is only when we are identified too closely with those parts that the play becomes intolerable. When we recall instead that we might play other parts, and that the natures we now wear are only borrowed glories, it is possible to greet all others as the spiritual equals—or superiors—that they are. Because I know I *might have been* a tramp, a leper, or a lord (or else a dog, a star, or a spider—or even a rapist or a rape-victim), I know that the ones who variously *are* those things (who wear those natures) are greater than the parts they play. It is possible to believe both that the various roles have their own duties, and are owed deference in the dance of time (as one dancer stands aside for another, or momentarily curtseys), and that the actual dancers have a worth that far transcends the dance.

Dancing indeed is one of Plotinus's favored metaphors, and one that outlasted him. The Delphic Oracle and Porphyry conclude their account of Plotinus's life with the expectation that he has gone to be a companion of those who "set the dance of immortal love."[24] "There the most blessed spirits have their birth and live a life filled full of festivity and joy; and this life lasts for ever, made blessed by the gods." Our task here-now, he thought, was to present at least an image of that dance. Even a tortoise, he jokingly remarks, could avoid being trampled on if it only managed to range itself with the movement of the dance (II.9 [33].7, 36f.). And that we can manage only if we look toward the leader and conductor of the chorus.

> That One, therefore, since it has no otherness is always present, and we are present to it when we have no otherness; and the One does not desire us, so as to be around us, but we desire it, so that we are around it. And we are always around it but do not always look to it; it is like a choral dance: in the order of its singing the choir keeps round its *koruphaion* but may sometimes turn away, so that he is out of their sight, but when it turns back to him it sings beautifully and is truly with him; so we too are always around him—and if we were not, we should be totally dissolved and no longer exist—but not always turned to him; but when we do look to him, then we are at our goal and at rest and do not sing out of tune as we truly dance our god-inspired dance around him.
>
> (VI.9 [9].8.34–45)

The leader of the dance is not, as both Armstrong and McKenna suggest, its "conductor," standing over us on his rostrum. The leader is the lead dancer. "If one takes away the leader," according to Demosthenes in an earlier century, "the rest of the chorus is done for."[25] Just possibly we are to think instead—or else as well—of the musician sitting at the center, in the place of Apollo (who is the god "who sits in the centre, on the navel of the earth, and is the interpreter of religion to all mankind").[26]

Looking Toward the One

We are to look "toward the One." But what is it in us that constitutes an "experience" of the One, when any such experience, setting oneself over against another object, is untrue to the very reason for positing that One? How can we look *toward* without also looking *away*—and how can we do that when the One is both everywhere and nowhere? How can we talk about something that, by hypothesis, cannot be meaningfully described or discriminated from anything else? "It is truly ineffable: for whatever you say about it, you will always be speaking of a 'something'" (VI.8 [39].16, 30–34). What is this wordless glimpse into a higher reality even than the infinite web of forms, and how—if we can't speak about it—do mystics (and Plotinus) fill so many pages? What do they carry away from the experience, and how might they advise we seek it? "How can the self that knows be known?"[27]

One answer—inadequate as it is—might be that we recognize that "knowing self" in others. Realizing that the world we inhabit is molded to our own preconceptions and interests may be occasioned by a prior recognition that other people, other creatures, are experiencing things very differently, that *their* worlds are likewise molded to their own preconceptions and interests, and that the World Itself is larger and more intricate than they—or we—imagined. That shock of recognition may lead us no further than a glimpse of the encompassing reality, and of our own involvement in it. On the one hand, everything is connected—as the Stoics also recognized—to everything else, and the sad attempt to disconnect ourselves so as to have our "private world" is bound to fail: as Heracleitus said, the world—for those who are awake—is single and in common, while each dreamer turns aside to a private world.[28] On the other, everything is, as it were, a version of some less transient form, arranged—in Plotinus's universe—in a hierarchy of being: everything, in summary, is an expression of an immortal beauty. The singleness of reality may be understood in both these ways: its interconnectedness and its underlying identity.

But there is still more to say. As far as I can tell, no one has picked up Martin Buber's echoing of Plotinus in his discussion of what he called the I-Thou relationship: "In every sphere, in every relational act, through everything that becomes present to us, we gaze toward the train of the eternal You; in each we perceive a breath of it, in every you we address the eternal You, in every sphere according to its manner. All spheres are included in it, while it is included in none. Through all of them shines the one presence."[29] The Other that we occasionally acknowledge is not another object in the world, conditioned and contained by our own viewpoint—or even by the real nature of the actual, natural objects: "Whoever says You does not have something for his object. For wherever there is something there is also another something; every It borders on other Its; It is only by virtue of bordering on others. But where You is said there is no something. You has no borders. Whoever says You does not have something; he has nothing. But he stands in relation."[30] A real encounter with any Other is the discovery of what is meant, in the Jewish tradition at least, by "God":

The sacred is here and now. The only God worth keeping is a God that cannot be kept. The only God worth talking about is a God that cannot be talked about. God is no object of discourse, knowledge or even experience. He cannot be spoken of, but he can be spoken to; he cannot be seen, but he can be listened to. The only possible relationship with God is to address him and to be addressed by him, here and now—or, as Buber puts it, in the present. For him the Hebrew name of God, the tetragrammaton (YHVH), means HE IS PRESENT. *Er ist da* might be translated He is there; but in this context it would be more nearly right to say: He is here.[31]

What is always and everywhere Here cannot be pointed to, cannot be discovered by its *absence* (since it is never absent). But though this Here cannot ever be really absent, it may be overlaid and forgotten. We forget that we too are Here, and need to be reminded to withdraw our attention from the panorama of seeming events "outside over there." We are still all Here together—though our souls' fall into seeming, into the illusion of separate identities, material distances, was the consequence of our being "tired of being together." The discovery—call it the revelation—that we have not escaped from Here, or from "the Presence of God," is also the discovery of its supreme generosity, its openness to whatever happens, its being—precisely—the "power of all things" (III.8 [30].10).

That generosity is both a cosmological and an ethical idea. Cosmologically, it is charmingly represented in one of Calvino's fables: "Naturally, we were all there [in the Beginning]—*old Qfwfq said*—where else could we have been?" The subsequent expansion is an effect of Mrs. Ph(i)Nk$_0$'s wanting room to feed all her boys tagliatelle.[32] Of course, this is a joke, a myth, a narrative expansion of an eternal truth—but it may convey rather more of Plotinus's own *playfulness* than any dry account of One and Intellect and Soul-as-Such. And even modern *scientific* cosmology, however well grounded in subtle observation, seems strangely to repeat the Bronze Age myth, by which the primordial mound, Atum, appeared in Emptiness and ejaculated eight paired principles from which the worlds were made. The older story—and Plotinus's—had a more clearly ethical dimension: we are all in this together, and together compose an *eikon aei eikonizomene*,[33] an image always being reimaged, a beauty resting in perpetual exchange.

Notes

An earlier version was presented at the American Philological Association Conference, San Francisco, January, 2–5, 2004. Some of the material is addressed in my *Plotinus: Myth, Metaphor, and Philosophical Practice* (Chicago: University of Chicago Press, 2016).

1. See Andrew Louth, *The Origins of the Christian Mystical Traditions from Plato to Denys* (1981; New York: Oxford University Press: 2007), 50: Christian commentators often prefer this translation, precisely to contrast a supposedly "philosophical" or "pagan" goal with the Trinitarian hope of Christendom. The contrast is at least

exaggerated: see Kevin Corrigan, "'Solitary' Mysticism in Plotinus, Proclus, Gregory of Nyssa, and Pseudo-Dionysius": *Journal of Religion* 76 (1996): 28–42, for further discussion of the meaning of *monos*.

2. The reference is to an episode in Homer's *Iliad* (I.197–98), in which Athena (the goddess of good sense) recalls Achilles from a murderous rage. Save for occasional emendations I have used A. H. Armstrong's version of *The Enneads*, Loeb Classical Library (Cambridge: Harvard University Press, 1966–88).

3. T. S. Eliot, "Little Gidding," in *Four Quartets* (London: Faber, 1944), 44.

4. Porphyry, *Life of Plotinus* 15.7ff.

5. Porphyry, *Life of Plotinus* 2.4–2.5; cf. Porphyry *On Abstinence from Eating Animals*, trans. Gillian Clark (London: Duckworth, 2000).

6. Porphyry, *Life of Plotinus* 9.14. The story is also told of other philosophers. It does not follow that Plotinus didn't say it.

7. See *Enneads* I.9 [16]; cf. I.4 [46].7–8. Armstrong (1:320) very oddly remarks that since I.9 [16] was written before Porphyry joined Plotinus "it cannot represent the arguments Plotinus used to discourage Porphyry from suicide" (Porphyry, *Life of Plotinus* 11). It is true that Plotinus does change tack a little between I.9 [16] and I.4 [46], which concedes that there will be occasions when suicide is at least permissible (when it is impossible to live well in slavery, or one's pains are entirely too much to bear), though not obligatory.

8. Porphyry, *Life of Plotinus* 12.4ff.

9. Diogenes Laertius, *Lives of the Philosophers* 10.22.

10. William Blake "The Human Abstract" (*Songs of Experience*), in *Complete Writings*, ed. G. Keynes (Oxford: Clarendon, 1966), 217; see Aristotle, *Nicomachean Ethics* 10.1178b7ff.

11. Aristotle, *Eudemian Ethics* 8.1249b20. See Clark, "Therapy and Theory Reconstructed," *Philosophy as Therapy*, Royal Institute of Philosophy Supplementary, volume 66, ed. Clare Carlisle and Jonardon Ganeri (Cambridge: Cambridge University Press, 2010), 83–102.

12. See Clark, "A Plotinian Account of Intellect," *American Catholic Philosophical Quarterly* 71 (1997): 421–32.

13. Which is why, *pace* Peter Adamson, in *The Arabic Plotinus* (London: Duckworth, 2002), 73, the Arabic adaptor was not un-Plotinian in declaring, with reference to V.1 [10].11, that the soul's virtue is derived from intellect, and so in turn from the First.

14. *Enneads* I.6 [1].9, 13ff., after Plato, *Phaedrus* 254b7.

15. After Homer, *Odyssey* 11.601ff.; see also IV.3 [27].32, 24f.; I.1 [53].12, 32–40.

16. See the story of the senator Rogatianus, "who advanced so far in renunciation of public life that he gave up all his property, dismissed all his servants, and resigned his rank" (Porphyry, *Life of Plotinus* 7.32ff.).

17. "Providence ought not to exist in such a way as to make us nothing. If everything was providence and nothing but providence, then providence would not exist; for what would it have to provide for?" (III.2 [47].9, 1ff.).

18. "For the activity of sense-perception is that of the soul asleep; for it is the part of the soul that is the body that sleeps; but the true awakening is a true getting up from the body, not with the body" (III.6.6, 69ff.).

19. See also Plato, *Laws* 1.624a–b, *Minos* 320b; Diodorus, *History* I.94, 1–2; see Jan Assmann, *Religio Duplex: How the Enlightenment Reinvented Egyptian Religion*, trans. Robert Savage (Cambridge: Polity, 2014), 56–59, on the trope's later history.

20. A. H. Armstrong and R. A. Markus, *Christian Faith and Greek Philosophy* (London: Darton, Longman and Todd, 1960), 27.

21. Armstrong prefers "escape in solitude to the solitary," but this is no improvement.

22. *Epistle* 52.5, cited by Margaret R. Miles, *Carnal Knowing: Female Nakedness and Religious Meaning in the Christian West* (Tunbridge Wells: Burns and Oates, 1989), 63.

23. *Ennead* V.3 [49].4.1–4.

24. "*khoron sterixan erotos athanatou*": Porphyry, *Life of Plotinus* 23.36–37, after 22.54ff. The words are not Plotinus's, but still Plotinian: *sterizein* means "to establish, or set firm," but what is thus established is a dance.

25. Demosthenes, *Against Meidias* 60, cited by Martin West, *Ancient Music* (Oxford: Clarendon, 1992), 46, who goes on to report from other ancient sources that "he gave the lead and did his best to keep his fellows to the proper rhythm, which they managed better when there were more of them. . . . [His] place was in the middle, while at the edges there might be two or three who could not sing at all, and who kept mum." My thanks to Sebastian Moro for two relevant references in Proclus's work: in his commentary *In Timaeum* II.208.9 he refers to Apollo Musagetes as the leader of the chorus of the Muses, and to the World Soul as *koruphaion* of the choir of the Sirens, in his commentary *In Rempublicam*, II.238.20.

26. Plato, *Republic* 4.427c; see also *Iliad* 18.567–72: "Young maidens and youths, gay of spirit, were carrying the fruit, sweet as honey, in woven baskets. And in their midst a boy played charmingly upon a clear-toned lyre, and sang sweetly in accompaniment, with delicate voice; and dancers followed along with him, leaping, with songs and shouts of joy."

27. Brihadaranyaka, *Upanishad* 4.5.15: Ananda Wood, *From the Upanishads* (Pune, India: Ananda Wood, 1996), 99.

28. Heraclitus 22B89 DK: Robin Waterfield, ed., *The First Philosophers: The Pre-Socratics and Sophists* (Oxford: Oxford University Press, 2000), 38 [T1].

29. Martin Buber, *I and Thou*, trans. Walter Kaufmann (1923; New York: Simon and Schuster, 1996), 150.

30. Buber, 55.

31. Walter Kaufmann, in Buber, 25.

32. Italo Calvino, *Cosmicomics*, trans. William Weaver (London: Cape, 1969), 43.

33. After II.3 [52].18, 17: the original phrase is "*ho kosmos eikon aei eikonizomenos.*"

CHAPTER 4

ONENESS, ASPECTS, AND THE NEO-CONFUCIANS

DONALD L. M. BAXTER

C onfucius gave counsel that is notoriously hard to follow: "What you do not wish for yourself, do not impose on others" (Huang 1997, 15.24).[1] People tend to be concerned with themselves and to be indifferent to most others. We are distinct from others so our self-concern does not include them, or so it seems. Were we to realize this distinctness is merely apparent—that our true self includes others—Confucius's counsel would be easier to follow. Concern for our true self would extend concern beyond the narrow selves we appear to be.[2]

The neo-Confucians held just such a view. They espoused an identity with the universe and everything in it, arguing that this identity explains a natural concern for everyone and everything, not just for our narrow selves. I will summarize their universal identity view as an example of the kind of oneness I am concerned with. The theme of the identity of the self with everything else is common among some adherents of many other religious traditions: Daoist, Hindu, Buddhist, Muslim, Jewish, and Christian.[3] A claim so widespread must be taken seriously, yet there is an obvious objection.

Many things in the universe differ from one another, that is, some have qualities others lack. If they are all one and the same thing, then that one thing differs from itself. But this seems to be a contradiction.[4] How then can such an identity in difference be made sense of? Unless the metaphysical problem can be resolved the neo-Confucian-type view is disproven and our distinctness from others remains a barrier to concern that must be overcome some other way.[5]

I will suggest that the objection can be answered with some metaphysical innovation. I will sketch a theory—call it the theory of aspects—that explains how numerically identical things can differ qualitatively (see Baxter 1999). I motivate the theory by examining the sort of internal conflicts that led Plato to divide the self into parts, while emphasizing the unity of the self found in Sartre and Descartes. One is the same self on both sides of the conflicts. One does not have numerically distinct parts; one has numerically identical but qualitatively differing "aspects." I defend the theory by arguing that Leibniz's Law (the Indiscernibility of Identicals) applies only to complete entities such as individuals, not to incomplete entities such as aspects. Given the theory of aspects, the oneness entailed by views like that of the neo-Confucians has the following consequence: there is only one individual—the One, the universe itself. Everyone and everything else, including oneself, are aspects of the One.

Note that I am not attributing belief in aspects to the neo-Confucians. I am rather suggesting a way to augment any such theory of universal identity to save it from the otherwise decisive objection against it.

I will end by discussing two apparent ethical problems with the view. The universal identity view seems to have trouble accommodating altruistic concern. Apparently there would be no others to receive altruistic concern, or if there were then our universal concern would extend even to the undeserving. I will argue first that altruism just is concern for other aspects of the One beyond the aspect that is the narrow self. I will argue second that concern for everyone and everything as aspects of the One need not entail equal concern for each of these aspects. The deserving may deserve more than the undeserving. Such hierarchy by no means suggests, however, that the narrow self is especially deserving. Far from it.

Neo-Confucians and Oneness

Under the influence of Buddhism, neo-Confucians came to regard the universe as a system of principles (li), such that each thing in the world contained all the principles of the universe, differently manifested depending on each thing's qi. Neo-Confucians then augmented this view of oneness with an elaboration that helped explain our natural concern with the well-being of everything. For Zhou Dunyi, Zhang Zai, and Wang Yangming, the self or mind was "coextensive with the universe" (Ivanhoe n.d., 8–10; 2002, 34). Note that the oneness here is something more than just connection with other people, creatures, and things. It is "something like" oneness in "the strongest sense in which two things can be 'one,'" namely, "by being identical, the way Bruce Wayne and Batman are one" (1998, 64). It is "a more robust and dramatic sense of oneness as a kind of identity between self and world" (n.d., 8).

It is important to be clear about the claim of being one body with the universe. The claim is not just that the universe is a body of which oneself is an organic part. Such a view would be a variation on a theme of being distinct from and connected to everything else in the universe—all its other parts—to jointly compose something distinct from each—the universe as a whole.[6] Such a view would not capture a key element of the neo-Confucian view, namely, that it provides "an expanded view of the self" (Ivanhoe n.d., 14): "The moral life involves realizing one's fundamental identity with all existence. However, rather than wearing away and eliminating the self, Wang's ideal was to expand one's sense of self until it embraced all of reality" (Ivanhoe 2002, 29). On the neo-Confucian view, the universe is somehow identical with the self while yet being beyond the narrow self of normal, everyday concern. The universe is not a whole distinct from the self, a whole of which the self is a part. Rather, the universe is one's broader self, one's true self.

Granted, the neo-Confucian view contains the claim that the narrow self is connected with everything else. Wang takes the narrow self's connections to other things in the universe to be like the connections between parts of a human body (Ivanhoe n.d., 10–11). "Wang's moral paragon was to see the entire universe as his body or, more precisely, to see himself as part of the universal body" (Ivanhoe 2002, 35; see also 24, 30). However, this claim about being connected does not exhaust the view that the narrow self is one with the universe. To see this point requires distinguishing two senses of being-one-with: what I'll call the "unitedness sense" and what I'll call the "identity sense."

> *Unitedness sense*: x is one with y when x and y are two distinct things that are united by some connecting relations.

In this sense of being one with, the things that are one with one another are still distinct things.

> *Identity sense*: x is one with y when x and y are numerically identical.

This sense is not compatible with their distinctness.[7] Oneness in the unitedness sense is not literally oneness because the things connected are two or more, not one. It is part of the neo-Confucian view that the self is one with the universe in the identity sense as well.

If one part of the universe—namely, oneself—is identical with the universe, then presumably its other parts would be as well. That would suggest that according to the neo-Confucian view the parts of the universe are identical with one another. This interpretation is confirmed by Zhou Dunyi's refusal to cut some grass saying, "I regard it in the same way I regard myself," and Zhang

Zai's similar regard of a braying donkey (Ivanhoe n.d., 10). For Wang Yangming, "There was no distinction between the self and the other, or between the self and things" (Chan 1963, sec. 142). In the identity sense of oneness, being one with the universe entails being identical not just with the universe, but also with each of its parts.

There is a temptation to read the neo-Confucian view in the unitedness sense nonetheless, because they emphasize a hierarchy of concerns about the parts of the universe. Just as we use the hands and feet to protect the head, we can tolerate differences in relative importance (Ivanhoe n.d., 11–12). So, for example, Wang says we can butcher animals to feed our parents, or prefer our parents over a stranger to mete out life-giving food (Chan 1963, sec. 276).

The differences underlying a hierarchy of concerns push against the literal identity of the different things. Any account of the literal identity of narrow self with the universe and with each of its parts must somehow also be able to accommodate the fact that there are differences between each of these. A defense of the neo-Confucian-type metaphysical view must therefore make sense of the identity of the narrow self with the universe and of the identity of the narrow self with each thing in the universe, and yet also of the fact that what is true of the narrow self can differ from what is true of the universe and what is true of each thing in the universe.[8]

The Objection from Leibniz's Law

There is thus an obvious objection to the neo-Confucian-type view of universal identity:

1. The narrow self is narrow.
2. The broader self is not narrow.
3. The narrow self is identical with the broader self.
4. If two things are identical then all the same things are true of them.[9]
5. Therefore, the narrow self is narrow and not narrow.

Leibniz's Law, as expressed by 4, seems to render the neo-Confucian view contradictory.[10]

I will argue, however, that 4 is ambiguous. It is true if "things" refers just to individuals, but false if "things" also includes what I will call "aspects." First, then, I will argue that there are aspects. The aspects of an individual are numerically identical with one another and the individual, yet not all the same things are true of them. With the theory of aspects in hand, we can answer the objection by saying that the universe is the only individual, whereas oneself is an aspect of the universe, numerically identical with it and with its other aspects.

Since Leibniz's Law does not extend to aspects, the contradictory conclusion does not follow.

Motivating Aspects

It will take a while to motivate and explain the theory of aspects. I will eventually return to talk of neo-Confucian-type oneness. To begin, let me motivate the idea that there are numerically identical things such that different things are true of them, in other words, that there is "qualitative self-differing." Consider cases in which someone is torn about what to do or how to feel. A dramatic case is that of Euridipes's Medea, who struggles with herself whether to kill her children to punish their father, Jason, who has abandoned her:

> Ah, Ah! Why do you gaze at me with your eyes, children? Why do you smile your last smile? Oh, what shall I do? My courage has gone, women now that I've seen the shining eyes of the children. I couldn't do it. Goodbye to my former plans! I'll take my children from this land. Why should I, in harming them to give their father pain, make myself suffer twice as much? I cannot. Goodbye plans!
>
> But what is happening to me? Do I want to make myself ridiculous, letting my enemies go unpunished? I must go through with this. What a coward I am—even to admit soft words into my mind! . . . I shall not weaken my hand.
>
> Ah, Ah! Don't, my heart, don't you do this! Leave them alone, wretched heart, spare the children! Living there with me they will give you joy.
>
> By the avenging furies down in Hades, I swear I'll never leave these children for my enemies to insult and torture! They must certainly die; and since they must, then I who gave birth to them shall kill them.
>
> (Excerpted and translated in Annas 2001, 111–12)

Insofar as Medea is enraged at the father, she wants to kill the children. Insofar as she loves them, she has no desire to kill them. She is torn. She is in conflict with herself. She differs from herself. Medea's struggle is between two aspects of her: Medea insofar as she is enraged at Jason *versus* Medea insofar as she loves her children.

There may seem to be a simple argument that no one can differ from herself. Here it is: there is no respect in which someone differs from herself.[11] This is true if it means there is no respect such that someone in that respect differs from herself in the same respect. However, it is false if it means that there is no respect such that someone in that respect differs from herself in some other respect. It is this latter formulation that is needed to capture what it is to be torn.

Such struggles with ourselves are all too common, even if less fevered than Medea's. Who has not been moved in opposite ways by love and anger in a custody dispute, or in child rearing, or in a close relationship? Self-differing is something we all experience.

But is this literal self-differing? Many will say that we merely have opposing desires—ones that cannot both be satisfied. The conflict is between them, not between one and oneself. However, this way to make theoretical sense of the self-differing is not true to the phenomenon.

First, the relevant conflict here is not just desiring to do incompatible things. The conflict is that one has a desire and lacks it. Though Medea insofar as she is enraged at Jason has a desire to kill her children, Medea insofar as she loves her children lacks all desire to do so. It is not that Medea insofar as she loves her children is moved to oppose another desire she has. Insofar as she loves her children she is not moved by the murderous desire at all.

Second, desires are not like quarrelsome children in being opponents one is merely related to. To have internal conflict like Medea's is like trying to move in opposite directions. Or it is "to take something to oneself and to cast it off," as Plato puts it. This internal opposition indicates a complexity in oneself, as argued in the *Republic* (1974, 435c–441c, esp. 437b).

The reality of the conflict has led a number of important authors to downplay the unitariness of the self. The operative principle seems to be that of Plato's: "It is clear that one thing cannot act in opposite ways or be in opposite states at the same time and in the same part of itself in relation to the same other thing; so if we find this happening we shall know that we are not dealing with one thing but with several" (Plato 1974, 436b). In consequence, after noting some conflicts, Plato concludes that there are three parts of the soul (439d–e).

Other important examples are St. Paul's distinction between flesh and spirit (Romans 7:14–25; Galatians 5:17), Goethe's Faust saying "Two souls, alas! reside within my breast" (Goethe 1994, 1:1112–17), Du Bois's talk of double-consciousness (1903, 3), and Fanon's talk of self-division (1967, 17).

As these authors convey, the internal conflicts are real and deep. Nonetheless, the talk of distinct parts of the soul or of distinct, cohabiting souls neglects the unitariness of the conscious self, the subject of thought. Sartre emphasizes this unitariness in his criticism of the Freudian interpretation of bad faith: "By the distinction between the 'id' and the 'ego,' Freud has cut the psychic whole into two" (Sartre 1956, 50) and would have it that self-deception is a case of one part deceiving another. However, when someone lies to himself, if there is a lying part conscious of the lying and a lied-to part that is not conscious of the lying, then the lying part is simply an Other to the lied-to part. This is not self-deception. Further, Sartre argues, on the Freudian scheme the lying could only happen by the operation of a censor that decides what is allowed into consciousness and what stays unconscious. The censor "must be the consciousness (of) being conscious of the drive to be repressed, but precisely in order *not be* conscious of it" (Sartre 1956, 53): "The very essence of the reflexive idea of hiding something from oneself implies the unity of one and the same psychic mechanism and consequently a double activity in the heart of unity, tending on the one hand to maintain and locate the thing to be concealed and on the other hand to repress and disguise it" (53). In other words there must be a "single consciousness," such that "I must know in my capacity as deceiver the truth which is hidden from me in my capacity as the one deceived" (49).

Sartre's talk of a single consciousness captures the unitariness of the self overshadowed by the previous dramatic appeals to two-ness. The subjects in these cases would say that it is I who desire to do something yet lack all desire to do so. It is I who move toward the pleasures of the world yet also move away from them. It is I who am attracted and repelled by the values of white America. It is I who am aware of the truth and who is not. The fact that it is me, even when I am in conflict with myself, must not be overlooked. It is I who am conscious on either side of these divides. Descartes brings our attention to this fact when he says in the sixth meditation that the mind, unlike the body, is "utterly indivisible": "For when I consider the mind, that is, myself insofar as I am only a thinking thing, I cannot distinguish any parts within me; rather, I understand myself to be manifestly one complete thing. . . . Nor can the faculties of willing, sensing, understanding, and so on be called 'parts' of the mind, since it is one and the same mind that wills, senses, and understands" (1984, 89). The appeal to Descartes and the other talk of soul should not mislead about the point. I am not arguing for a unitary immaterial entity that inhabits the body. I am simply arguing that the self on one side of the conflict is numerically identical with the self on the other side. The unitariness of the mind is the identity of the mind in one conscious action with itself in another. That is why, as Descartes says, "For we cannot conceive of half of a mind, as we can half of any body whatever, no matter how small" (1984, 13). If any remnant of your mind is you, then it is you and not half of you. If any party to an internal conflict is you, then it is you and not just part of you.

To conclude, I am taking such cases of internal conflict, of being torn, as cases of qualitative self-differing. It is easiest to capture the conflict by writing in terms of two distinct parts of a soul or two distinct souls. However there are not two numerically distinct things in conflict. There is just one self in conflict with itself.

In such a case of qualitative self-differing, call what differ the "aspects" of the individual that self-differs. For the case to be one of *differing*, one aspect must have a quality that somehow the other aspect lacks. For it to be a case of *self*-differing, the aspects must be numerically identical with the individual that self-differs. Noun phrases that include qualifiers such as "insofar as" and "to the extent that" will have the special semantic role of referring to aspects. So, for example, "Medea insofar as she loves her children" refers to one aspect of her and "Medea insofar as she is enraged at their father" refers to another. I think that these qualifier phrases sometimes work this way in natural language, but for now I am just stipulating how I will refer to aspects. I will call qualifiers used in noun phrases when referring to aspects "nominal qualifiers."

It is hard to distinguish aspects from other entities. Aspects are not qualities; they *have* qualities. They are not the individuals they are aspects of, even though numerically identical to those individuals, because they lack some of the qualities the individuals have. Aspects are not mereological parts of the individual because each aspect is numerically identical with the individual it is an aspect of; aspects of the same individual are therefore numerically identical with one another. Aspects of the same individual differ qualitatively but not numerically.

Aspects are abstract particulars in somewhat the same way that tropes were meant to be. Aspects are particulars in that they are numerically identical with particular individuals. They are abstract in the sense of not having all the properties that the particular individuals they are aspects of have. For instance, a lollipop may be round and sweet, but insofar as it is round it is not sweet and insofar as it is sweet it is not round. If an individual has a property, then one of its aspects has it, but not necessarily vice versa.[12] This sense of "abstract" as "pared down" was emphasized by D. C. Williams (1953, 6–7). However something's tropes are numerically distinct from it and one another. Not so with aspects. For the same reason, aspects should not be confused with Casteñeda's guises (1975), or Fine's qua-objects (1982), or other such attenuated entities.

The difference between two different aspects of the same individual, therefore, is a less-than-numerical distinction but more than a mere distinction of reason, as, for example, Dun Scotus's formal distinction and Suarez's modal distinction are supposed to be (Suarez 1947, 24, 27). The aspects are "two" only loosely speaking since they are not numerically distinct; strictly speaking they are one. Call the distinction between them an "aspectival" distinction.

Self-differing is not confined to the conflicts of conscious minds. I focus on them because considering such conflicts is the best way to motivate the concept of aspect. Cases of being torn give us the experiences by which we know that there are numerically identical, qualitatively differing aspects. We feel them.

Aspects and Leibniz's Law

Saying that there is self-differing sounds contradictory. This is the powerful and enduring objection to any proposal of a less-than-numerical distinction.

For instance, Ockham rejects Dun Scotus's formal distinction with these words, "But among creatures the same thing cannot be truly affirmed and truly denied of the same thing." [13] Likewise Bayle rejects Spinoza's monism, which he interprets as an existence monism, saying, "When one can affirm of a thing . . . what one cannot affirm of another, they are distinct" (1991, 306).

However, the use of nominal qualifiers such as "insofar as" removes explicit contradiction. I am not saying that Medea does and does not want to spare her children. Nor am I saying that Medea in one respect wants to spare her children and in no respect wants to spare her children. Either of those would be contradictory. I am saying that Medea insofar as she loves her children wants to spare them, but Medea insofar as she is enraged at their father does not want to spare them. The negation is internal, that is, has short-scope relative to the nominal qualifier and so there is no contradiction.

Even if I am not saying something explicitly contradictory, aren't I still violating Leibniz's Law—the principle that for any x and y, if they are numerically identical then all the same things are true of them? After all, I am suggesting that the nominally qualified phrases refer to aspects, where aspects qualitatively differ but are numerically identical. My response to this objection is that Leibniz's Law is silent about aspects.

Why would we think that Leibniz's Law applies to any entity whatsoever? My only guess is that we think that it captures the truth that nothing both has and lacks a property. There are no contradictions in the world.[14] However, what is true is that nothing both has and lacks a property in the same respect at the same time, as Aristotle says in *Metaphysics* IV.3 (1941, 1005b19–20). That truth leaves open the possibility that something in one respect has a property that it in another respect lacks. I'm not yet able to think of another reason for unqualified allegiance to Leibniz's Law. Certainly Leibniz's own reason cannot be what is motivating us: that a substance has a complete concept containing all its predicates such that being the same substance is a matter of having the same complete concept (1989, sec. 8). It is apparently part of this view that things that differ have different complete concepts and so are distinct substances.[15] However, we nowadays do not hold this view of substances. And aspects are supposed to differ from substances anyway. So we lack a reason to believe that Leibniz's Law applies to every entity whatsoever.

Consider the domain of quantification for Leibniz's Law. It is a principle concerning single things. The quantifier is a singular quantifier. Does it hold of pluralities, that is, what one quantifies over with a plural quantifier? Maybe, but the original principle is silent about that. I suggest that the original principle is silent about aspects as well. And the noncontradictory internal negation in claims about self-differing suggests that Leibniz's Law does not apply to aspects. Here is an account that would explain why.

Distinguish complete entities from incomplete entities, to borrow terminology from Descartes.[16] Complete entities are individuals that can exist on their own. Incomplete entities are dependent on complete entities. They are incomplete in having fewer properties than it takes to exist on one's own.

Leibniz's Law is certainly applicable to complete entities like individuals. The same thing can't be true and false of the same individual without contradiction. However, I am proposing that there are incomplete entities numerically identical with individuals, namely, aspects. Phrases such as "the white globe insofar as it is white" refer to aspects, not the individuals they are numerically identical with. Besides singular reference (reference to complete entities such as individuals) there is aspectival reference (reference to aspects). The former is not sensitive to the aspectival distinction; the latter is. The domain of quantification for Leibniz's Law includes all the complete entities, but does not include the incomplete entities numerically identical to some of them.

It follows that Leibniz's Law does not preclude a qualitative difference between aspects of the same individual, or between an individual and one of its aspects.

The distinction between singular and aspectival reference allows me to be more precise when I say that there is self-differing. When I say that something differs from itself, I am elliptically referring to some of its aspects. This can be interpreted three ways, all of which are intended. First, what I mean is that some individual has numerically identical aspects that qualitatively differ. By its having them, I mean its being numerically identical with them. In this case with "something" and "itself" I am singularly referring to the individual and "differ" implicates the aspects. Second, what I mean is that something in one respect qualitatively differs from itself in another respect. That is, numerically identical aspects qualitatively differ. With "something" and "itself" I am not singularly referring to one individual; rather I am elliptically aspectivally referring to one of its differing aspects, then another. Third, I mean that some individual differs from one of its aspects.

One's Narrow Self as an Aspect of the Universe

The theory of aspects enables a solution to the metaphysical objection that the neo-Confucian-type view of oneness is contradictory. Recall the argument:

1. The narrow self is narrow.
2. The broader self is not narrow.
3. The narrow self is identical with the broader self.
4. If two things are identical then all the same things are true of them.
5. Therefore, the narrow self is both narrow and not narrow.

Reformulated with an eye to the theory of aspects the conclusion no longer follows:

1'. An aspect of the universe is narrow (namely, the universe insofar as it has all the characteristics of the narrow self).
2'. The universe (that is, the broader self) is not narrow.
3'. This aspect of the universe is numerically identical with the universe.
4'. If two individuals are identical then all the same things are true of them.
5'. An aspect of the universe (namely, the universe insofar as it has all the characteristics of the narrow self) is both narrow and not narrow.

Since Leibniz's Law, 4', is silent about aspects, the contradictory conclusion, 5', does not follow.

This solution brings out a consequence of the theory. Not everything true of an aspect of an individual is true of the individual. For instance, one aspect of Medea has desire to kill her children. However, having the desire is not true of Medea as an individual, that is, of Medea unqualifiedly. It is only true of "part" of her as we say when speaking like Plato. Nor is lacking all such desire true of Medea unqualifiedly. So there can be qualitative self-differing, not just between differing aspects of an individual, but also between the individual and an aspect of it. This qualitative difference between an individual and an aspect of it is just what is needed to solve the metaphysical problem with the neo-Confucian view of oneness. The narrow self is numerically identical with the universe, though differs from it. Similarly, the narrow self is numerically identical with each other part of the universe, though differs from it.[17]

The Self and Altruism

The universal identity view seems to have trouble accommodating altruistic concern. Apparently, such concern either would be impossible, or, if possible, would extend too widely. I will show that neither of these alternatives is a successful objection to the universal identity view.

First, the view would seem to undermine the possibility of altruism by making selfless behavior impossible (Ivanhoe n.d., 20). Any behavior that benefits anyone or anything benefits one's broader self so it is not selfless. However, the view has the resources to answer the objection. The objection can be put as an argument.

1. Altruism benefits another person and not oneself.
2. Given the universal identity view, any other person is numerically identical with oneself.
3. Therefore altruism does and does not benefit oneself.

The response is to make use of the distinction between the narrow self and the broader self, and the proposal that the narrow self and others are aspects of the One.

1'. Altruism benefits another aspect of the One and not the narrow self.
2'. Given the universal identity view, any other aspect of the One is numerically identical with one's narrow self.
3'. Therefore altruism benefits an aspect of the One that differs from one's narrow self and does not benefit one's narrow self.

Given the theory of aspects, 3' is not a contradiction.

What drives the objection, I think, is a worry that the universal identity view encourages a kind of self-centeredness. It would seem to encourage the idea that the universe is just more you. Such an idea would militate against any appreciation of the reality and importance of others in their own right. Given the theory of aspects, the worry is that one would regard one's narrow self as encompassing the universe and would regard everything else in the universe as aspects of one's narrow self. The worry can be assuaged by noting that it is a misunderstanding of the universal identity view. On that view one's narrow self is merely an aspect of the universe, as is anything else in the universe. The One encompasses the universe; one's narrow self is just as far from being central as it deserves.

However, if altruism is possible then altruistic concern would seem to run amok. We apparently must have the same concern for an evil tyrant and even the Ebola virus as we have for ourselves and those we ought to love.[18] As Cheng, quoted in Angle, says, "The fault of recognizing no distinctions is that there will be impartial love for all without appropriateness (yi)" (2009, 68–69). I think the proponent of universal identity ought to appeal to a neo-Confucian-type hierarchy of importance to correct this fault. Just as Wang says we can endanger our hands to protect our eyes, we can endanger tyrants or viruses when protecting potential victims. Being concerned for all does not prevent some from being more important than others. Universal concern need not entail universal impartiality.

Opening the door to partiality might seem to reopen the door to partiality for the narrow self. But why would it? Our apparent distinctness from others was the major reason for our overweening concern with the narrow self. Absent that reason, it is hard to find another.

So the objections are answered. The universal identity view is compatible both with altruism and with appropriate partiality.

✳ ✳ ✳

The neo-Confucians hold that oneself is identical with the universe and everything in it in a way compatible with a hierarchy of importance. I have presented the theory of aspects—a theory of qualitative self-differing—in order to make literal sense of this view. On this interpretation I and everyone else and everything else are aspects of the One—the universe itself.

Notes

I'm grateful for comments from the participants in the "International Conference on Oneness in Philosophy and Religion," City University of Hong Kong, April 2015, especially Lawrence Blum, Sungmoon Kim, Jonardon Ganeri, Victoria Harrison, Owen Flanagan, and P. J. Ivanhoe. I'm grateful to Toby Napoletano for research assistance.

1. According to Karen Armstrong, "Confucius was the first to promulgate the Golden Rule." Further, "The Axial sages put the abandonment of selfishness and the spirituality of compassion at the top of their agenda. For them, religion *was* the Golden Rule" (2006, 208, 392).
2. For a related approach to the same sort of issue, see Baxter 2005.
3. Zhuangzi in Watson 1996, 39, 42. From the Isa Upanishad and the Chandogya Upanishad in Mascaró 1965, 49, 120. Samkara quoted in Deutsch and van Buitenen 1971, 63. Huayan Buddhism as characterized in Cook 1977, 2. Ibn Arabi quoted in Kakaie 2007, 185, 188. Moses Cordovera quoted in Matt 1995, 24. Meister Eckhart quoted in Kakaie 2007, 186–87. The numerous cultural differences between various mystical experiences emphasized by Katz cannot be denied (1983, 32–43). Nonetheless as James says, "there is about mystical utterances an eternal unanimity which ought to make a critic stop and think" (1982, 419).
4. Bayle makes the same criticism of Spinoza's monism (1991, 306–7).
5. One might wonder whether merely *perceived* identity with the universe would be enough to overcome the barrier. Perhaps. However the same metaphysical problem would attend the oneness perceived, requiring the same solution to make sense of what is being perceived. I'm grateful to Toby Napoletano for the question.
6. This view is closer to the one Paul expresses in 1 Corinthians 12:12–31.
7. It might seem that there is a middle sort of oneness between unitedness and identity, namely, interpenetration in Priest's (2015) very special sense. As Priest puts it, things x and y interpenetrate just in case each just is the structure of relations it stands in, and each structure is a substructure of the other. A more general notion of interpenetration would presumably be that each is a proper part of the other. However, the structures are either distinct from the substructures or not. The wholes are either distinct from the proper parts or they are not. If they are, the same impediment to universal concern exists. If they are not, then the oneness is oneness in the identity sense.
8. Given these constraints, none of the senses of "oneness" that Ivanhoe lists fully captures the neo-Confucian view, as he notes (n.d., 4–5; 1998, 63–65). All but the first are of oneness in the unitedness sense. The first is standard numerical identity without the possibility that something true of one is false of the other. Psychologists have also discussed various ways to characterize oneness; Tien summarizes these (2012, 64). Yet none of these ways is fully apt for capturing the oneness of the neo-Confucians. "Identity and psychological indistinguishability," "expansion of the self to include the other," and "merging" would each be a reduction of the ways the narrow self and the

universe differ; "confusion between self and other" would be failing to see the ways that the narrow self and the universe differ; "union" would not distinguish between the unitedness sense and the identity sense of oneness; "seeing part of oneself in the other" either is metaphorical or does not acknowledge the identity of the self and the other.

9. Or, perhaps more carefully but harder to understand, if something and something are identical, then anything true of either one is true of the other one.

10. That may be why in an earlier essay Ivanhoe says, "Clearly it is contrary to reality for me to think of myself as one with the world in the sense of an *identity* between self and world (i.e. in the way that Batman is 'one' with Bruce Wayne)" (1997, 113).

11. I'm grateful to Jonathan Schaffer for the objection.

12. In some cases, though, what is true of an aspect is true of the individual. If an aspect of Socrates is human, then Socrates is human. If an aspect of Socrates earns money, then Socrates earns money. It is an interesting question which predications work this way. For some discussion, see Szabo on "persistent predication" (2003, 400–1).

13. William of Ockham, *Ordinatio* I, distinction ii, qu. 6, in Spade 1994, 156.

14. Wiggins 1967, 4.

15. Feldman points out rightly that Leibniz does not state Leibniz's Law in the sense of the indiscernibility of identicals (1970, 511). However, I think it follows from his view that substances have complete concepts.

16. Descartes 1984, third and fourth replies, in *Objections and Replies*, pp. 130, 156–57.

17. Thus the view I am suggesting is an existence monism that shares the advantage with Schaffer's priority monism that it "does not conflict with Moorean banalities" such as the existence of our hands (2010, 66). Thus the view also enables me to claim in a way consistent with having a "sound mind" that "my right foot is literally and numerically identical with my left" without claiming that they are the same foot, contrary to Priest's contention (2014, xv). I say that hands and feet are differing, numerically identical aspects of the One. Despite our differences there is a deep similarity between my project and Priest's. We both see oneness as identity. We differ in the ways we address the seeming contradictions in such a view and defend restrictions on the substitutivity of identicals. Priest appeals to paraconsistency. I appeal to aspects.

18. Ivanhoe raised this second objection in comments on this essay.

References

Angle, Steven. 2009. *Sagehood: The Contemporary Significance of Neo-Confucian Philosophy.* New York: Oxford University Press.

Annas, Julia, ed. 2001. *Voices of Ancient Philosophy: An Introductory Reader.* New York: Oxford University Press.

Aristotle. 1941. *Metaphysics.* In *The Basic Works of Aristotle,* edited by Richard McKeon. New York: Random House.

Armstrong, Karen. 2006. *The Great Transformation: The Beginning of Our Religious Traditions.* New York: Knopf.

Baxter, Donald L. M. 1999. "The Discernibility of Identicals." *Journal of Philosophical Research* 24:37–55.

——. 2005. "Altruism, Grief, and Identity." *Philosophy and Phenomenological Research* 52:371–83.

Bayle, Pierre. 1991. *Historical and Critical Dictionary: Selections.* Translated by Richard H. Popkin. Indianapolis: Hackett.

The Bible. Revised Standard Version. New York: Thomas Nelson and Sons, 1952.

Casteñeda, H. N. 1975. "Identity and Sameness." *Philosophia* 5:121–50.

Chan, Wing–tsit, trans. 1963. *Instructions for Practical Living, and Other Neo-Confucian Writings by Wang Yang-ming*. New York: Columbia University Press.

Cook, Francis Harold. 1977. *Hua-Yen Buddhism: The Jewel Net of Indra*. University Park: Pennsylvania State University Press.

Descartes, René. 1984. *The Philosophical Writings of Descartes*. Translated by J. Cottingham, R. Stoothoff, and D. Murdoch. Cambridge: Cambridge University Press.

Deutsch, Eliot, and J. A. B. van Buitenen. 1971. *A Source Book of Advaita Vedanta*. Honolulu: University of Hawaii Press.

Du Bois, W. E. B. 1903. *The Souls of Black Folk*. New York: Dover.

Fanon, Frantz. 1967. *Black Skin White Masks*. New York: Grove.

Feldman, Fred. 1970. "Leibniz and 'Leibniz's Law.'" *Philosophical Review* 79:510–22.

Fine, K. 1982. "Acts, Events, and Things." In *Sixth International Wittgenstein Symposium*, Kirchberg-Wechsel, Austria, 97–105.

Goethe. 1994. *Faust*. In *Goethe's Collected Works*, vol. 2, edited and translated by Stuart Atkins. Princeton: Princeton University Press.

Huang, Chichung, trans. 1997. *The Analects of Confucius*. New York: Oxford University Press.

Ivanhoe, P. J. 1997. "Nature, Awe, and the Sublime." *Midwest Studies in Philosophy* 21 (1): 98–117.

——. 1998. "Early Confucianism and Environmental Ethics." In *Confucianism and Ecology: The Interrelation of Heaven, Earth, and Humans*, edited by M. E. Tucker and J. Berthrong. Cambridge: Harvard University Press.

——. 2002. *Ethics in the Confucian Tradition: The Thought of Mengzi and Wang Yangming*. Indianapolis: Hackett.

——. n.d. "Senses and Values of Oneness." Manuscript. www6.cityu.edu.hk/ceacop/kpcp /draft_paper/Oneness.pdf.

James, William. 1982. *The Varieties of Religious Experience: A Study in Human Nature*. New York: Penguin.

Kakaie, Ghasem. 2007. "The Extroversive Unity of Existence from Ibn 'Arabi's and Meister Eckhart's Viewpoints." *Topoi* 26:177–89.

Katz, Steven T. 1983. "The 'Conservative' Character of Mystical Experience." In *Mysticism and Religious Traditions*, edited by Steven T. Katz, 3–60. Oxford: Oxford University Press.

Leibniz, Gottfried Wilhelm. 1989. *Discourse on Metaphysics*. In *Philosophical Essays*, edited by R. Ariew and D. Garber. Indianapolis: Hackett.

Mascaró, Juan, trans. 1965. *The Upanishads*. London: Penguin.

Matt, Daniel, trans. 1995. *The Essential Kabballah: The Heart of Jewish Mysticism*. San Francisco: HarperSanFrancisco.

Plato. 1974. *Republic*. Translated by G. M. A. Grube. Indianapolis: Hackett.

Priest, Graham. 2014. *One: Being an Investigation Into the Unity of Reality and of Its Parts, Including the Singular Object Which Is Nothingness*. Oxford: Oxford University Press.

——. 2015. "The Net of Indra." In *The Moon Points Back*, edited by Koji Tanaka et al., 113–27. Oxford: Oxford University Press.

Sartre, Jean-Paul. 1956. *Being and Nothingness*. Translated by Hazel E. Barnes. New York: Philosophical Library.

Schaffer, Jonathan. 2010. "Monism: The Priority of the Whole." *Philosophical Review* 119:31–76.

Spade, Paul Vincent, ed. 1994. *Five Texts on the Mediaeval Problem of Universals*. Indianapolis: Hackett.

Suarez, Francis. 1947. *On the Various Kinds of Distinctions*. Milwaukee: Marquette University Press.

Szabo, Z. 2003. "On Qualification." In *Philosophical Perspectives* 17: *Language and Philosophical Linguistics*, edited by J. Hawthorne, 385–414.

Tien, David W. 2012. "Oneness and Self-Centeredness in the Moral Psychology of Wang Yangming." *Journal of Religious Ethics* 40:52–71.

Watson, Burton, trans. 1996. *Chuang Tzu: Basic Writings*. New York: Columbia University Press.

Wiggins, David. 1967. *Identity and Spatio-Temporal Continuity*. Oxford: Blackwell.

Williams, Donald C. 1953. "On the Elements of Being: I." *Review of Metaphysics* 7:3–18.

CHAPTER 5

ONE-TO-ONE FELLOW FEELING, UNIVERSAL IDENTIFICATION AND ONENESS, AND GROUP SOLIDARITIES

LAWRENCE BLUM

I am interested in four related themes involved in compassion or other forms of fellow feeling for other human beings, and in the sense of connectedness among human beings sometimes expressed in the language of "oneness." These are (1) whether compassion is seen as particularized to a specific human being versus being seen as directed to all human beings in a more universalistic way, (2) the degree of emphasis placed on the subject of fellow feeling's sense of a distinct identity from the target of fellow feeling, (3) group solidarities, such as of a racial or ethnic character, and how these relate to oneness, (4) the relation between metaphysics and ethics.

Schopenhauer: Phenomenal Compassion and Noumenal Oneness

I take Arthur Schopenhauer as an initial reference point, drawing on his book on ethics, *On the Basis of Morality*, from 1841. Criticizing, and contrasting his view systematically with, Kant's, Schopenhauer said that compassion, not reason or duty, is the fundamental moral motive. He does not explore the precise psychological character of compassion, but he means by it an affective phenomenon involving taking the weal or woe of another as a direct motive of action to assist the other. Taking a position unusual for philosophers in the Western canon, Schopenhauer explicitly mentions Hinduism and Buddhism as sources of ancient wisdom that promote compassion as the fundamental moral stance toward the world.[1]

Schopenhauer says that compassion as a psychological phenomenon is mysterious—"practical mysticism"—since in it we treat another's woe as a direct motive for our will in the way we normally do only for our own woe (212). He sometimes describe this phenomenon by saying that in compassion we make less of a distinction than do the uncompassionate between himself and others (204), or "another's ego is treated as equal with his own" (205), while in egoistic (or malicious) action we experience a distinction between ourselves and others. "For the egoist and the malicious, there is a wide gulf, a mighty difference, between the ego that is restricted to their own persons and the non-ego embracing the rest of the world" (204).

Schopenhauer sometimes expresses his description of compassion in a somewhat different way: that the compassionate person sees his own inner nature, his own true self, in all others, in fact in every living thing (213); "He always recognizes and loves his own inner nature and self in all others; the illusion that separated his consciousness from theirs vanishes" (213).

The worry about the latter formulation is that it edges toward a kind of egoism, in a way that the former does not. And this is a charge that has been made against the Buddhist and neo-Confucian doctrine of "oneness." If I love my own nature as I perceive or experience it in others, is this not a form of self-love? The metaphor of "making less of a distinction" between self and other is different. It preserves the idea that the suffering that the compassionate person responds to is perceived as in the other person, not in the self, but the agent feels that suffering in the other in the way that she normally perceives it in herself. She perceives it and is concerned about it as if it were her own but she is acutely aware that it is not.

Schopenhauer shares with Kant the view that, as he puts it, the human way of acting morally has metaphysical significance. He turns to metaphysics to explain the mystery of compassion. If we were confined to the world of appearances, where individual objects including persons are individuated by space and time, the egoist would in a sense be right—his woe is his, and yours is just yours: "The difference in space that separates me from him separates me also from his weal and woe" (205). But, Schopenhauer says, Kant has demonstrated the ideality of space and time and thus has shown that in the world of things in themselves there is no space and time, and thus no plurality or individuation. Kant himself did not draw this conclusion, but continued to individuate rational beings in the noumenal world; but Schopenhauer thought this was inconsistent of Kant (209). In the noumenal world, everything is one, a unity, so the compassionate person is in touch with the reality of that world because he makes no distinction between himself and others. In his defense of Kant against Schopenhauer on this point, Paul Guyer, the distinguished Kant scholar, says that Schopenhauer sees compassion as flowing from a theoretical appreciation of this deep metaphysical truth.[2] But at least in his ethics book, I read Schopenhauer as saying that merely by acting compassionately, the compassionate agent thereby expresses and reveals his knowledge of the fundamental unity of all being, even if he has not been explicitly exposed to this doctrine as such.[3]

But Schopenhauer bolsters his metaphysical view by again adverting to Hinduism and Buddhism, which, he says, propound the doctrine that all reality is one and that individuation and plurality are illusion.[4] The relationship between the noumenal and phenomenal realms is unclear in Schopenhauer. If all reality is one it is not clear that there is room for any kind of agency, especially individual agency, since there are no individuals. But perhaps agency should be conceived of as a purely phenomenal phenomenon, yet one that can manifest an understanding or *grasp* of noumenal reality, expressed in compassion.

Scheler: Fellow Feeling Requires Lived Sense of Distinct Identity

Let me turn now to Max Scheler, an early-twentieth-century German phenomenologist influenced by Schopenhauer. Scheler (in *The Nature of Sympathy*) emphasizes that the subject must feel the sorrow of the other *as being the other's sorrow, not her own*. (I will construe the subject of fellow feeling as female and the target as male.)[5] This is not contrary to Schopenhauer's understanding, but Schopenhauer does not give sufficient emphasis to it. For Scheler, the subject must have a clear, lived sense of herself as a distinct individual from the target, so that in fellow feeling for him, she is not in any way confusing her self with his. "True fellow-feeling is a genuine out-reaching and entry into the other person and his individual situation, a true and authentic transcendence of one's self" (46). This emphasis on compassion as a kind of activity and an outreaching is barely present in Schopenhauer. Scheler sees the significance of this point in light of a depth psychology influenced by Freud. (Hints of this direction are indeed present in Schopenhauer, as Freud recognized. Schopenhauer influenced Nietzsche in this regard and Nietzsche influenced Freud.) That is, Scheler sees that on deeper, lived levels, we can confuse our self with that of another. We can think that something that we would want were we to be in a situation similar to that of the other is what that other person wants; but, as Scheler says, with his particular character and temperament, the other actually wants something different.

Identity confusions of this sort are common and come in different forms. Jones may identify with Rodriguez in such a way that she in a sense loses her sense of being a distinctive self and takes Rodriguez's experiences, at least in the way she understands them, for her own. And she can do this without in any way being aware that she is doing so; indeed, it would be conceptually impossible for her to be aware of that form of self-deception. Scheler says that the fellow feeling that Jones may have for Rodriguez is not the genuine item since she lacks a clear sense of herself as a subject distinct from Rodriguez.

Schopenhauer sees the distinctness among persons as being due to their numerical, spatiotemporal distinctness. But the subjects whose defective or inadequate forms of separate identity Scheler notes do not lack Schopenhauer's form of recognition of individual difference. Jones is aware that she is a spatiotemporally distinct individual from Rodriguez. He is over there, she is over here. Yet she lacks a lived sense of distinct psychic identity required for genuine fellow feeling with its "authentic transcendence of one's self."

Scheler is explicitly critical of Schopenhauer on this very point. He sees Schopenhauer, plausibly, as saying that compassion involves an identification with the other, seeing oneself in the other, even if it is only in a noumenal realm (although we saw that Schopenhauer sometimes uses nonidentificationist metaphors to express the nature of compassion).[6] This is the view of fellow feeling that Scheler decisively rejects. We can only have fellow feeling with someone with whom we do not identify, someone for whom we are as clearly as possible separate and distinct from ourselves, with a temperament and character, a set of feelings and interests, and so on that might be very different from our own. Only then can fellow feeling be grounded in an understanding of the other's state *as other*.[7] For Scheler, it is only when we have the fellow feeling for the other as other that our action motivated by it can have moral worth. (In a sense Schopenhauer agrees with this and says so in his description of compassion in the empirical world; Scheler is saying that he violates this view when he moves to the metaphysical realm.)

So Scheler tunes us into how the achievement of a distinctive sense of identity can be a complex matter, not something simply given with spatiotemporal differentiation/individuation. Feminist philosophers and psychologists of the early second wave took up Scheler's insight (not necessarily as such) into a feminist framework.[8] They said that women often fail to develop the fully distinctive sense of self Scheler highlights because they are socialized and ideologized to subordinate their selves to those of particular men in their lives—partners, husbands, fathers, friends, even male children (or female children, for that matter).[9] Feminists of this strand recognized that a sense of a separate and distinct self was an important achievement that required countering the ideology of female subordination. These feminists were particularly attuned to the corruptions of fellow feeling involved in lacking a distinctive sense of self. Female caring can be bound up with a female's sense that she is not worthy of having her own needs and desires counted equally or adequately, so the caring is premised on thinking the male other to be worthier of having his needs met than her own.

Finally, I note that the kind of separateness involved in Schelerian fellow feeling is very different from the egoistical separateness that Schopenhauer characterizes in the noncompassionate (egoist or malicious). It does not involve a barrier between self and other, a sense that the other is alien. Rather it is open to a kind of connectedness that the feminist philosophers articulate more so than Scheler.

Iris Murdoch: Platonist Metaphysics and the Challenge of Seeing the Other Clearly

Iris Murdoch is another philosopher who has contributed to the recognition that we are subject to "identity confusions" that taint our ability to proffer appropriate help to other people. She also sees metaphysics as important for ethics. Murdoch says that our own fantasies about others, often founded on particular desires for something from the other person, constantly get in the way of our seeing others clearly, and thus knowing what they really need. Her novels are full of characters who exemplify this point, one that Murdoch takes to be Freudian in character. She often projects a strong sense of pessimism about ordinary humans' ability to avoid these distortions. Scheler does not go down that path, but rather simply explains the phenomenon in question. Some feminists have drawn on Murdoch's insights in this regard, especially insofar as she emphasizes personal relations as a central domain of morality, and is helpful in understanding in how personal relationships can go wrong.[10] Because feminists also have an ideological critique of the forces in society that produce these distortions, they in a way possess a greater range of resources for correcting these distortions than does Murdoch. She sees individual distortions as almost entirely a matter of individual pathologies and never articulates any sort of social critique.[11]

A noteworthy feature of Murdoch's views on these matters is an eschewing of the affective dimension involved in fellow feeling, emphasized strongly by Scheler and generally by the second-wave feminist philosophers as well. Murdoch does not talk of having empathy, compassion, or care for others. She frames the moral relationship in cognitive/perceptual and "moral realist" terms. The subject "sees" the target clearly, and is responding to the "reality," as she puts it, of the other. This formulation echoes Schopenhauer's notion that for the egoist, others are not entirely "real"; they are only "phantoms" seen as candidates for serving the subject's needs. For Murdoch, the response to the reality of the other is not always an action, such as helping. As she emphasizes in her famous example of a woman and her departed daughter-in-law, an "inner" action of seeing the other justly is a moral act and can be a moral achievement in itself, independent of any behavior to which it might lead.[12]

Murdoch's less affective orientation to the appropriate stance we take toward others in need than Scheler's and the feminists' is no doubt bound up with her more Platonic ethical metaphysics. She shares with both Kant and Schopenhauer, and with Buddhism, the idea that metaphysics is deeply connected with ethics, that metaphysics informs our understanding of ethics as a phenomenon, but also informs the actions of a moral agent.[13] She would agree with both philosophers that ethics in some sense requires metaphysics. As we saw, Schopenhauer sees his Hindu-/Buddhist-influenced metaphysics as essentially Kantian in character, although he thought that Kant failed to take the final step implied by his own doctrines of affirmatively denying the spatiotemporal character of ultimate reality, of noumena, and thus failed to see the Oneness of ultimate reality. But the metaphysics to which Murdoch is committed is Platonic, and so generates a cognitive/perceptual relation to a reality that is moral in character. Murdoch sometimes fully embraces something like Plato's form of the Good and speaks of Goodness in the abstract as having an attracting character; other times she describes the "moral reality" in question as individual other persons and their needs. Murdoch never quite resolves this duality in her version of Platonic metaphysics. But her cognitivism is not of a Kantian stripe. She does not think we normally act out of a *rational principle*, nor does she frame the moral pull of the reality of others as generating a *duty* to help. But for Murdoch/Plato, the cognitive/perceptual relation to an external moral or morally infused reality is the driving metaphor, quite different from Schopenhauer's. This metaphysic does not express the idea of fundamental connectedness among human beings, or all creatures, that Schopenhauer's Buddhist-like "oneness" metaphysic does, and that the feminist, less metaphysical notion of the connected self also does.

What Scheler, Murdoch, and the feminists share, which distinguishes them from Schopenhauer, is an acute focus on the individual as both subject and target of fellow feeling or helping motivation, and a consequent sensitivity to the requirement that the agent have a clear, lived (not merely intellectual or cognitive) sense of herself as distinct from the target—that she not confuse her identity with his in a lived sense. To summarize, this identity-confusion or failure to differentiate raises two different moral concerns. One is the straightforward egoist worry that if the subject does not distinguish herself from the target, if she confuses her identity with his, then her compassionate or concerned action is egoistic in character—she is really concerned about herself, not about him. The second is more subtle. It is that in order to help the other, and to possess appropriately directed fellow feeling that would motivate such help, it is necessary to see the other clearly as the distinct individual that he is. But there are many barriers or challenges to achieving such a recognition of the other, such as confusing what she wants and needs with what I might want and need, or would want and need were I in her circumstances. The first of these two forms of identity confusion operates in one way at a more conscious, and yet metaphysical, level. I am concerned about the other because I consciously see myself in the other and it is myself-in-the-other that is the intentional object of my concern. Thus the moral worry is that what looks like concern for the other is actually a form of self-concern—I care about myself in the other.

In this second form, I take myself to be recognizing the other as other, but at a less conscious level I am failing fully to see her in her distinct individuality; I am letting my fantasies about her get in the way of my seeing her clearly (Murdoch's emphasis) or at a deeper level I am not fully psychically distinct from her (Scheler's and the feminists' emphasis). In this case the moral worry is not that the motive in question is self-concern rather than other concern; it is that the agent has failed to see the other clearly, so as to be able to recognize what she needs, and what in particular the agent is able to provide for her.

Schopenhauer raises this issue only at a very formal level. He does not appear to recognize the kinds of self/other difficulties Scheler, the feminists, and Murdoch raise. This seems to me true of the Dalai Lama as well in *An Open Heart: Practicing Compassion in Everyday Life*, and of Jay Garfield's recent account of compassion and Buddhist ethics in *Engaging Buddhism*.[14]

Perhaps a feature of Buddhist metaphysics, partially adopted by Schopenhauer, renders the worry about the self-other differentiation required for knowing the other less significant. That feature is the view that suffering is the human condition, permeating all aspects of our life, even if we are not explicitly feeling it at a given time. If everyone is always suffering, then it is always appropriate to feel compassion for another particular person, and compassion is in a sense guaranteed its appropriate object. The agent does not need to have as differentiated a sense of self-and-other as Scheler, Murdoch, and the feminists are concerned with. The other's needs are not so individualized if the salient point is that the other is suffering and thus warranting compassion. When the Dalai Lama talks about cultivating compassion for every living being, he cannot have in mind an exquisitely individualized sense of each individual person. He must mean each-individual-insofar-as-he-is-a-sufferer. "Our compassion for all sentient beings must stem from a recognition of their suffering." And "eventually we should be able to relate to all beings [with compassion] seeing that their situation is always dependent upon the conditions of the vicious cycle of life."[15]

Group Solidarities

Let me now turn to group solidarities. Solidarities involve a kind of definitively nonmetaphysical oneness. I will focus on ethnic or racial group solidarities.

These are large groups in which no individual member can know personally every other, yet some other members are very likely to be personally known to any given individual member. One can feel solidarity with an unknown member of the group.

Earlier I noted that identifying with another person can involve a kind of identity confusion that taints the fellow feeling the identifier has with the identifiee. But some forms of identification, where this does not simply mean understanding the other, lack this distortion and can support appropriately informed and directed fellow feeling. For example, the agent can identify with the target because the target is going through some difficult experience that the agent has herself gone through in the past. While such a situation can blind the agent to differences between her past experience and the target's present one, it need not. The agent can identify with the target with respect to this experience while being entirely tuned in to the ways that the experience has a different meaning and quality from the target given differing circumstances and histories, of which the agent is fully aware.

Group identities can have this "appropriate identification" feature, in which one member identifies with another based on their shared group identity but is entirely aware of other differences between them. Yet group identities also raise a different issue regarding identification. Sometimes identification with the other proceeds entirely by way of the shared identity. Yvonne identifies with Reggie with because she is black and he is black. The shared identity forges the identification. But sometimes the shared identity, while present, does not play such a central role in the identification. The situation could be like the shared experience one. Suppose Delia comes to recognize that Yvonne is undergoing an experience that seems to her similar to one she herself has undergone—for example, Yvonne is being demeaned as a black woman in a way that Delia feels she has experienced also. The shared experience is the source of the identification, rather than the shared identity per se, although the shared identity plays a role since the experience is partly characterized in terms of that identity.

This distinction is orthogonal to the "tainted identification" issue. The identification can be either tainted or not tainted, and entirely based on shared group identity or based on something else but drawing on the shared group identity.

Solidarity involves a form of concern for a group and for members of the group as members of the group; but it is not an encompassing concern for their well-being in its totality but rather in light of a particular adversity facing them at a particular time.[16] Perhaps if the group suffers *general* adversity—for example, if it is a particularly disadvantaged group in a particular society, or is a general target of discrimination or stigma (as Muslims are in many Western societies, for example)—then the concern is of a more standing character, rather than localized to a particular time. Even then, however, solidarity would not seem directed to the others' overall well-being but only the relief of the adversity. In a way this does not differ so much from the Dalai Lama's compassion, which is directed toward the suffering of the other, but not necessarily toward improving the other's well-being apart from relieving suffering.

The African American Buddhist thinker Charles Johnson is interesting to bring in here, as a bridge between race issues and Buddhism.[17] Johnson says that African Americans have suffered more than many other groups. This distinctive suffering *could* be made a source or foundation of a distinctive racial solidarity that is directed toward relieving that suffering. The African American philosopher Tommie Shelby looks at black suffering, or, more precisely, black injustice-based suffering, in this way; he argues that it appropriately provides a basis and justification for black solidarity.[18] However, Johnson does not take this path. Rather, he sees black distinctive suffering as a source of insight into the human condition generally, but one that often escapes white people who are not in touch with suffering, even if they do suffer.[19]

Even if not as encompassing as overall concern for the other's well-being, solidarity of the most robust kind does involve a definite kind of "oneness." To have solidarity is to see the group identity shared with others as an important mutual identification. Some particular expressions of group solidarity especially reflect this sense of oneness. The American film *Selma*, released in 2014, about a march for voting rights led by Martin Luther King, Jr., in 1965 in Alabama, vividly re-creates the sense of solidarity among the marchers, all seeing themselves as part of a single entity, a movement, with which they all identify.[20] When some marchers are beaten, others rush to help them. They do not feel a sense of separateness from one another.

This sense of oneness in solidarity is not confined to race- or ethnicity-based forms of solidarity. The film and the real events on which it is based involve transracial solidarity as well. At first all the marchers are black. Then, for both strategic and moral reasons, King puts out a "call" for whites or nonblacks of good will to come to Selma to be part of subsequent attempts to march from Selma to the capital in Montgomery. Two subsequent marches bring together people of different races, powerfully portrayed in the film in these moments of solidarity.

Three Bases of Solidarity: Experience, Group Membership, Political Commitment

In-group and transgroup solidarities have different foundations. We can differentiate three bases of solidarity—experience, political commitment, and group membership. As mentioned earlier, we can feel solidarity with those who have had the same experience as we—for example, the experience of being discriminated against or stigmatized. That experience can, of course, cross ethnic or racial group boundaries, since people of many different groups can share that particular experience.

Shared political commitment is a different basis. It brings together people striving for the same political goal, where this may be people who have different experiential relations from that goal, and come from different identity groups. In the first marches in Selma, the black participants were mostly people who had all had the experience of living under segregation, with generally insuperable obstacles to voting put in their way (the focus of the film). In this case the experiential and identity bases of solidarity align. One might say that shared experiences *inform* the way the shared identity functions to create solidarity. It is black people who have experienced discrimination and segregation. The subsequent marches that involve whites as well still exemplify the sense of oneness in solidarity, but it is based only on shared political commitment, not on identity or experience, which the whites did not share with the blacks.

So experience, political commitment, and identity are distinct bases for solidarity, and often generate different groupings of persons. But the marches consisting of only black people can be regarded as all three coming together to inform and create the grouping in question—since those who chose to march were not only those blacks who suffered from segregation but, among them, those who chose to commit themselves to doing something about it through participating in the marches.[21]

All three of these bases of solidarity are exclusionary, in the sense that the group so defined is confined to people who satisfy the criterion for inclusion—having certain experiences, having certain political commitments, and being in an identity-defined group, in this case a racial one. But the political commitment criterion reaches out in a somewhat more universalistic way than do the other two—because anyone, no matter what their experiences or identity group, can choose to take up certain political commitments. The film attempts to capture this universality when it shows various people around the United States watching King's call for volunteers on television, after having seen footage of marchers being beaten, and then responding to that call by choosing to come to Selma. This universality can be regarded as analogous to or exemplified in both Schopenhauer's and the Dalai Lama's implication that anyone is capable of compassion for anyone else.[22] Scheler very definitively, perhaps even more than the Dalai Lama, articulates the view that the capability for fellow feeling is universal in humans, and that it is not limited by experience. Scheler affirms that we are each capable of understanding the experience of the other and having the appropriate fellow-feeling for her, even if we have not had the same experience ourselves (47). As mentioned earlier, this individualized dimension of fellow feeling is absent in the Buddhist writers, including here Schopenhauer, because the object of compassion is suffering, a condition assumed to be universal to human nature. We are meant to have compassion for each individual being as a sufferer, but not as an individual in Scheler's sense.

King's Universalism: The "Beloved Community"

A kind of universalism is expressed in Martin Luther King's vision of what he called "the beloved community," a vision of the future in which white, black, and others would live together in harmony, accepting one another as fellow citizens and fellow human beings in an overarching community of care and concern. But this vision did not, in King's mind, aim to erase racial identities. It was not what came later to be called "color blind" or "postracial." One line has been lifted from King's famous speech at the March on Washington for Jobs and Freedom in 1963 and wrongly "spun" to imply that King was invoking a world beyond racial identities entirely.[23] He was invoking a world beyond racism but *not* beyond racial identities. He saw American blacks as a distinct people, who would not lose that distinctiveness in a beloved community, but would bring it as a positive element in that interracial community. This retaining of a group distinctiveness is not incompatible with the Dalai Lama's vision of a universal compassion, but the recognition and retention of group identities that are positive for their members but also can be sources of division and have historically been so seem to me to go against both the Dalai Lama's and Schopenhauer's emphasis on the suffering of humanity as the most fundamental shared feature of existence. It is us as sufferers, not as black, white, Kurd, Turk, or Chinese ethnic, that really counts.

Interestingly, Charles Johnson, the African American Buddhist, says that Buddhist teachings may be the next step in spiritual evolution toward the "beloved community."[24] Johnson does not refer to King's sense of retention of a black or African American identity in the beloved community that he, Johnson, envisions. He sees the Buddhist letting go of the ego as something that can be especially valuable for American blacks. There is no explicit valorizing of a distinctive black identity and solidarity that can be brought to and coexist with a wider universality in the vision of the beloved community that he articulates, but on the other hand, Johnson does not take his Buddhism in an explicitly "postracial" dimension either, and often talks about black Americans as a distinct group that, the reader could infer, he would expect to retain their identity in the beloved community he envisions.

Finally, the notion of solidarity based on any of the three foundations mentioned—experience, identity, and political commitment—offers a partial, though only partial, buffer against the identity confusion that Scheler and Murdoch are concerned about. It does so because it is focused on particular concerns around which the solidarity is built. So the concern that individual members of the solidarity group have for one another is not open-ended but targeted to something—the achievement of civic equality, an end to racial discrimination—on whose character we can assume the parties to the solidarity agree. This is similar to the focus on suffering as the human condition in Schopenhauer and Buddhism that in a sense ensures that compassion will be properly directed.

This targeting, with its consequent buffering against identity confusion, is less true, however, of the identity-based form where there is more room for disagreement as to what members of the identity group need or what is good for them. This point relates to the way the form of solidarity exemplified in the Selma marches does not capture the full significance of racial solidarity, because solidarity involves a sense of connection with members of one's group unknown to one that may permeate one's life but not in an always conscious way. One feels a sense of connection to the racial or ethnic others in one's group and acknowledges them as a plurality of persons with their individual lives in a way that gets sidelined in a focused demonstration such as King's voting rights marches. But such whole group solidarity leaves room for significant unclarity on the part of one member of the group about what another wants or needs.

Racial and ethnic solidarity exemplifies an important form of nonmetaphysical oneness that differs in significant ways from its universal forms implied in the Buddhist tradition and in Schopenhauer. It also differs from the more individualized forms of fellow feeling highlighted by Scheler and feminist writers on this topic. Finally, it provides some but not unerring protection against Murdoch's and the feminist writers' concerns about the difficulties of knowing the other's needs, and the temptations of confusing one's own needs with those of the other.

Notes

1. Arthur Schopenhauer, *On the Basis of Morality*, trans. E. J. F. Payne (1841; Indianapolis: Bobbs-Merrill, 1965). Citations hereafter given parenthetically in the text.
2. Paul Guyer, "Schopenhauer, Kant, and Compassion," *Kantian Review* 17, no. 3 (November 2012): 403–29. Guyer refers to Schopenhauer's *World as Will and Representation* as a source of his interpretation.
3. "The beneficent, righteous man would express by his deed that knowledge only which is the result of the greatest intellectual depth and the most laborious investigation of the theoretical philosopher" (210). Schopenhauer's emphasis (in *On the Basis of Morality*) on the compassionate person's thereby revealing insight into the noumenal realm echoes Kant's similar view that the agent acting according to the moral law is manifesting her noumenal nature; but Kant's view does not allow for the definitive knowledge of the noumenal that Schopenhauer does.

     In holding this view Schopenhauer is like most neo-Confucian thinkers who believe we possess an innate faculty of moral sapience that spontaneously appreciates the metaphysical fact of our fundamental oneness and that, under the right circumstances, manifests such understanding without the need for deliberation or judgment. (I am indebted for this point to P. J. Ivanhoe.)

4. "This doctrine teaches that all plurality is only apparent; that in all the individuals of the world, however infinite the number in which they exhibit themselves successively and simultaneously, there is yet manifested only one and the same truly existing essence, present and identical in all of them. Such a doctrine, of course, existed long before Kant; indeed it might be said to have existed from time immemorial. In the first place it is the main and fundamental teaching of the oldest book in the world, the sacred Vedas" (207).

5. Max Scheler, *The Nature of Sympathy*, trans. Peter Heath (London: Routledge and Kegan Paul, 1954). Citations hereafter given parenthetically in the text.

6. Schopenhauer nevertheless often implies that each one of us possesses that noumenal nature individually, though he criticizes Kant for making that same assumption. We sometimes, even often, use the term *identify* or *identification* not to implicate lack of individuation or identity but simply to express common cause with or understanding of another.

7. "Schopenhauer's theory becomes a special case of the erroneous theory of fellow-feeling as identification, and a metaphysical version of this to boot. Now actually, as we have shown already, the sort of identification which Schopenhauer describes can only come about by way of some sort of emotional infection and identification, which would positively exclude an understanding of the other person's state; so that his theory implies a further confusion of moral pity with susceptibility to emotional infection and identification" (Scheler, *The Nature of Sympathy*, 55).

8. Sandra Bartky is the one feminist philosopher I have run across to explicitly draw on Scheler. Bartky, "Sympathy and Solidarity: On a Tightrope with Scheler," in *Feminists Rethink the Self*, ed. Diana T. Meyers (Boulder: Westview, 1997).

9. Diana T. Meyers, *Essays on Identity, Action, and Social Life* (New York: Rowman and Littlefield, 2004); Marilyn Friedman, *What Are Friends For: Feminist Perspectives on Personal Relationships and Moral Theory* (Ithaca: Cornell University Press, 1993).

10. Sara Ruddick, *Maternal Thinking: Toward a Politics of Peace* (Boston: Beacon, 1995).

11. For this critique of Murdoch for omitting social sources of distortions of moral perception, see L. Blum, "Visual Metaphors in Murdoch's Moral Philosophy," in *Iris Murdoch, Philosopher*, ed. Justin Broackes (Oxford: Oxford University Press, 2012).

12. Example is from Murdoch, "Idea of Perfection," in *Sovereignty of Good* (London: Routledge and Kegan Paul, 1970).

13. Murdoch discusses Schopenhauer extensively in her last book, *Metaphysics as a Guide to Morals* (New York: Penguin, 1993), based on her 1982 Gifford Lectures.

14. Dalai Lama, *An Open Heart: Practicing Compassion in Everyday Life*, ed. Nicholas Vreeland (New York: Back Bay, 2001); Jay Garfield, *Engaging Buddhism: Why It Matters to Philosophy* (Oxford: Oxford University Press, 2014).

15. Dalai Lama, *Open Heart*, 93, 105. If compassion is a general emotion-based attitude that is to be cultivated, the picture one is given of our caring relations with others is different than Murdoch's, in which the agent is confronted with an individual moral reality consisting in a particular other person and her needs. One responds to something one is confronted with in the moment. It is not a question of a standing general attitude that one cultivates. Perhaps in the final analysis these two states of mind are reconcilable. Perhaps the cultivated attitude of compassion could be construed as a disposition to respond to others as individuals when the situation arises. Perhaps, but this is not the impression one gets in *An Open Heart*.

16. For a discussion of this feature of solidarity, see L. Blum, "Three Forms of Race-Related Solidarity," *Journal of Social Philosophy* 38, no. 1 (Spring 2007): 53–72.

17. Johnson is best known as a novelist, having won the National Book Award, a prestigious American fiction award, for *Middle Passage*, published in 1990. But he has also had training in philosophy, and this comes through in his writings. His writings on Buddhism, from which I am drawing, are in *Taming the Ox: Buddhist Stories and Reflections on Politics, Race, Culture, and Spiritual Practice* (Boulder: Shambala, 2014).

18. T. Shelby, *We Who Are Black: The Philosophical Foundations of Black Solidarity* (Cambridge: Harvard University Press, 2005).

19. Johnson approvingly cites another African American Buddhist, Jan Willis: "People of color, because of our experience of the great and wrenching historical dramas of slavery, colonization, and segregation, understand suffering in a way that our white brothers and sisters do not. That understanding provides a kind of 'head start' in comprehending essential elements in Buddhist philosophy." Johnson, *Taming the Ox*, 70.

20. *Selma* (dir. Ava DuVernay, 2014).

21. Perhaps one needs a further distinction here. The whites who marched can indeed be seen as helping to constitute a political-commitment-based group with the blacks who are marching. But they can also be seen as expressing an "outgroup" solidarity with blacks (not only the marchers, but those on behalf of whom the marchers are marching) as sufferers of injustice. Outgroup solidarity does not involve a shared basis of solidarity among all members of the constituted solidarity group; it involves the outgroup *standing with* members of the in-group, where the latter are defined by experience and identity. In this respect outgroup solidarity has a different character than in-group solidarity, but both manifest "standing with."

22. This universalism is somewhat compromised in Schopenhauer's case, however, by his determinism—that people's characters are set and unchangeable and that many and indeed most people are not compassionate.

23. "I have a dream that my four little children will one day live in a nation where they will not be judged by the color of their skin, but by the content of their character." Martin Luther King, Jr., "I Have a Dream," in *A Testament of Hope: The Essential Writings and Speeches of Martin Luther King, Jr.*, ed. James Washington (New York: HarperCollins, 1986), 218.

24. Johnson, *Taming the Ox*, 73, 79.

CHAPTER 6

THE RELATIONALITY AND THE NORMATIVITY OF *AN ETHIC OF CARE*

EVA FEDER KITTAY

J oel Feinberg wrote that a person in a world without rights would be a "Nowhere Man." What, we might ask, would a person be in a world with care? One simply would not be, as a human being cannot survive beyond infancy without care. Nor can one thrive in such a world, even if one could miraculously survive. Indeed it seems extraordinary that Western philosophers have taken so long to consider care a central moral concept. A world without care would not only be a dismal world; it would be a world in which great harm would be done. A world in which nobody cared about anyone else would be a world in which those who could not attend to their own needs (and that is all of us at some point in our lives) would be neglected. It would be a world without compassion, without relationships that affirm our inherent connections, dependence, and interdependence. Although an implicit ethic of care has been indispensable to the survival and development of human society, its articulation as moral theory is still in its infancy. Western philosophy has been more concerned with being a nowhere, rather than a no-care, man.

As women, who have long been charged with doing carework, have entered philosophy, they have expressed two divergent attitudes toward care. One group has been anxious to disavow caregiving, dependency, and vulnerability, seeing instead their entrance into the mostly male world of philosophy as an escape from their gender-assigned place. Other women, however, have embraced care as an important, if neglected, value and have insisted that its devaluation arises from its being viewed as merely a natural sentiment and as a form of gender-specific labor, rather than as a practice from which we could garner ethically important concepts and relationships. Sarah Ruddick saw ethical values and practices in the work of maternal caregiving that she thought can and should be brought to bear on peacemaking. Carol Gilligan saw an entire ethical perspective revealed, one that was in contrast to an ethics based primarily on individual rights. What all who took on the question of an ethic of care saw was the relational nature of the self, and the moral significance of human connection to those for whom we care and to the world we inhabit. It is in the understanding of relationality and connection that the question of care meets the theme of Oneness. The self, from a perspective of care, is not a solitary and independent self whose interests and concerns primarily begin and end with the boundaries of one's skin. Instead selves are porous and connected, situated in a web of relationships where even those far from us are bound to us with invisible but morally important threads. We may be born and die in our own skins, but we live always in togetherness with others, and with our environment and the nonhuman world.

The vision of the human being as ideally independent, self-sufficient, and self-determining, a vision found in all the seventeenth- and eighteenth-century Western philosophers who shaped the Enlightenment and the liberal ideals so characteristic of Western philosophy, posed a problem. Why should such self-sufficient beings form social groups in which they have to be bound by the rules that govern all, if we are equally empowered and situated? We have adopted the mythical social contract, although the reason why we may want to do so relies on a just-so story. The more likely story is that the human are inherently social beings and develop in concert with one another, as beings who are born and remain dependent for long periods of time and develop social organizations to protect and provide for themselves in their dependency. The ethical view that embraces our dependency and our connectedness is an ethic of care.

Care as Descriptive and as Normative

Care is more than a necessary feature of the world. It is at the heart of our moral relationships with others. We can harm another not only by hurting or interfering with that individual; we also can harm someone through neglect, through a lack of concern and responsiveness. That care has not always been understood as the basis of a moral vision is partly due to an understanding of care as a merely natural disposition, one that is always embedded in practices that are carried out by those thought to be most naturally suited to care, for example, mothering, nursing, eldercare, or assistance for a disabled person. Thus care talk has largely been thought of as descriptive, part of an anthropology, not a morality. But practices are themselves sources of normativity. Practices, as Peter Winch first showed, provide the context by which we make claims of truth or falsity. Alasdair MacIntyre maintained it is within a practice that we exercise the virtues.

The telos of a practice is the regulative ideal by which we evaluate not only the behavior of individuals, but also the activities and structures, the rules and conventions that characterize the practice. Thus Ruddick derives the virtues of mothering from the telos of the practice, virtues that can be extracted and guide us to a peace politics. When rules of a hospital run counter to the telos of nursing, a nurse who wants to be a *good nurse* should be willing to break those rules.

Yet norms for specific practices and general moral demands are not always aligned. Killing someone who is your enemy is generally commendable in the practice of war, but killing someone who is your enemy, even your mortal enemy, is *generally* not a good or right action. The way we normally speak of caring is the way we speak of mothering or nursing. You can do it well or poorly; you can be a good carer or an inadequate one. You can care "too much" (for example, a parent constantly hovering over a child, what we in the US call a "helicopter parent") or "too little" (for example, being callous, negligent, or even abusive in carrying out presumed acts of care). This is a perfectly service-able way to speak of care most of the time.

However, in speaking of an ethic of care, we want to get at something less descriptive and more fully normative. We have to know that the practices of care and their regulative ideals themselves have moral validation. Thieving is a sort of practice. But honesty among thieves does not make a thief honest. A moral practice is one that, when meeting its regulative ideal, is a morally good or morally right practice.

What gives a practice such moral validation? Consider mothering. It may seem that a good mother can be one that does everything for her child regard-less of the cost to others. But one of the aims of mothering is to socialize her child, guide the child in becoming a member of her community. A mother that is ruthless in obtaining things for her own child will be doing a poor job, for such a parent does not model behavior that is acceptable. Mothering does not set its own aims apart from the world in which the child must live.

What caring practices share is an ideal that leaves no one's genuine and legitimate needs and wants, needs and wants that can result in real harm, unat-tended. More positively, caring practices attend to what I will call, somewhat distorting the normal usage of the term, people's CARES, that is, using the term to signify those things people care about, which figure in their flourishing and, in the case of persons who need care, which they cannot accomplish without the proper assistance. Avoiding harming another, allowing others to flourish are conceptions that are familiar to all moral theories. A moral theory based on care gives special consideration *to the avoidance of neglect, to the importance of attending to those who are inevitably dependent and so cannot attend to what they require themselves, and to a motivational structure based on affective ties and empathetic capacities.*

Our cares and concerns reflect our deep attachments, attachments that Western philosophers have struggled with, attachments that lead us to a partialist ethics, where those we care about or are assigned to care for receive more moral considerations than others. However, as Bernard Williams wrote so eloquently and insightfully: "Somewhere one reaches the necessity that such things as deep attachments to other persons will express themselves in the world in ways that cannot at the same time embody the impartial point of view, and that they also run the risk of offending against it. They run that risk if they exist at all; yet unless such things exist, there will not be enough substance or conviction in a man's life to compel his allegiance to life itself."[1] The trick is to extend the notion of care in such a way that the partialism ultimately produces a good for all. To do this, we can borrow a notion from the American philosopher Josiah Royce. Royce maintained that the chief good for humans was loyalty. If an eyebrow is raised, it is because we think: Is not loyalty to a cause or community what causes us to act badly when that community adheres to an unmoral or amoral creed; doesn't loyalty to one cause or group involve us in often violent disputes with other such groups? Partiality, like loyalty, unites those who work in concert but divides us and splits us off from others. Care appears to suffer from the same difficulty, if what it is to care is to honor those deep attachments that give us "enough substance or conviction" to "compel" our allegiance to life itself.

But Royce also shows us the way out of the dilemma of the partiality of loyalty and so also of care. Royce argues that we are all capable of loyalty and so loyalty is a good for everyone. Loyalties that cause us to engage in violence toward other groups or try to otherwise harm them bring about an great evil, not least because they destroy the cause for loyalty of others, and so deny them this supreme good. Thus the highest good is loyalty to loyalty.[2] If we likewise believe that care is a supreme good, one can make a similar argument for care. Efforts at care that destroy or create conditions that destroy the possibility of care for others destroy the very thing we honor about caring as a value when we care for another—that it promotes the flourishing of another.[3] Thus an ethics of care that is fully normative must care about care. Practices of care that do not care about care are not fully moral practices, just as loyalties to a cause or a group that intend on vitiating the loyalty of another group violate what is important in loyalty—that individuals are able to form attachments that matter. If we are correct about the moral validation of practices of care, then we have a basis for thinking that there is an ethic of care in the fully normative and not merely descriptive sense.[4] This is the ethic that expresses the moral values inherent in the fully normative conception of care, which I designate orthographically as care in small caps, CARE. The ETHIC OF CARE that I am formulating here then is an ethics based on a fully normative conception of care.

Caring about caring is not only inherent in the ideal of CARE as a supreme good that promotes our flourishing; it is also inherent in the ideal of CARE as connection and as requiring a relational conception of the self. We begin with the inevitability of human dependency that sits at the heart of the human condition. Unlike many other creatures, we are born in a state of utter dependence, and unlike most, our dependency lasts for a long time. Inevitable dependency is a state into which we return when we are ill and need care and when, in our late years, we become frail and lose capacities. Some people born with certain sorts of disabilities are inevitably dependent throughout their lives.

Those who care for dependents often have to turn their attention away from their own needs and wants to tend to the dependency needs of others. This dependency work makes them, at least to the extent that the demands of the dependent are urgent, derivatively dependent. The caregivers become dependent on others to provide for them and the dependents for whom they care. Even those who provide these resources, who I elsewhere call the providers, are dependent—on their employers if they are wageworkers, on their customers if they are self-employed, on their citizens when the state is the provider. The inevitability of human dependency brings with it a set of nested dependencies such that we are all engaged in inextricable human interdependencies. And we need not stop at the human world, as our inevitable dependencies extend to the air we breathe, the water we drink, the food we consume, the animals and creatures who share the world with us. When we begin with inevitable dependency, we soon discover the web of relations that sustain us all. And what sustains the web is CARE.

What I hope to present in this essay is the way in which an ETHIC OF CARE is deeply relational. Within some moral theories, whether or not we do the right thing is up to us alone. We accept the credit and the blame. Within an ETHIC OF CARE, to quote Nel Noddings, "How good I can be is dependent, is partly a function of how you—the other—receive and respond to me."

The Completion of CARE as Key to the Normativity of CARE

Descriptions of care usually begin with the obligations and responsibilities of the carer, at the front end—so to speak—of the caring relationship. If, however, we look at an ETHIC OF CARE from its end point, that is, from its reception, we can identify in in an ETHIC OF CARE the operative concept.

The way into the question comes from the nature of care alluded to in Noddings's quotation. Noddings wrote: "my caring has somehow to be completed in the other if the relation is to be described as caring." Tronto wrote: "The final phase of caregiving recognizes that the object of care will respond to the care it receives."

The reception of care has, however, received little attention. I do not know why others have missed its importance. But I do know why I failed to do so. The model that informed my thinking about care also shaped my views about its reception. That model was care for my daughter, Sesha. My criterion for the adequacy of any ethics—including care ethics—was whether it would be true to the care of Sesha and people with similar disabilities. Although now an adult woman of forty-five, she remains incapable of doing anything that falls within the conventional understanding of acknowledging or refusing another's care: she can neither say thank you nor flee or otherwise refuse the care she receives. It was absurd to say that because of her incapacities, what we do for her is not care because there is no way she is able to "complete our care."[5]

It was only when I found myself having to care for my ninety-two-year-old mother that I came to appreciate the idea that care needs to be completed in the other. Unlike my daughter, my mother would sometimes acknowledge my care with words of praise and thanks, but more often, she would fiercely resist my attempts to help her. Sesha's response to our caring presented a stark contrast to my mother's bitterness at her powerlessness and lost capacities. Faced with the intransigence of someone in need of care but who refuses it, I came to recognize that Sesha did in fact receive our care.

I realized that she could in fact turn away, could, even with her limited means, resist, get angry at her impotence, as some folks with her disabilities do. It suddenly became apparent that Sesha is much less passive than I had acknowledged. There are times when she makes it difficult for us to give her medication, when she turns away at something unpleasant we have to do, and there are other times when she clearly helps us to help her. I have come to see that Sesha's thriving is itself a responsiveness to our care, that the hugs, smiles, and her own distinctive "kisses" are still other forms of receiving our care. All this she does with a beautiful graciousness. It is precisely because Sesha receives her care with such grace that I was able to miss the fact that she does indeed complete our care. The general assumption is that to be a recipient is to be passive. To resist is instead a mark of agency. But this is false. To be receptive to care can itself be an active affirmation of a willingness to be helped and to embrace the relationship that care establishes. To refuse care may be a form of passivity in the face of suffering, and a refusal of care can be found in a passive resistance to actively engage with another. Care is not something we do *to* something or someone. It is something we do *for* another's benefit and *with* their engagement. There has to be an uptake on the other's part if our action is to count as a benefit for the other. If the other is not benefited—has taken up our actions as a good—we have failed to confer a benefit. To underscore the active element in the reception of care, I will speak of the completion of care as the "taking-up of care."

Most moral concepts we call "virtues" do not behave in this fashion. I can be prudent, gracious, honest, charitable, and temperate even if no one responds to my efforts as instances of such virtuous action. If I succeed in rescuing an unconscious person from a burning building, my courage is already demonstrated and it does not depend on the recognition from the person saved. The person might even not have wanted to be saved, but my action would still be courageous. For the most part, virtues are virtuous insofar as the person acts with a right intent and in the right manner.

There are, however, moral theories where the end point matters—utilitarianism being the prime example. Moral concepts such as "mercy" and "respect" also depend on their uptake. If an inmate on death row sees the commutation of his sentence as a form of torture, not mercy, then commuting the sentence may[6] not, in fact, be merciful. If I think it is disrespectful to ask about another's mortal illness because I believe such a question would be too personal and so presumptuous, but the afflicted person regards my silence as coldness and aloofness, then my attempt to be respectful has misfired. CARE, I believe, is this sort moral concept.[7]

As I begin here to consider the uptake as critical to CARE, we can see a number of things about CARE that otherwise might not be apparent. In this text, I will discuss only some of these, namely, why CARE is an ethic that requires action and is not based only on intention, that it should be distinguished from paternalism, and that it is inherently relational. I will end with a surprising implication: That we have a *duty to receive care graciously* when it is offered with a good will and with the requisite attention and competence, insofar as we are able to discharge such a duty.

The Logic of Care

How important is the taking-up of care to the act of care.[8] Let us begin by considering a very simple example: caring for a plant by watering it. Now suppose that unbeknown to me, I pick up a pitcher of *vinegar* instead of a pitcher of *water* to pour into a dry wilting plant. Predictably, the plant begins to wither instead of perk up. Have I cared for the plant? Most of us would answer, "No."[9]

Of course, pouring vinegar rather than water was an error on my part. Some errors result from incompetence or carelessness. But if I had no reason to suspect that someone would leave a pitcher of vinegar in my vicinity, the error was not due to my carelessness, thoughtlessness, or lack of competence. My action was not perfunctory. Yet even if my act was motivated by my love or concern for the welfare of the plant and my desire to see it thrive, it could not be said to be caring for the plant. Although I may not be blameworthy, I failed carry out a responsibility I took upon myself, namely, to care for the plant. If, as it appears, it is the case that pouring vinegar when I intended to water the plant was not care, then this simple case illustrates that *we have a strong intuitive sense that a thing's or person's well-being*[10] *must be positively affected by our actions if our actions are to be counted as care—at the very least, it ought not to be negatively affected.* This intuition helps to ground what I have called the fully normative sense of care. Of particular importance to the development of a fully normative account of care—CARE—are the following three claims:

Proposition 1. Caring requires action, or it is not yet CARING. This is because nothing can have the effect of CARE if it is not put into action.

Proposition 2. CARE is an achievement and "to CARE" is an achievement verb.

Proposition 3. CARE requires that the object of the care respond in some way that results in the achievement of the act—that is, CARING requires that the cared-for take up the action as care.

Let me take these considerations in turn.

CARING Is an Action or a Disposition to Act

The claim I wish to defend is that while the term *care* is used in many different ways, when it is used with normative content, "to care" is to *act* in a certain way, or to have the *disposition to act* in this manner. That is to say, care or caring is *not only* a frame of mind (though it is that as well), nor is it simply an intention. To be in a caring frame of mind or to have caring intentions would mean nothing at all if these were not tethered to a willingness to act in certain caring ways when the appropriate circumstance pertains.

Let us take a moment to consider Bernice Fischer's and Joan Tronto's phases of care and see if this claim is defensible.[11] "Caregiving" is the phase of care that clearly involves action. "Taking care" or "taking responsibility" similarly implies that we will act in such a way that the other's needs get met, whether we ourselves meet these needs or ensure that a third party does. We can't claim, for instance, that we are taking care of someone's financial matters, and do nothing to assure that their financial matters are taken care of.

"Caring about" less obviously involves action since that term is first of all attitudinal. We can care about many things without actually *doing something.* We believe we care about the hungry children in the world even if we do not travel the world feeding hungry children. But is this really care (that is, CARE), or merely a pretense, mixed perhaps with a bit of self-deception? If we never give a dime to organizations who try to feed the hungry, nor vote for the candidate who is most likely to pay attention to world hunger, nor engage in any action whereby we can say this is our small part in doing something to alleviate world hunger, then we vacate the claim that we care about world hunger.

CARE as an Achievement Term

Our withered plant thought experiment carried the implication that CARE is a particular kind of action, namely, one that is an achievement. The British ordinary language philosopher Gilbert Ryle drew a distinction between verbs that named tasks (for example, "running"), those that signaled failures (for example, "losing"), and those that marked achievements (for example, "winning"). The meaning of an achievement verb includes the idea that the action aimed for was successful. Achievement terms include the end result, and not merely the tasks or conditions needed to achieve the end.[12] Ryle writes: "For the runner to win, not only must he run but also his rivals must also arrive at the tape later than he; for a doctor to effect a cure, his patient must both be treated and be well again; for the searcher to find the thimble, there must be a thimble in the place he indicates at the moment when he indicates it."[13] Just as the doctor must not only treat a patient but the patient must be well again if we are to say that the doctor cured the patient, so must the carer not only attend to the cared-for, but the cared-for also has to receive these attentions as caring.

Within an ETHICS OF CARE, when the cared-for individuals are subjects, which is to say that they are capable of a subjective life, caring needs to contribute to their flourishing. In sum, *an action will count as CARE, if it contributes to the well-being, restoration, or flourishing of a thing or a subject.*[14] When we are dealing with a subject, because we are promoting the individuals' flourishing, the care must be for the sake of the individual cared for—not for the sake of the carer, a larger community, or some abstract conception of goodness. The concern takes the form of actions directed at the genuine and legitimate needs and wants of the individual requiring care.

Using the framework of Ryle's achievement verbs, we can see that caring carries a constraint on how the aim is legitimately achieved. Just as one does not win a race by knocking down opponents to ensure that one gets to the finish line first, so CARE is constrained by what a care ethics, based on caring practices, recognizes as moral harm, most importantly exploitation, domination, and the neglect of others' needs. Caring for one's own charge by inflicting injury on others is like "winning" a race by knocking down one's fellow runners.

Let me point out here that when I speak of CARE as requiring the uptake of care by the cared-for, I am not offering a merely stipulative definition. I am instead trying to identify a deep intuition, one that is widely held and is captured in the response to pouring vinegar, mistaken as water, on a wilted plant. That intuition is what, I believe, captures the true normativity of care, that care is a morally significant achievement that is accomplished only when care is taken up by the cared-for as care. Thus, an action that fails to achieve its end, even when it is carried out with the intention to care or with the attitude of care, is insufficient to make an action.

Perhaps this sounds too demanding. If we say, "Sue intended to care for her sister, Ann, but didn't succeed, because Sue did more harm than good," we can admit that Sue cares about Ann and tried to do what she thought would be best for her (and so went beyond mere feeling into action). The intent and the effort may have been admirable (even commendable),[15] but Ann did not get the care that she needed, and Sue did not provide it. There are important questions and one important qualification with respect to my hardline position on CARE as an achievement term.

The qualification first: Sometimes merely experiencing the other's *desire* to care for oneself—as clumsy and inadequate as these efforts may be—can be a contribution to one's flourishing. We can be moved—and feel cared for—by the evident tenderness and concern. However, a carer who feigns the intention to care for manipulative or exploitive reasons fails morally on several grounds: she has not met the cared-for's needs, she lacks the appropriate attitude for caring, and she may even envision using the deception for harm. The objective conditions under which the actions are carried out as well as the subjective response count toward the moral evaluation of the act as care.

To the questions: The hardline seems to imply, save for the qualification just given, that the carer is not to be *morally* commended for her attempts to care, and that she should not be given *moral* praise for being caring. This seems not only harsh but wrong. Thus the first question is whether we are wrong to insist that the *achievement* of care is part the *moral* content rather than more practical aspects of care.

To respond we need to consider the moral harm and the moral good of care. The harm we aim to avoid by caring for another is not only unwarranted interferences into another's life and affairs, as in most modern ethical theories. Rather, what is required is the active intervention on another's behalf.[16] If we fail to succeed in caring, we are willy-nilly causally implicated in an ethically important harm. A Kantian good will, which Kant maintained was the only unqualified good in the world, without the *successful* action does not feed a hungry infant, and a starved infant dies. Harm that results from a failure of care occurs not merely if we fail to act, but if we fail to succeed.

Second question: Is it then the case that within an ETHICS OF CARE moral motives accrue no moral credit, and a failure not of our own making makes us blameworthy?

We can mitigate the harshness of this moral view if we follow the views of those bothered by this feature of a consequentialist ethic, but who nonetheless want to remain consequentialists. G. E. Moore remarked, "that we didn't act other than how we acted, even though our actions did not result in right action, does not necessarily mean that we acted *wrongly*."[17] It is interesting to note that many carers, in fact, do feel this way when their caring efforts fail and are irked when people attempt to console them with praise precisely because they recognize that their actions did not warrant the praise, although trying was not blameworthy.

Is an ethic of care then not so new but merely another sort of consequentialism? And what about those intentions, and caring attitudes and dispositions, have they no place in an ethic of care?

An ethics of care is not simply a form of consequentialism—intentions, motivations, and such matter. That someone's needs are met without anyone's intent to give care signifies only that a need has been met, not that CARE was given. Consider a man who has lost all interest in the world, throws his money out of his window, and says to himself (as he watches the bedlam below), "look at the fools below picking up the useless paper!" This misanthrope has doubtless met the needs of many, but he will have cared for none, and no one who has benefited from his actions will feel cared for by him. What remains crucial to CARE is that the action is executed *out of concern for the other's welfare or the other's ability to flourish.*[18] This is a motivational constraint on the part of the carer that is essential to our evaluation of the outcome as CARE.[19]

Our CARING Must Be "Taken Up as Care"

What does the taking up of care on the part of the cared for look like? In the case of the plant, that participation is akin to a merely tropic response: that is, it is without intention, will, or agency of any sort, but it is a responsiveness that is inherent in that sort of being. As there is no subjectivity on the part of the plant, whether or not care has been given can be determined entirely from a third-person standpoint. Either the plant survives or it dies. I contend later that such purely objective measures of the success of caring are insufficient when the cared-for is a subject, and later I will consider the many different ways we might consider how beings, in different states of awareness and stages of development, take up care as subjects.

But first, I want to point out how the claims made here about the taking up of care exhibit the intimate connection between this conception of care and the normativity of care. I have suggested that one test of whether we can say we are using care in a fully normative sense is whether the claim that someone "cares too much" is incoherent, in a way similar to the claim that someone is "being too just" is incoherent.[20] A caregiver whose ministrations are rejected (or criticized as "caring too much") may tell herself that her charge in time will come to see that her actions were caring. Her longings to be seen as caring may be so powerful or her concern or love so strong that she cannot imagine that her actions may be anything but caring. Yet if we think of care in its normative sense, she may well be *wrong* in thinking that she is CARING at all.

The Requirement of Subjectivity

Let us now look more closely at the claim that caring for a subject there has to be a *subjective* taking up of care as care. Care, I have claimed, promotes another's flourishing. Although there are objective measures by which we can determine that a person is not flourishing, these cannot definitively tell us that a person *is* flourishing. To flourish as a conscious sentient being includes having the sense that we are flourishing, a sense that we are living the life we want to live, a sense of well-being, as we ourselves conceive of well-being. To live a life that others might think is a flourishing life and yet to have no sense of well-being or satisfaction with one's life is not yet to flourish. Similarly, one can lack what others think is a flourishing life, even have a life of deprivation—especially when the deprivations are self-chosen—and yet be flourishing nonetheless. The claim that a subjective element is *necessary* for flourishing, however, does not accept the view that subjective criteria are *sufficient*. We can care about things that are genuinely harmful either to others or us, and we will need to face the problem of adaptive preference formation. Yet even objective indicators of (or conditions for) flourishing, such as Martha Nussbaum's capability list, must be endorsed by the subject, if they are to figure in *this* subject's own sense of flourishing.[21] When one is unable to attend to one's most urgent CARES, to what makes one's life meaningful,[22] a carer serves as an affordance, enabling the person to engage in what she cares about and enables that person's ability to flourish.

The requirement that there is a subjective uptake of another's actions as caring is readily susceptible to objections. Most important are those objections that presume that care can be, and often is, paternalistic. Stephen Darwall's account of care builds paternalism into the concept. A person's welfare, he avers, is what a rational carer should want for that person. Wishing to attend to another's welfare, he maintains, arises from what he calls a "natural disposition" to care. The rationality in "rational care" comes from adhering to an objective conception of a person's good, which the carer *should* want for the cared-for, for cared-for's own sake. While care arises from a "natural disposition" there is another moral disposition that considers the person's own view on his good. This is "respect." It requires that we view the other as autonomous and an end in oneself with her own perspective of what is of value. Because, on Darwall's account, a carer has an objective standard for the other's good, the carer is justified in acting paternalistically and overriding the cared-for's own idiosyncratic view of what is good and right for herself. In doing so, we will be caring for her, but we will not necessarily be respecting her. Darwall reflects, I believe, a rather standard view of care as sanctioning paternalistic interference with another.[23]

Against this conception of care is the view that care has to be a moral concept and not merely a natural disposition, and that care is fundamentally opposed to a paternalistic imposition of a putative objective conception of a person's good. The carer who acts in accordance with the moral concept CARE, disciplines herself to have what I have called a "transparent self," a self that is respectful of the perspective of the other and the other's own conception of her needs and wants.

Who is right? Is care paternalistic; is it to be contrasted with the moral attitude of respect for the person's autonomy? Consider the following cases where it seems the paternalistic view should prevail.[24]

Case 1. The Child or Adult with a Judgment-Affecting Disability

My own experiences of caring for my daughter seem to condemn my theory. When I give my daughter her antiseizure medication—which is bitter and difficult to swallow—I do believe that I am CARING for her even if she tries to spit it out, and even if she hardly feels cared for at such times. In fact, not to give her this medicine would be negligent and morally culpable.[25] If the medication works, and she doesn't have seizures, I am CARING for her by any objective measure.[26] Where is the role of subjective uptake?

My response is that if the cared-for, Sesha, could understand, then she would endorse my actions as CARE. This is sometimes referred to as "hypothetical consent" in the bioethics literature. One has to take care with such counterfactuals. In principle they can be used to justify all sorts of coercion. In my daughter's case, she has two sorts of seizures. There are the small quick jerks often ending in her giggling, hedonic seizures she would have not interest in preventing. One could justifiably say that if I forced pills on her for these seizures (assuming that they do not cause additional brain injury), I would not be CARING. The other are grand mal seizures, which are frightening, leave her drained, and— were they possibly to get out of hand—could even be life-threatening. These are not events that she herself would want.

If Sesha and I could communicate better, not only would I be able to explain the importance of her taking the pills, but she would be able to explain her resistance to them. As it is, I must grope about and consider if the pills are too large, too distasteful or perhaps have an unpleasant side effect. The closer I come to discerning the reason for the resistance and avoiding coercion, the more fully I fulfill my obligation to CARE for her.

Case 2. The Mature, Conscious, Autonomous Subject Who Refuses to Act in Accordance with Her Objective Good

The following case, presented by Michael Slote, is perhaps most challenging: "If I prevent my adult child from riding helmetless on a motorcycle, he or she may never acknowledge the value of what I have done, but what one does is good for the child. Should that not count as care?"[27] Notice that respect for the autonomy of the decision-maker requires us to respect this decision to ride helmetless. Care and respect seem to come apart here.

I am willing to bite the bullet and say that without enlisting the adult child's willingness to take up our prohibition as care, our care can at best be partial.[28] If the adult child, having gotten into an accident in which the helmet prevented worse harm, later agrees that we did right to insist, he then takes up our admonitions as care. A parent may determine that she would rather have the adult child alive, and live with the child's disapprobation, than the reverse. But if living on the edge is part of the adult's child's idea of a flourishing life, then we have not fully fostered his flourishing, and we have not cared in the most complete sense.

Care as a Particularistic Ethic

Justifying paternalism in the name of care appears reasonable only if we consider care itself to be a nonmoral notion, a "natural disposition,"[29] while the respect that foreswears paternalism is the moral disposition. Caring, however, is not a "natural disposition" but a process of morally motivated attention, discernment, and response. CARING commits us to respond to the other when appropriate; respect commits us to avoid interfering with another. Both are moral responses.[30] There is no other way to determine right action within an ETHICS OF CARE except to try to see the situation and the good as the cared-for sees it.

As in any particularist ethics in which deliberation does not take us from general principles to particular instances, care involves attention and discernment to understand what right action is in *this* case.[31] Care also requires a mindfulness, that is, a presence of mind and awareness of one's surroundings, to avoid allowing harm to come to a dependent. These are not tools that come neatly packaged as moral principles and defy appeal to a singular objective rational good. The give and take in a caring relationship, along with self-reflection on the part of the carer and the cared-for (when the cared-for is capable of it), helps define what would constitute appropriate action in *this* particular situation with *this* particular cared-for.

We can see the plausibility of the view I am propounding when we consider that a person cannot take up the actions of a caregiver as CARE if she is left feeling disrespected. Care not administered in a way that preserves and respects the person's dignity is not a care most of us would desire. Indeed, it is a form of care we fear. And on my normative understanding of care, it is not CARE at all.

When we reserve the idea of respect for those who have autonomous decision-making ability, we fail to respect those whose dignity is most at stake, those who need both care and respect the most. Caring for my daughter has taught me that wherever there is a subject, there is agency that ought to receive respect and attention: there is a will, a way one wants to feel oneself in the world, an intuitive sense of what is good for oneself. One does not need to demonstrate autonomy to command respect.[32] However inarticulate the expression of this agency, "attention must be paid."[33] The carer must pay attention to discern her good, to respond to it, and not to impose an alien one. Another's good can be as ill fitting as another's garment, as Mill pointed out.[34] What Mill might or might not have seen—had he come into contact with individuals like my daughter—is that this pertains to her no less than to himself.[35]

Moral Luck

Focusing on the achievement of an act of care rather than the intention to care may provide grounds for developing a fully normative conception of care, but, as we see in the examples earlier, it can also lead us into quandaries about how to evaluate the moral good of an action. Often enough, the answers to questions we may pose about our attempts to care and our effective failure to care are indeterminate or underdetermined. We can find a neither a good resolution to the question of praise or blame, nor the source of the moral failure. Thus, when it comes to an ethic of care, in which intention cannot be all and a clear conscience is difficult to ensure, nagging guilt may be just one of the occupational hazards of caregiving. In this sense caregiving is morally hazardous.

Perhaps nothing that I have thus far argued is as difficult to accept as the role that moral luck has within an ethics of care. It is, I think, difficult to accept that someone who prima facie does what we expect of a carer can be deprived of her laurels because the individual for whom she cares fails to take up her acting as caring. That is to say, it may well be just a caregiver's bad luck to have chosen, or worse to have been assigned, to care for someone who cannot take up as care what she has done, and for this reason all her efforts at care remain efforts only and not CARE. As disturbing as this is, I shall insist upon it. Moral luck is as inevitable to an ETHICS OF CARE as care is indispensable to human life.[36]

Bad moral luck encompasses cases where certain background conditions required for successful care are not present: the parent lacks the resources to adequately feed her child because of poverty, and there is no third party to take up the responsibilities inherent in the dependency relationship; the caregiver of a disabled person gets no relief and so fails to be able to carry on successfully; the caregiver of a disabled person cannot obtain the needed equipment or other support to adequately care; the nurse is stuck in a bureaucracy that places obstacles between her responsibility to her patient and the successful execution of that responsibility—all these cases display what care ethicists have so often emphasized, namely, that rather than being a simply dyadic relationship, the relationship between a carer and a cared-for sits in a set of nested dependencies. These situations can also help us identify an injustice, and that is still another important reason to insist that—as sad as it may be to say—care was not given.

A Moral Obligation to Receive Care?

Now I want to force a moral question that arises from this analysis: Is there a moral responsibility or obligation (when the cared-for is capable of it) to accept care. The answer here is not always, as I explain later. However, when care is offered in good faith and with the suitable competence to answer a real need, I believe we do have a moral obligation—to the extent that we are capable of fulfilling it—to accept the care graciously, just as one is obliged to accept a gift offered in good faith graciously. But in the case of the gift, the offense is in politesse. The offense in the case of care deserves moral opprobrium. I believe it is a moral obligation because refusing care when it is offered in good faith and with requisite competence is harmful, both to myself and to the carer, as I will argue later. It is a *delimited* obligation because not all care that is offered is offered appropriately—that is, with the requisite competence and good faith—and care is often needed by those incapable of exercising moral agency.

What is the case for the cared-for's obligation? Because care is more complex than the coordinated action of two actors, the one I will call the "care-refuser" not only harms himself, but does an injury to the caregiver and to the relationship between them. When we refuse care offered in good faith and with the requisite competence, we refuse *this* relationship, and we effectively refuse the *good* of relationship. In the case of people to whom we are close, this can be a painful rejection of our expression of love and concern. One hears the plaint often in the adult children caregivers. The parent, used to being in a position of authority or being the carer, finds it difficult to hand over any responsibility for their well-being to their adult child. A lot of bitter feelings result and threaten the relationship that is especially important to maintain as the parent becomes increasingly incapacitated. Just as the adult child must sacrifice time, work, and their other familial obligations to care for the parent, it seems appropriate to expect the parent go some way to let go of the previous power dynamics or the excessive pride or even the fear of being dependent. Often, however, by the time the parent is in the position of requiring care, it is too late for the parent to change—there is too little vigorous moral agency as some cognitive capacities become compromised. But there may be a point to alerting ourselves prior to that point of need to the fact that we have a moral obligation to graciously receive care appropriately offered.

Not all care is offered by people previously in relationship. In the case of people who are giving care professionally, the refusal of care is still destructive to the carer as it is a frustration of their duty and obligation.

The Overdemanders: We can also fail to receive care graciously when we demand more than is reasonable. The overdemander subordinates the other's interests to his own. To borrow a phrase from Marilyn Frye, he grafts the substance of the other onto his own. When an elderly husband is unsatisfied with any hired help and demands to be cared for only by his wife—also elderly and with needs of her own—he fails to acknowledge the wife as having interests that are equally valid. The lack of graciousness can often show itself in a dismissive attitude toward the needs of the carer. Instead the cared-for believes himself entitled to impose his will on his caregiver, with little regard for her as a person in her own right. The caregiver's actions are thought of as not issuing from her willingness to care. Instead the cared-for sees the carer's actions as a mere extension of his own will. Lynn May Rivas called this appropriating the *authorship* of the caregiver's actions.[37]

The failure to take up care *graciously* is a moral lapse on the part of the cared-for. But it is one that is facilitated by certain structural social features. Consider the caregiving relationship between a husband and wife in a very traditional marriage. When the wife gives care to a husband who becomes dependent, the subordination of her will to his can be such a normal expectation that any additional efforts of the wife may be invisible to her spouse. The same situation is evident in the case of a paid female caregiver. The image of the cantankerous old man who is an overdemanding, never-satisfied patient is a caricature; but the real life instantiations hang on a scaffold of patriarchal relationships. The situation of the paid personal attendant to a disabled person who wants to be seen as independent, in the sense of self-sufficient, is similar. The scaffolding here is a society that refuses to acknowledge public responsibility for unavoidable dependencies and overemphasizes the importance of independence.

   In brief, the refuser and the overdemander each short-circuit, and so doom to failure, the ethical imperative of caring for the needs of those who cannot care for themselves. Caring for those who are meaningful in our lives is one of the most important ethical projects we undertake, and its failure is a great wound, a genuine harm. If the carer's success in caring hinges on the uptake of the cared-for, those cared-for have an obligation to receive care (to the extent to which they are in a condition to do so) when it is offered in good faith and with the requisite competence.

Final Remark

The final thoughts on the obligation to receive care graciously when appropriated offered are the logical outcome of a moral conception in which, to borrow from Nel Nodding, how moral I can be depends on how moral you can be. The possibility of creating a moral world depends on the giving and receiving of care, the acknowledgment that our ethical lives are intertwined, are one. The oneness that this contribution points toward is the relationships that constitute our selves, and our ability to be effective moral agents. It is the oneness of a connected and caring world.

Notes

1. Bernard Williams, "Persons, Character, and Morality," in *Moral Luck* (Cambridge: Cambridge University Press, 1981), 18.
2. Royce writes: "Suppose that my cause, like the family in a feud, or like the pirate ship, or like the aggressively warlike nation, lives by the destruction of the loyalty of other families, or of its own community, or of other communities. Then, indeed, I get a good for myself and for my fellow-servants by our common loyalty; but I war against this very spirit of loyalty as it appears in our opponent's loyalty to his own cause. And so, a cause is good, not only for me, but for mankind, in so far as it is essentially a loyalty to loyalty, that is, is an aid and a furtherance of loyalty in my fellows." Royce, *Philosophy of Loyalty* (New York: MacMillan, 1914), 118.
3. Note that care too involves loyalty, either to the person or to the idea of care itself.
4. A caregiver who cares well is one who cares about caring: she thinks that it is important for people to be cared for, and that not to care when one is in the best position to care is morally wrong. Alternatively (and sometimes in conjunction with the moral judgment just given), one may want to think of oneself as a caring person and have this characterological idea be the motivational one. For Nodding, the ideal of the caring person is what is most important in our morally driven motivation to care.
5. Although Tronto speaks of caring for things as well as people, there is no discussion of the reception phase that could clarify how those persons or things that could not acknowledge or refuse care could be involved in care's reception.

6. I say "may," not "will," because it can happen that the prisoner whose life is spared finds ways in which he can find happiness or meaning even though he did not think it was possible prior to the intended act of mercy.

7. I hope I will be forgiven for repeating some of their thinking as I integrate this notion into my own way of working through the idea of an ethic of care. A good idea is well worth repeating and worthy of new framings.

8. For the moment I drop the distinction between care and CARE. There is a deep logic to the general concept of care that concerns us here. The logic that will figure into the more precise sense I mean to capture in the use of the locution CARE is really a more general feature of the more generic term as well.

9. Since I first presented this thought experiment, the response of many and diverse audiences is overwhelmingly "No, I have not cared for the plant."

10. I use the term *well-being* here as a general term covering different notions such as welfare and flourishing.

11. Theorists of care have made important distinctions between the many ways in the term *care* is used. Bernice Fischer and Joan Tronto ("Towards a Feminist Theory of Caring," in *Circles of Care*, ed. Emily K. Abel and Margaret K. Nelson, 35–62 [Albany: State University of New York Press, 1990]) sequence some of these senses when they speak of the stages of care. According to their model, we first care about something, then we take responsibility to take care of it, and then we do the caregiving required. The care is completed when the cared-for receives the care. Fischer and Tronto distinguish taking care of and caregiving but frequently both are thought of as aspects of caring *for* another rather than caring *about* them. Even though it is useful to make the lexical distinctions that Fischer and Tronto make, I do not follow them in their sequencing of the "stages" of care. The sequencing is neither conceptually nor temporally necessary. Sometimes one is thrown into a situation where we must care for another without actually caring about that individual. What frequently will happen is that the relationship that forms gives rise to a "caring about," which then becomes a motivational attitude. Once such a bond is formed, we *want* to care for a person because we *care about* her.

12. Ryle tells us "some state of affairs obtains over and above that which consists in the performance, if any, of the subservient task activity." Gilbert Ryle, *Concept of Mind*, (London: Hutchinson University Library, 1949), 150.

13. Ryle, 150.

14. Some care theorists, such as Fiona Robinson (*Globalizing Care: Ethics, Feminist Theory, and International Relations, Feminist Theory and Politics* [Boulder: Westview, 1999]), maintain that we cannot care for entities that lack consciousness. I think the plant example makes it clear that we can and we do. We can, for example, care or fail to care for a painting, by ensuring that it remains well preserved or by subjecting it to conditions under which it will deteriorate. Fischer and Tronto's most expansive concept of care (which is too expansive for CARE)—that caring is any activity that maintains or repairs the world we live in—allows that we can care more broadly than for persons. Fischer and Tronto, "Towards a Feminist Theory of Caring."

15. I thank Michael Slote for this observation.

16. In Kantian terms, these are not the perfect duties but the imperfect ones. While the imperfect duties of benevolence are not required of anyone in particular, unlike perfect duties, which are required of all, the duties within a care ethics are more properly *responsibilities* that fall on whomever is in the appropriate role or the contingent situation of one in a position to assist.

17. G. E. Moore, *Ethics* (1912; New York: Oxford University Press, 1965). See also Derek Parfit on "blameless wrongdoing" (in *Reasons and Persons* [Oxford: Clarendon, 1984], 31ff.

18. Here I am not drawing a sharp distinction between welfare and flourishing.

19. Even actions one might have experienced as caring at the time they were carried out might be revalued as uncaring if it turns out that the motivations were not the appropriate ones. The point is nicely illustrated in a segment of the movie *Blind Side*. Big Mike is an African American teenager who is adopted by a white family when he is already in his early teens. With the help of their caring attention, Mike becomes a successful high school athlete with an academic record strong enough to make him an attractive recruit to many colleges. When someone suggests to him that all the efforts on the part of the mother were to groom him to become a player for her alma mater's team, he confronts her and asks her accusingly, "What was this all for? Was it for me or was it to acquire a winning football player for your school?" As implausible as that accusation is, the mere suspicion of such a motive was sufficient to throw into doubt all the manifestations of care: the sacrifices, efforts, apparent trust, and affection.

20. When I speak of caring too much, I am not speaking about a distributional matter. One can tend to "care too much" about people of one's own race and ignore the well-being of those of other races. But this is like saying wealthy whites are given "too much justice" compared to poor whites or people of color, when we mean to say that the legal system gives too much deference to wealthy persons who are accused of white collar crimes compared to other groups who are given "too little justice", that is, too little fair consideration by the justice system.

21. I am not proposing a view based on rational endorsement, as required by some views of autonomy. My daughter can endorse choices we make for her by registering her pleasure, by not resisting, and so on. Endorsement from someone nonverbal is more difficult to discern than from one who can speak and who clearly exhibits rational reflection, but it is not to be assumed that it need not be sought. See note 23.

22. I conceive of flourishing as given by these things one cares about. (See Harry Frankfurt, *The Importance of What We Care About: Philosophical Essays* [Cambridge: Cambridge University Press, 1988] and Agnieszka Jaworska, "Caring and Internality," *Philosophy and Phenomenological Research* 74, no. 3 [2007]: 529–69.) This conception of one's good takes us out of the confines of our own skin since much that we care about concerns the good of others and the things in the world that provide meaning in our lives. It is, of course, possible to care about things that are harmful to others, to care about harming others. Such objects of a person's care—cares that interfere with the cares of others—are ruled out by moral considerations and are incompatible with an ETHICS OF CARE. Flourishing at the expense of other's flourishing must be disqualified as a morally acceptable ideal in any ethical view, particularly in an ethical view that takes care as a fundamental value.

23. Injected in the moral codes of certain caring professions is the idea that we act "in the best interests" of a person who cannot make an autonomous decision. A paternalistic conception of medicine would hold that a physician can and should override the wishes of a patient, if the patient's view of their own good is, in the judgment of the physician, not in the patient's best interest. This is a view that is now generally held to be permissible only in the case of the "incompetent" patient, that is, the nonautonomous patient. According to the newer understanding of the physician's role, the health care provider respects the autonomy of the patient. I reject not only a paternalistic conception of care, but also a stark contrast between the autonomous patient and the

incompetent patient. All patients are better served by a nonpaternalistic conception of care that is based on the idea that the carer needs to make him or herself transparent to the needs of the other. (See Eva Kittay, "Beyond Autonomy and Paternalism: The Caring Transparent Self," in *Autonomy and Paternalism: Reflections on the Theory and Practice of Health Care*, ed. Thomas Nys, Yvonne Denier, and T. Vandevelde [Leuven: Peeters, 2007].)

24. In a longer version of this work, a chapter in a work in progress tentatively titled *Learning from My Daughter: Disabled Minds and Rethinking Things That Matter* (Oxford: Oxford University Press, forthcoming), I consider more cases, ones that pick out still more subtle objections.

25. For writing that problematizes this view of antiseizure medication, see Anne Fadiman, *The Spirit Catches You and You Fall Down* (New York: Farrar, Straus and Giroux, 1998).

26. Note that I am assuming that the reason she would try to spit it out would be because of the unpleasantness of the pill itself and not whatever effects it has on her other than subduing her seizures.

27. Personal correspondence. For Stephen Darwall (*Welfare and Rational Care* [Princeton: Princeton University Press, 2002]) this is a classic instance of caring for someone for their own sake, although Darwall may argue that here the attitude we should take toward the person is not care but respect.

28. I assume here that I prevent my child from riding a motorcycle without a helmet out of my concern for her well-being and not from a need to control her actions. Then, surely, the action is done from a *desire* to care for the child for the child's own sake.

29. I am not taking a position on the question of whether paternalism is ever justified, only that it is not justifiable in the name of care because when we think of care as a fully normative notion, we must take the perspective of the person in need of care, and that is opposed to paternalism, where another claims to know what *our* good is.

30. See Robin Dillon, "Respect and Care: Toward Moral Integration," *Canadian Journal of Philosophy* 22, no. 1 (1992): 69–81, for the concept of care respect. See also Sarah Miller's discussion of "dignifying care" in *The Ethics of Need: Agency, Dignity, and Obligation* (New York: Routledge, 2012). But neither author is using the term care as I suggest it can be used, namely, in its fully normative sense.

31. See Margaret Little, "Moral Generalities Revisited," in *Moral Particularism*, ed. Brad Hooker and Margaret Little, 276–304 (Oxford: Clarendon, 2000), for an excellent discussion on particularism in ethics.

32. An objection to this statement may be that while we care for a very young child or infant, it would stretch the meaning of respect to say that in caring for the infant we must respect him. In the case of an infant, what we no doubt should respect is the infants right to life, to be adequately fed, and to the sorts of things that are on any objective list of things we think infants universally need to survive and thrive. These do not involve us in discerning the particularity of *this* infants' wants and needs. In response, we can note that a very young infant does not (or may not) yet have *individualized* cares—cares that are particular to *that* individual. Once such more particular cares do start to manifest themselves, I don't see why we don't have an obligation to respect them, as long as they are not self-defeating, putting at risk goods we can anticipate the child having as she or he matures, or ones that are harmful to others. Our thinking about children and their rights has evolved, and we now think it is wrong for parents to treat their child's will as an extension of their own. Even as we deal with young children, we try to discern where their preferences and talents lie, and caring

that helps to foster the child's development tries to nurture preferences as long as they stay with the constraints I have mentioned earlier.

33. This is said by Willie Loman's wife Linda in *Death of a Salesman* speaking to her sons about her totally despondent husband. "But he's a human being, and a terrible thing is happening to him. So attention must be paid. . . . Attention, attention must be finally paid to such a person." In a passage pertinent to the discussion here, she speaks of her knowledge of her husband's toying with suicide by poisoning himself with gas and her struggle with whether or not to discard the rubber tube by which he might end his life. "Every day I go down and take away that little rubber pipe. But when he comes home, I put it back where it was. How can I insult him that way?"

34. John Stuart Mill writes: "A man cannot get a coat or a pair of boots to fit him, unless they are either made to his measure, or he has a whole warehouseful to choose from: and is it easier to fit him with a life than with a coat." Mill, *On Liberty* (1860; Indianapolis: Hackett, 1978), 121.

35. In this respect, one might say, ETHICS OF CARE is a liberal ethics, although the stress on relationality is a less liberal view.

36. Michael Slote, in a personal communication, noted that this "last point doesn't really make things much better." Agreed, but that it doesn't make things better doesn't make it less true.

37. Lynn May Rivas, "Invisible Labors: Caring for the Independent Person," in *Global Women: Nannies, Maids and Sex Workers in the Global Economy*, ed. Barbara Ehrenreich and Arlie Russell Hochchild, 70–84 (New York: Holt, 2002).

CHAPTER 7

ONENESS AND NARRATIVITY

A Comparative Case Study

MARK UNNO

Whatever "oneness" might mean to people, unless it carries some significance for a lived existence, it remains remote: a philosophical abstraction, a mystical experience, some metaphysical referent. One way to explore its relevance is to place "oneness" within the narrative context of a human life, as something that is activated in the context of a person's story. Whether fiction, biography, or autobiography, once placed within a narrative context, one can begin to see what potential significance it might have for a lived existence: What are the contours of "oneness" as it informs the narrative trajectory of a person's life? What does it tell us about the larger worldview—religious or philosophical—that informs that life and story? What is the impact of "oneness" upon a person's life story? As will become evident, such a narrative approach allows for examination of similarities and differences, and exploration of the lived consequences of "oneness," whatever significance that may carry within a given narrative.

For the purposes of the present, we select here three contemporary first-person narratives for examination: one Zen Buddhist, one Pure Land Buddhist, and one Protestant Christian. There is not space here to provide a full-fledged analysis of each narrative, only an episodic examination. Nevertheless, it will become evident that these narratives are telling in the diversity of their details, the range of significations "oneness" might carry, and the striking points of resonance they share. The first is the narrative of an Irish American woman, Maura O'Halloran (1955–82), who goes to Japan to study Zen Buddhism in a rural area of northern Japan. She is widely praised as a superior practitioner and is about to return to Ireland to open her own Zen center but dies tragically while touring Thailand on a bus. Second is the story of a Japanese man, Shinmon Aoki (b. 1937), who seemingly accidentally finds himself living the life of a mortician; unexpectedly, this leads him on a journey of Pure Land Buddhist awakening. Third is the tale of Michael Morton (b. 1954), who spends nearly twenty-five years in prison wrongfully convicted of murder, and his Christian journey of finding faith and encountering the light of the Divine.

Each became celebrated in their own right. A statue of Maura O'Halloran was dedicated and permanently installed in the Zen monastery of Kannonji. Shinmon Aoki's story became the inspiration for *Departures* (2008), which won the Academy Award for Best Foreign Film. Michael Morton's journey was chronicled in the award-winning documentary *An Unreal Dream: The Michael Morton Story* (2013).

The purpose of bringing these narratives together is not to distill some essential definition or formula for understanding "oneness." Rather, it is to engage in a conversation and dialogue that provides analogical markers and analytical tools, along with the stories themselves, to readers who can then enter the dialogue themselves. Each story is its own small language game, and, from an analytical standpoint, one can learn their rules, what makes them tick. To mix Wittgensteinian metaphors, each story is also, as language, a form of life. These stories, these forms of life, are related to one another, but are not the same. Perhaps they are like cousins. In sharing their lives, we can discover their shared interests as well as points of divergence. The discovery of commonalities enables sharing, helps form bridges to understanding; the discovery of difference, as long as one comes with an open mind, is enriching. It is somewhat like, or even a special case of, learning foreign languages. They serve to expand one's horizons, cultural, philosophical, religious, or otherwise.

One element that is common to these three stories is the use of "counterstory." In *Damaged Identities, Narrative Repair* (2001), Hilde Nelson introduces the idea of "counterstory." According to Nelson, when the narrative of the dominant culture, that is, the master narrative, ceases to work for a given individual or a group of people within the larger culture, it becomes necessary to formulate a "counterstory" that resists the force of the dominant story and begins to alter or overturn it. According to Nelson, counterstories can enable a person to

> resist the evil of diminished moral agency . . . by uprooting the harmful stories that constitute the subgroup members' identity from the perspective of an abusive, dominant group, . . . [and thereby] alter the dominant group's perception of the subgroup. [Furthermore], by uprooting the harmful identity-constituting stories that have shaped a person's own sense of who she is, counterstories aim to alter the person's self-perception.
>
> (Nelson 2001, xii)

In a word, "The immediate purpose of a counterstory is to repair [damaged] identities" (20). In each of the three cases examined in this essay, there is some element of the master narrative that proves oppressive or inadequate for the protagonist, leading to the creation of one or more counterstories that alter or overturn the master narrative. At critical junctures or turning points in the transformation of self-narratives, there is a realization of oneness that comes from "deep within" or from a "higher power" that allows the counterstory to emerge. It is as if there is a vertical or depth dimension to the self that facilitates the horizontal transformation of the life of the individual within society, from a maladaptive master narrative that is imposed on the person to one in which a counterstory more befitting him or her is allowed to emerge.

This approach to studying stories of oneness may be contrasted with a more thoroughly theoretical approach, for example, any attempt to provide an analytic definition, and then to classify various instances of "oneness" according to some differentiated understanding. This is a perfectly valid, perhaps even necessary approach. Unless one is careful, however, it can lead to some problems. Two of these are illustrative of a range of problems that might arise: reductionistic essentialism and radical contextualism. We have seen these kinds of problems before, for example, in the study of mysticism. Perennialist views of mysticism have been accused of denaturing their subject matter, artificially isolating certain cases or features, and creating an academic construct that has no referent in lived human experience. The likes of Williams James, W. T. Stace, and Mircea Eliade have been accused of this type of reductionistic essentialism (Katz 1978, 22–74). The rejection of the perennialist approach has led in some quarters to a radical contextualism, such as is found in the work of Steven Katz. In this approach, historical grounding and textual specificity are emphasized, often with the effect of debunking any attempt to form an overarching taxonomy or theory of mystical experience. Both by association and by analogy, one can see that the study of "oneness" can become subject to both reductionistic essentialism and radical contextualism. Mystical experiences are often described as involving something akin to the realization of oneness: oneness with nature, oneness with the divine, oneness with ultimate reality, and so forth. Oneness, like mysticism, is difficult to pin down.

As opposed to one another as they are, reductionistic essentialism and radical contextualism share a common problem: they are often focused on the attempt at explanation above all else, whether as theory or as historiography. Yet, in studying "oneness," is *explanation* necessarily the only or even primary goal? There is nothing wrong with explanation, of course, but might another way to approach the topic be as an exploration of *habitability*? Isn't the exploration of a livable "oneness" as compelling as or more compelling than finding an explainable one? Of course, livability and explainability are not mutually exclusive. One way to understand their mutual interrelation is to see explanation in the service of living, not the other way around: lived examples are not there merely to be dissected for the prize of an explanation; explanations are useful only insofar as they help us to live. Sharing, comparing, and, yes, analyzing stories of oneness might be one way to integrate explanation *in the service* of living. In our globalized world living stories are in constant interaction with one another to a degree hitherto unseen: in person, in the virtual world of digital technology, in the mobile web. What better way, then, to bring to bear our scholarly knowledge of "oneness" than to nurture and facilitate the interaction between diverse forms of the life of oneness, which promises to lead to further understanding, possibilities for lived experience, and perhaps new forms of the life of oneness?

There is a potential hazard in using the concept of "counterstory"; it might tilt the presentation of the three cases that serve as the focus of this study too much toward reductionistic explanation. However, as long as "counterstory" is understood, as intended, as a helpful aid in bringing the three cases examined here into further dialogue and conversation and not as providing an overarching explanation, this concept will have served its limited yet useful role.

Zen Buddhism and Active Oneness: "Care for Things Just Because They Exist"

Maura O'Halloran: Background

The first narrative comes from the life of Maura "Soshin" O'Halloran (1955–82). It is presented through the published record of her journals and letters, *Pure Heart, Enlightened Mind* (1994). She was born in Boston, Massachusetts, to an Irish father and American mother. After her father's untimely death in an auto accident in 1969, her mother moved her and her siblings to Ireland, where she eventually graduated with honors from Trinity College in Dublin, double-majoring in economics and sociology. On the one hand, she considered the possibility of postgraduate studies. On the other, her academic interests were tied to her concern for the real life problems people faced. After college, she demonstrated a strong sense of social responsibility, working in soup kitchens and traveling to South America, where she witnessed various dimensions of social and economic oppression. Seeking inner equilibrium and deeper resources to engage social issues, she turned to spirituality and was eventually drawn to Asian religions and philosophies. Thus, from the outset, it is clear that the master narrative of a global society and economy driven by free-market capitalism did not work for her.

With her background of personal interest in spirituality and social activism, she eventually made her way to Japan, where she sought out Zen masters, leading to a three-year period of intensive Zen practice at Kannonji in rural Iwate Prefecture. This marks her active integration of a counterstory that she hopes will empower her socially as well as spiritually. Kannonji, a Sōtō Zen monastery, was unusual in that it followed the Rinzai practice of assigning Zen problems, or *kōan*, to be tested in private interviews, *dokusan*, with the master, Ban Tetsugyū, also known as Go Rōshi. O'Halloran successfully passed a course of three thousand *kōan*, and her master gave her recognition as an awakened teacher at her completion ceremony, or *hishinsai*. She soon planned to return to Ireland to found her own Zen center. Tragically, during a trip through Asia, a tour bus she rode had an accident, and she died along with two others at the age of twenty-seven. In a eulogy to O'Halloran, her teacher wrote:

> Our grand master Dōgen went to China and to the Tendō mountain for one thousand days, working hard all day, he sat for meditation at night. He slept two or three hours in the sitting position. Maura did the same. She was the modern Dōgen. . . .
>
> There was a spring training at Kannonji from May 2nd for five days. Maura reached her enlightenment on the first day. She went in for meditations twice, three times a day, and solved all three thousand kōans. We had her Hishinsai . . . on August 7th, 1982. . . .
>
> She had achieved what took Shakuson [Shakyamuni Buddha] 80 years in twenty-seven years. She was able to graduate Dōgen's thousand-day training. Then she left this life immediately to start the salvation of the masses in the next life! Has anyone known such a courageously hard working Buddha as Maura? I cannot possibly express my astonishment.
>
> (1994, 298–99)

Such was the remarkable, brief career of O'Halloran that a memorial statue of her has been erected on the grounds of Kannonji. This eulogy and many of the journal entries and letters by O'Halloran herself convey the sense of a traditional Zen narrative in an authentic training monastery. There is a kind of "living museum" quality to the story as it unfolds. It is as if the reader is given a rare glimpse into a long-forgotten world, a gem of a traditional spiritual practice into which one is given an intimate, inside account. So compelling was her story, and apparently she herself, that after she left this world, her sister followed in her footsteps to enter full-time Zen practice herself. As a work that was likely never meant for publication, the journal of Maura "Soshin" O'Halloran offers a fresh and vivid account of one person's journey into the Zen Buddhist practice of oneness.

The Zen Practice of Oneness: Turning Points

Breaking Through the "Mu" Kōan

Zen Buddhism, as part of the larger movement of Mahayana Buddhism, subscribes to the twofold truth of conventional and highest truth (*samvritti-satya* and *paramartha-satya*; form and emptiness; the discursive world of appearances and concepts, on the one hand, and the world of oneness beyond words, on the other). It is suitably described as twofold, since form and emptiness, words and the oneness beyond words, are like two sides of the same coin. They are not two separate truths; rather, they are inseparable, nondual, such that the deepest truth of self is disclosed in the emptiness or illusory nature of any particular "self" concept, and words, like the poetry of love, become vehicles embodying the truth of a oneness beyond words.

Zen practice is body-practice: seated meditation, chanting, bowing, cleaning, cooking, gardening. As the Chinese master Baizhang Huaihai states, the essence of Zen is to "carry water, chop wood." In each moment of practice, the practitioner seeks to realize the oneness of reality devoid or "empty" of any discursive distractions. *Kōan* practice is the practice of receiving a Zen problem or puzzle whose resolution leads to the embodied practice of the twofold truth: carrying water (form) as the realization of the all-oneness of reality (emptiness), the form of seated meditation as the manifestation of cosmic oneness, and so forth.

Maura O'Halloran (Buddhist name "Soshin") receives from her master a typical first *kōan*, that of *mu*, or nothingness. To make a long story short, the essence of the *kōan* is to *become mu*, become nothingness, through prolonged chanting of this single syllable. Functioning like a mantra, the repetitive invocation of this simple syllable is designed to cut off the discursive train of thought, to lead to the realization of the emptiness or nothingness of any fixed notion of self, until one simply becomes one with *mu*, with nothingness.

Throughout her daily chores, during her practice of seated meditation, during intensive retreats, O'Halloran chants, sometimes silently, sometimes vocally, "*Muuuuuuu*," until she loses herself in her effort. As long as one is "trying to figure it out" intellectually, one is separated from the nothingness through the act of conceptual objectification. Only when she is able to abandon the desire or exhaust the need to grasp *mu* conceptually can she become one with *mu*. Her practice of the *mu kōan* follows a pattern that is not untypical. On the one hand, she gradually deepens her self-immersion in *mu*, body and mind. On the other, her frustration also mounts, as she is unable to abandon her thoughts about it. The skillful Zen master harnesses both the power of meditative immersion and mental frustration, coaxing the practitioner to go ever deeper into the practice of *mu* and assisting in the ego's process of self-destruction (103–4):

> "You must see *mu* in everything," [Go Rōshi says]. I leave *dokusan* (interview), crying and laughing [sensing both how far and near is my realization], with Tachibana Sensei [a lay practitioner] apologizing for his English translation [in the interview room]. That's okay. He encourages me.
>
> I go to dokusan with Kobai-san [so she can translate Rōshi's Japanese for me].
>
> "Where does mu come from?" [Go Rōshi asks.]
>
> "I don't know—how can it come from somewhere? It doesn't have a place," [I say]. . . .
>
> In we go again [for another dokusan]. Go Rōshi says, "*Zenzen wakaranai*" ["You don't understand at all"].
>
> I'm crushed, devastated. Rōshi says, "Next time, come alone."
>
> After lunch we rest. I'm crying, feel wretched, forlorn. . . .
>
> I'm called to dokusan. I feel so dejected, empty-minded. It doesn't even occur to me to wonder why Go Rōshi wants me to come alone.
>
> "*Mu—dō?*" ["How is your mu?"]
>
> I mu for him with all my strength, raising myself high and squeezing every bit of breath into mu until my head touches the floor.
>
> "Once more again," He says in English. (He doesn't speak English, but I don't register surprise.)
>
> I do so.
>
> Then, "Once more again."
>
> My first and only thought was "He may make me do this for ages." Then he jumped at me, grabbed me—"This body is *muji* [the character or figure of *mu*], this head, eyes, ears."
>
> Suddenly I'm laughing and crying muji. I don't even realize "Now I am muji," but I simply was muji and everything around me. . . .
>
> "*Kenshō shita* [You have realized your Buddha-nature]," says he.
>
> I'm surprised. I was too self-conscious even to know that it was kenshō. Only when I got outside and was looking at everything and really seeing mu did I finally know. Suddenly I understood why we must take care of things just because they exist; we are of no greater and of no lesser value.

Led by her teacher and her own powerful practice, O'Halloran in the story exhausts her ego-conscious desire to grasp nothingness/emptiness/oneness conceptually, letting go into *mu*, becoming nothing, and then realizing that everything is one with her: "Only when I got outside and was looking at everything and really seeing mu did I finally know."

The description of O'Halloran's realization of the *mu kōan* brings some features of her practice into relief as well as raises key questions. First, what her practice does is to bring to life emptiness/oneness as the deepest reality of Zen Buddhism. That is, she realizes what is already there in a foundational sense but which she must come to know through her practice. Second, this realization of nothingness/oneness has immediate ethical ramifications: "Suddenly I understood why we must take care of things just because they exist; we are of no greater and of no lesser value." There is no is/ought distinction operative here. Rather, "ought" issues spontaneously from "is"-ness. *Mahā-karuṇā* (Jpn. *daijihi, daihi*), great compassion, is the self-expression of the practitioner's own self-identity as inseparable from the world. The realization of oneness is the dissolution of the opposition between self and other, self and world, such that the natural power of interdependence and compassion is unleashed. This is a critical turning point in O'Halloran's story. It helps to free her from the master narrative defined purely in the discursive terms of a materialistic society. It also provides her with a "deeper" or "greater" sense of moral agency to reengage and reinterpret the world anew, a counterstory that resists the master narrative. Third, O'Halloran's experience of oneness, oneness with the *mu kōan*, oneness with her master Go Rōshi, and oneness with everything around her expressed in her sense of identity with her natural surroundings, is framed within a particular narrative context.

Prospectively, O'Halloran's breakthrough with the *mu kōan* represents just the beginning of her practice: she has nearly all of the rest of the three thousand *kōan* yet to solve until she has realized oneness deeply enough for her Zen practice to become the thoroughgoing basis of her life. The reader of her journal is led to see this vividly, as she continues to express all kind of frustrations, such as being burdened with more than her fair share of chores while her lazy fellow monks loaf, or the sexism she faces in the monastery as the only ordained female at Kannonji.

Retrospectively, she is a young Western woman, college-educated, who has made her way to a rural Zen monastery in Japan. She has primed her mind by reading Asian philosophy and books on Zen Buddhism, and has formed an image of herself that pops up at various points. Long before attaining *kenshō*, for example, she states, "I want to be a Zen master."

That is, narratively speaking, she has come to inscribe in her own mind the worldview of Zen Buddhism, expectations concerning Zen practice, and the various possibilities of what she might encounter in terms of Zen masters, Japanese culture, and so forth. During the moment of her *kenshō*, or breakthrough experience, she has such a profound experience that she loses consciousness of *mu*, nothingness, which she has been so intent on realizing. Yet, she does not lose consciousness as such. In fact, she is vividly aware of the moment, a moment that has been narratively prescribed and that will continue to unfold into the future. To the degree that she has internalized her Zen Buddhist worldview, its practices, and its expectations, how she interprets the moment of realization in ethical terms seems seamless, altogether natural: "Suddenly I understood why we must take care of things just because they exist" (104).

The ethical significance of the moment that she perceives to be *inherent* in the realization of oneness is one for which she has been thoroughly prepared *narratively*, by her study and practice of Zen. Yet, this does not necessarily mean that her sense of compassion for all things and beings is *external* to the moment, either. If she had not had this vivid moment of embodied realization, would she still have had the sense of profound compassion come over her?

It could be a mistake to attempt to determine whether the ethical outlook associated with the realization of the moment of oneness is either internal or external to the "oneness" itself. Perhaps an analogy may be helpful here, one taken from music. Suppose that the moment of realizing "oneness" is like a moment of silence that occurs in a musical performance, say, something like the grand silence that comes toward the end of Stravinsky's *The Firebird*. Like the realization of oneness, there is a certain lack of discursive differentiation, as there are no sounds at the moment. There is something opaque about "oneness" from the perspective of the purely discursive intellect, since "oneness" often indicates that which is beyond the grasp of conceptual distinctions. Yet, the power of the silence, its significance, derives from its being framed by the symphonic melody that comes before, and that continues unfold thereafter. That is, there are clear contours to the silence, shaped by the sounds that surround it. Likewise, depending on its narrative framework, "oneness" may take on very different significations. Silence is always silence, but no two silences are alike. Oneness is always oneness, but no two onenesses are alike. Thus, there are contours to the oneness/nothingness realized by O'Halloran in the context of her Zen practice, which help to shape her realization of the ethical ramifications of the moment of oneness.

Attachment, Gender Bias, and Expectations

One of the consistent themes throughout *Pure Heart, Enlightened Mind* is O'Halloran's struggles with the male-dominated, patriarchal culture of the Zen monastery at Kannonji. Although initially she is delighted that everything seems egalitarian and that the monks treat her just like "one of the lads" (17), she quickly comes to see that she had simply brought with her a naïve Western vision of an egalitarian spirituality to Zen Buddhism, which, really, she knew so little about and was thus largely a blank canvas for her projections. For her, true emptiness/nothingness meant that everything had to be equally empty, equal in nothingness, a conviction that she holds throughout the journal. Indeed, "emptiness" (*śūnyatā*) and "equality" (*samatha*) are often closely associated in Buddhism, for the very fact that "emptiness" often has a leveling effect on hierarchy, since everything is equally empty in Mahayana Buddhism.

Yet, historically, Buddhism, like many other religions, has had various androcentric biases, including Zen, with its "patriarchal" succession of male Zen masters.

O'Halloran's observations include such statements as "Women really are repressed here, forced into the mold of a giggling innocent" (108), and "I think it's part of the way Japanese men are raised to treat the women in their lives" (196). O'Halloran herself proves an exception; as a highly educated white Westerner, her subject positionality is one of privilege; she is the only fully ordained woman in an all-male monastery.[1] Yet, things are not so simple, as she feels as though she is often treated like a female servant by her (jealous) male counterparts. Eventually, she begins to recognize that even her beloved Go Rōshi, while lavishing attention on her as one of his prized pupils, does so with certain expectations. At one point, it dawns on her, "My purpose is to make kids" (194).

On the one hand, her sharp criticisms of the patriarchal attitudes of the Japanese men are expressions of her Western liberal feminist consciousness. On the other, as long as her attention is focused in a critically outward manner, it is difficult for her to realize emptiness/oneness beyond distinctions. Her ambivalence in this regard is apparent in the following passage:

> [Tetsugen] told me to plant *kiku* [*chrysanthemums*]. . . . I quite firmly said I'd go to Sasaki-san's and get them, but I'm not planting them today. He looked shocked and giggled nervously, a bit embarrassed. "Why?" I said I had other work to do. I didn't feel or sound annoyed. Pushing the wheelbarrow down to Sasaki's for the kiku, I felt, "Hee, hee, I'm a bitch, I'm terrible, but chuckle, chuckle, I enjoyed that." Then, I saw her—skinny, 70, down on the floor vigorously scrubbing the already gleaming wood with such earnestness she didn't even hear my call I felt ashamed. She trundled into the garden and dug me up kiku from the ends of the rows she'd already neatly trimmed, thinned, and transplanted. She motioned me into the shed, all the time half running. . . . Ashamed, thoroughly ashamed, I . . . pushed my barrow past the rice fields with the radios, the many bent bodies at their jobs. I wondered what they thought about, if they thought at all. Were they like so many Zen masters, living their kōans—digging and digging and only digging?
>
> (197)

Tetsugen is an older monk, in her eyes paternalistic and unlikeable, yet he is the one that her master Go Rōshi has selected for her to marry, so that she can bear children who will become monks. She is highly critical, but then, as she is mumbling these very criticisms, she notices lay Japanese Buddhist women working the fields tirelessly, "like so many Zen masters," without complaint, and she feels ashamed.

O'Halloran appears to be an ideal disciple: the first to be up and meditating, the last to be cleaning up and returning to her meditation. She exerts herself mind and body to the utmost, until she fully realizes Zen Buddhist oneness in breaking through the *kōan mu*. Yet, the ambivalence she feels toward the culture of Zen Buddhism shows that not all is smooth sailing thereafter. Interestingly, her teacher Go Rōshi seems to pick up on this. Not only that, he even seems to use her ambivalence to propel her further on her path of practice, insisting that she marry Tetsugen.

In her realization of the *mu kōan*, O'Halloran realizes, "We must take care of things just because they exist; we are of no greater and of no lesser value [than anything or anyone else]." Yet, she finds she is in fact not free to take care of things [and people] equally. She has her likes and dislikes, her own aspirations. She wishes to return to Ireland to open her own Zen center; she wants to fall in love, not be forced into an arranged marriage with a Japanese; she doesn't want to wait on an old paternalistic monk.

> In this overly sensitized state, I went to dokusan. Go Rōshi told me I was to marry Tetsugen-san on September 18th and stay in this temple. I said I didn't want to. He was pushing me, pushing me hard. It was killing me to refuse him. I love him so very, very much, and he was being so insistent, thinking of everything to induce me. I begged him not to ask, no not that. Finally, I broke down and told him something of . . . my dreams for Ireland [and of founding a Zen center there]. He said he'd think it over. I went out in tears, became quite hysterical. . . . I knew I was being ridiculous.
>
> All along I realized my reaction was out of proportion to the situation. We were walking back towards the zendō when my legs gave way. I fainted. . . . Something left me, some huge oppressive weight that I'd never known was there and only recognized in its lifting. . . . My mind never felt so clear or lucid. . . .
>
> Next day, Go Rōshi said, "Until last night you were human trying to become God; now you're God. I'm Buddha." He shook my hand. "We must help others." He said it would be all right for me to go back to Ireland after three years.
>
> (227–29)

Did Go Rōshi simply use the idea of an arranged marriage as a device to expose her ego attachments, or did he actually have this in mind, and only later come to the realization that, while it would not be appropriate to force her, the idea could be used heuristically? What of her Western feminist views, and her entrepreneurial spirit, to found a Zen center in Ireland? We will likely never know for certain; what is of significance is the narrative context that helps to frame these questions and bring them to life for the reader.

O'Halloran has had to confront the fact that traditional Zen Buddhist culture has its own master narrative, one that she variously tries to ignore, accept, or reject. Fortunately, according to the account we are given, her Zen master is able to use the conflict between her idealized Zen narrative and the actualities on the ground to deepen her Zen realization. Here, the clash between master narrative and counterstory helps to propel O'Halloran to a deeper resolution.

Letting Go of Expectations by Embracing Them

Paradoxically, now that she honestly expresses and owns her own emotions of dislike and aspiration, she is able to let go of her obsession with them: "I knew I was being ridiculous. All along I realized my reaction was out of proportion to the situation." Later on, she confirms this as she expresses the sense of freedom she feels: "Whether I'm here or in Ireland, married or not, none of it seems a big deal. It seems I should assent and truly throw my life away for training. . . . In the real world, Rōshi's and my ideas are so different. But it seems I have no criteria left by which to make a decision. Anything is okay" (276).

The sense of spiritual fulfillment and freedom she conveys is eerily prescient, as she describes a completeness beyond human constructs of life and death, less than a year before her fatal bus accident:

> Now I'm 26, and I feel as if I've lived my life. Strange sensation. Almost as if I'm close to death. Any desires, ambitions, hopes I may have had have either been fulfilled or spontaneously dissipated. I'm totally content. Of course, I want to get deeper, see clearer, but even if I could only have this paltry, shallow awakening, I'd be quite satisfied. . . . So in a sense I feel I have died; for myself there is nothing to strive after, nothing to make my life worthwhile or justify it. At 26, a living corpse and such a life! . . . To give myself is all I can do, as the flowers have no choice but to blossom. At the moment the best I can see to do is to give to people this freedom, this bliss, and how better than through zazen?"
>
> (232–33)

It is almost as if her initial realization of oneness through the *kōan mu* and this culminating realization of "becoming Buddha, becoming God" provide the narrative bookends of her brief but intense journey in Zen Buddhist practice.

Oneness as Freedom in Emptiness

Oneness in Zen Buddhism is grounded in the twofold truth of form and emptiness. The path of practice is to be able to realize emptiness/oneness in relation to every manifestation of form. It is one thing to realize oneness by losing self in chanting the syllable *mu*, nothingness. This does not mean that one has become free of attachments in the rest of one's life. It can be an arduous process to have the illusion of one's supposed spiritual attainment exposed, to have one's ego stripped away, to recognize that one still has strong attachments, likes and dislikes, hopes, fears, and aspirations. These attachments need to be illuminated from even deeper within, so that one achieves a greater freedom still, a greater range of emptiness—this is one way to read the story of Maura "Soshin" O'Halloran. Questions nevertheless remain: What becomes of social change when the greater emphasis is on the life of interiority? How should issues of social change be framed within the larger framework of nature and the cosmos? There are many questions that remain unexplored in her case because her life was tragically cut short. To a certain extent, responses to these questions can be found in the field of Engaged Buddhism, as can be seen in the work of such figures as the Vietnamese master Thich Nhat Hanh and the Dalai Lama. But, like O'Halloran's quandary in the face of unacceptable circumstances that seem inseparable from her love for her teacher, we as a species may be wedded to circumstances over which we have limited control. There are problems we may not be able to resolve satisfactorily, such as accelerating climate change, resource depletion, water crisis, population explosion.

It is interesting to think about O'Halloran in relation to her story as told in *Pure Heart, Enlightened Mind*: O'Halloran *as story*, as well as O'Halloran *and her story*. Ironically, we would likely not have her story in all of its vivid vulnerability had she survived. Only by virtue of her "untimely" passing are we given this account of her journey to be bodhisattva-like, to become one with all beings and bring to them the liberating path of emptiness: "Then she left this life immediately to start the salvation of the masses in the next life!" In a sense, her next life can be said to be the publication of *Pure Heart, Enlightened Mind*, through which she is reborn in the minds and hearts of her readers. Because her life was cut short, the story of O'Halloran's confrontation with the deepest issues of her self-identity may leave more questions for her readers than answers. Yet, the problems we face as a species may also leave us at this time with more questions than answers, questions that only become more profound the more deeply we inquire into them.

The fruition of O'Halloran's counterstory remains incomplete. Would she have gone on to found a socially and environmentally engaged Zen center? To what extent would her work as a Zen teacher have enabled her to transform the master narrative? Can a spiritually based practice become the basis for global transformation? These questions are relevant not only for a life that was cut short like O'Halloran's but for anyone who considers transformative moments of oneness to be relevant for life in society. In this way, her life and these unanswered questions become food for thought for anyone who finds that her life story resonates with theirs.

Pure Land Buddhism and Receptive Oneness: Infinite Light of Boundless Compassion

The Illumination of Boundless Compassion:
The Oneness of Foolish Being and Amida Buddha

Like Zen Buddhism, Pure Land Buddhism is part of the larger movement of Mahayana Buddhism and, as such, subscribes to the twofold truth. Whereas Zen Buddhism emphasizes realization of emptiness through form, and form as manifestation of emptiness, Pure Land Buddhism, a more lay-oriented form of Buddhism, takes a somewhat different approach. In particular, the Shin tradition of Pure Land Buddhism, the largest sectarian development of Japanese Buddhism, emphasizes the twofold truth in its problem aspect. That is, it focuses on the dynamic between blind passions and boundless compassion, foolish being and Amida Buddha, self power and other power.

Blind passion (Skt. *kleśa*; Jpn. *bonnō*) is desire blinded by attachment. In Mahayana Buddhism, there is nothing wrong with desire as an expression of form, as long as it is fulfilled in accord with and within natural limits. Thus, there is the Zen Buddhist saying "Eat when hungry; sleep when sleepy." Problems only arise when one becomes fixated on expectations, attached to external outcomes, blinded by greed and obsession. The release from this blindness comes through emptiness, or the emptying out of expectations and overweening ambition. Emptiness in and of itself has no characteristics, being beyond discursive identifiability; it is colorless, odorless, formless. Yet, the release from the bonds of blind passion is a positive movement, one that reflects a coming into congruence with the ever-changing landscape of reality; it is a "feeling with" reality, or "com-passion." In Shin Buddhism, emptiness, expressed as boundless compassion (*muen no daihi*), illuminates, envelopes, and dissolves the blind passion of the foolish being (*bonbu*). As the founder of Shin Buddhism, Shinran (1173–1261), states, "The greater the ice [of blind passion], the greater the water [of boundless compassion]." Blind passion is not eliminated. Rather, it is embraced just as is, and transformed into boundless compassion.

The realization of blind passion and the realization of boundless compassion occur simultaneously. Without the illumination of boundless compassion, there is not the freedom to recognize one's own blindness; without the recognition of blindness, the portal to boundless compassion remains closed. Because emptiness contains no discursive determination, this illumination is nonjudgmental. Like a mirror that simply illuminates without distortion, the action of boundless compassion releases the foolish being from the bonds of blind passion gently, without condemnation. Because this illumination occurs without qualification, the action of emptiness on the foolish being is an infinite awakening, the awakening of infinite light, or Amida Buddha (Skt. Amitābha Buddha), where "infinite" reflects the unqualified, unbounded nature of emptiness. In Shin Buddhism, then, the twofold truth of form as emptiness is realized as the oneness of the foolish being with Amida Buddha, blind passion, and boundless compassion.

In Zen Buddhism the central practice to manifest or embody the twofold truth is seated meditation; in Shin Buddhism it is the chanting of the Name of Amida Buddha, Namu Amida Butsu. This is the Sino-Japanese transliteration of the Sanskrit, Namō Amitābha Buddha, where "Namō" has the same root as *namas* in the South Asian greeting "*Namaste.*" *Namas* means "to bow"; *te* means "you"; thus, *namaste* means literally "I bow to you." The Name (Jpn. *myōgō*), Namu Amida Butsu, then, means "I, this foolish being, bow and entrust myself to the awakening of infinite light."

Like the repetitive action of seated meditation, or the chanting of *mu* in *kōan* practice, the chanting of the Name is designed to cut through the discursive meanderings of the calculating ego-mind and to release the unifying power of the oneness of reality as boundless compassion. Yet, ultimately, the chanting of the Name does not arise from the ego-consciousness of the Shin Buddhist practitioner who relies on her own self power. It issues forth from the other power of Amida Buddha as the power other than ego arising from emptiness. Thus, Shinran states, "true entrusting is buddha-nature," not human-nature. The modern Shin teacher and interpreter Kai Wariko (1964) composed the following verse to express the same point:

Mihotoke no na wo yobu waga koe wa	The voice with which I call Amida Buddha
Mihotoke no ware wo yobimasu mikoe narikeri	Is the voice with which Amida Buddha calls to me.

Shinmon Aoki: Coffinman

Approximately 360 miles southwest of Kannonji temple in Iwate Prefecture is the area of Toyama where Shinmon Aoki (b. 1937), the author of the memoir *Coffinman*, was born, raised, and lives to this day. Toyama is an area of devout Shin Buddhists, and Aoki is profoundly shaped by the influences of his local religious culture. In contrast to Zen Buddhism, which has a monastic ideal, Shin Buddhism is lay-centered. Intensive Zen practice entails disciplined commitment to a course of practice in which one is subjected to a rigorous regimen that is physically, emotionally, and spiritually demanding. As we saw in O'Halloran's case, the *kōan* practice is designed to unmask ego-attachments and lead the student into the realization of unbounded emptiness. Shin Buddhism, with its lay orientation, takes life as such as the arena of practice, and regards its many vicissitudes as more than enough without the need for introducing artificial challenges such as *kōan* practice. As will become evident, Aoki faced many difficulties in life.

Born into a landed family in Toyama Prefecture, Aoki is intellectually capable and attends Waseda University, one of the top private universities in Japan. However, Aoki becomes embroiled in the student protests surrounding the completion of the Treaty of Mutual Cooperation between the United States and Japan in 1960, and he never graduates. Returning to Toyama, Aoki continues to aspire to be a writer and poet, and opens a bar/restaurant in the hope that it will serve both as a source of income and as an intellectual salon. By this time, he has a wife and child, but he is not a good businessman and so becomes bankrupt. Desperate to find a job, he answers a help-wanted ad in the newspaper, only to find out after accepting the job that it is for a mortuary service, and that his job would be to clean and dress corpses for funerals.

For much of its history and into the early twentieth century, the Japanese custom was for the family to clean and prepare the corpse for the funeral (after which it would be cremated), but with modernization and its technological, antiseptic culture, a sense of defilement and taboo began to surround death, and families began to move away from this custom of attending to the corpses themselves. This created the need for a new kind of professional, the mortician, who would dress the body for the coffining. The term *coffinman* (*nokanfu*), more literally *coffiner*, was kind of an invention of Aoki himself, who found himself caught between traditional values and attitudes toward death in modern Japan.

As part of its lay orientation, Shin Buddhism has especially embraced those who live on the margins of society, subject to prejudice, and are often regarded as karmically impure or inferior. Among them were the outcasts (*hinin*) who were considered defiled due to their livelihoods deriving from the death of other people and creatures. These included butchers, gravediggers, and metal smiths who created weapons. Shinran considered such people to be precisely the object of boundless compassion; society could not function without them, yet the majority tended to shun them. Shinran saw them as unfairly carrying the burden of negative karma for a society that needed them, literally, for life and death. Yet, the priesthood, which also made its living off of the dead in the form of funerals and memorial services, was extolled as holy and as of the highest social status. Just as Shinran saw a certain irony in this and declared himself to be "neither monk nor layman," Aoki labored under the irony of having to serve a priesthood too often preoccupied with their many services to truly attend to the dead and grieving. It is under such circumstances of shame and humiliation that Aoki began his work as Coffinman.

Like the story of Maura "Soshin" O'Halloran, Shinmon Aoki's life narrative includes a rejection of the master narrative of the usual social and economic success story. Only in this case, it is not Aoki who rejects the life of the master narrative; he is the one who becomes excluded from the master narrative due to a life trajectory that he does not intend but that is largely of his own making. His having to take the job of a mortician or "coffinman" forces him to seek a counterstory that resists his rejection at the hands of the master narrative.

Shin Buddhist Oneness with the Awakening of Infinite Light: Turning Points

Unconditional Acceptance by the Other

Such was the taboo associated with livelihoods pertaining to death that virtually everyone in Aoki's immediate and extended family rejects him, including his wife, who refuses to sleep with him any longer. He does not give in to the prejudice and rejection he faces, but he also sees little in the way of a meaningful existence. One day, as he approaches the address that he is given for the next coffining procedure, he recognizes it as the residence of the parents of his ex-girlfriend, who he went out with while he was still a student at Waseda University. He had dropped her off there many times, and she had begged him to meet her father, but he had refused. At that time in Japanese society, meeting the parents, especially the father, entailed a much deeper level of commitment than just dating, and he had not been ready to make such a commitment at that time. Now, he was a lowly coffinman, and he simply hoped that she would not be there as he attended to the procedure.

> By now I had done so many cases that anyone watching how deftly I moved would surely see me as a pro at work. But there I was sweating profusely, the same as the first time, and this had come on as soon as I had the corpse and begun to work. The sweat on my brow was about to run down, and just when I was about to wipe my forehead with the sleeve of my white robe, there she was, reaching out to wipe my brow—how long she'd been sitting there I don't know. Tears welled up in those beautiful eyes. She sat next to me until the work was finished, mopping the sweat from my face.
>
> As I was taking my leave, the family representative, who seemed to be her younger brother, knelt on the tatami mat and politely bowed and expressed his thanks. Behind him I could see her standing there just like that, her eyes filled with so many things that needed to be said but would never come to pass. . . . But deep within the surprised look in her eyes there was something more. Even her sitting by me to wipe the sweat away, all the way through the procedure, was a gesture of no ordinary dimensions. . . . I felt there was something

there that transcended the trivial world of scorn or pity or sympathy, that even went beyond the relationship between man and woman.

I felt that she showed me she accepted my total existence just as I was, no more no less. And so thinking I began to feel good about myself. And I began to feel I could continue this line of work.

(20–21)

There is a striking similarity between Aoki's statement "She accepted my total existence just as I was, no more no less," and O'Halloran's statement "Suddenly I understood why we must take care of things just because they exist; we are of no greater and of no lesser value" (104). The difference, if there is one, is that in the case of the latter, O'Halloran is the practitioner who embraces, whereas in the former, Aoki is the foolish being who is embraced, just as he is. Aoki's ex-girlfriend becomes the conduit for boundless compassion, in which he is embraced, enabling him to embrace others.

In the case of O'Halloran, it is her master Go Rōshi who helps her to break down her ego and release the power of emptiness/buddha-nature through her *kōan* practice; in Aoki's case, it is social prejudice and isolation that reduce him to "just a coffinman." Yet, it is his virtually ego-less, single-minded devotion to this work that opens the way to a greater realization, in which his ex-girlfriend, as the conduit of boundless compassion, becomes one with him, and leads him to realize the dignity and worth of his existence.

Again, there is a break in the master narrative, in which a deeper or transcendent moment of oneness emerges to empower Aoki as the protagonist. This realization of oneness helps him to heal at a spiritual and emotional level, and to empower his counterstory in his life in society.

All Sentient Beings Glow with Infinite Light

The religious character of Aoki's awakening is apparent in its all-encompassing scope. It is not just people in whom Aoki begins to see this infinite light, a kind of glow, but in all sentient beings, even the apparently "lowliest" creatures. One day, Aoki is called to the house of an elderly person who had been deceased for quite some time:

I peeked in through a open window. . . . I could see the mound of the covers under which the corpse lay, but, squinting my eyes, I seemed to detect motion from the top of the covers. Not only that, it seemed there were tiny white beads scattered throughout the entire room. One good hard look and I finally realized they were maggots. . . .

A chill ran down my spine. . . . At any rate we couldn't get near the body until we did something about those maggots. . . . The guy who brought me the broom fled outside. There were countless maggots wriggling like waves in the rib cage. . . . Even after the coffin was on its way to university forensics, I was still cleaning up the maggots. . . .

As I was sweeping them together, I got a better look at the maggots as individual existences. I noticed some were trying to crawl up the pillars to get away. A maggot is just another life form. And just when I was thinking that, I was sure I saw one of them glow with light.

(44)

Through this and many similar experiences, Aoki gains intimate glimpses into a world that embraces both life and death, and that ultimately transcends distinctions of life and death. He likens this to *mizore*, Japanese for "sleet." In Aoki's view, people often seem to take "sleet" to mean a "mixture of rain and snow," whereas for him *mizore* is something in between: yes, both rain and snow, but also neither rain nor snow: "The relation of life to death is like the relation of rain to snow in sleet. In the singleness of LifeDeath = sleet, there can be no sleet if the rain is separated out from the snow" (31). In his coffining experiences, Aoki begins to enter a realm or state in which the distinction between life and death begins to blur, one that is enveloped in a gentle light that is not visible to the physical eye alone.

Light of Compassion: Reconciling with His Uncle

One of Aoki's harshest critics had been his uncle, who, speaking on behalf of the larger clan, had condemned Aoki for bringing shame upon the family: "You better quit [being a coffiner]. Right away. . . . All the relatives are so ashamed that we can hardly go out into the streets." "If you refuse to quit, then we will end all relations. I never want to see your face again."

Now, however, his uncle was on his deathbed, and Aoki's mother calls for him to go visit the uncle one last time.

"Can't you do it just this time? . . . "

"Hell, no. He's the one who told me not to show my face around here!"

"Well, you know your uncle looked after you when you were little. . . ."

As I listened to my mother's entreaties over the phone, I had a change of heart. . . .

I was rather tense when I knocked at the door of the private room, from behind which my aunt peered out.

"Ah, you've come at a good time," she said, welcoming me in a big voice, explaining that he had been under but had just regained consciousness a little while ago. . . .

My uncle was looking in my direction and was trying to say something. His face was completely different from the face he made when lecturing me. It was a soft and gentle face. From the corner of his eye a tear glistened. When I felt him grip my hands ever more slightly, I thought I heard him say, "*Arigato*," thank you. Then later again, still grasping my hands, he repeated in a voice barely audible, "*Arigato*." That face of his was so soft and gentle, it virtually glowed.

The next morning my uncle died. The resentment in my heart was gone. The only thing I felt building up was a sense of shame. At the funeral, as I offered incense, I said, "Uncle, I am so sorry. Please forgive me." The tears were rolling down my cheeks in a steady stream.

(56–57)

Just as in the case of his ex-girlfriend, the maggots, and now his uncle, Aoki's realization of oneness in the awakening of infinite light is described as coming to him, often unexpectedly, in a moment of receptivity. In this moment all oppositions seem to fall away: past and present, human and nonhuman, life and death: "The Light of Amida Buddha is not like candlelight or sunlight; it's not a light we can detect with our eyes. Nor is it like the first rays of the rising sun at New Year's that people pray to. . . . Shinran called it the light transcending sun and moon; thus, the Light is neither sunlight nor moonlight. A light beyond sun and moon would be the Light of eternity" (118).

As in the case of O'Halloran, there is more than one turning point in Aoki's story; in fact, there are multiple moments of oneness that break through the conventional or master narrative of social expectations, and that empower Aoki to propel his self-narrative in the form of counterstories. Even the failure of his initial attempts to become a writer is integrated into his new life narrative, such that *Coffinman* as his memoir comes to be the embodiment of his counterstory, one that transforms his total view of life, society, nature, and the cosmos, so that his story comes to the fore, and the oppressive master narrative seemingly fades into the background.

Christian Oneness: Divine Love

Michael Morton: Background

Michael Morton (b. 1954) was a supermarket manager in Williamson County, Texas, when in 1986, at the age of thirty-two, his wife Christine was brutally murdered due to blunt force trauma. Although it would eventually come out that the prosecution made many mistakes involving lack of evidence, suppression of exculpatory evidence, and failure to pursue alternative suspects, Michael Morton was nevertheless convicted of his wife's murder, was separated from his three-year-old boy, and spent the next twenty-five years of his life in prison. Only with the aid of the Innocence Project and DNA testing on key pieces of evidence was his conviction finally overturned, and Morton granted release from prison.

As one might imagine, Morton faced tremendous despair during those twenty-five years, nearly giving up on his life many, many times. Yet, it was in the midst of this enormous struggle that he would find the light: the light of truth, light of freedom, the light of the Divine.

This is a tale of the total loss or inability to live out the master narrative of a happy family, career, and life of freedom in American society. Everything Morton valued was stripped away from him; yet, paradoxically, this enabled the opening up of a religious dimension of which he had previously been unaware but which had always been underfoot.

Oneness in Faith: Turning Points

In both the case of Maura "Soshin" O'Halloran and Shinmon Aoki, their realization of oneness—with the depth of their own existence, with the world around them, between self and other, life and death—involves a process in which there are moments great and small, of grand epiphanies and more mundane flashes. Whether induced in the process of a formal practice as in the case of O'Halloran or more organically by life events as in the case of Aoki, both figures experience the stripping away of the illusion of ego as a workable basis of self-identity and are moved to discover a deeper, larger awareness of emptiness/oneness as the basis of their existence. In the case of Michael Morton, there is a similar process of suffering the destruction of his ego, but the effective cause is singular, insofar as it is the incarceration that follows from his false conviction that takes him into the depths of his own personal hell.

Cooped up in a concrete prison with little light and no air conditioning, living like sardines among the most violent offenders, was intolerable enough. One might think that being sent outdoors in work parties would be better, with at least fresh air, but this was not necessarily the case:

> My first day in the fields was instructive. We were up at the crack of dawn, piled onto wagons, and driven to what felt like the edge of the world, finally stopping at a series of very long, very deep drainage ditches. The banks were steep, muddy, and slippery—and home to the tallest weeds I'd ever seen, a small forest of greenery, taller than the men in my squad. Just maintaining a

footing was tough. Our job was to scrape off the thicket of tangled, tall grass and brambles, leaving behind only bare earth.

It seemed almost doable, if not necessarily survivable. Every single creature we encountered bit or stung or was eager to fill a person with poison. Sometimes, they could do all three.

(Morton 2014a, 154)

Year after year of grueling conditions took their toll, as did the unending series of failed appeals in the judicial system. One small consolation was the brief biannual visits he had with his son. These visits were not easy, as Eric was now being raised by his wife's sister's family, who did not have a favorable view of Morton's guilt or innocence, and they would not have brought Eric for even these brief visits had there not been a court order to do so. Over time, the connection between father and son became more tenuous, as there just was not enough shared time and experience to sustain and nurture the relationship. Eventually, Eric was formally adopted into his sister-in-law's family, and this entailed even a change in name from Eric Michael Morton to Eric John Olson (163). The visits, so infrequent as they were, became more sporadic until they stopped altogether:

I was unaware of Eric's life, out of every loop, deemed undeserving of the most basic inclusion. This news left me absolutely broken. My long-hoped-for life [with my son Eric] after [my hoped-for] vindication and release was gone— irretrievably gone. I hit rock bottom. And I went down angrily blaming everyone and everything: fate, my sister-in-law, [my deceased wife] Chris's entire family, my family, myself, the legal system, the universe—you name it.

(164)

Now there was nothing to look forward to, and "each day was just another gray day in prison" (166). What happened next would change everything:

With no warning whatsoever, a bright, blinding, golden light burst into the room. The light swallowed up everything; it enveloped me. I felt wrapped in that light—a warm, wonderful, comforting light. It was a sensation different from any I had ever known.

I felt like I was floating above my bunk—fearlessly, effortlessly, blissfully.

My ears were filled not with music but with an incomprehensible roar. I didn't know if it was the thunderous roll of a massive wind or the crash and rumble of great, rushing waters. I felt I was being lifted by a monumental power—by something mighty but gentle, formidable and yet more forgiving than anything I had ever experienced.

But most of all—more than the beautiful light or the roar of unseen winds or the pure pleasure this experience gave me—I remember the infinite peace and joy, the limitless compassion and the intense love I felt aimed right at me.

That night in my cell I hadn't sensed an individual vision of Jesus or seen the traditional icons of Christianity. No disembodied voice told me to build an ark because it was going to rain. What I had seen and felt and heard was divine light—and divine love—and the presence of a power that I had sought, in one way or another, all my life.

I explored the possibility that something else had triggered this—what had I eaten that day anyway? What had I done? But after months of questioning, after analyzing and reanalyzing everything I could, I found nothing concrete that would have induced that moment, nothing that could provide a reasonable earthbound explanation for what had happened to me.

In the end, I fell back on Occam's razor—the old philosophical theory that the simplest explanation is probably the best.

In other words, I realized I had cried out to God—and received exactly what I had asked for—a sign. Nothing more, nothing less. It was that simple and that profound.

I didn't change overnight. I was—and still am—a human being with deep flaws. Like everyone else on earth, I still have the capacity to make unfair judgments about others, an inherent tendency to make mistakes of pride, an ability to unthinkingly inflict casual cruelties on others. I am a work in progress. But I want to be a person who deserves to be in the presence of God.

(168–70)

There are some striking similarities between Morton's account of the unbounded, divine light that envelops him, and some of Aoki's descriptions of infinite light in *Coffinman*. It is a comforting, warm, compassionate light; it is unbounded or infinite, and it seems to be aimed directly at Morton, just as Aoki sensed the light of each creature and circumstance as intimately related to his own existence at each moment of realization.

It is a key narrative turning point, one in which Morton "hit bottom," in which the bottom then falls out to open a portal to the divine light, and the inauguration of a counterstory that he had not known was available to him. It is not unlike Aoki, who also had a kind of bottoming out when he took on his life as Coffinman.

Yet, there are significant differences as well. Beyond individual details such as the sounds that seem to be present in Morton's account but absent in Aoki's, the greater difference is evident in the narrative that frames the ineffable moment of encountering the infinite light. Morton, raised as a Baptist in a predominantly Christian setting, has been socialized to name the source of light as a means of empowering his own faith. Aoki (along with O'Halloran), in contrast, seeks to let go of any discursive determination in order to enter into and embody of the flow of emptiness/oneness/infinite light. For Morton, the experience of oneness with the divine light becomes the basis of *belief*; for Aoki, the awareness of infinite light opens the way to embodied *practice*. Certainly, there can be elements of each in both accounts, and the net effect may not be so different. Nevertheless, we can see how their realizations are framed differently. For Morton, belief comes to drive his actions. As he states,

> I have no specific mission or divine task. But I know that:
> 1. He exists [God].
> 2. He is wise beyond any human calculation, and
> 3. He loves me.
> Because those three simple, yet powerful truths, life makes sense to me now. I get it.
> (Morton 2014b)

Aoki, in contrast, speaks of a letting go into the formless flow of emptiness and boundless compassion:

> Shinran writes in his "Tract on the Spontaneity of Dharma-Nature" (*Jinen hōni shō*):
> "What is called the unsurpassed Buddha has no form. Due to having no form, it is called the spontaneous dharma-nature [*jinen hōni*]. . . . We learn to listen deeply [to the voiceless voice of] Amida in order to be led to the awareness of formlessness. Amida Buddha is the skillful means for us to realize [this formless] spontaneity. . . . One should not be constantly thinking about this matter of spontaneity. If one thinks about this spontaneity too much, one will take the meaning of what has no meaning, and turn it into something that appears to have [some specific] meaning. This is the inconceivable buddha-wisdom."
> (Aoki 1996, 130)

One cannot say which is better or worse, only that the narrative frameworks differ. Morton is enabled to move forward by distilling the basic beliefs that correspond to his experience of divine light and love. Aoki is always evoking a world in which boundaries dissolve, and he is led to slip into the intimate experience of an inconceivable light that embraces and goes beyond all oppositions.

For his part, Morton, once he is fully exonerated of any wrongdoing and declared innocent in 2011, is able to fully embrace life beyond the prison walls again. Due to his newfound faith, he can move forward without overwhelming resentment or the need for revenge. He helps to reform the Texas criminal justice system with what becomes known as the Michael Morton Act (SB 1611) so that the prosecution is responsible and liable to turn over any and all evidence in a criminal court of law. He reaches out to those who have been wrongly convicted and assists with the work of groups such as the Innocence Project to help overturn such convictions. Yet, he has patience and forgiveness even for overzealous prosecutors, even the very one who helped to put him jail. Barry Scheck, cofounder and codirector of the Innocence Project, who, as an atheistic existentialist, has a very different normative orientation from Morton himself, writes in the foreword to Morton's book:

> The story itself is so astonishing, especially the way Michael came to be exonerated, that it should induce an existentialist to literally get religion, a point Michael gently makes to me (existentialist) on occasion. You will pinch yourself at some of the stranger-than-fiction dramatic turns in this story. . . .
>
> Michael speaks truth to power with moral authority that cannot be questioned, with Christian forgiveness that comes from his core. He has, indeed, defined himself by the sum total of moral choices he has made, choices that inspire and that command respect.
>
> (Morton 2014a, ix)

Narratively, Scheck's foreword adds another element to the interplay between master narrative and counterstory. Morton initially embraces and partially succeeds in living the life of the master narrative, with family, career, and social expectations. When this is all taken from him, he must find a counterstory. The twist here, one that is implicit in his memoir, is that the Christian faith that is a part of the dominant culture remains dormant until he hits bottom, a turning point marked by the rejection by his only son. Although ever present, he does not pay much attention to the Christian narrative in which he had been encultured from his childhood. This faith narrative is spontaneously activated when he is forced to abandon the secular narrative of family, work, and human love.

Certainly, Morton's advocacy on behalf of the wrongly convicted is a counternarrative that is empowered by his newly found faith, but it is not as if the faith narrative is outside of the master narrative. In the liberal academy of North America, Christian narratives have an ambiguous status. On the one hand, the story of the white male Protestant is often depicted as part and parcel of an oppressive master narrative. On the other, mystical moments of redemption realized by the oppressed can easily be seen as turning points of the emerging counterstory.

Scheck's self-description of himself as an atheistic existentialist who is forced to respect and admire Morton's faith-narrative can be seen as reflecting the ambiguous status of the Christian narrative: part of both the master narrative and the counterstory. Scheck's brief narrative at this juncture also suggests another possibility, that there is a *human* narrative that can form a framework large enough for both existentialist and Baptist.

Conclusion: Stories of Oneness Untold, Unrealized

Still, the narrative analysis of Morton's story is just as significant for what it does not contain as for what it does contain. What Barry Scheck alludes to, "the stranger-than-fiction dramatic turns," includes so many remarkable moments, any one of which, had it been lacking, would have led to Morton either still being imprisoned or being not alive at all: the fact that he was not given the death sentence; the fact that he survived being assaulted in prison by those who were much stronger or had deadly diseases; the fact that key pieces of evidence were not discarded or existed at all, with key advances in DNA testing when he needed them; the fact that there were so many lawyers, Innocence Project workers and volunteers, and others who came forward at the moment of greatest need; the fact that his son was willing to form a relationship with someone whom he really did not remember having been a father in any significant way. No doubt Morton himself had more than a small part to play in the emergence and involvement of many of these circumstances and people, but so much had lain beyond his control.

For each person who survives long enough to come to a spiritual resolution about their plight as wrongly convicted, for each person whose wrongful conviction is actually overturned, how many thousands, even hundreds of thousands, remain incarcerated without any hope of release or of spiritual realization? While this is very dramatic in Morton's case, one could say something similar about O'Halloran and Aoki. O'Halloran, despite the brevity of her existence, fulfilled the dream of Zen awakening that not everyone is able to realize, an awakening that has gone on to inspire many others. Aoki, for all his early despair, actually became the writer he so earnestly desired to become as a young man, before he embarked on his journey as Coffinman; now, the world knows of his work through the English-language translation of his book, and award-winning film *Departures*. How many others had similar aspirations but ended their lives in despair or even took their own lives, as many of the most famous Japanese writers did, in the postwar period? That is to say, how many counterstories go unfulfilled, unrealized, unrecognized?

As diverse as they are, the narrative case studies examined here, of Maura "Soshin" O'Halloran, Shinmon Aoki, and Michael Morton, represent the stories of three people who, confronted with the unmasking of their ego-centered selves, discovered a greater aspiration to realize a oneness that took them beyond the binary oppositions of self and other, self and nature, self and world, mundane and supramundane, even life and death. O'Halloran is gone from this world. Aoki is elderly in Japan. Morton is still learning to enjoy life in this world. They will not meet in this world, and yet they have already met here in these pages, and we are invited to join their stories of oneness. What kind of "oneness" is that?

Note

1. Anne Klein describes her own experience of studying Tibetan Buddhism in the Himalayan region in a similar manner, as an honorary "male" (Klein 2008).

References

Aoki Shinmon. 1996. *Nōkanfu nikki*. Rev. expanded ed. Bunshun Bunkō A-28–1. Tokyo: Bungei Shunjū.

——. 2002. *Coffinman: The Journal of a Buddhist Mortician*. Anaheim, CA: Buddhist Study Center.

Kai Wariko. 1964. *Shinshū kusakago*. Edited by Tesshin Sasaki. Kyoto: Hyakkaen.

Katz, Steven. 1978. *Mysticism and Philosophical Analysis*. New York: Oxford University Press.

Klein, Anne Carolyn. 2008. *Meeting the Great Bliss Queen: Buddhists, Feminists, and the Art of the Self*. Ithaca: Snow Lion.

Morton, Michael. 2014a. *Getting Life: An Innocent Man's 25-Year Journey from Prison to Peace*. New York: Simon and Schuster.

——. 2014b. "Forgiveness and Three Powerful Truths." *Beliefnet*. www.beliefnet.com/Faiths /Articles/Forgiveness-and-Three-Powerful-Truths.aspx?p=2.

Nelson, Hilde. 2001. *Damaged Identities, Narrative Repair*. Ithaca: Cornell University Press.

O'Halloran, Maura. 1994. *Pure Heart, Enlightened Mind: The Zen Journals and Letters of *Maura "Soshin" O'Halloran*. Boston: Tuttle.

CHAPTER 8

KANT, BUDDHISM, AND SELF-CENTERED VICE

BRADFORD COKELET

Immanuel Kant famously identifies an ethically good agent as one who treats people as ends in themselves and never as mere means. The intuitive appeal of this ideal—and of Kant's secular articulation of its content and justification—does much to explain the continued popularity of Kantian ethics. However, even if we agree that the ideal of treating people as ends and never means is attractive and fits our intuitions about important cases, we should not assume that this ideal is best articulated within a Kantian framework. It may turn out that while Kantians should be thanked for getting us to appreciate the ideal, we must move to a different framework (for example, a broadly virtue ethical or utilitarian one) to best articulate it. In fact, that is the view for which I will argue here: the Kantian conception of treating people as ends in themselves and not mere means (hereafter "treating people as final ends") is inadequate and Buddhist philosophy has resources—in particular its teachings about the self and the related conception of oneness—that can help us construct a viable alternative.

The idea that an ethically good agent is one who treats people as ends in themselves and never as mere means is appealing for a number of reasons, but centrally because it yields intuitive results when we think about the ethical excellence of those who admirably inhabit their identity-defining roles. Good parents, friends, and teachers, for example, help their children, friends, and students flourish and their motivations are not merely instrumental. They want those they love (or to whom they are devoted) to live good human lives—to actualize their human potential, we might say—and they either want this for its own sake or for the sake of those they love. Conversely, lackluster or deplorable parents (or friends or teachers) are often less than good because they either treat their kids as mere means or fail to adequately treat them—or their human potential—as ends in themselves. It is morally bad, for example, when a parent pushes his kids to accomplish things in order to buttress his self-esteem or otherwise "feed his ego"; and there is something morally wrong with the neglectful parent who doesn't help his daughter develop rationally and morally because he is too focused on his career. In the former case, we could say that the parent treats his child as a mere means. In the latter, he fails to treat her (or her human potential) as an end in itself.

Moral philosophers who agree that the ideal of treating people as final ends is appealing will want to develop a philosophic conception of that ideal. First, we want a positive account of the ideal of treating people as final ends. Following Kant, I will assume that the ideal calls on us both to reach out to others in a positive way (to treat others as ends in themselves) and to exercise self-restraint in our interactions with others (to never treat them as mere means). Roughly, and again following Kantians, we can say that the ideal calls on us to act with both *love/devotion* and *respect*. Giving an account of these two aspects and their interplay in different contexts is certainly a complicated affair and will minimally involve giving some account of the distinctive features of persons to which the well-motivated respond when they act with love and respect and a characterization of those modes of apt responsiveness to persons. Kantians, for example, typically focus on our powers to engage in rational reflection and end-setting and hold that well-motivated agents respect these or the dignity that they ground, and Kantians understand love as a practical attitude requiring us to adopt other people's happiness as an end.

Second, an account of the ideal of treating people as final ends will provide some account of the main negative motivations or vices that are ruled out by our ethical ideal. It will explore common or salient cases in which we fail to treat people as ends and are responsible for those failures, and explain how positive motivation can rationally overcome the problems present in these negative ones. For example, Kantians typically focus on failures to treat others with respect that are the result of self-conceit and they then explain how respect rationally strikes down self-conceit. Third, a conception of treating people as final ends should tell us something about the scope and normativity of the ideal. Does the ideal require that we treat all people as ends or only some? And are we morally obligated or rationally compelled to treat people as ends or is it merely an appealing ideal that one could reasonably reject in order to pursue other ideals (or one's own good)?

In this essay, we will be focusing on the first two tasks, and I will be assuming that common sense cases involving parents, friends, and teachers provide paradigm instantiations of the ethical ideal in which we are interested. I will assume that a conception of treating people as final ends is adequate only if it yields plausible results in most, if not all, of these paradigm cases, and I will be mainly concerned with the positive aspect of the ideal that calls on us to treat others as ends in themselves by acting out of love or devotion. With this framework as a background, I argue that Kantian conceptions are inadequate and that we should look to traditions such as Buddhism when constructing a plausible alternative.

My basic argument against the Kantians hinges on an account of self-centeredness and the claim that to treat people as final ends we must overcome self-centeredness. This may strike some readers as an obvious truth, but I flesh it out and then argue that Kantian conceptions of treating people as final ends are problematic because they imply that self-centered people, who we intuitively think of as failing to treat others as ends in themselves, can be perfectly morally motivated. Part of the problem is Kant's conviction that good moral motivation does not require any sort of contingent character or insight—any moral cultivation or improvement of the self. Roughly, he thinks that if we set our minds (or wills) to it we can immediately start treating others as ends in themselves, regardless of our past histories and the different forms of personal baggage that color our experiences, mental lives, and interactions. But reflection on cases involving vicious self-centeredness suggests otherwise. In addition, Kant's general framework implies that we treat people as ends in themselves if and only if we respect their rational capacities for end-setting and fulfill our wide duty of beneficence, but someone who is viciously self-centered can successfully treat others with respect *and* fulfill that wide duty, so Kant doesn't have the normative resources to support or elucidate the thought that self-centered people who fail to treat others as final ends exhibit defective human moral motivation. By extension, I argue that his account of motivational improvement (respect rationally striking down self-conceit) cannot be applied to all the relevant cases involving self-centeredness.

After making my case against the Kantian conception, I will turn to Buddhism and discuss the possibility that by appropriating certain Buddhist ideas we can construct a more viable, non-Kantian conception of treating people as final ends. In short, I think that Buddhist moral psychology provides us with a plausible framework for understanding self-centered vice and that by appropriating aspects of a Buddhist account of enlightened compassion we might be able to construct a more plausible conception of treating people as final ends.

Self-Centeredness: Its Nature and Cost

To begin, I want to sketch out some aspects of human self-centeredness and discuss how various types of self-centeredness characteristically get in the way of our treating our relational partners (friends, parents, and the like) as ends in themselves. First, we can usefully consider some points that P. J. Ivanhoe (2013) makes when discussing the senses and values of oneness in neo-Confucian thought, a tradition that was deeply influenced by Buddhist philosophy. In the last sections of his paper, Ivanhoe distinguishes selfishness from self-centeredness and gives us a couple of examples of undue self-centeredness. In describing the distinction he plausibly suggests that self-centeredness involves taking "the self as the center of one's thoughts about the world." As examples, he mentions a generous woman who "thinks of her attitude and actions as expressions of her remarkable compassion toward the world," and parents who would insist on paying their child's tuition so that they can enjoy reflecting on what remarkably self-sacrificing parents they are. These examples are intended to show that selfishness and self-centeredness are distinct, because they show that one can be problematically self-centered while acting altruistically. I think they also suggest that self-centered people are characteristically concerned with the esteem or approval that they get or merit, but before getting to that issue, I want to reinforce Ivanhoe's contention that selfishness and self-centeredness are distinct by pointing out that sometimes our self-centered tendencies are bad for us.

For example, consider Bill, whose tendency to put himself at the center of his cognitive and emotional life is impeding his ability to found and maintain intimate reciprocal relationships. In virtue of how much it is costing him, we might rightly conclude that Bill's narcissistic tendencies are very bad for him; they are robbing him of valuable relationships that he needs to have in order to truly flourish. Because it is in his self-interest to become less self-centered, it seems implausible to think that he is being selfish if and when he falls into his old narcissistic patterns (for example, he does not notice when his wife Hilary is down after reading the new book about her that came out).[1]

In response to this case, one might claim that although Bill's self-centered focus on his own problems and his related failure to notice and respond well to others' struggles are not objectively in his self-interest, his focus can nonetheless be selfish if he is not cognizant of that fact—and if his failure to change is motivated by sensitivity to the subjective cost of his changing. This might be unconscious or conscious. For example, we can imagine Bill refusing to go to therapy because it will be time-consuming and impede his ability to go on some planned speaking tour. We may deny that he is making an objectively prudential decision here, of course, but that does not undercut the claim that he is selfishly choosing to stay self-centered. In fact, I think we should grant that in this case Bill is selfishly staying self-centered, but still resist the idea that being or staying self-centered is always selfish. To see why consider two more cases. In the first, Bill comes to see that the lack of close relationships is very bad for him and enters therapy. He is working to uproot or curtail his self-centeredness in order to promote his good, but his old habits die hard. When they pop up, it is hard to see how they, or the behaviors they motivate, count as selfish. Second, consider the fact that some people are self-focused but have low self-esteem. They may even despise themselves and think they deserve to suffer. Some people like this "can't get out of their heads," as people say, because they are obsessed with the idea that they are bad or worthless, and when these people exhibit self-centered tendencies, these are almost never in their objective or subjective self-interest.

With these points out of the way, we now turn to some different aspects of self-centeredness themselves. After charting out some of its different dimensions, we will be able to better recognize its prudential and moral costs.

First, being self-centered is often a matter of one's motives or reasons for acting. Ivanhoe's examples of off-putting self-centeredness nicely illustrate this. In one of these, we are invited to consider the parents who insist that they be the ones to pay for their kids' education when a stranger offers to pay. They are very concerned to be the ones to help because they know that if they do help they will merit esteem for being good parents. Now I agree that this is off-putting, but I also want to suggest that the problem crops up because of the parents' desire to be, or be seen as, good parents, rather than their desire to be the ones to help their kids (instead of a stranger). To see the difference, consider a case in which someone wants to be the one to act virtuously (rather than some relevant strangers), but in which she is *not* moved by any self-centered desire to merit praise or approval. Take a mother who sees her kid go down in a soccer game from a painful slide tackle. As he writhes in pain on the field, she rushes out to comfort him. So does the father of another teammate. I think that the mother quite naturally prefers to be the one to comfort her son ("Thanks, but I have this covered"), even if the other father might do well enough in her stead. In fact, I think that desiring to be the one to help might make her a better mother. My main point, however, is that the mother can desire to be the one to help without desiring to be the one to help because that makes her a better mother (in fact or in other's eyes). This illustrates the general point that self-centered motivation is often or mainly problematic because it involves an undue concern with getting or meriting approval, esteem, and pride; adapting some language from Kant, we can say that while self-centered people are inordinately concerned with or have false beliefs about the worth of their self, selfish people are inordinately concerned with the worth of their condition.

Next, consider some of the ways in which inordinate concern with, or false beliefs about, the worth of one's self can be manifest in self-centered patterns of thought and behavior. We can roughly divide these into three categories: self-centered attention, self-centered judgment, and self-centered interpersonal interaction.

Self-centered attention can be manifest, in the first place, in facts about what one does and does not notice in one's experience. For example, we may be unduly self-centered when we are so focused on our own projects or problems that we simply do not notice the suffering or the success of others around us. Or we may fail to notice (or foresee) how our actions will affect others because we are so focused on our projects, problems, or standing. In addition, self-centered attention is often manifest in dispositions to think or guide discussion. We are all familiar with people (including perhaps ourselves) who tend to bring their thoughts, and the conversations they have with others, back to themselves and their experiences.

Next, consider self-centered judgment. This is manifest when the way that we interpret and judge things in our experience is unduly colored by our own interests or concerns, especially our desires to get or merit approval. Iris Murdoch's famous example of the mother who judges her daughter-in-law illustrates this.[2] As I imagine it, the upper-class British mother initially judges her young American daughter-in-law to be crude and impertinent. On Murdoch's telling she is able to revise this interpretation by paying concentrated attention to the daughter-in-law's actual behavior and adopting a loving, just gaze. This results in the mother thinking that the daughter-in-law is refreshingly forthright and unconventional. My point here is that we naturally imagine that the mother's initial interpretation of the daughter-in-law is motivated by her concern to get and merit the approval of her peers. She might initially judge that the daughter-in-law is crude and unrefined because she is concerned about what her peers will say about the daughter-in-law, her son, the family, or her. If she is only concerned about what her peers or others will say, her motives need not be self-focused, but we can imagine that she is concerned about losing face herself and this is what drives her negative interpretation of the daughter-in-law. If so, this would be a case in which her judgment is distorted by self-centered considerations, and coming to see things aright would involve overcoming these effects of, as Murdoch colorfully puts it, the big fat ego.

There are other forms of self-centered judgment, but I want to move on to self-centered interpersonal interaction. There are at least three subforms of self-centeredness here that I think we can roughly distinguish: self-centered negligence, self-centered reactivity, and self-centered demands/needs. Self-centered negligence has already been mentioned earlier and it involves a failure to notice, aptly interpret, or respond to the struggles, successes, needs, or valid demands of others because one is unduly focused on one's own projects, problems, or standing. People who exhibit robust self-centered negligence are often said to be living in a bubble.

Self-centered reactivity involves oversensitivity to how things will affect one's own projects, problems, or standing. People who exhibit robust self-centered reactivity are often said to take things too personally. And as with the other forms of self-centered interpersonal interaction, reactivity will involve self-centered attention and judgment. People who are overly sensitive about how things will affect their own social standing, for example, will often have trouble noticing how others are being affected by their actions because they are so centrally concerned with protecting their own standing and they will also often interpret people who they take to threaten their social standing with an evil, self-centered eye.

Last, but not least, there are self-centered demands/needs. First, there are self-conceited people who believe they already are more important or worthy of esteem and benefits than others and who are obsessed with getting esteem or benefits. Second, there are people who want to be, or to be taken to be, more important and worthy than others and focus unduly on getting benefit and esteem in order to have evidence that they are getting what they want. They may also want benefits or esteem in order to feel good about themselves, in which case we might say they are thirsty for approval or validation from others. They want to prove themselves. Third, there are people who don't believe or feel that they have some relatively basic modicum of worth or esteem, and who focus on getting approval or benefits to assuage their fear of being worthless or shameful. This illustrates the important point that self-centeredness need not always be driven by an overly high opinion of oneself.

With this rough overview of some aspects of self-centeredness in mind, we will be turning to Kant and then Buddhism and asking how we should normatively evaluate and overcome our all-too-human tendencies to be self-centered. But before doing that, it will be helpful to consider more carefully how our self-centeredness can impede our treating others as ends in themselves and our enjoying good relationships, which are key contributors to the good life.

First, being self-centered will often reduce one's tendency to empathize and empathize well with others. Someone with self-centered attention, for example, will have a reduced tendency to empathize simply because he or she will not notice others or what is happening to them. And even if one notices another person and how she is doing, self-centered judgment may inhibit the ability to empathize well. Returning to our Bill and Hilary example, we can imagine Bill noticing that Hilary is down but his misunderstanding what is making her upset and what might help her feel better because he can only think about how he would feel if he were in that situation. Or perhaps his thinking about things from her point of view would be distorted by his concern about how the new book about her will make *him* look and affect *his* popularity. Last, consider my Murdoch-inspired mother case. If the mother is thinking about the daughter-in-law as a crude and unrefined American, she may then think it would be best for the daughter-in-law to take night classes at a finishing school when she empathizes with the daughter. So even if her self-centered tendencies do not lead her to heartlessly not care about the daughter-in-law, it can distort her thinking about what would be best for the daughter-in-law.

These points about how self-centeredness affects our tendency to empathize and do it well support the claim that self-centeredness often impedes virtue, but they also remind us that being self-centered impedes our ability to develop and maintain healthy, reciprocal relationships. Unsupportive or otherwise "dysfunctional" relations between friends, parents and children, teachers and students, and so forth are often marred by self-centered negligence, reactivity, demands/needs, and subpar empathy, and the people who exhibit these tendencies fail to treat their partners as ends in themselves. Some forms of self-centeredness involve arrogance or self-conceit and this can lead people to *disrespect* others or to enable others to disrespect themselves. Other forms of self-centeredness involve failures to positively treat others as final ends—overly self-involved parents are notorious for *failing to love* and support their kids and for failing to nurture a nonneurotic sort of independence and confidence.[3]

Last, but not least, it is worth noting that self-centeredness can inhibit the achievement of so-called flow states. These are states in which an agent is pleasurably drawn on into a good activity for its own sake and is not caught up in thinking about what she is doing or how well she is doing it. Of course this is not a satisfying account of flow, but I hope that with only that much said we can see that someone who exhibits a self-centered tendency to worry about their self and whether it will get or merit esteem or praise will have a hard time dropping these hang-ups and getting into a flow state. If this is right, and flow states are very good for us, then being self-centered can be bad for us. In addition, if flow states are a part of many excellent joint activities and practices, as it seems plausible to assume, the self-centered impediments to flow threaten our ability to bond with others by participating in flow-fueled joint activities and practices.[4]

Kant and Self-Centeredness

Now that we have brought to mind some of the various ways in which people can be self-centered and noted some of ethical and prudential costs of self-centeredness, I want to turn to Kant and his account of treating people as final ends. We have seen that to treat others as ends in themselves one needs to overcome self-centeredness so we can test the adequacy of Kantian conceptions of treating people as final ends by considering what they can say about the cases discussed earlier.

To sharpen our discussion, we can narrow our focus to some variations on the Iris Murdoch example discussed earlier. The mother-in-law who initially judges her daughter-in-law to be impertinent and crude but then comes to see her as refreshingly forthright and unconventional gives us a good example of someone whose self-centered vice initially blocks her from positively treating another person as an end in herself, but who then shifts and is able to relate to this person in a more loving way. Murdoch's own discussion of the case suggests a broadly Platonic conception of positive moral motivation on which ethically well-motivated agents are moved by love of a transcendent Good to overcome their self-centered tendencies. She emphasizes that this involves (i) paying attention to people and situations as they really are and (ii) imagining others and their situations realistically, and in each case (when attending to what is directly present in experience and imaging what is not) Murdoch thinks we must exercise discipline in order to resist self-centered "fantasies." This presumably would involve resisting many of the more specific aspects of self-centeredness that we identified earlier.[5] Of course this sort of discipline does require a *willful* resistance to fantasy and *willed* attempts to attend and imagine realistically, but we should keep in mind that in Murdoch's account these willed activities are ultimately motivated by love of the Good—be it embodied in the full reality of some person to whom one attends, embodied in the noble and realistic vision that one aspires to achieve,[6] or understood along theistic lines.[7]

I mention Murdoch's love-of-the-Good conception of ethical motivation not in order to develop and assess it here, but because it provides a nice contrast to Kant's conception of treating people as final ends. The first thing to note is that Kant has no use for the concept of an attractive, lovable Good that motivates and justifies our struggles to overcome self-centeredness; for Kant, the two fundamental forms of value that move morally responsible agents are happiness and ethical goodness or worth, and good moral motivation is a matter of willing in a way that aptly responds to the objectively greater significance of ethical goodness. In developing this view, Kant connects the idea of ethical goodness with the idea of moral worth and argues that our conception of moral worth should be grounded in the idea of a moral and rational law that is binding on all agents, a law that human beings experience most clearly when it constrains their desire to be happy. Kant thinks that if we will in a way that is aptly responsive to the objective value or rational significance of the moral law, we thereby actualize our potential for rational freedom, and that we will also respect other people and their humanity as ends in themselves and not mere means. More concretely, Kant thought that people who will in a way that responds correctly to the moral law are bound to will benevolently (that is, will to promote others' welfare or happiness) and respect the dignity of persons; he holds that if we have a good will, which rightly adopts these ends, then we will treat other people, and their humanity, as ends in themselves.

Given the basic structure of his theory, there are two main ways that Kant could try to capture the ethical defects that show up when self-centered people fail to treat their friends, children, parents, and the like as ends in themselves. In general he holds that ethically culpable failures to treat others as final ends involve irrational forms of willing that do not aptly respond to the objective value and rational significance of the moral law, but in thinking about cases it is better to focus on the idea that self-centered people can fail to treat others as ends because they either fail to *respect* the other person's dignity or fail to treat the person in a *loving* way. By extension, Kant thinks that we can reorient our will and become well-motivated agents by adopting and acting on commitments to respect and love. But, in part because he believes that we are not ethically culpable for what is not under our volitional control, he argues that a well-motivated agent need only manifest *practical love*, roughly the intentional promotion of others' happiness or welfare, in order to treat others as ends. He contrasts this with *pathological love*, which would involve emotions or affects (*pathos*) that we cannot control at will, and holds that we treat persons as final ends if and only if we are willingly benevolent and respectful to persons. So to capture the thought that self-centered friends, parents, teachers, and the like often fail to treat others as ends and that a well-motivated Kantian person will do better, Kant must argue that the relevant self-centered people are either not respectful or not practically loving in the way that a well-motivated Kantian person would be.[8]

Returning to Murdoch's example of the judgmental mother-in-law with this background in mind, we need to ask whether she is plausibly thought of as failing to respect the dignity that her daughter-in-law has in virtue of her powers of rational reflection and end-setting, and whether her change of heart can be aptly understood as her adopting the Kantian ends of benevolence and respect with respect to her daughter-in-law. Before we directly answer that question, however, it will be useful to think about Kant's account of ethically defective motivation or vice and how this might explain the motivation behind the mother-in-law's initial, self-centered verdict. In short, Kant holds that all culpable moral failures reflect an agent's disordered will. More specifically, he thinks that moral failures always result from a decision to comply with morality only if doing so is compatible with pursuit of one's happiness; he thinks immorality always traces back to a merely conditional commitment to act morally, where the condition is compatibility with one's happiness. Given this background, Kant would explain the mother-in-law judging her daughter-in-law to be crude and impertinent by appeal to her conditional commitment to morality and the fact that her concern for her own happiness is what leads her to make this judgment. More generally, Kant would explain self-centered vice by appeal to the fact that self-centeredness is motivated by the agent's concern for her happiness.

At first glance it might seem implausible to claim that the mother-in-law's self-centered judgment is motivated by a desire for happiness, because, as noted earlier, being self-centered is often at odds with one's self-interest. For example, the mother-in-law's judgment is presumably part of a larger pattern that may strain her relationship with her son and her daughter-in-law and that may cause her significant grief. Regardless of one's conception of personal well-being, it is plausible to think that her self-centeredness and its expression in this judgment may be quite bad for her because it detracts from the quality of her experiences and her relationships. By extension, it is implausible to think that agents who are self-centered, and for that reason fail to treat others as ends in themselves, must always believe that they will gain benefits by being self-centered or by making specific self-centered judgments.

I believe that the foregoing points are correct, but it is important to note that Kant has further resources on which to draw. The challenge at hand is to explain how self-centeredness could be grounded in the desire for happiness, so it will presumably help to focus in on what Kant says about happiness and the immoral (Kant says "evil") temptation to act in accord with the moral law only if doing so is compatible with one's pursuit of happiness. Now Kant's claims about happiness are somewhat opaque and underdeveloped, but three things are clear. First, he thinks that the desire for happiness centrally involves the desires to feel content with one's condition and to feel pleased with oneself. Second, he holds that happiness is an indeterminate and moving target—it lies beyond our powers to form a rational conception of it that could guide our deliberations or modes of activity. Third, Kant holds that our *rational* capacities actually make it harder for us to be happy and that awareness of this fact can tempt us to hate our rational capacities and wish that we were less reflective, like nonrational animals. We can usefully reconstruct Kant's way of thinking about the desire for happiness if we keep these three basic points in mind and consider how the moral-psychological views that Kant develops in his later works can support and elucidate them.

In *Religion Within the Limits of Reason Alone*, *The Metaphysics of Morals*, and other late works and lectures, Kant develops a nuanced account of the various types of desires that human beings have, discusses which desires typically tempt people to adopt a merely conditional commitment to being moral, and develops psychologically substantive accounts of good moral motivation, moral improvement, and virtue. First, he distinguishes three types of desires that are rooted in three basic "predispositions" that he takes to be innate. He associates unreflective bodily desires that do not depend on our capacity to reason, for example, hunger, thirst, and sexual desire, with the predisposition to animality, but he denies that these desires are the ones that motivate people to be immoral. Instead, he points the finger at the desires that he associates with the predisposition to humanity. These are desires that depend on our capacity to reason, but they do not include respect for the moral law, which Kant takes to be an especially pure rational motive, and he associates it with the separate predisposition to personality. Given this typology it makes sense to think that happiness involves contentment and that this involves satisfaction of one's animal desires (for food, water, sex, sleep, and so forth), but if we want to understand how the desire for happiness motivates people to be immoral, why Kant thinks happiness is an indeterminate and moving target, and why Kant thinks reason makes it hard for us to be happy, we need to focus on the distinctively rational desires that Kant associates with the predisposition to humanity.

Kant clearly thinks that human desires are based in reason in a way that animal desires are not, and while it is not entirely clear what "reason" means in this context or in what sense the desires are based in reason, Kant seems to be thinking that our human reason enables us to be self-aware, to compare our condition with that of others, and to be aware of how others judge us. Without going into unnecessary detail, we can note some of the central ways that exercise of these capacities could affect our conception of happiness (in addition to affecting who strongly we are motivated by considerations of happiness).

Most simply, rational comparison with others and awareness of their judgments of our condition can affect what we want and how content we are with what we have. So our degree of contentment with our condition can depend on how others around us are faring and how they judge our condition—factors that are out of our control, subject to regular change, and hard to predict. Next, probably under the influence of Rousseau, Kant notes that interpersonal comparison and self-awareness lead human beings to care a lot about how others judge *them* and their relative status. For example, even if someone envies your *condition* you may feel discontent because she thinks *you* have a bad or flawed character that makes you a fit target for mockery or denigration (or that just causes her to reduce her degree of good will toward you). More generally, whether we are pleased with ourselves is often affected by what others think of us and by how we fare relative to the social conventions that we embrace or that are embraced by those whose approval we care about. Moreover there is often a competitive aspect in play here, as people jockey for social status and prestige, with people kissing up to those above them and kicking down their peers and rising underlings. These factors all introduce new reasons for our happiness to be out of our control, subject to regular change, and hard to predict.

The foregoing remarks about how Kant thinks of our distinctively human desires are no doubt schematic, but I think they also help us understand Kant's claims about happiness being an indeterminate and moving target and about reason making it harder for us to be happy. Presumably Kant is thinking that human happiness is indeterminate and moving because our contentment and self-satisfaction are affected by various contingent, unpredictable factors, such as those just canvassed, and he thinks these features persist because our contentment and self-satisfaction are largely staked on our success or failure in fulfilling our human, rationally based desires. If we had only animal desires, our contentment and self-satisfaction would hinge on factors that are easier to control and predict, so we can see how these reflections might lead one to hate one's reason or humanity.

Now that we have a better grasp of Kant's conception of the human desire for happiness, we can turn to his claim that it is the specifically human desires, not the animal ones, that motivate us to immoral action, and to his idea that respect for the law motivates a moral agent by striking down her self-conceit and curbing her self-love. Simply put, Kant thinks that the human desire for happiness, especially the desire to be pleased with oneself, leads some people to think they are more worthy of respect than others or that they are more deserving of happiness than others because of their nonmoral excellences. Alternatively, the desire to be pleased with oneself can lead one to disrespect oneself or another, either in order to gain social esteem or approval or because oneself or the other person has some nonmoral defects. Those desires tempt us to disrespect people or treat them in a nonbenevolent manner in order to further our pursuit of happiness, and Kant holds that our inherent respect for the moral law, which is associated with our predisposition to personality, can motivate us to resist these temptations and to choose to pursue our happiness only if in doing so we are able to treat people respectfully and benevolently. To reign in our natural desire for happiness in this way, however, we must make our pursuit of happiness conditional on our adherence to morality rather than vice versa.

With this Kantian model of immorality and moral motivation in mind, we can now return to our guiding question and ask how this model might apply to the self-centered mother-in-law who judges her daughter-in-law to be crude and impertinent. Murdoch holds that these judgments are false and reflect the mother-in-laws' bad (mean or vicious) motives or character. She also holds that love of the Good can move the woman to become aware of those facts and improve. Our question now concerns what Kant could say in this case. Despite the lack of any explicit discussion of such cases by Kant, it is hard to see how he could accept Murdoch's claim that the mother-in-law's initial judgment was false and that her later judgment was true. Kant does hold that there are non-relative evaluative facts about what has *moral worth* and what does not, but he does not have any clear resources for building a nonconventionalist, nonrelativist account of judgments like the one that the mother-in-law makes (for example, about whether someone's behavior is crude). Still, Kant could adopt a conventionalist and relativist view when it comes to such judgments and still hold that the mother-in-law's change in view is an instance of moral improvement. First, he could argue that the daughter-in-law is crude and impertinent relative to the social standards that the mother-in-law's peers embrace but that she is *also* refreshingly youthful and unconventional from the point of view of someone who rejects those standards and embraces more romantic ones.

Second, he could argue that while both standard-relative claims about the daughter-in-law are *true*, it is morally or ethically better for the mother-in-law to make, and approach the situation in the light of, the second, more romantic judgment.

To establish that the mother-in-law's self-centered judgment is morally worse than her revised one, the Kantian will presumably argue that the initial judgment is motivated by her desire for happiness but that it involves either disrespect or a lack of benevolence. The first part of this proposed explanation is plausible. The basic idea would be that the mother-in-law judges her daughter-in-law to be crude and impertinent because her own happiness hinges to a significant extent on how the daughter-in-law fares relative to the social standards against which those judgments are framed.[9] It is natural to imagine that the mother-in-law cares a lot about the approval or judgment of her peers who embrace those standards and that she will be less pleased with herself and her condition if her daughter-in-law provokes her peers to look down their noses at her or pity her. And the mother-in-law may have herself internalized the relevant standards and feel ashamed to have such a daughter-in-law or at least feel sorry for herself in that condition. As this case illustrates, concern for happiness, understood in the Kantian way I have sketched, does often motivate self-centeredness because it often motivates us to worry about how our self and our condition compares with and will be judged by others. The standards relative to which we will be judged are often set by others' judgments, by social competitions for status or recognition, by collectively evolving expressions of approval or esteem, and so forth. It makes sense that one would be anxious about these factors because they are constantly changing, involve competition, and are hard to control and predict; and this anxiety presumably often motivates self-centeredness in all of its various forms.

I think we should grant that self-centeredness is characteristically based in a Kantian desire for happiness in something like the way I just suggested, but this is only the first part of the story that Kantians need to tell. They have a plausible account of what motivates self-centered vice, but they also need to explain why it counts as vice and they need to show that an ethically good person, who embodies their conception of good moral motivation, will not exhibit self-centered vice. To accomplish these tasks, the Kantian must argue that in cases like Murdoch's the person's self-centeredness is at odds with her duties to treat others respectfully and benevolently. And this is where I think the Kantian argument falters. To see why, we can helpfully attend to relevant details of the Kantian response to Murdoch developed by Bagnoli (2003). As she mentions, Kant's central example of respect striking down an out-of-line desire for happiness involves someone who is arrogant and *self-conceited*.

Self-conceited people come in two grades, but they all have a high opinion of themselves and believe, or act as if they believe, that their needs, desires, and projects are more important than others' because of their greater personal worth. We can think of a CEO or famous painter who thinks that it is more important for him to have his coffee just as he likes it than for his intern to get through the day without being harshly told to remake the coffee because his desire to feel good at work is more important than hers (because he is a great man and she is a mere intern). Someone who is self-conceited in this sense thinks *he* has more reason to satisfy, and focus on the satisfaction of, his own desires and projects than others, and he presumably thinks that the same is true of *others*. This does not by itself settle, however, how he thinks of and reacts to others who do not treat his desires and needs as more important. Some self-conceited people may simply think that others are too stupid, blind, or crude to appreciate their greater worth, while others may *demand* that others recognize their greater worth. For example, the CEO may think he has the authority to demand that the intern recognize his greatness and stop complaining after he yells at her. In addition, in some cases conceited people act as if their worth provides reasons for others to forgo their *happiness* and in other cases they act as if their worth provides reasons for others to put up with vicious treatment and sacrifice their *self-respect*. For example, a CEO who yells at his intern for not getting his latte right is one thing, but a CEO who expects his interns to put up with sexual harassment is another. They might both act as if their great worth makes their desires more important than others and demand that others treat them accordingly but the former CEO is less bad because he does not expect others to put up with vicious treatment and sacrifice their self-respect.

Kant thinks that respect for the dignity of persons and the moral law strikes down self-conceit because this respect reflects a recognition that while we are naturally inclined to pursue our own happiness and that is perfectly rational, it is *never* rational to think that we have some sort of personal worth that gives others reason to disrespect themselves (let alone that this is something we have the authority to demand of others). The self-conceited CEO who expects his intern to put up with sexual harassment would be acting rationally if his high social and economic status or power made his desires so important that the intern had reason to sacrifice her self-respect in order to help satisfy them, but this supposition is false because the intern has a rationally compelling duty to treat herself with self-respect and to stand up to his insulting behavior. Moreover, the Kantian can help us understand why harassment is insulting; it implies that the person being harassed does not deserve respect when they most certainly do in virtue of their powers of rational reflection and end-setting.

While this Kantian story about how respect for dignity and the moral law can correct arrogant self-conceit is promising, I don't think that it applies to all of the relevant cases of self-centered vice. For example, the mother-in-law's initial judgment may well be based on her concern for her happiness, but it need not involve any form of self-conceit. The mother-in-law may be quite firmly committed to respecting her daughter-in-law's dignity and merely be upset about, and caught up in, how poorly her new relation fares relative to the social norms that loom large in her social circles and mental life. She need not, furthermore, think that the daughter-in-law is worthy of contempt or that she may be treated cruelly because she is crude and impertinent; perhaps the mother just does not want her son to be married to this woman and greatly dislikes being around her. She might even defend the woman's moral right to live however she wants and deny that there is anything morally bad about her; she just very strongly wants her son be married to someone else and finds it painful to be around a daughter-in-law that she dislikes and finds embarrassing. In my view this just illustrates that self-centered people can fail to treat others as ends in themselves without thereby disrespecting them.

In addition to these doubts about whether the mother-in-law's initial judgment is disrespectful, we should note that Kant will have a hard time explaining how respect for the law can motivate the mother-in-law to adopt her second judgment. Murdoch can sensibly hold that love of the Good will motivate the mother-in-law to judge the daughter-in-law to be refreshingly youthful and unconventional, because love can move one to focus on the standards against which people and their actions look good and because she thinks love motivates us to see people as they really are. It is hard to see, however, how respect for the moral law or the daughter-in-law would require or motivate the mother-in-law to view the daughter-in-law in the light of some more romantic standard. After all, that is presumably not a standard that the mother-in-law otherwise embraces or that is embraced by the people whose approval the mother-in-law cares about. Moreover, that romantic standard is not one that respect requires us to use whenever we are forming our opinions of people and their conduct; presumably in some other context the mother-in-law could judge that someone else is crude and unrefined relative to her upper-crust social standards, and that would not be morally bad on Kant's account. For example, she might make that judgment of her recently arrived cousin from America and then give the newcomer benevolent pointers about how to change her ways and achieve the social success she desires. In this case it would be very odd to think that respect requires the woman to change her judgments and focus on the romantic judgments that render her less able to help her cousin navigate the social ladder in her new land.

We have considered a version of Murdoch's case in which the mother-in-law sticks with her initial judgment, fails to treat the daughter-in-law as an end in herself, exhibits self-centered vice, and yet is motivated by a Kantian desire for happiness (she wants to be pleased by her self, as that is reflected in the eyes of her social circle). As we have seen, this mother-in-law can be regarded as possessing a Kantian good will because she treats the daughter-in-law with respect and benevolently wishes that she ends up happy (albeit *elsewhere*). If this is correct, then we can conclude that good Kantian moral motivation is insufficient for treating people as ends in themselves.

Buddhism

Having pressed my worries about the adequacy of Kant's conception of treating people as final ends, I want to devote this last section to Buddhist philosophy and the prospects it holds for developing a more adequate conception.

One initial point is that although Buddhism traces suffering to belief in the self and attachment based on that belief, it is unclear whether this view has anything to say about self-centeredness. On one standard telling, the Buddhist doctrine of no-self centrally involves denial that there is a temporally enduring (or extended) self or subject that would figure in an account of personal identity across time. Once we realize this fact and take it to heart, the story goes, we will, on pain of irrationality, no longer care more about the future and past states that we would conventionally call "ours" than about the states that are conventionally attributed to other people.[10] Now even if this were true and it could lead us to become radically altruistic, it is not clear that it tells us anything about self-centeredness. As we have seen, selfishness and self-centeredness are distinct, and since this Buddhist argument aims at eliminating any sense of self, it does not seem amenable to accommodating any morally significant distinction between these two concerns. Of course if self-centeredness causes suffering and we are radical altruists, we will aim to eradicate it, but one can imagine circumstances where self-centeredness will be beneficial and then a radical altruistic Buddhist might promote it.[11] This just underscores the main point: that the no-personal-identity-across-time version of the Buddhist doctrine of no-self does not seem to support any claim about self-centered vice being a particular moral failing, resulting from a false belief about the self.

In what remains of this chapter, I turn to some other Buddhist ideas, or at least attributed views, that might be more relevant to thinking about what is wrong with self-centeredness. Specifically I have in mind Zen views of nonduality, emptiness, and without-thinking. Although his interpretations are no doubt contentious, I will take my bearings here from T. P. Kasulis's book *Zen Action, Zen Person*. There are two key ideas that I will take from this book. First, a three-way distinction between thinking, not-thinking, and without-thinking found in Dōgen. Second, the idea that Dōgen's concept of without-thinking can be fruitfully understood as combining Madhyamaka views about emptiness and the limits of conceptual thinking with Daoist ideas. Roughly, Kasulis argues that we need first to appreciate that our conceptual self-understanding is always limited and then to attempt to achieve some sort of nonconceptual self-appreciation that we can use as a basis for action.

Kasulis's Dōgen holds that not-thinking, thinking, and without-thinking are different ways in which we can we engage in activities, and that when we are engaged in the without-thinking mode we are in touch with our most fundamental or true nature, which cannot be conceptually described or understood. Of course if we think about what we are doing, have done, or will do, we will be deploying concepts and Kasulis holds that this will inevitably involve our distorting or limiting our appreciation of the relevant activities and what we are most fundamentally like. He does not think the solution is to think more and improve our concepts, as if there were a more complete account that would allow us fully to appreciate our activities or ourselves. Kasulis tries to mount an argument that this is in principle impossible, which I find unconvincing, but I think we can shelve that issue and simply grant that it is practically impossible and imprudent to try to achieve full propositional knowledge of all of the most subtle aspects of our activities or selves; we should accept that our propositional self-understanding is always bound to be partial and limited.

According to Kasulis's Dōgen, we need to be constantly reminded of the limits of our propositional self-understanding, and then be encouraged to try to achieve some sort of nonpropositional self-appreciation. This is not easy to do and it might be tempting to try to achieve this by inhibiting conceptual, propositional thought—by making our minds blank. But this aspiration to achieve a state of *not-thinking* is, the argument runs, no wiser than aspiring to achieve full and complete propositional self-understanding. If one aims to appreciate the nature of the sky after realizing that the clouds are not the sky, it is not a good strategy to spend all one's time working to clear the sky of clouds. Instead one should presumably learn to appreciate the sky directly.

Now I don't want to get bogged down in confusing questions about how to achieve this appreciation (of what is already present but unappreciated). Instead, I want to focus on Kasulis's claim that *without-thinking* is the mode of activity that obtains when one "achieves" the "goal" and appreciates one's true nature while being engaged in an activity. One might still be having propositional thoughts while in this mode, but one does not take them to be capturing the full nature of one's activities or experiences.

I am rehearsing all of these ideas drawn from Dōgen because I think they provide one way of understanding oneness and the way it might help us overcome self-centeredness. I say that achieving the mode of without-thinking can be thought of as involving insight into oneness for two reasons. First, because it is said to involve overcoming the assumption that our true nature can be understood propositionally and this entails overcoming the assumption that we can adequately be understood as subjects who bear propositional attitudes.

Second, Buddhist insight is supposed to involve seeing past the dualism of subject and object in the sense that when we attain a mode of without-thinking we appreciate that we are not separate from our environment in the way that propositional thought suggests. Sometimes Zen teachers talk explicitly in this context about our achieving insight into our identity with the environment or things in it, but I do not currently see how to understand these claims propositionally.[12]

In any case, my final goal here is to say something about how Buddhist insight into oneness—Buddhist appreciation of one's true nature—might help us overcome self-centeredness. To lead up to that, I am going to have to speculate some more about Buddhist insight into oneness and its internalization. The first thing to point out is that if we accept the Buddhist view then we should think we are disposed to make two mistakes. First, we are disposed to form propositional beliefs about our experiences and to assume that these are adequate. Second, we are disposed to form propositional beliefs about ourselves and to believe that they are adequate. In each case, we have to recognize the error of our ways and work to appreciate the fact that our experiences and self elude any sort of adequate propositional understanding. However, when it comes to the second mistake—the belief that our propositional beliefs about the self are adequate—there seems to be a special kind of error. When we form beliefs about ourselves, we use concepts and form judgments that fail to capture the whole truth about their object, but we also assume that we are selves of the sort that figure in the judgments. For example, if Jane is upset because her friends think she is a loser and she suspects she is, then she assumes that she is someone—a self—who could be a winner or a loser relative to whatever standard her friends are deploying. Moreover, she cares about how this self fares relative to those standards; she may thirst for success and feel an intense aversion to failure.

I believe that Buddhist insight into oneness is supposed to reveal that one is not a self of the sort that figures in judgments like "Jane is a loser" and that internalization of this insight would involve uprooting the tendencies to think, act, and feel as if one were a self of that sort. This would presumably change the content of one's experience, for example, by modifying the efficacy (if not undercutting the existence) of self-interpreting emotions such as pride and shame,[13] but I think it might also undercut self-centered vice of the sort that we have been discussing. To see why, recall the story that was recounted earlier about how the Kantian desire for happiness could explain most cases of self-centered vice. The Kantian story emphasizes that our human concern for happiness centrally involves a desire to reach contentment with our selves and that this involves caring about how we fare relative to social norms and how others judge us. Against this backdrop we could say that, on the Buddhist view, insight into oneness could undercut self-centered vice because it would undercut the all-too-human desire to reach contentment with our *selves* where those are understood as the things that figure in the judgments that others make of us and that also figure in our self-interpreting emotions. The basic idea is that those selves are socially and conceptually constructed fictions and that it is a mistake to think they are real and to identify with them. This leaves room for Buddhists to still hold that there are persons or selves in some other sense, and Buddhist teachers do often talk about the Big or Real self that is discovered upon internalization of insight.[14]

Finally, I think that the more simple Buddhist insight into the limits of one's propositional understanding of oneself, one's experiences, and other people should help mitigate the problems of self-centered judgment and attention I identified in the first section. If one knows that one's propositional understanding is limited and is working to mitigate this fact and achieve without-thinking modes of activity, one is presumably more likely to notice that one is only thinking about some aspects of one's environment. And if one is thinking of others, one is presumably disposed to doubt that one's judgments are adequately capturing what others are like.

To end, I want to mention how the Zen Buddhist–inspired view I have sketched suggests a different way of overcoming blinkered interpretations of others than the one that Iris Murdoch famously suggests. In the case of the mother and the daughter-in-law mentioned earlier, Murdoch suggests that the mother will be able to overcome her prejudiced interpretation of the daughter-in-law as crude and impertinent by carefully attending to the daughter-in-law's actual behavior and viewing it justly and lovingly. This will lead her, Murdoch suggests, to thinking the daughter-in-law is refreshingly unconventional.

On the Zen view, however, this would still look like a mistake. It is simply replacing one fundamentally inadequate view of the daughter-in-law with another fundamentally inadequate one, and it would be better to see that no propositional evaluation of the daughter-in-law will be fully adequate. Moreover, on the Zen view, as I have sketched it, it is simply a mistake for the mother to think of the daughter-in-law who figures in her experiences as a self that could figure in judgments like "she is crude and impertinent." Assuming that she is unenlightened this is indeed how the daughter-in-law thinks of herself and she probably has a desire to reach contentment with herself. But on the Buddhist view this desire and the suffering it generates are the result of an erroneous assumption,[15] so if the mother-in-law internalizes insight, her way of relating to the daughter-in-law will not be shaped by beliefs about what kind of self she has. To advance further, we would have to consider the idea that to treat the daughter-in-law as an end in herself the mother must relate to her in ways that will help her achieve insight, and think about whether the mother will do this necessarily and naturally if she achieves insight. But these will have to remain topics for another occasion.

Notes

1. The narcissism illustrated in this example highlights the way that an unrealistic and unhealthy conception of the self can be both bad for the narcissist and a source of moral failure. Interesting studies of narcissism in contemporary American culture, which are sensitive to these issues, include Twenge and Campbell 2010 and Lasch 1991.

2. Murdoch 1985.

3. For an interesting survey of different forms of neurosis, see Horney 1991. Horney was interested in Zen Buddhism and may have been influenced by it in developing her conception of the "real self" that one must develop in order to overcome neuroses.

4. For interesting discussions of fading self-centeredness and its benefits, see Ivanhoe 2010 and 2011 and Leary 2004.

5. Murdoch also mentions the need to resist the influence of social norms and prejudices, but there is dispute about whether she had a realistic sense of how pervasive their influence is or whether her account provides a helpful way of thinking about how to resist the influence of norms and prejudices. See Blum 2012, Holland 2012, and Clarke 2012.

6. Murdoch thought we could get a grasp on the noble appeal of clear vision and the struggle to achieve it by reflecting on the analogous struggles that artists, philosophers, and scientists must undergo to produce beautiful and insightful works or to discover and justify conclusions or theories.

7. Adams (2002) provides the most worked-out theistic conception that fits much of what Murdoch says in her essays.

8. I am just granting for the sake of argument that Kant's wide duty of benevolence generates a specific duty to treat one's friends, loved ones, and so on benevolently. Kant's conceptions of wide and imperfect duties are hard to understand but most interpreters seem to agree that the duty of beneficence is not a duty to *maximally* promote *every* person's happiness (within the bounds of respect). For debate about relevant interpretive issues, see Baron 1995 and Cummiskey 1996.

9. In the real world our motives are of course more complex and our judgments and actions may be overdetermined. Real world narcissists may be motivated by inapt concern for their own standing or happiness *and* the welfare of their loved ones, and we might imagine the mother-in-law in a Murdoch-inspired example in this way too. In this discussion I am focusing on a pure narcissist who is motivated only by her concern for her happiness, not by concern for her son or her family.

10. See, for example, Goodman 2009.

11. Julia Driver's consequentialist virtue theory implies that self-centeredness could be a virtue for this reason and presumably, as a Buddhist consequentialist, Goodman would be sympathetic to her view.

12. An example is Thich Nhat Hahn's claim in *The Miracle of Mindfulness* that insight into nonduality should lead us to think, on seeing a bird flying in the sky, "That bird is me." Perhaps we should interpret these utterances expressively, that is, as not making propositional claims but as expressions of nonpropositional insight. One's experience of seeing the bird is presumably partially constituted by the bird's flight and nonpropositional insight involves appreciation of one's experience and the ways it transcends propositional description, so perhaps saying "That bird is me" is a way of expressing awareness of some aspects of experience that are misrepresented when we think about ourselves as subjects that are independent of, and the bearers of, experiences.

13. It is worth mentioning in this context, however, that contemporary Buddhists have had trouble dealing with people who have a fragile and negative sense of self-worth and this is one of the things that has led to calls to combine Buddhism with psychoanalysis. So even if, in principle, internalized Buddhist insight into oneness should undercut tendencies to believe one is a self that is shameful, it may be that this insight is not psychologically accessible to people with such tendencies, and that Buddhist practices of cultivating insight may therefore be ineffective at reducing such people's self-centeredness.

14. For example, see Kosho Uchiyama 2005 and Shunryu Suzuki 2010.

15. For example, the suffering that Kant thinks can lead us to hate our humanity and wish we were more like brute animals.

References

Adams, Robert Merrihew. 2002. *Finite and Infinite Goods: A Framework for Ethics.* Oxford: Oxford University Press.

Bagnoli, Carla. 2003. "Respect and Loving Attention." *Canadian Journal of Philosophy* 33 (4): 483–515.

Baron, Marcia. 1995. Kantian Ethics Almost Without Apology Cornell: Cornell University Press.

Blum, Lawrence. 2012. "Visual Metaphors in Iris Murdoch's Moral Philosophy." In Broackes 2012.

Broackes, Justin, ed. 2012. *Iris Murdoch, Philosopher: A Collection of Essays.* Oxford: Oxford University Press.

Clarke, Bridget. 2012. "Iris Murdoch and the Prospects for Critical Moral Perception." In Broackes 2012.

Cummiskey, David. 1996. *Kantian Consequentialism.* Oxford: Oxford University Press.

Driver, Julia. 2001. *Uneasy Virtue.* Cambridge: Cambridge University Press.

Goodman, Charles. 2009. *Consequences of Compassion: An Interpretation and Defense of Buddhist Ethics.* Oxford: Oxford University Press.

Hanh, Thich Nhat, and Dinh Mai Vo. 1987. *The Miracle of Mindfulness: An Introduction to the Practice of Meditation.* Boston: Beacon.

Holland, Margaret. 2012. "Social Convention and Neurosis as Obstacles to Moral Freedom." In Broackes 2012.

Horney, Karen. 1991. *Neurosis and Human Growth: The Struggle Towards Self-Realization.* 2nd ed. New York: Norton.

Ivanhoe, Philip J. 2010. "The Values of Spontaneity." In *Taking Confucian Ethics Seriously: Contemporary Theories and Applications,* edited by Yu Kam-por, Julia Tao, and Philip J. Ivanhoe, 183–207. Albany: State University of New York Press.

——. 2011. "The Theme of Unselfconsciousness in the *Liezi*." In *Riding the Wind with Liezi: New Essays on the Daoist Classic,* edited by Ronnie Littlejohn and Jeffrey Dippmann, 129–52. Albany: State University of New York Press.

——. 2013. "Senses and Values of Oneness." In *The Philosophical Challenge from China,* edited by Brian Bruya. Cambridge: MIT Press.

Kasulis, Thomas P. 1985. *Zen Action, Zen Person.* Honolulu: University of Hawaii Press.

Kosho Uchiyama. 2005. *Opening the Hand of Thought: Foundations of Zen Buddhist Practice.* Somerville, MA: Wisdom.

Lasch, Christopher. 1991. *The Culture of Narcissism: American Life in an Age of Diminishing Expectations*. Rev. ed. New York: Norton.

Leary, Mark R. 2004. *The Curse of the Self: Self-Awareness, Egotism, and the Quality of Human Life*. New York: Oxford University Press.

Murdoch, Iris. 1985. *The Sovereignty of Good*. London: Ark, Routledge and Kegan Paul.

Suzuki, Shunryu. 2010. *Zen Mind, Beginner's Mind*. Boston: Shambhala.

Twenge, Jean M., and W. Keith Campbell. 2010 *The Narcissism Epidemic: Living in the Age of Entitlement*. New York: Free Press.

CHAPTER 9

FRACTURED WHOLES

Corporate Agents and Their Members

KENDY M. HESS

The very word *whole* carries a kind of normative force. Making something whole is presumptively good and right, a return to a natural state, and this aura of goodness surrounds many of the discussions of unity and oneness. Wholeness, unity, oneness—they all sound so lovely. Wholesome, in every sense of the word. And yet we unite around fear and hatred as easily as we unite around love and compassion—perhaps more easily, and certainly more reliably—and wholes can be created and maintained by violence. We can simply stipulate that "oneness" (and "wholeness" and "unity" and all the rest) is *only* good, that it's a misuse of the words to use them in reference to anything ugly or violent, but then we're just arguing about semantics. I want to look at the facts, and the fact is that we *can* come together around ugly purposes and under ugly circumstances in order to perform ugly, violent actions. The unity of a whole does not guarantee anything good. There are ways of forming wholes and "being one" that are not wholesome, and these are increasingly common and increasingly problematic.

In this essay, I want to look at one particular version of this: the way in which we come together to create new social "wholes"—the collectives that are increasingly identified as "corporate agents." The modern business entity is the paradigm of the type, but they arise in other contexts as well. The agents we create this way tend to be large, powerful, and productive, but also remarkably destructive and apparently indifferent to the harmful impacts associated with their productivity. Much of my work has focused on arguing that there's nothing *necessary* about this, that we can and should come together to create corporate agents that are more sensitive to externalities and more prone to avoid them. I generally talk about them as moral agents bound by moral obligations, but in a sense I guess I've been arguing that we should finish what we've started, creating "wholesome wholes" rather than the incomplete and fractured wholes we've usually created thus far. What I want to look at here, though, goes beyond the fractured wholes we create to the fractured selves that we use to create them.

First, I will introduce the idea of corporate agent. I will not argue for any of the claims outlined here, or address criticisms (of which there are many). Instead, I will simply provide a brief history and outline some of the basic claims to give the reader a sense of the position, taking my own account as a model. With that shared understanding of "corporate agents" in place, we can move on to some of the mechanics by which we generally create and maintain them. The most important of these mechanisms is the demand for "professional" behavior, which has come to imply behavior that is rational, goal-oriented, and unaffected by other concerns.[1] It is, essentially, a demand for a fractured self. Next, I will quickly consider some of the costs of approaching the creation of corporate agents in this way. It is difficult to say who has suffered more from this practice: the people inside the corporate agent, who have to leave so much of themselves behind in order to participate, or the people outside the corporate agent who experience the often unrestrained impacts of its pursuit of its goals.[2] One obvious way to address the costs of using fractured selves to creature fractured wholes is to stop the fracturing, to demand that members bring their "whole selves" to the corporate agents and let that remedy the analogous "fractures" that mark the corporate whole. Next, however, I discuss how this obvious solution runs into problems of its own. I tentatively and rather reluctantly conclude that we can better address the fractures of the corporate agent by an external, "technical" fix, and that the members themselves are ultimately better off "fractured." The best option there is an ameliorative compassion.

Corporate Agents

The history of Western moral theory is overwhelmingly individualistic. This is especially true after the Enlightenment; even before that time, however, the paradigmatic moral action was that of a rational, autonomous agent facing a rather sharply defined scenario, contemplating alternatives, and then choosing on the basis of any of a number of different principles. Moral obligations are understood as belonging to individuals and directed at individuals, and responsibility is bound up in individual choice. The moral agent has responsibilities regarding other agents, of course, but she is not responsible *for* them (except in the most unusual of cases) and is certainly not responsible for what *they* might do. The fact that "someone else did it" is almost always exculpatory.

Beginning in the mid-1900s, however, we start to see an increasing recognition that groups occupy a significant niche in the moral landscape.[3] Groups often do things that no individual did, or indeed could have done, and these actions are often morally significant: storming the Bastille, for example, or committing genocide. In many cases, these actions cannot be comfortably "reduced" to the disparate actions of the individual members because the various contributing actions are so profoundly interwoven and interdependent, both in practice and in purpose. There were, of course, innumerable individual actions that went into storming the Bastille or perpetrating the Holocaust, but many theorists argue that the simple recitation of those individual actions fails to adequately capture the fullness of the event that was "storming the Bastille" or "perpetrating the Holocaust." To do that, we have to talk about "the group"—now, "the collective"—in its own right, recognizing it as something more (or other) than just the individuals who make it up.

Theorists who fall into this camp are called collectivists (as opposed to "individualists"), and there's been an enormous amount of work over the last sixty to seventy years or so to try to adequately theorize these kinds of collectives and the "collective actions" in which they engage. Much of that work has focused on the question of moral responsibility in collective contexts. Most of the literature on collective responsibility has focused on backward-looking issues like blame, debating the extent and grounds upon which moral responsibility for past collective actions can be "distributed" to the members of the collective, and whether there is a remainder that belongs to the collective itself. A smaller portion of the literature has focused on forward-looking issues about whether and how a collective might have a moral obligation to act in certain ways. Underlying the moral issues are the metaphysical questions of *when* a group of people form a collective—a significant new thing in the world—and what kind of unity must obtain before there is a new whole. While theorists have differed, the overwhelming consensus has gathered around "shared intentions."[4] These come in a variety of flavors and go by a number of different names, but the general idea is that a group forms a whole when the members share certain mental states: beliefs, ends, intentions, sometimes a certain understanding of themselves as unified in certain ways. Classic examples include two people moving a couch, the members of an orchestra performing a symphony, or spectators at a sports event doing "the wave." A group of people waiting at a bus stop is not likely to form a collective in this sense, as there is no shared purpose or shared understanding of themselves *as unified*. They may know that they are "unified" in a certain sense—they know they're all waiting at the same bus stop—but this knowledge carries no significance for them. It does not unite them, or lead them to act as a unity. If we looked inside their heads, they wouldn't "match" the way the couple moving the couch, the orchestra, or the fans doing the wave would "match." On these theories, the unity that establishes the collective as a "whole" is an intimate one, built from shared personal understandings and commitments, and the collective action that issues from it closely tracks the shared preferences of the members.

More recently (starting in the 1980s), a group of scholars has begun arguing that there is another kind of collective that can't be understood or approached in this way. In fact, the shift is sufficiently recent that scholars are just now beginning to acknowledge that this *is* "a different kind of collective"—that the differing descriptions are not disagreements about one thing, but accurate descriptions of two different things. The terminology is unsettled, but the literature seems to be moving toward identifying the other kind of collectives as "corporate agents."[5] A corporate agent is (usually) a large, highly organized collective—something with established hierarchies, practices, and culture that endures through massive (even complete) changes in membership. Typical examples include universities and colleges, governments, religious orders, branches of the military, and of course business entities, whether legally incorporated or not. In what follows I will generally talk about "firms," because it is the business entities that I am most familiar with and most concerned with, but the claims made apply to corporate agents wherever they are found.

Corporate agents have a number of distinctive characteristics that set them apart from other collectives, but the most significant is the fact that their behavior is governed by a set of commitments that is not necessarily shared by their members. These "commitments" include basic commitments of fact and value—commitments about how the world is and what matters—as well as larger commitments to long-term goals. Thus, it is possible to have a corporate agent that is committed to environmental responsibility while being made up entirely of members who couldn't care less about the environment; similarly (and more familiarly), it is possible to have a corporate agent committed to "maximizing profit at any cost" made up of members who do not, in fact, want to maximize profit at any cost.[6] There are a number of mechanisms by which this divergence almost invariably comes about,[7] but what I want to point out here is the simple *fact* of this divergence. The fact that a corporate agent regularly violates human rights does not entail that the members want to do so, or even know that the corporate agent they constitute has done so.[8] The causal chain from member commitments to corporate commitments and action is long and complex, and such simplistic equivalencies do a disservice to the members and distract us from other factors that play a significant role in generating these kinds of corporate behavior (in business and elsewhere).

Having pointed all of this out, it probably seems obvious. All of us are familiar with the experience of stepping into a new institution (whether in business, academia, or elsewhere) and conforming our behavior to existing practices and policies, welcome or not. In many cases, we have no idea what kind of corporate action our collective compliance with existing practices and policies will yield, nor are we aware of how our own idiosyncratic choices about how and when to conform will influence the corporate action that results.[9] People often seem to assume that the "higher-ups" must know all of this, and that the organization conforms unfailingly to executive directives that take all of this into account, but a moment of reflection should make it clear that this is not likely to be the case in an organization of any size. Large organizations operate by a logic of their own, embodied in and guided by long-established practices and procedures and bound by tacit expectations and cultural norms, and the members from top to bottom generally conform to that logic; they can make changes, of course, but those changes have to be made from within that existing logic and structure—even (or especially) when they come from the top. There is nothing mystical or mysterious about any of this. It's a familiar fact about the world, but one with four significant implications that are rarely appreciated.

First, these familiar "commitments" that guide corporate action qualify as beliefs, desires, and intentions on standard philosophical accounts. Second, they are generally integrated into a coherent whole. While there will be some inconsistencies (as there are in the commitments of any agent), there is an enormous amount of pressure to rationalize them so that the corporate agent is not pursuing contradictory goals or acting on the basis of contradictory beliefs.[10] Together these commitments form what Carol Rovane calls a "rational point of view," or "RPV"; she describes this as "the point of view from which [practical] deliberation proceeds" and it sets the standard against which an agent's actions can be judged as instrumentally rational or irrational.[11] Possession of an RPV, together with the ability to act on it, is the hallmark of an agent on most accounts of agency (though, of course, different philosophers use different terminology). Third, this RPV—this logically integrated set of beliefs, desires, and intentions—belongs to the corporate agent itself. It does not typically match the RPVs of the members, it can and does survive changes in membership, and it can and does survive changes in the RPVs of the members; it thus is not the RPV of the members (of any level). These commitments are thus *corporate* beliefs, desires, and intentions—not because they have to do with business or with a legally incorporated entity, but because they belong to a "corporate agent." The possession of an effective RPV marks the corporate entity as an agent (and arguably a moral agent) in its own right. Fourth, all of this allows us—arguably requires us—to recognize the firm (college, government, and the like) as a thing, a *res*, a new "whole."[12]

There are a number of different directions to go from here, but now I want to focus on the ontological implications. What we see here is a true unity, a new whole, and in fact a very sophisticated one. Moreover, this "whole" is a social entity—a collective—that does *not* arise out of the kind of shared mentality assumed in the collectivist literature. It is true that the majority of the members must share certain commitments or expectations about membership (and possibly work, professionalism, and the like) that lead them to join a corporate agent and conform to the practices they find there, but none of those commitments is specific to the individual corporate agent they now constitute. These shared, generic expectations about "membership" are not analogous to the unifying "shared intentions" that unite a collective to move a couch, perform a symphony, or do the wave. Moreover, it is true that all of the members of the corporate agent (probably) know that they are members of the corporate agent; I'm reasonably confident that the members of Exxon know that they are members of Exxon. As with the people waiting for the bus, though, it does not follow from this knowledge that all the members of Exxon understand themselves as a unity, that they consider themselves united in the pursuit of shared goals or brought together by shared commitments. It is just as likely (more likely?) that many of the members of Exxon feel no real sense of membership, unity, belonging, or shared fate—of "doing something together." Instead, for many (most?) of the members of Exxon, their participation in Exxon is instrumental to unique, individual goals that have no direct connection to Exxon, the other members, or their activities there.

Thus, the unity of a corporate agent is not the intimate, internal unity of most collective endeavor, driven by the distinctive, shared commitments of their members. As a result, the agency of a corporate agent is not the agency of a typical collective, bound by the commitments of the members and closely linked to the members' own goals and preferences. Instead, corporate agents have commitments—goals and preferences—of their own. Given that they can't rely on shared goals and intentions to motivate member behavior in accordance with those corporate goals and preferences, they have structures of imperatives and incentives that coopt the individual (unshared) goals and preferences of their members for corporate purposes. They connect with the members via the member's self-interest, offering to satisfy certain needs in exchange for the necessary behaviors.

Two things about these corporate "structures" before we move on to discuss some of the mechanics of all this: First, these structures are not neutral—they are aimed at specific goals and embody the commitments about fact and value that define the corporate RPV—and they are immensely complex. They include explicit incentive schemes like raises, promotions, and awards (and pay cuts, demotions, and other penalties) and explicit demands laid out in contracts, policies, and published "standard procedures," but they are not limited to the things laid out in official documents. The corporate structures that unify the members also include tacit incentive schemes bound up in culture and peer expectations, and tacit demands embodied in office politics and unpublished "actual practices." Second, crucially, all these structures evolve over time. They can be intentionally, officially amended, of course; none of these things is set in stone. But they can also evolve in the absence of strategic member behavior, nudged along by unintended results and implications or larger (but unacknowledged) shifts in member behavior.[13] Too much disruption of these structuring elements will destroy the agent, and it will dissolve into its component members and resources; gradual evolution, on the other hand, is almost inevitable, and members can adapt to changing structures without even realizing that they have done so.

It is this goal-oriented, value-driven, evolving structure—internal to the corporate agent, external to the members—that creates and maintains the unity of the whole. The corporate agents that are unified in this way are the "fractured wholes" of the title. They are true social wholes, sustained and active unities, held together *from the outside*—a contrast to the more intuitively familiar collective, held together from the inside (as it were). I have argued elsewhere that this whole qualifies as a moral agent in its own right, bound by much the same moral obligations as the human moral agents who share so many of their capacities—but my concern here is different. Instead I now focus on some of the internal mechanics that facilitate the formation and functioning of corporate agents, and the implications these processes have for the members.

The Mechanics—Making and Maintaining

Corporate agents need members. The members provide the physical base for the corporate agent—the "body," if you will—and the impetus for action, while the corporate agent (through the RPV and supporting structures) coordinates member activity and directs that impetus toward corporate ends. More traditional collectives coalesce around a shared goal, with both goal and collective emerging simultaneously; in such cases, the members are already motivated to work toward the collective goal, as it was this motivation that led them to form the collective in the first place. In contrast, corporate agents already *have* the goal;[14] what they need are members who will contribute necessary skills and resources toward corporate goals that are not their own. Thus, corporate agents have to provide incentives. Most corporate agents acquire their members via contract. The corporate agent offers to provide what the members need— money, of course, but also status, power, opportunity, challenge, a social circle, identity, even meaning—if the members will contribute the skills and expertise that the corporate agent requires. *And nothing else.* It's that last bit that concerns me here. (In what follows I will limit my discussion to situations in which the members are employed by the corporate agent; the difficulties are starker there, where jobs are at stake, than in more casual or purely voluntary settings.)

At a time, a corporate agent generally has a full complement of rationally integrated commitments (the RPV) and a full array of established structures designed to encourage the implementation of that RPV. Again, any piece of this can be changed—or can change—at any time, but most of it doesn't change all that often. Just like human agents, the vast majority of a corporate agent's beliefs, desires, and intentions are quite stable; significant change is disruptive and unpleasant for both kinds of agent, and hardly "the normal course of things." If the RPV and its supporting structures are to remain stable, then it is important that the members generally fit themselves into that existing framework, and of course this is what usually happens. Even at the highest ranks, members join the corporate agent to fill an existing, already defined role, and they are expected to step into that role and to begin contributing their particular skills and expertise toward an already established set of tasks aimed at an already established set of goals. Again, any piece of this *can* be changed, and often will be changed over the course of the corporate agent's existence. But the corporate agent does not adapt itself to every new member that joins its ranks. The members adapt themselves to the corporate agent. Part of maintaining the functional existence of a corporate agent, then, is establishing the incentives that will encourage members to not only join the corporate agent but conform to its existing commitments and structures as well. Only then can the member's contributions be reliably directed toward corporate ends.

That brings us to the first general requirement of membership in a corporate agent: the contribution of specific skills and expertise. Corporate agents require a wildly complex array of things from their members, but most of that complexity boils down to a surprisingly short list. In general, corporate agents seem to require six things from their members: physical actions, information gathering and analysis, interfacing with other agents, rationality (means-ends reasoning), self-interest, and of course conformity. Regarding the first, again, the members are the physical aspect of the corporate agent (analogous to the body of a human agent), so of course the members have to provide all of the necessary physical actions. Regarding the second, every agent needs to be able to gather information about the world, in order to develop successful strategies and adjust strategies that aren't working, and the bits of information gathered by the various members can be synthesized into astonishingly nuanced and comprehensive representations of the world. With this, the corporate agent can have access to a much deeper and encompassing knowledge of external situations than that possessed by any individual member.[15] Regarding the third, every *social* agent needs to be able to navigate the social sphere in pursuit of its goals, and members can typically provide a much more flexible and effective interface for other agents than technological alternatives. Regarding the fourth, of course the agent needs to be able to draw conclusions about the information gathered by its members, and the bits of means-end reasoning performed by individual members can be (again) synthesized into much larger and more sophisticated plans regarding the pursuit of corporate goals than those developed by any individual member. Regarding the fifth and sixth, as already noted, the entire mechanism is premised on the idea that the members are self-interested—that's what spurs them to join the corporate agent in the first place—and that they are able and willing to conform to corporate requirements.

At this point, it may sound like the members provide everything and that there is really nothing left for this so-called corporate agent to contribute to the establishment and pursuit of the (so-called) corporate ends. As a reminder, though, the corporate agent provides at least three crucial things: (1) The corporate agent provides the incentives, which bring the members together and motivate them to contribute to the accomplishment of ends that none of them had as individuals. (2) The corporate agent provides the structures, which synthesize the many contributions from the members into a single, unified whole. This is what makes it possible for a corporate agent to know things that none of its members (individually) knows, and to take actions that none of its members (individually) could take. (3) Finally, most of all, the corporate agent provides the RPV that governs all of this—the overarching beliefs that guide corporate action, and the larger desires and intentions that the corporate actions aim to fulfill. Without those three things—most especially the last—there would be no new agent in the world, pursuing *its own* ends in accordance with *its own* beliefs, desires, and intentions.

All of that brings us to the second general requirement of membership in a corporate agent: that the members *not* contribute anything else. It's the corporate agent that provides the RPV—the larger ends to be pursued and the general commitments about how the world is, what matters, and the manner in which those ends are to be pursued. The members are not asked to offer up their own values, emotions, or personal commitments about "how the world is and what matters in it." Nor are they asked to offer up the complexities of their personal identities—deep loyalties to friends and family, rich details of difference associated with race, class, gender, religion, and the rest. In fact, as a rule they are specifically being asked *not* to offer those things up, *not* to bring them to the corporate agent, *not* to let these things unduly influence their membership-related actions.[16] All of the things that distinguish us one from another, all of the things that make us uniquely ourselves, distinct wholes, are generally unwelcome in this setting, and for good reason: they undermine the integrity of the corporate whole.

Again, corporate agents are unified by a set of commitments and structures, which can be remarkably robust; many corporate agents survive for decades, and some for centuries. But this unification holds only as long as the members abide by them and conform to them. The more the members deviate from the commitments and procedures that define the corporate agent, while acting in their role as members, the weaker that unification becomes. In the end, if too many members are introducing too many divergent aspects of themselves, too many pieces that are not consistent with or do not further the corporate project, the corporate agent will cease to exist. Thus, while it is important to the corporate agent that the members offer up the desired skills and their distinctive expertise in valuable areas, it is *crucial* that they not offer up more than that.

Thus, the "fractured wholes" of the title comprise "fractured selves." The members of corporate agents need to sever (or at least repress) those aspects of themselves that run counter to the corporate project and "leave them at home," bringing only that part of the self that fits with and is valued by the corporate agent. Membership in corporate agents is an increasingly inevitable part of modern life, and most people (at least in the developed world) have long since resigned themselves to this kind of fracturing. In fact, to many it seems perfectly natural and unobjectionable, even admirable: dividing oneself in this way is the mark of the professional, and there is something juvenile and embarrassing about people who violate these norms and introduce "personal" concerns into these "corporate" settings (in business and elsewhere).[17] I nonetheless find it troubling.

Fractured Wholes

There are at least two problems with the corporate agents that we make and maintain in this way. First, of course, is the cost to the members. None of the major Western moral traditions is particularly concerned with "wholeness" (though there are hints in Aristotle, and especially in Aquinas), but it plays a central role in some of the Eastern traditions—most particularly in the philosophy of *ahimsa*. The self is meant to be whole and complete, and the fracturing required by contemporary ideals of professionalism is a particularly intimate kind of violence practiced against the self.[18] Moving away from philosophy and theology, even mainstream psychology recognizes the costs of this kind of harsh repression and denial. The point hardly needs to be belabored: this is not a good way for human beings to live.[19] Second, however, there's the nature of the corporate agents that we produce in this way.

Again, corporate agents as I have described them here are extremely sophisticated. They can believe, desire, and intend; they possess a first-person perspective, the ability to learn, distinctive characters, and free will; and they are capable of "thought," reasoning, and reactive attitudes.[20] With all of this, they are capable of immense feats of information gathering and analysis, and capable of action on an enormous scale. For all of this sophistication, however, they lack a number of qualities that most human agents possess to at least some degree. For one thing, they are not phenomenally conscious and thus cannot feel or experience anything. They feel no pleasure or pain, of course, and they cannot *feel* emotions (which is not to say that they can't act angrily, compassionately, respectfully, and the like).[21] That much, at least, seems inevitable. But they also tend to be overwhelmingly motivated by self-interest, and their drive to achieve their goals seems woefully unmoderated by concerns about impacts to other agents, to communities, to the environment, or indeed to *anything* outside themselves.[22] We rarely see them doing "good things" like going out of their way to help the disadvantaged, fight corruption, preserve animal welfare, protect the environment, support local communities, and the like. I would suggest that this is partly because we rarely *look* for instances of corporate agents doing such things; when we do find them, we dismiss them as "enlightened self-interest" and thus not truly moral or compassionate actions. To the extent that "true" moral or compassionate action requires certain phenomenal experience or feeling, this is fair enough (though I doubt it matters that much to the recipients). Still, even if it is recognized that corporate agents may do more good than is often acknowledged, it remains the case that they do an enormous amount of harm.

Look more closely at exactly what seems to be missing from the "fractured wholes" just described. For one thing, they seem to lack moral principles or values: there is no apparent effort to "maximize pleasure and minimize pain," "treat others respectfully," "act on universalizable principles," and so on. Further, they seem to lack familiar moral virtues. They possess many of the intellectual virtues—curiosity, rationality—but the moral virtues of honesty, generosity, and the rest seem to be absent. Beyond that, they seem to lack emotions, or, at least, what we might call "emotional action." Of course they can't *feel* things like respect, care, or compassion, but we human agents are certainly capable of *acting* with respect, care, and compassion whether we actually feel them or not. It is at least theoretically possible that corporate agents could do the same, but it seems that they generally do not. I've listed these as four separate things, but they all seem to identify the same basic lack: corporate agents seem to have no moral *presence*, no moral identity that shapes their actions in the way their (clearly present) self-interest shapes their action. Put another way, they seem to have no *conscience*. (Baron Thurlow famously said in the early 1800s, "Did you ever expect a corporation to have a conscience, when it has no soul to be damned, and no body to be kicked?") Having listed them separately, though, we can see that this list also matches the previous list of qualities that the members are required to "leave at home" when they enact their membership. In this sense, corporate agents are perhaps twice-fractured: once in the lack of deep, organic unity among the members and again in the lack of a moral presence, which would arguably be part of any truly "whole" agent.

It may seem that there is a simple, obvious solution to this problem: heal the fractures! Let the members make themselves whole and then bring their *whole selves* to work—their principles and values, their virtues, their emotions, all of it! Then all of that goodness can be taken up by the corporate agent—drawn up through the same network of structures that currently gathers rational, self-interested input—to influence the development of *moral* corporate commitments and goals that will then lead to moral corporate actions. This will make the corporate agent "whole" in the sense of having developed the missing piece, the moral aspect. More, perhaps this will lead to the development of a deeper, more organic unity among the members, thus healing *both* of the fractures that plague the corporate agent. Even allowing for the imperfect implementation of the real world, it seems that this could address the concerns identified in this section, making all of the fractured wholes "wholesome" again.

The Cost of Wholesome Wholes

I'd like to begin this final section by acknowledging that the foregoing may very well be the right answer. It certainly sounds nice. But I have doubts.

For one thing, the quick solution I sketched at the end of the previous section misrepresents the inner workings of a corporate agent. As outlined earlier, the actions and intentions of a corporate agent are not just "sum totals" of the actions and intentions of its members, so a bunch of "good" (moral) individual actions and intentions will not necessarily "add up" to good (moral) corporate actions and intentions. "Good" inputs in a random scattering are as likely to cancel one another out as they are to support one another: if half of the people engaged in a project simply "do something good" instead of one of the actions consistent with that project, they're more likely to achieve nothing at all than to achieve "something good." Getting good (moral) results at the corporate level will require attention to systems-level dynamics, not just member inputs, so "fixing" the member-level inputs in the manner just suggested is unlikely to be effective. I return to this point later. For another thing, there are reasons for the corporate demand for a limited, "fractured" self—reasons that go beyond the simple convenience of not being burdened by moral commitments or constraints. The corporate demand for a fractured self achieves efficiency, stability, and most of all a kind of neutrality[23] that may be very important for the members.

The first point, regarding efficiency, is a simple one. When the members are acting as members, the corporate agent wants them to be focused on their tasks and comfortably settled into their roles. To the extent that members have personal practices or commitments that are inconsistent with the practices, culture, and commitments of the corporate agent, the corporate agent generally wants the members to leave them at home. Such things are a distraction for that member (and potentially for others), and introduce a kind of "grit in the gears" for the corporate agent. The second point, regarding stability, is relatively straightforward as well. Again, in an important sense the corporate agent *is* its commitments—its RPV, as embodied by its members—and this is the primary source of its unique identity. While change is possible and often appropriate, the stability of the RPV is important and disruption carries a heavy cost. If the members are constantly allowing their behavior to be guided by unrelated or contrary commitments and values, this can ultimately threaten the unity of the whole as well as its efficiency. The third point is more interesting, and involves an illuminating parallel with political philosophy.

There's an extraordinarily powerful set of moral and (especially) political systems associated with the Enlightenment, all of which are based on a distinctive paradigm of the person. This is the paradigm that underlies contemporary liberalism and libertarianism; it drives most contemporary efforts to develop a "cosmopolitan" ethics and politics; it stands as the justification for most contemporary discourse about international human rights; and it even undergirds most contemporary efforts to articulate a case for sustainability and environmental protection.[24] There's a reason it shows up in precisely those contexts, and I will return to that later.

This paradigm of the person is often called "the abstract individual" because it is achieved by a process of abstraction.[25] The general approach is to take real, complicated, idiosyncratic human persons and strip away all of the contingent particularities—likes and dislikes, bonds of family and friendship, details about social status and education and religious beliefs and gender and race, the irrational details of emotional attachment, and so on. What remains are the things that we all have in common, the significant universal attributes that are present in all and—importantly—*equally* present in all. Historically, this process of abstraction has yielded a paradigm of the person as rational, autonomous, and free, capable both of setting ends for itself and of binding itself via agreements with other agents. The abstract individual is "social" in the sense that it exists in and must navigate a social setting, dealing with other agents, but its primary (or sole) significant character trait is that it is self-interested—not necessarily selfish, but primarily concerned with its own ends. (The fact that the agent is physically embodied is rarely acknowledged but always assumed.)

This paradigm provides both the thrust and the justification for moral and legal systems that protect the exercise of precisely these universal aspects. In each domain, moral and political, they create a kind of privileged sphere around the individual—a sphere within which she can act upon her own idiosyncratic likes and dislikes, mores and values, at the cost of accepting that a similar privileged sphere surrounds other individuals. She cannot be imposed upon and she cannot impose, beyond those restrictions necessary to guarantee precisely these (universally valuable) protections. As John Rawls noted with respect to his own (liberal) theory of justice, systems based on this paradigm can claim to guarantee "the right" while remaining neutral with respect to "the good."[26] In smaller and more homogenous societies, where people actually share a conception of the good, richer and more burdensome obligations may be appropriate. In more diverse contexts, however—like most modern nation-states, or with respect to any global issues—this limited Enlightenment system provides a valuable framework for engagement without agreement. It's a kind of fallback system of rules of engagement for those scenarios where people do not share a conception of the good—where, to put it another way, people lack a shared end, or shared intentions.

This is, of course, a perfect description of a corporate agent. Most corporate agents operate in exactly such a diverse context, of course, but more importantly—as discussed at length earlier—most corporate agents *embody* precisely this kind of diversity, and they are defined by the lack of a shared end. Again, the members of corporate agents (like the members of a modern nation-state) are not unified by deeply held convictions or a shared sense of identity or purpose. They are unified by a corporate structure that appeals to their individual self-interest—one that stimulates and coopts precisely that drive. This isn't necessarily selfish, but it is not "shared" or unificatory in its own right; it's the corporate structure that harnesses this drive in a mutually beneficial exercise, if not toward a "shared end."[27] Here, as in the modern nation-state, what all of the members have in common is their capacities for reason, agency, action, and above all self-interest—that, and their consent to be bound to the corporate agent. It is thus unsurprising to find that (1) these are precisely the characteristics that the corporate agent requires from its members, essentially the "six contributions" discussed earlier, and (2) other characteristics are generally unwelcome. In essence, the corporate agent asks its members to *become* the abstract individual of Enlightenment theory, at least while acting as members: they are asked to contribute the characteristics of the abstract individual (rationality and autonomy, physical activity and interaction with other agents, self-interest and binding consent) and the characteristics that they are asked to abandon or suppress are precisely the ones stripped away by the traditional process of abstraction.[28]

If anything, the exclusion of potentially competing or complicating characteristics is even more important in a corporate agent than in the governance of a modern state. Most of the time it is easy enough to live in the neutral state, to enjoy your protective bubble (in which you can express most of your personal preferences) and simply not deal with people whose particularities don't jibe with your own. It is difficult to entirely opt out of the modern state, but not too difficult to live unengaged within it. This is not the case with corporate agents. First, at least in the developed world, this is where the jobs are; it is exceedingly difficult to avoid joining *some* corporate agent, and it's the fortunate person who even has attractive options about *which* corporate agent to join. Second, after having joined a corporate agent, it is not possible to "live unengaged within it." Corporate members have to work closely with people "whose particularities don't jibe with their own" day after day, week after week, even year after year. It is thus crucial that this setting remain as neutral as possible, both for the sake of the members who have to work so closely together and for the sake of achieving the ends at which the corporate agent aims. In some cases these ends are rather trivial (do we really *need* swizzle sticks?) but in others they are quite significant: education, health care, national defense. Regardless of the value of the end sought, there is at least some value in pursuing it effectively, and that will not be possible if the members are not united under the corporate RPV.

Part of the power (and glory) of the neutrality of the Enlightenment systems is the way they make all of this *possible*—both the diverse and energetic mix that is the modern nation-state and the diverse and energetic mix that is the modern corporate agent. By adhering to these strictures, leaving the things that divide us at home, and focusing our shared capacities and shared efforts on mutually beneficial activities, we can participate in fruitful relationships with people we could never be friends with. This is as true of corporate matters as of civic matters, and perhaps more so. Thus, by asking for only those six contributions and *allowing* only those six contributions, corporate agents can unite truly enormous numbers of people in the pursuit of ends that (in most cases) end up making valuable contributions. People outside of the corporate agent benefit by receiving goods and services—everything from swizzle sticks to the most advanced medical care—and the members manage to meet needs of their own.

The "fracturing" of the self that is required of the members is a way of establishing a neutral context in which the members can interact with one another, and while this certainly benefits the corporate agent, it also provides significant benefits for the members. The corporate agent benefits by having its own commitments (as incorporated into the RPV) complied with—not lost under the noise of a million competing commitments introduced by the diverse members—and it benefits from having a membership not distracted by conflicts arising from their diversity. The members, on the other hand, can be allowed to maintain their diversity. There is no need for deep engagement, no need to engage seriously with other members so as to generate the deeper, shared unity more typical of smaller wholes; there is no need to "buy in" to the corporate project, or to either generate or feign a deep congruence with the whole. Moreover, the members can maintain their *privacy*. With the demand that (so-called) personal matters remain outside, the members can maintain impersonal, arms-length relationships with colleagues; given that colleagues are chosen for expertise rather than personal compatibility, this can be a blessing indeed. The vast majority of corporate agents are employers to their members, and membership typically comes in the form of a job. It doesn't seem that anybody should be *required* to bring "their whole self" to a corporate agent just to keep their job.

***

So what do we do? I've suggested that our current approach to constructing corporate agents leads to significant costs. For one thing, as outlined earlier, it imposes costs on the members, who are required to sever or repress many of their deepest and most personal commitments in order to meet expectations of neutrality and conform to corporate commitments. For another thing, current practices have shown a distressing tendency to turn out rapacious, immoral corporate agents who cause a great deal of harm to the world outside of themselves—people, communities, and the environment. It seems plausible that the insistence on "fractured members" plays at least some role in the creation of the "fractured whole" that results. Given the latter possibility, it seems that the appropriate response would be to stop the fracturing—to amend current conceptions of membership so that members bring their whole selves to the agent. This will certainly relieve the members of the need to fracture themselves, and might plausibly play a role in creating a more "wholesome" whole at the corporate level. As discussed earlier, however, I think this is problematic.

For the reasons outlined, I rather hesitantly conclude that the members themselves may be better off under the current approach. I've treated "fracturing" as if it's an all-or-nothing thing, and of course that's not the case. The kind of fracturing I'm talking about comes in degrees, and the degree required will vary from person to person and corporate agent to corporate agent; it strikes me that basic kindness and compassion may be a better way to address some of the harshness that accompanies this fracturing than a huge overhaul.

That still leaves the second difficulty, that our current methods seem to generate unnecessarily destructive corporate agents. To echo Baron Thurlow, again, corporate agents seem woefully lacking in conscience. As I have argued at length elsewhere, however, I think the best approach here is simply to modify the existing RPV *without* asking for any deep, personal change from the members—a technical change, from the top down, as it were, rather than from the inside out.[29] If we do the technical and managerial work of incorporating moral principles, values, and virtues into the corporate structure itself, then we can simply let the members continue to implement it as they always have. This makes no extra, invasive demands on the members but still works to address external harms, and the external harms are in some ways more important, as they are typically imposed without consent and without compensatory benefits. In the fractured world in which we live, this may be the best we can do.

Notes

1. Kenneth Goodpaster describes this hyperfocus on goals as "teleopathy" or "goal-sickness." See Goodpaster, *Conscience and Corporate Culture* (Hoboken, NJ: Blackwell, 2007), esp. chap. 1, for a fascinating discussion of teleopathy at both the individual and the organizational level. See Bernard Baumrin and Benjamin Freedman, eds., *Moral Responsibility and the Professions* (New York: Haven, 1983) for interesting contemporary discussions of the professionalism, especially section 1.
2. At the same time, it is important to remember the many, many benefits that both insiders and outsiders reap from the power and effectiveness of these agents. We don't make them because we're stupid; we make them because they are incredibly powerful and effective. For better and worse.
3. See, for example, H. D. Lewis, "Collective Responsibility," *Philosophy* 24 (1948): 3–18; D. E. Cooper, "Collective Responsibility," *Philosophy* 43 (1968): 258–68; A. Quinton, "Social Objects," *Proceedings of the Aristotelian Society* 76 (1976): 1–27; and works cited therein. The articles anthologized by May and Hoffman provide an excellent overview of the development of the debate: L. May and S. Hoffman, eds., *Collective Responsibility: Five Decades of Debate in Theoretical and Applied Ethics* (New York: Rowman and Littlefield, 1992). It is interesting to note that the impetus for much of the early work arose from concerns about whether and how individual Germans could be morally responsible for the Holocaust.
4. See, for example, R. Tuomela and K. Miller, "We-Intentions," *Philosophical Studies* 53, no. 3 (1988): 367–89; M. Gilbert, *On Social Facts* (Princeton: Princeton University Press, 1992); M. Gilbert, "Who's to Blame? Collective Moral Responsibility and Its Implications for Group Members," *Midwest Studies in Philosophy* 30, no. 1 (2006): 94–114; M. Bratman, "Shared Intention," *Ethics* 104, no. 1 (1993): 97–113; S. Miller, *Social Action: A Teleological Account* (Cambridge: Cambridge University Press, 2001); S. Miller, "Collective Moral Responsibility: An Individualist Account," *Midwest Studies in Philosophy* 30, no. 1 (2006): 176–93.
5. Peter French's "The Corporation as a Moral Person" is generally recognized as the seminal work in this literature, and he followed that with the book-length treatment: P. A. French, *Collective and Corporate Responsibility* (New York: Columbia University Press, 1984); see also D. Copp, "The Collective Moral Autonomy Thesis," *Journal of Social Philosophy* 38, no. 3 (2007): 369–88; Isaacs, *Moral Responsibility in Collective Contexts* (Oxford: Oxford University Press, 2011); C. List and P. Pettit, *Group Agency:*

The Possibility, Design, and Status of Corporate Agents (Oxford: Oxford University Press, 2011); P. Pettit, "Groups with Minds of Their Own," in *Socializing Metaphysics*, ed. Frederick F. Schmitt (New York: Rowan and Littlefield, 2003), 129–66; D. Tollefsen, "Organizations as True Believers," *Journal of Social Philosophy* 33, no. 3 (2002): 395–410.

6. It is perhaps less obvious that this is true even of members at the higher levels of a firm (university, order, and so on). People often seem to assume that CEOs, presidents, and the like can simply impose any set of commitments or policies that they want, and this is simply not true. Even the most aggressive executives are enormously constrained by preexisting commitments, structures, and culture; as a result, even the new set of commitments that a firm (and the like) may develop under their guidance is still unlikely to match their own.

7. For a moderately detailed discussion, see Kendy M. Hess, "Because They Can: The Basis for the Moral Obligations of (Certain) Collectives," *Midwest Studies in Philosophy* 38, no. 1 (2014): 203–21; Kendy M. Hess, "The Free Will of Corporations (and Other Collectives)," *Philosophical Studies* 168, no. 1 (2014): 241–60; Gunnar Björnsson and Kendy Hess, "Corporate Crocodile Tears? On the Reactive Attitudes of Corporations," *Philosophy and Phenomenological Research* 94, no. 2 (2017): 273–98.

8. Again, this is not to say that they bear no moral responsibility for their participation.

9. Again (and again and again), this is not to say that we are not responsible for our contributions in these contexts. The responsibility—causal and moral—of members of corporate agents is an extremely complicated matter that I set aside here.

10. See Pettit, "Groups with Minds of Their Own," on this point.

11. C. A. Rovane, *The Bounds of Agency: An Essay in Revisionary Metaphysics* (Princeton: Princeton University Press, 1998).

12. *Pace* Miller and Makela, there is nothing spooky or mysterious about any of this, nor—*pace* Velasquez—does it involve anything "ghostly." The corporate agent is just another agent: it is a material object partially constituted by its physical base (its members), and its capacities to believe, desire, and act are firmly grounded in the proper functioning of that physical base. The corporate agent cannot believe, desire, intend, decide, or act in the absence of appropriate contributions from its members. These "contributions" are not themselves beliefs, desires, or intentions. Instead, the members contribute their actions—actions that may or may not have any obvious connection to the relevant belief, desire, or intention. The members act in ways that are shaped by, and in turn ultimately shape, the complex of corporate beliefs, desires, and intentions that is the corporate RPV. But the fact remains that the corporate agent is entirely dependent on its physical base, its members, for the existence, development, and effectiveness of its RPV. In all of this it is, of course, much like a human agent, who is likewise profoundly dependent on her physical base (her body) for the existence, development, and effectiveness of her own RPV. (It is an interesting exercise to reread this paragraph and substitute "human agent" for each mention of the corporate agent and "body" for each mention of the base.) Seumas Miller and Pekka Makela, "The Collectivist Approach to Collective Moral Responsibility," *Metaphilosophy* 36, no. 5 (2005): 634–51; Manuel Velasquez, "Debunking Corporate Moral Responsibility," *Business Ethics Quarterly* (2003): 531–62.

13. Again, see Hess, "Because They Can," and Hess, "The Free Will of Corporations (and Other Collectives)," and Björnsson and Hess, "Corporate Crocodile Tears?," for details.

14. Obviously, corporate agents also have a beginning, a time when at least some of the members came together around a shared goal. I set aside the complexities of initial formation here, but see Hess, "Because They Can," for discussion.

15. See Hess, "The Free Will of Corporations (and Other Collectives)," for more detailed discussion, with examples.

16. I am not suggesting that there is never any room in any work context for members to express these things, nor am I suggesting that the presence or expression of these pieces of personal identity would immediately destroy the corporate agent as if they were some kind of corporate kryptonite. I am simply pointing out that in the overwhelming majority of cases, behavior specifically associated with these aspects of the members will be in tension with corporate goals and practices, if not in direct conflict with them.

17. This is not absolutely necessary even today, of course. To the extent that a member's "personal" self is truly in sync with the corporate agent of which she is a member, there will be no need for fracturing. Values, emotions, personal concerns, and the rest are welcome (in limited amounts) to the extent that they further the corporate project. Still, it is hard to imagine that many people will find this kind of synchronicity. For the rest, it is just a question of how much of yourself you have to leave at home, and how able you are to reconnect with it at the end of the day.

18. See discussion in Kendy M. Hess, "Violence in the Practice of Law: The View from Here," in *Nonviolence as a Way of Life: History, Theory, and Practice*, ed. Predrag Cicovacki and Kendy Hess (Delhi: Motilal Banarsidass, 2017), 499–513. See other essays in these volumes regarding *ahimsa* more generally.

19. Marx in particular voiced concerns along these lines, but he was not alone. Even conservative philosophers like Adam Smith, Georg Hegel, and Matthew Arnold, writing in the late 1700s to late 1800s, expressed concerns about how workers forced into meaningless piece-work would be damaged by it—their intellects stunted, their characters warped, and their spirits broken. See the chapters on these philosophers in Jerry Z. Muller, *The Mind and the Market: Capitalism in Western Thought* (New York: Random House, 2007).

20. See Kendy M. Hess, "The Modern Corporation as Moral Agent: The Capacity for 'Thought' and a 'First-Person Perspective,'" *Southwest Philosophy Review* 26, no. 1 (2011): 61–69, and other cited works.

21. For a more detailed exploration of this possibility with regard to the reactive attitudes, at least, see Björnsson and Hess, "Corporate Crocodile Tears?"

22. Again, see Goodpaster, *Conscience and Corporate Culture*, esp. chap. 1, regarding the modern problem of teleopathy, in individuals and organizations.

23. As discussed at some length earlier, the corporate agent itself is not neutral. It is most emphatically aimed at specific goals by specific means, and it has a number of systems in place to encourage its members to conform to that program. Corporate agents nonetheless tend to be "neutral" on just about everything *not* involved in achieving those goals by those means—for example, questions of morality, politics, and religion that don't touch on the corporate project. Corporate actions can undoubtedly have profound impacts on political and religious issues and institutions, but they are unlikely to have a true political or religious identity *of their own*—to be liberal, socialist, or conservative, for example, or to (themselves) be Hindu or Christian. It's not impossible for them to be these things, at least to some extent; it's just extremely unusual (but see discussions around the recent US Supreme Court holding in *Burwell v. Hobby Lobby*, regarding the possibility of corporate rights to freedom of religion).

24. While this paradigm has been hugely popular and powerful, it has also been roundly criticized from both the left (especially feminist scholars) and the right (conservative scholars). An alternative paradigm drawn from the Aristotelian tradition by Amartya

Sen and Martha Nussbaum, especially, has been gaining ground in many of these contexts.

25. See Onora O'Neill, *Towards Justice and Virtue: A Constructive Account of Practical Reasoning* (Cambridge: Cambridge University Press, 1996); Alisa L. Carse, "The Liberal Individual: A Metaphysical Or Moral Embarrassment?," *Noûs* 28, no. 2 (1994): 184–209.

26. John Rawls, *A Theory of Justice* (Cambridge: Harvard University Press, 1971); see also Michael J. Sandel, "The Procedural Republic and the Unencumbered Self," *Political Theory* (1984): 81–96.

27. This language may sounds familiar, from Adam Smith's fascination with markets and the way they turn the pursuit of self-interest to *social* ends—ends that benefit of all of society.

28. We can also read this as an unusually blunt statement of the contemporary ideal of professionalism, as it is actually practiced. I set that topic aside for another time, but see the essays in Baumrin and Freedman, *Moral Responsibility and the Professions*, for interesting discussion, especially those in the first section.

29. For an excellent discussion of how to approach this, together with real world examples, see Goodpaster, *Conscience and Corporate Culture*.

CHAPTER 10

RELIGIOUS FAITH, SELF-UNIFICATION, AND HUMAN FLOURISHING IN JAMES AND DEWEY

MICHAEL R. SLATER

A s fellow pragmatists, it should come as little surprise that William James (1842–1910) and John Dewey (1859–1952) held similar views on a wide range of philosophical issues. To give but a few salient examples, both philosophers defended an expansive conception of pragmatism as a practical method for resolving traditional philosophical problems, in contrast to the narrower and strictly semantic conception of pragmatism developed by Charles S. Peirce.[1] James and Dewey both argued, furthermore, that philosophy itself needed to become more empirical and experimental in its methods, while at the same time becoming less focused on the solution of theoretical puzzles and more focused on the practical concerns of human beings. And both also affirmed a distinctive combination of empiricism, fallibilism, and verificationism in epistemology, a pragmatic view of the nature of concepts and theories, and broadly Darwinian views of the nature of mind and the basis of morality. On the issue of religion, however, James and Dewey held remarkably different views, with James defending the legitimacy and practical value of supernatural religious experiences, beliefs, and practices, and Dewey defending the need to naturalize and secularize traditional forms of religion in order to make them epistemically and morally justifiable. These are deep and important differences, to be sure, yet even here one finds notable similarities within differences and differences within similarities, to borrow Lee Yearley's helpful model for comparative study. For both philosophers regarded their views as thoroughly "pragmatic" and fully in line with their larger defenses of pragmatism; indeed, both understood themselves as having been led to their respective conclusions by considering the practical consequences of holding and acting on religious commitments. James and Dewey also agreed at a general level that religious faith could play a uniquely important role in helping individuals to achieve a more unified sense of self—and, with it, certain distinctive forms of human flourishing—by ordering and integrating their ideals, and by uniting them in turn with those ideals. And yet, James and Dewey disagreed over such fundamental issues as the nature of the object of religious faith, the nature of faith in or commitment to that object, and the desirability of moral transformation through personal religious experience, and these substantive differences in their pragmatic accounts of religion arguably reflect underlying differences in their respective conceptions of pragmatism.

My aim in this essay will be to explore these differences and similarities in more detail, with a particular focus on James's and Dewey's respective views on the connections between religious faith, self-unification, and human flourishing. As we shall see, both philosophers endorsed a religious version of the oneness hypothesis, insofar as each maintained, first, that human beings are capable of realizing a more expansive sense of self by making connection with, and understanding their personal identity as inextricably intertwined with, an object of faith that exceeds and transcends themselves (a descriptive claim), and, second, that realizing an expanded sense of self of this kind is an important, and possibly even an essential, ingredient in human flourishing at both the individual and the social levels (a normative claim). To anticipate my conclusions, I hope to show that the differences in their pragmatic accounts of oneness largely stem from differences in their metaphysical views and their positions on the epistemology of religious belief (which inform their understanding and application of their respective versions of pragmatism), and that each account—in spite of its shortcomings—captures something important about the relationship between religious faith and the widespread human longing for happiness and a sense of wholeness.[2] Although I do not think that either account is wholly unproblematic, much less that either is fully commensurable with the other, I nevertheless believe that a comparative study of James's and Dewey's accounts of oneness can help us to understand each of their views more fully than if we considered them independently of each other, and can possibly assist us in working out our own views on the nature of oneness in the process.

James's Account of Self-Unification Through Religious Faith

James was unique among the classical pragmatists in making the study and defense of religious faith a central feature of his pragmatism. Although it would be a mistake, in my view, to reduce his many interests in the subject of religion to a single feature or issue, even a cursory glance at James's religious writings reveals that one of his chief interests in religious faith was its capacity to meet certain important human needs and improve the quality of individual human lives. As most readers of James know, one of the most pronounced features of his major work on religion, *The Varieties of Religious Experience* (hereafter *Varieties*), is its deliberate focus on the empirically observable and testable practical effects of religion—its "practical fruits"—and its corresponding deemphasis on theoretical questions concerning the "roots" or causes of religious beliefs, experiences, and attitudes.[3] Such an approach is informed by James's view that religion itself is primarily practical as opposed to theoretical in nature, and that its most valuable function in human life is to provide a means of securing happiness, understood in the eudaimonic sense of that term as human well-being or flourishing (VRE, 44–51, 71–72, 122–23, 139, 382–83, 400–1, 405, 413).[4] Although James acknowledged the importance of theoretical questions concerning the truth of religious beliefs and the scientific value of attempts to explain religion, his own interests as psychologist and philosopher of religion were primarily therapeutic in nature, and were focused on the aim of understanding and providing an ethical justification for those forms of religion that were capable of fulfilling that practical function in the lives of particular human beings. If we are interested in those questions, he believed, and if we furthermore take an empirical, cross-cultural, and historical approach to answering them that draws upon our best science and is not beholden to the teachings or assumptions of any particular theological or religious tradition, we find that there is considerable evidence in support of the following claims.

First, that religion, on the whole, is a vital means of securing happiness for a majority of human beings, and that this happiness is typically achieved when an individual believes (usually on the basis of her personal religious experiences and as a consequence of having engaged in religious practices such as prayer or meditation) that she has gotten into a proper relationship—or, more specifically, a state of union or harmonious relation—with an "unseen order," or a transcendent higher power that is continuous with us and friendly with us and our ideals (VRE 51, 382–83, 400–2, 409–13). And second, that there is no good reason to think—as many religions maintain—that there is one religion or one type of religious attitude that is uniquely capable of or objectively better at fulfilling that function, or that is capable of satisfying all of the various religious needs that human beings have (VRE 383–85, 401–2). I think James is right on both counts, but for reasons of space I will confine my discussion in this essay only to the first of these claims.

One of James's larger aims in *Varieties* was to use the methods of empirical psychology—in conjunction with his pragmatism and a broad sample of firsthand reports of religious experience and religious autobiographies—to arrive at a tradition-independent appraisal of the practical value of religious faith.

Rather than taking religious traditions or communities and their own self-appraisals as his focus, James instead focused his attention on a widespread kind of religious attitude, which he variously termed the "faith-state" or the "state of assurance," which one finds among both traditionally religious and nontraditionally religious persons (VRE 201–2, 397–401).[5] Although this psychological attitude or state typically took either a "healthy-minded" or a "sick-souled" form, he believed, in both cases it was usually preceded by a period of division within the self ("the divided self") followed by a process of conversion (which could be either sudden or gradual), and it displayed a fairly definite set of phenomenological characteristics that we can discern across many different times and cultures. James gives at least three different but overlapping formulations of these characteristics in *Varieties*, but in his most comprehensive formulation he states that it includes a set of very general beliefs and a set of general psychological characteristics. These include the following:

1. The belief that the visible world is part of a more spiritual universe from which it draws its chief significance.
2. The belief that union or harmonious relation with that universe is our true end.
3. The belief that prayer or inner communion with the spirit thereof—be that spirit "God" or "law"—is a process wherein work is really done, and spiritual energy flows in and produces effects, either psychological or material, within the phenomenal world.
4. A new zest which adds itself like a gift to life, and takes the form either of lyrical enchantment or of appeal to earnestness and heroism.
5. An assurance of safety and a temper of peace, and, in relation to others, a preponderance of loving affections (VRE 382–83).

On James's view, then, what it means to be a person of faith, in the most general terms, is to hold a set of beliefs concerning the reality of an unseen order (or of a higher or larger power, as he adds on VRE 400 and 413) and concerning our need to get into a proper union or relationship with that order, and to hold that there are certain practices such as prayer or meditation that we can engage in to effect that union or relationship (see also VRE 411–12). And once we have made a proper connection with that unseen order, furthermore, there are certain experiences and changes of character that we should expect to have, including a new zest for life, an increase of loving affections for others, and a psychological state of assurance, which involves "the loss of all the worry, the sense that all is ultimately well with one, the peace, the harmony, the *willingness to be*, even though the outer conditions [of life] should remain the same" (VRE 201).[6] At least in the case of religions that promise some form of salvation or liberation, which is by far the most prevalent type of religion today, James thinks that we can identify a two-stage psychological process in which the individual moves from a state of uneasiness, or a sense that there is "*something wrong about us* as we naturally stand," to a state of solution in which the individual believes herself to be "*saved from the wrongness* by making proper connexion with the higher powers" (VRE 400). As he continues, in one of the most well-known passages in *Varieties*:

> The individual, so far as he suffers from his wrongness and criticizes it, is to that extent consciously beyond it, and in at least possible touch with something higher, if anything higher exist. Along with the wrong part there is thus a better part of him, even though it may be but a most helpless germ. With which part he should identify his real being is by no means obvious at this stage; but when stage 2 (the stage of solution or salvation) arrives, the man identifies his real being with the germinal higher part of himself; and does so in the following way. *He becomes conscious that this higher part is coterminous and continuous with a more of the same quality, which is operative in the universe outside of him, and which he can keep in working touch with, and in a fashion get on board of and save himself when all his lower being has gone to pieces in the wreck.*
>
> (VRE 401)

The process of moral self-transformation through religious experience that James describes is similar in a number of respects to his earlier discussion in *The Principles of Psychology* (hereafter *Principles*) of how human beings manage to pursue ends or lead lives that violate established social norms by identifying themselves with a potential or ideal social self, a higher and possible self against which they measure their own thoughts and conduct, as well as prevailing social norms and the thoughts and actions of others (PP 300–2). By imagining themselves as being approvingly judged by future generations, or by God, many persons are able to pursue ideals or to adopt new worldviews or ways of life that might earn them the disapproval or censure of their families, communities, and societies.[7] In such cases, James thinks, "I am always inwardly strengthened in my course and steeled against the loss of my actual social self by the thought of other and better *possible* social judges than those whose verdict goes against me now" (PP 300). Indeed, he adds a little later on that "probably no one can make sacrifices for 'right,' without to some degree personifying the principle of right for which the sacrifice is made, and expecting thanks from it" (PP 301–2).

One of the more fascinating and surely controversial features of James's account of the ideal social self in *Principles* is his view that this psychological process, which he thinks can be explained along purely naturalistic lines, can also lead us—if pursued sufficiently far—to the idea of God or an Absolute Mind, "a highest *possible* judging companion, if such companion there be"

(PP 301). This sounds a bit like an incipient piece of natural theology, and it is one of several places in *Principles* where James appears to have some difficulty in sticking to the strictly empirical and nonmetaphysical point of view that he promises to take at the outset of the work (see PP 6). James does not develop this suggestive line of reasoning very far, however; and equally significantly, he does not argue that God's existence can be *proved* in this way, nor does he give any indication that he is trying to provide rational support for belief in God. Yet, James also clearly thinks that this way of extending our powers of moral imagination to their furthest conceivable limit is a natural one for reflective people to make, and that it bears directly on the question of why many people persist in holding religious beliefs and engaging in religious practices such as prayer in a scientific age. He observes:

> We hear, in these days of scientific enlightenment, a great deal of discussion about the efficacy of prayer; and many reasons are given us why we should not pray, whilst others are given us why we should. But in all this very little is said of the reason why we *do* pray, which is simply that we cannot *help* praying. It seems probable that, in spite of all that "science" may do to the contrary, men will continue to pray to the end of time, unless their mental nature changes in a manner which nothing we know should lead us to expect. The impulse to pray is a necessary consequence of the fact that whilst the innermost of the empirical selves of a man is a Self of the *social* sort, it yet can find its only adequate *Socius* in an ideal world.
>
> (PP 301)

As others have pointed out, the notion of a *Socius* that James develops in *Principles*—or, more specifically, his psychological view of God as an ideal social self against whom we can evaluate our thoughts and conduct and to whom we can pray for assistance—is noticeably similar to his notion of a "wider self" in *Varieties*. Indeed, in both works James argues that for most persons identification of the self with an ideal and higher self is indispensable for achieving happiness, and that without a process of self-identification of this sort most people would be unable to lead psychologically healthy, much less flourishing, lives.[8] Yet there are also some important differences between the accounts that he gives in these works. First, James's account of the various forms that this process of self-identification can take is much richer and more extensively developed in *Varieties* than in *Principles*. Second, and perhaps more importantly, in *Varieties* James argues that belief in the reality of an unseen order or higher power, and having unifying religious experiences of that order or power, seems to be required in order to realize the full, practical benefits of religious faith, which he now describes in terms of an influx of "energy" from the subconscious or subliminal mind that can empower us morally and spiritually and can produce "regenerative effects" in our character; indeed, he clearly regards these characteristics as defining features of religious faith itself (VRE 400–13).[9] Belief in a *merely* ideal *Socius* or wider self, in other words, is not enough to achieve the happiness that is characteristic of religion in its most developed forms, and in order to realize the full practical benefits of religion one must believe (1) that the wider self exists, (2) that it produces real effects in the world, and (3) that it has some bearing on how we should lead our lives. As James explains this "thoroughly 'pragmatic' view of religion," the world interpreted religiously "is not the materialistic world over again, with an altered expression; it must have, over and above the altered expression, *a natural constitution* different at some point from that which a materialistic world would have. It must be such that different events can be expected in it, different conduct must be required" (VRE 408).

On the pragmatic view of religion that James defends in *Varieties*, then, one of the essential functions of religion is to realize certain important practical goods in the lives of human beings, which I have elsewhere described in terms of the possession of a *morally strenuous attitude* and the achievement of *metaphysical intimacy*, a saving or liberating sense of union with an unseen order or wider self.[10] While the empirical evidence does not clearly or uniquely support the truth-claims of a specific religious tradition or theological view, he believed, much less the claim that one religion is practically superior to another on the whole, it does nevertheless provide considerable support for the view that religion functions to secure the earlier-mentioned goods for many human beings. James personally believed that religious faith was *necessary* to secure both of these practical goods, but his arguments regarding the first are not very well developed or supported. In the case of the second, however, he is surely right in thinking that a practical good of this sort—one that seems to be inherently religious or metaphysical by its very nature—cannot plausibly be realized without holding supernatural religious beliefs and having religious experiences, ones that appear to unite the believer (in one way or another and from the believer's point of view) with the object of her faith.[11] To believe, as most religious people do and as James himself did, that there is a knowable, really existent unseen order or higher power of some sort, one that is "ideal" but that also has efficient causality and produces real effects in the world and the lives of human beings, is to affirm a very general religious view that he terms "piecemeal supernaturalism" (VRE 409–14).

Although most traditional religious believers have much "thicker" theological views than this, James himself believed that the practical needs and experiences of religion were "sufficiently met by the belief that beyond each man and in a fashion continuous with him there exists a larger power which is friendly to him and to his ideals" (VRE 413). By believing or disbelieving in the existence of a supernatural power or order of this sort, or in a more specific set of beliefs about that power or order, we commit ourselves to what James calls an "overbelief," or a metaphysical belief that is compatible with—but that cannot be confirmed by—the available empirical evidence (VRE 402–14). Under the terms of such a view, both naturalists and supernaturalists are committed to various overbeliefs in the matter of religion, but neither can justifiably claim—at least in a neutral, non-question-begging way—to have a demonstrably true belief, or to have drawn the inference to the best explanation, or something similar. Both sorts of believer, as James sees it, can appeal to various forms of evidence in support of their preferred view. Yet they are unlikely to agree completely about such matters as what should count as evidence, about which background assumptions may or should be privileged, or about how to determine the relevant probabilities when arguing for their preferred view (or against rival views, for that matter).[12] In the end, each believer is engaged in a "faith-venture" that cannot be settled at present by appealing to strictly objective reasoning or evidence, and these different ventures have definitely different practical effects on the kinds of lives we lead. As James explains:

> By being faithful to [my own overbelief], I seem to myself to keep more sane and true. I *can*, of course, put myself into the sectarian scientist's attitude, and imagine vividly that the world of sensations and of scientific laws and objects may be all. But whenever I do this, I hear that inward monitor of which W. K. Clifford once wrote, whispering the word "bosh!" Humbug is humbug, even though it bear the scientific name, and the total expression of human experience, as I view it objectively, invincibly urges me beyond the narrow "scientific" bounds. Assuredly, the real world is of a different temperament—more intricately built than physical science allows. So my own objective and subjective conscience both hold me to the overbelief which I express.
>
> (VRE 408)

James believed that piecemeal supernaturalism has a number of theoretical and practical advantages over its rivals, although in his brief discussion of those advantages in the postscript to *Varieties* it is—unsurprisingly—the latter that take pride of place. Unlike naturalism, piecemeal supernaturalism does not seek to debunk the religious believer's understanding of her religious experiences or insist that she give up her supernatural beliefs, both of which are incompatible with most forms of religious faith (and which consequently pose a threat to many people's ability to have their religious needs met). And unlike "refined" versions of supernaturalism, which deny that we can know or stand in causal relations with the supernatural realm (a view that many philosophers and some theologians in James's day subscribed to, largely due to the influence of Kant and absolute idealism), piecemeal supernaturalism does not rule out the possibility of our having genuine religious experiences, nor does it seek to reform the nature of faith itself so as to eliminate supposedly incredible or indefensible religious beliefs and practices such as belief in miracles or "providential leadings" or petitionary prayer (VRE 409–11).

Contemporary naturalists, of course, will likely have a number of objections to realistic religious views of this sort, and James himself was well aware that it is one thing to show that religious believers tend to understand their faith along realistic lines, and another to show that their realistic religious beliefs are true. To show the latter would be an exceedingly tall order, and to James's credit he does not presume to have done anything of the sort in *Varieties*, or in any of his other religious writings for that matter. As for his reasons for defending piecemeal supernaturalism, James says the following:

> If asked just where the differences in fact which are due to God's existence come in, I should have to say that in general I have no hypothesis to offer beyond what the phenomenon of "prayerful communion," especially when certain kinds of incursion from the subconscious region take part in it, immediately suggests. The appearance is that in this phenomenon something ideal, which in one sense is part of ourselves and in another sense is not ourselves, actually exerts an influence, raises our centre of personal energy, and produces regenerative effects unattainable in other ways. If, then, there be a wider world of being than that of our every-day consciousness, if in it there be forces whose effects on us are intermittent, if one facilitating condition of the effects be the openness of the "subliminal" door, we have the elements of a theory to which the phenomena of religious life lend plausibility. *I am so impressed by the importance of these phenomena that I adopt the hypothesis which they so naturally suggest.* At these places at least, I say, it would seem as though transmundane energies, God, if you will, produced immediate effects within the natural world to which the rest of our experience belongs.
>
> (VRE 411–12, emphasis added)

Such an argument is unlikely to convince James's contemporary naturalist critics, no matter how friendly they might be, as it asks for concessions that most naturalists would be unlikely to make. Nevertheless, this frank and humble admission nicely captures the heart of James's pragmatic approach to defending the practical value and legitimacy of religious faith, I think, for it shows that James did not base his defense of piecemeal supernaturalism on an impartial and objective consideration of the available evidence, which in any case he believed to be too indeterminate to play the supporting role that many critics and defenders of religion want, and too colored by individual temperaments to qualify as impartial and objective in the first place. Rather, he defended that view on account of its practical importance to the lives of most religious people, whose faith would not be sustainable apart from the convictions it describes.

What we have in James's pragmatic account of religion, then, and his con-comitant defense of piecemeal supernaturalism, is an empirical and pluralis-tic framework for evaluating religious beliefs, experiences, and practices on essentially practical and nontheological grounds, with the aim of providing empirical support for the view that religious faith—in a remarkably wide variety of forms—is an important and possibly irreplaceable good in the lives of many human beings.

Dewey's Account of Self-Unification Through Religious Faith

William James was John Dewey's philosophical hero, but before his conversion to pragmatism he was as a Hegelian, and Hegel remained a lifelong influence on his thinking.[13] As Richard Gale has recently (and I think convincingly) shown, one of the most pervasive and neglected features of Dewey's version of pragmatism was a basically Hegelian concern with the ideal of self-unification, and the various ways in which art, religion, and philosophy—the classic Hege-lian trio—could serve as instruments for promoting the growth of human values, ideals, and relationships.[14] As Gale observes of Dewey's pragmatist-cum-Hegelian view of growth as self-unification:

> Growth involves the realization by an individual of ever richer and more extensive unifications, both within herself and with other persons, as well as with her natural environment, each of these unifications being dependent on the other two. This naturalizes the Hegelian dialectical development by hav-ing human beings replace the Absolute or God as the determiners of the his-torical process in which more widespread and rich syntheses are achieved. It is something that we must earn through our own free endeavorings rather than have imposed on us by some behind-the-scenes machinations by the Absolute or God.[15]

All human action, on Dewey's view, should ultimately aim at the achievement of this kind of growth, which involves not merely the overcoming of obstacles to growth but also their ongoing dialectical "sublation." As Dewey himself writes, there is "but one issue involved in all reflection upon conduct: The rectifying of present troubles, the harmonizing of present incompatibilities by projecting a course of action which gathers into itself the meaning of them all."[16]

Dewey's marriage of pragmatism and left-wing Hegelianism is an interest-ing topic in its own right, to be sure, but it is largely ancillary to my interests in this essay. In what follows I will pass over some of the problems surrounding his view of growth as self-unification, most notably what Gale has termed

Dewey's "growth fanaticism," as well as certain features of that view which lie outside the scope of this essay, such as how the idea of growth connects with other important ideas in Dewey's philosophy like inquiry, democracy, and education, and I will focus instead on how this view informs his distinctive understanding of religious faith.[17] For reasons of space, I will confine my discussion to *A Common Faith* (1934), where Dewey offers his most extensive statement of his views on religion and where, more importantly, he undertakes to justify a naturalistically reconstructed conception of faith on pragmatic grounds on account of its capacity to unify the self and to strengthen our commitment to secular moral values and ideals.[18]

If we want to understand Dewey's views on self-unification through religious faith, we first need to situate those views within the context of his pragmatic and naturalizing reconstruction of religious faith, which has a number of interrelated aims. I will highlight just two of these here. The first is Dewey's aim of occupying a viable middle ground between two opposed camps, both of which Dewey finds objectionable. For the sake of convenience, we might call these *Camp Supernaturalism* and *Camp Militant Atheism*. The former camp is occupied by traditional religious believers, or those who hold supernatural religious beliefs, engage in religious practices connected with those beliefs, and are affiliated with religious institutions such as churches and synagogues that conserve and transmit those beliefs and practices from one generation to the next. In spite of their many differences, Dewey thinks, traditional religious believers share an underlying commitment to supernaturalism, which typically includes such things as belief in the existence of a transcendent, supernatural being or beings and some sort of belief in afterlife (CF 1).[19] This is true not only of religious fundamentalists, but even of liberal Protestants who have "largely abandoned the idea that particular ecclesiastical sources can authoritatively determine cosmic, historic and theological beliefs" (CF 30). Camp Militant Atheism, in contrast, is occupied by atheists who are hostile or unfriendly to religion as such, and who think not only that religious beliefs, practices, and institutions have been completely discredited by modern science and modern cultural norms, but also that "with the elimination of the supernatural not only must historic religions be dismissed but with them everything of a religious nature" (CF 1).

What Dewey proposes is to avoid both camps by rejecting an assumption that they share in common, namely, "the identification of the religious with the supernatural" (CF 2). By rejecting supernaturalism and separating "the religious" from its unnecessary association with "religion," Dewey argues that we can affirm what is valuable about religious ideals, attitudes, ways of living, and so on while dispensing with those aspects of religion that conflict with modern science and hinder the full realization of secular humanist values and ideals. Summarizing his basic line of argument, he writes:

In the discussion I shall develop another conception of the nature of the religious phase of experience, one that separates it from the supernatural and the
things that have grown up about it. I shall try to show that these derivations
are encumbrances and that what is genuinely religious will undergo an emancipation when it is relieved from them; that then, for the first time, the religious aspect of experience will be free to develop freely on its own account.

(CF 2)

By emancipating the "religious aspect of experience" from religion, Dewey
believes, this valuable function in human life will be free to develop of its own
accord for the first time, having been relieved of the burden of supernatural
commitments that has until now limited its therapeutic possibilities. What
Dewey is proposing is that there is no essential connection between "religion"
in the traditional, supernatural sense of the term and "religious" attitudes or
aspects of experience, which essentially concern ethical attitudes that "may be
taken toward every object and every proposed end or ideal" (CF 10). While such
attitudes have historically tended to take supernatural forms, Dewey thinks
that it is not only possible but also desirable to "emancipate" this therapeutic
function from religion, and to enlist it in the service of purely natural and secular humanist ends.

The major advantage of this secularized or naturalized conception of faith,
as Dewey sees it, is that it allows us to jettison those aspects of traditional religion that are a hindrance to the full realization of natural or secular values and
ideals, or are intellectually suspect, or both, while also preserving a sense of
reverence or "natural piety" that is lacking in militant atheism, which rejects
religion but typically leaves us unable to account for a profound sense of connection, "in the way of both dependence and support," between ourselves and
the universe (CF 29–57). As he explains:

Natural piety is not of necessity either a fatalistic acquiescence in natural hap-
penings or a romantic idealization of the world. It may rest upon a just sense
of nature as the whole of which we are parts, while it also recognizes that we
are parts that are marked by intelligence and purpose, having the capacity to
strive by their aid to bring conditions into greater consonance with what is
humanly desirable. Such piety is an inherent constituent of a just perspective
in life.

(CF 25–26)

So long as we conceive of faith along naturalistic lines as "the unification of the
self through allegiance to inclusive ideal ends, which imagination presents to
us and to which the human will responds as worthy of controlling our desires
and choices" (CF 33), Dewey thinks, there is nothing morally or intellectually

objectionable about faith, and indeed there are very good practical reasons to do so.[20] I will have more to say about Dewey's naturalized reconstruction of religious faith later in this section.

The second aim of Dewey's account of religion that I want to emphasize is its proposed accommodation of religious ideals and values to secular humanist ones, which comes most clearly into focus in lecture 3 of A Common Faith, "The Human Abode of the Religious Function." Here Dewey observes that his distinction between religion and the religious and his prescription of a secularized version of the latter have the added benefit of not requiring us to draw an invidious division between a religious sphere and a secular or profane social sphere (CF 66). The future of "the religious function," he believes, "seems preeminently bound up with its emancipation from religions and a particular religion" (CF 67), and one consequence of this process of secularization is a sense of confusion over how to integrate religious meanings and values into "normal social relations" (CF 70). This is one of the most pressing intellectual and social problems of our time, as Dewey sees it, and what he encourages us to do is to abandon the attempt to give religious meanings and values a supernatural foundation, and to base them instead in what has been their true source and ground all along: the human abode or realm (CF 70–87). If we can bring ourselves to accept this disorienting but ultimately liberating truth, and affirm that the "goods actually experienced in the concrete relations of family, neighborhood, citizenship, and the pursuit of art and science are what men actually depend upon for guidance and support, and that their reference to a supernatural and other-worldly locus has obscured their real nature and has weakened their force," then we will be able for the first time to affirm purely natural social values and relations as the highest values and relations (CF 71). This revolutionary "revaluation of values," to borrow Nietzsche's phrase, is necessary on Dewey's view if we are to avoid devaluing the only values there really are, and if we are to realize the full potential of natural human social relations, or what Dewey calls "the values of natural human intercourse and mutual dependence" (CF 71–87).[21] He writes:

> What would be the consequences upon the values of human association if intrinsic and immanent satisfactions and opportunities were clearly held to and cultivated with the ardor and the devotion that have at times marked historic religions? The contention of an increasing number of persons is that depreciation of natural social values has resulted, both in principle and in actual fact, from reference of their origin and significance to supernatural sources.
> (CF 71)

Dewey thus views supernatural religions at once as obscuring the real source and ground of our values and ideals, as siphoning off energies that might be put to better use in the pursuit of realizing purely natural values or human social ideals, and as a hindrance to the effective realization of those values and ideals. Indeed, he makes clear a few pages later that his basic objection to supernaturalism is that it "stands in the way of an effective realization of the sweep and depth of the implications of natural human relations. It stands in the way of using the means that are in our power to make radical changes in these relations" (CF 80). Although Dewey concedes that traditional religions have made important contributions to the progress of human values and social ideals, he thinks that this has largely been in spite of—and not on account of—their supernatural commitments. These religions have often sought to develop and promote important human qualities and values such as affection, compassion, justice, equality, and freedom, but they have erred in directing their efforts toward "a less promising object" than humanity itself—namely, the supernatural (CF 81).

Having completed this admittedly brief sketch of Dewey's account of religion, I now want to consider his views on self-unification through religious faith in more detail. As we have already seen, Dewey conceives of faith—or, rather, reconceives it—as "the unification of the self through allegiance to inclusive ideal ends, which imagination presents to us and to which the human will responds as worthy of controlling our desires and choices" (CF 33). This "persuasive definition" of Dewey's requires a bit of unpacking.[22]

As I have already mentioned, one of the obvious features of Dewey's conception of faith is that it is a moral or ethical conception, in which faith is to be understood in terms of an individual's commitment to certain moral values or ideals, specifically ones that are "worthy of controlling our desires and choices." Dewey does not specify the content of such a moral faith in much detail, perhaps due in part to the supreme value that he places on growth (which on his view is an intrinsically valuable end, and, more controversially, one that precludes having fixed moral principles, a fixed account of the virtues, or a fixed conception of human nature and the good life for human beings). But he nevertheless indicates that moral feelings, emotions, and values such as affection, compassion, justice, equality, and freedom are the sorts of things he has in mind, and what is needed, on his view, is something that can "weld all these things together" (CF 81). In the past that thing has tended to be a supernatural object of some sort such as God, but, given Dewey's rejection of supernaturalism, that will not do. But a commitment to promoting moral ends such as the perpetual increase of compassion, or justice, or equality, or freedom, or something similar is not inclusive or holistic enough to do the work that Dewey thinks needs to be done; rather, faith must have an object that somehow includes all of these ends and integrates them, presumably in much the same way that a person can possess and exemplify all of these moral qualities. As he explains, "in a distracted age, the need for such an idea is urgent. It can unify interests and energies now dispersed; it can direct action and generate the heat of emotion and the light of intelligence" (CF 51–52). Without such a unifying object, Dewey believed that a purely secular or naturalized faith could not avoid the pitfalls of militant atheism, which suffers from a lack of natural piety and too often takes the nihilistic attitude of human beings "living in an indifferent and hostile world and issuing blasts of defiance" (CF 53). If he is right about all of this, then what is needed is a clear and compelling alternative to both supernatural religions and militant atheism, and what Dewey proposes is that we take the traditional concept of a personal God and reconceive it along purely ethical lines, by regarding God as a symbolic representation and synthesis of our highest moral ideals—variously, as "the unity of all ideal ends arousing us to desire and action" (CF 42) and the "*active* relation between ideal and actual" (CF 51), an idea that is "connected with all the natural forces and conditions—including man and human association—that promote the growth of the ideal and that further its realization" (CF 50).

Putting all of this together, then, to have faith in God on Dewey's proposed reconstruction of faith is to express one's moral commitment to the earlier-mentioned ideals—indeed, to *all* worthy ideal ends, presumably including even ideals that one hasn't yet thought of, let alone committed oneself to—and to the collaborative human project of realizing those ideals in ever-increasing ways. To possess such a faith, Dewey thinks, can unify a person's various moral commitments into a single moral vision, and indeed bring about a kind of harmony or unity in herself, with her fellow human beings, and even with the natural world. In short, we get to enjoy the best features of both religious and naturalist or secular humanist views of the world, while overcoming the theoretical and practical disadvantages of supernatural religions and the practical disadvantages of militant atheism.[23]

It is reasonable, however, to ask some hard questions of Dewey's view, such as what exactly it means, how it works, who might find it convincing, and whether it is even necessary for the defense and advance of secular humanism. Unfortunately, Dewey does not really address these questions, and this presents a rather serious problem—or rather a set of problems—for understanding and evaluating his view. I have no great difficulty understanding what it might mean to think of God as a symbolic representation of our highest moral ideals, and by drawing an analogy with Hegel's concept of Absolute Spirit (which isn't entirely clear to me, either) I think I have some sense of what he means by claiming that the idea of God is "connected with all the natural forces and conditions—including man and human association—that promote the growth of the ideal and that further its realization" (CF 50). But I find Dewey's claim that this *idea* of God could serve as the "*active* relation between ideal and actual" (CF 51) extremely puzzling, especially given his avowed rejection of supernaturalism. This makes Dewey's God sound like an agent who realizes or actualizes ideals in the world and in the lives of human beings, but Dewey explicitly denies that God should be thought of as a real or actually existing divine being who produces real effects in the world. The trouble, though, is that an idea of God all by itself does not plausibly have the power that Dewey wants to ascribe to it, any more than the idea of Batman all by itself could frighten criminals or make a large city a safer place to live. A *real* Batman could accomplish those tasks, of course, and so too, perhaps, could people who were inspired by the idea of Batman and began dressing up and fighting crime by night (though I suspect they would look a lot sillier and get hurt much more often). But in those cases it would be *persons*, and not ideas, that were realizing the ideals of justice and freedom that Batman stands for—or to use Dewey's language, functioning as "the active relation" between those ideals and their actualization. Even if one grants that ideas can function as causes (say, Aristotelian formal causes), it is very hard to see how ideas all by themselves can produce real effects, any more than the idea of a statue all by itself can carve a block of stone.

This presents a rather serious problem for Dewey's defense of his common faith, and for at least two reasons. First, the success of his argument depends in part on convincing atheists who are also secular humanists that they either need to have faith in his "God" if they are to achieve the aims of secular humanism and lead a spiritually fulfilling life, or at least would be better able to achieve those ends by doing so (it is hard to tell whether Dewey is making the stronger or the weaker of these claims). But if human beings can achieve those ends satisfactorily without believing in Dewey's God, then that God seems to be a fifth wheel to the coach. Indeed, many of these atheists will likely find Dewey's continued flirtation with theism, even in this naturalized form, an unnecessary distraction that impedes rather than aids the cause of secular humanism. Second, the success of Dewey's argument also depends in part on convincing theists and other traditional religious believers that they are losing nothing of practical or theoretical value by giving up their supernatural religious beliefs. But if a real God can produce real moral effects in the world and can provide an objective basis for moral values and obligations, and an imaginary or purely ideal God can do neither of those things, then, all other things being equal, Dewey's purely ideal God seems to be deficient by comparison.

Presumably one of Dewey's reasons for retaining the concept of God as the object of his "common faith" is that the concept of a divine person seems to be well (if not uniquely well) suited to the job of providing a perfect moral standard by which we assess our moral beliefs and actions, and because the belief that one stands in a proper relationship with such a being, or is loved, or commanded, or assisted by such a being, or something similar, can have powerful and positive transformative effects on an individual or group of individuals, such as inspiring them to labor for the kingdom of God on earth (or the Kantian kingdom of ends or whatever secularized substitute one prefers). How the latter process works, exactly, is not entirely clear—and to be fair, there don't seem to be any detailed and testable supernatural explanations for this either— but presumably Dewey thinks that there is, or at least could be, a sufficient naturalistic explanation for this process. As we have already seen, however, in the case of Dewey's common faith the divine person must be understood by the believer as an imaginative unification and projection of her own highest moral values and ideals—and imaginative projections do not provide a plausible basis for objective moral values, and are notoriously unable to love, command, or assist us.

Once again, I suspect that most theists would probably view Dewey's God as a poor and decidedly inadequate substitute for the God they already believe in, and most atheists would probably find it unnecessary or even harmful to the cause of promoting secular humanism. If the secular humanist is already committed to noble moral ideals such as the promotion of compassion, justice, equality, and freedom, and if she derives a deep sense of fulfillment and purpose in life by working to realize those ideals—including a stable and unified sense of self and an ethical orientation toward other human beings and the natural world—then why, exactly, does she need to personify them? And what practical or theoretical benefits would she obtain by doing so? Furthermore, if the secular humanist takes an attitude of reverence toward the natural world and the human social world and acknowledges her dependence upon them, can she not have a form of natural piety without believing (if that is the right word) in Dewey's God? I think there are better contemporary alternatives to Dewey's common faith for secular humanists of this sort, and in the absence of a compelling argument for the necessity of belief in a quasi-religious object such as Dewey's God, it is not clear why contemporary secular humanists should accept it.[24]

As we observed in the previous section, James's views on the religious unification of the self might be convincing to many traditional religious believers, but they are likely to be dead on arrival for most contemporary naturalists. What we can now observe of Dewey's views is that they are likely to be dead on arrival for most traditional religious believers *and* for most contemporary naturalists, who are likely to find Dewey's proposed naturalistic reconstruction of religious faith unpersuasive and unnecessary. Perhaps some very liberal Christians or Jews might be persuaded to adopt Dewey's religious vision, in particular those who have been influenced by the writings of religious thinkers like Paul Tillich or Mordecai Kaplan, but it is difficult to imagine that a majority of theists or atheists would ever be converted to Dewey's common faith.

✳ ✳ ✳

So where does this leave us, and what valuable insights, if any, can we take from James's and Dewey's pragmatic accounts of self-unification through religious faith?

In response to the first question, what we are left with is the insight that a commitment to pragmatism can support a remarkably wide range of views on this topic, and that it can be adapted to suit the practical needs of both traditional religious believers and committed naturalists or secular humanists. And this is chiefly because pragmatism is compatible with a wide range of metaphysical views, including James's "piecemeal supernaturalism" and Dewey's rejection of supernaturalism in any form. Rather than seeing this diversity as a weakness or shortcoming of pragmatism, however, I happen to see it as one of its strengths, and as fully consistent with pragmatism's insistence that practical philosophical issues not only do but also should have primacy over theoretical ones. What James and Dewey both held, in their respective and frequently differing ways, was that religious faith or commitment can have a powerfully unifying and positive effect in the lives of human beings, that it can be justified under certain conditions on this basis, and that the loss of this great good in human life has far-reaching and potentially serious implications at both the individual and the social level—and I am inclined to agree with them. Furthermore, what both philosophers sought to do, in their own ways and in line with their own particular metaphysical beliefs, was to defend this practical good in human life against the criticisms of certain religious skeptics, such as the "medical materialists" and scientific positivists that James criticized in *Varieties* or the militant atheists that Dewey criticized in *A Common Faith*.[25] These are both admirable aims, and while I am personally more sympathetic to James's views on the whole I also think there is much to like about Dewey's account of natural piety, which describes a kind of ethical and (for lack of a better word) spiritual attitude or orientation that is, or at least could be, widely shared by many traditional religious believers and many nonreligious people alike, and which potentially might help some individuals to achieve a unified worldview and sense of self without holding what P. J. Ivanhoe calls "heroic" supernatural religious or metaphysical commitments (including quasi-supernatural religious commitments such as faith in Dewey's God).[26]

In response to the second question, I would submit that James can help us to see that scientific inquiry and philosophical inquiry into the nature of religious belief—or religious disbelief, for that matter—have their uses as well as their limits and, perhaps even more importantly, to see where those limits lie. Dewey, in turn, usefully draws our attention to the social function and value of religious faith, which James never denied but tended to give relatively less attention to than his fellow pragmatist. He also helps us to see some of the inadequacies of militant versions of atheism, and to see that there are possible alternatives to traditional supernatural religions on the one hand and the outright rejection of religious faith on the other, even if his own religious alternative is not fully viable at the end of the day. At a time when militant versions of atheism have come to dominate popular reflection on and discussion of religion (not to mention the best-seller lists), and when scientific positivism seems to be enjoying something of a contemporary renaissance, James and Dewey can both provide important correctives and help us to see other possibilities that we might otherwise have missed.

Notes

1. Dewey's version of pragmatism (which he variously termed "instrumentalism" and "the method of intelligence") was, if anything, even broader and more ambitious than James's, insofar as it aimed to resolve not only the traditional problems of philosophy but also "the problems of men," or the various social challenges that human beings confront. In contrast, Peirce—who was the originator of pragmatism—insisted that pragmatism (or "pragmaticism," as he later called it) should be thought of simply as a method for clarifying the meanings of unclear terms, one to be used in the service of scientific inquiry and toward the end of making philosophy a more scientific discipline.

2. I am not particularly interested in the question of which, if either, of these philosophers had the better or more correct understanding of pragmatism, because I do not think that there is a single, widely agreed upon conception of what pragmatism is, and because I think that the differences in James's and Dewey's views on religion have relatively little to do with their views on the nature of pragmatism. Although I do not have the space to argue this point here, I have argued elsewhere that pragmatism is compatible with a wide range of views on metaphysical and religious issues, and that the pragmatist tradition exhibits much more diversity on these issues than is commonly recognized. See, in particular, the introduction to *Pragmatism and the Philosophy of Religion* (Cambridge: Cambridge University Press, 2014), 1–7.

3. I have argued elsewhere that this strategy of James's is a perfectly defensible one, and that it should not be taken as evidence that he had some sort of principled hostility to attempts to investigate religion using the tools of the natural and social sciences. Rather, his minimization of attempts to explain religion scientifically follows from his view that explanations of religion—whether of the naturalistic or the supernatural variety—inevitably beg the question on a range of important metaphysical and epistemological questions and are themselves expressions of particular philosophical "temperaments," which load the empirical evidence in advance in favor of a particular interpretation. See *Pragmatism and the Philosophy of Religion*, chapters 1 and 7.

4. All references to James's works are to *The Works of William James*, ed. Frederick H. Burkhardt, Fredson Bowers, and Ignas Skrupskelis (Cambridge: Harvard University Press, 1975–88). I will use the abbreviation "VRE" for references to *The Varieties of Religious Experience* (1985, originally published in 1902), and "PP" for *The Principles of Psychology*, (1981, originally published in 1890), followed by the page number.

5. James is not entirely consistent in his use of these terms, but I am not sure that this greatly affects the larger argument that he wants to make concerning the practical value of such states for life. On page 201 of *Varieties*, for example, he draws a distinction between the faith-state and the state of assurance when discussing the work of the psychologist James Henry Leuba, and uses the latter term to refer to the affective experience of faith as opposed to its cognitive or doxastic content. Yet when James summarizes his previous conclusions on pages 397–99 of *Varieties* he omits this distinction, and reverts to using Leuba's term *faith-state* in such a way that it includes the state of assurance. (Indeed, he draws a different contrast here between the faith-state,

which he now takes to consist essentially of religious feelings and conduct, and creeds, or the positive intellectual content of particular religions, which when taken together form "religions.")

6. In his previous discussion of the state of assurance in lecture 10, James adds that it also typically involves the sense of perceiving truths not known before, and the sense that the world has undergone an objective and positive change (VRE 201–2).

7. One friendly amendment to James's view would be to add ancestors and past moral exemplars such as sages to this list. In any case, these would seem to be two other types of "ideal social selves" that many human beings, both past and present, have measured their thoughts and actions against, particularly in the traditional cultures of East Asia.

8. As James writes in *Principles*, "The humblest outcast on this earth can feel himself to be real and valid by means of this higher recognition. And, on the other hand, for most of us, a world with no such inner refuge when the outer social self failed and dropped from us would be the abyss of horror" (PP 301).

9. James develops his views on how contemplative practices such as prayer, meditation, and yoga can increase our moral and spiritual "energies" at greater length in two essays written after *Varieties*, "The Energies of Men" (1907) and "The Powers of Men" (1907), although even here his views remain quite speculative.

10. See Slater, *William James on Ethics and Faith* (Cambridge: Cambridge University Press, 2009), esp. 7–8.

11. James took a pluralistic view of the kinds of religious union that are or could be practically efficacious in this way, including not only mystical experiences (whether of the monistic or the dualistic variety) but also more commonplace religious experiences such as the state of assurance, which could be realized by engaging in religious practices such as prayer and meditation. And he took this view, at least in part, because the available empirical evidence does not support specific theological claims about the nature of the unseen order (or "wider self," "higher power," and so on), such as that it is really a personal, omnipredicate God. Rather, the only thing that the evidence "unequivocally testifies is that we can experience union with *something* larger than ourselves and in that union find our greatest peace" (VRE 413).

12. James thus would be critical, I think, of contemporary Christian philosophers who use logical formulas such as Bayes's Theorem to argue that their preferred religious beliefs and hypotheses are more probably true than rival beliefs and hypotheses, such as atheism or naturalism. From James's point of view, such arguments—like the traditional arguments for God's existence—are likely only to convince those who are willing to grant certain crucial assumptions from the outset, such as the probability calculations upon which such arguments are based. They are, in other words, simply more sophisticated ways of preaching to the choir, and are unlikely to convince religious skeptics to change their beliefs.

13. For an extensive and carefully researched historical account of Hegel's influence on Dewey, see James A. Good, *A Search for Unity in Diversity: The "Permanent Hegelian Deposit" in the Philosophy of John Dewey* (Oxford: Lexington, 2006).

14. See Richard M. Gale, *John Dewey's Quest for Unity: The Journey of a Promethean Mystic* (Amherst, NY: Prometheus, 2010).

15. Gale, *John Dewey's Quest for Unity*, 11.

16. John Dewey, *Human Nature and Conduct* (1922), in *The Middle Works of John Dewey*, vol. 14, 1899–1924 (Carbondale: Southern Illinois University Press, 1983, 2008), 146; quoted in Gale, *John Dewey's Quest for Unity*, 89.

17. Gale argues, among other things, that Dewey's obsession with growth at the expense of other goods imposes some impossible demands for many moral choices, and that it leads him to hold some "perversely silly" views about the nature of good human beings. I am sympathetic to these criticisms, but for reasons of space I cannot rehearse them here. See Gale, *John Dewey's Quest for Unity*, 90–91.

18. I offer a more extensive discussion of Dewey's account of religion in chapter 4 of my *Pragmatism and the Philosophy of Religion*.

19. John Dewey, *A Common Faith* (New Haven: Yale University Press, 1934). All references to this work in the text are abbreviated as "CF," followed by the page number.

20. Dewey also remarks at one point that the very idea of a whole—whether of a unified self or world, or of the unification of the self with the world—is an ideal and imaginative construction that we project upon ourselves or the world. "The *whole* self is an ideal, an imaginative projection. Hence the idea of a thoroughgoing and deep-seated harmonizing of the self with the Universe (as a name for the totality of conditions with which the self is connected) operates only through imagination—which is one reason why this composing of the self is not voluntary in the sense of an act of special volition or resolution" (CF 19). This is especially significant in the case of various ways of unifying the self or the self with the world, Dewey thinks, because it entails that such unification cannot be attained simply in terms of itself. "The self is always directed toward something beyond itself and so its own unification depends upon the idea of the integration of the shifting scenes of the world into that imaginative totality we call the Universe" (CF 19). This recognizably Hegelian feature of Dewey's account of religious faith is perhaps most pronounced in his idea of natural piety, and in his naturalized "reconstruction" of the concept of God as the unification of ideal values or ends and the active relation between these ideals and the natural forces and conditions (including human beings) that "promote the growth of the ideal and that further its realization" (CF 43–52).

21. Nietzsche's views regarding the need to "revalue" our inherited moral values have received far more attention from contemporary philosophers than Dewey's, which is unfortunate for several reasons, not the least of which is that Dewey, unlike Nietzsche, championed the democratic ethical and political values that most contemporary Westerners—and most contemporary philosophers—actually tend to affirm. This is pure conjecture on my part, but I suspect that this phenomenon can be partly explained by the fact that Nietzsche's views on this topic are much "edgier" and more iconoclastic than Dewey's, and by the fact that many philosophers place a high (I am tempted to say *inordinate*) value on those qualities.

22. As Richard Gale has observed, Dewey frequently employed "persuasive definitions" in his writings, or "unannounced linguistic innovation[s] whose purpose was to inculcate in the reader an attitude toward the referent of the definition that would aid the establishment of a moral democracy." See Gale, *John Dewey's Quest for Unity*, 10. I thank David Solomon for pointing out to me that Charles Stevenson was the first to use this term of art.

23. Dewey usually gives the impression that militant atheism has only practical disadvantages, in contrast to supernaturalism, which has both practical and theoretical disadvantages. What he does not seem to consider is that some versions of militant atheism might also have theoretical disadvantages, especially those that accept or entail what Owen Flanagan calls an "imperialistic" version of ontological naturalism, which among other things wrongly assumes that we can *know* that the natural world is the only world there is, and has difficulty accounting for things like moral properties because

it assumes that they are necessarily "spooky." For Flanagan's discussion of this version of ontological naturalism and his defense of a nonimperialistic alternative, see "Varieties of Naturalism," in *The Oxford Handbook of Religion and Science*, ed. Philip Clayton (Oxford: Oxford University Press, 2006), 430–52.

24. For a recent defense of secular humanism that derives inspiration from Dewey's views in *A Common Faith* but that dispenses with what we might call his "quasi-theism," see Philip Kitcher, *Life Without Faith: The Case for Secular Humanism* (New Haven: Yale University Press, 2014). Interestingly (and fittingly), both works were originally delivered as the Terry Lectures at Yale.

25. I discuss these features of James's philosophy of religion at greater length in chapter 5 of *William James on Ethics and Faith*, and chapter 1 of *Pragmatism and the Philosophy of Religion*.

26. Heroic meaning that they call upon us to live up to high ideals but require belief far in excess of what evidence supports. For this idea, see Ivanhoe, "Senses and Values of Oneness," in *The Philosophical Challenge from China*, ed. Brian Bruya (Cambridge: MIT Press, 2015), 231–51.

CHAPTER 11

THE SELF AND THE IDEAL HUMAN BEING IN EASTERN AND WESTERN PHILOSOPHICAL TRADITIONS

Two Types of "Being a Valuable Person"

CHO GEUNG HO

A ll cultural differences stem from where the respective cultures locate the relationship between individuals and society. Here, there are only two fundamental choices: either the individual comes before the collective, or the collective comes before the individual (Greenfield 2000). The former is characteristic of the culture of individualism, which is the cultural type dominant in North America, Oceania, and Northern Europe (Hofstede 1980, 1991). In contrast, the latter is characteristic of the culture of collectivism, which is the cultural type dominant in the Chinese-speaking world—including China, Taiwan, Hong Kong, and Singapore—and in the East Asian countries of Korea and Japan, which have been under continuous Chinese influence (Hofstede 1980, 1991).

The West identifies a person as an independent and individual entity. Priority is given to the purpose of the individual rather than to that of the collective, and the motive of social behavior is found in the inner qualities of a person, such as the person's temperament, competence, emotion, and motivation. In contrast, in East Asia, a person's ontological significance is found in the ties between the self and others. Priority is given to the purpose of the collective rather than to that of the individual, and the motive of social behavior is found not in the inner qualities of a person, but in relational and situational factors, such as social norms, duties, and responsibilities (Triandis 1995). This difference in the perception of the relationship between the individual and the collective has led to the development of different concepts of selfhood (Markus and Kitayama 1991) as well as different worldviews (Nisbett 2003) in East Asia and the West. Furthermore, it has been shown that these cultural differences are borne out in various ways through the personal characters and behaviors of individuals living in the respective cultures.

In the background of this cultural tendency of the West, one finds the mainstream of Western history and Western philosophy, long steeped in the values of *personalization*, since classical Greek times (Lukes 1973, Nisbett 2003). Historically, this Western individualism, or the idea of placing the individual before the collective, reached its peak in the Western philosophy of liberalism, which championed the universality of reason and the inalienable rights of liberty for all human beings, who, liberals believe, are all born equal, independent, and autonomous. In short, the ideological backdrop of Western individualism is liberalism (Noh 1991, Cho 2003, 2006, 2007, 2008, 2012, Gray 1985, Laurent 1993, Lukes 1973). In contrast, East Asian collectivism gives priority not to individuals, but to the collective to which they belong. Here, social relations are given priority. Its philosophical background can be found in Confucianism, which emphasizes the importance of taking interest in and being considerate of others, and which gives priority to social responsibility and being ethically upright (Cho 2003, 2006, 2007, 2008, 2012, Bond and Hwang 1986, Kagitcibasi 1996, 1997, Markus and Kitayama 1991, Nisbett 2003, Tu 1985, 1996).

There are two parts to this essay. First, it examines the fact that the cultural differences between Western individualism and East Asian collectivism have their ideological roots in liberalism and Confucianism, respectively (Cho 2003, 2006, 2007, 2008, 2012). These two philosophies differ fundamentally in their understanding of the nature of being human, and the difference is manifested through the character and behavior of the people living in their respective cultural spheres, including their perceptions, emotions, and motivations. Second, Western liberalism and East Asian Confucianism conceptualize an ideal human being differently (Cho 2006). This essay examines how this difference in the conception of an ideal human being leads to different views on what is a valuable life and different conceptions of what constitutes a "valuable person" in the two cultural spheres.

On Being Human: Different Views of Liberalism and Confucianism

In the West, individualism has long been the dominant attitude in life, and its roots can be traced to the seeds of the respect for personality sown by classical Greek civilization; these seeds were nurtured in the strong wind of individualism brought on by the Renaissance and the Protestant Reformation movements; by the seventeenth century in Europe, liberalism was fully developed, and individualism bloomed in full force. The liberal movement that peaked in the seventeenth century spread to all sectors of life following the popular revolutions in America and France, followed by the Enlightenment movement and the Industrial Revolution. By the end of these periods, individualism had firmly taken place in the consciousness and attitudes of the people of the West (Noh 1991, Dumont 1970, Dülmen 1997, Gray 1995, Laurent, 1993, Lukes 1973).

Liberalism is a belief system in which "the individual is seen as coming before the social system or structure, and therefore as being more real and more fundamental than society" (Noh 1991, 31). In other words, liberalism is a belief system in which the individual, living as an independent entity, is seen as the basic unit of society. By thinking that "the individual comes before society, that the individual is more urgent than society," Westerners came to see that, "logically speaking, society was only a fiction that was no more than the sum total of individuals" (Noh 1991, 43). In the liberal worldview, the individual is the irreplaceable center, and liberalism thus serves as the ideological background of individualism.

In this context, the individualist view of a human being can be inferred from the values pursued by liberalism. According to the shared opinions of many scholars (Noh 1991, Dumont 1970, Dülmen 1997, Gray 1995, Laurent 1993, Lukes 1973), the values pursued by liberalism can be summarized as personal freedom and rights, reason and rationality, and human equality and dignity. These are the three value systems from which liberals and individualists draw their view of being human in terms of (a) the source of the human ontological significance, (b) the core human characteristics, and (c) the changeability of a human being. In other words, liberals found human ontological significance in the individuality of a person as the subject of freedom and rights; they found the core human characteristic in reason, which is the basis of rational decision-making; and they found all human beings to be a fully self-contained entities in that each human being is a rational subject with stable capabilities and character.

In contrast, the ideology that has dominated East Asian nations for centuries is Confucianism. Confucianism was the ruling ideology at the highest levels of state governance for two thousand years in China (since Emperor Wu of Han introduced the civil service exam), for a thousand years in Korea (since King Gwang [光宗] of Goryeo introduced the civil service exam and in particular for the five hundred years of the Joseon dynasty, during which neo-Confucianism served as the state ideology), and for four hundred years in Japan (after the establishment of the Tokugawa Shogunate). With this background, "Confucian habits of the heart" are still at work in East Asian nations, and they still maintain a collectivist consciousness and attitude toward life (Tu 1996, 343).

The values pursued by Confucian ideology are the social aspects of human life, moral uprightness, and the human capacity to change. Confucian scholars saw that from womb to tomb, human beings live and die within social relations. In other words, they saw a person as a social *relatum*, an embodiment of social relations. Thus, they found human ontological significance in human sociality and core human characteristics in morality, or the system of a person taking interest in and being considerate toward others. Furthermore, they saw that a person is not born morally perfect, but only as potentially moral, and that a person can change according to the efforts exerted by that person in the course of her social life (Cho 2003, 2006, 2007, 2008, 2012).

The East-West ideological differences discussed so far can be summarized as follows: (a) the individual-oriented Western human view contrasts with the sociality-oriented East Asian human view, which reveals a difference of perception at the level of where to find human ontological significance; (b) the reason-oriented (that is, rationality-oriented) Western human view contrasts with the morality-oriented East Asian human view, which reveals a difference of thinking at the level of what is considered a core human characteristic; and (c) the entity-oriented (that is, self-containment-oriented) Western human view contrasts with the progress-oriented (that is, changeability-oriented) East Asian human view, which reveals a difference of perspective at the level of whether or not a person can change in the lived world of space and time.

Human Ontological Significance: Individuality vs. Sociality

The central difference between liberalism and Confucianism, or between the individualism and the collectivism begotten in Western and East Asian cultures, respectively, has to do with the question of where to find human ontological significance. Liberalism, which fully matured during the Renaissance and Protestant Reformation eras, is a system of thought that attempts to find human ontological significance in the individuality of persons who are independent and have clear boundaries from one another. In this system, society is no more than an aggregate of independent and equal individuals. In other words, the basic liberal argument is that human ontological significance cannot but be revealed through the manifestation of personal independence and uniqueness as its axis.

In this liberal frame of ideology—the prism through which human ontological significance is identified—is, more than anything else, the concept of a person as "the bearer of freedom and rights." This ideology of personal freedom, which includes the notions of religious freedom, freedom of conscience, freedom of expression, political freedom, economic freedom, and freedom of privacy, has been dominant in the West since the seventeenth century, and the notion of these freedoms forms the foundation of liberal ideology. The most exalted ideology pursued by liberalism was the securing of personal freedom, and what was behind this notion of personal freedom was the notion of natural rights. In other words, liberal philosophers believed that a person is born with the basic and inalienable rights to pursue life, property, and happiness, and that personal freedom is the essential mechanism by which these basic rights are executed and protected. What is at the base of this liberal notion is the belief that a person may independently and autonomously choose a faith, conscience, ideology, moral principle, political belief, or political system that is most advantageous, suitable, or appropriate for himself (Noh 1991, Dülmen 1997, Gray 1995, Laurent 1993, Lukes 1973).

In contrast, Confucian philosophy, long the ideological backbone of East Asian cultures, is a theoretical system whose goal is to find human ontological significance in the sociality of a person. In Confucian thought, a person exists within social relations, and outside of such relations, the person loses her very ontological significance. In this system, society is not a set of *individuums* but a large *organismus*, whose compositional units are interpersonal relations. Accordingly, the basic position of Confucianism is that human ontological significance resides within social relations that individuals have with others, that is to say, in human sociality, at the core of which is human interdependence.

In contrast with liberal ideology, in which a person is perceived as the bearer of freedom, Confucian philosophy sees a human being as a social *relatum*, and thus its perspective is firm on regarding a person as "a complex of roles, responsibilities, and concern and sensitivity for others" that inevitably stem from social relations. The basic units of society in Confucian philosophy are interpersonal relations, such as father and son, the sovereign and subject, husband and wife, the old and the young, and friends. Here, an ideal society, one that is harmonious and peaceful, is one in which harmony and order in interpersonal relations are achieved through successful fulfillment of the duties by the principal parties involved in bilateral relations. In Confucian philosophy, the motive of a person's social behavior is found in a person's social roles and responsibilities; consequently, great importance is attached to what serves as the basis of such roles and responsibilities, which is the interconnectedness of the principal parties in a relationship, or their concern and sensitivity for one another.[1]

The Core Human Characteristic: Rationality vs. Morality

Another central difference between Western liberalism and the East Asian Confucian philosophy is that each takes a different position on what is considered the core human characteristic, or the characteristic that is uniquely human and therefore absent in animals. In the West, from the classical Greeks onward, the tripartite theory of soul has been dominant; here, the soul consists of intellect, emotion, and desire. It was believed that, of these three, animals share with humans emotion and desire but not intellect (reason). Thus, in the Western philosophical tradition, intellect (reason) was the most superior characteristic, one that was uniquely human. This approach to understanding what is considered human from the perspective of the supremacy of reason has long been a characteristic of the Western philosophical tradition (Bordt 1999, Guthrie 1960, Hilgard 1980, Ricken 1988). Western liberal thinkers have wholly inherited this tradition; they believe that human beings are the agent of reason, and thus they prize human rationality as the core human characteristic.

From the perspective of identifying a person as an agent of freedom, liberal ideology hinges on the belief that a person is born to pursue his or her happiness and satisfaction, in other words, that a person must act and live according to his or her selfish passions and desires. However, when all human beings thus pursue selfish desires, desires will inevitably clash. It is precisely at this point that the power of reason, inherent in all human beings, comes through, according to liberal thinkers. In other words, as the agent of reason, each person would avoid any catastrophe that might arise from the clash of desires; at the same time, as a collective, individuals will agree to create a system of regulating their desires in such a manner as to maximize individual benefits. In the end, what emerges as the result of this process is a state system based on a social contract. It is the belief of liberal thinkers that, thus, state and society are the products of personal reasoning and that this rationality is manifested through people's capacity to rationally calculate and choose what is good for themselves (Noh 1991, Cho and Kang 2012, Lukes 1973).

In comparison, the East Asian Confucian theory of human character has four elements; it argues that intellect, emotion, desire, and morality comprise human character. In this theory, the first three parts are shared by animals, whereas morality is a uniquely human characteristic; thus, a person must be identified mainly on the basis of his morality. This view of the supremacy of morality was the basic framework through which Confucian philosophers understood humanity. This was a position not only taken by advanced Confucian scholars, but also inherited by neo-Confucians, making it a long-held tradition in Confucianism; in other words, Confucianism is a theoretical system in which innate human morality constitutes the core of the system. Not surprisingly, in East Asian countries, to be a human means to be an agent of moral virtue, and showing concern and sensitivity for others or the collective is emphasized as the core characteristic that sets humans apart from animals.

In contrast to liberal ideology, where a person is recognized as an agent of rationality, what best defines human agency and subjectivity in Confucianism is human morality, which is defined as showing concern and sensitivity for the well-being of others. For Confucian scholars, who identified the human being as an agent of moral virtue, human agency and subjectivity meant being

self-aware that all persons are innately equipped with the foundational elements of morality—such as humaneness, righteousness, propriety, and wisdom (仁義禮智)—and then putting these elements to practice in actual life.[2]

Human Changeability: Self-Containment vs. Variability

The third difference between Western liberalism and East Asian Confucianism in terms of their perspectives on human nature is the difference in their
understanding of a human being as either *a stable entity* that is fully contained
and unchanging or *a variable being* that is in a constant process of changing. It
has been the tendency of the Western philosophical tradition since the classical Greek civilization to view all individual objects comprising this world as
having fixed and self-contained properties in and of themselves and, accordingly, to view all persons living in the world in the same way (Nisbett 2003).
Liberal thinkers believe that all persons are self-contained entities with fixed
and stable properties with which to self-direct their actions. They also believe,
given that all persons are equipped with autonomy to develop the properties
inherent in themselves to achieve self-realization, that all persons are equal and
that all human beings are dignified, in that their particular inherent properties are unique to each individual (Lukes 1973). In other words, they sought
to find the basis for equality and dignity for all human beings in the self-
contained nature of all human beings or in the supposition that every human
being is a self-contained entity with stable properties.

The Western view of objects in the world, from ancient Greece to today, is
that objects have fixed properties, that all their properties are stable, and that
they do not change over time or under changing circumstances. This belief also
carries over to their view of the human subject. Liberal thinkers, in particular,
believe that all human beings have uniquely individual internal dispositions
(character, capacities, motivation, and so on) and that such dispositions are
fixed and stable entities, just as the objects in the world are. In other words,
they believe that every individual has characteristic dispositions and capacities that are fixed, and such fixed qualities take on stability that does not change
(Dweck 1991, Dweck, Hong, and Chiu 1993).

In contrast, Confucianism is a system aimed at cultivating virtue (成德); its
premise is that a human being is by nature equipped with infinite possibilities
and that anyone can cultivate virtue through education (教) and learning (學).
Confucian thinkers believe that a person can learn according to the teachings
of her predecessors (先人) or those who have already achieved the Dao (道) or
thereby achieved self-reflection and self-improvement, that a person is a variable being who can thereby eventually transform the self from a "small person"
(小人) into an ideal man, or "gentleman" (君子), and that human life is a process

of cultivating oneself toward the ultimate state of virtue. In other words, Confucian philosophers believe that a person is a variable being and a being in process and never an unchangeable or fixed being.

It is characteristic of Confucianism to identify a person as a variable being and a being in process; through learning, a person can become a gentleman. Confucianism also identifies a human being as being relational by nature, and, in accordance with this view, it emphasizes not only the changeability of a person's moral maturity, but also the flexibility and variability of a person's identity, as it would change according to the different roles and responsibilities a person takes on in the course of his life.[3]

Cultural Difference Between Western Individualism and East Asian Collectivism

As we have seen thus far, from the standpoint of liberalism, the ideological backbone of Western individualism, a person is endowed with freedom and rights and is self-contained as the source of all his or her behaviors, an agent of rationality who is equipped with rational thinking and the capacity to choose and a fully contained entity equipped with stable and consistent qualities. In contrast, from the standpoint of Confucianism, the ideological backbone of East Asian collectivism, a person is a complex of roles and responsibilities, which arise from the person's social relations in the world, an agent of moral virtue, or a person who shows concerns and sensitivity toward others and the community, and a variable, who is born a small person but who can develop into a gentleman.

These different viewpoints on human nature are at the base of more general differences such as focus of attention, mode of self-expression, and belief in human changeability among people in the West and in East Asia. These aspects, in turn, operate as the source of different manifestations in all spheres of life among Westerners and East Asians, including personal evaluation, attribution, emotion, and motivation.[4]

In terms of the focus of attention, the East-West difference stems from whether a culture privileges the individual characteristics or the socioontological characteristics of a person. This difference determines whether the attention is focused on the individual as a person who is fully equipped with self-motivation for all his or her behaviors (individualism), or on the circumstances and social relations of a person that serve as the source of the person's behaviors (collectivism).

In terms of modes of self-expression, the East-West difference stems from whether a culture sees the core human characteristic as rationality, the foundation for making rational decisions, or as morality, the foundation for exhibiting concern and sensitivity for others and the community. These differences determine whether a culture encourages revealing or hiding the self as agency. They also determine whether it is desirable for a person to change the environment to suit the needs of the self, according to rational choices the self makes, and thus actively manifest the self in the process (individualism), or to change the self to fit the environment or the relationship the self is engaged in, and consequently to withdraw oneself within society (collectivism).

In terms of belief in the human ability to change in the lived world of space and time, the East-West difference stems from whether a person is seen as a fixed and stable entity or as a variable being always in the process of changing. The difference here determines whether a person is identified as a seeker of consistency who has fixed and stable characteristics (individualism), or as a flexible changer who can change him- or herself according to different circumstances or changing social relations (collectivism).

Cultural Differences at the Level of Focus of Attention: Emphasis on Independence, Autonomy, and Originality vs. Emphasis on Connectedness, Harmony, and Similarity

The different viewpoints discussed earlier concerning where one finds human ontological significance or whether it is found in human individuality or in human sociality, gives rise to different viewpoints regarding the focus of one's attention in life. This difference, in turn, leads people in the two different cultures to emphasize different aspects of their social lives.

The perception of a person as the bearer of freedom engenders the attitude of privileging personal independence and autonomy in life. Ultimately those who hold such an attitude prize independence and autonomy, and they show psychological and behavioral profiles of pursuing independence and autonomy in their everyday activities. They find the motives for their social behaviors in the unique inner qualities (personality, skills, desires, emotion, and so on) of the individual, the bearer of freedom. Accordingly, in an individualist society, attention naturally is focused on an individual person and on his or her inner qualities, and consequently this leads to the self-centered psychological and behavioral characteristics that exaggerate individual uniqueness.

On the other hand, the perception of a person as a social *relatum*, and therefore as a complex of roles, responsibilities, and concern for others, engenders an attitude of emphasizing connectedness and harmony. Those who hold such an attitude place a high value on interconnectedness and harmony and carry within them a psychological and behavioral tendency to pursue them in their everyday activities. Their emphasis on connectedness and harmony would bring about the result where the focus of attention is given to others and the communities to which they belong (rather than to themselves) and to public norms and the demands of the circumstances (rather than to their own inner qualities). Ultimately, this is connected to other- or collective-centered psychological and behavioral characteristics that pursue the similarity between oneself and others excessively.

Personal Evaluation

Because of the difference in focus of attention, the two cultures have different standards for evaluating the self and others, different contents to emphasize for socialization, and different characteristics to underscore for personal evaluation. For example, in the individualist society, the *self* is the standard by which to evaluate oneself and others. In such society, people exaggerate their uniqueness; emphasis for socialization is placed on the question of "What can I do?" (identifying skills and pursuing uniqueness). Consequently, accumulation of personal possessions (including skills and achievements) becomes the basis for positive self-evaluation. Accordingly, these subjects not only exert efforts to identify and develop their unique skills and talents, but in the process of personal evaluation they also place high value on characteristics (extroversion, aggressiveness, leadership, volubility, and so on) that could actively manifest their skills and talents.

In contrast, in collectivist society, the other is the standard by which to evaluate oneself and others. In such society, similarities between the self and others are exaggerated; emphasis for socialization is placed on the question of "Who am I?" (confirming position in a group and identifying with members of the group). Consequently, formation of harmonious relations with members of the group becomes a channel for a positive self-evaluation. Accordingly, these subjects exert efforts to cultivate characteristics (kindness, consideration for others, gentleness, modesty, generosity, and so on) for pursuing relational harmony, and they place high value on these characteristics in personal evaluation (Bond and Hwang 1986, Fiske et al. 1998, Heine and Lehmam 1997, Kitayama et al. 1997, Markus and Kitayama 1991, Rhee et al. 1995, Srull and Gaelick 1983, Triandis 1995).

Attribution

In an individualist society, a person is identified as an independent being separate from his or her external circumstances and thus as a bearer of a stable, innate disposition. Here, a person's innate qualities (disposition) are seen as the motive for the person's behaviors. Accordingly, the source of action is attributed not to external factors, but to the person's inner qualities, which is a form of attribution whose distinguishing mark is *dispositional bias*.

In contrast, in a collectivist society, a person is identified based not on the individual's inner qualities, but on situational factors and relations external to the inner qualities of a person. Accordingly, social roles and pressures predicating the person's circumstances and social relations are seen as the source of the behavior. Here, *situational bias* is revealed as the characteristic mode of attribution, where the cause of action is attributed not to personal inner qualities, but to situational factors (Choi and Nisbett 2000, Fiske et al. 1998, Markus and Kitayama 1991, Miller 1984, Morris and Peng 1994, Nisbett 2003, Nisbett et al. 2001).

Emotions

In individualist society, emotions that are helpful for pursuing individual autonomy and uniqueness are valued highly, and consequently individualists become sensitive to such emotions as pride, a sense of happiness, and anger, which encourage division among individuals and personal independence. Accordingly, in individualist society, where the inner qualities of an individual are taken as the primary reference point, *differentiating emotions* are encouraged and often experienced.

In contrast, in collectivist society, emotions helpful for caring and attaining harmony with others are valued highly, and consequently collectivists become sensitive to such emotions as compassion, sympathy, and a sense of shame, which are helpful in building relationships among people. Accordingly, in collectivist society, where others are taken as the primary reference point, *integrating emotions* are encouraged and often experienced (Markus and Kitayama 1991, 1994, Matsumoto 1989).

Motivation

In individualist society, *motivation of agency* is emphasized: this is "related to the behavior of separating an individual from his or her immediate community, and of trying to secure personal benefits independent of regard for others in the social environment, even at the cost of sacrificing others" (Geen 1995, 249). Such motivations of agency privilege the self over others and the collective; they are motivations for pursuing personal autonomy and independence. This category of motivation includes seeking autonomy, triumph, domination, self-display, and independence.

In contrast, in collectivist society, *motivation of communion* is likely to be emphasized; this "leads a person to have close ties with others and produces behaviors that promote a sense of communion between a person and the person's social environment" (Geen 1995, 249). Such motivation of communion is a motivation that privileges the interest of others and the collective, rather than the interest of the self, and as such it aims for belongingness in the collective. This category of motivation includes belongingness, respect, imitation, intimacy, and social acceptance (Geen 1995, Markus and Kitayama 1991, Wiggins 1992).

Cultural Differences at the Level of Mode of Self Expression: Emphasis on Self-Assertion vs. Emphasis on Self-Restraint

The question here is whether core human characteristics are to be found in reason, the basis of human rationality, or in morals, the foundation for having concern and sensitivity for others and the collective community. Answers to this question have implications for whether it is the external environment vis-à-vis the self or the self and its private desires and feelings that need to be controlled in life. The difference of viewpoint on this question leads to cultural differences on what is considered a proper mode of self-expression.

Liberals, who see a person as a rational subject, emphasize human rationality. Their belief in the power of reason is so strong that it has become a tenet of life for them. They believe that, as agents of reason, humans can control the world of external environment, and the external environment then becomes the object of control for them. Because they are the agents of reason, they are aggressive in expressing themselves; they try to augment their personal attributes (such as their strengths, positive characteristics, skills, and emotions) that would bring them benefits; and their optimism for their present and future tends to be exaggerated. Accordingly, the distinguishing feature of their psychological and behavioral characteristics is that they place high value on aggressive self-expression.

In contrast, to Confucians, human agency is directly related to taking on responsibility for everything as a moral subject. Accordingly, for them, controlling one's selfish and personal desires and feelings is equivalent to exercising human agency and subjectivity, or a shortcut to becoming morally virtuous, their goal in life. As a result, in Confucian societies, the object of control is the self, the subject of cultivating moral virtues; thus they lay stress on modesty and self-restraint. The distinguishing feature of their psychological and behavioral characteristics is that they place high value on self-restraint; the self must not actively reveal itself but, rather, should withdraw inward.

Personal Evaluation

The difference in the viewpoints of what is considered a proper mode of self-expression is also revealed in the different modes of resolution for personal conflicts. In individualist society, direct confrontation through competition and confrontation is preferred. In collectivist society, resolution through concession and mediation, thereby avoiding direct confrontation, is preferred (Nisbett 2003, Peng and Nisbett 1999, Triandis 1989). This difference in the modes of conflict resolution in the two cultures reflects the difference in what each culture pursues as an important characteristic. In other words, in individualist society, assertiveness, forthrightness, competition, and extroversion are valued, as they reveal personal uniqueness and supremacy; on the other hand, in collectivist society, concession, cooperation, and introversion are valued, as they contribute to building harmony in social relations (Barnlund 1975, Bond and Hwang 1986, Markus and Kitayama 1991).

Attribution

In causal reasoning for success or failure, *self-serving bias* is prominent among individualists, who attribute their success to their own innate personal qualities, such as their personal excellence, while attributing failure to external factors, such as bad luck. In contrast, *modesty bias* is prominent among collectivists, who attribute success to external factors, such as good luck and help from others, while attributing failure to internal factors, such as insufficient capacity or effort (Davis and Stephan 1989, Fiske et al. 1998, Heine and Lehman 1997, Markus and Kitayama 1991).

Emotion

"Display rules" for manifesting emotions exist in every society in order to control and regulate emotional expressions within social boundaries (Ekman 1982). In individualist society, emotional expression is about being straightforward and honest, and thus anger and pride are encouraged to be readily expressed. Furthermore, in such a society, repression of emotion is thought to lead to psychological maladjustment so that even negative emotions, such as anger, are actively expressed, because it is believed that they are beneficial in adjusting interpersonal relations. In contrast, in collectivist society, expression of allocentric emotions, such as compassion and sympathy, is recommended; self-centered emotions such as pride and anger are thought to harm interpersonal relations and harmony of the collective and are thus actively suppressed (Markus and Kitayama 1991, 1994, Matsumoto 1989, Matsumoto and Juang, 2004).

Motivation

In individualist society, personal capacity is experienced through expression of one's inner desires, emotions, and abilities, and through resistance efforts against social pressure. Here, control ultimately means changing social conditions or external restrictions (obstacles) in order to achieve individuality and autonomy. Accordingly, in this society, uniqueness, excellence, competence in self-expression, and freedom from external restraints are sources of pride, and thus motivation to control the external environment is strong. In contrast, in collectivist society, personal capacity is experienced through showing sensitivity toward others, through adaptation to the needs and demands of the situation, and through efforts toward self-suppression and modulation. Here, control ultimately means suppressing inner qualities, such as personal desires and goals and private feelings, in order to realize interdependence and connectedness. Accordingly, in this society, self-suppression, adaptation to the environment, and maintenance of harmony in interpersonal relations are sources of pride, and thus motivation to control inner desires is strong (Markus and Kitayama 1991, Morling 1997, Morling, Kitaama, and Miyamoto 2002, Rothbaum, Weisz, and Snyder 1982, Weisz, Rothbaum, and Blackburn 1984).

Cultural Differences at the Level of Belief in Human Changeability: Emphasis on Stability, Consistency, and Expansion of Merits vs. Emphasis on Variability, Flexibility, and Self-Improvement

Westerners today have inherited the long tradition of identifying a person as a fixed and stable entity, and they show a strong belief structure in *entity theory*, which assumes that a person's character and capacity do not change over time or over a change of circumstances (Dweck 1991, Dweck, Hong, and Chiu 1993). Accordingly, Westerners show a tendency to identify the existence of a stable and immutable consistency between inner dispositions, between external behaviors, and between an inner disposition and an external behavior. Consequently, they show strong psychological and behavioral characteristics of pursuing stability and consistency; they see themselves achieving self-development through expansion of merits, identifying merits and expanding upon them. In contrast, from the perspective of Confucianism, which sees a person as in process of becoming and variable, a person may verify and accept his or her shortcomings and improve upon them through learning. Thus, they emphasize self-improvement. East Asians today have inherited the long Confucian tradition of emphasizing human variability and self-improvement, and they show a strong belief in *incremental theory*, which assumes that a person's character and capacity can change dynamically over time or over a change of circumstances (Dweck 1991, Dweck, Hong, and Chiu 1993). Accordingly, East Asians show a tendency to tolerate and accept their own negative factors (shortcomings, negative characteristics, and emotions), to consider it valuable to improve upon them, and to prize efforts more than capacity with regard to achievement. As a result, they show strong psychological and behavioral characteristics emphasizing variability and flexibility according to changing circumstances, and accept and improve upon personal shortcomings.

Personal Evaluation

In comparison to individualists, collectivists have a stronger faith in the variability of a person's character over time and over a change of circumstance; they also have a stronger tendency to see that human behaviors are triggered solely not by inner characteristics, such as a person's character, but through interaction with external situations (Choi and Nisbett 1998, 2000, Nisbett 2003, Norenzayan, Choi, and Nisbett 2002). Such differences lead to differences of self-narration between individualists and collectivists. In other words, one of the self-concept characteristics of individualists (Americans and Western Europeans) is that positive characteristics exceed negative characteristics by four to five times; thus, they perceive themselves mainly through positive characteristics. However, in the case of collectivists (Koreans, Chinese, and Japanese), the ratio is either the same, or negative characteristics exceed positive characteristics. This shows the tendency of collectivist society to tolerate negative characteristics. The result shows that the Barnum effect—the self-perception of oneself as possessing both positive characteristics (for example, politeness) and negative characteristic (for example, rudeness)—is more pronounced among collectivists than among individualists (Bond and Cheung 1983, Choi 2002, Choi and Choi 2002, Heine and Lehman 1995, 1997, Heine et al. 1999, Stigler, Smith, and Mao 1985).

Attribution

In individualist society a person's constant and stable qualities are perceived as the motive for all his or her behaviors. Thus individualists place a higher value on personal capacity, rather than on personal efforts; the former is fixed and stable and does not change due to circumstances, while the latter could change in another situation. Thus, individualists have a strong tendency to attribute success to personal capacity. In contrast, in collectivist society, the emphasis is on variability, or on adjusting one's behavior appropriately according to varying circumstances. Collectivists place a higher value on personal efforts, rather than on personal capacity, and have a strong tendency to attribute success to personal efforts rather than to personal capacity (Mizokawa and Ryckman 1990, Stevenson and Stigler 1992).

Such differences in the attribution for the cause of achievement lead to the East-West divergence in achievement model. In the West, achievement is conceptualized in a multiplying model (Achievement = Capacity × Effort), where capacity is more important than effort. In this model, it is assumed that if one does not have capacity in a particular field, there is no amount of effort that would lead to any achievement. In contrast, in East Asia, achievement is conceptualized in an additive model (Achievement = Capacity + Effort), where effort is more important than capacity. In this model, it is assumed that even without capacity one could achieve some results by exertion of effort. Such difference in achievement model is well illustrated in the fierce fervor for education in East Asia (Markus and Kitayama 1991, Nisbett 2003, Norenzayan, Choi, and Nisbett 2002, Singh 1981, Triandis 1995).

Emotion

In individualist society, independence and uniqueness are a cultural imperative; thus aggressive self-assertion and self-expression are considered desirable. Consequently, such a society aims for the pursuit of positive self-image and positive emotions. In other words, individualists are sensitive to positive emotions—such as pride, happiness, joy, and pleasantness; they have a high frequency of experiencing such emotions; and while they are agreeable in accepting such emotions, their reception level for negative emotions is very low. In contrast, in collectivist society, social connectedness is a cultural imperative; thus concern for others and maintenance of group harmony are emphasized. Ultimately, such society places high value on self-restraint and on discovering one's negative characteristics and on efforts to improve upon them. Consequently, such society is more receptive to negative characteristics or negative emotions than to one's own positive characteristics and positive emotions, and they are more ready to accept experience of such emotions and characteristics. In other words, collectivists have a relatively higher frequency of experiencing negative emotions—such as humiliation, sorrow, pity, and regret—and a stronger tendency to accept them as desirable (Bagozzi, Wong, and

Yi 1999, Diener et al. 1995, Kitayama and Markus 2000, Markus and Kitayama 1991, 1994, Suh and Diener 1995).

Motivation

In individualist society, a person's behavior is seen as a manifestation of the person's stable inner qualities, and thus any discordance between the person's inner qualities and behavior, or discordance from one situation to another, brings about severe confusion. Ultimately, individualist society shows a strong motivation for pursuing consistency. In contrast, in collectivist society, that character and behavior can change depending on the situation is accepted and encouraged. Thus, any incongruence between a person's inner qualities and his or her behavior, or incongruence of one's social behavior from one situation to another, does not pose a problem. Accordingly, in this society, there is not much motivation for pursuing consistency (Choi, Choi, and Cha 1992, Choi and Nisbett 1998, Fiske et al. 1998, Heine and Lehman 1997, Markus and Kitayama 1991, Nisbett 2003, Nisbett et al. 2001).

East-West Differences on the View of the Ideal Human Being

So far, the liberal and Confucian differences on what it means to be a human have been examined from three viewpoints: where each culture found the source of human ontological significance; what each culture considers core human characteristics that distinguish humans from animals; and whether or not each culture believes that humans can change over space and time. Then, how these differences of viewpoints were translated into real world differences of people's behaviors in the two cultures have been explored. Based on the differences of the characters and behaviors exhibited by people living in these two cultures, it is possible to arrive at the different images of the ideal human being espoused by the two cultures. This difference of viewpoints on the ideal human being reveals divergent attitudes on what is considered a valuable life; from this, one can postulate the different concepts of self-making and being a valuable person as espoused in the West and in East Asia.

The Ideal Human Being in the West: A Self-Actualizing Person

In the West, due to the liberal ideological tradition, it is viewed that the ultimate ontological unit of society is the equal and independent individual and that society is no more than a collective sum of these individual entities. In this view, an individual is perceived as the bearer of freedom, the subject of reason, and a stable and fixed entity. Here, the departure point for any social institution is the individual, or a person who is self-contained, with the skills, motivations, emotions, and characteristics necessary to be a whole being, who is separate and independent of circumstances or other people. Accordingly, the normative units of social behavior are basically found in the fixed, inner qualities of the nonsocial individual. The result is that a situation-disconnected and individual-centered view of a human being stands out, and the individualist position, in which the manifestation of the individuality of a person becomes the purpose of any social relationship, gains prominence.

Westerners perceive a person as the bearer of freedom and rights; thus, a person with independence, autonomy, and uniqueness is esteemed. They perceive a person as the subject of reason; thus, a person who has strong opinions and who aggressively expresses himself or herself based on rational judgment is appreciated. And they perceive a person as a self-contained entity; thus, a person equipped with stability and consistency who exerts efforts to expand his or her merits is valued.

Such a portrait of an ideal human being as perceived in the West is plainly reflected in modern Western psychological theories. While modern personality psychology suggests a portrait of an ideal person from a number of different perspectives—including self-actualization (Adler, Jung, Maslow), productivity (Fromm, Rogers), adaptability (Erikson, Lawton), integrity (Cattel, Elkin, Seeman), maturity (Allport), and autonomy (Riesman)—Kim (1976, 1989) has classified them collectively as a "theory of mature personality." He has identified fifty-two characteristics of the "mature personality" that Western psychologists describe and, through cluster analysis, has further sorted them into five clusters of similar characteristics. In other words, in modern Western psychology, an ideal human being can be conceptualized in five clusters of personality characteristics.

The clusters are *subjectivity, self-acceptance, self-integrity, problem-centeredness*, and *warm personal relationship*. Here subjectivity refers to "clearly recognizing one's own skills, and exerting efforts to actualize one's in-born potentials." Self-acceptance refers to "effectively recognizing one's reality, objectifying oneself in it, and accepting reality and self as they are." Self-integrity refers to "living a life of firm and valid goals, setting a unified world-view, and thus behaving autonomously." Problem-centeredness refers to "feeling satisfied from solving problems in reality firsthand and focusing on work not in a self-centered but in a problem-centered manner." "Warm personal relationship" refers to the characteristic of maintaining close relationships with others "with love, understanding, and accepting attitude" (Kim 1976, 1–27; 1989, 199–243).

Except for the characteristic of having a warm personal relationship, the four other personality clusters are drawn from interest in the person as an individual entity. Whether it is the recognition of one's own capacity and potentiality (subjectivity), recognition and acceptance of the reality surrounding oneself (self-acceptance), objective definition of one's course of life and life goal (self-integrity), or orientation toward achievement that is focused on actualizing one's potentials in everyday life (problem-centeredness), these are characteristics that are deeply related to establishing and achieving the identity of a person as an individual entity. A sense of identity comprises objective and accurate understanding and acceptance of one's abilities and potentials, of objective and accurate understanding of one's situation, and of the recognition of self-sameness and self-continuity comprising objective and accurate establishment of a life goal and course that are based on the first two understandings (Erikson 1959, 102). Self-actualization is achieving all of one's potentialities in reality by pursuing this sense of identity (Rhi 2002, 90–93).

Thus, in the individualist Western conceptualization of an ideal human being, self-actualization is at its core, while warm interpersonal relationship is secondary. In other words, A person who has established self-identity, exerts efforts in everyday life to realize one's own potentials, and builds warm personal relationship with others in life is a person who has actualized himself (Jung, Maslow), who is creative (Adler), productive (Fromm), healthy (Erikson), and mature (Allport), who has integrity (Cattell), and who is fully functioning (Rogers), well adapted, and independent (Riesman). This view of an ideal human being, or the characteristics of a self-actualized person, established by modern personality psychology, has direct bearing on Westerners' view of the self.

Subjectivity is first and foremost an awareness of one's own abilities and potentials; this is linked to the notion of a person as the bearer of freedom and rights; thus, it is pertinent in seeking human ontological significance in the person's individuality. It is pertinent because a subjective person would pursue originality of the self independently and autonomously.

Self-acceptance involves being accurately aware of and accepting the reality that surrounds oneself. Problem-centeredness is an attitude in which one is focused on problem-solving as a means of fully realizing one's own potential in everyday life. These characteristics are closely linked to the notion of the human being as a subject of reason, or a rational being. This is because both the attitude of accepting reality as is and problem-centeredness are products of rational self-understanding.

Self-integrity means defining the course of one's life and its goals objectively. This is linked to the view of a person as a stable entity and therefore lays emphasis on consistency and stability. This is because people who have solid and reasonable life goals, and a unified view of the self based on a unified worldview, are those who would pursue consistent and stable life goals.

The Ideal Human Being In East Asia: An Ontologically Expanding Person

In the Confucian tradition, a person exists and is defined within his or her social relationships with others, and that, accordingly, society is maintained as a result of everyone faithfully carrying out the roles and responsibilities implicated in those relationships. In other words, this view holds that the ultimate unit of society is the unit of interpersonal relationship, or a primary group such as a family, the archetype of such relationship; apart from such relationships, an individual is only an imaginary atom and loses ontological significance. As such, a person in East Asia is perceived as a complex of responsibilities, roles, and consideration for others, as a subject cultivating virtue, and as a variable being and a being in process. In such a system, interpersonal relationships are the departure point for any social institution; accordingly, the normative units of social behavior are found in the social roles and interconnectedness of a person. Consequently, a situation-dependent and relationship-centered view of human beings stands out, and the collectivist position, in which the purpose of social relationships is to pursue harmony and order, gains prominence.

East Asians perceive a person as a social *relatum*; thus, a person pursuing connectedness, harmony, and similarity is esteemed. They perceive a person as the subject of cultivating virtue; thus, a person who is deeply concerned about others and the community, and who is outstanding in self-control is appreciated. And they perceive a person as a variable being and a being in process; thus, a person who is flexible and who can change oneself according one's situation and one who tries to find one's own shortcomings and improve upon them is valued.

Such a portrait of the ideal human being as perceived in East Asia is plainly reflected in the Confucian "gentleman" (君子) and "sage" (聖人), which represent the concept of the ideal human being. Confucian scriptures suggest various characteristics of the gentleman, or *gunja*, but what has become the foundation of the discourse on the ideal person for all Confucian scholars since the time of Confucius is the following discourse on gentleman, as set out in the *Analects* 14.42:

> Zilu asked about the *junzi*. The Master said, "One should cultivate oneself to be reverent." "Is that all there is to it?" "Cultivate oneself to bring comfort to others." "Is that all there is to it?" "Cultivate oneself to bring comfort to the people. Even Yao and Shun were apprehensive about cultivating themselves to bring comfort to the people."

In this exchange of question and answer with Zilu, one of his disciples, Confucius states that the "gentleman" is one who "cultivates oneself to be reverent" (修己以敬), one who "cultivates oneself to bring comfort to others" (修己以安人), and one who "cultivates oneself to bring comfort to the people" (修己以安百姓); thus, the three characteristics of the gentleman as established by Confucius are self-cultivation (修己), having harmonious relations with others (安人), and undertaking and fulfilling obligations to society (安百姓).

To "cultivate oneself to be reverent" is for the gentleman to restrain his personal desires and emotions, to not shift any of his responsibilities to others, and to cultivate himself and seek self-improvement, thereby achieving a firm awareness of himself as a moral subject. In other words, a person who cultivates in himself respectful attentiveness is one who has achieved perfect personality as a person.

To "cultivate oneself to bring comfort to others" is for the gentleman to cultivate his body based on benevolence and righteousness, thereby cultivating the morals, and leading others to comfort in everyday life. In other words, this refers to perfection of harmony in interpersonal relations or having achieved relational perfection.

To "cultivate oneself to bring comfort to the people" is for the gentleman who has achieved cultivation through self-improvement not only to embrace family, friends, and others around him and to achieve harmony only with them, but also to lead all people under the sky, or the entire nation, to comfort by voluntarily imposing social duty on himself. In other words, this refers to an attitude of taking on social responsibilities and exerting efforts to fulfill them.

This position of Confucius as recorded in the *Analects* was carried forward intact by later Confucian scholars, such as Mencius. For example, Mencius said, "Po Yi among the sages was the pure one; Yi Yin was the one most inclined to take office; Hui of Liuxia was the accommodating one," suggesting three characteristics of an ideal human being as "holding on to purity of the sages" (聖之清), "achieving the harmony of the sages" (聖之和), and "fulfilling the responsibilities of the sages" (聖之任).[5]

As observed earlier, the ideal human being commonly conceptualized by Confucian scholars has three aspects: self-improvement through self-cultivation and firm self-awareness as a moral subject; self-restraint and pursuit of harmony in personal relations; and taking interest in others and in society, voluntarily taking on social duties and having an attitude to implement them in practical life. Thus, the ideal human being postulated by Confucian scholars is a self-expanding person who does not stop at achieving his or her own personal maturity as a moral subject, but one who builds upon his or her own self-cultivation to take interest in and show consideration for the well-being of others, and take on social duties, and thereby create harmony with other people and be socially accountable; in other words, it is a self-expanding person. This model of an ideal human being as a self-expanding person is a model that is drawn directly from the Confucian view of what constitutes a human being.

The basic characteristic of being a valuable person for both the gentleman and the sage is self-cultivation; this plainly reflects the faith of Confucian scholars in the infinite potential of a human being. This Confucian emphasis on self-cultivation is based on the Confucian faith in human plasticity, commensurate with human endeavors. In this context, it can be deduced that the characteristic of the gentleman, which is the perfection of self as a person through self-cultivation, is intimately related to the variability and self-improvement that are emphasized by East Asian collectivists when they consider human changeability.

Another characteristic of being a valuable person for both the gentleman and the sage is harmonious personal relations; this characteristic stems from the subjective identification with the view that a person is inherently fully equipped with a moral foundation and that an individual is a moral subject. It is assumed that the gentleman and the sage are well aware that other people have the same morals, desires, tastes, and feelings that they do; it is because of this that in relationship with others they are able to restrain themselves, and to be proactive in showing consideration for others. In this context, it is clear that the characteristic attributed to the gentleman, the forming and maintaining harmonious personal relations, triggered the self-restraint that East Asians emphasize when they consider modes of self-expression. It can be concluded that the characteristic attributed to the Confucian gentleman, that of pursuing harmony in personal relations, is deduced from the view of a human being as a moral subject.

Also, the core characteristic of being a valuable person for the gentleman and the sage is voluntarily taking on and carrying out social duties; this characteristic stems from identifying a human being as a social *relatum*, from understanding a person in the context of connectedness with others, and from the attitude of living a life in which one tries to achieve harmony in one's relationships with others. The gentleman and the sage see that human ontological significance lies in relations people have with others and thus emphasize the importance of the social nature of life. Accordingly, Confucian scholars argue, one should always secure harmonious connectedness with others and not avoid but incorporate social duties arising from such relations into one's life. In this context, it can be seen that the characteristic attributed to the gentleman, or taking on and carrying out social duties, is deeply related to connectedness and harmony that the East Asian collectivists emphasize when they consider the level of focus of attention.

Two Types of "Being a Valuable Person"

As shown earlier, there is a sense of subjectivity with which Westerners take in their reality as is. They define an ideal human being as a self-actualizing person; such a person is one who, based on a unified outlook on life, immerses herself in work with a problem-focused approach, and thereby accomplishes achievements in the real world by proving her uniqueness and potential. This notion of the ideal human being in the West originates from the liberal view of a person, which, based on its assumption of human individuality, rationality, and substantiality as a fully self-contained entity, emphasizes personal independence, autonomy, originality, active self-assertion, rational thinking, judgment, and the pursuit of stability and consistency in its understanding of what constitutes a human being.

In contrast, East Asians postulate an ideal human being to be a self-expanding person, who accomplishes self-perfection as a moral person through a process of self-cultivation, or self-improvement upon discovering and correcting flaws within oneself, who pursues harmonious social relations by expanding her concerns and sensitivity for others, and who exerts efforts to voluntarily take on and fulfill social duties. This notion of the ideal human being in East Asia originates from the Confucian view of a person, which, based on its assumption of human sociability, morality, and variability, emphasizes connectedness, harmony, similarity among people, consideration for others, self-restraint, and variability and flexibility in accordance with change of circumstances. From these two models of an ideal person—the Western self-actualizing person and the East Asian self-expanding person—we can move further to consider the East Asian and Western ideas about being a valuable person or self-making as meaningful oneness.

Fortification of Individuality and Enhancement of Self

In the individualist society, where human ontological significance is sought in the individuality of a person as the bearer of freedom, the self (the driver of behavior) emerges as the focus of attention. Ultimately, people who live in such a society emphasize the importance of personal independence, autonomy, and uniqueness, and they pursue these qualities in the course of their lives. Westerners, therefore, find standards for evaluating self and others within themselves: they exaggerate individual uniqueness, show a clear tendency to find the causes of their own and others' behaviors in the unique inner characteristics of a person, have a high frequency of experiencing ego-focused emotion such as pride, and show strong individual-oriented motives.

In addition, in the individualist society, where the core human characteristic that differentiates the human from the animal is found in human rationality, the object of control is one's external world, or the environment. In such a society, individuals try to change the environment to conform to themselves, and consequently people in such a society value and pursue self-assertion and self-enhancement. Thus, Westerners have a strong tendency to resolve conflicts through competition and confrontation, a strong tendency to find the cause of behavior of themselves and others from the viewpoint of self-enhancement and believe in openly and actively expressing their emotions, even if an emotion such as anger could jeopardize personal relations, and they are strongly motivated to adjust the external environment to fit themselves.

Furthermore, in the individualist society, where a person is conceptualized and accepted as a fully contained entity equipped with overall causal characteristics of human action, ways for self-improvement are found in identifying and expanding various merits the person has. Consequently, people in such a society value and pursue stability and consistency, or that which remains constant regardless of temporal or situational variation. It is in this context that Westerners believe that personal characteristics and abilities are quite stable, that they do not significantly change with either time or personal effort; they think self-improvement is accomplished through expansions of one's inborn merits; and they have a strong tendency to value and pursue their own positive characteristics and positive feelings. Also, they view that the world around them is relatively consistent and stable; they have a strong tendency to assign the end result of any achievement to their ability; and they show strong motivation for pursuing consistency in everyday life.

As can be seen in these results, the attention of Westerners throughout their lives is generally focused on identifying and showcasing the individuality, uniqueness, and supremacy of an independent self. They find the meaning of being human or self-making in discovering the difference between self and others and in increasing satisfaction toward themselves by identifying their uniqueness and actively expanding upon it.

Thus, for Westerners, the foundation of self-esteem is the singularity and supremacy of self and self-satisfaction. This is evident in the fact that, from early on, all the questions in the Rosenberg Self-Esteem Scale (SES; Rosenberg 1965), a tool widely used in psychological studies of self, were based on addressing the self-estimation of one's uniqueness, supremacy, and self-satisfaction.[6] The results of studies using the SES show high levels of self-esteem among Westerners. For example, in their many studies, Heine et al. (1999) conducted meta-analyses of scores measured by SES. Their studies show that the self-esteem curve among Westerners (mostly Americans and Canadians of European ancestry) is generally (approximately 93 percent) distributed above the arithmetic mean, while only 7 percent are distributed below the arithmetic mean (Heine et al. 1999, figure 1, p. 776). In contrast, among Japanese, the same curve is distributed slightly below the arithmetic mean (figure 2, p. 777). Furthermore, in many self-esteem studies of Westerners that do not use the SES but other measuring tools, the average or the median value of their self-esteem is distributed above the arithmetic mean, regardless of the measuring tool used in studies (Baumeister, Tice, and Hutton 1989).

There is another fact indicating that the self-image of Westerners is mainly shaped by their sense of self-uniqueness. It is the fact that Westerners show an excessive tendency to have false uniqueness perception, in which the subject exaggerates his own abilities and positive characteristics of uniqueness beyond what is real. In a study (Myers 1987) where the subjects were US college students, 70 percent said their leadership was above average; 60 percent said their ability to mingle with others was in the top 10 percent; and 25 percent even said that their social skills belong to the top 1 percent. Such perceptions of excessive false uniqueness operate as the source of Westerners falling into "unrealistic optimism" (Heine and Lehman 1995).

These facts let us know that for Westerners, self-making is achieved on the foundation of self-satisfaction, which, in turn, is hinged on their sense of their own uniqueness and excellence. They look for their own ontological significance as valuable persons by discovering and expanding upon their uniqueness and by thus positively discriminating themselves from others, as they believe they are self-contained, independent, and autonomous individuals (Markus and Kitayama 1991). Through this process, an individual becomes a separated person, whose border with others becomes further and further fortified; and the pursuit of self-satisfaction through such a self-fortification and self-enhancement process is what, for Westerners, is the heart of the journey toward becoming an ideal person.

Expansion of Interconnectedness and Self-Improvement

In Confucian philosophy, where a person is seen as a social *relatum* and where human ontological significance is thus sought in the social nature of human beings, it is not an individual but the others around the individual, or the collective, who are highlighted as the focus of attention. Accordingly, people who live in such a society lay emphasis on interconnectedness, harmony, and similarity among individuals, and they show a strong tendency to pursue these qualities. East Asians, therefore, find standards for evaluating self and others in the other; they exaggerate their similarity with others, show a strong tendency to find cause for action not within but outside themselves, have high frequency of experiencing other-focused emotions such as empathy and sympathy, and show strong group-oriented motives.

In addition, in the collectivist society, where the exclusively human characteristic is found in the moral character of the human being (the subject of the cultivation of virtue), the object of control is one's own self. Members of such a society try not to reveal their own private desires and emotions, and, accordingly, they show a strong tendency to value and pursue self-restraint and modesty in the course of their lives. Thus, East Asians have a strong tendency to resolve conflicts through concession and mediation; they have a strong tendency to find the cause of behaviors of self and others modestly, from the viewpoint of lowering themselves and raising others; they do not easily show personal emotions, especially such emotions as anger, which could potentially jeopardize relations with others; and they are conspicuously motivated to have self-control in order to restrain their own desires and to adapt themselves to others as well as to external conditions.

Furthermore, in the collectivist society, where, according to its incrementalist belief system, a person is seen as a being-in-process that can change according to changing times and spaces, the path to self-improvement is seen as the path to identifying and improving upon one's shortcomings. People in such a society pursue and place a high value on human variability and flexibility. It is in this context that East Asians perceive personal characteristics and abilities as that which can change with time and exertion of individual effort, and they believe that self-improvement is accomplished when a person recognizes her own shortcomings and remedies them. Thus, these people have a strong tendency to easily accept their own shortcomings and negative emotions. Also, they have a strong tendency to assign the cause of the end result of any achievement to a personal effort, which is a variable, not a constant; and they do not show a strong tendency to pursue consistency between private and public self, or in the attitudes and actions of everyday life.

What these results show is the fact that in their everyday lives the attention of East Asians is generally focused on confirming the connectedness among those with whom they have a social relationship, and on maintaining harmonious relationships with them. By finding similarity between self and others and confirming the mutual dependence among the parties thus involved, they try to solidify harmonious relationships with others; by doing so they try to be recognized and accepted by others and the community. It is in this notion of self-expansion that they find the meaning of being human or self-making.

For East Asians, uniqueness or supremacy of self does not constitute the foundation of self-esteem. Westerners, who find the driving force of social behaviors in the inner qualities of a person, value and pursue personal independence and autonomy; for this reason, the pursuit of one's own uniqueness, as in the identification and active expression of one's own inner characteristics, becomes the foundation of self-esteem for Westerners. In contrast, East Asians find the driving force of social behaviors in situational factors, such as the roles and responsibilities a person has socially, and they value and pursue interdependence and connectedness; for this reason, recognition and acceptance from others, self-regulation, restraint, and the maintenance of harmony in social relations emerge as foundations for self-esteem among East Asians (Fiske et al. 1998, Heine 2012, Kitayama et al. 1997, Kunda 2000, Markus and Kitayama 1991, Matsumoto and Juang 2004).

This conclusion is also supported by a comparative study of Westerners and East Asians conducted by Sedikides, Gaertner, and Toguchi (2003). The study concludes, on one hand, that Westerners lay importance on personal factors such as autonomy, independence, individuality, and uniqueness, and that these factors are accepted as the building blocks of self-esteem among Westerners. On the other hand, it concludes that East Asians lay importance on relational factors, such as kindness, willingness to compromise, modesty, and harmony, and that these factors are accepted as the building blocks of self-esteem among East Asians. There is also another study (Heine and Lehman 1995) that further supports this conclusion. On one hand, it shows that, for Westerners, happiness and a sense of self-satisfaction are closely related to pride in oneself and achievement of self-uniqueness; on the other hand, it concludes that, for East Asians, happiness has nothing to do with one's sense of pride and uniqueness, but much to do with acceptance from others. Given that East Asians depend on their relations with others for self-esteem, it is not surprising that they scored low (Baumeister, Tice, and Hutton 1989, Heine et al. 1999) on self-esteem tests (for example, Rosenberg 1965) that are based on the Western notion that self-esteem is derived from perfection of self-containment.

Because East Asians thus find the basis of self-esteem and self-satisfaction in social relational factors, such as interconnectedness and acceptance from others, they have a tendency to exaggerate similarities between the self and others (Holyoak and Gordon 1983, Srull and Gaelick 1983). According to a study conducted in Korea (Cho 2005), among those Koreans who tend to be more group-oriented than self-oriented, the recognition of their similarity with friends, measured in terms of opinions, tastes, hobbies, and values, was much higher than among Koreans with the reverse tendency.

Such findings show that, for East Asians, self-making is based on relational satisfaction, that is, the satisfaction derived from being similar to and interconnected with others, and from being accepted by others. They perceive themselves and others to be part of a social *relatum*, and they try to maintain their social relations in harmony; for them what is important, in their longlong process, is that they identify and improve upon their shortcomings in order to maintain this harmony. It is in this context that East Asians lay emphasis on similarity with others so as to embrace others as part of themselves, and they exert efforts on self-improvement so that they themselves may be recognized and accepted by others. Through such a process, an East Asian becomes a harmonious person, or an ensembled person. The expansion of interconnectedness in such a manner and the pursuit of self-improvement are the materials that pave the road for becoming an ideal human being, as postulated by East Asians; in other words, in East Asia, they are the building blocks of self-expansion.

Is Cultural Difference Destiny?

It is important not to fall into an ecological fallacy when one discusses cultural differences. An ecological fallacy occurs when a difference found at a group level is generalized and assumed to apply to every individual in that group (Smith, Bond, and Kagitcibasi 2006, 43). For example, it would be committing an ecological fallacy to assume, because the United States is an individualistic society and Korea is a collectivist society, that all Americans are more individualistic than any Korean, or that all Koreans are more collectivist than any American.

Cultural differences only reflect average differences between cultures. Thus, a cultural difference is a relative difference between cultural groups, not a difference that applies uniformly to all individuals in the respective cultures. There are Westerners who are more collectivist than an East Asian, and East Asians who are more individualist than a Westerner. Thus, the discussions in this essay must be taken as relative conclusions. Clearly, the differences discussed do not reflect any absolute differences between the West and East Asia.

Having said that, the cultural differences observed are based on real data. The question is, Will the differences continue? Some people say that with globalization East Asian cultures will be absorbed into Western cultures. Others say that East-West cultural competition will only intensify and that the cultural differences cannot but continue. Still others say that each culture will open itself up more to the other, and that the two cultures will *converge* somewhere in the middle (Holton 1998, 167–80, Nisbett 2003, 219–29).

Among these three opinions, psychological studies support the conclusion that the two cultures will be integrated and converge somewhere in the middle (Nisbett 2003). For example, one study concluded that those who have lived in another culture, even if it is for a short duration, adopted the cognitive style of the host culture and that such cognitive style grew on the subjects' worldview (Kitayama et al. 2002). Other studies conclude that East Asians who migrated to the West show a cognitive style that is somewhere in the middle between what are typically Western and East Asian styles (Heine and Lehman 1997, Nisbett 2003, Peng and Knowles 2003). These studies corroborate the convergence claim.

With globalization, East Asia and the West are becoming more familiar with each other, and they are each embracing the other's culture from within the heart of their own traditions. Already, the educational system in East Asia follows that of the West, in terms of both structure and content, and the values and behaviors of East Asian students educated under such a system are very similar to those of students in the West (Nisbett 2003, Peng, Nisbett, and Wong 1997). The rate of students receiving higher education in East Asia is one of the highest in the world; in 2010 the combined high school entrance rate in Korea, China, and Japan was 8 percent to 99 percent, while the rate for college was 50 percent to 80 percent. That is to say, East Asians, in particular the young, are not only well aware of Western cultures, but they are also familiar with them.

Conversely, in the West, appreciating and admiring East Asian culture has become a trend that cannot be ignored. Westerners rave over East Asian food, religions, medicine, and health practices. Many Westerners who believe that excessive individualism in the West has resulted in widespread alienation are now trying to deal with some of the social issues in the West by forming communities with Eastern values (Nisbett 2003).

It is possible to infer from these circumstances that a significant number of people in both the West and East Asia are now bicultural and that this trend will become only more entrenched in the future, as globalization continues and contact between cultures increases. The biculturalists not only have values and convictions that reflect a convergence of the two cultures, but they also have the flexibility of choosing only one side under particular circumstances.

Due to their unique historical experience, Hongkongers have become the typical biculturalists. When they are shown images that are representative of the West, such as the White House or the Statue of Liberty, thus primed by Western culture, they attribute the cause of others' behaviors in a typically Western manner. However, when they are shown images of China, such as the Great Wall or Tiananmen Square, thus primed by East Asian culture, they attribute the cause of others' behaviors in a typically East Asian manner (Hong, Chiu, and Kung 1997). Recently, a number of studies have been carried out where students in the West and students in East Asia were each primed by collectivist cultural tendencies and individualist cultural tendencies, respectively, through various questions (for example, they were asked to put a parenthesis around first-person plural words [we, our, us] and first-person singular words [I, my, me] in a text). In these experiments, students exhibited cultural values, selfhood values, or behavioral modes of the culture in which they were primed in the experiment, regardless of their own cultural origin (Hong et al. 2000, Kühnen, Hannover, and Schubert 2001, Lee, Aaker, and Gardner 2000).

Given these circumstances, we do not believe that Westerners and East Asians are bound by any fate to abide by the notions of selfhood and being a valuable person that are prevalent in the cultures they are born in. All people living today are to some degree biculturalists. Westerners do not always try to attain selfhood through fortification of individuality and enhancement of the self simply by virtue of being Westerners; likewise, East Asians do not always try to attain selfhood through expansion of interconnectedness and self-improvement, simply by virtue of being an East Asian. The differences between the two cultures are based on general trends in each culture; however, depending on the circumstances, an individual in East Asia or the West may exhibit the Western style of attaining selfhood (for example, competition in a debating contest) or the East Asian style of attaining selfhood (for example, rooting for the other country, not one's own, in a national sport competition), respectively. This is because a human being essentially exists both as an individual being and as a collective being.

Notes

1. The Confucian treatises on humaneness (仁說) and rectification of names (正名論), Mencius's treatises on five relationships (五倫說) and completely fulfilling the Way (盡道論), and Xunzi's treatises on great foundation (大本說) and clear distinctions (明分論) illustrate the Confucian view of the human being as a social *relatum*.
2. Such arguments for the innateness of morality in humans and the supremacy of moral virtue are supported by the Confucian theories that the practice of humaneness comes from a man himself (爲仁由己說) and that a man seeks within himself (求諸己論), by Mencius's Four Principles (四端說) and his theory of finding fault in oneself (反求諸己論), and by Xunzi's theories of hierarchy (位階說) and the Way of humans (人道論).
3. Confucian theories on teaching and learning (教學說) and reformation (改過論), Mencius's treatises on compulsory education (教育義務說) and self-enlightenment (自得論), and Xunzi's treatises on encouraging learning (勸學說) and physical disposition (體道論) illustrate Confucian views on human variability.
4. See Cho 2007, 98–142; 2008, 43–95; and 2012, 48–140 for a comparison of the Western liberal and Confucian views of the human being, and for a study of the cultural differences stemming from the differences.
5. See *Mencius* 5B1.
6. For example, the SES measures the subjects' responses to statements such as the following: "I feel that I have a number of good qualities," "I feel that I am a person of worth, at least on an equal plane with others," and "On the whole, I am satisfied with myself."

References

Bagozzi, R. P., N. Wong, and Y. Yi. 1999. "The Role of Culture and Gender in the Relationship Between Positive and Negative Affect." *Cognition and Emotion* 13:641–72.

Barnlund, D. C. 1975. *Public and Private Self in Japan and the United States.* Tokyo: Simul.

Baumeister, R. F., D. M. Tice, and D. G. Hutton. 1989. "Self-Presentational Motivations and Personality Differences in Self-Esteem." *Journal of Personality* 57:547–79.

Bond, M. H., and T. S. Cheung. 1983. "College Students' Spontaneous Self-Concepts: The Effect of Culture Among Respondents in Hong Kong, Japan, and the United States." *Journal of Cross-Cultural Psychology* 14:153–71.

Bond, M. H., and K. K. Hwang. 1986. "The Social Psychology of Chinese People." In *The Psychology of Chinese People*, edited by M. H. Bond, 213–66. New York: Oxford University Press.

Bordt, M. 1999. *Platon.* Freiburg: Herder. [Translation: Han Seok-hwan, trans. 2003. *Cheolhakjia Peulaton (Plato the Philosopher).* Seoul: Ihaksa.]

Cho, Geung Ho 조긍호. 2003. 한국인 이해의 개념틀. 서울: 나남출판. *Hangukin ihaeui gaenyeom teul [A Conceptual Framework for Understanding Koreans].* Seoul: Nanam Chulpan.

——. 2005. 문화성향에 따른 유사성 판단의 비대칭성. 한국심리학회지: 사회 및 성격, 19 (1): 45–63. "Munhwa seonghyane ddareun yusasong pandanui bidaechingseong" [The Asymmetry of Similarity Judgments According to Cultural Tendencies]. Hanguk simrihakhoeji: Sahoe mit seonggyeok [*Journal of Korean Psychological Association: Society and Personality*] 19 (1): 45–63.

——. 2006. 이상적 인간형론의 동·서 비교. 서울: 지식산업사. *Isangjeok inganhyeongron ui dong-seo bigyo [An East-West Comparison of Theories of Ideal Human Being].* Seoul: Jisiksaneopsa.

——. 2007. 동아시아 집단주의의 유학사상적 배경. 서울: 지식산업사. *Dongasia jipdanjuui ui yuhak sasangjeok baegyeong [The Confucian Background of East Asian Collectivism].* Seoul: Jisiksaneopsa.

——. 2008. 선진유학사상의 심리학적 함의. 서울: 서강대학교 출판부. *Seonjin yuhak sasangui simrihakjeok hameui [Psychological Implications of Advanced Confucian Philosophy].* Seoul: Sogang University Press.

——. 2012. 사회관계론의 동·서 비교. 서울: 서강대학교 출판부. *Sahoe gwangyeronui Dong-Seo bigyo [An East-West Comparison of Social Relations Theory].* Seoul: Sogang University Press.

Cho, Geung Ho, and Kang Jeong-in 조긍호·강정인. 2012. 사회계약론 연구. 서울: 서강대학교 출판부. *Sahoe gyeyakron yeongu [A Study of Social Contract Theory].* Seoul: Sogang University Press.

Choi, I. 2002. *Who Trusts Fortune Telling? Self-Concept Clarity and the Barnum Effect.* Unpublished manuscript, Seoul National University, Seoul, Korea.

Choi, I., and Y. Choi. 2002. "Culture and Self-Concept Flexibility." *Personality and Social Psychology Bulletin* 28:1508–17.

Choi, I., K. W. Choi, and J. H. Cha. 1992. *A Cross-Cultural Replication of Festinger and Carlsmith (1959).* Unpublished manuscript. Seoul National University, Seoul, Korea.

Choi, I., and R. E. Nisbett. 1998. "Situational Salience and Cultural Differences in the Correspondence Bias and Actor-Observer Bias." *Personality and Social Psychology Bulletin* 24:949–60.

——. 2000. "The Cultural Psychology of Surprise: Holistic Theories and Recognition of Contradiction." *Journal of Personality and Social Psychology* 79:890–905.

Davis, M. H., and W. G. Stephan. 1989. "Attributions for Exam Performance." *Journal of Applied Social Psychology* 10:235–48.

Diener, E., E. Suh, H. Smith, and L. Shao. 1995. "National and Cultural Difference in Reported Subjective Well-Being: Why Do They Occur?" *Social Indicators Research* 34:7–32.

Dülmen, R. V. 1997. *Die Entdeckung des Individuums, 1500–1800*. Frankfurt: Fischer. [Translation: Choe, Yoon-yeong, trans. 2005. *Gaein ui balgeyon: Eotteotke gaeineul chaja ganeunga, 1500–1800*. Seoul: Hyeonsilmunhwa yeongu.]

Dumont, L. 1970. *Homo Hierarchicus*. Chicago: University of Chicago Press.

Dweck, C. S. 1991. "Self-Theories and Goals: Their Role in Motivation, Personality, and Development." In *Perspectives on Motivation: Nebraska Symposium on Motivation, 1990*, edited by R. A. Dienstbier, 199–235. Lincoln: University of Nebraska Press.

Dweck, C. S., Y. Hong, and C. Chiu. 1993. "Implicit Theories: Individual Differences in the Likelihood and Meaning of Dispositional Inference." *Personality and Social Psychology Bulletin* 19:644–56.

Ekman, P. 1982. *Emotions in the Human Face*. 2nd ed. Cambridge: Cambridge University Press.

Erikson, E. H. 1959. "Growth and Crisis on the Healthy Personality." *Review of Existential Psychology and Psychiatry* 1:50–100.

Fiske, A. P., S. Kitayama, H. R. Markus, and R. E. Nisbett. 1998. "The Cultural Matrix of Social Psychology." In *The Handbook of Social Psychology*, 4th ed., vol. 2, edited by D. T. Gillbert, S. T. Fiske, and G. Lindzey, 915–81. Boston: McGraw-Hill.

Geen, R. G. 1995. *Human Motivation: A Social Psychological Approach*. Pacific Grove, CA: Brooks/Cole.

Gray, J. 1995. *Liberalism*. London: Open University Press. [Translation: Son, Cheol-seong, trans. 2007. *Jayujuui*. Seoul: Ihu.]

Greenfield, P. M. 2000. "Three Approaches to the Psychology of Culture: Where Do They Come From? Where Can They Go?" *Asian Journal of Social Psychology* 3:223–40.

Guthrie, W. K. C. 1960. *The Greek Philosophers: From Thales to Aristotle*. New York: Harper and Row. [Translation: Park, Jong-hyeon, trans. 2003. *Hirap cheolhak ipmun: Tales eseo Aristoteles kkaji (Introduction to Greek Philosophy: From Thales to Aristotle)*. Seoul: Seogwangsa.]

Heine, S. J. 2012. *Cultural Psychology*. 2nd ed. New York: Norton.

Heine, S. J., and D. R. Lehman. 1995. "Cultural Variation in Unrealistic Optimism: Does the West Feel More Invulnerable Than the East?" *Journal of Personality and Social Psychology* 68:595–607.

——. 1997. "The Cultural Construction of Self-Enhancement: An Examination of Group-Serving Biases." *Journal of Personality and Social Psychology* 72:1268–83.

Heine, S. J., D. R. Lehman, H. R. Markus, and S. Kitayama. 1999. "Is There a Universal Need for Positive Self-Regard?" *Psychological Review* 106:766–94.

Hilgard, E. R. 1980. "The Trilogy of Mind: Cognition, Affection, and Conation." *Journal of the History of the Behavioral Sciences* 16:107–17.

Hofstede, G. 1980. *Culture's Consequences: International Differences in Work-Related Values*. Beverly Hills: Sage.

——. 1991. *Cultures and Organizations: Software of the Mind*. London: McGraw-Hill. [Translation: Cha, Jae-ho, and Eun-yeong Na, trans. 2014. *Segyeui munhwa wa jojik (Cultures and Organizations of the World)*. Seoul: Hakjisa.]

Holton, R. J. 1998. *Globalization and the Nation-State*. London: Macmillan.

Holyoak, K. J., and P. C. Gordon. 1983. "Social Reference Points." *Journal of Personality and Social Psychology* 44:881–87.

Hong, Y., C. Chiu, and T. M. Kung. 1997. "Bringing Culture Out in Front: Effects of Cultural Meaning System Activation on Social Cognition." In *Progress in Asian Social Psychology*, vol. 1, edited by K. Lenng, U. Kim, S. Yamaguchi, and Y. Kashiman, 139–50. Singapore: Wiley.

Hong, Y., M. W. Morris, C. Chiu, and V. Benet-Martinez. 2000. "Multicultural Minds: A Dynamic Constructivist Approach to Culture and Cognition." *American Psychologist* 55:705–20.

Kagitcibasi, C. 1996. *Family and Human Development Across Cultures: A View from the Other Side*. Hillsdale, NJ: Erlbaum.

——. 1997. "Individualism and Collectivism." In *Handbook of Cross-Cultural Psychology*, 2nd ed., vol. 3, edited by J. W. Berry, M. H. Segall, and C. Kagitcibasi, 1–49. Boston: Allyn and Bacon.

Kim, Seong-tae 김성태. 1976. 성숙인격론. 서울: 고려대학교 출판부. *Seongsuk ingyeokron* [*Mature Personality Theory*]. Seoul: Korea University Press.

——. 1989. 경과 주의 (증보판). 서울: 고려대학교 출판부. *Gyeonggwa juui* [*Progress Attention*]. Rev. ed. Seoul: Korea University Press.

Kitayama, S., S. Duffy, T. Kawamura, and J. T. Larsen. 2002. "Perceiving an Object in Its Context in Different Cultures: A Cultural Look at the New Look." *Psychological Science* 14:201–6.

Kitayama, S., and H. R. Markus. 2000. "The Pursuit of Happiness and the Realization of Sympathy: Cultural Patterns of Self, Social Relations, and Well-Being." In *Culture and Subjective Well-Being*, edited by E. Diener and E. M. Suh, 113–61. Cambridge: MIT Press.

Kitayama, S., H. R. Markus, H. Matsumoto, and V. Norasakkunkit. 1997. "Individual and Collective Processes of Self-Esteem Management: Self-Enhancement in the United States and Self-Criticism in Japan." *Journal of Personality and Social Psychology* 72:1245–67.

Kühnen, U., B. Hannover, and B. Schubert. 2001. "The Semantic-Procedural Interface Model of the Self: The Role of Self-Knowledge for Context-Dependent Versus Context-Independent Modes of Thinking." *Journal Personality and Social Psychology* 80:397–409.

Kunda, Z. 2000. *Social Cognition: Making Sense of People*. Cambridge: MIT Press.

Laurent, A. 1993. *Historie de l'individualisme*. Paris: Presses Universitaires de France. [Translation: Kim, Yong-min, trans. 2001. *Gaeinjuui ui yeoksa* (*History of Individualism*) Seoul: Hangilsa.]

Lee, A. Y., J. L. Aaker, and W. L. Gardner. 2000. "The Pleasures and Pains of Distinct Self-Construals: The Role of Interdependence in Regulatory Focus." *Journal of Personality and Social Psychology* 78:1122–34.

Lukes, S. 1973. *Individualism*. New York: Harper and Row.

Markus, H. R., and S. Kitayama. 1991. "Culture and the Self: Implications for Cognition, Emotion, and Motivation." *Psychological Review* 98:224–53.

——. 1994. "The Cultural Construction of Self and Emotion: Implications for Social Behavior." In *Emotion and Culture: Empirical Investigations of Mutual Influence*, edited by S. Kitayama and H. R. Markus, 89–130. Washington, DC: American Psychological Association.

Matsumoto, D. 1989. "Cultural Influence on the Perception of Emotion." *Journal of Cross-Cultural Psychology* 20:92–105.

Matsumoto, D., and L. Juang. 2004. *Culture and Psychology: People Around the World*. 3rd ed. Belmont, CA: Wadsworth.

Miller, J. G. 1984. "Culture and the Development of Everyday Social Explanation." *Journal of Personality and Social Psychology* 46:961–78.

Mizokawa, D. T., and D. B. Ryckman. 1990. "Attributions of Academic Success and Failure: A Comparison of Six Asian-American Ethnic Groups." *Journal of Cross-Cultural Psychology* 21:434–51.

Morling, B. 1997. "Controlling the Environment and Controlling the Self in the United States and Japan." Paper presented at the Second Conference of the Asian Association of Social Psychology, Kyoto.

Morling, B., S. Kitayama, and Y. Miyamoto. 2002. "Cultural Practices Emphasize Influence in the U.S. and Adjustment in Japan." *Personality and Social Psychology Bulletin* 28:311–23.

Morris, M. W., and K. Peng. 1994. "Culture and Cause: American and Chinese Attributions for Social and Physical Events." *Journal of Personality and Social Psychology* 67:949–71.

Myers, D. G. 1987. *Social Psychology*. 2nd ed. New York: McGraw-Hill.

Nisbett, R. E. 2003. *The Geography of Thought: How Asians and Westerners Think Differently and Why*. Thousand Oaks, CA: Sage.

Nisbett, R. E., K. Peng, I. Choi, and A. Norenzayan. 2001. "Culture and Systems of Thought: Holistic vs. Analytic Cognition." *Psychological Review* 108:291–310.

Noh, Myeong-sik 노명식. 1991. 자유주의의 원리와 역사: 그 비판적 연구. 서울: 민음사. *Jayujuui ui weolliwa yeoksa: geu bipanjeok yeongu* [*The Principle and History of Liberalism: A Critical Study*]. Seoul: Minumsa.

Norenzayan, A., I. Choi, and R. E. Nisbett. 2002. "Cultural Similarities and Differences in Social Inference: Evidence from Behavioral Predictions and Lay Theories of Behavior." *Personality and Social Psychology Bulletin* 28:109–20.

Peng, K., and E. Knowles. 2003. "Culture, Ethnicity and the Attribution of Physical Causality." *Personality and Social Psychology Bulletin* 29:1272–84.

Peng, K., and R. E. Nisbett. 1999. "Culture, Dialectics and Reasoning About Contradiction." *American Psychologist* 54:741–54.

Peng, K., R. E. Nisbett, and N. Wong. 1997. "Validity Problems of Cross-Cultural Value Comparison and Possible Solutions." *Psychological Methods* 2:329–34.

Rhee, E., J. S. Uleman, H. K. Lee, and R. J. Roman. 1995. "Spontaneous Self-Descriptions and Ethnic Identities in Individualistic and Collectivistic Cultures." *Journal of Personality and Social Psychology* 69:142–52.

Rhi, Bou-Young 이부영. 2002. 자기와 자기실현. 서울: 한길사. *Jagiwa jagi silhyeon* [*The Self and Self-Attainment*]. Seoul: Hangilsa.

Ricken, F. 1988. *Philosophie der Antike*. Berlin: W. Kohlhammer. [Translation: Kim, Seong-jin, trans. 2000. *Godae Geuris cheolhak* (*The Greek Philosophy of Antiquity*). Seoul: Seogwangsa.]

Rosenberg, M. 1965. *Society and the Adolescent Self-Image*. Princeton: Princeton University Press.

Rothbaum, F., J. R. Weisz, and S. S. Snyder. 1982. "Changing the World and Changing the Self: A Two-Process Model of Perceived Control." *Journal of Personality and Social Psychology* 42:5–37.

Sedikides, C., L. Gaertner, and Y. Toguchi. 2003. "Pancultural Self-Enhancement." *Journal of Personality and Social Psychology* 84:60–79.

Singh, R. 1981. "Prediction of Performance from Motivation and Ability: An Appraisal of the Cultural Difference Hypothesis." In *Perspectives on Experimental Social Psychology in India*, edited by J. Pandey, 31–53. New Delhi: Concept.

Smith, P. B., M. H. Bond, and C. Kagitcibasi. 2006. *Understanding Social Psychology: Living and Working in a Changing World*. London: Sage.

Srull, T. K., and L. Gaelick. 1983. "General Principles and Individual Differences in the Self as a Habitual Reference Point: An Examination of Self-Other Judgments of Similarity." *Social Cognition* 2:108–21.

Stevenson, H. W., and J. W. Stigler. 1992. *The Learning Gap*. New York: Summit.

Stigler, J. W., S. Smith, and L. Mao. 1985. "The Self-Perception of Competence by Chinese Children." *Child Development* 56:1259–70.

Suh, E., and E. Diener. 1995. "Subjective Well-Being: Issues for Cross-Cultural Research." Translated in *Hanguk Simrihakhoeji: Salmui jilui simrihak* [*Journal of the Korean Psychological Association*], 147–65. Seoul: Korean Psychological Association.

Triandis, H. C. 1989. "The Self and Social Behavior in Differing Cultural Contexts." *Psychological Review* 96:506–20.

——. 1995. *Individualism and Collectivism*. Boulder: Westview.

Tu, Wei-Ming. 1985. "Selfhood and Otherness in Confucian Thought." In *Culture and Self: Asian and Western Perspectives*, edited by A. J. Marsella, G. A. DeVos, and F. L. K. Hsu, 231–51. New York: Tavistock.

——. 1996. *Confucian Tradition in East Asian Modernity*. Cambridge: Harvard University Press.

Weisz, J. R., F. M. Rothbaum, and T. C. Blackburn. 1984. "Standing Out and Standing In: The Psychology of Control in America and Japan." *American Psychologist* 39:955–69.

Wiggins, J. S. 1992. "Agency and Communion as Conceptual Coordinates for the Understanding and Measurement of Interpersonal Behavior." In *Thinking Clearly About Psychology*, edited by W. M. Grove and D. Cicchetti, 89–113. Minneapolis: University of Minnesota Press.

CHAPTER 12

HALLUCINATING ONENESS

Is Oneness True or Just a Positive Metaphysical Illusion?

OWEN FLANAGAN

Twenty-First-Century Oneness

The year 2015 was important for oneness. The United Nations agreed on seventeen Sustainable Development Goals (SDGs) for the entire globe, every country on earth signed the Paris Climate Accords, and Pope Francis issued an encyclical *Laudato Si': On Care for Our Common Home* in which he called for a "global ecological conversion" (2015, 5). The "global ecological *conversion*" would be one in which the oneness and indivisibility of the natural, social, and spiritual realms are fully recognized and then acted upon.[1] Each of these documents was motivated by and is replete with claims that all aspects of the health and well-being of the planet, sentient beings, and future generations are interconnected. All is one, and it is a scientific, ethical, political, and spiritual mistake to think and act otherwise.

The necessity of what Pope Francis calls an "integral ecology" (137) has urgency in the twenty-first century as environmental catastrophe looms. But the core ideas that "everything is interconnected," that the well-being of each depends on the well being of all, and that fate is shared are not new ideas. They are ancient and familiar in the philosophies of many indigenous peoples, as well as in Daoist, Buddhist, and neo-Confucian sources.

In this chapter I discuss several conceptions of oneness, and explore the question how believing in some sort of scientific or metaphysical oneness might warrant and motivate a "global ecological *conversion*." Taken together, the United Nations' SDGs, the aims of the Paris Accords, and the papal oneness agenda claim that there is a moral imperative of individuals and nation-states to work to achieve the inextricably linked goals of ending war, ending corporate greed, eliminating poverty and economic and political inequality, bringing heath care and education to everyone, and aiming for environmental sustainability for future generations. How might a belief in oneness morally motivate these kinds of heroic integrated action? My overall thesis is that the true belief that all is one and even the entire set of true beliefs that reveal the interdependency of all things are not in themselves sufficient to motivate heroic action. I explore the additional ingredients besides believing in oneness that are necessary. These include moral commitment, such states as faith and hope, certain positive metaphysical illusions, and perhaps at the limit some sort of complex quasi-creedal, morally inspiring, imaginative, even fantastical state I dub a metaphysical hallucination.

Varieties of Oneness

Most religions and most philosophies one could live by, philosophies that attempt to provide a genuine way of life, a comprehensive way of being in the world (and thus not most contemporary philosophy), link a metaphysics, a story about what there is and how it is, with endorsement of an ethical vision, a picture of a good person, and an excellent human life. Once in place, the typical relationship between the metaphysic and the morals is one of mutual support. Here I am interested in cases where a certain one-directional epistemic relation is thought to obtain, specifically cases where the metaphysics is supposed to supply a reason—especially cases where it is thought to supply sufficient reason—for the morals, where the theory about what there is and how it is is supposed to warrant or justify a certain way of being in the world. The morals must fit with the metaphysics; it is after all warranted or endorsed by it. But it doesn't provide reason in the other direction for it. The relationship between getting the metaphysics right and the morals right is thought to involve some sort of relation between seeing or grasping or understanding things as they really are and being good and acting well. There are sacred and secular traditions that claim that the metaphysical interconnectedness of all that is and ever will be is true in some way that—if we grasp it properly—gives us reason to want to be expansively compassionate, loving, and selfless. Grasping interconnectedness provides reason for caring about the whole of which one partakes, as well as acting for its good. Oneness as conceived in the twenty-first century is put forward as a metaphysical thesis that is continuous with the best science and with the wisdom of the ages.

I am interested in theories that make the link between the grasping of metaphysical interconnectedness and the morals it motivates or sustains noninstrumentally. I am less interested here, but not uninterested overall, in theories that explicitly make the fact that "what goes around comes around" the reason to be good. Hinduism, Buddhism, Jainism, Daoism, and neo-Confucianism endorse wide compassion and selflessness for reasons of a noninstrumental kind. And the philosophies of indigenous people in the Americas, Africa, and Oceana emphasize the intrinsic significance of harmonious relations with all between heaven and earth. The noninstrumental reasons typically involve a move from right seeing, right perception, and right grasping to right valuing and right acting, not because one wants something but because one is then rightly and harmoniously aligned with what there is. Perhaps harmonious alignment is conceived both as an intrinsic propensity and as intrinsically motivating. Some utopian brands of communism, communitarianism, and deep ecology offer naturalistic metaphysics of morals that might have the right sort of structure. But they also might not, especially if they are understood as conceiving moral goodness and social solidarity as instruments of individual and small group well-being.

Buddhism provides a useful example of an ancient tradition that has theorized the metaphysics of oneness and explored its relation to a life of maximal compassion. Looked at in a clear-eyed way, the entire philosophical picture, the metaphysic, which is to become the philosophical background, the surround, the horizon, the penumbra, the habits of a Buddhist heart, can be framed in terms of oneness, which can be glossed in several not incompatible ways (there are only Buddhisms, so what I offer here is a philosophical reconstruction of one kind). I'll call the view depicted by these five theses Oneness (1–5).[2]

1. *Cosmic Oneness*: I am part of everything that unfolds. My arising depends on everything that has arisen before, and my being and my passing will affect the quality of what comes after; it will affect the goodness of the world after I am gone.
2. *Sentient Being Oneness*: All "I"s," all "selves" are impermanent, but there is a common feature that makes all sentient beings one, a common creature: we all are the same in having experiences of pain, suffering, ill-being, and well-being.
3. *Historical Oneness*: The well-being of all sentient beings now depends on the actions of sentient beings that are long gone. The well-being of future beings will depend on what we do now, how we live at this time in the unfolding of the cosmos.
4. *Shared Fate Oneness*: The ill-being and well-being of impermanent selves now depend on other contemporary sentient beings, especially those nearby and those near and dear.
5. *Care Oneness*: I naturally care, as we all do, about the weal and woe of others. I have some natural motivation that others not suffer.

These five ways of describing oneness differ in this way. *Cosmic Oneness* depicts the maximal metaphysical interconnectedness of everything that there is. *Historical Oneness* speaks of my (and everyone's) causal dependency on everything, including all those sentient beings that have come before me, and that of future creatures on the doings of those now existing. Whereas *Historical Oneness* marks long-term diachronic dependencies, *Shared Fate Oneness* marks the synchronic, contemporaneous features of flourishing. Whether and how I fare depend on how well my contemporaries, family, friends, and other citizens of my nation-state and the world are faring. *Sentient Being Oneness* speaks of our common, unified predicament, that we are (all) creatures who are impermanent and suffer. *Care Oneness* depicts a universal and natural human motivational concern for the weal and woe of other beings, not just the self. *Care Oneness* says nothing about our causal interdependencies; but it speaks about a relation that is just as fundamental to who and what we are as any causal relation. We are the kinds of creatures who have care or concern that others not suffer. We are caring beings (to a point).

My self, really, my no-self, is deflated once it is seen truthfully as something impermanent and interdependent. The deflation involves seeing my dependency relations to the cosmos, and especially to the weal and woe of fellow sentient beings with whom I share a common plight. Seeing things this way makes me less self-obsessed because the self with which I am obsessed, who needs what it wants, now will pass. What is of greater concern to me, now seen in the light of oneness, is to make a contribution to the well-being of the unfolding of the whole of which I partake, from which I am made, and to whose going forward I contribute. Compassion and loving-kindness are the highest Buddhist virtues and are motivated from within a philosophical background of oneness.

Buddhist oneness, as I have been emphasizing, is only one kind of oneness metaphysics. David Tien (2012) and P. J. Ivanhoe (2014) have written profitably about the distinctive neo-Confucian *li-qi* oneness metaphysics. There are others, Neoplatonic, Epicurean, Advaita Vedanta, Block Universe, and "Blobject" views (Horgan and Potrc 2000).

The question arises: Insofar as Oneness of the 1–5 sort is true, is it true in a way that naturally entails or motivates maximal love and compassion—the kind that a bodhisattva vows to enact or the kind that Pope Francis calls for in *Laudato Si'*? The answer I think is "no" unless we endorse an even stronger version of oneness where my well-being is ONE with the fate of the entire universe, and according to which ideas such as the flourishing of any individual or partial ecosystem is an illusion. Individual well-being, the flourishing of some parts or systems or subsystems, seems to happen, but it doesn't happen really. It can't happen because what there is and all there is is the ONE. And either it flourishes or it doesn't. Well-being is all or none. Call this view ONE-NESS*. It is what Ivanhoe calls a heroic conception.

Why is it that Oneness 1–5 is not enough? The answer is that Oneness 1–5 is compatible with responses of this sort:

- Yes, I am part of a great cosmic unfolding, but my life as a conscious being is now; the parts of the cosmos that came before are gone, and the parts that will come after will not affect me one iota.
- Yes, everyone suffers. We are ONE in that way. That is really unfortunate for them. I feel bad about that for everyone that suffers. But I can only do so much. I am naturally concerned with the suffering of myself and my loved ones.
- The universe will die a cold death. I am either an aspect of the sum, the "blobject" that will have that fate or, perhaps by some weird logic, I am ONE with the sum of everything that will have that fate. But that motivates nothing, exactly zero. What does it even mean to think that I play a role in the well-being of a universe that is aimed at that absurd telos? And why should I care one lick for that kind of ONE?
- The fact that I am an aspect of the ONE does not mean I am identical to the ONE. My toes are part of me but they are not ONE with me, nor I am I ONE with them. My toes cannot go on without me, but I can go on without them. And so it is with me, however deflated I am metaphysically. I am going on now, as a temporarily unified event or process, and I am going on without my *Dasein* being constituted in any significant way by what went on in the Garden of Eden or even what is now happening at Thirteenth and Main in Hoboken, New Jersey, or what will happen in six billion years in another galaxy.

Many say that Oneness of the 1–5 sort gives powerful reason to be maximally compassionate and loving-kind. But suppose you think, as I do, that the responses to this Oneness 1–5 that I just sketched show that some more powerful views are necessary to motivate great compassion. Leave to one side what exactly the more powerful version of ONENESS* would look like. We might think that whatever exactly the view is like, it would be good to make people believe that this stronger version, ONENESS*, is true or to be motivated by the thought that it might be true or that it is true in the best of all possible worlds or in God's mind.[3] The next question would be how, if it is existentially important enough, we can induce the relevant metaphysical illusion or hallucination.

Metaphysical Hallucinations

Positive illusions are ordinary false beliefs that have good-making features (Taylor and Brown 1988). People who are taught that the average person has a certain objective chance of getting a certain disease, being in a bad accident, or involved in a painful betrayal, and who think that the poor odds do not apply to them, are generally happier and more pleasant to be around than people who think that the poor odds apply to them. The people who believe that the bad objective probabilities apply to them tend to be moderately depressed and self-centered. Positive illusions are epistemically negative, but existentially positive.

One thought engendered by the discussion of the heroic kind of ONENESS* is that it might require something even stronger than a metaphysical illusion, something like a transformative hallucination, which might genuinely mark, announce, or motivate the life of a bodhisattva, or a Christian saint, or make possible the sort of grassroots global ecological conversion Pope Frances seeks. I am sure the distinction I have in mind between a positive metaphysical illusion and a positive metaphysical hallucination is imprecise, but the idea is something like this: a metaphysical illusion would be a kind of positive illusion, but consist in, or involve, false beliefs about *Being*, about *What There Is*, which have good existential effects. A metaphysical hallucination would involve an altered state of consciousness in which the shape of reality and the structure of values are envisioned in a fantastical but entirely appealing and transformative way.

One possibility is "making believe" that certain metaphysical theses that pertain to oneness (for example, Oneness 1–5 or ONENESS*) that are false are true or, what is different, are worth aiming at, committing to, trying to make so. For reasons I have alluded to, I am not at all sure whether the states of mind I am thinking about are primarily creedal, really believing that something that is likely false is true, or more akin to an expansive hope or commitment or aspiration or some admixture.

One thought is that the attitude of "make-believe" required for a true positive metaphysical illusion is familiar in children but unusual for grownups. It involves a creedal attitude toward propositions that are logically possible, but that, like beliefs in the tooth fairy or Santa Claus, are highly implausible, much more likely literally false than true given the evidence. This much makes them illusions—perhaps, depending on how one uses words, fantasies, hallucinations, or even delusions, false beliefs that one won't or can't ever give up.

For a metaphysical illusion to be good-producing in the right way requires more than simply thinking a certain set of propositions that are most likely false are true. It involves embracing the relevant beliefs and then trying to imaginatively project oneself into a world in which the relevant beliefs seem as true as true can be, and are thus action-guiding. It involves working one's way into or achieving a certain kind of strong noetic confidence that reveals itself in how one lives one's life. One thinks that a certain likely false proposition is true and then lives as if it is as true as true can be. And so it is with oneness, at least the kind of ONENESS* that could ground, seed, warrant, or otherwise motivate a life of maximal compassion.

Hallucinating No-Self

Let me give a specific example of what might be a positive metaphysical illusion that involves oneness (perhaps it is a hallucination). As I have said, Buddhism doesn't normally use a language of oneness, but it does entertain a variety of Onenesses (1–5) by way of, speaking anachronistically, a process metaphysics of cosmic interpenetration. What there is and all there is is one unfolding event or process. The one is empty (*sunyata*) in the sense that there seem to be particular separate things or parts, for example, individual selves, but really there are no such things. Insofar as we are real at all, we possess an aspectual reality. Either we are persons who possess no-self (*anatta, anatman*), selfless persons, or we are only conventionally persons, but not really persons. Really we—each one of us—are an empty node in a great cosmic unfolding. What there is and all there is is the cosmic unfolding. It is the ONE.

Buddhism teaches that most people are confused in thinking that things have intrinsic nonrelational properties, and specifically that they have a self or are a self or some such. The mistake is not merely metaphysical. Believing in the self is connected to selfishness. We believe that each and every self is a metaphysically separate individual with a separate fate, and we act then as if this is true. The belief in self, really in selves, separates each of us from every other, and it is the source of selfishness by way of setting up the conviction that each thing achieves its fate or telos for itself and on its own. We believe that we are many and separate, not one, and we act as such. But there is no-self (*anatta, anatman*), no permanent diamond-in-the-rough that is me, or you, or even that makes each seemingly separate individual thing what it is. Understanding, knowing, getting, or grasping no-self encourages or motivates lives of great compassion and loving-kindness, possibly for all sentient beings. The metaphysics of no-self motivates or seeds dispositions to care about the whole, for all sentient beings, to end suffering whenever and wherever it occurs, not just when it occurs in (what seems to be) me or to mine. There are three questions: Is no-self true? How, given that no-self is hard to comprehend conceptually and grasp nonconceptually, can I understand it, grasp it, and sustain my grasp of no-self? What are the consequences of believing no-self and getting that belief onto the motivational circuitry; how, if it does, does the belief in no-self link to selflessness

Noetic Confidence

Imagine that no-self is taught as a piece of Buddhist philosophy to a twenty-year-old Catholic American philosophy student in some canonical Buddhist way. The student gets what no-self means propositionally, what it means as a piece of Buddhist philosophical wisdom, how it makes sense inside Buddhist metaphysics. She understands no-self at this point in roughly the way she understands the doctrine of the Trinity—that there are three persons in one God. She can state the relevant truths, but she hasn't cracked the mystery. She understands also that the doctrine of no-self provides a reason to be less selfish, for example, to apply a discount rate to her own pressing desires since she will not be the same self if and when those desires are realized as the self that has the desires now. Imagine she also read David Hume, Derek Parfit, and Galen Strawson for ways of putting no-self in terms congenial to her analytic philosophical training, and sees how it has some sort of implications for how she should weight her own present and future desires versus the weal and woe of others. But she hasn't overcome the illusion of the self. She intellectually grasps no-self (to a point) but can't enact that truth or, what may come to the same thing, deactivate the delusion of self.

Catholic theology says the doctrine of the Trinity is a mystery; Buddhist soteriology, however, says that no-self can be grasped in meditative enlightenment. So now she meditates with experts, and she grasps nonpropositionally her very no-selfness. Imagine that this is enough. She is now enlightened, existentially compelled to follow the bodhisattva path. She has experienced her own maximally compassionate selfless personhood, and she is committed to enacting her Buddha nature for the sake of all sentient beings.

The philosopher Miri Albahari describes the relevant phenomenology of achieving "insight" (*vipassana*) this way:

> [Her] theoretical understanding of the proposition that 'there is no self' (and by implication that she is not such a self) is being coupled with the overcoming of a powerful and pervasive delusion—the delusion that she is a self. Overcoming this delusion imbues her with a genuinely accurate feeling of noetic resonance: of having dispelled a cognitive error—analogous, it is sometimes said, to awakening from a dream. The depth and pervasiveness of the error overcome explains and grounds her feeling that the insight is profound and irreversible, resulting in a more accurate mode of cognition.
>
> (2014, 14)

Now here's the rub: Buddhists will say that no-self is true. Others will say that no-self is not true, at least not in any interesting form that is stronger than something like a psychobiological continuity view familiar from thinkers who deny that humans possess eternal Platonic or immortal Hindu (*atman*) or Abrahamic souls and claim instead that humans are finite, sentient, gregarious animals. On this view if meditation produces a grasp that one is no-self, which is entirely possible, it produces the grasp of a falsehood.

However, believing that no-self is false and that meditation produces the erroneous grasp is compatible with thinking that it is good to believe (or as I should say "make believe") in no-self, and that it might be even better, morally good, for everyone to adopt the attitude, the positive metaphysical illusion that there are no selves, none at all. If believing or hallucinating no-self is possible even though there really are selves (and even if, as seems likely, I am one of them), and if in addition it is good to so believe or hallucinate, then we have an example of a positive metaphysical illusion, a false metaphysical belief that pertains to oneness, perhaps to ONENESS*, and that can be inculcated and that has good effects. The fact that noetic confidence attaches to the false belief, the mistaken grasping, the hallucinatory experience is just good cosmic luck.

The Ethics of Belief

For those familiar with the debate between William Clifford (1877) and William James (1896) about the ethics of belief in the last quarter of the nineteenth century, you might think I am endorsing James's view. Actually I am endorsing, well, at least seriously considering, a much stronger view. I am endorsing make-believe, illusion, hallucination, metaphysical fantasy, and self-hypnosis that will result in feeling attuned to a way of conceiving things that is somewhere along the line of the extremely unlikely or probably false. I am endorsing metaphysical illusions or hallucinations in the oneness vicinity because they might have really good-making moral effects.

Clifford argued, "It is wrong always, everywhere, and for anyone, to believe anything upon insufficient evidence." And in addition, "It is wrong always, everywhere, and for anyone, to form beliefs without seeking any readily available evidence that is relevant to them." James meanwhile argued that there are certain momentous beliefs that will always be underdetermined by the evidence, but that nonetheless a person can will rationally to believe because sometimes the meaning and significance of life for that individual depend on the belief. In the case of beliefs in oneness of the sort that might engender maximally expansive moral thinking and acting, specifically, believing in ONENESS*, I think the evidence is not just insufficient; it is not really there at all. So you shouldn't believe in ONENESS* on Clifford's stringent standards, and you shouldn't believe in it on Jamesean standards. ONENESS* is possible logically, but it is really rather incredible given the evidence. Still it might be a good idea to project yourself into a notional reality that would make it seem as if it is true and worth believing.

By adopting ONENESS* one chooses or commits to live or imagine living in the possible world where ONENESS* is true as a way of constituting that very world. The metaphysical illusion would engender expansive ethical concern, but also at the same time it might be experienced as intrinsically pleasant, positive, uplifting, worthy. If the positive metaphysical illusion is worth it, it is worth it because the good matters, at least in this case, more than the true.

Positive Hallucinations

There is a budding industry nowadays of what is being called by its advocates "contemplative neuroscience." Evan Thompson explains the agenda of contemplative neuroscience in *Waking, Dreaming, Being* (2014) as an attempt to blend the wisdom of the ages with contemporary neuroscience, and as involving inquiry into

- the effects of yoga and meditation on the brain, body, health, and well-being;
- phenomenological revelation of the true nature of awareness, its layers, and its deep structure;
- seeing reality in general—one's own mind, other minds, and world—more clearly, as it really is, as they really are;
- the effects of yoga and meditation on reducing ego-fixation and enhancing compassion and loving-kindness.

In accordance with this agenda, yoga and meditation are put forward as multipurpose techniques and practices. Sometimes they are recommended as vehicles for high-resolution phenomenology, as methods for accurately revealing the ultimate nature of mind and world. Other times, as in some examples of dream yoga, they are offered as techniques that might be, as the kids say, really cool or fun. Still other times, they are recommended as ways of learning such truths as impermanence, no-self, and so on. Finally, as in some dying yoga, they can be viewed as inducing hallucinations that have good effects.

These multiple uses, some phenomenological, some that are vehicles for ethical or epistemic self-cultivation, and some that are like tripping on LSD, will have to be carefully distinguished if contemplative neuroscience is to become respectable. For present purposes, I am interested in the claim, in this case common inside the Buddhisms (as well as many other Indic traditions), that certain practices reveal the truth of oneness (1–5) or even ONENESS*, whereas when considered from another skeptical point of view these practices could be read just as inducing false beliefs in no-self, in some of the varieties of oneness (1–5), or even in ONENESS*.

Contemplative neuroscience is a location where we see differences of opinion about the legitimacy of certain meditation techniques and methods for discovering metaphysical truth, and where both advocates and skeptics might agree that believing in no-self or oneness (1–5) as discovered or experienced in meditation might have positive effects. This forcefully raises the prospect that the beliefs acquired in some of the more metaphysically momentous meditation practices involve good techniques not just for acquiring positive metaphysical illusions but actually for inducing metaphysical hallucinations. Can the belief in ONENESS*—the kind that could really make sense of, that possibly could motivate, radical deflation of self and inflation of care for all sentient and, perhaps, nonsentient beings as well—be induced even though it is false, and might doing so be good?[4]

It is useful to distinguish between (1) a grasp of a variety of oneness that is true, for example, that things are causally interdependent, (2) a grasp of a variety of oneness that is a positive metaphysical illusion comprising a false but optimistic belief, for example, that all sentient beings naturally care for all other sentient beings, and (3) a grasp of a variety of oneness, even ONENESS*, that is a positive metaphysical hallucination, where the mental state involved is one of conative, cognitive, affective absorption, akin to entry into an alternative reality altogether. In a *New Yorker* article (February 9, 2015), Michael Pollan reports on new—really renewed—research on hallucinogens at top medical centers like Johns Hopkins and NYU. Psilocybin, the key ingredient in magic mushrooms, is now being given to patients with terminal illnesses and the results so far reveal that the well-controlled daylong trips are normally pleasant, interesting, and enjoyable, not at all like the bad trips of the days of yore with unpleasant flashbacks. Unlike REM dreams, the trips are well remembered, and thus they are subsequently available for revisitation and fine-grained analysis. Most importantly, as far as the patients go, the trips reduce fear and anxiety about dying, and produce a kind of acceptance, even contentment about their impending death. Remarkably, even for individuals at death's door, the experience is judged as in the very top group of existentially meaningful experiences in their lives.

A common feature of the phenomenology is described in terms of "completeness," where this involves "feelings of unity, sacredness, ineffability, peace, joy, as well as the impression of having transcended space and time and the 'noetic sense' that the experience has disclosed some objective truth about reality. A 'complete' mystical experience is one that exhibits all six characteristics."

The so-called astronaut effect (also called the overview effect) of seeing the world from above, where one feels minute and experiences awe, ego dissolution, oneness, and expansive love, is another way that the experiences are commonly described. Interestingly, around the same time as the *New Yorker* article, Oliver Sacks wrote a moving op-ed in the *New York Times* (February 19, 2015) about receiving news that he was terminally ill. He writes, "over the last few days, I have been able to see my life as from a great altitude, as a sort of landscape, and with a deepening sense of the connection of all its parts."

Notice that the confidence of the psilocybin patients of possessing unshakeable objective truth when they experience ego dissolution and oneness is very similar to what Miri Albahari describes as the experience produced by meditation on no-self: "Overcoming this delusion imbues her with a genuinely accurate feeling of noetic resonance: of having dispelled a cognitive error—analogous, it is sometimes said, to awakening from a dream. The depth and pervasiveness of the error overcome explains and grounds her feeling that the insight is profound and irreversible, resulting in a more accurate mode of cognition" (2014, 14).

There are several interpretations of what is happening that do not claim truth for the relevant insights, just good effects. One might think that various confirmation biases overdetermine meditative insight and thus that noetic confidence is best explained in terms of leading the witness or in terms of self-hypnosis. One might think also, given the history of metaphysics, that we ought not to have confidence that any conceptual scheme can capture mind or world, as they really are, that all ways of seeing reality are instruments, to be judged in terms of their good or bad effects.

The facts are that these trips are experienced as revelatory of the way things really are, not as hallucinatory, at least not if hallucinatory means inaccurate. Of course, thinking that one has seen reality as it is is not the same as having seen reality as it is. Pollan asks:

> How are we to judge the veracity of the insights gleaned during a psychedelic tour? It's one thing to conclude that love is all that matters, but quite another to come away from a therapy convinced that "there is another reality awaiting us after death," as one volunteer put it, or that there is more to the universe—and consciousness—than a purely materialistic view of the world would have us believe. Is psychedelic therapy simply foisting a comforting delusion on the sick and dying?

Why would Pollan let the psilocybin-induced thought that "love is all that matters" slide but worry about people who claim to see what heaven is like. I think his response reflects our epistemic permissiveness with good-producing false beliefs.[5] In fact, he goes on to discuss William James's view that we can judge mystical experiences not by their objective truth-value, but by their fruits, by whether they have positive effects, results.

I claimed that Buddhist Oneness of the 1–5 sort is supposed to be true, really true, and, in addition, is supposed to have some fairly strong link, both rational and motivational, to a life of maximal compassion. Buddhists claim that they are concerned with both seeing things as they really are and alleviating suffering. But I have said—I haven't really argued it adequately here (see Flanagan 2011)—that the Oneness hypothesis (1–5) is not enough to warrant a life of maximal compassion and loving-kindness, whereas a view like ONENESS* that might be enough would likely be false or fantastical. For example, I might really need to believe I am literally ONE, identical with ALL that there is, to be properly motivated to be maximally compassionate and loving-kind. Put another way, insofar as Oneness of the 1–5 sort is true, it is not true in a way that grounds or motivates maximal moral oneness or for that matter maximal prudential concern for all. To do either we would have to expand Oneness (1–5) into ONENESS* where my well-being is literally conceived as one with the fate of the universe or, better perhaps, where there is only the well-being of the entire universe, where my well-being or the well-being of any other seeming proper parts of the universe is an illusion.

Late in his life, when he was already in his nineties, Bertrand Russell wrote this about overcoming the fear of death:

> The best way to overcome it . . . is to make your interests gradually wider and more impersonal, until bit by bit the walls of the ego recede, and your life becomes increasingly merged in the universal life. An individual human existence should be like a river: small at first, narrowly contained within its banks, and rushing passionately past rocks and over waterfalls. Gradually the river grows wider, the banks recede, the waters flow more quietly, and in the end, without any visible break, they become merged in the sea, and painlessly lose their individual being.

This seems like good advice. The "should" recommends a deflation of ego and an absorption or immersion into a shared medium of being.[6] But note that Russell is speaking about adopting a certain attitude that helps one accept that death, in all likelihood, is the end of me for all eternity. He may also be understood as speaking about what it feels or seems like to adopt that attitude, and thus in a certain sense as a careful phenomenologist. Is he saying anything about the way reality is, or the way consciousness normally is, about the way the metaphysical facts really line up? I don't think so.

And so it is with oneness. There is a connection between a metaphysics that emphasizes interdependency and shared fate and experiencing both the consolation that one's life matters and a calling to expansive love and compassion. Truth, consolation, and goodness are excellent, great things.

Believing in a view that approximates Oneness (1–5), while acknowledging the objections to it, and also believing that we ought to live in accord with our beliefs, would be enough to permit us to call our selves out for being selfish creeps, uncaring, and inconsiderate when we are. If we really believed in that variety of Oneness (1–5) we would no doubt be better than we are now. But we would not, I suspect, be all that far from something like a sensible commonsense morality. I do not think that Oneness (1–5) is remotely strong enough to motivate the bodhisattva ideal; it is not strong enough to motivate a life of great compassion and loving-kindness. Maybe such lives are unrealistic, are not in the cards for animals like us. But if we think it good to work toward becoming saints, sages, arhats, bodhisattvas, or something in their vicinity, then we might need to believe, really believe, in something like ONENESS*, the heroic conception. How could that happen? Well, ONENESS*—whatever its exact shape—is incredible, likely false, a fantasy. But we could decide to hallucinate it, to adopt a certain incredible way of seeing and believing what reality demands, and then work to enact its truth, to make it so. Would that be a good idea? Maybe.

Notes

I am grateful to Miri Alhabari, Victoria Harrison, and P. J. Ivanhoe for helpful criticisms.

1. See www.un.org/sustainabledevelopment/sustainable-development-goals/ and https://ec.europa.eu/clima/policies/international/negotiations/paris/index_en.htm.
2. I mean these five kinds of oneness to express and reflect the core tenets of Buddhist philosophy: (i) *Impermanence*: Everything is impermanent. Nothing lasts forever. Good things pass; bad things happen. (ii) *Dependent Origination* and *Dependent Being*: Everything is interdependent; there is no such thing as independent being; everything is becoming, an unfolding in a field of causes and effects. (iii) *No-Self*: A person is one of the dependently originating things, one of the constituents of the ever-changing flux that is the world, the sum of everything that is changing. A person, like all other things that seem to exist as independent substances (think diamonds that are said to last forever but came from coal and don't last forever), has only conventionally or pragmatically endowed stability. And thus personal identity is not an all-or-none matter; it is a matter of psychobiological continuity and connectedness. There is no permanent diamond in the rough that is me, that makes me exactly the same person over time. (iv) *Emptiness*: There are no things as they seem or appear; indeed there are no things at all, where "thing" means an independent subject or object.
3. One possibility I do not take up here but that is wide open and that I am very interested in is straightforward therapy of desire, Buddhist-style. Think of *metta* meditation or Tibetan *tonglen* meditation, where one works on developing compassion, loving-kindness, and their suite. One could try this without any cognitive or conceptual metaphysical ground whatsoever, but instead just because one takes it to be foundational to living a good life that one try to be this way, maximally compassionate and loving-kind. If one believes that sooner or later one will have to take something as axiomatic, as foundational—a belief, a desire, a set of either or both, an orientation, a way of being in the world—then this approach that takes wanting to act as if one's own fate and well-being just are tied to the fate and well-being of all else is entirely open. If the question is raised why think this, one reply is that there is no reason; I enact its truth, and I will that it be so. I am not sure doing this requires or enacts a metaphysical hallucination, but it requires something in its vicinity that rationalist

philosophers won't like—a baseless commitment to be a way that is compelling and then practices to be that way, to keep one's eye on that prize, however hard to defend it might be.

4. Besides ONENESS*, panpsychism, and vitalism might be other expansive metaphysical views that are false or, what is different, fantastical, but that, if believed, might have positive moral effects. Galen Strawson (2012) thinks that the best way to be a "real materialist" and to avoid radical emergence of sentience (ruptures in the causal fabric of the sort that traditionally God is imported to explain) is to introduce sentience into reality at the start with the bosons and fermions that emerged when the Big Bang banged. This is panpsychism. I think panpsychism is unwarranted, false; most days I think it crazy. But I can see still how embracing it as a metaphysical hallucination—imagine I practice believing it, developing noetic confidence in it, even though I think it unwarranted, false, crazy—might have good effects on my environmental ethics. It is hard to care for nature noninstrumentally if I think it totally insensate and incapable of suffering. But if I spread sentience throughout the fabric of the universe and care about any and all suffering, I might be able to sustain deep care for all that there is. One reason I think panpsychism crazy, when I do, is because our best science teaches that once upon a time, say, fourteen billion years ago, the universe consisted of only the singularity that banged. The elements in the periodic table did not exist until certain thermonuclear reactions took place after the bang. Ten billion years passed and then on Earth life, plants, and bacteria emerged. Before then there was nothing alive. Sometime later—a billion years—conscious life emerged among certain animals. No one who knows the science thinks we possess either a full explanation of how life emerged or a reduction of the life sciences to inorganic chemistry and physics. Nor does anyone who knows the science think that we have a full explanation of sentience or a reduction of the mind sciences (psychology and cognitive neuroscience) to molecular biology and that to physics. If we worry too much about emergence, we have as much reason to impute life to the singularity as sentience. This matters to the topic at hand: even though it is unwarranted by physical science and by metaphysics to think that the singularity that banged fourteen billion years ago was alive and sentient, it might be a good idea to hallucinate it. Why? Because, it is easier to love living sentient things than nonliving, insensate things. Believing what is false—believing in vitalism and panpsychism—might get us over certain motivational humps that lie between us and expansive love for all being.

5. "Love is all that matters" is pretty transparently false. Suffering matters, justice matters. Even if there were no love left, we would still care about suffering and pain. Is love the greatest good, the most important thing, the best thing in life? Maybe.

6. One might read Russell as saying that the proper attitude will happen naturally to a certain extent due to development and age. A young person, perhaps because of what the world demands and partly because of psychobiological imperatives, will have fire in the belly to accomplish personal things. With age the fire of ego diminishes, the sense of urgency for me, myself, and I dissipates.

References

Alhabari, Miri. 2014. "Insight Knowledge of No Self in Buddhism: An Epistemic Analysis." *Philosophers' Imprint* 14 (21).

Clifford, W. K. 1877. "The Ethics of Belief." *Contemporary Review*.

Flanagan, O. 1991. *Varieties of Moral Personality*. Cambridge: Harvard University Press.

——. 2007. *The Really Hard Problem: Meaning in the Material World*. Cambridge: MIT Press.

——. 2011. *The Bodhisattva's Brain: Buddhism Naturalized*. Cambridge: MIT Press.

Flanagan, O., and G. Graham. 2016. "Truth and Sanity: Positive Illusions, Spiritual Delusions and Metaphysical Hallucinations." In *Extraordinary Science: Responding to the Crisis in Psychiatric Research*, edited by J. Poland and S. Tekin. Cambridge: MIT Press.

Flanagan, O., and P. J. Ivanhoe. 2016. "Metaphysical Habits of the Heart: Moderating Ego in East and South Asia." In *The Oxford Handbook of Hypo-Egoic Phenomena*, edited by Kirk W. Brown and Mark Leary. Oxford: Oxford University Press.

Horgan, Terry, and Matjaz Potrc. 2000. "Blobjectivism and Indirect Correspondance." *Facta Philosophica* 2:249–70.

Ivanhoe, P. J. 2014. "Senses and Values of Oneness." In *The Philosophical Challenge from China*, edited by B. Bruya. Cambridge: MIT Press.

James, W. 1896. *The Will to Believe*. Cambridge: Harvard University Press.

Pope Francis. 2015. *Laudato Si': On Care of Our Common Home*. Vatican City: Liberia Editrice Vaticana.

Russell, B. 1950. *Portraits from Memory, and Other Essays*. New York: Simon and Schuster.

Strawson, Galen. 2008. *Real Materialism*. Oxford: Oxford University Press.

Taylor, S., and J. Brown. 1988. "Illusion and Well-Being: A Social Psychological Perspective on Mental Health." *Psychological Bulletin* 103 (2): 193–210.

Thompson, Evan. 2014. *Waking, Dreaming, Being*. Cambridge: MIT Press.

Tien, D. W. 2012. "Oneness and Self-Centeredness in the Moral Psychology of Wang Yangming." *Journal of Religious Ethics* 40.

CHAPTER 13

EPISODIC MEMORY AND ONENESS

JAY GARFIELD, SHAUN NICHOLS, AND NINA STROHMINGER

Oneness and No-Self

The idea of oneness is that "human beings are intricately and inextricably intertwined and share a common destiny with the other people, creatures, and things of this world" (Ivanhoe 2017). A central obstacle to achieving oneness in this sense is egocentricity, the focus on oneself. Buddhism promises a way of defeating this obstacle, by leading the practitioner to recognize that, ultimately, there is no self. The recognition that there is no self, many Buddhist philosophers argue, undermines egocentricity. But one must attend carefully to Buddhist accounts of just how that undermining occurs, and just what is required to achieve the kind of selflessness that is the goal of Buddhist moral practice. Perfection is not as easy to achieve as it might appear.

The locus classicus in the Indian and Tibetan Mahāyāna Buddhist tradition is *How to Lead an Awakened Life* (*Bodhicāryāvatāra*) by the eighth-century Buddhist philosopher Śāntideva. The book is a detailed exposition of Mahāyāna ethics, with instructions on how to cultivate the moral attitude of *bodhicitta*. Bodhicitta is the central conative state in Mahāyāna Buddhist moral psychology. It is the aspiration to attain awakening in order to benefit all sentient beings. In successive chapters, Śāntideva presents more specific accounts of the nature and means of cultivating the set of moral perfections to be cultivated by the bodhisattva: generosity, introspective awareness, patience, effort, meditation, and wisdom. This book is the most widely read and oft-cited ethical texts in Tibet, and is the subject of several important Indian and Tibetan commentaries.

Śāntideva distinguishes in chapter 1 of *Bodhicāryāvatāra* (on cultivating the moral attitude) between "aspirational" and "engaged" bodhicitta.

> 15. In brief, one should understand that
> Bodhicitta has two aspects:
> Aspirational *bodhicitta*,
> And engaged *bodhicitta*.

> 16. The wise should understand these two,
> Just as one understands the difference
> Between one who desires to travel and one who has traveled,
> Recognizing the differences between them and the order in which they arise.

> 17. Aspirational *bodhicitta* brings about great results,
> Even as we continue to circle within *saṃsāra*;
> Yet it does not bring about a ceaseless stream of merit,
> For that requires engaged bodhicitta.

Śāntideva argues that moral progress begins with aspirational *bodhicitta*, the cultivation of this goal and resolve to attain awakening prior to having achieved a direct understanding of emptiness and selflessness. Since one who has merely cultivated aspirational *bodhicitta* (still a significant moral accomplishment) has not yet realized the emptiness of all phenomena and in particular the lack of any self in the person, such an agent's cognitive and conative states are still pervaded by an instinctive ego-grasping that she or he nonetheless knows—at a more reflective level—to be deluded. This aspirational bodhicitta, he argues, while ultimately deficient, is necessary at the beginning of the path.

When one achieves a direct realization of emptiness and selflessness—very late on the path—one generates engaged *bodhicitta*, which is a completely impersonal commitment involving an experience of the world that does not represent a self at its center. Importantly, the difference between aspirational and engaged *bodhicitta* is characterized neither by the *content* of the commitment nor by degree of understanding one has of selflessness, but rather by the *mode of apprehension* of selflessness. The difference is between an inferential, or merely cognitive, understanding and an immediate awareness of selflessness that frames experience.

Śāntideva's elegant analogy is that aspirational bodhicitta is like the understanding one has of a place having read a guidebook, while engaged bodhicitta is like the experience of being there; so, he draws the distinction in terms of inferential knowledge, which is of limited effectiveness, and direct perception, which is cognitively more powerful.[1] But in any case, he argues that full moral effectiveness demands an attitude in which innate self-grasping is extirpated, but that that extirpation comes late in one's development.

In chapter 6 (on patience), Śāntideva connects the understanding of interdependence and the absence of ego to the ability to distance oneself from anger. Consider these verses from chapter 6:

> 22. Although such things as bile cause suffering,
> One doesn't get angry at them.
> Why get angry at sentient beings?
> They are all completely governed by conditions?

> 24. One does not think, "let's get angry,"
> And thus intentionally cultivate anger.
> Nor does anger intentionally
> Arise in a person.

> 25. All of the misdeeds
> And all of the various vices
> Arise as a result of conditions.
> None arise independently.

> 26. Collections of conditions
> Do not think, "let's produce something."
> Nor does that which is produced think,
> "Let me be produced."

Here Śāntideva is arguing that anger is fueled by the identification of an agent of harm; to the extent that we can see agency not as located in a personal self, but rather as the consequence of a confluence of causes and conditions, we can depersonalize the *objects* of our reactive attitudes, thus generating greater patience. He concludes this argument by remarking that to be angry at a person for hitting one with a stick is as irrational as blaming the stick; it suggests a center of agency, but none is there, only an indefinite web of causes and conditions:

> 41. Instead of the principal agent, such as a stick,
> I develop aversion to the one who wields it.
> But it would make more sense to cultivate aversion
> To aversion itself, since it impels him.

In chapter 8 (the meditation chapter), Śāntideva turns from the objects of our attitudes to the subject side, exploring the consequence of realizing the selflessness of the person for ameliorating egoism. In verses 90–103 we find the central argument that egoism is irrational: in the absence of a self, there is no reason to prefer oneself over others, and indeed there is no self.

The first verse states the conclusion, the irrationality of egoism:

> 90. "Self and other are the same,"
> One should earnestly meditate:
> "Since they experience the same happiness and suffering,
> I should protect everyone as I do myself."

Śāntideva then immediately connects this to the idea that insight into the lack of self should lead one to see oneself as part of a greater whole, and not an individual whose own interests are paramount:

> 91. Divided into many parts, such as the hands,
> The body is nonetheless to be protected as a whole.
> Just so, different beings, with all their happiness and suffering,
> Are like a single person with a desire for happiness.
>
> 92. Even if my own suffering
> Does no harm to anyone else's body,
> It is still my own suffering.
> Since I am so attached to myself it is unbearable.
>
> 93. Just so, even though I do not experience
> The sufferings of others,
> It is still their suffering.
> Since they are attached to themselves, it is hard for them to bear.
>
> 94. I must eliminate the suffering of others
> Just because it is suffering, like my own.
> I should work to benefit others
> Just because they are sentient beings, as am I.

This point is important. Śāntideva emphasizes that the reason for eliminating suffering cannot be that it is *my* suffering per se, but that suffering is *bad*. And if suffering is bad per se, then it is bad no matter whose it is, and so there is good reason to eliminate it no matter whose it is. For this reason as well, the idea that there is a self is irrelevant to moral motivation. But attachment to self is a cause of suffering, and therefore is something to be eliminated.

> 98. The idea that this very self
> Will experience that suffering is false:

Just as when one has died, another
Who is born is really another.

99. If another should protect himself
Against his own suffering,
When a pain in the foot is not in the hand,
Why should one protect the other?

In these two verses Śāntideva emphasizes the impact of the view of no-self on egoism. If I do not endure, what happens in the future to the personal continuum of which I am now a part should not be of special concern to me; and since I am as different from others around me as my foot is from my hand, I should show the same concern for others and lack of focus on myself that my hand shows to my foot when it reaches for a sore spot. Śāntideva develops this point further in the following verses. One should, he argues, abandon the habit of taking a personal continuum to be a unitary self; like an army or a forest, we are merely collections of constantly changing, causally interacting phenomena with no essential core; as a consequence, because suffering itself is what is to be abandoned, we should be equally concerned with suffering wherever it is manifested, and not concerned with our own well-being or suffering per se.

100. One might say that even though it makes no sense,
One acts this way because of self-grasping.
That which makes no sense with regard to self or others
Is precisely the object you should strive to abandon.

101. The so-called continuum and collection,
Just like such a thing as a forest, or an army, are unreal.
Since the sufferer does not exist,
By whose power does it come about?

102. As the suffering self does not exist,
There is no distinction among anyone.
Just because there is suffering, it is to be eliminated.
What is the point of discriminating here?

103. "Why should everyone's suffering be alleviated?"
There is no dispute!
If it is to be alleviated, all of it is to be alleviated!
Otherwise, I am also a sentient being![2]

The fact that this discussion is located in the meditation chapter of *How to Lead an Awakened Life* reflects the importance attached to meditative practice in the Buddhist tradition for internalizing this view, which is defended in more detail in chapter 9, the emptiness chapter. It is common in this tradition to distinguish between two sources of egoism, or "self-grasping": *Conceptual self-grasping* is the view that there is a self developed as a consequence of philosophical reflection (say, taking Plato's *Phaedo*, Descartes's *Meditations*, or the *Bhagavad-gītā* too seriously). As Tsongkhapa remarks, views caused by bad philosophy can be refuted by doing good philosophy. *Innate self-grasping*, on the other hand, is a deep cognitive reflex, an instinct for regarding ourselves as persisting unitary subjective centers. This innate self-grasping is a cognitive illusion and, like many illusions, not so cognitively penetrable; its extirpation, most Buddhist philosophers—Śāntideva included—think, requires extended meditative practice to reorganize one's psychology so that one *sees* the world through the lens of selflessness, as opposed to the lens of self. Buddhist soteriology is hence achieved through a transformation of phenomenology, and Buddhist ethics is best seen as a kind of moral phenomenology (Garfield 2015, 4, 9). Buddhist ethical attitudes are hence grounded in a metaphysical theory of the self and of reality more generally; Buddhist ethical cultivation begins with the *aspiration* to see the world free of the cognitive illusion of self, but is thought to be only complete once one cultivates a way of *seeing* the world free of that illusion.

Episodic Memory and Egocentricity

Although the no-self view promises to facilitate oneness, there seem to be several psychological factors that persistently reaffirm to the individual that there *is* an enduring self. Perhaps the most obvious of these psychological factors is episodic memory—memory of experiences. It's widely thought that when a person remembers an experience, she remembers the experience as having happened to *her*. Theorists in both Eastern and Western traditions maintain that episodic memory involves representing an event as having happened to one's *self*.[3] The memory has to present the experience as having happened to *me*.

We find an articulation of this in Reid: "The remembrance of a past event is necessarily accompanied with the conviction of our own existence at the time the event happened. I cannot remember a thing that happened a year ago, without a conviction as strong as memory can give, that I, the same identical person who now remember that event, did then exist" (2002, 202). We find it in James Mill:

> I remember to have seen and heard George the Third, when making a speech at the opening of his Parliament. . . . In this remembrance there is, first of all, the mere idea, or simple apprehension—the *conception* as it is sometimes

called—of the objects. There is combined with this, *to make it memory,* my idea of my having seen and heard those objects. And this combination is so close, that it is not in my power to separate them. I cannot have the idea of George the Third—his person and his attitude, the paper he held in his hand, the sound of his voice while reading it, the throne, the apartment, the audience—without having the other idea along with it, that of my having been a witness of the scene.

 (Mill 1869, 328, 330)

We also find the view in William James: "Memory requires more than the mere dating of a fact in the past. It must be dated in my past. In other words, I must think that I directly experienced its occurrence" (1890/1950, 650). Indeed, James even suggests that such memories are required for the sense of personal identity: "If a man wakes up one fine day unable to recall any of his past experiences, so that he has to learn his biography afresh . . . he feels, and he says, that he is a changed person" (336). The idea that the self is represented in episodic memory is also a staple of contemporary theorizing in cognitive psychology. As Harlene Hayne and colleagues note, the prevailing view is that an episodic memory "is accompanied by conscious awareness that the event happened to 'me' or will happen to 'me' that does not accompany retrieval of other kinds of memories" (Hayne et al. 2011, 344).

We also find the idea that episodic memory carries with it a representation of self in Eastern philosophers. For instance, Uddyotakara offers a "memory argument" against the Buddhist view that there is no self. Monima Chadha characterizes the argument as follows:

My present desire and a certain past experience are unified insofar as they concern the same object; I recognise that the thing I desire now is of the sort I experienced to be a cause of pleasure in the past. Recognition requires a persisting unitary agent, the referent of "I" since that which does not have the same agent is never recognised. For example, I can never recognise my friend's cognitions; therefore, recognition cannot be explained without postulating a persisting unitary agent, i.e., a self.[4]

 (Chadha 2014)

Dignāga, in *Encyclopedia of Epistemology* (*Pramāṇasamuccāya*), offers a related argument for the necessary reflexivity of awareness.[5] As a Buddhist, he does not take this to be an argument for a self, but rather for the necessity of a kind of apperceptive consciousness in perception as a necessary condition for memory. Dignāga argues that when I remember a sunny day last week, and remember seeing a sunny day last week, that is the same memory. So, any memory of a sunny day is a memory of *my seeing* a sunny day, and since I can only remember what I saw when I see a sunny day, I see *myself seeing* a sunny day. Dignāga's argument is important in the Buddhist tradition, and initiates a long debate concerning whether, or in what sense, awareness is reflexive (Garfield 2006; 2015, 135–49).

Not all Buddhist philosophers accepted the thesis of the reflexivity of awareness. Candrakīrti and Śāntideva in India and Tsongkhapa and his followers in Tibet, in particular, criticized this view, arguing instead for a higher-order view of apperception. They each argue that Dignāga's introduction of reflexivity in awareness amounts to the claim that awareness itself requires the cognitive illusion of self-grasping, with an identified and reidentified ego as the subject of experience. Instead, they each argue that episodic memory can be explained simply as the veridical awareness at a moment of something that happened at a prior moment that is caused by a sequence of psychological events beginning with the initial perceptual experience.

Śāntideva, in the ninth chapter of *How to Lead an Awakened Life*, introduces the analogy of a bear who is bitten on the foot by a rat while hibernating, and awakens with a septic wound. The bear comes as a consequence of noticing the painful bite to believe that he was bitten by a rat in the past. Śāntideva draws the analogy as follows: the bear was not aware of being bitten at the time of the bite, but nonetheless, because of the sequence of events intervening between the bite and the formation of the belief that there was a bite in the past, forms a belief intentionally directed upon the past bite. Similarly, he argues, I can, without having been aware of my seeing a sunny day in the past, as a result of a sequence of events intervening between some past perception of a sunny day and the formation of belief now that there was an experience of a sunny day in the past, have a state intentionally directed upon that very day, caused in the right way, and so have episodic memory of that sunny day without any reflexivity. So, there are within the Buddhist tradition conceptual resources to understand episodic memory in the absence of self or of self-consciousness, even in the minimal sense suggested by the reflexive awareness doctrine.

Experience Memory Without Self-Representation

As we saw in the previous section, philosophers from both Eastern and Western traditions maintain that episodic memory involves self-representation. While it is true that episodic memory often involves self-representation, there can be experience memories without explicit self-representation. For experience memories are likely present in animals that lack a concept of self like rats (see, for example, Crystal et al. 2013). Neuroscientists who work on rat memory often characterize episodic memory without explicit representation of self (for example, Hasselmo 2011). In this section, we want to explore this in more depth.

Ultimately, we think, the suggestion from Śāntideva in the previous section—that memory doesn't require a representation of self—is sustainable.

Egocentric Spatial Memory

Although rats presumably lack an explicit concept of self, it's plausible that at least many experience memories in rats are egocentric in an important way. For instance, rats deploy egocentric spatial memory in maze tasks. If a rat is put in a Y-maze several times (with different start points) and repeatedly experiences reward when it goes left and no reward when it goes right, the rat will soon start going to the left. Plausibly, the rat remembers the experience that *going left led to pleasure*. What counts as "left" is obviously egocentric—it depends on the position of the organism having the recollection. But this kind of egocentricity doesn't require a representation of self. To see the point, consider how one might use a prominent kind of AI programming—production systems—to model the cognition. Roughly speaking, production systems are made up of conditional statements, such that the consequent is an action, and if the antecedents are represented as satisfied, the program generates the act specified in the consequent. Thermostats provide a familiar example (for example, Newell 1990). A partial production system for a thermostat could include the following: "if the temperature is below 64 degrees and the heater is off, then turn on heater." A thermometer provides data for the antecedent in this case, for example, by broadcasting when it registers a temperature of 64 degrees. Notice that this system doesn't explicitly specify *whose* temperature is being registered or what heater is being turned on. There is no mention that the thermometer is measuring "*my* temperature" or that the heater to turn on is "*my* heater." Why is that? Because it's hard-coded into the system that it is only measures the ambient temperature, and it's hard-coded into the system that it only controls one heater. Now consider a production system for egocentric navigation in the rat (cf. Byrne 2000, 513). Her decision-making might be partly model with the conditional "if going left produced pleasure, then go left." Just as in the thermostat case, there is no need to specify *whose* pleasure or *whose* left is at issue. Egocentric directions like Right and Left can be dedicated to the organism so that self-representation isn't necessary. That is, there might be a hard-coded connection between Left and the organism. The system doesn't need to specify "My Left" since the default for Left will just be the organism navigating the maze. So, while there is probably not a self-representation here, there is still an important kind of egocentricity.

Note that, without this egocentric spatial memory, rats would be severely impaired in navigation (indeed, lesions to medial prefrontal cortex regions produce this deficit [Kesner et al. 1989]). Humans, of course, plausibly have this egocentric navigation system as well. And any individual will fare worse if this system is damaged.

Although there is a kind of experience memory that is inevitably egocentric, Buddhist philosophers have argued that this kind of egocentricity does not interfere with the view that there is no self. For the egocentricity here is tied to the *organism*, and Buddhists, like those in many other philosophical traditions, reject the idea that the organism is the self. Indeed, in *Introduction to the Middle Way* (*Madhyamakāvatāra*), Candrakīrti, in his famous sevenfold analysis (Garfield 2015, 111–16; Huntington and Wangchen 1989, 171–77), argues directly that we do not regard the body as the self. We talk instead about *having* bodies, and we imagine having *different* bodies. Indeed, when we imagine having different bodies we can easily imagine that the egocentric spatial relations switch—that in the new body, the food is to the *right*—without this having any important effect on one's personal identity. Thus, the *kind* of egocentricity at issue in spatial memory is very different from the kind of egocentrism that threatens oneness.

The real problem posed by experience memory (and the memory argument discussed earlier) is that when we *reflect* on our experiences—something rats can't do—we naturally represent the experiences as having happened to the self. Indeed, this is true even when we reflect on the kinds of navigational experiences that we share with rats. If I had an experience of going left and getting food, and then I reflect on that experience, it seems like I am bound to think of that left-going experience as an experience that happened to *me*.

As we emphasized earlier, Buddhist thought about the self and about self-consciousness is grounded in the idea that we are subject to profound cognitive illusions, and one of those is that we are distinct selves. That illusion grounds our instinctive conative orientation to the world, and a rational conative and ethical orientation to the world, Buddhists argue, would be one freed from that illusion. If Buddhist philosophy had evolved in the context of evolutionary psychology, we could imagine Candrakīrti or Śāntideva arguing as follows: just because some cognitive process contributes to our fitness doesn't mean that the process will track the truth.

Instead, we evolved to have quick strategies to keep us alive long enough to reproduce and to raise our young. Sometimes those track truth; sometimes they do not, and generate cognitive illusions (like the tendency to misidentify objects as guns in situations of high threat, or to distrust those perceived as outsiders, which are adaptive but not truth-tracking). The Buddhist can allow that the cognitive illusion of self is adaptive—it leads us to act to preserve ourselves as organisms and to raise our young. But, if Buddhists are right, it is hardly truth-tracking, and, like the illusions better known to modern psychology that underlie implicit bias, it is neither an unalloyed good, nor easy to transcend.

Reflection and Self-Representation

Buddhists maintain that there is a cognitive illusion of a persisting self, and they recommend that we rid ourselves of the illusion. But to what extent is this possible? This is an empirical question, of course. And we propose to apply empirical conditions to the question.

Earlier, we saw that even though rats have egocentric spatial memories, this doesn't yet generate a problematic (from a Buddhist perspective) sense of identity with a past self. The problem emerges when one reflects on one's experiences. Because when I reflect on a past experience had by this organism, it seems inevitable that the result is the sense that I—my self—had that experience. This sense of a persisting self is, of course, exactly what the Buddhist wants to claim is illusory. So we first want to ask whether it is possible for an organism to reflect on the past experiences of that organism *without* having the sense of identity.

Neurology provides several cases that indicate that it is indeed possible to recall an experience without having the sense of identity. The most extensive description comes from the case of R. B., who suffered head trauma from a bike accident at age forty-three (Klein and Nichols 2012). After the accident, R. B. could still recall experiences from the past, but he said that the recalled experiences didn't seem like they were experiences that happened to *him*. Here is R. B.'s description of one such memory: "I could clearly recall a scene of me at the beach in New London with my family as a child. But the feeling was that the scene was not my memory. As if I was looking at a photo of someone else's vacation." R. B. also described a memory from college: "I can picture the scene perfectly clearly . . . studying with my friends in our study lounge. I can 'relive' it in the sense of re-running the experience of being there. But it has the feeling of imagining, [as if] re-running an experience that my parents described from their college days. It did not feel like it was something that really had been a part of my life. Intellectually I suppose I never doubted that it was a part of my life. . . . But that in itself did not help change the feeling of ownership." Thus, R. B. seemed able to reflect on memories of past experiences had by that very organism, but his reflection on the experiences did not bring with it the sense of personal identity (Klein and Nichols 2012). As Monima Chadha has argued, this kind of case suggests that it is in fact possible to have experience memories without running afoul of the no-self doctrine (Chadha 2014).[6] The original discussion of R. B. (Klein and Nichols 2012) was quite explicitly informed by questions about the sense of personal identity. But there is a broader disorder—*depersonalization*—that shares important features with R. B.'s cases. One symptom of depersonalization disorder is "The subjective feeling of not being able to recall things (e.g., memory episodes) or having the feeling that the person was not part of the episode" (Sierra and Berrios 2001, 631).

One patient with this symptom is described as follows: "When he recalled events in his life, he felt as though he was 'not in them'" (Sierra and Berrios 2001, 631). This kind of symptom is incorporated into the diagnostic measures, reflected in the following item: "I feel detached from memories of things that have happened to me—as if I had not been involved in them" (Sierra and Berrios 2000).

Combating Egocentrism

Buddhist Strategies

The Buddhist tradition comprises two classes of strategies for extirpating the illusion of self: analytical and meditative, and we see each in place from the very beginning of the Buddhist tradition. We see the analytical strategy developed in the earliest strata of the Pāli suttas, in which the person is decomposed into five *khandhas* (Skt: *skhandas*), or *heaps*, of phenomena: material form; sensation or hedonic tone; perception; dispositions or personality traits; and consciousness. Siddhartha Gautama—the historical Buddha—and his followers repeatedly argue that there is no more to the person than these constantly changing, causally interacting aggregates of phenomena that themselves can be decomposed into subheaps and so on and on. When one strips the person of these heaps of phenomena, we find nothing left—no owner, no core.

As the *Abhidharma* (advanced doctrine) develops, the person—and especially the cognitive aggregates—is further decomposed into a complex classification of momentary mental states and mental processes: we naïvely take ourselves to be directly aware of our mental life as it is; but many Buddhist philosophers argue that the mind and mental life with which we take ourselves to be so intimately acquainted are in fact an illusory construct grounded in countless evanescent processes far too subtle to introspect. None of these is endurant; none of these is a self; and there is nothing to us beyond these. These strategies ramify in the Mahāyāna tradition through analyses such as Candrakīrti sevenfold analysis.

Meditative strategies are also present from the beginning. From early suttas like the *Greater Discourse on Mindfulness* (*Mahasatipatthana-sutta*) to the Mahāyāna meditation manuals such as the ninth-century philosopher Kamalaśīla's *Stages of Meditation* (*Bhāvanākrama*) we find a range of techniques for directing introspective attention to our psychological processes and finding only states and events, no substance in which they inhere or subject to whom they appear. Repeated practice is intended to settle the view that there is no self at all, and to undo the cognitive habit of positing one.

In the work of Śāntideva, particularly in the eighth chapter of *How to Lead an Awakened Life*, this meditative practice is given an ethical direction, with an emphasis on making the transition from meditation on selflessness to meditation on the ethical consequences of selflessness with the goal of the transformation of our ethical perception of the world. One can see this as an attempt to undermine a natural implicit bias in favor of self and to replace it with an equanimous attitude of care for all.

Retrieval Strategies

The Buddhist strategies for eliminating the illusion of self are philosophical in nature. But psychologists have been exploring more practical ways of combatting self-focus. These techniques do not promote the view that there is no self. But they do encourage resistance to a certain kind of egocentricity. And the effects of these techniques resonate with some of what Buddhism seeks. They all seek to circumvent a *first-personal* orientation in recollection (and prospection).

Although we usually remember experiences from a first-person perspective—from the original perspective of the experiencer—classic experiments show that experiences can be recalled from a third-person perspective (Nigro and Neisser 1983, Robinson and Swanson 1993, McIsaac and Eich 2002, 2004, Libby Eibach, and Gilovich 2005). Third-person recollection is characterized as follows: "In your memory, you imagine the scene as an observer might see it. Such an observer would see you as well as other aspects of the situation" (Nigro and Neisser 1983). In fact, some kinds of experiences tend to be recalled from the third-person perspective, for example, when people recall an episode of swimming laps they often recall it as from above, seeing their body in the water rather than the original perspective that might have experienced a blurry distant pool wall. The fact that we can recall from the third-person perspective does not contradict the claim that experience memory is naturally from the first-person perspective. Rather, the fact that it's possible to have a third-person perspective on a past experience is taken to provide evidence of the reconstructive capacities of memory (see, for example, Loftus and Palmer 1974). It is because reconstruction is implicated in memory that we can come to have a memory from an observer perspective even though, of course, the actual experience was not from that perspective (for example, McIsaac and Eich 2004, 248).

One way to lead people to adopt a third-person perspective is by telling people to recall the past event as if they were viewing the scene as a detached observer (McIsaac and Eich 2002, 147; see also Mischkowski, Kross, and Bushman 2012). People who are given this instruction are more likely to mention personal appearance and less likely to use first-person pronouns (McIsaac and Eich 2002, 148). So the manipulation seems to work. More importantly, taking the detached perspective has emotional benefits.

People suffering from PTSD (posttraumatic stress disorder) were instructed to recall a traumatic event from either the third-person or the first-person perspective; those who recalled the event from the third-person perspective found the recollection less anxiety-provoking (McIsaac and Eich 2004, 250). Even for a very recent event, using a third-person perspective reduces anger and aggressive behavior (Mischkowski, Kross, and Bushman 2012).

Empirical Results on Attitudes on the Self and Death

The previous sections provide some reason to be optimistic that episodic memory does not provide any kind of insuperable obstacle to egocentrism. While reflection on episodic memories typically brings with it a sense of personal identity, this is not inevitable. Moreover, there are Buddhist strategies and practical techniques for reducing self-focus.

It was with this optimism that we conducted studies on attitudes about death among monastics in the Tibetan Buddhist tradition. We wanted to examine whether the inculcation of the doctrine of no-self would have the beneficial effects advertised by Buddhist teachings.

On all of the explicit measures regarding the no-self doctrines, we found strong agreement among the Tibetan monastics. They almost uniformly maintained that there is no core self and there is no person that stays the same across time. On these questions they differed dramatically from Christian and Hindu samples. In addition, the Tibetan monastics showed a significantly reduced essentialism, as compared to Christians and Hindus. Finally, we asked whether one strategy they used to cope with death was thinking that there is no self that persists anyway. On this question, almost every single monastic said "yes," and almost every single Christian said "no."

Our primary interest in the study was whether the monastics would exhibit less fear of death of self. One of the primary outcomes of extirpating the illusion of self is that it will reduce fear of death. Thus, we had participants indicate the extent to which they feared the death of self. To our great surprise, we found that the Tibetan monastics reported *greater* fear of death of self than the other participants. In addition, the monastics showed greater selfishness than Christians and Hindus in decisions about whether to sacrifice part of their life so that another person could live longer. Thus, despite the explicit commitment to the no-self doctrine, we find evidence that the monastics still exhibit considerable egocentricity (Garfield et al. 2015, Nichols et al. Forthcoming).

Tibetan Autobiographies

Our results suggest that the Tibetan monastics have not extirpated the sense of personal identity that is rejected by Buddhist teachings. In the terms of the tradition, they seem not to have overcome innate self-grasping. Thus, it turns out to be harder than one might have thought to uproot this sense of personal identity, harder to evade this key obstacle to achieving oneness.

Why is it so difficult to uproot this sense of personal identity? We think part of the answer is the insistence of episodic recollection. While it is possible to reject or blunt the sense of personal identity that episodic memory generates, this likely requires considerable effort. Insofar as episodic recollection is naturally from the first-person perspective, it will take cognitive resources to recode it from a detached perspective. Instead, one's natural reflections on one's past experiences will tend to trigger the sense of personal identity. That's our current speculation in any case. Although we don't have any experimental evidence on this issue, we do think that there is a very suggestive source of evidence provided by Tibetan autobiographies, which are a major genre in Tibetan literature. Autobiographies are written by individuals who have reached a high level of high spiritual attainment (for example, Gyatso 1998, 103). It might seem paradoxical for an enlightened Buddhist to produce an autobiography—how can one compose an autobiography while maintaining that the self is an illusion? The explanation is that one can speak of the self in a conventional way without endorsing the idea that there is an enduring ultimate self.

It's possible to treat persons as a merely conventional notion, but when we consult the autobiographies, it often seems otherwise. Not surprisingly, the autobiographies recount past experiences. But the important point for us is that these recollections do not seem to present a distanced perspective of the sort associated with the view that there really is no persisting self. Rather, the recollections often suggest a robust identification with the past experiencer. Consider, first, the most famous work in this tradition, *The Life of Milarepa*. At one point the author describes a scene from years earlier in which there was an experience of walking into a building and finding human bones among a heap of rags. He writes, "When I realized they were the bones of my mother, I was so overcome with grief that I could hardly stand it. I could not think, I could not speak, and *an overwhelming sense of longing and sadness swept over me*" (Quintman 2010, 118, emphasis added). How different this is from a detached reportage of there being some previous set of experiences. Nor is this kind of emotion-ridden episodic memory unusual in this literature. Indeed, in every major autobiography that has been translated into English we find these expressions. Several more examples follow:

Because my relatives rose up as enemies against us, mother and son were separated in misery while I was still young, and we never met again. *This filled me with immeasurable sorrow.* I called out the names of my mother and sister and wept. When I awoke my pillow was damp with tears. Thinking this over brought my mother to mind. I shed many tears and resolved to do whatever I could to see my old mother again."

(Quintman 2010, 103)

When I turned twenty-one I thought, "Now I must begin to practice Dharma right away, and do so in a perfectly pure way. In order to urge those who cling to permanence to do spiritual practice, even my most kind root guru Jamyang Gyatso Rinpoche has shown the passing into nirvana of his physical manifestation. Someone like me is bound to die soon, needless to say. Abandoning concern for my native land, for my family and friends, and for this life's affairs, I must go to some place far away, and practice the Dharma truly. I must do this, and it is already late." *An unbearable sadness arose in my mind.*

(Shabkar 1994)

When I crossed the door of the tent and looked up at his face, seeing it filled with tears, *I couldn't bear to go any farther.*

(Shabkar 1994)

When I arrived at Ngamong plateau, I saw that the camp fires of other travelers had set the grass afire. Scattered over the plateau were perhaps a hundred fires, resembling hundreds of smoke-offerings. Curious, I walked around and discovered that these were anthills that had caught fire. Flames were consuming the ants; the ground was aglow with burning embers. *Seeing this, I felt great compassion.* There was no water on that vast plateau, but I stayed there for the whole day, doing everything I could to accumulate merit and purify obscurations—taking refuge, generating Bodhicitta, making the seven-branch offering, and so on. Visualizing a rain of purifying nectar, I prayed to the guru and the Three Jewels, "May you guide these dying ants to the Pure Realms."

(Shabkar 1994)

> There I was, in a state of unbearable veneration.
> How the waves of tears flowed from my eyes!
> Remembering Father Orgyan, I don't stand it.
> "If only I could get to that place right now." I thought.
> (Jigme Lingpa in Gytaso 1998)

> I thought, in my residual fleshly form's mind,
> "The unreal mind is without such designations as "birth" or "death."
> Since I've seen the truth, bliss and sorrow are false. . . ."
> At that moment, I awoke from sleep,
> and was absorbed in a state of bliss-clarity.
> (Jigme Lingpa in Gytaso 1998)

On the evening of the either day of the ninth month, I had a dream in which I experienced something very much like actually dying, *which saddened me greatly.*

(The autobiography of Jamgon Kontrul in Barron 2003, 38)

On the fifteenth day of one month, there appeared to me in a dream one who was in essence a *dakini* of enlightened awareness, but in form was a flesh-eating *dakini* with the body of a human woman; *she gave me an unshakeable experience of great bliss.*

(The autobiography of Jamgon Kontrul in Barron 2003, 66)

I awaited the day of departure with a mix of anxiety and anticipation. On the one hand, I was very unhappy at the prospect of abandoning my people. I felt a heavy responsibility towards them. On the other hand, I eagerly looked forward to traveling.

(Dalai Lama 1990, 59)

We were all exhausted. But I felt a tremendous sense of excitement.

(Dalai Lama 1990, 60)

In 1948 Washington had welcomed a trade delegation [with China], which even had a meeting with the Vice-President. So they too had obviously changed their minds. I remember feeling great sorrow when I realized that this really meant: Tibet must expect to face the entire might of Communist China alone.

(Dalai Lama 1990, 60)

So although it might be possible to have experience memories without the sense of personal identity, this seems to be a remarkably difficult feat to accomplish in an enduring way. Although this might seem antagonistic to Buddhism, we have already seen that the Buddhist tradition has the resources to explain it. Śāntideva notes that one can acknowledge the truth of the no-self view, and aspire to lead others to recognize it as well. But this is not enough to actually have a truly engaged recognition of no-self. That engaged form of the no-self view is opposed by a deep force—instinctive self-grasping. Episodic memory, we've argued, provides one powerful and persistent basis for such self-grasping, and thus a powerful and persistent obstacle to achieving the kind of oneness at which Buddhism aims.

Notes

1. Most Buddhist epistemologists distinguish two epistemic instruments: perception (*pratyakṣa/mngon gsum*) and inference *(anumāṇa/ rje dpag)*. Perception engages with

particulars, and does so immediately and nonconceptually; inference engages with universals, and does so conceptually. Other Indian schools (and *some* Buddhist philosophers) add other instruments to the list, such as testimony (*śabda/gra*) and analogy (*upamāṇa/dpe*), but Dignāga and Dharmakīrti reduce these latter instruments to inference. Śāntideva has this dichotomy in mind when he distinguishes aspirational from engaged bodhicitta on the basis of the mode of its epistemic engagement with its object.

2. For more detailed discussions of this passage in *How to Lead an Awakened Life*, see Cowherds 2016, 55–76, Garfield 2010/2011, and Garfield 2015, 299–313.

3. The term *episodic memory* came into usage with Endel Tulving. But it's clear that the earlier philosophers had this kind of memory in mind in the passages to follow.

4. In another context in that same commentary, Uddyotakara argues that the integration of information from multiple sensory modalities requires a unitary self: that if there were no unitary self, sight, sound, smell, and so on, each might be experienced, but could not be referred to as the same object or integrated in the same conscious field. His argument anticipates Kant's argument for a transcendental unity of apperception. This argument is criticized by the Buddhist philosophy Śāntarakṣita, who replies that all that is needed is an apperceptive consciousness, not a self to be perceived. See Garfield 2015, 102–4.

5. Buddhist arguments about reflexive awareness have a long history, and continue to the present day among Buddhist scholars and scholars of Buddhist studies (and indeed among contemporary Western philosophers of mind). Things are complicated by the fact that there are multiple versions of the reflexive awareness thesis, and it is put to multiple uses. According to Dignāga, every intentional moment of consciousness has two intentional objects: the object on which the act is directed, and the act itself. So, for instance, when I think about Dignāga, my thought is necessarily directed not only to Dignāga, but to the thought itself. For more on this, see Garfield 2006, 2015, Mackenzie 2007, 2008, Thompson 2014, and Williams 2000.

6. Roache 2016 offers a competing interpretation.

References

Barron, R. 2003. *The Autobiography of Jamgon Kongtrul: A Gem of Many Colors.* Ithaca: Snow Lion.

Byrne, R. 2000. "How Monkeys Find Their Way." In *On the Move: How and Why Animals Travel in Groups*, edited by S. Boinski and P. Garber, 491–517. Chicago: University of Chicago Press.

Candrakīrti. 1992. *dBu m la 'jug pa'i bshad pa. (Madhyamakāvatāra.)* Sarnath: Kagyud Relief and Protection Society.

Chadha, M. 2014. "A Buddhist Explanation of Episodic Memory: From Self to Mind." *Asian Philosophy* 24 (1): 14–27.

Cowherds. 2016. *Moonpaths: Ethics and Emptiness.* New York: Oxford University Press.

Crystal, J. D., W. T. Alford, W. Zhou, and A. G. Hohmann. 2013. "Source Memory in the Rat." *Current Biology* 23 (5): 387–91.

Dalai Lama. 1990. *Freedom in Exile.* New York: HarperCollins.

Garfield, J. 2006. "The Conventional Status of Reflexive Awareness: What's at Stake in a Tibetan Debate?" *Philosophy East and West* 53:201–28.

——. 2010/2011. "What Is It Like to Be a Bodhisattva? Moral Phenomenology in Śāntideva's *Bodhicāryāvatāra*." *Journal of the International Association of Buddhist Studies* 33 (1–2): 327–51.

——. 2015. *Engaging Buddhism: Why It Matters to Philosophy*. New York: Oxford University Press.

Garfield, J. L., S. Nichols, A. K. Rai, and N. Strohminger. 2015. "Ego, Egoism and the Impact of Religion on Ethical Experience: What a Paradoxical Consequence of Buddhist Culture Tells Us About Moral Psychology." *Journal of Ethics* 19 (3–4): 293–304.

Gyatso, J. 1998. *Apparitions of the Self: The Secret Autobiographies of a Tibetan Visionary*. Princeton: Princeton University Press.

Hasselmo, M. 2011. *How We Remember: Brain Mechanisms of Episodic Memory*. Cambridge: MIT Press.

Hayne, H., J. Gross, S. McNamee, O. Fitzgibbon, and K. Tustin. 2011. "Episodic Memory and Episodic Foresight in 3- and 5-Year-Old Children." *Cognitive Development*.

Huntington, C., and N. Wangchen. 1989. *The Emptiness of Emptiness: Candrakīrti's Madhyamakāvatāra*. Honolulu: University of Hawaii Press.

Ivanhoe, P. 2017. *East Asian Conceptions of Oneness, Virtue, and Human Happiness*. New York: Oxford University Press.

James, W. 1890/1950. *Principles of Psychology*. Vol. 1. Mineola, NY: Dover.

Jamgon Kongtru. 2003. *The Autobiography of Jamgon Kongtru*. Translated by R. Barron. Ithaca: Snow Lion.

Kesner, R. P., G. Farnsworth, and B. V. DiMattia. 1989. "Double Dissociation of Egocentric and Allocentric Space Following Medial Prefrontal and Parietal Cortex Lesions in the Rat." *Behavioral Neuroscience* 103 (5): 956.

Klein, S., and S. Nichols. 2012. "Memory and the Sense of Personal Identity." *Mind* 121 (483): 677–702.

Libby, L. K., R. P. Eibach, and T. Gilovich. 2005. "Here's Looking at Me: The Effect of Memory Perspective on Assessments of Personal Change." *Journal of Personality and Social Psychology* 88 (1): 50.

Loftus, E. F., and J. C. Palmer. 1974. "Reconstruction of Automobile Destruction: An Example of the Interaction Between Language and Memory." *Journal of Verbal Learning and Verbal Behavior* 13 (5): 585–89.

Loftus, E. F., and D. C. Polage. 1999. "Repressed Memories: When Are They Real? How Are They False?" *Psychiatric Clinics of North America*, edited by P. Resnick, 22:61–71.

Mackenzie, M. 2007. "The Illumination of Consciousness: Approaches to Self-Awareness in the Indian and Western Traditions." *Philosophy East and West* 57 (1): 40–62.

——. 2008. "Self-Awareness Without A Self: Buddhism and the Reflexivity of Awareness." *Asian Philosophy* 18 (3): 254–66.

McIsaac, H. K., and E. Eich. 2002. "Vantage Point in Episodic Memory." *Psychonomic Bulletin and Review* 9:146–50.

——. 2004. "Vantage Point in Traumatic Memory." *Psychological Science* 15:248–53.

Mill, James. 1869. *Analysis of the Phenomena of the Human Mind*. London: Longmans, Green, Reader and Dyer.

Mischkowski, D., E. Kross, and B. J. Bushman. 2012. "Flies on the Wall Are Less Aggressive: Self-Distancing 'in the Heat of the Moment' Reduces Aggressive Thoughts, Angry Feelings and Aggressive Behavior." *Journal of Experimental Social Psychology* 48 (5): 1187–91.

Newell, A. 1990. *Unified Theories of Cognition*. Cambridge: Harvard University Press.

Nichols, S., N. Strohminger, A. Rai, and J. Garfield. Forthcoming. *Death and the Self*.

Nigro, G., and U. Neisser. 1983. "Point of View in Personal Memories." *Cognitive Psychology* 15:467–482.

Quintman, A., trans. 2010. *The Life of Milarepa.* New York: Penguin.

Reid, T. 2002. *Essays on the Intellectual Powers of Man.* Edited by D. R. Brookes. University Park: Pennsylvania State University Press.

Roache, R. 2016. "Memory and Mineness in Personal Identity." *Philosophical Psychology* 29 (4): 479–89.

Robinson, J. A., and K. L. Swanson. 1993. "Field and Observer Modes of Remembering." *Memory* 1 (3): 169–84.

Śāntideva. 1999. *Byang chub sems pa'i spyod pa la 'jug pa's rnam bshad rgyal sras 'jug ngogs (Bodhicaaryāvatāra with rGyal tshabs commentary).* Sarnath: Gelugpa Student Welfare Committee.

Shabkar, T. 1994. *The Life of Shabkar.* Translated by Mathieu Ricard. Albany: State University of New York Press.

Sierra, M., and G. E. Berrios. 2000. "The Cambridge Depersonalisation Scale." *Psychiatry Research* 93 (2): 153–64.

——. 2001. "The Phenomenological Stability of Depersonalization: Comparing the Old with the New." *Journal of Nervous and Mental Disease* 189 (9): 629–36.

Thompson, E. 2014. *Waking, Dreaming, Being: Self and Consciousness in Neuroscience, Meditation and Philosophy.* New York: Columbia University Press.

Williams, P. 2000. *The Reflexive Nature of Awareness: A Tibetan Madhyamaka Defence.* London: Curzon.

CHAPTER 14

CONFUCIUS AND THE SUPERORGANISM

HAGOP SARKISSIAN

Seeing ourselves as part of a superorganism allows us to understand our actions, choices, and experiences in a new light. If we are affected by our embeddedness in social networks and influenced by others who are closely or distantly tied to us, we necessarily lose some power over our own decisions. Such a loss of control can provoke especially strong reactions when people discover that their neighbors or even strangers can influence behaviors and outcomes that have moral overtones and social repercussions. But the flip side of this realization is that people can transcend themselves and their own limitations.

—Christakis and Fowler 2009

How does one acquire a sense of oneness? An obvious answer is through religion or religious texts. One might read of the notion of Brahman in the Vedanta school of Hinduism—pure consciousness or bliss—which is the unified and singular true nature of reality, of which we are but temporary manifestations (apparent but not real). Hence we are all ultimately one, though temporarily we are not. Or one might read of neo-Confucians thinkers claiming that every creature, every single specimen under the stars, forms one body with every other (天地萬物為一體). Of course, such notions are quite distant from where I now sit in my office in mid-Manhattan, typing this essay. They are distant in an obvious and trivial sense—namely, that they represent ideas written in contexts far removed from our own, both spatially and temporally. However, they also advert to metaphysical beliefs that are difficult to take on board.

Nonetheless, feeling connected to others, as though one is part of a larger plan or goal, or feeling a kinship with all living things—these need not stem from extraordinary metaphysical views. They might, instead, express values that individuals affirm, which factor into their well-being and psychological economy—contributing, say, to their overall sense of belonging or meaning. But even while this may be true of scores of individuals, it is not obvious how affirming one's values through expressions of oneness might have purchase for those who are not inclined to think in these terms, and who might take such language as, at best, expressing relatable values using strong metaphysical language or, at worst, expressing "heroic" metaphysical beliefs (to borrow a euphemism) using clichéd language.[1]

In what follows, I will describe a sense of oneness that, while having its roots in a tradition of thought far removed from our own, might nonetheless be accessible to many persons. It is a sense of oneness that is, admittedly, smaller in scope than the two options just canvassed. It is not a oneness with all of humanity, let alone with all the creatures under the sky or all the elements of the cosmos. Nevertheless, it is recognizably a sense of oneness that transcends one's own person and connects one to a larger whole.

I will be calling this conception that of a *superorganism*, to borrow another phrase, this time from the natural and social sciences, where it finds paradigmatic application to collectives of eusocial animals—for example, an ant colony, which consists of numerous individual members yet which also constitutes an entity with properties that go beyond that of any of its members. There are obvious and significant discontinuities between ant colonies, on the one hand, and human societies, on the other. I don't mean to suggest that human beings are mindless agents, or that human societies are superorganisms in the exact same way ant colonies are. Nonetheless, human societies are entities that transcend their individuals. In the words of Borgatti et al., "the idea is that social ties can bind nodes together in such a way as to construct a new entity whose properties can be different from those of its constituent elements" (Borgatti et al. 2009, 894). I will be exploring, then, a conception of oneness not by canvassing spiritual views of connectedness or metaphysical views about the ultimate nature of reality, but instead by seeing groups of entities as forming a new, super entity. It's a view that arises when thinking in network or collective terms as opposed to node or individual terms.

I find this particular sense of oneness in classical Confucian conceptions of society, though without the explicit (and robust) metaphysics of the later neo-Confucians. Though this sense of oneness is not stated in explicit terms, it is nonetheless one that can be easily reconstructed out of certain views of individuals and collectives in classical Confucian texts. I begin with passages from the *Analects* that can be interpreted as containing within them such a sense of oneness as superorganism. Later, I present what I take to be stronger evidence of a more explicit kind in the *Daxue* and *Zhongyong* chapters of the *Liji*. I then conclude by arguing that thinking of Confucian social and political philosophy in terms of a superorganism can be helpful in understanding why the entire project may have been ill founded.

The Zhou Superorganism

In *Analects* 19.22, Zigong, a student of Confucius, is asked the following question: whence his teacher's knowledge of the *dao* of sage kings of the past, who flourished centuries before he was even born (ca. 551 BCE)? The answer Zigong gives is noteworthy:

> *Analects* 19.22: Gongsun Chao of Wei asked Zigong, "From whom did Confucius acquire his learning?" Zigong replied, "The *dao* of Kings Wen and Wu has not yet sunken into the ground—it still exists in people. Those who are worthy understand its greater aspects, while those who are unworthy understand its lesser aspects. There is no one who does not have the *dao* of Wen and Wu within them. From whom did the Master not acquire his learning? And what need was there for him to have a formal teacher?"[2]

The sage kings Wen and Wu, founding figures of the Zhou dynasty, are long since dead. Confucius could not learn from them directly, or from any of the other towering figures of this era (such as the Duke of Zhou). But their teachings remain embedded in what I'll call the latent Zhou superorganism that remained nascent in the state of Lu. Lu was Kongzi's home state and where the high culture of the Zhou dynasty had managed to persist in spite of the very real and precipitous decline of the power of the Zhou kings starting in 771 BCE. That superorganism might not have been revived were it not for one particular individual—Confucius—who would stitch it back together.

Brook Ziporyn (2012) places special emphasis on this passage, and his reading of it bears similarities to my own (even while he does not use the image of a superorganism in his explication). As Ziporyn notes, in this passage,

> We are presented with a sense in which a certain *specific cultural tradition*, to which special *value* is attached, is omnipresent within the members of a particular community. We are told that it can be found everywhere in that community, but the decisive thing here, the turning of the tables, is that what really

actualizes this omnipresence is Confucius himself, that is, his ability to recognize the coherence of these various cultural forms, to ask the right questions, to "thread them together," to borrow a trope he uses elsewhere.

The presence of the particular concerns, values, and projects of Confucius is what makes this omnipresence effectively present around him. What actualizes this presence as something readable, the Way of Wen and Wu, is the way it is connected to, interacts with, *coheres* with, the dispositions, cognitive and ethical, of a certain human being, Confucius. . . . And this Way is neither purely internal to Confucius nor existing independently outside him. He does not invent it ex nihilo, but nor does it simply impose itself upon him. If he were not there to see it that way, the fragments of the Way of Wen and Wu, though present everywhere, would not cohere into anything intelligible. It is the focus provided by his own activity and presence, his own orientation and disposition of character, that make it come together sustainably and discernibly around him, to be seen as, and indeed to genuinely function as, a resource for his own particular inquiry. The things out there in the world are neither the same as what Confucius sees, nor different from it. He sees an aspect of what is there, and by so seeing makes this aspect, as present in many places, cohere into a particular presence.

(Ziporyn 2012, 94)

Ziporyn does not speak of a superorganism, nor does he use resources from network theory. However, we do see here a sense of a collective that contains, within it, knowledge that any particular member lacks, and Kongzi as the person who is able to see its coherence.[3] Confucius becomes a new node through which the superorganism is reinvigorated. He is able to become a central conduit through which its various parts interact and communicate to one another. Importantly, Confucius sees himself as playing this precise role.

Analects 9.5: The Master was surrounded in Kuang. He said, "Now that King Wen 文 is gone, is not culture (*wen* 文) now invested here in me? If Heaven intended this culture to perish, it would not have given it to those of us who live after King Wen's death. Since Heaven did not intend that this culture should perish, what can the people of Kuang do to me?"

Networks, Nodes, and Influence

A social network consists of all the connections and ties within a collection of individuals, or nodes. A node (or self) is constituted by the larger network while also constituting it. To be a self in a network is to be a particular point upon which network forces impinge (in both manifest and imperceptible ways), while also impinging upon others similarly in turn. This notion finds expression throughout classical texts in the Confucian philosophical tradition, which often discuss how individuals and groups influence and shape one another.

One of the powerful roles that networks play is to build a bridge from the local to the global—to bridge from individuals to groups, or from nodes to networks—and back again. In this way, explanations can be provided for how simple processes at the level of individual nodes and links can have complex effects that ripple through a population as a whole. That early Confucians saw individuals as deeply affected by their social environments is well known, as discussed in a number of recent papers (for example, Hutton 2006, Sarkissian 2010b, Slingerland 2011). Ziporyn makes similar claims.

> Confucius is nonnegotiably a member of a group, prior to any choice, and yet at the same time decisively constitutes the nature of the group of which he is a part, from which he can only depart in terms of his prior commitment to that group, but which nonetheless requires his own present deed to be actualized in a particular way. He cannot choose not to be a member of this group, but he can choose what sort of group it is that he is a member of. Just which forces of world, nature, culture, and deceased semi-personal spiritual powers are considered to be contributing members to the collective body of which he considers himself a part depend on his own "take" on the trajectory of the tradition he connects to. He is educated in this tradition, and selectively emphasizes those aspects to which he, in both the literal and figurative senses, "connects."
> (Ziporyn 2012, 97–98)

For the early Confucians, no person is an independent actor in any interesting sense. The classical texts characterize individuals as acting on their own choices and deliberations, and assuming responsibility for the course of their lives, while also acknowledging that any particular person's behavior is continually shaped by the behavior of others in his or her midst, by the objects and variables in their immediate environments and, ultimately, by the various other nodes that comprise her larger network of relations. This assumption formed the basis of much else in early Confucian thought. Network theory provides a way to bring such notion of influence, shaping, and constitution into sharper focus, by providing more robust theoretical resources to understand the relationship between individuals and the collectives in which they participate.[4]

The key notion representing the influence of individual nodes on other nodes in the classical texts is *dé* 德, which, at its core, refers to a person's ability to influence others through noncoercive means. In the words of A. C. Graham, it had traditionally represented "the power, whether benign or baleful, to move others without exerting physical force" (Graham 1989, 13). The importance of "effective power" or "power over others" in understanding *dé* is recognized by nearly everyone. For example, Arthur Waley translates *dé* as "moral force"

(Waley 1938), Graham as "potency" (Graham 1989), Philip Ivanhoe as "moral charisma" (Ivanhoe 1999), Bryan Van Norden as "a sort of 'ethical force' that a person has, which can have a transformative effect on others" (Van Norden 2007, 21). In addition, scholars also agree that this power seems, for the Confucians, to be the prerogative of morally upright or charismatic individuals, lending them authority in the eyes of others. David Nivison was characteristically perceptive in noting that the concept of *dé* "has implications, not easily analyzed, that make mature and sophisticated moral-philosophical discussion by the Chinese philosophers complex and fascinating—even when the word and syllable de has been left behind, and these philosophers are talking about *rén* 仁 ("benevolence"), *yì* 義 ("duty"), *xìn* 信 ("trust"), *lǐ* 禮 ("propriety"), *liáng zhī* 良知 ("moral intuitions"), etc." (Nivison 1996, 17).

In previous work, I have tried to explicate one sense of *dé* by discussing the attractive power that accrues to individuals owing to the scrupulous way they mind their impact over others, including not only their honing the accuracy of their moral inclinations and reactions over time (2010a), but also their minding features of their self-presentation (2010b) and regulating themselves when they are the site of others' scrutiny (2015). The *jūnzǐ* (nobleman/moral exemplar) in classical Confucian texts is represented as capable of cultivating himself along these lines and thereby wielding influence over others, who find the *jūnzǐ* to be both agreeable and authoritative—someone to cooperate with or yield to. Indeed, a prominent aspect of *dé* in the *Analects*—besides its characteristic power—is its linkage to self-cultivation (*xiū* 修—for example, 7.3, 12.10, 12.21, 16.1). Since moving others (or influencing them) to make social and political changes was the ultimate goal of Confucius and his disciples, cultivating *dé* or "effective nodal influence" was one of their chief aims. It is discussed in several passages in the text.

> *Analects* 4.24: The master said, "One who possesses *dé* is never solitary; he is certain to have neighbors."

> *Analects* 9.14: The master expressed a desire to go and live among the Nine Yi Barbarian tribes. Someone asked him, "How could you bear with their uncouthness?" The Master replied, "If a gentleman were to dwell among them, what uncouthness would there be?"

> *Analects* 12.19: The *dé* 德 of a gentleman is wind, the *dé* of a petty person is grass—when the wind blows, grass bends.

> *Analects* 2.3: The master said, "Guide them with governance (*zhèng* 政), regulate them with punishments, and the people will evade them with no sense of shame. Guide them with *dé* 德, regulate them with ritual propriety, and the people will have a sense of shame and be orderly."

These effects flow from one person to another, which is also known as dyadic spread (Christakis and Fowler 2009). What can spread from one node to another is not just influence or mood or behavior but also information, materials, or other resources.[5]

However, there is also hyperdyadic spread, which characterizes the tendency of effects to spread from node to node to node outside of a person's direct social ties and thus to ties of those ties. The more someone has ties to others, the more susceptible is one to the flows of information within it. Some passages in the classical Confucian literature express this relationship between the individual and the greater whole as going through several intermediary nodes or subnetworks, evoking a sense of oneness or unity greater than the self. We find this expressed in the *Daxue* 大學 (Great Learning), a chapter in the *Liji* 禮記 (*Book of Ritual*), an important early source of Confucian writings.

> The ancients who wanted to manifest radiant *de* first ordered their states.
> Wanting to order their states they first aligned their familial clans.
> Wanting to align their familial clans they first cultivated their persons.
> Wanting to cultivate their persons they first set their minds straight.
> Wanting to set their minds straight they first made their intentions sincere.
> Wanting to make their intentions sincere they first reached understanding.
> Reaching understanding lies in getting a handle on affairs.[6]

Consequences at the level of the network (ordering the state) are linked to the influence of a particular node (the cultivated mind of the ruler, its central node). The passage continues:

> So you get a handle on affairs and only then reach understanding,
> You reach understanding and your intentions become sincere,
> When your intentions are sincere your mind straightens.
> Your mind straightens and your person becomes cultivated
> Your person is cultivated and your family becomes harmonized.
> Your family is harmonized and your state becomes ordered
> Your state is ordered and there is tranquility under the skies
> From the node of the king to the nodes of the common people, all must take
> the cultivation of their own persons as the root (of everything else).[7]

It should be emphasized that such scrupulous self-attention was counseled not for everyone, but rather for those who sought positions of authority. As De Bary notes while discussing this theme in the *Analects*, "when Confucius speaks of the *chun-tzu* [*jūnzǐ*] as someone especially careful and restrained, one who is punctilious about not overstepping the bounds of what is right, it is not because he expects ordinary men to exercise the same circumspection or constrain themselves to the same degree, but because those he addresses have a heightened visibility and potentially more far-reaching influence on others" (De Bary 1991, 29). Self-regulation is especially important when one is the main focus of an entire group's attention.

The importance of self-regulation is heightened in proportion to the greater impact one can have on others through their shared focus (Sarkissian 2014). Because they occupy a stratum of society that has the possibility to influence the whole network, they believe they will be modeled by others, and so they perceive themselves from the point of view of the network, regulating their intentions and conduct by anticipating larger, wider network effects.

Put another way, if one both understands behavior as being obviously and significantly sensitive to immediate situational factors, *and* if one also wants to shape human behavior toward the end of social harmony, then one would do well to attempt to control those signals that promoted harmony and marshal them toward this end. So the emphasis on norms of self-scrutiny, personal decorum, and cultivated influence is intricately connected with certain entrenched views concerning the working of moral psychology.

The Sagely Node

The early Confucians believed in *virtue politics*—the idea that bringing about a state of harmony in the general population required a commitment to placing virtuous individuals in positions of power. Virtuous individuals would affect others through their *dé*, which would resonate out from the ruling class through the rest of the network, binding and shaping the superorganism. Of course, the Confucians themselves sought positions of power to embed themselves as key nodes within the network, yet a virtuous ruler was vital for the Confucian vision to succeed. A truly cultivated, virtuous, and charismatic ruler was believed capable of transforming the entire world by sheer power of his *dé*.

> *Analects* 2.1: The master said, "One who governs by means of his *dé* is comparable to the Pole Star, which occupies its place and receives the homage of the myriad lesser stars."

> *Analects* 8.18: The master said, "Majestic! Shun and Yu[8] possessed the whole world without even managing it."

> *Analects* 15.5: The master said, "Someone who ruled without even acting (*wu-wei* 無為)—was this not Shun? What did he do? He made himself reverent and took his proper position facing south—that is all!"

Here we find the telltale effects of *dé* on a grand scale. Rather than simply affecting those in his immediate presence, a ruler with *dé* was thought to affect an entire nation.

Indeed, one of the fundamental axioms of network theory is that the opportunities and constraints of any particular node—the degree to which it is both susceptible to network effects and capable of affecting the network—hinges on its *position* within the network (Borgatti et al. 2009, 894). The outsized effects of *dé* noted in the passages can be explained by the fact that they stemmed from a central position where resonance was most potent, keyed to the centrality of the ruler's node.

Following Freeman (1978), we can discriminate between three distinct measures of centrality in networks. The first concerns *degree*, or the extent to which a given node is directly connected to other nodes. The ruler, being at the center of the superoganism, is well positioned to be connected to more nodes more directly than most any other node in it. The second concerns *betweenness*, or the extent to which a node falls between pairs of other nodes within the network. The ruler, receiving tribute from the various noble houses in the realm, lies in between them all, for the ruler occupies the central node through which all resources and information follow. The third is *proximity*, or the number of nodes that any other node must go through to reach any other point in the network. It is thus a measure of access. The ruler has access to any other node through fewer intermediaries than any other node (say, a member of a noble house of a particular fiefdom). A ruler with *dé*, then, would influence and transform his senior ministers, who in turn would influence their subordinates, creating a linked chain of virtuous behavior that would be modeled down through the ranks of officials to village and clan leaders. Through ritual performance, personal excellence, and scrupulous devotion to the superorganism, the ruler would bind the network together.[9]

We find this reflected in passages even where the notion of a collective is not even salient, and even where the notion of *dé* is not even tokened. Consider, for example, *Analects* 13.3:

> *Analects* 13.3: Zilu asked, "If the Duke of Wei were to employ you to serve in the government of his state, what would be your first priority?" The Master answered, "It would, of course, be the rectification of names (*zhengming* 正名)." Zilu said, "Could you, Master, really be so far off the mark? Why worry about rectifying names?"
>
> The Master replied, "How boorish you are, Zilu! When it comes to matters that he does not understand, the gentleman should remain silent. If names are not rectified, speech will not accord with reality; when speech does not accord with reality, things will not be successfully accomplished. When things are not successfully accomplished, ritual practice and music will fail to flourish; when

ritual and music fail to flourish, punishments and penalties will miss the mark. And when punishments and penalties miss the mark, the common people will be at a loss as to what to do with themselves. This is why the gentleman only applies names that can be properly spoken and assures that what he says can be properly put into action. The gentleman simply guards against arbitrariness in his speech. That is all there is to it."

Here, I suggest that we have a striking example of the effect a single, weighty, embedded node can have on an entire network. It's imperative that information is passed along without degradation or noise from this node.

Confucius is, of course, speaking counterfactually. He was not in a position to rule. And, as we noted in the quotations at the outset of this section, the ruler was not supposed to actively manage the state. Instead, the ruler was meant to attract other individuals of virtue to take up positions in his government, manning posts and embedding themselves in positions of influence. For example, we find the following passage in "The Doctrine of the Mean," another chapter in the *Liji*: "Therefore the administration of government lies in procuring proper men. Such men are to be procured by [the attractive power of] the ruler's own person. His person is to be cultivated by following the right *dào*, and he cultivates the right *dào* by means of his humankindness."[10] According to this passage, a virtuous ruler attracts good men by his side, who would, in turn, work tirelessly for the benefit of the ruler and his people. These ministers would be weighty nodes themselves, serving to enable the ruler to exercise his benevolent will while also constraining him by advising and exhorting him and thus providing for checks on mistakes.

Such a structure would allow the ruler to govern "effortlessly"—by just sitting on the throne (as it were), the heaviest, weightiest, most influential node in the network. After all, the ruler occupied the top position of a thoroughly hierarchical network system that demanded loyalty to those above, and powerful examples from above might have significant effects below. In the words of Bruce and Taeko Brooks, "if the ruler has the right qualities, those below will *spontaneously* acquire those qualities. We might call this the *assent* of the governed; their capacity to respond to good influence" (Brooks and Brooks 1998, 94).

Moving the Superorganism from the Periphery

We can understand this process of attracting individuals as one of constructing, node by node, the state superorganism. However, there was a fundamental structural challenge to the hopes of this model working. Becoming good *itself* (and in the first place) required influence from the right kinds of experienced mentors, who were customarily *above* one in the social hierarchy. If the ruler was starkly deficient in virtue (as was the norm), who does he model? There is no one above him, no one to whom he ought to defer. Of course, Confucians such as Mencius would argue vehemently that the ruler ought to comply with his ministers (for example, *Mencius* 4A1, 6B8), but this was more aspiration than reality. In Wm. Theodore De Bary's memorable characterization, Mencius better exemplified "the fearlessness of the teacher in a classroom than that of the minister at court or the soldier in battle" (De Bary 1991, 16).[11] In practice, the Confucians had to defer to (and await recognition from) the rulers of the time, and otherwise lacked institutional support to remonstrate with them in any effective fashion.

Put another way, this is the problem of moving the superorganism by influencing the central node from the periphery. This highlights a concession or severe limitation in the Confucians' conception of cultivating *dé*—namely, the influence that accrues to an individual node by virtue of his or her position in the network. In a hierarchical system (such as the Confucians endorsed), one typically holds sway over one's peers and those beneath one in the social hierarchy. So it is likely that rulers were largely immune from the example of the nobleman, no matter how cultivated, owing to their superior position. The ruler would be tone-deaf to influence because others were expected to yield to him. Indeed, all of the paradigmatic examples of *dé* in the *Analects* have this very feature of working *down* the social ladder—from *jūnzǐ* to barbarian, from *jūnzǐ* to petty person, and from rulers to everyone else.

Experiments on social networks seem to provide us with some vindication of this. In an experimental study using a representative sample of 1.3 million Facebook users, Aral and Walker (2012) found that younger users of the platform were more susceptible to influence than older users, that men were more influential than women, that women influenced men more than they influenced other women, and that influential individuals were less susceptible to influence than noninfluential individuals were. Influential individuals cluster together in the network, whereas susceptible individuals do not. So influential people are instrumental in the spread of information throughout the network. Influential people are therefore instrumental in the spread of information throughout the network while also, and simultaneously, not being as susceptible to influence within it. They are loci of influence. They are sources of potency. They drive the superorganism.

De Bary called the problem of influencing bad rulers a key aspect of *The Trouble with Confucianism* (1991). If a system is strictly hierarchical, then who leads or guides the person at the apex? Various models were proposed in the classical period: Heaven (for the Mohists), the inheritance of the ancient Sage Kings (for Xunzi), the Dao (for Laozi). But these are all rather impersonal, abstract models. In practice, a ruler occupied power by virtue of occupying the seat at the apex, and transforming *him* proved to be a thorny and delicate task. Indeed, the very fact that Mencius speaks so boldly with the various rulers of his time has been taken by some as prima facie evidence of the fictional status of these dialogues (Brooks and Brooks 1998). Petty persons might bend to the noblemen like grass to wind, but rulers were an entirely different story.

This doesn't impugn the general model of *dé*, or the idea of nodes influencing networks. However, it must be considered a fatal flaw in classical Confucianism political philosophy. A Confucian nobleman's goal was to wield influence and have real impact over social policies and practices, and knowing that such influence was often highly improbable led to much consternation about whether or not a Confucian should accept an official title; if one could not hope to transform one's ruler, should one accept the job? "In general, the noble man assumes office only when he can hope to influence the rulers. To accept office with an unsavory ruler whom one cannot possibly influence to the good is to justify the suspicion that one is motivated by a desire for emoluments and fame and not by the ideal of service. . . . [Yet] is it not the duty of the *shih* [scholar-official] to *attempt* to influence them?" (Schwartz 1985, 112). Seeking such influence and then failing at it could easily make one a tool for those in power, serving individuals with questionable or even immoral ends. The problem of wanting to serve and fulfill one's ethical obligation, but only when one can have some real expectation of exerting influence, and only in a way that will preserve one's own integrity, plagued Confucian philosophy from the *Analects* onwards. It is perhaps for these reasons that throughout the *Analects* there is an insistence that it's OK to be a political loser (so to speak) so long as one maintains one's integrity (for example, 1.1, 1.16, 4.5, 4.14, 11.19, 14.30, 15.19).[12]

Finally, it is not at all clear that, *even if* a virtuous ruler were to take the throne, the network model of *dé* could work on a scale envisioned by the early Confucian thinkers. Though Confucian, Mohist, and Legalist texts alike emphasize the ruler's crucial duty to place meritorious individuals in administrative posts and properly manage the kingdom's affairs, the means by which the ruler was to secure such individuals and assure their performance was a matter of dispute. Many, such as Han Fei, would come to doubt that the ruler's moral excellence could serve any useful role in the process of filling administrative posts and properly managing the kingdom's affairs.

Hanfeizi: When a sage governs a state, he does not wait for the people to be good in deference to him. Instead he creates a situation in which people find it impossible to do wrong. If you wait for people to be good in deference to you, you will find that there are no more than ten good people within the borders of your state. But if you create a situation in which you find it impossible to do wrong, the entire state can be brought into compliance. In governing, one must use what is numerous and abandon what is scarce. Therefore, the sage does not work on his *de*, he works on his laws.

(Sahleen 2006, 354)

As others have noted, these and related passages in the Han Fei constitute a basic (and forceful) critique of the Confucian view of top-down, *dé*-inspired rulership models. The crux of Han Fei's criticism seems to be that such models, resting on the attractive and transformative power of moral example, are "impossibly idealistic, because they hopelessly over-estimate the number of people who can be transformed and made good through the power of virtue" (Hutton 2008, 429). Basing one's political philosophy on the appearance of such a ruler has been described as "ludicrous" (Liu 2006, 188–89). Hence, Han Fei and others emphasized clear laws and standards with manifest rewards and punishments. Put another way, such thinkers believed it was better to have a population that was law-abiding and compliant rather than to wait for a population to be transformed to the good because a virtuous ruler sat on the throne.

***

The sage kings were the central nodes of the early superorganisms. So long as a sage did not reappear, it could not be fully reconstituted. However, even though this ideal would not be realized, thinking of oneself as a node of influence on one's network can have purchase for us today. It can serve as a reminder that one may continuously exert influence over the broader course of one's social network just by occupying one's position in one's own distinctive way. We might tend to think of how we influence those around us in volitional terms, through discrete, agential actions. The early Confucians remind us that this is perhaps an overly simplistic view of things. We cannot be a node in a network without shaping it to one degree or other. And some of our networks (for example, our classrooms, our students, our families) will be influenced by us continually and in significant ways. Herbert Fingarette expresses this point nicely in a discussion of *ren* (what I've been translating as humankindness) that could just as well be a discussion of *dé*.

> Let us attempt finally to place Confucius's own way of seeing *ren* in focus . . . and try to find an image that both distinctively and truly reflects Confucius's way of seeing *ren*. Such an image must suggest a power emanating from the actor. . . . Finally, this power is to be essentially human power; that is, it is a power of human beings (when they are truly human) and it is directed toward human beings and influences them. . . . It seems to me that the Western image that would serve best is one drawn from physics—the vector. In the case of *ren*, we should conceive of a directed force operating in actions in public space and

time, and having a person as initial point-source and a person as the terminal point on which the force impinges. The forces are human forces, of course, not mechanical ones.

(Fingarette 1972, 36–37)

Thinking through these issues from the Confucian perspective can serve to remind us of the forces that emanate from our own persons, and how they might be impinging upon others. This is a first, and necessary, step in uncovering, understanding, and ultimately shaping one's own *dé*.

Notes

1. P. J. Ivanhoe refers to neo-Confucian metaphysics as "heroic" while explicating the sense of oneness that can be found in their writings. He explains his choice of term as follows: "I mean by [heroic] that such beliefs would be very difficult for a modern person to embrace, since they cannot be reconciled with views that are now widely accepted by science. I find these traditional metaphysical views implausible, just as I find many of Plato's views about value or Aristotle's views about human nature, untenable" (2015, 231–32). I take it, then, that "heroic" may be amenable to a euphemistic reading. See Ivanhoe (2016) for further discussion of this term, in particular how it also reflects the strong ethical demands that such a metaphysical view entails.
2. Translations follow Slingerland 2003, with some modification.
3. Ziporyn draws support for his reading here by a particular interpretation of *tian* 天, or "Heaven," as a kind of superorganism as well. As Ziporyn notes, the way that *tian* is presented in the *Analects* reflects some middle position between referring to a personal agent as found in the *Mozi* (a contemporary rival school of thought), on the one hand, and referring to a thoroughly naturalized conception of nature or natural progression as we find in the *Xunzi* (a later Confucian text), on the other (2012, 95). He cites Ivanhoe for inspiration: "There are a number of ways in which one might attribute agency but not personality to Heaven. One way would be to see Heaven as a kind of collective will—a conception that as noted earlier can be found in the early Zhou sources. A jury can make judgments and assign guilt without being a single person or being of any kind. At a minimum though, Kongzi and Mengzi did regard Heaven as what Daniel Dennett calls 'an intentional system'" (Ivanhoe 2007, 217n11). Ziporyn develops this idea in a particular direction, arguing that heaven "would be conceived along the lines of the collective body of ancestors . . . thought to maintain their personalities, their concern with specific purposes in the world, and their consciousness of their earthly life in inverse proportion to the length of time they had been dead" (Ziporyn 2012, 95).
4. So far as I know, no one has used resources from network theory to understand classical Confucian thought, though Karyn Lai has noted the appropriateness of thinking of the relationality of selfhood in the tradition in node-and-network terms: "The idea that people within a community participate in its moral life and enrich each other is a theme of profound significance in Confucian thought. In the Confucian scheme, each individual is a necessary and distinct node within a web-like network of different relationships. Engagement with others in society presents opportunities for self-fulfilment and development in that context. The harmonies that are created rely on

the concerted effort of people who are fine-tuned to each other and who are mutually responsive" (Lai 2006, 155). Similar statements are likely to be found in the secondary literature.

5. Cf. *Analects* 6.30: "Now he who exemplifies humankindness—by wanting to establish himself thereby establishes others, by wanting to advance himself thereby advances others."

6. 古之欲明明德於天下者、先治其國。欲治其國者先齊其家。欲齊其家者先脩其身。欲脩其身者先正其心。欲正奇心者先誠其意。欲誠其意者先致其知。致知在格物。My translations of the final two lines follow a suggested reading by Steve Angle and Justin Tiwald.

7. 物格而后知至。知至而后意誠。意誠而后心正。心正而后身脩。身脩而后家齊。家齊而后國治。國治而后天下平。自天子以至於庶人、壹是皆以脩身爲本。

8. Mythical heroes and sage-rulers of antiquity, venerated by the Confucian and Mohist schools.

9. A ruler might quickly cultivate his *dé* by bestowing favors on his subjects, who would in turn feel "generosity-gratitude" toward him (Nivison 2002, 234). These feelings of gratitude and indebtedness would be amplified by socialization forces in Chinese culture demanding that individuals display gratitude and respect whenever favors are bestowed upon them. In this way, a natural sense of gratitude would be amplified by social norms and serve as powerful sources for a ruler's accumulating moral power through a grateful and lovingly obedient population.

10. 故為政在人，取人以身，修身以道，修道以仁。

11. The problem extends to other social relations as well. Consider the family: children may remonstrate with their parents when appropriate, but if their counsel falls on deaf ears they must desist and obey without resentment (*Analects* 4.18). Indeed, a filial son must cleave to the ways of his father even after the latter has passed away, and for the entirety of the three-year mourning period; only then could he consider departing from his father's example (*Analects* 1.11).

12. There is the separate question of whether the fact that most of Confucius's disciples failed to achieve office impugns Confucius's teachings. Confucius himself was a failure in this regard, and at times appears to admit that his work is doomed (5.27, 14.38). Elsewhere, he expresses doubts as to whether Heaven has abandoned him and his mission (9.9, 11.9), and is subject to mocking by his contemporaries (3.18, 14.32). The issue of his disciples' failures has received comparatively little scholarly attention, but is given excellent treatment in Wong and Loy (2001).

References

Aral, S., and D. Walker. 2012. "Identifying Influential and Susceptible Members of Social Networks." *Science* 337 (6092): 337–41.

Borgatti, Stephen P., and Ajay Mehra, Daniel J. Brass, and Giuseppe Labianca. 2009. "Network Analysis in the Social Sciences." *Science* 323:892–95.

Brooks, E. Bruce, and A. Taeko Brooks. 1998. *The Original Analects: Sayings of Confucius and His Successors.* New York: Columbia University Press.

Christakis, Nicholas A., and James H. Fowler. 2009. *Connected: The Surprising Power of Our Social Networks and How They Shape Our Lives.* New York: Little, Brown.

De Bary, Wm. Theodore. 1991. *The Trouble with Confucianism.* Cambridge: Harvard University Press.

Ekman, Paul. 2002. "Are There Basic Emotions?" *Psychological Review* 99:550–53.

Fingarette, Herbert. 1972. *Confucius: The Secular as Sacred.* New York: Harper and Row.

Freeman, Linton C. 1978. "Centrality in Social Networks: Conceptual Clarification." *Social Networks* 1 (3): 215–39.

Graham, A. C. 1989. *Disputers of the Tao*. LaSalle, IL: Open Court.

Hutton, Eric. 2006. "Character, Situationism, and Early Confucian Thought." *Philosophical Studies* 127 (1): 37–58.

——. 2008. "Han Feizi's Criticism of Confucianism and Its Implications for Virtue Ethics." *Journal of Moral Philosophy* 5 (3): 423–53.

Ivanhoe, P. J. 1999. "The Concept of *De* ('Virtue') in the *Laozi*." In *Religious and Philosophical Aspects of the Laozi*, edited by M. Csikszentmihalyi and P. J. Ivanhoe. Albany: State University of New York Press.

——. 2007. "Heaven as a Source for Ethical Warrant in Early Confucianism." *Dao* 6 (3): 211–20.

——. 2015. "Senses and Values of Oneness." In *The Philosophical Challenge from China*, edited by Brian Bruya. Cambridge: MIT Press.

——. 2016. *Three Streams: Confucian Reflections on Learning and the Moral Heart-Mind in China, Korea, and Japan*. New York: Oxford University Press.

Lai, Karyn. 2006. *Learning from Chinese Philosophies: Ethics of Interdependent and Contextualised Self*. Aldershot, UK: Ashgate.

Liu, JeeLoo. 2006. *An Introduction to Chinese Philosophy: From Ancient Philosophy to Chinese Buddhism*. Hoboken, NJ: Wiley-Blackwell.

Nivison, David. 1996. "Virtue in Bone and Bronze." In *The Ways of Confucianism: Investigations in Chinese Philosophy*, edited by B. Van Norden. La Salle, IL: Open Court.

——. 2003. "De (Te): Virtue or Power." In *Encyclopedia of Chinese Philosophy*, edited by A. S. Cua. London: Routledge.

Sahleen, Joel. 2006. "Han Feizi." In *Readings in Classical Chinese Philosophy*, edited by B. Van Norden and P. J. Ivanhoe. Indianapolis: Hackett.

Sarkissian, Hagop. 2010a. "Confucius and the Effortless Life of Virtue." *History of Philosophy Quarterly* 27 (1): 1–16.

——. 2010b. "Minor Tweaks, Major Payoffs: The Problems and Promise of Situationism in Moral Philosophy." *Philosopher's Imprint* 10 (9): 1–15.

——. 2014. "Is Self-Regulation a Burden or a Virtue? A Comparative Perspective." In *The Philosophy and Psychology of Character and Happiness: An Empirical Approach to Character and Happiness*, edited by Nancy E. Snow and Franco V. Trivigno, 181–96. London: Routledge.

——. 2015. "When You Think It's Bad It's Worse Than You Think: Psychological Bias and the Ethics of Negative Character Assessments." In *The Philosophical Challenge from China*, edited by Brian Bruya. Cambridge: MIT Press.

Schwartz, Benjamin. 1985. *The World of Thought in Ancient China*. Cambridge: Belknap Press of Harvard University Press.

Slingerland, Edward G. 2003. *Confucius Analects*. Cambridge: Hackett.

——. 2011. "The Situationist Critique and Early Confucian Virtue Ethics." *Ethics* 121 (2): 390–419.

Van Norden, B. 2007. *Virtue Ethics and Consequentialism in Early Chinese Philosophy*. New York: Cambridge University Press.

Waley, A. 1938. *The Analects of Confucius*. New York: Vintage.

Wong, B., and H. Loy. 2001. "The Confucian Gentleman and the Limits of Ethical Change." *Journal of Chinese Philosophy* 28 (3): 209–34.

Ziporyn, Brook. 2012. *Ironies of Oneness and Difference: Coherence in Early Chinese Thought: Prolegomena to the Study of Li*. Albany: State University of New York.

CHAPTER 15

DEATH, SELF, AND ONENESS IN THE INCOMPREHENSIBLE ZHUANGZI

ERIC SCHWITZGEBEL

The ancient Chinese philosopher Zhuangzi defies coherent interpretation. This is an inextricable part of the beauty and power of his work. The text—by which I mean the "Inner Chapters" of the text traditionally attributed to him, the authentic core of the book—is incomprehensible as a whole. It consists of shards, in a distinctive voice—a voice distinctive enough that its absence is plain in most of the "Outer" and "Miscellaneous" chapters—and which I will treat as the voice of a single author. Despite repeating imagery, ideas, style, and tone, these shards cannot be pieced together into a self-consistent philosophy. This lack of self-consistency is a *positive* feature of Zhuangzi. It is part of what makes him the great and unusual philosopher he is, defying reduction and summary.

We don't know the order in which the Inner Chapters were originally written (the text didn't take its current form until around 300 CE), but the opening passage of the text as we now have it is a striking introduction.

There is a fish in the Northern Oblivion named Minnow, and Minnow is quite huge, spanning who knows how many thousands of miles. He transforms into a bird named Breeze, and Breeze has quite a back on him, stretching who knows how many thousands of miles. . . .

The Tales of Qi, a record of many wonders, reports: "When Breeze journeys to the Southern Oblivion, the waters ripple for three thousand miles. Spiraling aloft, he ascends ninety thousand miles and continues his journey for half a year."

—It's a galloping heat-haze!—It's a swirl of dust!—It's some living creature blown aloft on a breath of air! And the blue on blue of the sky—is that the sky's true color? Or is it just the vast distance, going on and on without end, that looks that way? When Breeze looks down, he too sees only this and nothing more.[1]

(3–4)

Let's suppose it's an important part of the text's design that it starts this way. An odd start for book of philosophy!

For one thing, it's false. Of course, there's no such fish that turns into a giant bird, nor was there ever (probably) a text called the *The Tales of Qi* that Zhuangzi supposedly drew this story from. It's absurd!

It's also a parable. A bit further along, the passage continues:

The cicada and the fledgling dove laugh at him, saying, "We scurry up into the air, leaping from the elm to the sandalwood tree, and when we don't quite make it we just plummet to the ground. What's all this about ascending ninety thousand miles and heading south?" . . .

A small consciousness cannot keep up with a vast consciousness; short duration cannot keep up with long duration. How do we know? The morning mushroom knows nothing of the noontide; the winter cicada knows nothing of the spring and autumn. This is what is meant by short duration. In southern Chu there is a tree called Dark Genius, for which five hundred years is a single spring and another five hundred years is a single autumn. In ancient times, there was even one massive tree whose spring and autumn were each eight thousand years long. And yet nowadays, Pengzu [reputed to have lived eight hundred years] alone has a special reputation for longevity and everyone tries to match him. Pathetic, isn't it?

(4)

As I read it, this passage serves at least the following three functions.

First function: It signals that what Zhuangzi says is not to be taken at face value. Zhuangzi emphatically does *not* do philosophy in the way Mozi, Aristotle, or Kant does philosophy, by laying out a series of statements presented as truth. In fact, throughout the text Zhuangzi uses a wide variety of devices to dislodge the typical reader's general assumption that philosophical texts are in the business of stating truths.[2] He makes seeming assertions, then raises objections or questions about those assertions, then fails to resolve those questions. Much of the text is in quotation from people whose wisdom we might wonder about: a butcher, a speaking tree, a "madman," a convicted criminal with an amputated foot, a hunchbacked woman, miscellaneous dubious sages with funny names, and especially "Confucius," who says a mix of things, some of which Zhuangzi would presumably reject and some seemingly closer to what Zhuangzi might accept. Zhuangzi uses humor, parody, paradox, absurdity. He explicitly contradicts himself. He seems to say almost nothing with an entirely straight face. The giant flying minnow-bird is only the start of this.

Second function: The principal import of the parable seems to be this: Small things cannot comprehend large things; and just as short-lived insects cannot understand the change of seasons, we human beings should not be able to understand things vastly larger than ourselves. And the world does contain things vastly larger than ourselves, even if not exactly the ones Zhuangzi mentions. Now it's crucial to understanding the bearing of this parable on the remainder of the text to know whether Zhuangzi includes *himself* among the small beings with limited understanding. You might read him otherwise. You might read him as setting himself up as a sage whose wisdom is beyond ordinary human understanding. You might read him as saying: Reader, you are like the cicada and this book is like the giant bird. You will not understand it, at least not in your first, second, or third read, but that is because you are small and limited and have not yet achieved my level of wisdom. I do think philosophers often try to intimidate readers into thinking that if there is something the reader doesn't understand or something that seems mistaken, the reader must be the one at fault, rather than the philosopher whose text it is. I understand the temptation! But to yield to that temptation is both authoritarian and cowardly.[3] I don't think this is what Zhuangzi is doing. Rather, I propose, Zhuangzi regards himself too as one of the cicadas—though perhaps one more humbled by greatness than the one in his parable.

If so, this would explain the first feature of the text that I pointed out: his constant self-undermining. Zhuangzi does not want the reader to take his words as authoritative. Just the opposite. Presumably, he wants the reader to find some philosophical value in reading the text, but he works constantly against the human tendency, when we are reading philosophy we enjoy, to accept the text we enjoy as truth. The text is too full of explicit self-doubt, too absurd, too self-contradictory for it to be truth. It is literally, as a whole, incomprehensible—as incomprehensible as the world itself, at least to little doves like us. If I am right, there is not, beneath the text, a single coherent message that could have been said plainly, if only Zhuangzi had wished to do so. I will develop this point more, in connection with Zhuangzi's passages about death, self, and oneness. For now, just consider this: Zhuangzi is presumably presenting himself, in this passage, either as a limited animal baffled by the greatness of things or as someone of great understanding by whom we of lesser understanding will be baffled. There are at least tentative reasons to favor the former view.

Third function: The passage introduces two themes that recur throughout the text, in addition to the recurring theme of limited human knowledge: self and death. In the first two sentences of the text, a giant minnow transforms into a giant bird. This is only the first of several cross-species transformations in the Inner Chapters, and it raises the question of what, if anything, remains constant in such transformations, whether we ourselves could undergo radical transformations while continuing to exist. Thus, the question of self, of what makes us the beings we are, is broached, and a liberal attitude toward transformation is hinted at but not explicitly developed. On the topic of death, Zhuangzi seems to be doing at least two things. One is to admire the long-lived, at least for their broad vision and possibly for their longevity itself. Another is to challenge our own attitudes toward longevity: viewed in a large enough perspective, even an eight-hundred-year life is not that long, not really much different from what we would normally regard as a brief life.

Might that large perspective also be limited but in a different way? When Breeze looks down, he too sees only blue on blue, missing the details—failing to see, perhaps, some details important to us, but too minor for him to bother about, like the difference between a twenty-year and an eight-hundred-year life? If so, there may be no single perspective from which everything is visible.[4]

***

Zhuangzi seems to think it's a good thing to "live out your years" rather than dying early through strife or self-exhaustion. This view is, I believe, a genuine strand in the text, though some other strands problematize it. When I say that the text is "incomprehensible," this is the sort of issue I have in mind. I don't mean that individual passages are incomprehensible, or that all ways of reading Zhuangzi on death are equally good or bad. Let's walk through the case.

Ziporyn translates the title of chapter 3 as "The Primacy of Nourishing Life" (21). It begins with a passage that seems to recommend us "to maintain our bodies, to keep the life in them intact, to nourish our parents, and to fully live out our years" (22).[5] It continues with a story about a butcher so skilled that after nineteen years of cutting oxen his knife is still sharp as if straight from the whetstone. On this, a king comments, "Wonderful! From hearing the cook's words I have learned how to nourish life!" (23). Zhuangzi appears to advocate that you "live out all your natural years without being cut down halfway" (39). Zhuangzi celebrates trees that are big and useless and are thus never chopped down (8, 30–31). Zhuangzi seems to prefer the yak who cannot catch mice over the weasel who can and who thus, hurrying about, dies in a snare (8). In the voice of "Confucius," Zhuangzi seems to think it bad if a disciple is killed by a tyrant (25; similarly, 29–30). The Inner Chapters conclude with the story of an emperor who lacks the seven holes in his head that the rest of us have, and who dies when his well-meaning friends drill him holes—a story both sad and funny, and in which presumably the emperor's death implies that something has gone wrong (54). In light of these passages and others, it seems reasonable to suppose that Zhuangzi, or at least one strand of Zhuangzi, shares with most of us the rather unradical view that living out one's full life-span is a good thing, and preferable to dying young.

Yet, though "the sage" likes growing old, the sage equally likes dying young (43). And Zhuangzi's Confucius, confronted with two men evidently more wise than he, who have been singing a goofy, joyous song to a friend's corpse, says that "Men such as these look upon life as a dangling wart or swollen pimple, and on death as its dropping off, its bursting and draining" (46–47). Zhuangzi also says: "The Genuine Human Beings of old understood nothing about delighting in being alive or hating death. They emerged without delight, submerged again without resistance. Swooping in they came and swooping out they went, that and no more" (40). Royal Relativity, who seems to speak for Zhuangzi, says that "even death and life can do nothing to change" (Kjellberg: "make no difference to"; Watson: "have no effect on"; Graham: "alter nothing in") the "Consummate Person" (18).[6]

On the face of it, it seems like Zhuangzi is saying or assuming, in some places, that we should prefer living out our years to being cut down early, while in other places he seems to be portraying sages and other sorts of superior people as *not* preferring long life over death. How might we reconcile these apparently conflicting strands in the text? I will review some possibilities drawn from the recent Anglophone literature on Zhuangzi.

One possibility is suggested by A. C. Graham: Phrases like "nourishing life" and "living out one's years" are familiar from the Yangist school of philosophical thinking in ancient China (best represented in selected "Yangist" chapters identified by Knoblock and Riegel (2000) in their translation of *The Annals of Lü Buwei*, written in the third century BCE). According to the Yangists, one's primary aim should be to nurture the body and preserve life, especially one's own body and life. The Yangist-seeming strands and phrases in the text might be a residue of Zhuangzi's thinking earlier in his career, possibly reflecting Yangist schooling, before he matured into equanimity.[7]

Another possibility is suggested by Robert E. Allinson (1989): Different strands in the text might speak to readers at different levels of understanding. Passages about nurturing life might be directed toward readers of lower understanding, for whom nurturing life would be a step forward; passages about sages' indifference to death might be directed toward readers at a more advanced stage.

Nothing in the texts, I think, compels us to reject either of those approaches. However, neither matches my own sense of the text. One consideration against Graham's view is that both the preferring-life passages and the not-preferring-life passages are scattered through the whole of the "Inner Chapters." There would have to be quite a lot of temporal mangling of the text for the strands to reflect different stages in Zhuangzi's development. One consideration against Allinson's view is that it seems to give us a Zhuangzi who sees himself as so superior to the reader that he is ready to dispense pablum advice to that segment of his readership who would do well to advance even partway toward his own level of understanding. This is not the self-doubting, antiauthoritarian Zhuangzi I see in the text, who treats the reader as an equal.

Another possible interpretation is this: Skillful action requires equanimity, including equanimity in the face of risks to one's life. Skillful responsiveness to one's circumstances can help one live out one's years rather than being cut down early. Semiparadoxically, then, if one hopes for longevity, one ought not care too much about it. Perhaps something like this fits with interpretations of Zhuangzi that emphasize the importance, for him, of skillful, spontaneous responsiveness without critical linguistic judgment (Graham 1989, Hansen 1992, Ivanhoe 1993, Carr and Ivanhoe 2000).

There are two main difficulties with the skill interpretation as a means of resolving the apparent tension in Zhuangzi's remarks about death. One difficulty is that many of the most important skill passages in the Zhuangzi are outside of the Inner Chapters, and thus of dubious authenticity. The Inner Chapters themselves contain one clear celebration of skillfulness, the butcher's skill in carving oxen, offered as a means of "nourishing life" (22–23), but elsewhere skillfulness is not marked for praise: the weasel's skill in catching rats leads to its death (8), Huizi's logical skill ends in obscurities about "hard" and "white" (15) and maybe harms his life (38), and games of skill are said to lead to competitive strife (28); simultaneously, Zhuangzi praises useless, unskilled trees and yaks, and also people with disabilities that limit their skill at commonly valued tasks.

The other main difficulty with the skill interpretation is that if equanimity about death is subsidiary to some greater aim of preserving life, then Zhuangzi's sages and Consummate People have strangely lost track of their priorities, for it seems that they no longer care about this greater aim. Perhaps they live longer as a result, but it is only by having forgotten what really, on this interpretation, has value. It is actually we, with our more conventional valuing of life over death, who better know the proper value of things.

Still another resolution emphasizes the following passage: "The Great Clump burdens me with a physical form, labors me with life, eases me with old age, rests me with death. So it is precisely because I consider my life good that I consider my death good" (43). This sounds like an argument. A first-pass thought might be this: life is impossible without death. So if I value life I must therefore also value death. But if this is the argument, it is a poor one. Perhaps life as we know it is impossible without death at some point, as a resolution. Nonetheless, a long, healthy life of eighty years is perfectly conceivable as a valuable life; and nothing about the necessity of death prevents one from strongly preferring that type of life over a short life of twenty years. But if we take at face value the passages about the sage liking dying young, the sage does not appear to prefer long over short lives, which is exactly the oddity to be explained. Another possible reading of this passage emphasizes that physical form is a "burden," life is a "labor," old age is "ease," and death is a way of "resting." This sounds a bit like the pessimistic view that life is an unpleasant hassle that one is well rid of; but that doesn't fit so well with the upbeat and joyful attitude that Zhuangzi seems to favor elsewhere.

The passage continues, ending with a remark that I had briefly paraphrased earlier:

> You may hide a boat in a ravine or a net in a swamp, thinking it is secure there. But in the middle of the night, a mighty one comes along and carries it away on his back, unbeknownst to you in your slumber. When the smaller is hidden within the larger, there remains someplace into which it can escape. But if you hide the world in the world, so there is nowhere for anything to escape to, this is an arrangement, the vastest arrangement, that can sustain all things.
>
> This human form is merely a circumstance that has been met with, just something stumbled into, but those who have become humans take delight in it nonetheless. Now the human form in its time undergoes ten thousand transformations, never stopping for an instant—so the joys must be beyond calculation! Hence, the sage uses it to roam in that from which nothing ever escapes, where all things are maintained. Early death, old age, the beginning, the end—this allows him to see each of them as good.
>
> (43)

With this passage in mind, Chris Fraser (2013) suggests that Zhuangzi is embracing an "aesthetic attitude" that celebrates the constant stream of transformations that is the Dao, the way of things—the stream of transformations that gives you life and then, soon or not quite as soon, gives you death.[8] Similarly, Roger Ames (1998) sees Zhuangzi as inviting us to reconceptualize life as "life-and-death," a series of transformations, in a "ceaseless adventure" (1998, 66).

Despite the merit of these interpretations, especially as approaches to this particular passage, they strain against the substantial thread in Zhuangzi that seems to favor nurturing life and living out one's natural span of years rather than being chopped down early. If every transformation is as good as every other, why not see the chopping as just another exciting transformation? Why not celebrate the weasel's being caught in the snare, the tree's being shaped into boards by an energetic carpenter and becoming someone's house?

Still another possibility might be drawn from Amy Olberding's (2007) reading of passages from the Outer and Miscellaneous Chapters describing Zhuangzi's reaction to the death of his wife and his friend Huizi. (See also Wong 2006.) Whereas Graham sees the different strands in Zhuangzi as reflecting different phases in his philosophical career and Allinson sees them as speaking to different target audiences, Olberding suggests that Zhuangzi's attitude might vary during the process of personal mourning for loved ones. Olberding suggests that Zhuangzi reacts to death by recognizing its disvalue, but only briefly, before shifting to a recognition of death as part of what gives life its value and interest, in a series of transformations that is overall to be celebrated.

Olberding thus appears to attribute conflicting attitudes to Zhuangzi— interpreting him as embracing one attitude in some moments (that death is bad, his feeling in moments of immediate personal grief) and another attitude in other moments (that death is not bad but another transformation to be celebrated, his feeling as he distances himself from personal grieving). If so, this puts her view close to my own: I read Zhuangzi as genuinely expressing both of these conflicting opinions about death.

But there are, I think, at least two more dimensions of complexity to this picture. First, we have not yet seriously confronted the strangeness of the metaphysical view that Zhuangzi seems to be embracing in this last passage and in some others—that human form is simply a circumstance that you are temporarily met with. More on this later. And second, there are Zhuangzi's skeptical remarks about death, to which I now turn.

$$* * *$$

Zhuangzi sometimes expresses radically skeptical views—especially but not exclusively in chapter 2, "Equalizing Assessments of Things." When Toothless asks Royal Relativity, who seems to speak for Zhuangzi, "Do you know what all things agree in considering right?" Royal Relativity replies, "How could I know that?" When Toothless then asks if he knows that he doesn't know, Royal Relativity again replies, "How could I know that?" (17). In the voice of Master Long Desk, Zhuangzi asks: "Suppose you and I get into a debate. If you win and I lose, does that really mean you are right and I am wrong? If I win and you lose, does that really mean I'm right and you're wrong? Must one of us be right and the other wrong? Or could both of us be right, or both of us wrong? If neither you nor I can know, a third person would be even more benighted" (19). In both of these passages, the seeming assertion of skepticism is tempered both by placing it in another's mouth—someone it's natural to regard as speaking for Zhuangzi, but who might not—and by posing skeptical doubts as questions rather than positively asserting the truth of skepticism.[9] However, in a way this makes the passages even more skeptical: like Royal Relativity, Zhuangzi here seems unwilling to assert anything, not even that he lacks knowledge.

Two other skeptical passages bring us directly into issues of death and self. The first is, again, in the voice of Master Long Desk:

> How, then, do I know that delighting in life is not a delusion? How do I know that in hating death I am not like an orphan who left home in youth and no longer knows the way back? Lady Li was a daughter of the border guard of Ai. When she was first captured and brought to Qin, she wept until tears drenched her collar. But when she got to the palace, sharing the king's luxurious bed and feasting on the finest meats, she regretted her tears. How do I know the dead don't regret the way they used to cling to life? . . .
> Perhaps a great awakening would reveal all of this to be a vast dream.
> (19)

The second passage is probably the most famous passage in the *Zhuangzi*:

> Once Zhuang Zhou dreamt he was a butterfly, fluttering about joyfully just as a butterfly would. He followed his whims exactly as he liked and knew nothing about Zhuang Zhou. Suddenly he awoke, and there he was, the startled Zhuang Zhou in the flesh. He did not know if Zhou had been dreaming he was a butterfly, or if a butterfly was now dreaming it was Zhou. Surely, Zhou and a butterfly count as two distinct identities! Such is what we call the transformation of one thing into another.
> (21)

The Lady Li passage starts with Master Long Desk seeming to admit that he hates death. He then raises doubts about the grounds of his hatred. It is possible, in fact I think natural, if one jettisons commitment to seeing Zhuangzi as entirely self-consistent across passages, to interpret this as a confession on Zhuangzi's part: Zhuangzi, too, hates death, wants to nourish life and live out his years. He is *not* like the "Genuine Human Beings" he celebrates elsewhere in the text, who emerge without delight and submerge without resistance, or the men who see life as a swollen pimple and death as draining it.

In this passage, Zhuangzi does not say that he (or Master Long Desk) is wrong to have such an attitude. He only expresses the more skeptical thought that he *might* be wrong, that he *might* be like Lady Li when first captured, that he *might* wake up and find his new situation to be a vast improvement over the current situation that he normally regards as waking life.

So I believe I hear not just two but three distinct attitudes in the text: one that takes for granted that nourishing life and living out your years are preferable to being cut down early, one that sees wisdom in valuing life and death equally and thus nothing to regret in dying young, and one that hates death but entertains doubts about the wisdom of that hatred. I am not proposing that these are three different authors. There is a commonality of philosophical style among them, and all three attitudes weave together throughout the text. I am proposing instead that Zhuangzi, like many of us, is ambivalent, inconsistent, and confused and cannot quite see how everything hangs together, and the text reflects this in an open, self-revealing way. Zhuangzi is not offering us a unified vision of the True Theory of Things and the One Right Way to Live. He is sharing his wonder and bafflement.

✳ ✳ ✳

Let's take Zhuangzi at his word in the butterfly passage: He thinks it at least *possible* that he is a butterfly dreaming that he is a human. Setting aside Kripkean (1980) worries about metaphysical vs. epistemic modality, this passage suggests that Zhuangzi does not regard himself as necessarily human or essentially human. This, of course, fits with Zhuangzi's remark, quoted earlier, that "human form is merely a circumstance that has been met with" (43). Another related passage is in the voice of Master Arrive:

> Now, suppose a great master smith were casting metal. If the metal jumped up and said, "I insist on being nothing but the great sword Moye!"[10] the smith would surely consider it to be an inauspicious chunk of metal. Now, if I, having happened to stumble into a human form, should insist, "Only a human! Only a human!" then the maker of changes would certainly consider me an inauspicious chunk of person. So now I look upon all heaven and earth as a great furnace, and the maker of changes as a great blacksmith—where could I go that would not be all right? All at once I fall asleep. With a start I awaken.[11]
> (46)

Master Arrive is portrayed as saying these words as he is at the very edge of his own death. Shortly before, his friend Master Plow has already commented similarly, "Do not disturb his transformation! . . . What will it make you become; where will it send you? Will it make you into a mouse's liver? Or perhaps an insect's arm?" (45).

These passages envision radical changes in physical form while the self or the "I" (or something like that)[12] continues to exist: "I" might wake and find myself a human, which I was not before, and then "I" might wake again and find myself something else, such as a bug's arm. Taking the passages at face value, Zhuangzi seems to be envisioning a reawakening of consciousness after these changes. The Lady Li passage suggests there might even be memory of one's previous form, regret for the way I previously clung to life.

We have a choice, I think, between treating these passages as "heroic metaphysics" (in Ivanhoe's [2010] memorable phrase for a common way of interpreting some other authors) and treating them as what I will call *real possibilities*. If we read Zhuangzi as a heroic metaphysician, then we read him as committed to a metaphysical system containing not only an agent who intentionally executes the transformations (the "Great Clump" who has burdened us with our temporary human forms) but also, more radically, conscious selves that run through mouse livers and bug arms, possibly recalling their previous lives. (Elder's [2014] interpretation of the death passages seems "heroic" in roughly this sense.) I see two reasons to resist reading Zhuangzi as a heroic metaphysician. One is that he spends no time developing and defending such a metaphysics. You'd think that if Zhuangzi literally thought that bugs' arms were conscious, he'd give us a better sense of how this works, how this fits into a larger (panpsychic?) picture, and why we should accept such an unusual picture as true. However, he does no such thing. The other reason to doubt the heroic interpretation is Zhuangzi's skepticism: Heroic metaphysics is an enterprise of the boldly self-assured, who think they have discerned the ultimate structure of reality, whereas Zhuangzi seems to think that the ultimate structure of reality is elusive, possibly beyond human comprehension. Zhuangzi says many absurd, or at least absurd-seeming, things that he presumably doesn't expect us to take seriously as the literal truth—the opening passage about the giant fish-bird among them. Perhaps these passages are the same.

And yet I doubt that Zhuangzi offers these ideas as *mere* absurdities. Maybe the idea that one might literally waken after death to discover that one is a bug's arm is a bit of colorful fun, but the idea that our consciousness might in some way survive our bodily death, merging somehow into nature or arising in a new form, is not a historically unusual view; and it's a defensible-enough skeptical thought that what one now regards as waking life might indeed be a dream from which one will waken to a very different reality. Although I think it loads Zhuangzi with too much confident metaphysics to insist that he is committed to the truth of awakening to continued survival either as another piece of this reality or in some higher reality—and notice that these are different metaphysical options that don't fit comfortably together—it seems entirely consistent with Zhuangzi's skepticism to allow that these are for him real possibilities, possibilities that can give genuine comfort in the face of death.

Similarly, some passages of the Inner Chapters invite magical or mystical interpretation. For example: "There is a Spirit-Man living on the distant Maiden Mountains with skin like ice and snow . . . [who] rides upon the air and clouds" (7; cf. Leizi on p. 5, the Consummate Person on p. 18). "That is what allows the joy of its harmony to open into all things . . . taking part everywhere as the springtime of each being . . . your own mind becomes the site of the life-giving time. This is what is called keeping the innate powers whole" (37). "Xiwei got it and thereby put the measure around heaven and earth. Fuxi got it and thereby inherited the matrix of vital energy. . . . Pingyi got it and thereby inherited the power of Mt. Kunlun. . . . Pengzu got it any thereby remained alive all the way back from the time of Shun Youyu down to the time of the Five Tyrants" (44). We might connect these passages with passages that appear to hint of meditative techniques, such as Yan Hui's "fasting of the mind" (26) and his ability to "just sit and forget" (49). Engage in the right meditative or mystical practices and achieve longevity, insight, and spiritual power! Harold D. Roth is among those who have recently emphasized the mystical (less so the magical) dimension of the text (Roth 1999, 2003).

I favor treating such passages like the "bug's arm" passage. Zhuangzi, the same skeptic who thinks we might wake up to find that this has all been a dream, would also, I think, not rule out the possibility that connection with a mystical energy or life force *might* deliver powers or longevity far beyond our mundane experience. Some people believe in such things; and I see no reason to suppose that Zhuangzi would insist that the world is mundane and non-magical. He might be inviting the reader to reconsider mystical and magical folk traditions devalued by the Confucians and logicians he seems to have regarded as his primary interlocutors. We can allow Zhuangzi to take the mystical and magical seriously as possibilities without reading him as fully accepting the truth of such claims or as fully endorsing the aim of transforming oneself into a magical being through the right spiritual practice. Indeed, he seems sometimes to exaggerate the claims to the point of silliness; and he reminds us that even Pengzu's eight hundred years look pathetic from a large-enough perspective.

Thus, we might see in these passages a trio of attitudes similar to the trio I've argued are at work in the passages about death: a strand that genuinely embraces the search for mystical transformation, another strand that pokes fun at the absurdity of such a search, and a third strand (which needn't be final or privileged over the other two) that doubts the wisdom of both of those other strands. I see no reason to insist that a single author or narrative voice must achieve a resolution among these competing thoughts.

* * *

Zhuangzi speaks repeatedly of "oneness." If you begin with those passages, it's tempting to think he must have a theory of oneness or at least a consistent view about it. His remarks about oneness, though puzzling, are neither as baldly contradictory as his remarks about death nor as patently strange as his remarks about the self, though the three topics are closely related. You might think he's trying to convey a profound truth that he knows, a truth about the deep oneness of things, a truth that is, however, difficult to express in words and that thus sounds strange or paradoxical.

I don't think it does violence to the text, exactly, to read Zhuangzi in that way. But I don't think that we *must* read him in that way; and I think declining to read him as univocally aiming toward mystical profundity yields a more interesting text.

Here's a sample of Zhuangzi on oneness:

1. "Heaven and earth are born together with me, and the ten thousand things and I are one. But if we are all one, can there be any words? But since I have already declared that we are "one," can there be no words?" (15–16).

2. "So no thing is not right, no thing is not acceptable. For whatever we may define as a beam as opposed to a pillar, as a leper as opposed to the great beauty Xishi, or whatever might be strange, grotesque, uncanny, or deceptive, there is some course that opens them into one another, connecting them to form a oneness" (13).

3. "Therefore his liking was one and his not liking was one. His being one was one and his not being one was one. In being one, he was acting as a companion of Heaven. In not being one, he was acting as a companion of man."[13]

And my favorite:

4. "Making a point to show that a point is not a point is not as good as making a nonpoint to show that a point is not a point. Using a horse to show that a horse is not a horse is not as good as using a nonhorse to show that a horse is not a horse. Heaven and earth are one point, the ten thousand things are one horse."[14]

Now wait. Stop! If you're trying to fit these passages into a theory, trying to figure out how this can all make consistent sense, that's exactly what I *don't* want you to do.

Notice the surface of the text: Zhuangzi asks how there can be words if everything is one, but also how there can be no words if he's already said something. He offers no good answer to this dilemma. He says, "His being one was one and his not being one was one." At least superficially, this is either nonsense or plain logical contradiction. He says, "The ten thousand things are one horse." This is the absurd conclusion of what I read as a jovial parody of the logicians of Zhuangzi's era, like Gongsun Long, who argued in all seriousness that a white horse is not a horse. We are not meant to sit down and figure out how the entire universe is in fact one horse.

Consider this passage, where Zhuangzi's Confucius character is talking about a one-footed convict, Royal Nag [King Worn-Out Horse: 王駘], whom he admires as a great sage:

Life and death are a great matter, but they are unable to alter him. Even if Heaven and earth were to topple over, he would not be lost with them. . . . Looked at from the point of view of their differences, even your own liver and gallbladder are as distant as Chu in the south and Yue in the north. But looked at from the point of view of their sameness, all things are one. If you take the latter view, you become free of all preconceptions about which particular objects might suit the eyes and ears. You just release the mind to play in the harmony of all Virtuosities. Seeing what is one and the same to all things, nothing is ever felt to be lost. This man viewed the chopping off of his foot as nothing more than the casting away of a lump of soil.

(33)

In this passage, selfhood and oneness meet. Here's a possible reading: Looked at from a narrowly specific perspective, I am not really the same person as the ten-year-old boy who was called "Eric Schwitzgebel." Looked at from a much broader perspective, the thoughts and feelings and ideas that I think of as central to myself are repeated with variations in all of you, in a way that might be interpretable as a matter of overlapping identities. Looked at from one perspective, I lose nothing of myself when my foot is removed. My foot is as far from me as the state of Chu. Looked at from another perspective, everything around me is part of me, and I lose a crucial part of myself when I lose treasured objects or when a beloved friend dies. We are not compelled to regard the boundary of the skin as the one true boundary of the self. We are not compelled to regard the date the baby emerges in 1968 and the date the man dies, hopefully at a ripe age in the 2050s, as the one proper set of temporal boundaries in conceiving the self. We might go narrower; we might go broader.

Is the broader perspective better overall—perhaps even so broad a perspective that the entire cosmos is just my own body? Though the Inner Chapters as a whole tend to value the broad over the narrow, I see no reason to suppose that Zhuangzi definitely resolves in favor of a broad view, especially once he has put us on the slippery slope toward the most radically broad view of all. But neither does Zhuangzi definitely resolve in favor of the equality of all perspectives, or in favor of a somewhat broader but not radically broad view.

Notice that there are two layers of separation between Royal Nag's view and Zhuangzi's authorial perspective. First, Zhuangzi has his "Confucius" character speak these words. Confucius is not a reliable bearer of truth in the Inner Chapters. Second, Confucius does not embrace this view as his own. Rather he says that it is *Royal Nag*'s view—and although he plainly admires Royal Nag, Royal Nag also sounds a lot like those sages and Consummate People I discussed earlier who are startling indifferent to death and who, I've argued, constitute only one strand in Zhuangzi's thinking.

I suggest that we don't try to tame, or render sensible, or render coherent with the rest of the text Zhuangzi's radical, bizarre, and sometimes incomprehensible claims about oneness. Zhuangzi is not a heroic metaphysician developing the one correct mystical metaphysics of universal unity. He espouses different conflicting positions, constantly contradicting and undermining himself. I suggest that we see Zhuangzi's remarks about oneness as the radical edge, or rather one of several partly conflicting radical edges, of his intellectual diversity—of his singular lack of oneness.

* * *

If we insist on seeing the vision of the Inner Chapters as a coherent vision, then whenever Zhuangzi appears to be endorsing a radical, far-out position, we will face a tension between three strands similar to those I have identified in the passages on death and oneness. There will be a strand that accepts the radical claim at face value ("dying young is no worse than living to old age," "everything is literally part of my body"), there will be a more moderate vision that seems to fit with a more mundane and charitable reading of the Inner Chapters as a whole (maybe something like "it's better to live to old age, but people get too emotionally fussed up about it," "the line between myself and other things or people is blurry and overemphasized"), and there will be a skeptical strand that doubts both the radical and the moderate positions ("*maybe* death is actually better than life," "*maybe* I can leave my body behind entirely and become something else or somehow flow into a great oneness with creation").

To render the radical, the moderate, and the skeptical strands coherent with one another requires compromising at least two of the three.[15] But why should we compromise? Maybe we can instead just let Zhuangzi remain incomprehensibly incoherent. In my work as a philosopher of psychology, I have highlighted our splintering tendencies to speak and act in ways that conflict with one another. Such splintering is, I think, a central part of the human condition, especially in the matters we care about most (for example, in professing high moral principles, in our attitudes toward things like money and reputation, in disavowed implicit prejudice of various stripes, in our religious attitudes: Schwitzgebel 2010, 2013). When philosophers seem to be incoherent, maybe that's just because they're like the rest of us. Zhuangzi might be in the unusual position of taking that fact about himself in stride rather than seeing it as a failure.

* * *

One idea that seems to shine through the Inner Chapters, especially chapter 2, is the inadequacy of philosophical theorizing. Words, Zhuangzi suggests, lack fixed meanings, distinctions fail, and well-intentioned philosophical efforts end up collapsing into logical paradoxes and the conflicting rights and wrongs of the Confucians and the Mohists (esp. 11–12).

If Zhuangzi does indeed think that philosophical theorizing is always inadequate to capture the complexity of the world, or at least always inadequate in our small human hands, then he might not wish to put together a text that advances a single philosophical theory. He might choose, instead, to philosophize in a fragmented, shard-like way, expressing a variety of different, conflicting perspectives on the world—perspectives that need not fit together as a coherent whole. He might wish to frustrate, rather than encourage, our attempts to make neat sense of him, inviting us to mature as philosophers not by discovering the proper set of right and wrong views, but rather by offering us his hand as he takes his plunge into wonder and doubt.

That delightfully inconsistent Zhuangzi is the one I love—the Zhuangzi who openly shares his shifting ideas and confusions, who will not stay put with any idea, who playfully frustrates the reader's attempts to imbue his words with sagely seriousness. I hope that was the real, historical Zhuangzi; I think I hear him in the text. I prefer this Zhuangzi to the Zhuangzi that most other philosophical interpreters seem to see, who has some stable, consistent position beneath, which for some reason he chooses not to display in plain language on the surface of the text.

Notes

For helpful discussion, thanks especially to Liam Kofi Bright, Kelly James Clark, Christopher Gowans, Jenny Hung, P. J. Ivanhoe, Daniel Korman, Amy Olberding, Mary Riley, Hagop Sarkissian, Kwong-loi Shun, readers at *The Splintered Mind*, and audiences at the "Varieties of Self" conference at Scripps College, the conference "Oneness in Philosophy and Psychology" at City University of Hong Kong, the Columbia Society for Comparative Philosophy, and Occidental College.

1. Except where specified, I use the Ziporyn translation (Zhuangzi 2009), modified by following Kjellberg's (Zhuangzi 2005) literal translations of nonhistorical characters' names. Here, I have replaced Ziporyn's translation of the text's name as *Equalizing Jokebook* with Kjellberg's more neutral *Tales of Qi*.
2. For more on this point, see Schwitzgebel 1996 and Wang 2004.
3. For more on this issue, see Sperber 2010 and Schwitzgebel 2011.
4. On "perspectivism" in Zhuangzi, see Ziporyn 2003, Lai 2006, Connolly 2011. One concern I have about perspectivism as an approach to Zhuangzi is that it sounds a bit too much like a philosophical doctrine of the sort that Zhuangzi might want to resist. However, stripped of its doctrinality, reduced to the more minimal interpretative idea that Zhuangzi finds philosophical value in expressing a variety of (inconsistent) perspectives, a perspectival approach might be similar to the approach I favor in this essay.

5. Replacing Ziporyn's "those near and dear to us" with the more Confucian "parents," following Watson (Chuang Tzu 1968, 50) and Graham (Chuang Tzu 1981, 62). Kjellberg has "raise your family" (224). Original: 可以養親.

6. The original Chinese phrase that I have presented the four translations of here is 死生無變於己.

7. See Graham's commentary from pp. 116–18 of his *Chuang-tzu* (Chuang Tzu 1981). This might not be Graham's final considered opinion about the Inner Chapters: In *Disputers of the Tao* (1989, 202), he seems to prefer something like the skill interpretation that I offer later.

8. In earlier work, Fraser (2011) suggests something like the equanimity-for-skillful-responding interpretation discussed earlier. In that work, he allows that this interpretation introduces a "fundamental tension" between different parts of the text. However, it's unclear whether Fraser would embrace the views I express here regarding that fundamental tension.

9. Compare Moser 1999 and Wong 2005 on "interrogative" vs. "declarative" skepticism.

10. Replacing Ziporyn's Westernized "an Excalibur."

11. Following Kjellberg's "maker of changes." Ziporyn: "Creation-Transformation." Watson: "the creator." Graham: "he that fashions and transforms."

12. Maybe an "arena of presence and action" (Cheng 2014, drawing the concept from Johnston 2010).

13. For this passage, I use Watson's translation, which seems to me plainer than Ziporyn's (Chuang Tzu 1968, 79–80). Kjellberg's translation is similar. Ziporyn has "Thus, what they liked was the oneness of things, but what they disliked was also the oneness of things. Their oneness was the oneness, but their non-oneness was also the oneness. In their oneness, they were followers of the Heavenly. In their non-oneness, they were followers of the Human" (42). Graham interprets it in still a different way ("they were one with what they liked"). The original is:

    其好之也一，其弗好之也一。其一也一，其不一也一。其一，與天為徒；其不一，與人為徒。天與人不相勝也，是之謂真人。

14. Here I use Kjellberg's translation (218). Where Kjellberg has "a point" for 指, Ziporyn has "this finger" (12), Watson has "an attribute" (40), and Graham has "the meaning" (53).

15. In Schwitzgebel (1996) I compromised the radical and the skeptical in favor of the moderate. If pushed to settle upon one coherent interpretation, the moderate Zhuangzi (who says radical things mainly to knock you out of your dogmatism) is still the one I would choose. But today I am trying out a different interpretative approach, despite the fact that it renders my readings of the Zhuangzi inconsistent with each other. See also Hansen (2003) on not needing to treat the Inner Chapters as coherent. (But then Hansen does come close to favoring a coherent interpretation, I think, by compromising the skeptical and radical strands in the text.)

References

Allinson, Robert E. 1989. *Chuang-Tzu for Spiritual Transformation.* Albany: State University of New York Press.

Ames, Roger T. 1998. "Death as Transformation in Classical Daoism." In *Death and Philosophy*, edited by J. Malpas and R. C. Solomon. New York: Routledge.

Carr, Karen L., and Philip J. Ivanhoe. 2000. *The Sense of Antirationalism*. New York: Seven Bridges.

Cheng, Kai-Yuan. 2014. "Self and the Dream of the Butterfly in the *Zhuangzi*." *Philosophy East and West* 64:563–97.

Chuang Tzu. 1968. *The Complete Works of Chuang Tzu*. Translated by B. Watson. New York: Columbia University Press. Originally published in the fourth century BCE.

——. 1981. *Chuang-tzu: The Seven Inner Chapters, and Other Writings from the Book Chuang-tzu*. Translated by A. C. Graham. London: George Allen and Unwin. Originally published in the fourth century BCE.

Connolly, Tim. 2011. "Perspectivism as a Way of Knowing in the *Zhuangzi*." *Dao* 10:487–505.

Elder, Alexis. 2014. "Zhuangzi on Friendship and Death." *Southern Journal of Philosophy* 52:575–92.

Fraser, Chris. 2011. "Emotion and Agency in *Zhuāngzǐ*." *Asian Philosophy* 21:97–121.

——. 2013. "Xunzi Versus Zhuangzi: Two Approaches to Death in Classical Chinese Thought." *Frontiers of Philosophy in China* 8:410–27.

Graham, A. C. 1989. *Disputers of the Tao*. La Salle, IL: Open Court.

Hansen, Chad. 1992. *A Daoist Theory of Chinese Thought*. New York: Oxford University Press.

——. 2003. "Guru or Skeptic? Relativistic Skepticism in the *Zhuangzi*." In *Hiding the World in the World*, edited by S. Cook. Albany: State University of New York Press.

Ivanhoe, Philip J. 1993. "Zhuangzi on Skepticism, Skill, and the Ineffable Dao." *Journal of the American Academy of Religion* 61:639–54.

——. 2010. "Lu Xiangshan's Ethical Philosophy." In *Dao Companion to Neo-Confucian Philosophy*, edited by J. Makeham. Dordrecht: Springer.

Johnston, Mark. 2010. *Surviving Death*. Princeton: Princeton University Press.

Knoblock, John, and Jeffrey Riegel, eds. 2000. *The Annals of Lü Buwei*. Stanford: Stanford University Press.

Kripke, Saul A. 1980. *Naming and Necessity*. Cambridge: Harvard University Press.

Lai, Karyn Lynne. 2006. "Philosophy and Philosophical Reasoning in the *Zhuangzi*: Dealing with Plurality." *Journal of Chinese Philosophy* 33:365–74.

Moser, Paul K. 1999. "Realism, Objectivity, and Skepticism." In *The Blackwell Guide to Epistemology*, edited by J. Greco and E. Sosa. Malden, MA: Blackwell.

Olberding, Amy. 2007. "Sorrow and the Sage: Grief in the *Zhuangzi*." *Dao* 6:339–59.

Roth, Harold D. 1999. *Original Tao*. New York: Columbia University Press.

——. 2003. "Bimodal Mystical Experience in the 'Qiwulun' Chapter of the Zhuangzi." In *Hiding the World in the World*, edited by S. Cook. Albany: State University of New York Press.

Schwitzgebel, Eric. 1996. "Zhuangzi's Attitude Toward Language and His Skepticism." In *Essays on Skepticism, Relativism and Ethics in the Zhuangzi*, edited by P. Kjellberg and P. J. Ivanhoe. Albany: State University of New York Press.

——. 2010. "Acting Contrary to Our Professed Beliefs, or the Gulf Between Occurrent Judgment and Dispositional Belief." *Pacific Philosophical Quarterly* 91:531–53.

——. 2011. "Obfuscatory Philosophy and Intellectual Authoritarianism and Cowardice." Blog post at *The Splintered Mind*, October 19. http://schwitzsplinters.blogspot.com/2011/10/obfuscatory-philosophy-as-intellectual.html.

——. 2013. "A Dispositional Approach to Attitudes: Thinking Outside of the Belief Box." In *New Essays on Belief*, edited by N. Nottelmann. New York: Palgrave Macmillan.

Sperber, Dan. 2010. "The Guru Effect." *Review of Philosophy and Psychology* 1:583–92.

Wang, Youru. 2004. "Strategies of 'Goblet Words': Indirect Communication in the *Zhuangzi.*" *Journal of Chinese Philosophy* 31:195–208.

Wong, David B. 2005. "Zhuangzi and the Obsession with Being Right." *History of Philosophy Quarterly* 22:91–107.

——. 2006. "The Meaning of Detachment in Daoism, Buddhism, and Stoicism." *Dao* 5:207–19.

Zhuangzi. 2005. "Zhuangzi." Translated by P. Kjellberg. In *Readings in Classical Chinese Philosophy*, 2nd ed., edited by P. J. Ivanhoe and B. W. Van Norden. Indianapolis: Hackett. Originally published in the fourth century BCE.

——. 2009. *Zhuangzi: The Essential Writings.* Translated by B. Ziporyn. Indianapolis: Hackett. Originally published in the fourth century BCE.

Ziporyn, Brook. 2003. "How Many Are the Ten Thousand Things and I? Relativism, Mysticism, and the Privileging of Oneness in the 'Inner Chapters.'" In *Hiding the World in the World*, edited by S. Cook. Albany: State University of New York Press.

CHAPTER 16

IDENTITY FUSION

The Union of Personal and Social Selves

SANAZ TALAIFAR AND WILLIAM B. SWANN, JR.

I magine that you were introduced to a group of ten transgender individuals, that is, people who want to be identified with the cross-
gender group. Imagine further that you were asked to predict which
members of the group would undergo gender-reassignment surgery within the
next two years. On what basis would you make this prediction? The age at
which the individual first reported his or her gender dysphoria? Socioeconomic
variables such as income or education? In our research, we have found that
neither of these variables is very predictive. Instead, we discovered that a feeling of "oneness" or "identity fusion" with the cross-gender group was critical.

To put this finding in context, let us tell you a little bit about the construct
of "identity fusion" that inspired it (Swann et al. 2012). Identity fusion rests on
a distinction that has a long history in the behavioral sciences, the distinction
between personal and social identities (for a philosophical exploration of individuation versus plurality see Lawrence Blum's essay in this volume). Personal
identities refer to the traits and characteristics that make people distinct from
others. In contrast, social identities are those aspects of ourselves that link people to others, especially groups. Identity fusion involves the union of personal
and social identity. In the transsexual study, we were interested in the extent
to which people's personal identities were fused with their cross-gender identity (male for natal females and female for natal males).

The transsexual study took place in Barcelona, Spain (Swann et al. 2015).
A member of our research team who was a psychiatrist at a gender identity

clinic collected the data. At the beginning of the study, she asked some of her transsexual patients to complete a measure of identity fusion with the cross-gender. Whereas nonfused patients indicated little overlap between their personal selves and their cross-gender identities, strongly fused people indicated that their personal identities were completely overlapping with their cross-gender identities. After patients completed the measure, they indicated what sacrifices they would be willing to make to attain their cross-gender sex. We then followed them for two years to determine whether they had gender-reassignment surgery. We discovered that those who were strongly fused with the cross-gender group at the beginning of the study were especially likely to indicate that they would sacrifice their close relationships to change their sex. More strikingly, strongly fused participants were particularly likely to have had a sex-reassignment surgery two years later, even when controlling for various socioeconomic and clinical variables.

The study of transsexuals is part of a larger program of research on identity fusion that we will be describing in this chapter. To understand how this work builds upon earlier research, we begin by placing it in historical perspective.

Historical Overview of Personal and Social Identity

The distinction between personal and social identities goes back to William James (1890), who fathered modern psychology. He devoted an entire section of his book to the self. Not long after James's initial foray into the psychology of the self, the subarea was vanquished from the field by mainstream American psychology's obsession with overt behavior (for example, Watson 1913). As the Second World War drew to a close, however, behaviorism lost steam and the self reemerged as a viable area of study. When it did, however, the personal self emerged alone (likely due to emphasis on individualism in America at the time). Constructs such as self-esteem, self-efficacy, and self-awareness commanded considerable attention while the social self was largely neglected.

It was not until the late 1970s that the social self regained a foothold in the psychological mainstream with the publication of social identity theory (Tajfel and Turner 1979). The primary architect of the theory, Henri Tajfel, based the theory at least partially on his experiences during the Second World War. A Polish Jew, he was fortunate to be studying in France at the beginning of the war, as it allowed him to pass as a French Jew (Polish Jews were routinely murdered). When he was captured by the Nazis in 1940, he was struck by the fact that his captors reduced him to nothing more than a member of a social category (that is, the French Jew whom they mistakenly believed he was). Tajfel noted that aspects of his personal self (related to his idiosyncratic qualities) were of no interest to his captors; his category membership was all that mattered (Turner 1996). These experiences inspired his appreciation for the power of social categories.

Tajfel's interest in the influence of social categories motivated his classic experiments on the minimal group effect (Tajfel 1970). In these studies, he and his colleagues showed that mere group membership biased people toward members of their in-group: even though they understood that group membership was completely arbitrary and random (hence the term *minimal group*), they discriminated against "outgroup members." The minimal group paradigm is a simple but powerful manipulation: even when group assignments are made on the basis of shirt color or some other arbitrary basis, people consistently display a preference for their own group. These findings and Tajfel's wartime experiences shaped the development of social identity theory, which proposed that identity was mentally represented on a continuum that ranged from personal to social identity. The theory assumed that the two types of mental representations were mutually exclusive, so that attending to one diminished attention to the other. Social identity theory was enormously important, as it made a strong case for recognizing social identity as an important and legitimate area of scientific study.

In their zeal to highlight the unique qualities of social identities, Tajfel and Turner (1979) emphasized the ways in which social identities competed with personal identities. We suggest that it is also possible to conceive of the two forms of identity as *complementary* aspects of self-knowledge. This is one of several ideas that inspired the development of identity fusion theory. "Identity fusion" occurs when someone's personal identity unites with a social identity. When such a union occurs, the personal identity remains salient despite being thoroughly integrated with the social identity. In contrast to the scenarios highlighted by social identity theory, here there is no subjugation of the personal self by the social self, as may occur in the case of people who are brainwashed by cults. Rather, in identity fusion, the personal self remains a potent force that combines synergistically with the social self to motivate behavior.

One of the defining features of identity fusion is a *visceral* sense of union, or oneness, with a group. These feelings of oneness are marked by a perception that the self and group members are kindred spirits who share deep essential qualities and strengthen one another. The perception of shared essence motivates strongly fused persons to make extreme sacrifices for the in-group "family."

Recent research has established that people who are strongly fused with their country are more likely to endorse extreme pronational behaviors (for example, fighting and dying for the country) in more than ten countries across six continents (Swann et al. 2014a). Moreover, strongly fused persons do not merely *say* that they will engage in extreme behavior; they actually enact these extreme behaviors in the real world. In a study of 179 Libyan revolutionaries working to oust the Gaddafi regime during the revolution in 2011, we found extremely high levels of fusion with the battalion among members actively engaged in the conflict (Whitehouse et al. 2014). In fact, some of the front-line fighters were more strongly fused to their battalion than to their own families. By contrast, a comparison group of revolutionaries who volunteered to provide logistical support (a less dangerous role than fighter) was more strongly fused with their natural families than to their battalion.

In light of this evidence that identity fusion motivates extreme actions, it is imperative to understand some of the mechanisms that underlie it. In what follows, we examine the emotional and cognitive processes that give rise to extreme behavior. Specifically, we will discuss how the moral reasoning of strongly fused individuals may differ from that of other individuals and how such reasoning influences behavior.

Fusion and Moral Decision-Making

How do fused individuals make moral decisions? Many past analyses of group processes have emphasized the role of cognitive processing and cost-benefit, utilitarian principles in morality-related decision-making (for example, Kohlberg 1969). Recently, however, some have challenged the emphasis on cognitive, utilitarian reasoning in moral decision-making, arguing instead for the importance of intuitive, emotional processes (Graham et al. 2013, Haidt and Kesebir 2010, Iyer, Jetten, and Haslam 2012). In this same vein, others have argued that consequential moral decisions are based on other "intuitive" mental structures such as "sacred values" (Sheikh, Ginges, and Atran 2013) or "moral mandates" (Skitka 2010).

We acknowledge the existence of both "deliberative" and "intuitive" pathways to moral behavior, but suggest that strongly fused persons are particularly inclined to follow the path of intuitive, deontological reasoning in their moral decision-making (see also Greene et al. 2001, Greene et al. 2004). Consider analyses of retrospective reports of extreme behaviors ranging from the efforts of combat troops to save their compatriots (Cashman 2014, Junger 2010, State of Israel 2010) to the self-sacrificial behaviors of Carnegie hero medal recipients (Rand and Epstein 2014). Note that all of these individuals are likely to be strongly fused to their group. Their commentaries regarding their actions reveal that systematic assessment of the costs and benefits of their actions played little role in motivating their actions. Instead, such individuals report that in the moments leading up to their heroic acts, they knew intuitively what to do and acted spontaneously. When reflection did occur, it occurred when they attempted to analyze their behavior later on rather than before the action.

Our research on intragroup versions of the trolley dilemma (Swann et al. 2014b) likewise casts doubt on the primacy of conscious reasoning as the exclusive cause of endorsement of self-sacrifice. In one study, participants responded to a dilemma in which five in-group members would die unless they sacrificed themselves (a train was approaching five Spanish workers and would kill them unless the participant self-sacrificed by summoning the "death" train to his or her own track). While most people acknowledged that the "correct" or "moral" course of action was to sacrifice him- or herself, only strongly fused persons reported that they would sacrifice themselves. Therefore, almost all of our participants appeared to know what was the "right" or moral thing to do, but it was only the strongly fused participants who actually endorsed doing it. This finding is consistent with research showing that empathic concern increases altruistic helping only through empathy's relation to perceived oneness (Cialdini et al. 1997). Moreover, it was not that strongly fused people lacked regard for their own lives. To the contrary, a follow-up study demonstrated that the presence of a concern with saving group members, rather than the absence of a concern with self-preservation, motivated strongly fused participants to endorse sacrificing themselves for the group.

Another follow-up experiment examined the thoughts and feelings of people while they were in the process of making moral decisions. To this end, we had people think aloud as they responded to a moral dilemma involving their in-group (the "summoning the death train" scenario described earlier). Analyses of audio recordings of their verbalizations suggested that for strongly fused participants, the thought of their compatriots being endangered triggered strong distress reactions. Specifically, as strongly fused participants navigated the psychological path leading to possible endorsement of self-sacrifice, they displayed signs of tension, distress, and anxiety. In contrast, weakly fused persons appeared to be relatively unemotional and were instead compelled by utilitarian considerations ("better that I should die rather than five others") in the (relatively rare) instances in which they endorsed self-sacrifice.

The results of yet another experiment tested our assumption that the immediate, emotional responses of strongly fused persons shape their responses to the dilemma (see also Suter and Hertwig 2011). We reasoned that if the immediate reactions of strongly fused persons are critical, hurrying the responses of strongly fused persons should increase self-sacrifice. In contrast, among weakly fused persons, self-sacrifice presumably grew out of conscious reflection. As a result, hurrying the responses of weakly fused persons decreased self-sacrifice (Swann et al. 2014b). When under time pressure, 100 percent of participants were willing to self-sacrifice, up from 67.9 percent in the control condition. By contrast, only 6.7 percent of weakly fused participants were willing to self-sacrifice under time pressure, down from 48.5 percent in the control condition.

A final set of studies indicated that identity fusion influenced the degree to which participants were sensitive to identity-based versus utilitarian manipulations. We discovered that the moral decisions of strongly fused persons were acutely sensitive to activating their personal identity (by having them write down what they were personally like) but immune to a utilitarian manipulation (whether self-sacrifice would save five as compared to one in-group member). That is, activating the personal identities of strongly fused persons by asking them to think about their personal selves increased their endorsement of self-sacrifice, but the utilitarian manipulation had no impact. In contrast, among weakly fused persons, activating their personal identities had little impact on their endorsement of self-sacrifice but telling them that self-sacrifice would save five as compared to one person increased their endorsement rates. This supports the notion that in their moral decision-making, weakly fused individuals rely on utilitarian thinking while strongly fused individuals rely on intuitive, identity-driven reasoning in the group-related moral decision-making paradigms we have investigated.

What processes give rise to the reflexive reactions that motivate strongly fused persons to endorse self-sacrifice? As noted earlier, one key factor appears to be the tendency for strongly fused individuals to think of the group as family. There is a widely shared consensus in many if not most societies that family ties transcend all other human connections. For example, the US legal system accords privileged status to family loyalty by stipulating that spouses cannot be compelled to testify against each other in court. As such, when a moral dilemma involves the in-group "family," fused persons become highly emotional—much as if their own personal fate were on the line. These emotional reactions motivate them to display unquestioned allegiance to those considered family (that is, "family comes first," "family is special"). The allegiance of strongly fused persons to in-group members makes perfect sense when the group includes genetically related kin. After all, evolutionary theory states that people should sacrifice themselves for genetic relatives—those for whom they develop familial ties (Hamilton 1964). Less obvious is why strongly fused individuals in large groups would make the ultimate sacrifice for group members with whom they have little or no contact. How can such "extended fusion" exert powerful effects in the absence of relational ties?

We proposed that individuals who are strongly fused project the relational ties they feel toward group members they *do* know onto those with whom they are unacquainted, thereby transforming members of large groups into fictive kin (Vázquez et al. In press). To test this reasoning, we conducted a series of studies. In the initial investigation, we asked participants if they would be willing to die to save members of their family versus members of relatively large groups (for example, nation or religious group). Regardless of the country they came from, family was the group for which most people endorsed dying (Swann et al. 2014a).

Even so, additional studies demonstrated that people project familial ties onto large, heterogeneous groups insofar as they believe that group members share core characteristics. That is, encouraging strongly fused persons to focus on shared core characteristics of the people from their country increased their endorsement of extreme sacrifices for their country (Swann et al. 2014a). Respondents from China, India, the United States, and Spain displayed this effect whether the core characteristics were biological (genes) or psychological (core values). We also discovered that priming shared core values increased the feeling of oneness among strongly fused group members and these feelings, in turn, mediated the influence of fusion on endorsement of extreme sacrifices for the country. Apparently, for strongly fused persons, recognizing that other group members share core characteristics makes larger extended groups seem "family-like" and worth dying for.

Clearly, researchers are just beginning to understand the relationship of identity fusion to moral behavior. One of the most important remaining issues is how strongly fused persons walk the line between loyalty to the group as a whole versus to the individual members of the group. For example, analyses have attributed the Enron debacle to the enormous pressure that management placed on employees to conform to group norms of turning a blind eye to malpractice and irregularities (for example, Sherman 2002, Tourish and Vatcha 2005). Conceivably, fused individuals may resist such pressure from individual group members and blow the whistle in an effort to do what they believe is in the best interest for the group as a whole. For example, in one study university undergraduates witnessed a fellow student engage in unethical conduct that was personally beneficial to the student but might damage the university (Buhrmester 2013). Those who were strongly fused to the group reported the unethical conduct to university officials. Nevertheless, at other times strongly fused persons may engage in morally dubious progroup action such as covering up evidence of wrongdoing (Besta, Gómez, and Vázquez 2014). One key moderator may be whether the moral action (reporting wrongdoing) risks destroying the "family" that strongly fused persons are striving to protect. If so, this phenomenon may offer an important example of the ways in which contextual factors (that is, the anticipated consequences of various actions for the fate of the in-group) interact with characteristics of identity (for example, strength of fusion) to shape moral action.

Concluding Thoughts: Transcending Tribalism

The case studies of transsexuals with which we opened this chapter offered compelling testimony to the sacrifices people make in the service of their identities. It also provides an example as to how fusion may thus satisfy several crucial needs at once, including personal agency (Ryan and Deci 2000), affiliation and belongingness (Baumeister and Leary 1995, Williams 2007), and meaningfulness and epistemic certainty (Kruglanski et al. 2002). Fusion may help individuals pursue a meaningful existence and a high quality of life (Jetten, Haslam, and Haslam 2011, Jones and Jetten 2011). In these ways and related ones, fusion may represent an asset to individuals as well as the group. Nevertheless, the powerful connections people form to social groups can be costly. Witness, for example, the carnage wrought by terrorists and modern warfare.

While it is overly simplistic to argue that fusion is either good or bad (see also Putnam 2000), we believe that social connections become costly primarily when the quest for feelings of oneness fosters exclusiveness rather than inclusiveness. While exclusivity may seem to some to be inevitable, other researchers have argued that humans actually have an intrinsic motivation to expand the self to include others (Aron and Aron 2001). In addition, advocates of social categorization theory (Turner et al. 1987) extended social identity theory by adding the superordinate category of the self as a human being (Hornsey 2008) to personal identity and social identity (cf. Gaertner and Dovidio 2000). We would add that it is not only membership in the human category that is important but also the idea that the personal self remains a potent force even as it becomes one with the superordinate human group.

Fusion may take two forms: local and extended. Local fusion refers to oneness with small groups comprising members we know well, while extended fusion refers to oneness with much larger groups of people, the vast majority of whom we can never meet. While local fusion and extended fusion are certainly not mutually exclusive (and may in fact be mutually reinforcing), fusion with humanity is the ultimate form of extended fusion. An unexplored but intriguing possibility is that the desire for oneness becomes more and more expansive, with fusion with humanity being the logical extreme. As the group becomes more expansive and divisions less salient, individuals may find that they have fewer reasons to fight with one another and more reason to work together toward mutually beneficial goals. In fact, this was partly the logic behind the creation of supranational entities like the United Nations and the European Union. While such institutions are far from perfect and the notion of oneness based on our shared humanity may seem idealistic, striving for fusion with humanity seems a more likely pathway to peace than fueling the flames of tribalism. This makes it a worthy, if lofty, goal.

References

Aron, A., and E. N. Aron. 2001. "The Self Expansion Model of Motivation and Cognition in Close Relationships and Beyond." In *Blackwell Handbook in Social Psychology*, vol. 2, *Interpersonal Processes*, edited by M. Clark and G. Fletcher, 478–501. Oxford: Blackwell.

Baumeister, R. F., and M. R. Leary. 1995. "The Need to Belong: Desire for Interpersonal Attachments as a Fundamental Human Motivation." *Psychological Bulletin* 117:497–529. doi:10.1037/0033-2909.117.3.497.

Besta, T., A. Gómez, and A. Vázquez. 2014. "Readiness to Deny Group's Wrongdoing and Willingness to Fight for Its Members: The Role of Poles' Identity Fusion with the Country and Religious Group." *Current Issues in Personality Psychology* 2:49–55.

Blum, L. 2017. "One-to-One Fellow-Feeling: Universal Identification and Oneness, and Group Solidarities." In *Oneness in Religion, Philosophy, and Psychology*. New York: Columbia University Press.

Buhrmester, M. D. 2013. "Understanding the Cognitive and Affective Underpinnings of Whistleblowing." PhD diss. http://repositories.lib.utexas.edu/bitstream/handle/2152/21278/BUHRMESTERDISSERTATION-2013.pdf?sequence=1.

Cashman, G. F. 2014. *Jerusalem Post*. December 15. www.jpost.com/Israel-News/Two-almost-simultaneous-events-related-to-Operation-Protective-Edge-384699.

Cialdini, R. B., S. L. Brown, B. P. Lewis, C. Luce, and S. L. Neuberg. 1997. "Reinterpreting the Empathy-Altruism Relationship: When One Into One Equals Oneness." *Journal of Personality and Social Psychology* 73:481–94.

Gaertner, S. L., and J. F. Dovidio. 2000. "Reducing Intergroup Bias: The Common Ingroup Identity Model." Philadelphia: Psychology.

Graham, J., J. Haidt, S. Koleva, M. Motyl, R. Iyer, S. P. Wojcik, and P. H. Ditto. 2013. "Moral Foundations Theory: The Pragmatic Validity of Moral Pluralism." *Advances in Experimental Social Psychology* 47:55–130. doi:10.1016/B978-0-12-407236-7.00002-4.

Greene, J. D., L. E. Nystrom, A. D. Engell, J. M. Darley, and J. D. Cohen. 2004. "The Neural Bases of Cognitive Conflict and Control in Moral Judgment." *Neuron* 44:389–400.

Greene, J. D., R. B. Sommerville, L. E. Nystrom, J. M. Darley, and J. D. Cohen. 2001. "An fMRI Investigation of Emotional Engagement in Moral Judgment." *Science* 293:2105–08. doi:10.1126/science.1062872.

Haidt, J., and S. Kesebir. 2010. "Morality." In *Handbook of Social Psychology*, 5th ed., edited by S. Fiske, D. Gilbert, and G. Lindzey, 797–832. Hoboken, NJ: Wiley.

Hamilton, W. D. 1964. "The Genetical Evolution of Social Behavior: I." *Journal of Theoretical Biology* 7:1–16. doi:10.1016/ 0022-5193(64)90038-4.

Hornsey, M. J. 2008. "Social Identity Theory and Self-Categorization Theory: A Historical Review." *Social and Personality Psychology Compass* 2:204–22. doi:10.1111/j.1751-9004.2007.00066.x.

Iyer, A., J. Jetten, and A. S. Haslam. 2012. "Sugaring O'er the Devil: Moral Majority and Group Identification Help Individuals Downplay the Implications of In-Group Rule-Breaking." *European Journal of Social Psychology* 42:141–49. doi:10.1002/ejsp.864.

James, W. 1890. *The Principles of Psychology*. New York: Dover. doi:10.1037/11059-000.

Janis, I. L. 1972. *Victims of Groupthink: A Psychological Study of Foreign-Policy Decisions and Fiascoes*. Oxford: Houghton Mifflin.

Jetten, J., C. Haslam, and S. A. Haslam, eds. 2011. *The Social Cure: Identity, Health and Well-Being*. Hove, UK: Psychology.

Jones, J. M., and J. Jetten. 2011. "Recovering from Strain and Enduring Pain: Multiple Group Memberships Promote Resilience in the Face of Physical Challenges." *Social Psychological and Personality Science* 2 (3): 239–44.

Junger, S. 2010. *War.* London: Fourth Estate.

Kohlberg, L. 1969. "Stage and Sequence: The Cognitive-Developmental Approach to Socialization." In *Handbook of Socialization Theory and Research*, edited by D.A. Goslin. Chicago: Rand McNally.

Kruglanski, A. W., J. Y. Shah, A. Pierro, L. Manetti. 2002. "When Similarity Breeds Content: Need for Closure and the Allure of Homogeneous and Self-Resembling Groups." *Journal of Personality and Social Psychology* 83:648–62. doi:10.1037/0022-3514.83.3.648.

Putnam, R. 2000. *Bowling Alone: The Collapse and Revival of American Community.* New York: Simon and Schuster.

Rand, D. G., and Z. G. Epstein. 2014. "Risking Your Life Without a Second Thought: Intuitive Decision-Making and Extreme Altruism." *PloS One* 9:e109687. doi:10.1371/journal.pone.0109687.

Ryan, R. M., and E. L. Deci. 2000. "Self-Determination Theory and the Facilitation of Intrinsic Motivation, Social Development, and Well-Being." *American Psychologist* 55:68–78. doi:10.1037/0003-066X.55.1.68.

Sheikh, H., J. Ginges, and S. Atran. 2013. "Sacred Values in the Israeli-Palestinian Conflict: Resistance to Social Influence, Temporal Discounting, and Exit Strategies." *Annals of the New York Academy of Sciences* 1299:11–24.

Sherman, S. 2002. "ENRON." *Columbia Journalism Review* 40:22–28.

Skitka, L. J. 2010. "The Psychology of Moral Conviction." *Social and Personality Psychology Compass* 4:267–81.

State of Israel, Ministry of Defense. 2010. *Private Epstein, Shlomo ("Mumah").* www.izkor.gov.il/HalalKorot.aspx?id=46037.

Suter, R. S., and R. Hertwig. 2011. "Time and Moral Judgment." *Cognition* 119:454–58.

Swann, W. B., Jr., M. Buhrmester, A. Gómez, J. Jetten, B. Bastian, A. Vázquez, . . . A. Zhang. 2014a. "What Makes a Group Worth Dying For? Identity Fusion Fosters Perception of Familial Ties, Promoting Self-Sacrifice." *Journal of Personality and Social Psychology* 106:912–26.

Swann, W. B., Jr., A. Gómez, M. D. Buhrmester, L. López-Rodríguez, J. Jiménez, and A. Vázquez. 2014b. "Contemplating the Ultimate Sacrifice: Identity Fusion Channels Pro-Group Affect, Cognition, and Moral Decision-Making." *Journal of Personality and Social Psychology* 106:713–27.

Swann, W. B., Jr., A. Gomez, A. Vázquez, E. Gomez-Gil, S. Segovia, B. Carrillo, and A. Guillamon. 2015. "Fusion with the Cross-Gender Group Predicts Genital Sex Reassignment Surgery." *Archives of Sexual Behavior.* doi:10.1007/s10508-014-0470-4.

Swann, W. B., Jr., J. Jetten, A. Gómez, H. Whitehouse, and B. Bastian. 2012. "When Group Membership Gets Personal: A Theory of Identity Fusion." *Psychological Review* 119:441–56. doi:10.1037/a0028589.

Tajfel, H. 1970. "Experiments in Intergroup Discrimination." *Scientific American* 223:96–102.

Tajfel, H., and J. C. Turner. 1979. "An Integrative Theory of Intergroup Conflict." In *The Social Psychology of Intergroup Relations*, edited by W. G. Austin and S. Worchel, 33–47. Monterey, CA: Brooks-Cole.

Tourish, D., and N. Vatcha. 2005. "Charismatic Leadership and Corporate Cultism at Enron: The Elimination of Dissent, the Promotion of Conformity and Organizational Collapse." *Leadership* 1:455–80.

Turner, J. 1996. "Henri Tajfel: An Introduction." In *Social Groups and Identities: Developing the Legacy of Henri Tajfel*, edited by W. P. Robinson. UK: Hartnolls.

Turner, J. C., M A. Hogg, P. J. Oakes, S. D. Reicher, and M. S. Wetherell. 1987. *Rediscovering the Social Group: A Self-Categorization Theory*. Oxford: Blackwell.

Vázquez, A., A. Gómez, J. R. Ordoñana, and B. Paredes. In press. "From Interpersonal to Extended Fusion: Relationships Between Fusion with Siblings and Fusion with the Country." *International Journal of Social Psychology*.

Watson, J. B. 1913. "Psychology as the Behaviorist Views It." *Psychological Review* 20:158–77. doi:10.1037/h0074428.

Whitehouse, H., B. McQuinn, M. D. Buhrmester, and W. B. Swann, Jr. 2014. "Brothers in Arms: Libyan Revolutionaries Bond Like Family." *PNAS* 111:17783–85.

Williams, K. D. 2007. "Ostracism." *Annual Review of Psychology* 58:425–52. doi:10.1146/annurev.psych.58.110405.085641.

CHAPTER 17

TRIBALISM AND UNIVERSALISM

Reflections and Scientific Evidence

DIMITRI PUTILIN

All things are linked with one another, and this oneness is sacred; there is nothing that is not interconnected with everything else. For things are interdependent, and they combine to form this universal order.

—Marcus Aurelius, *The Spiritual Teachings of Marcus Aurelius*

Tribalism is built deeply into the human psyche, as evidenced by Henri Tajfel's research using the so-called minimal group paradigm. In Tajfel's experiments, participants arbitrarily divided into two groups immediately behaved preferentially toward members of their own group and discriminated against the other group (that is, the outgroup). When choosing between maximizing the benefit to the in-group or maximizing the difference in benefit between the in-group and the outgroup, participants chose the latter—even at the cost of reducing their own group's rewards. Moreover, they expected outgroup members to behave as they did. Tajfel (1978, Tajfel et al. 1971) identified two motives at play in his studies, which he termed "groupness" and "fairness." In allocating resources between groups, "groupness" (that is, in-group favoritism) dominates; fairness comes into play primarily when allocating resources within one's in-group.

Given how little it takes to initiate intergroup conflict, it is perhaps unsurprising that much of history has been characterized by violence and oppression manifested in war, slavery, and countless other forms of strife and exploitation. Nearly twenty-five hundred years ago, as the Athenian army was invading the island nation of Melos and offering the Melians enslavement as a compromise, the Melians appealed to the famously democratic Athenians' sense of fairness and justice. When the Athenian generals replied, "you know as well as we do that right [that is, justice], as the world goes, is only in question between equals in power, while the strong do what they can and the weak suffer what they must," they could have been summarizing Tajfel's conclusions: fairness is reserved for the in-group; domination and exploitation for the outgroup (Thucydides 2009).

If the problem of group relations is ancient and global, so is the proposed solution. Writing nearly two and a half millennia ago, the Chinese sage Mozi considered selfishness and partiality, that is, tribalism, to be the cause of all conflict, and argued that regarding others as self is the antidote:

> If there were universal mutual love in the world, with the love of others being like the love of oneself, would there still be anyone who was not filial? If one were to regard one's father, older brothers and ruler like oneself, how could one not be filial towards them? . . . Would there still be thieves and robbers? If there were regard for the households of others like one's own household, who would steal? If there were regard for the persons of others like one's own person, who would rob? Therefore, thieves and robbers would also disappear. Would there still be great officers who brought disorder to each other's households or feudal lords who attacked each other's states? If there were regard for the households of others like one's own household, who would bring about disorder? If there were regard for the states of others like one's own state, who would attack? Therefore, there would be no instances of great officers bringing disorder to each other's houses or of feudal lords attacking each other's states. If the world had universal mutual love, then states would not attack each other, households would not bring disorder to each other, there would be no thieves and robbers, and rulers, ministers, fathers and sons could all be filial and loving. In this way, then, there would be order in the world.
>
> (Mozi 2013, 14.3)

The appeal of these ideas has not diminished in the intervening centuries. The contemporary philosopher Peter Singer argues that inclusivity of moral regard is the essence of moral progress, inevitably culminating in the ascription of equal weight to our own interests as well as those of all other sentient beings: "The circle of altruism has broadened from the family and tribe to the nation and race, and we are beginning to recognize that our obligations extend to all human beings. The process should not stop there. . . . The only justifiable stopping place for the expansion of altruism is the point at which all whose welfare can be affected by our actions are included within the circle of altruism" (2011, 120). Like Kant and Rawls before him, Singer suggests that impartiality is the only standpoint from which truly ethical decisions can be made, overcoming our natural tendencies to favor ourselves and the in-groups that serve as extensions of our individual identities:

> When my ability to reason shows me that the suffering of another being is very similar to my own suffering and matters just as much to that other being as my own suffering matters to me, then my reason is showing me something that is undeniably *true*. . . . The perspective on ourselves that we get when we take the point of view of the universe also yields as much objectivity as we need if we are to find a cause that is worthwhile in a way that is independent of our own desires.
>
> (2000, 238)

The universalist perspective advanced by Singer and Mozi stands in direct conflict with the automatic (that is, instinctive) tribalist tendencies documented by Tajfel. Whereas the inclusivity motive promotes cooperation and mutual support and respect, tribalism reserves these goods predominantly for the inner circle from which others may be excluded.

Between the age of Mozi and Singer's modern treatment of the same idea, its central aspect—impartially valuing the well-being of all others as one's own, also known as the Golden Rule—has found its way into religions and philosophies around the world. It is sometimes stated as "do unto others as you would have them do unto you." A naïve interpretation of this might suggest that the rule is advocating imposing one's desires upon others; however, that is a mistake. Interpreted that way, the rule becomes self-contradictory. People generally do not enjoy having others' wishes imposed on them, in contravention of their own desires, and therefore by doing to others what I would wish done to myself in the concrete sense (for example, feeding BBQ chicken to a vegetarian, if that happens to be what I am craving at that moment), I am in fact *not* doing to others what I would wish done to myself (respecting their wishes and preferences). Rather, the rule is more reasonably, commonly, and coherently interpreted as advocating for equality in the consideration that we show to ourselves and to others—a counterweight to our natural self-favoring tendencies.

The importance ascribed to the Golden Rule across cultures is attested to not only by its ubiquity, but also by the fact that we are able to be aware of its ubiquity today: the mere fact that it has been preserved in oral and written traditions for millennia and into the present day. In many of these traditions, the Golden Rule has been emphasized as the very essence of right conduct and moral thought. To cite only a few examples, the Talmud records Rabbi Hillel

(110 BCE–10 CE) as stating, "What is hateful to yourself, do not do to your fellow man. That is the whole of Torah and the remainder is but commentary" (quoted in Allinson 2003). In the Bible, Jesus emphasizes the Golden Rule as one of the two core commandments: "'Love the Lord your God with all your heart and with all your soul and with all your mind.' This is the first and greatest commandment. And the second is like it: 'Love your neighbor as yourself.' All the Law and the Prophets hang on these two commandments" (Matthew 22:37–40). It was emphasized in ancient Rome by Epictetus ("What you shun enduring yourself, attempt not to impose on others"; 1935) and when Confucius was asked for the single word that can guide one's entire life, the Golden Rule was his reply. Recognizing it as a shared thread in the diversity of the world's religious thought, the World Congress of Religions in 1993 produced a statement that reads, in part, "There is a principle which is found and has persisted in many religious and ethical traditions of humankind for thousands of years: What you do not wish done to yourself, do not do to others. Or in positive terms: What you wish done to yourself, do to others! This should be the irrevocable, unconditional norm for all areas of life, for families and communities, for races, nations, and religions" (Council for the Parliament of the World's Religions 1993, 23).

Clearly, the idea of equal concern for oneself and all others as the guide to life has historically been a tremendously compelling one. But is it plausible as a practical guide to behavior—is it realistic? In this essay, I will address some of the psychological facilities and barriers that are relevant to the demands of attempting to live in accord with the Golden Rule. First on the agenda: the Golden Rule asks us to care about others' needs equally with our own. But are we psychologically capable of truly caring about another's needs at all? This simple question has been a surprisingly contentious one in both psychology and philosophy. I shall summarize the relevant empirical evidence next.

Evidence for Altruism

Defining altruism as "a motivational state with the ultimate goal of increasing another's welfare," Daniel Batson (2011) sought to determine whether it is a psychological possibility using a series of more than thirty cleverly designed experiments. He recognized that it is not sufficient to observe overt helping behavior, however heroic or self-sacrificial it may appear, in order to determine whether its motive is altruistic or selfish. Fortunately, if one suspects that helping behavior is selfishly motivated, it is possible to discern this by varying the contingencies under which the behavior occurs. Altruistic behavior is costly, and if a given self-focused goal is its true objective, then providing a less costly means of achieving the same self-focused goal should decrease the rates of helping. On the other hand, helping (or having someone else help) is the only means to attain the altruistic goal of improving the other's well-being, and therefore the ready availability of easier ways to reach self-focused goals should not deter altruistically motivated individuals from helping.

Batson further proposed that empathic concern—the emotional state associated with valuing the well-being of another who is in distress—produces altruistic motivation. The expectation, then, is that people experiencing empathic concern would be more likely to help whether or not an easier way to obtain self-focused rewards is available, whereas those not experiencing empathic concern would be more likely to take the easier, nonhelping path toward self-focused goals.

To test this hypothesis, Batson identified the self-focused goals that could motivate helping behavior. These included (a) reduction of aversive inner states, that is, the sadness or distress one feels when confronted with another's distress, (b) avoidance of negative evaluation by others for not helping, (c) avoiding negative self-evaluation (for example, pangs of conscience, guilt, having acted inconsistently with one's positive self-image), and (d) seeking rewards for helping, which could be material rewards, social rewards (praise, honor), or self-rewards (satisfaction, sympathetic joy).

It is important to note that the core issue at stake is not whether these benefits can occur as a result of helping—clearly, they can. Rather, it is whether at the time one chooses to help, she or he is motivated by those consequences—or by the aim of reducing another's distress. The two motives are not incompatible: one can both wish to help and wish to feel good as a consequence of that helping, for example. However, as long as altruistic motivation is present—whether alone or together with self-focused motives—it can only be satisfied by helping, and not by any easier route if that route only provides self-focused benefits.

To appreciate the research evidence, it is helpful to consider the procedural details of Batson's approach. A sample experiment consisted of participants observing an interview with "Katie Banks," a senior at their university, who described her struggle to support her surviving younger siblings after the death of their parents and sister (Batson et al. 1988). Participants were randomized into two groups, one of which was told to watch the interview while imagining how Katie feels (in order to induce empathic concern), while the other was told to remain objective and detach from Katie's feelings. Both groups were randomized further: half were told that most of the previous students watching the interview did not help Katie, while the other half were told that the majority had chosen to help. This served to manipulate perceived behavior norms, providing the former group but not the latter with justification for not helping. Helping opportunities required investment of hours of one's time or, in other studies, willingness to take the place of another participant (actually a research confederate) who was apparently receiving painful electric shocks.

If empathic concern produces altruistic motivation, then the group undergoing empathic concern induction should be less sensitive to the presence or absence of justification for not helping. Within this group, both the high-justification and low-justification subgroups would be expected to help at high and roughly equal rates. In contrast, the group told to remain objective would be more likely to avoid helping when provided with a justification for doing so (that is, the information that the majority of previous participants had not helped), but the rates of helping would be higher if the justification for not helping was withheld. In other words, their behavior would be under the control of manipulated norms rather than the altruistic goal of alleviating Katie's distress.

The results precisely conformed to the prediction. In the objective/high-justification group, only 15 percent of participants helped Katie, compared to 55 percent in the objective/low-justification group. However, in the empathic concern conditions, the presence of justification had little impact: 60 percent and 70 percent of participants in the two justification conditions elected to help her, with no significant difference between the two values. These results supported the hypothesis that empathic concern produced a genuine desire to benefit Katie, rather than the self-serving motivation of avoiding guilt and shame.

Although this study alone does not address all the possible self-serving motives for helping behavior, Batson's systematic approach across the spectrum of such goals has consistently found support for the empathy-altruism hypothesis. Across these studies, researchers varied the following conditions designed to differentiate between altruistic and self-focused motivations (Batson 2011, Batson, Lishner, and Stocks 2015):

1.   Ease vs. difficulty of escape from exposure to suffering. If participants' goal is to escape the personal distress caused by witnessing the suffering of the victim, then they will be less likely to help when escape is easy than when escape is more difficult. This indeed occurred in the low empathic concern condition, but there were no differences in the high empathic concern condition, where high rates of helping occurred regardless of ease of escape.

2.   Justification for ineffective helping. If one's motive for helping is egoistic, having an excuse for having failed to help effectively should produce minimal distress, whereas not having an excuse (and thus being culpable) should produce significantly greater distress. If the motive is altruistic, learning that one has failed to help should produce increased distress regardless of excuse availability, and this is what occurred.

3.   Public knowledge (others know) vs. private knowledge (no one except the participant can possibly know) whether any given participant helped. In these tests of social rewards or punishments as the nonaltruistic motive for

helping, the highest rates of helping occurred in the high empathic concern, private condition. This once again supports the altruistic explanation.

4. Expectation of positive feedback about one's helping efforts. If helping behavior is motivated by the expectation of empathic joy due to having helped, helping should be greater when positive feedback will be provided than when it is not. If the motivation is altruistic, high levels of helping attempts should occur regardless of feedback, which was the result.

5. After hearing about someone's need, learning that the need either continues to exist or not, and that one will be able to offer help or not. If one is motivated by the rewards of helping, reduced positive affect should occur if one is blocked from offering help, whether or not the target remains in need. If the motive is altruistic, reduced positive affect should occur only if the need for help remains, as was found to be the case.

6. Availability of alternative means of improving one's own mood. Following the induction of low mood, participants were led to either expect a subsequent induction of positive emotions or not. They were then offered the opportunity to help a target in need. Self-focused motivation for helping (as a means to improve one's mood) would predict that inducing empathy would produce little to no increase in helping (a costly behavior) among participants expecting their mood to be improved at no cost. Altruistic motivation predicts that inducing empathy will increase helping, which is what occurred.

To summarize this literature, Batson and his colleagues have successfully demonstrated that, when exposed to a person in need and instructed to consider how that person is feeling, people are more likely to value his or her well-being as an end in itself, to experience the emotional state of empathic concern, and to be increasingly willing to engage in helping behavior at a cost to themselves. Providing an easier means of obtaining self-focused goals makes little to no impact on their rates of helping. In contrast, the availability of alternative ways to obtain self-focused benefits has a substantially stronger impact on the helping rates of individuals who are not experiencing empathic concern. Batson (2011) concludes that humans are, indeed, capable of altruism.

Altruism or Oneness?

In follow-ups to Batson's research, Cialdini et al. (1997) and Maner et al. (2002) showed that the degree of kinship or perceived similarity of the participant to the victim simultaneously increased empathic concern, helping behavior, and what they called "oneness." "Oneness" was also found to be a stronger predictor of helping behavior than empathic concern. Arguing that "oneness" represented a loss of distinction between the participant and the victim, they concluded that by helping the victim the participants were in fact selfishly helping themselves.

There are several problems with this logic; to understand them, it is necessary to understand the relevant measure. "Oneness" was measured by a combination of two items: participant's degree of willingness to describe the victim and self using the word *we*, and the Inclusion of Self in Other (IOS) scale—a series of seven increasingly overlapping sets of two circles from which the participant must choose the set that most accurately represents the relationship between self and other (Aron, Aron, and Smollan 1992). Both were measured on a scale from one to seven.

To claim, as Cialdini, Maner, and their colleagues do, that participants became unable to distinguish between themselves and the victim requires reaching significantly beyond the evidence. The creators of the IOS describe it as "a single item, pictorial measure of closeness," and for conceptual clarity I will retain that term rather than "oneness," which carries different connotations. Even in the condition where the highest degree of perceived oneness was obtained, the average level ($M = 3.98$, $SD = 1.52$) corresponded to the midpoint of the scale—the set of IOS circles with only approximately 35 percent overlap, and moderate (again, midpoint of the scale) willingness to use "we" to describe participant and victim (Maner et al. 2002). This suggests that participants saw both the majority of their own identity and that of the victim as unique and separate from whatever it was they shared in common.

Furthermore, even if Batson's perspective-taking instructions led participants to see the victim's problems as to some extent their own, a very important asymmetry persists. Whereas the actual victim has no choice but to deal with the aversive circumstances in which she finds herself, the potential helper (that is, the participant) has the ability to walk away from the problem, avoiding both the emotional costs and burdens of helping. There is an inherent difference in perspectives between the two people, and nothing in the data or common human experience suggests that the participant becomes so merged with the victim that he or she ceases to perceive choosing to take care of one's individual self rather than the victim as an option—in fact, a substantial percentage of participants in all conditions chose to do just that by refusing to help.

Batson also notes that even when empathic concern is activated, people nonetheless weigh costs to self as part of the decision on whether to help—and it is this ability to continue experiencing ourselves as emotionally connected to yet distinct from the victim that facilitates (that is, lowers the barrier to) but does not compel altruistic action (Batson 2011). For the drowning man, struggling to survive is not an option; for the bystander, however merged, the choice remains—emotional closeness does not rule out selfishness. Thus, it appears that whatever type of self-other merger or closeness occurs as a consequence of Batson's perspective-taking instructions, it does not preclude altruism. The participants experiencing closeness with the victim are in fact electing to remain and to help, and—as the data suggest—are guided in part by the altruistic goal of benefiting the victim when they do.

Although Maner, Cialdini, and colleagues' conclusion that altruism does not exist is not borne out by the data, their work does highlight the inherently tribalistic nature of our default programming as human beings, if our instincts can be considered as such. The closer we feel to another person, the more readily we are predisposed to help them; psychological closeness (sometimes called psychological distance) appears to reduce our automatic selfish bias toward strangers (for a review, see Davis 2015). Why should that be the case? By exploring this question, we may gain useful insight into the compatibility of our instinctive behavioral inclinations with the Golden Rule.

Closeness, Interdependence, and the Origins of Tribalism

Psychologically, emotional closeness signals interdependence. The prototypical example is the bond of emotional closeness between mother and child, but closeness exists to varying degrees in all forms of kin and nonkin relationships. From the perspective of evolution, genetic kinship is not necessary in order for a relationship to be interdependent and valuable for one's survival and reproductive success: in human societies, friendships are also essential, and we have evolved the capacity to feel emotionally close to both friends and relatives. In other words, we feel close to people whose well-being is relevant to our own happiness and perhaps even survival—whose well-being we ignore only at our own risk and detriment. To quote the country singer Tracy Byrd, "when mama ain't happy, ain't nobody happy." Therefore it makes perfect sense from the perspective of evolutionary theory that closeness with others should automatically predispose us to take their needs seriously and to act altruistically toward them. Consistent with this, emotional closeness was found to mediate the relationship between genetic relatedness and altruism (Korchmaros and Kenny 2001).

In other words, although the motivation produced when we feel empathic concern for another is altruistic—that is, focused on increasing their well-being, rather than attaining some benefit for oneself—such motivation is most likely to arise when we are exposed to the suffering of another with whom we are interdependent: a member of the in-group. Our altruistic intentions are most likely to arise spontaneously when having them is to our long-term advantage. In this way, nonpsychopathic humans are biologically prepared to form successful interdependent social units such as the family or the tribe, with the degree of automatic concern for the needs of its other members being proportionately related to our degree of emotional closeness with them.

Conversely, it makes a great deal of evolutionary sense for this altruistic machinery to fail to engage as readily when interacting with distant others—those categorized into the outgroup. There are several reasons for this. First, if one is not interdependent with certain others, sharing scarce resources with them may disadvantage the survival of one's own group and, ultimately, one-self. Second, whereas emotional closeness signals the availability of reciprocal help when needed, there is no such expectation of reciprocity when dealing with the outgroup. Resources allocated to outgroup members are, in this sense, wasted.

The third and final reason I shall propose is that outgroups represent a potential source of valuable resources for the in-group. These can be obtained through cooperation (for example, trade) or force; however, experiencing auto-matic empathic concern for the outgroup would inhibit one of these two strat-egies. Without the possibility of discounting the outgroup members' emotions and needs—what has become known as dehumanization and infrahumaniza-tion in the group conflict literature—the exploitation of outgroup members for the in-group's benefit is severely impeded, creating an adaptive disadvantage compared to other groups without such qualms. As a consequence, the empathic concern that automatically predisposes humans to altruism when interacting with close others is reduced or even reversed when encountering members of the outgroup (Cikara, Bruneau, and Saxe 2011, Tajfel 1971).

However, this status quo is neither inevitable nor ideal. A trait evolved under one set of conditions may become maladaptive when environmental circum-stances change. Among geographically isolated tribes, viewing contact with other groups primarily in terms of potential benefit or threat to the in-group may have been a viable survival strategy. However, given today's unprecedented levels of global connectedness and interdependence, continued tribalism reflects a situation akin to a family in which every member is only out for them-selves and on guard against the others. The constant friction thus produced exacts ongoing costs in stress and mutual harm that threaten to overwhelm the potential gains of this approach.

It appears that evolution has provided us with a mechanism for genuinely caring about others—but has restricted it primarily to close others by default. This serves to decrease conflict within groups, but may increase the potential for conflict between them. In a massively cross-cultural program of research, Schwartz has identified a circumplex of values present in all societies (Schwartz and Bilsky 1990, Schwartz et al. 2012). Although a full review of the theory is beyond the scope of this essay, two values it describes are directly relevant: benev-olence and universalism. Benevolence captures concern for the well-being of close others, while universalism reflects the same concern directed toward all.

On the surface, it may appear that both of these values are entirely prosocial; however, they differ in one crucial respect. Whereas benevolence allows for the existence of outgroups that may enter into moral consideration to varying degrees or not at all, universalism (in its full expression) does not. As a result, benevolence may facilitate intergroup conflict by transforming individual conflict tendencies into group conflict tendencies—for example, "an attack on one of us is an attack on all of us." In contrast, universalism eliminates the concept of an outgroup entirely, and with it, the possibility of perceiving an exploitable or expendable other.

Our evolutionary disinclination to altruism with outsiders can be further strengthened by what I shall call misguided pragmatism. When choosing whether to cooperate or compete with another, we are essentially playing a variant of the Prisoner's Dilemma, an economic game that illustrates why people who don't know each other's intentions often do not cooperate, even when it would be in their mutual best interest to do so. It boils down to fear of having one's good intentions or generosity exploited by a more selfish other. Until everyone cooperates, it seems disadvantageous to risk being the first. As a reminder, Tajfel found that arbitrary division of participants into groups was sufficient to produce expectations of receiving unfair treatment from the outgroup, which undoubtedly makes a cautious and suspicious approach to interacting with outgroup members seem particularly prudent.

In summary, our automatic cognitive processes effortlessly divide the world into "us" and "them," *and* make us less likely to feel empathic concern when faced with the suffering of distant others. This is experienced as differences in the natural inclination to help (or avoid harming) them. A second, conscious cognitive process further reinforces this pattern by making partiality appear to be the rational and optimal approach to dealing with uncertainty regarding others' intentions—that is, "a healthy dose of suspicion."

The Way Out of Tribalism

Fortunately, there is a way out of this predicament. Writing more than a century ago, William James observed that our relationship with objects in our world (objects in the psychological sense, including people, physical objects, and even intangibles) can vary along a continuum of antipathy or indifference on the one hand, and a merging of the object into our self on the other; varying degrees of psychological distance or closeness lie in between:

> The Empirical Self of each of us is all that he is tempted to call by the name of me. But it is clear that between what a man calls me and what he simply calls mine the line is difficult to draw. We feel and act about certain things that are

ours very much as we feel and act about ourselves. Our fame, our children, the work of our hands, may be as dear to us as our bodies are, and arouse the same feelings and the same acts of reprisal if attacked. And our bodies themselves, are they simply ours, or are they us? Certainly men have been ready to disown their very bodies and to regard them as mere vestures, or even as prisons of clay from which they should someday be glad to escape.

We see then that we are dealing with a fluctuating material. The same object being sometimes treated as a part of me, at other times as simply mine, and then again as if I had nothing to do with it at all.

(James 2012)

If, as James states, our degree of closeness with others can fluctuate significantly over time, and if we may be able to exercise conscious control over how close or distant we feel toward others, then we may be able to redirect our evolved, tribalistic altruism toward more universally inclusive ends.

Evidence certainly points in this direction: we do have the capacity to include others in self, and to adjust the degree of that relationship. This is the case even in our relationship with that most essential core of what James calls our "empirical self": the body. We have the capacity to experience foreign objects as parts of ourselves—but also to disown and wish to annihilate our own flesh. The so-called rubber hand illusion—where a healthy participant's real hand is hidden from view and replaced with a visible fake rubber hand and both hands are stroked simultaneously with a brush—shows that our brains possess the capacity to psychologically adopt an inanimate and unfeeling object. During the illusion, participants report and fMRI scans show a fear response when the rubber hand is threatened (Ehrsson, Spence, and Passingham 2004, Ehrsson et al. 2007). At the opposite end of the closeness continuum, chronic pain patients can perceive their affected limb as a foreign object, and express "a desperate desire to amputate [the affected] part despite the prospect of further pain and lack of function" (Lewis et al. 2007, 133). To quote one study participant, the afflicted body part is "just like this foreign body you were carrying around with you cause it didn't feel like it was part of you."

Our relationships with groups can also span the entire length of the closeness continuum. The tendency to automatically devalue the outgroup was described earlier; yet we are also able to reverse this by incorporating outgroups into the in-group via recategorization—a change of group boundaries whereby "us" and "them" become "we" (Gaertner et al. 1989). This process reduces all forms of in-group bias, leading former outgroup members to be evaluated as more likeable, valuable, cooperative, and honest, and improving the emotional tone of interpersonal interactions. Through recategorization, the benefits of in-group membership—including greater automatic empathy and altruism—become available to former outgroup members.

Identity fusion—"a visceral sense of union, or oneness, with a group" (Talai-far and Swann in this volume)—has been another fruitful conceptual frame-work for understanding how humans relate to groups. Strong identity fusion can motivate the sacrifice of one's life for the group's benefit—yet through our conscious choices we can separate even from groups we've been fused with from birth. A dramatic (although anecdotal) example of this, Megan Phelps-Roper had been indoctrinated from birth into the ideology of the Westboro Baptist Church—an organization combining three powerful inducements to fused in-group loyalty: family, religion, and a cult-like demand for obedience under the threat of severe punishment or excommunication (Chen 2015). Cre-ation of family-like bonds may explain the strength of commitment to the group in fused individuals; but in Phelps-Roper's case, the group actually *was* the family (Whitehouse et al. 2014). She had participated in the group's picket-ing activities since age seven and describes having enthusiastically worked to spread its message on the Internet. Despite this, Phelps-Roper was able to con-sciously and successfully choose to divest herself from the group (that is, her family) and its ideology.

Yet, despite this evolutionary heritage, we are—or, rather, can choose to be—masters of how our instincts and evolved proclivities are to be channeled. Batson's experiments spanning four decades have demonstrated that the sim-ple instruction "Try to imagine how the person who is being interviewed feels about what has happened and how the events have affected her life. Try to feel the full impact of what this person has been through and how she feels as a result" triggers the biological program of empathic concern and altruism—even when the victim is a stranger in a relative outgroup, such as a rival college (Batson et al. 1988, 61). A simple instruction to remain objective had the oppo-site effect. The striking differences in the helping rates between the perspective-taking and objective conditions obtained in these studies demonstrate not only the existence of the two programs, but also our capacity to engage them at will, should we so choose.

The Benefits of Universalism

Even if we can, why would we want to engage empathy universally, if the prag-matic considerations discussed earlier suggest that it could place us at a com-petitive disadvantage? This raises the question of what is truly pragmatic (that is, benefits ourselves) versus what only appears to do so. The benefit derived from a good—its utility—can be divided into two distinct types, which I will call subjective (or psychological) utility and objective (or material) utility. Subjective utility is measured in the units of happiness: the psychological goods that directly impact the quality of lived experience. Objective goods (for instance, wealth), on the other hand, produce their impact indirectly through subjective goods. The variables that impact one of the two types of utility may or may not impact the other, or might impact them in opposite directions. For example, a promotion at work may significantly increase objective utility in the form of higher pay, increasing the availability of subjective goods in the form of expensive positive experiences that are now more affordable and available to be indulged in with greater frequency (for example, gourmet restaurant meals or vacations). However, if the new job carries a stronger negative impact on subjective utility in the form of greater stress and conflict, the overall change to well-being could be negative. Focusing solely on objective utility when assessing the job change would produce misleading conclusions in this scenario. The recognition of the imperfect correlation between objective and subjective utilities has led to the establishment of alternative means of measuring progress to the traditional GDP, such as Bhutan's Gross National Happiness index, and to calls for a more widespread adoption of such measures by the United Nations (UN General Assembly 2011). Therefore, when discussing pragmatic considerations, it is necessary to be explicit with regard to the type of utility in question.

Objective utility follows the simple math of zero-sum relationships between using one's resources to benefit self, or others, that is, spending a dollar on someone else, in the absence of an expectation of reciprocity, is equivalent to losing a dollar's worth of utility to oneself. It is increasingly clear, however, that this model entirely fails to consider the very different mathematics governing the psychological realities of subjective utility: by benefiting others, we derive benefit for ourselves. For instance, Anik and colleagues (2009) and Dunn, Aknin, and Norton (2008) found that spending money on oneself had no correlation with happiness, whereas spending money on others increased it. Notably, people intuitively expect the opposite to be the case (Dunn, Aknin, and Norton 2008). These relationships were found in diverse cultures, across levels of income, and at ages as young as two. Objective and subjective utilities appear to be governed by different rules, and maximizing the former at the expense of the latter may produce a net decrease in the overall quality of life.

Following the Golden Rule may help to maximize subjective utility, and Putilin and Costanzo (2015) explored whether this might explain its ubiquity in world philosophies. Could it be that like the eye, which evolved independently in multiple unrelated organisms, the Golden Rule arose independently across cultures and civilizations because of its usefulness? Observing that the Golden Rule is most commonly embedded in religious teachings, we looked at the extent to which its perceived centrality to the faith of a given member of our combined sample of over five hundred Indian Hindus, Christians, Muslims, and Sikhs predicted various indicators of well-being.

As expected and regardless of the religion followed, the centrality of the Golden Rule (measured more broadly as concern for all others) consistently correlated with all other indicators in the direction of greater psychological and social health—the constellation of psychological benefits I refer to as "subjective utility." The more strongly participants endorsed that caring for all others was central to their religion, the more likely they were to enjoy higher levels of happiness and well-being, to experience more meaning and purpose in their lives, and to have more satisfying, supportive relationships. They also were more likely to have better self-reported physical and mental health, including fewer days on which physical or mental problems interfered with their daily lives. They felt and expressed more gratitude to others, and—consistent with our characterization of the inclusivity of care perspective as inhibiting cycles of aggression—were less willing to seek revenge against those who had harmed them in the past. Their attitudes toward themselves were more harmonious, characterized by higher self-compassion—a trait associated in other studies with less anger, anxiety, narcissism, and negative affect, and more positive affect and optimism (for a review, see Barnard and Curry 2011). Notably, this occurred in India—a collectivist culture with rigidly defined hierarchical and in-group/outgroup boundaries, as exemplified by the caste system (Hofstede 2015). The effects were robust to controlling for socially desirable responding.

These results contribute to a broader literature demonstrating the benefits of prosocial attitudes and behaviors for emotional and physical health. For instance, a series of studies conducted by Jennifer Crocker identified two types of motivation: "egosystem" (for example, self-image) goals and "ecosystem," that is, compassionate, other-focused goals. Endorsement of egosystem motivation was associated with impoverished relationship quality, increased depression and anxiety, and lower psychological well-being; conversely, compassionate goals were associated with the opposite effects (Crocker and Canevello 2012). In another relevant program of research, Kasser and his colleagues have consistently found that self-focused, materialistic goals are associated with psychopathology and decreased well-being; these relationships have been most recently confirmed in a cross-cultural meta-analysis of 259 independent samples (Dittmar et al. 2014, Kasser 2011).

Ecosystem motivation may further contribute to subjective utility via the socially contagious nature of goals. Crocker and Canavello (2012) found that, over time, participants' endorsement of compassionate goals increased endorsement of compassionate goals by their relationship partners, and the opposite was true for egoistic goals. In this manner, compassionate attitudes not only benefit oneself and others directly, but also maximize the probability that compassionate behavior will be reflected toward oneself from one's immediate social environment.

Contrary to the predictions of economic theory, it appears that investing one's resources—whether psychological or material—into caring about others produces a wide range of benefits. Altruism may not be the optimal way of amassing material fortunes, but it provides wealth of a different kind. Therefore, rationing empathy in the way to which we are automatically predisposed by evolution may well be self-defeating rather than pragmatic in the sense of maximizing subjective utility. Surprisingly, altruism turns out to not be a sacrifice, despite being perceived as such in what is clearly a paradox of human cognition. Our intuitive blindness to the true state of things, in combination with the Western cultural bias toward valuing objective utility over subjective, may explain why it has taken psychology as a field more than one hundred years since its inception to discover that treating others well produces greater happiness than does treating ourselves well at others' expense.

Oneness in Its Full Manifestation

We have now gathered all the ingredients required to put the Golden Rule into practice, namely, the human capacity for altruism, the ability to choose whom to include in our circle of altruistic concern, the understanding of why we don't naturally do so with distant others, and both the capacity and reasons for shifting away from that default. In this final section, I will briefly share some thoughts on the manifestations of a universally inclusive perspective.

As the research we have reviewed suggests, oneness (that is, closeness) and altruism are directly linked. In our previously described study (Putilin and Costanzo 2015), we found that individuals who saw concern for all others as central to their religion and experienced high levels of well-being were also more likely to endorse statements such as "all life is interconnected" and "on a higher level, all of us share a common bond" (Piedmont 2001). Their universalism was also reflected in their view of God as having the same universally inclusive attitudes as themselves, as evidenced by their endorsement of "God loves, and wants the best, for every single living being" and disagreement with "God favors some countries over others."

Endorsement of these statements suggests a mindset where the circle of moral regard has been extended to all human beings. Just as closeness or merger with in-group others promotes altruism toward them, this universally inclusive attitude may naturally predispose individuals to make extraordinary moral commitments to promoting the rights of all others—and to do so using means that respect the rights of all involved. Consider the following quotations:

- "It really boils down to this: that all life is interrelated. We are all caught in an inescapable network of mutuality, tied into a single garment of destiny. Whatever affects one directly, affects all indirectly" (Washington 1986).

- "How can there be room for distinctions of high and low where there is this all embracing, fundamental unity underlying the outward diversity? . . . The final goal of all religions is to realise this essential oneness" (Miller 2007).

Both statements were spoken by individuals who dedicated their lives to—and died in the service of—their efforts to help others: Rev. Dr. Martin Luther King, Jr., and Mahatma Gandhi. Their statements echo Rousseau's description of "some great souls, who consider themselves as citizens of the world, and forcing the imaginary barriers that separate people from people, after the example of the Sovereign Being from whom we all derive our existence, make the whole human race the object of their benevolence" (1761, 139).

Dr. King in particular was prone to stating that oneness of all mankind was a religious truth, and proceeded to explore the ways in which this truth could be realized in America in the 1950s. This was not a small task, given the obstacles he faced in the form of segregation along racial lines, and opposition to any alteration to the status quo that existed. However, he strongly opposed any efforts, advocated by others, to use violence as the means to achieving the goal of equality. Similarly, Mahatma Gandhi stated, "violent means will bring violent self-rule." Gandhi chose on four separate occasions to fast unto death, if necessary, to promote equality or to prevent others from using violence on his behalf, or on behalf of the causes he championed. The extraordinary resolve displayed by these individuals in both their commitment to the fight for equality of all and their rejection of seemingly more expeditious aggression in that fight may be a natural logical consequence of seeing all as part of self.

These individuals' oneness-based strategies stand in stark contrast with the typical, tribalism-based approaches to conflict. Even when engaged in the service of ideals such as justice, freedom, or democracy, their usual pattern is to identify the perpetrator and the victim, disempower or eliminate the perpetrator, often by force, and aid the victim. More often than not, however, Gandhi's words of warning resonate loudly as the oppressed become the oppressors, and violent means initiate cycles of violence. This dynamic has been witnessed, to cite just a few examples, in Germany's resentment at the indignities imposed on it after World War I, leading to the rise of fascism and World War II, in the brutality of the Russian revolution of 1917 and the succeeding repressions, and the origin of the Khmer Rouge in response to the tyranny of Lon Nol. In the criminal system, the "us vs. them" perspective produces retributive justice as a natural consequence, where the criminal "other" is dehumanized and brutalized. Equally naturally, the idea of restorative justice follows from the inclusive "us and them" view.

We have summarized evidence that suggests that we all have the capacity for oneness—that is, for seeing others not as indifferent objects or resources, but as parts of a larger Self whose needs and wishes deserve consideration. This suggests that the gulf between ourselves and the exceptional individuals mentioned earlier may not be as unbridgeable as it appears at first glance: it may be one of degree, rather than kind. Whereas the majority of mankind extends the self in a limited fashion, they chose to exclude no one.

Whether or not oneness exists as some sort of metaphysical reality (as described in Eastern religions, for example) I cannot say, and will leave, with the utmost respect, as a question of discussion for my philosopher colleagues. Concepts do not have to be objectively real to have psychological potency, however; to a significant degree, our choices of volitional behavior are motivated not by objective reality, but by our subjective and imperfect mental models of it, which include not only our perceptions and interpretations of facts but also affective and value dimensions. As a psychological reality, oneness appears to naturally engender the empathic concern and perspective-taking that increase altruism and allow no one to be perceived as merely an obstacle or an exploitable resource.

References

Allinson, R. 2003. "Hillel and Confucius: The Prescriptive Formulation of the Golden Rule in the Jewish and Chinese Confucian Ethical Traditions." *Dao* 3 (1): 29–41. doi:10.1007/BF02910339.

Anik, L., L. B. Aknin, M. I. Norton, and E. W. Dunn. 2009. "Feeling Good About Giving: The Benefits (and Costs) of Self-Interested Charitable Behavior." *Harvard Business School Marketing Unit Working Paper* (10–012).

Aron, A., E. N. Aron, and D. Smollan. 1992. "Inclusion of Other in the Self Scale and the Structure of Interpersonal Closeness." *Journal of Personality and Social Psychology* 63 (4): 596.

Barnard, L. K., and J. F. Curry. 2011. "Self-Compassion: Conceptualizations, Correlates, and Interventions." *Review of General Psychology* 15 (4): 289.

Batson, C. D. 2011. *Altruism in Humans*. Oxford: Oxford University Press.

Batson, C. D., J. L. Dyck, J. R. Brandt, J. G. Batson, A. L. Powell, M. R. McMaster, and C. Griffitt. 1988. "Five Studies Testing Two New Egoistic Alternatives to the Empathy-Altruism Hypothesis." *Journal of Personality and Social Psychology* 55 (1): 52.

Batson, C. D., D. Lishner, and E. Stocks. 2015. "The Empathy-Altruism Hypothesis." In *The Oxford Handbook of Prosocial Behavior*, edited by D. A. Schroeder and W. G. Graziano, 259–81. Oxford: Oxford University Press.

Batson, C. D., K. Sager, E. Garst, M. Kang, K. Rubchinsky, and K. Dawson. 1997. "Is Empathy-Induced Helping Due to Self-Other Merging?" *Journal of Personality and Social Psychology* 73 (3): 495.

Chen, A. 2015. "UNFOLLOW: How a Prized Daughter of the Westboro Baptist Church Came to Question Its Beliefs." *New Yorker.*

Cialdini, R. B., S. L. Brown, B. P. Lewis, C. Luce, and S. L. Neuberg. 1997. "Reinterpreting the Empathy-Altruism Relationship: When One Into One Equals Oneness." *Journal of Personality and Social Psychology* 73 (3): 481.

Cikara, M., E. G. Bruneau, and R. R. Saxe. 2011. "Us and Them: Intergroup Failures of Empathy." *Current Directions in Psychological Science* 20 (3): 149–53.

Council for the Parliament of the World's Religions. 1993. *A Global Ethic: The Declaration of the Parliament of the World's Religions.* New York: Continuum.

Crocker, J., and A. Canevello. 2012. "Consequences of Self-Image and Compassionate Goals." In *Advances in Experimental Social Psychology*, vol. 45, edited by D. Patricia and P. Ashby, 229–77: Amsterdam: Academic.

Davis, M. H. 2015. "Empathy and Prosocial Behavior." In *The Oxford Handbook of Prosocial Behavior*, edited by D. A. Schroeder and W. G. Graziano, 282. Oxford: Oxford University Press.

Dittmar, H., R. Bond, M. Hurst, and R. Kasser. 2014. "The Relationship Between Materialism and Personal Well-Being: A Meta-Analysis." *Journal of Personality and Social Psychology* 107 (5): 879–924.

Dunn, E. W., L. B. Aknin, and M. I. Norton. 2008. "Spending Money on Others Promotes Happiness." *Science* 319 (5870): 1687–88.

Ehrsson, H. H., C. Spence, and R. E. Passingham. 2004. "That's My Hand! Activity in Premotor Cortex Reflects Feeling of Ownership of a Limb." *Science* 305 (5685): 875–77.

Ehrsson, H. H., K. Wiech, N. Weiskopf, R. J. Dolan, and R. E. Passingham. 2007. "Threatening a Rubber Hand That You Feel Is Yours Elicits a Cortical Anxiety Response." *Proceedings of the National Academy of Sciences* 104 (23): 9828–33.

Epictetus. 1935. *The Golden Sayings of Epictetus.* Translated by H. Crossley. London: Macmillan.

Gaertner, S. L., J. Mann, A. Murrell, and J. F. Dovidio. 1989. "Reducing Intergroup Bias: The Benefits of Recategorization." *Journal of Personality and Social Psychology* 57 (2): 239.

Hofstede, G. 2015. "The Hofstede Centre: India." http://geert-hofstede.com/india.html.

James, W. 2012. *The Principles of Psychology.* New York: Dover.

Kasser, T. 2011. "Cultural Values and the Well-Being of Future Generations: A Cross-National Study." *Journal of Cross-Cultural Psychology* 42 (2): 206–15.

Korchmaros, J. D., and D. A. Kenny. 2001. "Emotional Closeness as a Mediator of the Effect of Genetic Relatedness on Altruism." *Psychological Science* 12 (3): 262–65.

Lewis, J. S., P. Kersten, C. S. McCabe, K. M. McPherson, and D. R. Blake. 2007. "Body Perception Disturbance: A Contribution to Pain in Complex Regional Pain Syndrome (CRPS)." *PAIN* 133 (1): 111–19.

Maner, J. K., C. L. Luce, S. L. Neuberg, R. B. Cialdini, S. Brown, and B. J. Sagarin. 2002. "The Effects of Perspective Taking on Motivations for Helping: Still No Evidence for Altruism." *Personality and Social Psychology Bulletin* 28 (11): 1601–10.

Miller, J. P. 2007. *The Holistic Curriculum.* Toronto: University of Toronto Press.

Mozi. 2013. *The Book of Master Mo.* Translated by I. Johnston. London: Penguin.

Piedmont, R. L. 2001. "Spiritual Transcendence and the Scientific Study of Spirituality." *Journal of Rehabilitation* 67 (1): 4.

Putilin, D., and P. Costanzo. 2015. "The Golden Rule Ethic, Its Measurement, and Relationships with Well-Being and Prosocial Values Across Four Religions in India." PhD diss. http://hdl.handle.net/10161/10492.

Rousseau, J. J. 1761. *A Discourse Upon the Origin and the Foundation of the Inequality Among Mankind.* London: Dodsley.

Schwartz, S. H., and W. Bilsky. 1990. "Toward a Theory of the Universal Content and Structure of Values: Extensions and Cross-Cultural Replications." *Journal of Personality and Social Psychology* 58 (5): 878.

Schwartz, S. H., J. Cieciuch, M. Vecchione, E. Davidov, R. Fischer, C. Beierlein, . . . M. Konty. 2012. "Refining the Theory of Basic Individual Values." *Journal of Personality and Social Psychology* 103 (4): 663–88.

Singer, P. 2000. *Writings on an Ethical Life*. 1st ed. New York: Ecco.

——. 2011. *The Expanding Circle: Ethics, Evolution, and Moral Progress*. Princeton: Princeton University Press.

Tajfel, H. 1978. *Differentiation Between Social Groups: Studies in the Social Psychology of Intergroup Relations*. London: Academic.

Tajfel, H., M. G. Billig, R. P. Bundy, and C. Flament. 1971. "Social Categorization and Intergroup Behaviour." *European Journal of Social Psychology* 1 (2): 149–78.

Thucydides. 2009. *The History of the Peloponnesian War*. Translated by R. Crawley. Boston: Digireads.com.

UN General Assemby, 65th Session. 2011. Resolution 65/309. *Happiness: Towards a Holistic Approach to Development*. www.un.org/Docs/journal/asp/ws.asp?m=A/RES/65/309.

Washington, J. M., ed. 1986. *A Testament of Hope: The Essential Speeches and Writings of Martin Luther King, Jr.* San Francisco: Harper and Row.

Whitehouse, H., B. McQuinn, M. Buhrmester, and W. B. Swann. 2014. "Brothers in Arms: Libyan Revolutionaries Bond Like Family." *Proceedings of the National Academy of Sciences* 111 (50): 17783–85.

CHAPTER 18

TWO NOTIONS OF EMPATHY AND ONENESS

JUSTIN TIWALD

This essay is about the relations between two different types of empathy and two different conceptions of oneness. Roughly, the first type of empathy is what is sometimes called "other-focused" or "imagine-other" empathy, in which one reconstructs the thoughts and feelings that someone else has or would have. The second conception, "self-focused" or "imagine-self" empathy, is the sort of emotional attitude someone adopts when she imagines how *she* would think or feel were *she* in the other person's place. Some philosophers and psychologists have taken note of this distinction (Batson 2009, Darwall 2002). To my knowledge, none has linked them with one of the more important reemerging religious and philosophical issues of the day, which has to do with the ethical significance of seeing oneself as part of a larger whole, or its proper role in moral motivation and other-directed moral concern. As it happens, there are some long-overlooked materials in neo-Confucian philosophy that attend closely to these very linkages, drawing out the morally salient differences between self- and other-focused empathy in light of their implications for the virtue of benevolence, understood by many mainstream neo-Confucians as including or causing a feeling that one is related to others as though different parts of the same body. Here I will unearth some of the most important ideas and arguments in this debate, fill in some gaps in the arguments, and draw out their moral implications.

The philosopher who makes most explicit the connections between the feeling of oneness and the two kinds of empathy is Zhu Xi朱熹 (1130–1200), who believes, in the final analysis, that other-focused empathy is more virtuous or "benevolent" (*ren* 仁) than self-focused empathy, in large part because the latter tends to undermine a sense of oneness with others. But Dai Zhen戴震 (1724–77), ever the critic of orthodox neo-Confucianism, makes a powerful case for self-focused empathy, and I hope to show that it fits well with a conception of oneness that is implicit in his own understanding of virtue and human relationships.

Zhu Xi's Conception of Oneness

Regarding oneself as "being one with a larger whole" can be construed in a number of different ways. I will start with the construal presupposed by Zhu Xi, which he characterizes as "forming one body with Heaven, Earth, and the myriad things."[1] In the first instance this type of self-regard is about part-whole relations—virtuous people see themselves as parts alongside others, all of which belong to the same whole. But as Philip J. Ivanhoe has observed, the significance of seeing oneself as part of a larger whole depends greatly on the kind of connection between individual parts and between the parts and their whole. Parts of ecosystems aren't as closely connected as different parts of a body—ecosystems can survive the loss of individuals relatively unchanged, but a body is dramatically changed by the loss of its head or arms, and in some cases, obviously, it can't survive without them (Ivanhoe 2015). Another indicator of closeness in part-whole relations is the degree to which parts are constituted by their wholes. We might say that the very nature or core significance of a living heart is the part it plays in supporting the body to which it pumps blood, whereas the role that a rock on Mars plays in supporting life on earth is peripheral. I take Zhu Xi to be suggesting that by the lights of the benevolent person, his connection to others is much stronger, more closely approximating the relationship between the hands and eyes of the same body. On Zhu's view, and on most mainstream neo-Confucian views, our relationship to the cosmos and its many constituents is much stronger and more intimate than it appears, being more family-like or body-like than we assume, which implies that we have stronger moral obligations than it otherwise seems (Chen 2010, 46–55).

By virtue of what circumstances, processes, or states of affairs can we regard ourselves as one with Heaven, Earth, and the myriad things? Zhu Xi thinks that contributing to and caring about what I'll call "widespread life production" is what makes us one with them, and thus warrants seeing oneself as one with them. There are two ideas at work in this. The first has to do with the role of making contributions to others or benefiting others. If I benefit the cosmos and its denizens, their welfare comes to depend more on me, and furthermore, the role that I play in sustaining their welfare becomes a core part of my self. The second idea is about the significance of life production in particular.

Contributions to the life, growth, and reproduction of others are more central and important than contributions to, say, their wealth or appearance.[2] For Zhu, it is also relevant that life is a good of this world, not a good that transcends this world or awaits us in the next life. By Zhu's lights, this sets his view apart from Buddhist ones, as it gets to the heart of what matters most for our welfare and continuity, and does not depend on speculative theories about nirvana and rebirth.[3]

The view that "being one" is closely related to caring about and contributing to widespread life production is not Zhu's alone. It is shared by a number of philosophers in the neo-Confucian tradition broadly construed. But the ways in which this sort of activity is related to oneness can vary. For Zhu, it is by virtue of caring and contributing in this way that we are one. A subtly different view says that this sort of caring and contributing is a natural consequence of being one, not oneness itself. Furthermore, the kind of care one has for widespread life production can vary: it can be primarily sensory, as when it pains me to see someone else in pain, or it can have more cognitive content, as when I also conceive myself as an extension of the person in pain and have some understanding of what unites us. Some neo-Confucian philosophers adopted these other positions, but Zhu rejected them, and it is useful to see why. In the interest of better understanding what motivates and justifies the notion of oneness that he adopts, and to indicate some of the richness of theories about oneness in the neo-Confucian era, I will briefly describe these two rival theories and explain why he dismissed them.

One rival view is that we become one with others by virtue of having certain immediate, ethical sensitivities to or awareness of (jue 覺) others. This can include sensitivities to others' interests or feelings, as when we feel joy at their success or pain at their suffering. It can also include sensitivities that reflect and reinforce our relationships with others, exemplified by feelings of respect for one's elder siblings or the natural desire to serve and care for one's parents.[4] On my reading of Zhu, he offers two notable arguments against this sort of account. First, Zhu assumes that we're capable of uniting not just with sentient things like human and nonhuman animals, but also with nonsentient parts of the grand environment like mountains. Zhu implies that the sensitivity theory excludes nonsentient things, which by his lights is both wrong and inconsistent with the views of Confucius himself.[5] Second, Zhu thinks that mere sensations are too superficial to sustain a durable sense of care for others, which is necessary for becoming one with them.[6] For Zhu, what provides the better foundation is the realization that all things essentially have the same nature (in a sense of "same" yet to be spelled out) and that this nature has to do with life production: it's in our shared nature to want to contribute to processes of living, growing, and procreation. This gives us a more robust root system from which to develop the virtue of benevolence and, by implication, the feeling of oneness. Among other things, it implies that it's natural for me to be one and contribute to the life-production of others, and developing this tendency comes naturally—not something that has to be forced.[7]

Another popular view in Zhu Xi's era is more mysterious, and perhaps best described as mystical. It holds that there is no particular content or way of spelling out how we are one with the world. Our oneness is a fact about us that we discover in ourselves, in our nature at its most tranquil moments, but not something we can articulate. Even to praise this state in ethical terms (for example, as being "good") mischaracterizes it.[8] Zhu thinks this puts the cart before the horse, presupposing that we are already one and therefore able to care and contribute in the right ways, when in fact it's the caring and contributing that makes us one.[9] Zhu also criticizes this account for providing too little guidance, for leading to confusion and recklessness, apparently because it says too little about the particular types of things we should realize and do in order to be one.[10] By contrast, Zhu's own view that we become one by contributing to widespread life production gives us a sense of what attitudes we ought to have (care for the life in others) and what we ought to do (promote birth, growth, and the preservation of life). Zhu also argues somewhat elliptically that the mystical account of oneness leads people to another error, which is "to regard other things as oneself" (*ren wu wei ji* 認物爲己).[11] It's not clear why this counts against the mystical view and not Zhu's own. Zhu himself also allows that we can form one body with others, so couldn't we level the same criticism against Zhu? My hunch is that Zhu is paying close attention to different ways and senses in which we could be one with other things, some of them apt and others not. I can share a mutual identity with, say, a monkey or tree, in roughly the same way that my eye and my hand share a mutual identity with each other—they're not numerically identical or qualitatively identical, but they belong to the same body. Perhaps Zhu's point is that his account provides enough content to help us see how we can be "one" in the sense of having a mutual identity but "not one" in the sense of being numerically and qualitatively distinct, whereas the mystical view tends to blur the latter distinctions.

Against Self-Abnegationist Conceptions of Becoming One

Although Zhu Xi generally condemns accounts of oneness that smack too much of Buddhism, there is at least one notable similarity with Chinese Buddhist explanations of how we attain a sense of oneness with others. We do so by putting the interests of others before our own, by eliminating self-centeredness or self-interest (*wusi* 無私).[12] Zhu realizes that this is a tall order, so he mitigates it somewhat: he says that we can't help but pursue the ends of self-serving desires that are basic and irrepressible, such as the desires for food, drink, and companionship, and he allows that we can want what's in our own interest for the sake of others, as when one seeks a well-compensated job in order to support one's needy parents. But presumably one shouldn't want an interesting career for one's own sake, and sometimes he suggests that we shouldn't desire, say, that our food and drink taste good.[13] In any case, no matter how much Zhu may carve out space for some self-interested desires, the more basic point is that he characterizes the achievement of "being one" with the world in self-abnegationist terms. On his view, attaining oneness with Heaven, Earth, and the myriad things requires that we eliminate attachments to one's own interests as such, a primarily subtractive project directed at oneself, rather than the more constructive, bi-directional project of building relationships in which one becomes more attached to others in light of the fact that contributing to their well-being tends to enhance one's own.

This brings us to the second philosopher featured in this chapter, Dai Zhen, an eighteenth-century Confucian thinker who made his name in part by criticizing Zhu Xi's philosophical views and interpretations of the Confucian canon. Dai shares Zhu's distaste for mystical accounts of oneness, and he agrees that we become one with others by playing a part in widespread life production. But his view stands apart from Zhu's in vital ways. For one thing, while Dai agrees that playing a part in life production is necessary to feel a sense of mutual identity with other things, he understands that part differently. He characterizes it as "mutual nourishment" and "mutual growth," proposing that we are united through relationships in which each party benefits from the other, and not exclusively through self-abnegation.[14]

A second point of departure has to do with the metaphysical picture that underwrites Zhu's notion of oneness. Zhu thinks that achieving oneness requires that we awaken to a certain profound connection between our nature and the nature of others. In an important sense, Zhu thinks, the innermost contents of our natures are actually the same. By discovering how other things work we find the same virtues and patterns or principles (li 理) of life-production that we already have in ourselves, fully formed. For example, we can see certain virtues at work in the behavior of ants, bees, trees, and people, and in written works like poetry, histories, and letters.[15] Because the patterns in all of these other things are the same as our own, when properly grasped we feel a deep resonance with them, as though we've discovered ourselves in them. Dai Zhen has no patience for this view. He thinks it implausible that these patterns are fully formed in our own nature, and a thing's nature, he argues, distinguishes it according to its own kind, which necessarily assumes that the natures of trees and oxen differ from our own.[16]

Dai tends to be suspicious of the language of oneness. He says that those who talk about "embracing the one" (bao yi 包一) or awakening to our oneness tend to assume that this is accomplished by eliminating desires.[17] But he espouses the view that we develop relationships of mutual fulfillment, which has certain formal similarities to Zhu Xi's understanding of achieving oneness. The formal similarities are these: (1) We come to be connected to the larger world by seeing ourselves as contributing to life production more generally. (2) Through mutual fulfillment we develop a sense of mutual identity, regarding ourselves as parts that fit naturally with others into a larger whole.[18] (3) Mutual fulfillment creates a deeper sense of attachment to others, which in effect helps us to see some of ourselves in others.[19] (4) The more we become attached, the more aware we become of our shared interests in living, developing, and self-preservation.[20]

Most scholars of Dai Zhen would be hesitant to say that he sees a conception of oneness as playing a strong role in ethics. More often they say that for him, in the respects that matter most, wholes are reducible to the sum of their parts. As Zheng Jixiong 鄭吉雄 puts it, Dai adopts a "the one of the many" (*duo zhi yi* 多之一) framework to explain part-whole relations, which assumes that the whole just consists of or is reducible to its various parts. More specifically, the defining features of the whole can be fully accounted for by appealing to the features of the parts that comprise it. Zheng appears to associate this view about defining features with a similar view about value: what's valuable for the whole is determined by what's valuable for the parts individually.[21] He contrasts all of this with a "the many of the one" (*yi zhi duo* 一之多) framework that he associates with Zhu Xi, the Cheng brothers, and Buddhists, according to which wholes are somewhat independent of their parts in the respects that mirror Dai's position (that is, in terms of their defining features and in terms of what's valuable for them).[22]

I think Zheng overstates Dai's aversion to the ethics of oneness. Much depends on what sort of reduction from whole to parts he has in mind. One option is what we could call summative reductionism, according to which we can determine how much good a certain state of the whole provides (say, the flourishing of a family, the thriving of a university) by adding up how much good it provides to its members. A second sort of reductionism has more metaphysical commitments, saying that there's no *subject* for which a state of affairs can be good above and beyond its members. Someone who embraces the second sort of reductionism would say, for example, that there is no such thing as "helping the family" independent of helping the individual members of the family, because the family just is its members. Someone who *denies* the second sort of reductionism might contend, in the manner of a feudal patriarch, that people should make sacrifices "for the family" that do not ultimately redound to the benefit of its members, perhaps for the sake of protecting the family's legacy at its members' expense. For lack of a better term, let us call this an ontological reductionism. There are other possible kinds of reductionism in play but these should be sufficient to show the limitations of Zheng's view.

Perhaps Dai thinks that the benefits derived from certain relationships—for example, more transactional business relationships or friendships of convenience—are just the sum of the benefits to their individual members. But I see no reason to think that he believes the good of more intimate or organically interrelated units, such as families or species, is mere sums of the good of individual members. Perhaps the most powerful evidence for this is his interest in life-continuity. It is good, he thinks, for types of living things to continue.[23] On the whole it is better that the human species exist centuries from now than vanish. No doubt this requires that we take some measures to ensure that distant future generations have a world on which they can survive, and it would be odd to say that this is only as good as the benefits it provides to us, the currently living. At best, those measures provide a little comfort to those who are future-oriented enough to care, which is unlikely to outweigh our pressing concerns about survival, shortages of food and water, and so on. Of course, one could argue that the continuity of the human species is good for the people who would eventually be born, but then we venture into the vexed territory of the moral claims of counterfactual people, territory that is better left alone. In any case, it seems a good bet that Dai would have no patience for it. The more elegant explanation is just that there's some good in continuing humanity that can't be fully accounted for by adding up the good of its members.

In light of this claim, it might be tempting to say that Dai also posits irreducible wholes in the ontological sense, that there is, for example, this thing we call the human species that can be made better or worse, independently of making individual human beings better or worse. I admit I'm not sure what Dai would say about this proposal. I think Zheng and other scholars of Dai Zhen are right to detect a kind of constitutional aversion to positing such entities. On the other hand, Dai is comfortable with the idea that the cosmos, Heaven and Earth, has a certain virtue (the virtue of ceaseless life production) and certain imperatives (*biran* 必然) of its own.[24] If he's comfortable with the idea that the cosmos has virtues and imperatives, it doesn't seem a great stretch to make it an irreducible subject of benefit and harm, something that can be made better or worse.

Zhu Xi's Two Kinds of Empathetic Concern

For present purposes, "empathy" refers to that which consists in reconstructing the salient features of another's psychological state, variously understood as something that one does in one's imagination, by simulation, or by vicarious experience of the other's thoughts and feelings—all overlapping permutations of what's sometimes called "perspective-taking." But most of the discussion will be about what I'll call empathetic *concern*, which consists of both the perspective-taking and care or concern for the person in question. We sometimes use empathy to understand or imagine what's going on inside other people's heads, so to speak, but without much concern about their welfare (consider an empathetic sadist).[25] Other terms are often used to refer to the sort of phenomenon I'm calling empathetic concern, including "sympathy," "sympathetic understanding," "compassion," and "pity." I've found that there is no consensus about how these terms are understood and distinguished in philosophy, psychology, or natural language. At present, the best we can do is define by stipulation and try our best to pick natural language terms that get the point across.[26]

Two of the founding figures of mainstream neo-Confucianism, the brothers Cheng Hao 程顥 (1032–85) and Cheng Yi 程頤 (1033–1107), were interested in the connections between the virtue of benevolence (*ren*) a certain kind of empathic state described in ancient texts as *shu* 恕. By their time, *shu* had long been associated with Confucius's formulation of the Golden Rule: "Do not do to others as one wouldn't want done to oneself."[27] On its face this description might appear to suggest that *shu* is just a decision procedure or principle of action, but most Confucians, including the Cheng brothers, also understood it as the emotional state or attitude that positions us to better understand and simulate the feelings of others in the first place. On most readings, that emotional attitude requires that we imagine what it is like to be someone else, such that we can know and simulate feelings that are more apt for the other's situation than one's own. For this reason, many have translated *shu* as "sympathy" or "empathy." As I will explain, however, the neo-Confucians tended to see it as empathy of a certain kind.

It is clear from the recorded conversations with the Cheng brothers that they saw *shu* as the means by which we can acquire the virtue of benevolence. But it's also clear that they saw it as deficient in crucial respects, so that it must be either superseded or transformed before one can have benevolence proper. On their view, *shu* is the method by which benevolence can be implemented (*ren zhi fang* 仁之方), and comes close to true benevolence (*jin hu ren* 近乎仁), but does not enable us to achieve a state of oneness, which they characterized as forming one body with Heaven, Earth, and the myriad things.[28] Multiple generations of disciples were intrigued by the suggestion that *shu* fell short of true benevolence, but there was not a great deal of consensus as to how and in what respects it fell short. The Cheng brothers evidently thought that true benevolence comes easily, whereas *shu* is, for the agents that adopt it, more like an imperative—"do not do to others what you do not desire for yourself"—and this implies that *shu* takes effort or feels forced.[29] But this didn't clearly or obviously explain what *shu* is, such that effort would be required (can't empathetic perspective-taking come effortlessly?), or why *shu* would inhibit or stand in the way of becoming one with the world.

Almost a century later, Zhu Xi came upon an interpretation of *shu* that seemed a promising explanation of how *shu*-type empathy differs from the virtue of benevolence, one that he thought wasn't explicitly articulated by the Cheng brothers but that was nevertheless consistent with their view.[30] In an earlier paper I reconstructed the main points of Zhu's interpretation by drawing on lessons and conversations recorded by his students.[31] To describe these findings in a nutshell, Zhu sees the principal difference between *shu* and proper benevolence as turning on the issue of how much it involves and depends on drawing inferences from one's own self—one's own feelings, dispositions, and experiences—in order to instantiate the appropriate empathetic feelings for the other. When we use *shu*, he suggests, we need to compare others to ourselves in order to elicit the right feelings and motivations. In the case of proper benevolence, this isn't required. Zhu sometimes elucidates this distinction by building on a famous passage from the *Analects*, which describes someone who, "desiring to establish himself, helps to establish others; desiring to succeed, helps others to succeed."[32] Here is how Zhu says that it works when using *shu*: "One takes [the feelings] that he finds nearby in himself and draws analogies to those of the other. . . . One desires to succeed, comes to fully understand that others also desire to succeed, and *only then* assists others to succeed."[33] And here is how it works for the benevolent moral agent: "Just by wanting to succeed, one helps others to succeed, and does so without applying any additional effort."[34]

In one of Daniel Batson's reviews of the psychological literature on empathy, he observes that researchers frequently conflate a number of different phenomena that sometimes go by that name. Two that he mentions are worth noting here: empathy as "imagining how another is thinking and feeling" and empathy as "imagining how one would think and feel in the other's place."[35] Batson credits Ezra Stotland for noticing the difference between these two forms, which the latter distinguished by coining the terms "imagine-other" and "imagine-self" to describe two kinds of perspective-taking.[36] Another psychologist who attends to the distinction is Martin Hoffman, who calls the first "other-focused" empathy and the second "self-focused" empathy.[37] Roughly, I take *shu* to be constituted in part by self-focused empathy and proper benevolence to replace self-focused empathy with other-focused empathy.

As mentioned earlier, Zhu's predecessors weren't decided about why *shu*, unlike benevolence, prevents or inhibits the feeling or state of forming one body with others. At the time that I wrote my article on Zhu's two types of empathy I could only answer speculatively. I think I may now have a better-informed answer, or at least a clearer picture of Zhu's answer (but hopefully both). As we have seen, neo-Confucians before Zhu thought that *shu* falls short of benevolence in part because it requires exertion. But the crucial issue for Zhu is not so much the fact that exertion is required, but the specific activity or function the exertion is applied to. Zhu says that the "point at which effort is applied" is when one exercises one's "ability to take [the feelings] that he finds nearby in himself and analogize them [to those of the other]."[38] Put more succinctly, it's the work of projecting ourselves into others that wearies us. My modest proposal is that Zhu believes that once we've started thinking about our own concerns and needs, we'll resist thinking about how others would feel when similarly situated. Having elicited concerns about oneself, it becomes a burden to care about others.

Martin Hoffman has studied a phenomenon that might seem to be a close approximation of the one that Zhu is concerned about. He describes a tendency in self-focused perspective-taking that he calls "egoistic drift." When subjects start to relate the experiences and concerns of others to their own, eliciting feelings about themselves, the "image" of the other person "fades away, aborting or temporarily aborting the empathic process" (2000, 56). I think Zhu has something different in mind. He's not worried that the image of the other will fade away. Rather, he's worried that we'll see the other's concerns as making demands on us, so that we'll start to see our interests as being at odds with theirs. When one starts to see one's own interests as being at odds with another's, one has already shut the door to oneness, and foreclosed the possibility of forming one body with the other.

Zhu makes other observations about *shu* that bear this out. For example, he says that when people apply *shu*, they act out of a sense of obligation or commitment. The obligation in question is the imperative to be "fair" (*ping* 平) to others, understood as giving each his or her appropriate share.[39] Here again the labor in *shu* appears to arise from the expectation that, having dwelled for a moment on one's own needs and interests, one then must take an interest in someone else's welfare.

Dai Zhen's Alternative

Dai Zhen openly embraces self-focused empathetic concern. Even paragons of benevolence must imagine themselves in the circumstances of others, asking questions like "what would *I* want?"[40] He explicitly rejects the view that *shu* must be superseded for full and proper benevolence, in direct opposition to theories of *shu* that date back to the Cheng brothers.[41] And he characterizes *shu* in terms of making inferences from oneself (especially one's own desires and needs) to others.[42]

To my mind, Dai offers powerful justifications for self-focused empathy. If we really want to use empathy to understand and be motivated to act upon the interests of others, we need to simulate not just their first-order desires for things like food and shelter, but their broader-scope and often higher-order desires that their lives go well in various respects. Being exposed to the elements on a winter night is bad, but not usually so agonizing as being exposed to the elements and thinking that one may never have warm shelter again, for we desire not just to be protected from the cold but to have the sort of life in which this hardship is rare. The fear of death itself may depend largely on such broader-scope, higher-order desires for one's own life-fulfillment as such. On my reading of Dai, he is making the claim that we can only empathize with these greater agonies if we can fully appreciate what it's like to want something— such as shelter or avoidance of premature death—for one's own sake, or for the sake of having a life that is reasonably good for oneself, and for that we need to imagine ourselves in the place of the other.[43] I also detect a worry in Dai that other-focused empathy, by itself, is a poor guarantor of the fairness (*ping*) that Zhu prizes.[44] When a person develops the habit of ignoring her own desires and concerns in deciding how she'll respond to others, she'll be predisposed to give her own interests very little weight by comparison.[45]

However, as we have seen, Zhu maintains that self-focused empathy is fundamentally flawed because, after considering one's own desires, one will see one's own interests as being at odds or in tension with the interests of others, so that one regards it as a burden to undergo the process of imagining oneself as the other, which makes it difficult (or perhaps impossible) to regard oneself as forming one body with them. Let me respond to this worry on Dai's behalf.

Zhu appears to believe that adopting another's point of view will necessarily or usually come as a burden to those who are dwelling on their own needs and interests. I'm not sure that this is right. Sometimes our own needs and interests converge with those of others, because we want what they want. Moreover, as we will see shortly, there are automatic processes by which we empathize with others in a self-focused or "imagine-self" way without really dwelling on our own needs and interests as such (see the discussion later on Hoffman and "scripts").

Perhaps Zhu would respond that "seeing how my interests converge" with someone else's interests falls short of a true feeling of oneness, because a true feeling of oneness consists in seeing the whole as being primary or more fundamental, maybe because the whole is ontologically irreducible to its parts. To this I say that it depends on the notion of oneness that we have in mind. Dai's notion of oneness as relationships of mutual fulfillment or mutual nourishment is consistent with both ways of thinking, in fact it requires both ways of thinking: I see myself as one with my family, but I wouldn't be able to appreciate how our relationships are mutually fulfilling unless I also saw each of us as individuals. Dai also thinks that the common bond achieved through relationships of mutual fulfillment makes other-directed care and action come more naturally and effortlessly, so that we're actually less inclined to feel tensions between our interests and theirs.[46] Here I think Dai would appeal to the psychological proposition that close attachment and the consequent tendency to see oneself in others are more likely than mere empathy to motivate altruistic behavior, a view defended by Cialdini, Brown, Lewis, Luce, and Neuberg.[47] But I am not certain. Dai tends to say that we see ourselves as *like* others, not *as* others.[48]

Perhaps the distinction between Zhu's and Dai's preferred variants of empathy has been drawn too sharply, and there are ways to make Dai's start to look like Zhu's. If Martin Hoffman is right, we often learn to empathize through perspective-taking, but after a while it becomes more automatic, so that we can model our feelings on another's situation without imagining things from her position. This begins at an early age, when parents ask questions like "how would you feel if someone made fun of your acne?" In Hoffman's nomenclature, we acquire "scripts" that make empathizing more effortless and less reliant on re-creating someone's point of view.[49] If this is accurate, then maybe the self eventually drops out of the well-developed moral agent's empathizing, so that she can feel a sense of unease just knowing that her behavior has shamed someone for features of his face or body without her putting herself in his shoes, in either the self-focused or the other-focused way.

I think Dai would readily concede that we often acquire scripts, and thus automatic empathizing processes, such that we can empathize without occurrent perspective-taking. In fact, I suspect that he took this into account, as I'll explain shortly. But this doesn't imply that self-focused empathy collapses into other-focused empathy. There are ways for different kinds of perspective-taking to frame and reinforce scripts. In fact, it's hard to imagine a sophisticated empathizer without framing and reinforcing. How we acquire scripts can affect the sort of feelings and attitudes it reproduces. Someone who has been teased specifically for having acne will likely better empathize, and feel the other's shame more acutely, because she has so often imagined herself in the other's place. Furthermore, although we may rely on scripts (or automatic processes) to do much of the work of routine empathizing, we still need to broaden, refine, and give more nuance to our empathy, and this requires that we regularly fall back on perspective-taking empathy. Perhaps I have a good sense of what it's like to be teased for acne, and this also gives me a sense of what it's like to be teased for mousy hair or freckled skin, but being teased for one's name is different, more appropriate to different sorts of shame and embarrassment of different intensities. In Dai's parlance, there are the kinds of moral deliberation where the situation is standard or routine and thus easily assessed, but frequently the situation varies from the standard, such that we need to stop and engage in discretion or "weighing" (*quan* 權) to reconsider how important or trivial some consideration in this variant situation is.[50] We have to engage in weighing to appreciate how and in what ways being teased about one's name is different from being teased about one's physical features, and I think for this weighing Dai assumes that we often need to turn back to nonautomatic, deliberate perspective-taking, with self-focused perspective-taking being preferred for its depth and richness of insight.

In fact, the phenomenon of empathic scripts can work in Dai's favor. As we saw, one of Zhu's objections to self-focused empathy is that it comes as a burden and an imperative, which comes about because concerning ourselves with the interests of others seems more demanding after we've put our own needs and desires in focus. But as Hoffman's work on scripts helps to show, not every instance of empathy—self-focused or otherwise—requires perspective-taking at all. Most sophisticated instances of empathy are informed by it, but quite often the occurrent process is automatic. I needn't recollect my years without romantic attachments to feel great sympathy for a forlorn friend, and that means that I can adopt a benevolent attitude toward the friend without internal resistance.

In conclusion, I have reviewed two ways of conceiving ourselves as being one with others and explored a long-neglected debate connecting these two ways to two different kinds of empathy. On Zhu Xi's view, regarding one's self and others as belonging to a larger whole requires other-focused empathy, and self-focused empathy inhibits that feeling of oneness. But Zhu presupposes a strong conception of oneness as mutual identity. We can see some of the weaknesses of Zhu's argument by developing an implicit conception of oneness in Dai Zhen, in which feelings of oneness are instantiated in relationships of mutual life-fulfillment, and by explicating Dai's arguments for self-focused empathy, which suggest both that self-focused empathy is more conducive to feelings of oneness and, just as importantly, that it isn't nearly as liable to Zhu's major objection to self-focused empathy—namely, that self-focused empathy makes it a burden to imagine oneself in another's circumstances. This is hardly the end of the debate, but I hope it is enough both to elucidate the tremendous importance of these connections between feelings of oneness and the two kinds of empathy, and to show that there are historical resources that address these issues with great subtlety, subtlety unmatched by contemporary treatments of the issue.

Notes

For their insightful feedback on an earlier draft of this essay I thank Philip J. Ivanhoe, Hagop Sarkissian, Eric Schwitzgebel, and the participants in the "International Conference on Oneness in Philosophy and Psychology" at City University of Hong Kong, May 2016.

1. Zhu 1986, 117 (*juan* 6) and 819 (*juan* 32).
2. "Life" and "life production" are translations of the Chinese character *sheng* 生, which refers to the state of being alive, birth, and growth or development.

3. The neo-Confucians in general, including Zhu Xi, often distinguished their views about the nature and sources of value from Buddhist views. In the eyes of neo-Confucians like Zhu Xi, one of the most succinct formulations of the difference between Buddhists and Confucians is to say that the Buddhists prized personal salvation and transcending the cycle of life and death, while the neo-Confucians instead prized "ceaseless life production" (*sheng sheng bu xi* 生生不息) (Tiwald 2018).

4. Zhu associates this account with a school of neo-Confucians descending from Xie Liangzuo 謝良佐 (1050–1120) (Zhu 1996, 3543–44 [cf. Chan 1963, 595–96]; Chen 2010, 67–71), although Xie himself used it primarily as an account of the virtue of benevolence and only occasionally associated it with achieving oneness (Chen 2010, 70). It also shares some resemblance to Cheng Hao's and Wang Yangming's views (see Ivanhoe 2002, 27–29).

5. Zhu 1996, 3544 (cf. Chan 1963, 596); *Analects* 6.21. As Owen Flanagan observes, there could well be advantages in thinking or hallucinating that nonsentient things have sentience. For example, this might be the best way to motivate ethical behavior toward the environment (see Flanagan's note on panpsychism, on p. 283, in his contribution to this volume). Zhu appears to think that we can be sufficiently motivated to care for the environment in the appropriate ways without this hallucination.

6. Zhu 1996, 3544 (cf. Chan 1963, 596); Zhu 1986, 478–79 (*juan* 20).

7. Zhu 1996, 3543–44 (cf. Chan 1963, 595–96); Chen 2010, 92–98.

8. This view is associated in Zhu's time with Buddhists and more Buddhistic Confucians like Yang Shi 楊時 (1053–1135). See Chen 2010, 83–116.

9. "Only after there is benevolence will there be [forming] one body with Heaven, Earth, and the myriad things" (Zhu 1986, 117 [*juan* 6]).

10. Zhu 1996, 3543–44 (cf. Chan 1963, 595–96).

11. Zhu 1996, 3544 (cf. Chan 1963, 596).

12. Zhu 1986, 117 (*juan* 6).

13. Chan 1989, 197–211.

14. Dai 2009a, 273–76 (*Mengzi Ziyi Shuzheng*, no. 10–11; cf. Ewell 1990, 146–61); Dai 2009b, 332 (*Yuanshan* 1.3). Dai also takes it for granted that there are other goods to be had. If relationships of mutual fulfillment are not available to us, for whatever reason, it would still make us better off to have more food and modest comfort for ourselves, but less so.

15. Zhu 1986, 161–75 (*juan* 10).

16. Dai 2009a, 294–96 and 302–03 (*Mengzi Ziyi Shuzheng*, nos. 21 and 27; Ewell 1990, 242–47 and 284–86).

17. See Dai's criticisms of Laozi and Zhou Dunyi in Dai 2009a, 274 (*Mengzi Ziyi Shuzheng*, no. 10; cf. Ewell 1990, 148).

18. Dai 2009a, 312 (*Mengzi Ziyi Shuzhen*, no. 32; cf. Ewell 1990, 325–26).

19. Dai 2009a, 284–85 (*Mengzi Ziyi Shuzheng*, no. 15; Ewell 1990, 199).

20. Dai 2009a, 293–96 (*Mengzi Ziyi Shuzheng*, no. 21; Ewell 1990, 240–47).

21. Zheng 2008, 38–39.

22. Zheng 2008, 38–41.

23. Dai 2009a, 311 (*Mengzi Ziyi Shuzhen*, no. 32; cf. Ewell 1990, 322).

24. Dai 2009a, 317 (*Mengzi Ziyi Shuzheng*, no. 36; cf. Ewell 353); Dai 2009b, 334 (*Yuanshan* 1.6).

25. Nussbaum 2001, 329–33.

26. One final clarification: We don't always need to reconstruct someone's actual psychological state in order to have adequate empathetic concern for her. It's often enough to imagine successfully how she *would* feel under certain circumstances, and sometimes

the best way to empathize with someone is by imagining a somewhat better-informed or idealized version of her. If Zhang goes about his days blissfully ignorant about the nasty and unfounded rumors circulating about him, there's not much empathetic concern in vicariously experiencing his blissful ignorance on its own.

27. *Analects* 15.24.
28. Cheng and Cheng 1981, 15 and 97 (*juan* 2A and 7). As Philip J. Ivanhoe has pointed out to me, it is telling that so many neo-Confucian philosophers think the basis of our unity with others should be conceived as a single body. A great deal of the conflict we feel with others arises from the fact that we are stuck in separate bodies, which leads us to attend to our own needs and regard the needs of others as extraneous.
29. Nivison 1996, 69–70.
30. Zhu 1986, 850–51 (*juan* 33).
31. Tiwald 2011b.
32. *Analects* 6.30.
33. Zhu 1986, 690 (*juan* 27, my emphasis). There is a worry here, because it seems that two people might have desires that are so fundamentally different that no analogies between them would be informative. I have responded to this problem on behalf of both Zhu Xi and Dai Zhen (Tiwald 2011b). Briefly, Dai tends to assume that the desires whose satisfaction matters most will necessarily have a close connection to birth, growth, and self-preservation—sufficiently close that astute and empathetic people can understand such desires even if they are not satisfied by exactly the same objects or states of affairs. One can know what it's like to want a great number of friends even if one only wants a few, assuming that all of these desires arise out of needs and interests in birth, growth, and self-preservation. Zhu is aware of this problem and proposes, intriguingly, that it applies to *shu* but not to benevolence proper. For more on this, see the discussion of what I call the "defective desires problem" in Tiwald 2011b, 667–69.
34. Zhu 1986, 846 (*juan* 33).
35. Batson 2009.
36. Stotland 1969.
37. Hoffman 2000.
38. Zhu 1986, 850–51 (*juan* 33). I have supplied "to those of another" because it is implied by the phrase "take [the feelings] that are nearby in oneself and analogize them," as Zhu makes clear elsewhere (Zhu 1986, 845 [*juan* 33]).
39. Zhu 1983 (*Daxue* 16); Zhu 1986, 364–65 (*juan* 16); Tiwald 2011b, 666–67.
40. Dai 2009a, 265–66 (*Mengzi Ziyi Shuzheng*, no. 2; cf. Ewell 1990, 106–09).
41. See Dai 2009a, 324–35 (*Mengzi Ziyi Shuzheng*, no. 41; Ewell 1990, 394–95), where Dai gives an alternative to the Cheng-Zhu interpretation (without naming them) of Mengzi's claim that "nothing comes closer in seeking benevolence" than "the vigorous application of *shu*" (*Mengzi* 7A26). Since the time of the Cheng brothers, mainstream neo-Confucians took the phrase "coming close" (*jin* 近) to indicate that *shu* falls short of proper benevolence and must ultimately be jettisoned or transformed (Cheng and Cheng 1981, 275–76 [*juan* 21]). Dai proposes that vigorous application of *shu* falls short insofar as one lacks the wisdom and strength of character to apply it reliably, suggesting that it merely needs to be enhanced and not superseded.
42. *Yi ji tui zhi* 以己推之 (Dai 2009a, 285 [*Mengzi Ziyi Shuzheng*, no. 15; Ewell 1990, 199]). Zhu marks the distinction between other-focused and self-focused empathy by describing self-focused as "inferring from the self" (*tuiji* 推己), a characterization of benevolence that Dai openly embraces (Tiwald 2011b).

43. Dai 2009a, 273 (*Mengzi Ziyi Shuzheng*, no. 10; Ewell 1990, 146–47); Tiwald 2011a. Perhaps this claim is too strong. There might be some routes—traveled by saints, for example—by which to arrive at a robust concern for others' homelessness or terminal illnesses even if one cares little about suffering from such things for her own sake. Even so, it likely requires psychological heroics to reach that sort of sainthood, and we would probably be right to suspect that they come at great cost to the saint's psychological health and well-roundedness of character.

44. Dai 2009a, 265–66 (*Mengzi Ziyi Shuzheng*, no. 2; cf. Ewell 1990, 106–9).

45. This alludes to another familiar fear about ethical prescriptions to see ourselves as part of a greater whole—at times the demands of the whole engulf the interests of their most righteous members.

46. Dai 2009a, 275–76 (*Mengzi Ziyi Shuzheng*, no. 11; Ewell 1990, 157–58).

47. Cialdini et al. 1997.

48. Dai 2009a, 285 (*Mengzi Ziyi Shuzheng*, no. 15; Ewell 1990, 199). I can't tell whether the procedure used by Cialdini et al. distinguishes between these two ways of conceiving the connection between ourselves and those to whom we are attached. To be sure, their *interpretation* of the evidence clearly does so distinguish them—they purport to study a phenomenon that they call "self-other merging."

49. Hoffman 2000, 159–64.

50. Dai 2009a, 321–23 (*Mengzi Ziyi Shuzheng*, no. 40; Ewell 1990, 384–88).

References

Batson, C. Daniel. 2009. "These Things Called Empathy: Eight Related but Distinct Phenomena." In *The Social Neuroscience of Empathy*, edited by Jean Decety and William Ickes, 3–16. Cambridge: MIT Press.

Chan, Wing-tsit. 1963. *A Source Book in Chinese Philosophy*. Princeton: Princeton University Press.

——. 1989. *Chu Hsi: New Studies*. Honolulu: University of Hawaii Press.

Chen, Lai 陳來. 2010. 中國近世思想史研究 [*Studies on the Intellectual History of China's Early Modern Period*]. Beijing: Sanlian shudian.

Cheng, Hao 程顥, and Cheng Yi 程頤. 1981. 河南程氏遺書 [*The Extant Works of the Chengs of Henan*]. In 二程集 [*The Collected Works of the Cheng Brothers*]. Beijing: Zhonghua shuju.

Cialdini, Robert B., Stephanie L. Brown, Brian P. Lewis, Carol Luce, and Steven L. Neuberg. 1997. "Reinterpreting the Empathy-Altruism Relationship: When One Into One Equals Oneness." *Journal of Personality and Social Psychology* 73:481–94.

Dai, Zhen 戴震. 2009a. 孟子字義疏證 [*Evidential Commentary on the Meanings of Terms in the Mencius*]. In 戴震集 [*The Collected Works of Dai Zhen*], 263–329. Taipei: Taiwan shangwu yinshuguan.

——. 2009b. 原善 [*On Goodness*]. In 戴震集 [*The Collected Works of Dai Zhen*], 330–50. Taipei: Taiwan shangwu yinshuguan.

Darwall, Stephen. 2002. *Welfare and Rational Care*. Princeton: Princeton University Press.

Ewell, John W. 1990. *Reinventing the Way: Dai Zhen's Evidential Commentary on the Meanings of Terms in Mencius (1777)*. PhD diss., University of California, Berkeley.

Hoffman, Martin L. 2000. *Empathy and Moral Development: Implications for Caring and Justice*. Cambridge: Cambridge University Press.

Ivanhoe, Philip J. 2002. *Ethics in the Confucian Tradition: The Thought of Mengzi and Wang Yangming*. 2nd ed. Cambridge: Hackett.

——. 2015. "Senses and Values of Oneness." In *The Philosophical Challenge from China*, edited by Brian Bruya, 231–51. Cambridge: MIT Press.

Nivison, David S. 1996. *The Ways of Confucianism: Investigations in Chinese Philosophy*. Edited by Bryan W. Van Norden. Chicago: Open Court.

Nussbaum, Martha C. 2001. *Upheavals of Thought*. New York: Cambridge University Press.

Selover, Thomas W. 2005. *Hsieh Liang-tso and the* Analects *of Confucius: Humane Learning as a Religious Quest*. New York: Oxford University Press.

Stotland, Ezra. 1969. "Exploratory Investigations in Empathy." In *Advances in Experimental Social Psychology*, edited by Leonard Berkowitz. New York: Academic.

Tiwald, Justin. 2011a. "Dai Zhen's Defense of Self-Interest." *Journal of Chinese Philosophy* 38s:29–45.

——. 2011b. "Sympathy and Perspective-Taking in Confucian Ethics." *Philosophy Compass* 6 (10): 663–74.

——. 2018. "Zhu Xi's Critique of Buddhism: Selfishness, Salvation, and Self-Cultivation." In *The Buddhist Roots of Neo-Confucian Philosophy*, edited by John Makeham. New York: Oxford University Press.

Zheng, Jixiong 鄭吉雄. 2008. 戴東原經典詮釋的思想史探索 [*An Exploration of the History of Thought in Dai Zhen's Interpretations of the Classics*]. Taibei: Guoli Taiwan daxue chuban zhongxin.

Zhu, Xi 朱熹. 1983. 中庸章句集注 [*Collected Commentaries on the Four Books*]. Beijing: Zhonghua shuju.

——. 1986. 朱子語類 [*Topically Arranged Conversations of Master Zhu*]. Eight vols. Edited by Li Jingde 黎靖德. Beijing: Zhonghua shuju.

——. 1996. "仁說 [*Treatise on Humaneness*]." In朱熹集 [*The Collected Works of Zhu Xi*], edited by Guo Qi 郭齊 and Yin Bo 尹波. Chengdu: Sichuan jiaoyu chubanshe. *Juan* 67:3542–44.

CONTRIBUTORS

Donald L. M. Baxter is Professor and Department Head in the Department of Philosophy at the University of Connecticut. He specializes in metaphysics and early modern Western philosophy. He is the author of *Hume's Difficulty: Time and Identity in the* Treatise (2008) and coedited *Composition as Identity* (2014) with A. J. Cotnoir.

Lawrence Blum is Emeritus Professor of Philosophy and Distinguished Professor of Liberal Arts and Education at the University of Massachusetts Boston. He is the author of *Friendship, Altruism and Morality* (1980) and *"I'm Not a Racist, But . . .": The Moral Quandary of Race* (2002),as well as three other books, and works in race studies, moral philosophy, social and political philosophy, and philosophy of education.

Geung Ho Cho is Professor Emeritus in the Department of Psychology of Sogang University, Republic of Korea. He has published extensively in Korean on the psychology of the Korean people and comparative psychology.

Stephen R. L. Clark is Emeritus Professor of Philosophy at the University of Liverpool, and an Honorary Research Fellow in the Department of Theology at the University of Bristol. He continues to manage an international e-list for philosophers and to serve as associate editor of the *British Journal for the History of Philosophy*. His books include *The Mysteries of Religion* (1984); *A Parliament of Souls* (1990); *God, Religion, and Reality* (1998); *Biology and Christian Ethics* (2000); *Understanding Faith: Religious Belief and Its Place in Society* (2009); *Ancient Mediterranean Philosophy* (2013); and *Plotinus: Myth, Metaphor, and Philosophical Practice* (2016).

His chief current interests are in the philosophy of Plotinus, the understanding and treatment of nonhuman animals, philosophy of religion, and science fiction.

Bradford Cokelet is a Visiting Assistant Professor of Philosophy at the University of Kansas. His work focuses on the nature of virtue and good human lives, with an emphasis on cross-cultural and empirically informed philosophic inquiry.

Owen Flanagan is James B. Duke Professor of Philosophy at Duke University and codirector of the Center for Comparative Philosophy. He works in the philosophy of mind and ethics and is the author of *The Geography of Morals: Varieties of Moral Possibility* (2017).

Jay Garfield is Doris Silbert Professor in the Humanities and Professor of Philosophy, Logic, and Buddhist Studies and director of the Buddhist Studies and Logic programs at Smith College. He is also Visiting Professor of Buddhist Philosophy at Harvard Divinity School, Professor of Philosophy at Melbourne University, and Adjunct Professor of Philosophy at the Central University of Tibetan Studies. He has taught in Australia, Singapore, Japan, and Germany and is a regular lecturer at major universities, Buddhist studies centers, and research institutions around the world. Professor Garfield is author or editor of 25 books and over 150 articles and book reviews. Professor Garfield's research addresses topics in the foundations of cognitive science and the philosophy of mind; the history of Indian philosophy during the colonial period; topics in ethics, epistemology, and the philosophy of logic; methodology in cross-cultural interpretation; and Buddhist philosophy, particularly Indo-Tibetan Madhyamaka and Yogācāra.

Victoria S. Harrison is Professor of Philosophy in the Faculty of Humanities, University of Macau, SAR. From 2009–2016, she directed the Forum for Philosophy and Religion at the University of Glasgow. Her books include *Religion and Modern Thought* (2007) and *Eastern Philosophy: The Basics* (2012). She has edited, with Charles Taliaferro and Stewart Goetz, *The Routledge Companion to Theism* (2013) and, with Jake Chandler, *Probability in the Philosophy of Religion* (2013). She specializes in the philosophy of religion, both Eastern and Western.

Kendy M. Hess is the Brake Smith Associate Professor of Social Philosophy and Ethics at the College of the Holy Cross in Worcester, Massachusetts. She has a JD from Harvard Law School and practiced corporate environmental law for fifteen years before finishing her PhD in philosophy at the University of Colorado-Boulder. Her research has focused on the development of a metaphysically robust account of group agency that will support the imposition of traditional moral obligations on firms and other highly organized groups; new projects include exploring contemporary conceptions of work and challenging the increasingly popular idea that firms should be politically active.

Philip J. Ivanhoe is Chair Professor of East Asian and Comparative Philosophy and Religion at City University of Hong Kong, where he also serves as director of the *Center for East Asian and Comparative Philosophy (CEACOP), the Laboratory on Korean Philosophy in Comparative Perspectives,* and the project *Eastern and*

Western Conceptions of Oneness, Virtue, and Human Happiness. He specializes in the history of East Asian philosophy and religion and its potential for contemporary ethics.

Tao Jiang is Associate Professor in the Religion Department at Rutgers University, New Brunswick, New Jersey, where he also serves as director of the Rutgers Center for Chinese Studies. His primary research interests are classical Chinese philosophy, Mahāyāna Buddhist philosophy, and comparative philosophy. He is the author of *Contexts and Dialogue: Yogācāra Buddhism and Modern Psychology on the Subliminal Mind* (2006) and the coeditor of *The Reception and Rendition of Freud in China: China's Freudian Slip* (2012). He codirects the Rutgers Workshop on Chinese Philosophy and cochairs the Neo-Confucian Studies Seminar at Columbia University.

Eva Feder Kittay is Distinguished Professor Emeritus of Philosophy at Stony Brook University/SUNY. She is the recipient of an NEH and a Guggenheim Fellowship for *Learning from My Daughter: Disabled Minds and Rethinking What Matters*, to be published by Oxford University Press. Her previous publications include *Love's Labor: Essays on Women, Equality, and Dependency; Cognitive Disability and the Challenge to Moral Philosophy;* and *Blackwell Guide to Feminist Philosophy.* She is a past president of the Eastern Division of American Philosophical Association.

Shaun Nichols is a Professor of Philosophy at the University of Arizona. He works at the intersection of philosophy and psychology. Among his publications are the monographs *Sentimental Rules* (2004) and *Bound: Essays on Free Will and Moral Responsibility* (2015).

Dimitri Putilin is on the faculty of the Department of Psychiatry and Behavioral Sciences at Duke University Medical Center.

Hagop Sarkissian is an Associate Professor of Philosophy at the City University of New York, Baruch College, and the CUNY Graduate Center. His research is located at the intersection of cognitive science, ethics, and classical Chinese philosophy: he draws insights from the cognitive and behavioral sciences to explore topics in moral psychology, agency, and the status of morality, with an eye toward seeing how culture shapes cognition in these domains. In addition to drawing from the empirical sciences, he also uses the tools of experimental psychology in some of his research.

Eric Schwitzgebel is Professor of Philosophy at University of California at Riverside. He writes on philosophy of mind, moral psychology, epistemology, and Chinese philosophy—especially concerning our poor self-knowledge, our dubious philosophical expertise, our inconsistency and inconstancy, and the often-weak relationship between explicit moral cognition and real-world moral behavior. His most recent book is *Perplexities of Consciousness* (2011), and he blogs at The Splintered Mind.

Michael R. Slater is Associate Professor of Theology at Georgetown University. He specializes in American philosophy and the philosophy of religion. Among his publications are *William James on Ethics and Faith* (2009) and *Pragmatism and the Philosophy of Religion* (2014).

Nina Strohminger is an Assistant Professor of Legal Studies and Business Ethics at Wharton University of Pennsylvania. She holds a BA in Cognitive Science from Brown University and a PhD in Psychology from the University of Michigan. She has held postdoctoral fellowships at Duke University and Yale University. Profesor Strohminger's research approaches key questions in business ethics through the lens of psychology.

William B. Swann is a professor of social and personality psychology at the University of Texas at Austin. He is best known for his work on self-verification, identity negotiation, and identity fusion. He has been elected Fellow of the American Psychological Association, the Society of Experimental Social Psychology, the American Psychological Society, the Society for Personality and Social Psychology, and the International Society of Self and Identity. He also served as the president of the Society of Experimental Social Psychology. He received the Distinguished Lifetime Career Award awarded by the International Society for Self and Identity in 2016.

Sanaz Talaifar is a graduate student in the Psychology Department at the University of Texas at Austin. Her areas of interest include the self, group identity, morality, and well-being. She also has a background in political science, having served as a research assistant at the Woodrow Wilson International Center for Scholars and studied at the London School of Economics and Political Science.

Justin Tiwald is Professor of Philosophy at San Francisco State University. He has published on classical Confucian, Daoist, and neo-Confucian accounts of moral psychology, well-being, and political authority, as well as the implications of Confucian views for virtue ethics, individual rights, and moral epistemology. His books include *Neo-Confucianism,* with Stephen C. Angle (2017); *Ritual and Religion in the* Xunzi, with T. C. Kline III (2014); and *Readings in Later Chinese Philosophy*, with Bryan W. Van Norden (2014).

Mark Unno is Associate Professor of East Asian Buddhism in the Department of Religious Studies at the University of Oregon. His research is in classical Japanese Buddhism, Buddhism and psychotherapy, comparative religious thought, and interrreligious dialogue. He is the author of *Shingon Refractions: Myoe and the Mantra of Light* (2004) and editor of *Buddhism and Psychotherapy Across Cultures* (2006), as well as articles on a wide array of topics. He serves on the boards of the Center for East Asian and Comparative Philosophy, the International Association for Shin Buddhist Studies, and the Society for Buddhist-Christian Studies.

INDEX

Abhidharma, 296
"achievement terms," 128–30
Adler, Alfred, 251, 252
Advaita Vedanta, 52*n*33, 272
afterlife, 44, 222, 384*n*3. *See also* Heaven
agents, 143, 245; caregiving, 125–26;
    corporate, 18–20, 192–208; freedom
    of, 239; moral, 54, 60, 193–94, 208;
    motivations of, 244–45, 247, 250; *Mozi*
    on, 318*n*3
ahimsa, 201
Albahari, Miri, 276, 280
alienation, 110, 262
Allinson, Robert E., 325, 326, 328
Allport, Gordon W., 251, 252
altruism, 100–1, 344, 352–59; Batson on,
    32, 35, 354–58; Baxter on, 9–10, 91;
    definition of, 354; Ivanhoe on, 17, 74*n*13;
    Putilin on, 32–33; Singer on, 352–53;
    Tiwald on, 382
Ames, Roger, 327
Amida Buddha, 155–56, 165
Analects, 308, 316; on *de*, 310, 312–13, 315; on
    "gentleman," 253–54, 310–16; on Golden
    Rule, 61–66, 379; on Heaven, 318*n*3; on
    oneness as superorganism, 307; on "petty
    men," 57, 60, 310, 315, 316; *ren* as justice

in, 53–61; on sage kings, 307, 308, 312–14;
    virtue in, 72*n*1
anātta. See no-self
Anik, L., 364
Annals of Lü Buwei, The, 325
Aoki, Shinmon, 15–16, 143, 156–61, 167–68;
    Morton and, 164–65; O'Halloran and,
    159, 162
Aquinas, Thomas, Saint, 201
Aral, S., 315
Aristotle, 4, 45, 227; on human nature,
    318*n*1; on justice, 73*n*4; on wholeness,
    201; *Metaphysics*, 98
Armstrong, A. H., 85, 88*n*7
Armstrong, Karen, 102*n*1
Arnold, Matthew, 210*n*19
artificial intelligence (AI), 293
aspects, theory of, 10, 91–102
"astronaut effect," 279
atheism, 166–67, 166; Dewey on, 21, 222, 223,
    226–30, 232*n*23; James on, 231*n*12
autobiographies, Tibetan, 298–301
autonomy, 23, 196; Cho Geung Ho on,
    235, 238–44, 247, 251–52, 256, 258–60;
    Darwall on, 131–32; Hess on, 204, 205;
    Kittay on, 132–34, 139*n*21, 139*n*23. *See also*
    individualism